AC

Time Out Washington

Penguin Books

PENGUIN BOOKS

Published by the Penguin Group
Penguin Books Ltd, 27 Wrights Lane, London W8 5TZ, England
Penguin Putnam Inc., 375 Hudson Street, New York, New York 10014, USA
Penguin Books Australia Ltd, Ringwood, Victoria, Australia
Penguin Books Canada Ltd, 10 Alcorn Avenue, Toronto, Ontario, Canada M4V 3B2
Penguin Books (NZ) Ltd, 182-190 Wairau Road, Auckland, New Zealand

Penguin Books Ltd, Registered offices: Harmondsworth, Middlesex, England

First published 1999
10 9 8 7 6 5 4 3 2 1

Colour reprographics by Precise Litho, 34–35 Great Sutton Street, London EC1
Printed and bound by William Clowes Ltd, Beccles, Suffolk NR34 9QE

Edited and designed by
Time Out Guides Limited
Universal House
251 Tottenham Court Road
London W1P 0AB
Tel + 44 (0)171 813 3000
Fax + 44 (0)171 813 6001
Email guides@timeout.com
www.timeout.com

Editorial
Editorial Director Peter Fiennes
Editor Ruth Jarvis
Deputy Editor Cath Phillips
Consultant Editor Brett Anderson
Listings Editor Alita Byrd
Proofreader Lisa Osborne
Indexer Jackie Brind

Design
Art Director John Oakey
Art Editor Mandy Martin
Senior Designer Scott Moore
Designers Benjamin de Lotz, Lucy Grant, Thomas Ludewig
Picture Editor Kerri Miles
Picture Researcher Olivia Duncan-Jones
Picture Admin Kit Burnet
Scanning & Imaging Chris Quinn

Advertising
Group Advertisement Director Lesley Gill
Sales Director Mark Phillips
Advertisement Director North American Guides
Liz Howell (808 732 4661)
Advertising co-ordinated in the US by
***Time Out New York*:**
Alison Tocci (Publisher), Andy Gersten (Advertising Production Manager)

Administration
Publisher Tony Elliott
Managing Director Mike Hardwick
Financial Director Kevin Ellis
Marketing Director Gillian Auld
General Manager Nichola Coulthard
Production Manager Mark Lamond
Accountant Bridget Carter

Features in this guide were written and researched by:
Introduction Ruth Jarvis. **History** Mark Jenkins (*We the people* Steve Ellman). **Washington Today** Mark Jenkins (*Washington by numbers* Steve Ellman). **Government in Action** Steve Ellman. **Architecture** Mark Jenkins (*Ten storeys and counting...* Steve Ackerman). **Tips & Tours** Steve Ackerman. **The Monumental Centre** Courtney Rubin. **Central DC** Steve Ackerman. **DC Neighbourhoods: Northwest** Amanda Ripley; **Northeast** Mark Jenkins; **Southeast** Mark Jenkins; **Southwest** Steve Ackerman (*The MLK riots* Amanda Ripley; *Alleyways and Avenues* Steve Ackerman; *I, Spy* Amanda Ripley; *Washington's Waterways* Steve Ackerman). **X-Files DC** Steve Ellman, Josh Green. **Virginia & Maryland** Steve Ackerman, Alita Byrd (*The other Washington Monument* Steve Ellman). **By Season** Sarah Wildman. **Museums & Galleries** Jessica Dawson. **Accommodation** Tina Davis. **Cafés & Coffeehouses** Lucy Powell. **Restaurants** Lucy Powell. **Bars** Courtney Rubin. **Shopping** Holly Bass (*Shopping with Monica* Courtney Rubin). **Children** Sandra L Hughes. **Culture** Holly Bass. **Film** Mark Jenkins (*Unpleasantville?* Steve Ellman; *The popcorn presidents* Matthew Crist, Ruth Jarvis). **Media** Mark Jenkins. **Nightlife** Steve Gdula (*Desperately seeking* Courtney Rubin). **Sport & Fitness** Emily Harris. **Trips Out of Town** Don Graff (*Crab culture* Steve Ackerman). **Getting Around** Emily Harris. **Directory** Alita Byrd (*Back to your roots* Courtney Rubin; *Diplo driving* Emily Harris). **Business** Don Graff. **The US System of Government** Steve Ellman. **Presidents of the USA** Steve Ellman. **The cradle of satire** Steve Ellman. **A-Z of politikspeak** Steve Ellman.

The Editor would like to thank the following:
Frances Anderton, Nicole Arthur, Andrew Coburn, Neeru Dhawan, Paige Dunn, Alexander Gardiner, Diane Granat, Rebecca Milner, Nina Negretti, Chris Niles, Gail O'Hara, Paul Hennemeyer, Mary Rega, Cyndi Stivers, Harriet Swift, Caro Taverne, Marie Tibor at Washington DC Convention and Visitors Association, Shallah Weiss, Sharon Wright.

The Editor flew to Washington with Virgin Atlantic (reservations UK 01293 747 747; US 1-800 862 8621)

Maps by JS Graphics, 17 Beadles Lane, Old Oxted, Surrey RH8 9JG.

Photography by Ian Teh except: pages 5, 9 Hulton Getty; pages 13 & 15 Popperfoto; page 11, 24 Corbis; pages 7, 10, 35 AKG; pages 44 & 46 Telegraph Colour Library; pages 55, 97 Associated Press; pages 84, 85, 200 Twentieth Century Fox; page 115 National Gallery of Art; page 116 Clark & Hogan; page 119 MH Photography; page 191 Rhoda Baer; page 200 Warner Brothers, Universal, Castle Rock, Paramount; pages 204 & 5 DOONESBURY © 1994 G. B. Trudeau reprinted with permission of UNIVERSAL PRESS SYNDICATE. All rights reserved. Page 213 Redferns/John Kirk; page 230 Bill Wood Photo; page 232 Steven Freeman/NBA Photos; page 235 Charisma PR/Middleton Evans; page 242, 250 Charisma PR; page 246 Communication Concepts; page 249 Annapolis & Anne Arundel County Conference and Visitors Bureau.
The following photographs were supplied by the featured establishments: pages 121, 215, 224, 239, 241.

Contents

About the Guide

This is the first edition of the *Time Out Guide to Washington, DC*, the latest in Time Out's expanding series of guides to cities around the world. It has been compiled by a team of resident experts, who have brought to it the same inside knowledge and attention to detail that Time Out's successful listings magazines in London and New York have founded their reputations on.

DETAILED DESCRIPTION

Above all, we have tried to make this book as useful as possible. Addresses, cross streets, telephone numbers, transport details, opening times, admission prices and credit card details are all included in our listings, along with websites, email addresses and fax numbers where relevant. To help those not familiar with the city to locate the places we've listed, we always give an area name, even if the postal address is technically just 'Washington, DC'. (Conversely, for anywhere you might want to write to, we have given the full postal address, including zip code.) Many of our chapters are divided according to these areas, so you should never have to look far for a restaurant or café. The area names we have used are mostly in common use, but not all are official appellations. They are defined on the maps on pages 292 to 297.

TALKING TELEPHONE NUMBERS

The area code for the District of Columbia is 202. All telephone numbers are given as dialled from DC; that is, as seven figures for within the District, an area code plus seven figures for local Virginia and Maryland numbers (in counties adjoining DC) and as 1 plus the area code plus a seven-figure number for long-distance calls. To make international calls to DC, dial your country's exit code, then 1 for the US, followed by 202 and the number. Note that you can now dial most – but not all – 1-800, 1-888 and 1-877 numbers from outside the US, although calls will be charged at the usual international rates.

CREDIT CARDS

The following abbreviations have been used for credit cards: **AmEx** American Express; **DC** Diners' Club; **Disc**: Discovery; **JCB** Japanese credit cards; **MC** Mastercard; **V** Visa.

Virtually all shops, restaurants and gas stations will accept dollar travellers cheques issued by American Express or Thomas Cook.

PRICES

The prices we've given should be treated as guidelines, not gospel. Seasonal variations and inflation can cause them to change rapidly, especially in the case of accommodation.

CHECKED & CORRECT

All listings information and other factual details have been thoroughly checked. However, inevitably businesses open and close, change their hours, relocate or alter their service in some other way. Public buildings frequently change their access arrangements at the last minute. We strongly recommend that you phone ahead before setting out. While every effort and care has been made to ensure the accuracy of the information contained in this guide, the publishers cannot accept responsibility for any errors it may contain.

RIGHT TO REPLY

It should be stressed that all the information we give is impartial. No organisation has been included in this guide because it has advertised in any of Time Out's publications, and all opinions given are wholly independent.

We hope you enjoy the *Time Out Guide to Washington, DC*, but we'd also like to know if you don't. We welcome tips from readers – feedback on current entries and suggestions for new ones – and take them into account in subsequent editions. There's a reader's reply card for your comments at the back of the book.

There is an online version of this guide, as well as weekly events listings for over 30 international cities, at http://www.timeout.com

Introduction

Wherever the capital of the USA was built, and whatever its physical form, certain qualities would inevitably come to be associated with it. To the patriot, it would be a shrine to American history and democracy; to the cynic a monolith of governmental excess. To the paranoid, the lair of cabals and conspiracists; to the activist, a place where real change could be achieved. It would attract idealists and opportunists; the power-hungry, the ambitious and the just plain greedy. It would be revered and reviled in equal measure. And its physical embodiment would become inseparable from the symbolism of nationhood.

And so it is with Washington, DC. But if such abstractions were determined by its birthright, Washington's founding fathers did all they could to give their capital a physical identity suited to its rôle. Their plan, for a city of neo-classical dignity with the institutes of government – the tallest buildings in a low-rise city – ranged around a stately sweep of parkland, has, thanks to a little vigilance during its two-century life, worked well. The layout not only succeeds in its appearance of grace and grandeur but in making the capital of the United States both accessible and enjoyable for its citizens to roam: almost everything of importance is concentrated on and around the National Mall. Here are America's proudly republican crown jewels: the articles of its founding, the institutions of its government; the monuments of its history; and, in the various Smithsonian museums, its cultural record. All are freely open to the public – and free of charge.

There are other advantages to Washington's capitalhood. The huge amounts of events and programmes run by its cultural institutions, the internationalism – and the politics. Serene though the Capitol and the White House may seem, their business reverberates around town, amplified by an obsessed media. You will pick up the buzz in overheard conversations, the flash-past of a motorcade, the opining of your taxi driver. If you're a political junkie, you'll be in candy. You can even sit in on a session and see legislation in the making, if you don't bore easy.

And what of the city beyond the politics? The Washington urban area has far outgrown its original District of Columbia boundaries. Over four million people live here and 80 per cent of them work in the private sector. That's hardly a one-horse, single-industry town. It might not be a metropolis to compete with London or New York, but it does have its neighbourhoods and its subcultures, a vibrant nightlife and a restaurant scene to compare with any world city.

The District of Columbia itself – notoriously – has its problems. Its lack of voting representation in Congress makes it hard for it to fight its corner, and yet it faces all the problems of the inner city core of a wider urban area: racial division, crime, lack of investment, depopulation. But currently things are looking up, with a new mayor, a falling crime rate and signs of regeneration in Downtown.

The average visitor need never travel far beyond the National Mall. But if you've come to look for America, you won't find it unless you do.

In Context

Key Events

circa 700 Indians use the confluence of the Potomac and Anacostia Rivers as a meeting place.
1608 Captain John Smith is the first known European to explore the Potomac, although he was apparently preceded by fur traders.
1749 Alexandria founded by Scottish settlers.
1751 Georgetown chartered by the Maryland Assembly.
1790 The US Congress votes to establish a Federal City and to move the capital there from Philadelphia.
1791-92 Pierre-Charles L'Enfant plans the new city, but is soon fired.
1800 President John Adams moves to the District of Columbia, the new capital.
1802 The city of Washington is incorporated, with local government by an elected council and a mayor appointed by the president.
1814 British troops invade Washington.
1820 Congress allows Washington's 30,000 residents to elect the city's mayor.
1829 Englishman James Smithson leaves his estate to the new nation for the founding of an educational institution.
1846 The portion of the District south of the Potomac is ceded back to Virginia.
1850 Congress abolishes slave trade in Washington, but not slave ownership.
1861-65 The Civil War greatly expands Washington's influence and size.
1862 Congress bans slavery in the District.
1865 President Lincoln is assassinated at Ford's Theatre.
1871 Congress converts Washington to a territorial government.
1874 Congress abandons territorial government, eliminates local voting rights and gives control of the city to three presidentially appointed commissioners.
1881 President Garfield assassinated. Flood-control project creates Hains Point and West Potomac Park.
1888 Electric streetcars begin operation.
1889 National Zoological Park established.
1890 Rock Creek Park established.
1902 The McMillan Commission begins to restore the L'Enfant Plan.
1908 Union Station opens.
1912 The first of 2,000 cherry trees, a gift from Japan, are planted near the Tidal Basin.
1917 America's entry into World War I spurs another population and building boom.
1919 Inflamed by false rumours of a black man's rape of a white woman, white rioters attack black neighbourhoods. Nine people are killed.
1922 In the city's worst natural disaster, 97 people are killed when the roof of the Knickerbocker Theater collapses during a 26in snowfall.
1924 The Washington Senators baseball team wins the World Series for the first and last time.
1926 The Federal Triangle building programme begins.
1928 The first licensed TV station in the US opens in Washington on an experimental basis.
1932 The federal government grows dramatically under Franklin D Roosevelt's New Deal. Jobless World War I veterans camp in Washington and are eventually dispersed by troops, killing four.
1941 National Airport opens.
1943 The Pentagon is completed.
1950 During the Korean War, the population of the District grows to 800,000, its highest point.
1954 DC schools and recreation facilities desegregated.
1961 A Constitutional amendment gives Washington residents the right to vote in presidential elections.
1962 The last lines of the local trolley system, shut down by Congressional edict, close.
1963 Martin Luther King Jr delivers his 'I have a dream' speech at the Lincoln Memorial.
1964 The Capital Beltway is completed.
1967 Congress re-establishes the mayor and council system of government for the city, but with all officials appointed by the president.
1968 Riots follow Martin Luther King Jr's assassination. Twelve people are killed.
1970 Several anti-Vietnam War protests.
1971 The Kennedy Center opens.
1972 Burglars working indirectly for President Richard Nixon are arrested during a break-in at the Watergate Office Building.
1975 Walter Washington becomes the city's first elected mayor of the twentieth century and its first African-American one.
1976 The first segment of the Metro rapid-rail system opens.
1981 President Reagan is wounded by a would-be assassin outside the Washington Hilton Hotel.
1990 Mayor Marion Barry is arrested in an FBI sting after being videotaped smoking crack.
1994 After serving prison time for a misdemeanour, Marion Barry is re-elected mayor.
1995 Congress appoints a control board to run most of the city government.
1997 The MCI Center opens in Downtown.
1999 Anthony Williams becomes mayor.

History

The life-story of the West's first purpose-built capital city.

British troops invade Washington in 1814 and torch the White House, so...

Washington, appropriately enough, began as a political compromise. After the Revolutionary War, the Northern states were left with substantial debts that they pressed the new federal government to assume. In order to get the Southern states to agree to this, they had to barter the location of the capital. Despite their desire to locate the government in a large Northern city – such as New York or Philadelphia, each of which served as the capital for a time – the Northerners agreed to a site on the border between north and south. The actual choice was left to President George Washington, who chose a spot less than 20 miles from his Virginia plantation, Mount Vernon.

THE NEW CAPITAL

The first president was not the first person to notice the confluence of the Potomac and Anacostia Rivers. Archaeologists have found artefacts indicating that the area was an Indian meeting and trading place a millennium before the Federal City was conceived. Still, the Algonquin Indians who lived in the area when Europeans first arrived in the early seventeenth century left little besides the names of the two rivers.

Within the new city were two port towns that had been founded in around 1750: Georgetown on the Maryland side and Alexandria in Virginia. Both were incorporated into the new District of Columbia, a diamond-shaped 100-square mile precinct that took 70 square miles from Maryland and 30 from Virginia. But the new capital, which came to be known as Washington, would be built from scratch on land that was mostly farmland or forest – contrary to the popular belief that the city is built on a swamp, hence the summer humidity. Washington hired a former member of his army staff, Pierre-Charles L'Enfant, to design the new city (*see page 8* **The L'Enfant Plan**).

Construction of the White House and Capitol began in 1792-93, but neither was finished when John Adams, the country's second president,

...President Madison flees to the **Octagon**.

arrived in 1800. Adams and other members of the new government were merely the first to notice the gap between the grandeur of L'Enfant's plan and the reality: a muddy frontier town of a mere 14,000 inhabitants, most of them living in Georgetown and Alexandria.

After 1801, residents of the District of Columbia lost their right to vote in Maryland or Virginia. The city of Washington was incorporated, with an elected city council and mayor appointed by the President. In 1820, the city's residents were allowed to elect the mayor as well. This was the first of many tinkerings with the local form of government. (However, the city's lack of voting representation in Congress remains unchanged two centuries later.)

What progress had been made in creating the new capital was largely undone during the War of 1812. In 1814, after defeating local resistance at the battle of Bladensburg, British troops marched unopposed into the city and burned most of the significant buildings. President Madison fled the White House for the Octagon, the nearby home of Colonel John Tayloe. It was there that he ratified the Treaty of Ghent, which ended the war. Among the things destroyed by the British was the original Library of Congress; former president Thomas Jefferson sold the nation his library as the basis for a new collection.

After the War of 1812 established American sovereignty, European visitors began to arrive to inspect the new capital. They were seldom impressed. Visiting in 1842, Charles Dickens provided the most withering sobriquet for pre-Civil War Washington: 'the city of magnificent intentions'. It was another Englishman, however, who made the greatest impact on the city in this period. In 1829, James Smithson, a professor of chemistry at Oxford who never visited the United States, left his estate to the new nation for the founding of an educational institution. Congress was so bewildered by this bequest that it didn't act on it for more than a decade, but the Smithsonian Institution was finally founded in 1846. Its original building opened in 1855.

While the Smithsonian laid one of the earliest foundations for Washington's late twentieth-century position as an information hub, the city showed few signs of becoming a centre of commerce. In an attempt to increase trade, the Chesapeake & Ohio Canal was built, paralleling the Potomac River for 185 miles to Cumberland, Maryland. Ground was broken in 1828, and the canal's Georgetown terminus opened in 1840. The canal continued to operate into the early twentieth century, but its importance was soon diminished by the Baltimore & Ohio Railroad, the country's first railway, which began operation in 1830 and arrived in Washington in 1835.

The other event of this period that had long-range significance for Washington was the 1846 retrocession to Virginia of the southern third of the District; the area now encompasses Arlington County and part of the city of Alexandria. Interestingly, the US Constitution was never amended to reflect the change, leaving the retrocession's legal status ambiguous. (When the give-back was challenged, however, the US Supreme Court declined to consider the case.)

Among the once and future Virginia residents' grievances was Congress's refusal to loan money to construct a Virginia-side canal connecting Alexandria to the west. Virginia was more inclined to support the project than Congress, which has always been reluctant to spend money on people without any voting representatives in the Capitol. (The canal project was ultimately reduced to an aqueduct connecting Alexandria to the C&O Canal.) An underlying issue, however, was some Virginians' anticipation that Congress would soon restrict the slave trade in the District.

From its founding, Washington had a large African-American population. By 1800, approximately one-quarter of the city's population was African-American, and most of those were slaves. By 1840, the ratio of white to black was similar, but there were almost twice as many free blacks as slaves. Free blacks and runaway slaves arrived in Washington to escape the horrors of life on Southern plantations, and quickly set up institutions to help their compatriots. Washington became a more attractive destination in 1850, when Congress did ban slave-trading (but not slavery itself). A year before Abraham Lincoln's 1863 Emancipation Proclamation, Congress abolished slavery in the District.

Despite the presence of some relatively prosperous free blacks, Washington was hardly a safe haven for former slaves. African-Americans were sometimes kidnapped off the city's streets and sold into slavery, the papers certifying their free status having been destroyed by their captors. Those who escaped this fate still had to live under the onerous 'black codes' adopted by Congress from the laws of Virginia and Maryland. These restricted African-Americans' property ownership, employment and trades, public meetings and even use of profane language. Being arrested for an infraction of these laws could result in a permanent loss of liberty, since jail wardens were authorised to sell their black prisoners to pay the cost of their incarceration.

CIVIL WAR CONSEQUENCES

The Civil War transformed Washington from a sleepy part-time capital into the command centre of an energised country – the first (but not the last) time that a national crisis actually benefited the city. New residents flooded into the city, and such DC inhabitants as photographer Matthew Brady became nationally known for their war work. Among the new Washingtonians was poet Walt Whitman, who initially came to care for his wounded brother and then became a volunteer at the makeshift hospitals in the converted Washington Armory & Patent Office. (Whitman remained in the city for 12 years, working as a clerk at various federal agencies; he was fired from the Bureau of Indian Affairs when the new Secretary of Interior deemed *Leaves of Grass* to violate 'the rules of decorum & propriety prescribed by a Christian Civilization'.)

Several Civil War battles were fought near Washington, notably the two engagements at Manassas, now a local commuter-rail stop. A string of forts was built to protect the District, but only one saw action: Fort Stevens, site of a 1864 skirmish. The city's most significant war-related incident, the 1865 assassination of President Lincoln at Ford's Theatre, actually occurred five days after the South surrendered.

After the war, a Congress dominated by 'radical Republicans' made some efforts to atone for slavery. The Freedman's Bureau was established to help former slaves make the transition to freedom, and in 1867 Howard University was chartered for African-American students. All adult male DC residents were granted local suffrage in 1866, and 9,800 white and 8,200 'colored' men registered to vote.

Congress, however, did not address Washingtonians' lack of Congressional representation. In 1871, it reclassified the city as a territory, but quieted the latest round of rumours that it would move the capital west by authorising the construction of the massive State, War & Navy Departments Building (now the Old Executive Office Building). A prominent local real-estate developer, Alexander Shepherd, was appointed to the territory's Board of Public Works, which he soon dominated. 'Boss' Shepherd began an ambitious programme of street grading and paving, sewer-building and tree-planting, transforming the city but also quickly bankrupting it.

Only three years after establishing the territorial government, Congress abandoned it, putting the city under the control of three presidentially appointed commissioners. Local voting rights were eliminated, a move that one local newspaper welcomed as ending the 'curse' of African-American suffrage. President Grant, still a Shepherd supporter, nominated the 'Boss' to be one of the three new commissioners, but the Senate wouldn't confirm him. In 1876, Shepherd moved to Mexico, leaving behind a city that was beginning to look like modern Washington.

The next major round of civic improvements was inspired in 1881 by severe flooding. A land-reclamation and flood-control project created Hains Point and West Potomac Park, quite literally creating the ground that would become the home

President Lincoln is shot by John Wilkes Booth in Ford's Theatre, 1865.

of such Washington landmarks as the Lincoln and Jefferson Memorials. That same year, President Garfield was shot at the Baltimore & Potomac Railroad station (now the site of the National Gallery of Art) by a disgruntled job-seeker. Garfield died two months later in New Jersey, where he had been taken for the supposedly rehabilitative effect of sea air.

Following Shepherd's modernisation of the city, many improvement projects were undertaken. The Washington Monument was finally finished in 1885, and electric streetcars began operation in 1888, opening the areas beyond Boundary Street (now Florida Avenue) to development as suburbs. In 1889, the National Zoological Park was founded in Rock Creek Park, which was officially established the following year.

NEW CENTURY & NEW DEAL

Major plans to remake the city came with its 1900 centennial. Under the influence of the 'City Beautiful' movement, the Congressionally chartered McMillan Commission proposed restoring the primacy of the oft-ignored L'Enfant Plan and developing the neglected Mall and nearby areas along the river. Some of the city's poorest and most dangerous neighbourhoods were to be removed to create a grand greensward, and such unseemly intrusions as the Baltimore & Potomac Railroad station were to be banished from the Mall. The result of the latter dictum was Union Station, which upon its 1908 opening consolidated the city's several downtown railroad stations on a site north of the Capitol. In 1910, the Fine Arts Commission was established to ensure the aesthetic worthiness of new federal structures, and an act was passed to limit the height of buildings.

A practical challenge to the McMillan Plan came with World War I, which prompted another Washington building boom. Dozens of 'temporary' structures were erected, including some built on the western part of the Mall. Many of these buildings were used not only during World War I but World War II as well. (The last of them was torn down in 1971, and part of the space they occupied became Constitution Gardens, which opened in 1976.)

The L'Enfant Plan

The fountainhead of Washington's physical existence was the street layout conceived by Pierre-Charles L'Enfant, a young Frenchman who had been a member of George Washington's army staff. The resulting 'L'Enfant Plan' is the city's single most influential architectural document – even though no one alive has ever seen a copy of it.

Washington hired L'Enfant in 1791, but was forced to fire him a year later because the Frenchman overspent his budget and dealt too imperiously with some of the city's largest landowners. L'Enfant took his plan with him; the version that exists today was probably drafted by his assistant, Benjamin Ellicott. Most historians of the document think the adopted plan differs only slightly from L'Enfant's intentions.

The baroque scheme attributed to L'Enfant is a rectangular street grid with broad avenues radiating from ceremonial circles and squares and from the two fundamental structures, the White House and the Capitol. The plan is often likened to Paris, although L'Enfant conceived his 100-foot-wide avenues a half century before Baron Haussmann began redefining the French capital by driving grand boulevards through neighbourhoods of narrow medieval streets.

The original plan dictated the layout of only the City of Washington, which is defined by the Potomac and Anacostia Rivers and Florida Avenue (originally Boundary Street). As the city expanded beyond these borders, attempts were made to follow L'Enfant's method, although difficult topography and sheer disinterest sometimes overcame deference to the plan. L'Enfant's avenues were named after the 15 states of the Union as of 1790; streets have subsequently been chosen to bear the names of the other 35, although some are quite modest.

At the city's first centennial, Washington rededicated itself to the L'Enfant Plan with the McMillan Commission Plan, which banished such intrusions as a railroad line and station on the Mall. Today the National Capital Planning Commission watches over the L'Enfant Plan, while the 1910 Height Limitation Act continues to prevent buildings from towering so high that they overwhelm the plan's horizontal emphasis. The maximum height is 150 feet, and that only on Pennsylvania Avenue, although such non-functional embellishments as spires are allowed to go higher.

Unfortunately, L'Enfant didn't live to see how influential his scheme would become. Washington was still a very humble place when the designer died in 1825, penniless after refusing the offer of $2,500 for his services. In 1909, his remains were transferred to Arlington National Cemetery, the final resting place of the country's most revered heroes.

The large numbers of unemployed sailors and soldiers demobilised in Washington after World War I are often cited as one of the causes of the race riots that convulsed the city in the summer of 1919. Nine people were killed in the worst disturbance, which began after false rumours spread that a black man had raped a white woman. Much of the violence spread from the Navy Yard into the predominantly African-American neighbourhoods nearby in Southwest.

Race relations were strained by the riots, but in truth they were precarious even before them. Most of the advances for African-Americans in the post-Civil-War era had been turned back by the early twentieth century, and President Woodrow Wilson, hailed as a visionary in foreign policy, was a reactionary on matters of race. Federal government agencies were rigidly segregated, as were most of the capital's public facilities, although its trolleys and buses, libraries and baseball stadium (but not the teams that played there) were integrated.

In 1922, when the Lincoln Memorial opened, the man who freed the slaves was commemorated by a racially segregated crowd; Tuskegee Institute President Robert Moten, an official invitee, was brusquely ushered to the 'Negro' section. Three years later, 25,000 hooded Ku Klux Klansmen marched down Pennsylvania Avenue, although the founding of a local Klan chapter drew little support. In 1926, the local superior court upheld the legality of voluntary covenants designed to prevent blacks from buying property in predominantly white neighbourhoods.

Women won the vote in 1920, although not if they were DC residents. Meanwhile, separate and unequal African-American Washington boomed, with the age of the Harlem Renaissance mirrored on U Street, known as the 'Great Black Way'. The Howard and other theatres frequently presented such performers as Ella Fitzgerald, Eubie Blake and Washington native Duke Ellington. The city's African-American neighbourhoods were swelled by dispossessed Cotton Belt agricultural workers, and the Depression was soon to send more Southern blacks to town.

In central Washington, the work begun by the McMillan Commission continued. Beginning in 1926, the building of the Federal Triangle displaced the city's Chinatown and one of its roughest neighbourhoods, 'Murder Bay', while creating an area of monumental federal office buildings unified by their Beaux Arts style. Other events boosted the capital's national prestige: in 1924 and 1925, the Washington Senators baseball team (now defunct) made the first two of three trips to the World Series. (They won only in 1924.) In 1927, the first Cherry Blossom Festival was held, calling attention to the city's new ornamental riverfront.

The Depression soon ended the major civic improvement projects and made Washington the focus for a different sort of national attention. In 1931, a group called the Hunger Marchers arrived in the city; it was followed by some 20,000 jobless World War I veterans who became known as the 'Bonus Army'. They encamped at various places around the city, sometimes with their families, waiting for Congress to pass legislation awarding them back pay. Eventually troops under the command of General Douglas MacArthur dispersed the camps with bayonets and tear gas. Four people were killed, two of them young children.

The 'Bonus Army' by the US Capitol, 1932.

In 1932, Franklin D Roosevelt was elected president and his 'New Deal' created new programmes and jobs. Again, Washington benefited from national adversity. Local construction crews began to work again, erecting the National Archives and the Supreme Court, both finished in 1935. Meanwhile, some of the president's cabinet members and top advisers discovered Georgetown, which fitted the 1930s vogue for the colonial style; the old port town, which then had a large African-American population, became the first Washington neighbourhood to be gentrified.

The New Dealers took a more liberal stand on racial issues. Although the Roosevelts were reluctant to antagonise segregationists with major changes, they did sometimes invite black leaders to receptions – and black musicians to perform – at the White House. In 1939, when the Daughters of the American Revolution refused to let famed African-American contralto Marian Anderson perform at the group's Constitution Hall, Secretary

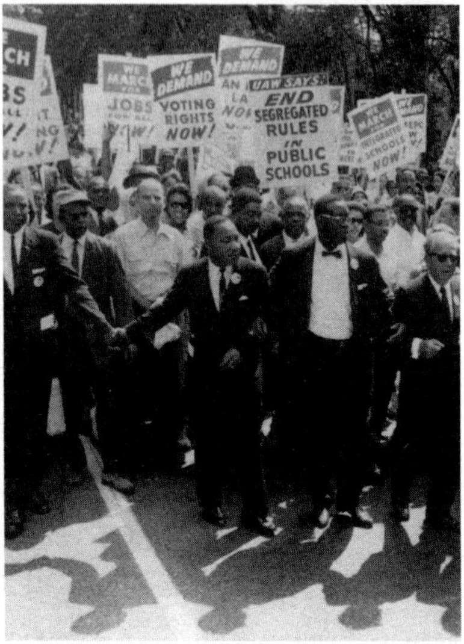

Martin Luther King civil rights march, 1963.

of the Interior Harold Ickes immediately approved a concert at the Lincoln Memorial. Anderson performed there for an integrated crowd of 75,000.

World War II added to the city's bustle, as thousands of workers and volunteers arrived to further the war effort. National Airport opened in 1941, and the Pentagon (still the largest federal office building) was rapidly constructed for the military command. (The Pentagon was built with separate bathrooms for white and black employees, but, after FDR protested, signs distinguishing the facilities were never added to the doors.) Also opening in this period were two less martial structures, the Jefferson Memorial and the National Gallery of Art. The arts kept a low profile for the remainder of the war, however, as such institutions as Dumbarton Oaks were requisitioned by wartime agencies.

Despite fears of a post-war depression, the city continued to boom in the late 1940s. As the Korean War began, the 1950 census put the District's population at 800,000, its highest point. Washington's new position as an imperial capital was emphasised by a series of controversial hearings on alleged Communist infiltration of the federal government as well as two attacks by Puerto Rican nationalists. In the first, gunmen tried to shoot their way into Blair House to kill President Truman (he was living at the property, normally used for visiting dignitaries, during White House renovations). In the second, attackers wounded five Congressmen on the floor of the House of Representatives.

In the 1950s, suburbanisation began to transform the land around Washington, most of it farms or woodland. Aided by new highways and federally guaranteed home mortgages, residential developments grew rapidly in the inner suburbs, followed by commercial development. Congress authorised the Interstate Highway System and supported plans for an extensive system of urban freeways for Washington that would destroy neighbourhoods and overwhelm the proportions of L'Enfant's plan.

Automobile, petroleum and rubber interests that worked quietly to destroy transit systems in other American cities had no need for subtlety in DC, which still had no elected local government. Corporate envoys influenced law makers to eliminate trolleys in favour of 'modern' cars and buses. Under Congressional pressure, streetcar lines were abandoned throughout the decade, and the final routes were cut in 1962.

While the suburbs grew, Congress turned again to remaking embarrassing examples of poverty in the vicinity of the Capitol. Thousands of working-class inhabitants were displaced from Southwest Washington in a process that was called 'urban renewal'. Southwest also became a focus for federal development, with massive new headquarters buildings erected near the new L'Enfant Plaza.

RIGHTS & RIOTS

The city's white population began to decline precipitously in 1954, after the Supreme Court outlawed racial segregation. While many jurisdictions resisted the ruling, Washington quickly came into compliance. It was soon a majority black city, with a poverty rate that embarrassed federal officials. Under Presidents John F Kennedy and Lyndon Johnson, the capital became both the symbolic focus and a conspicuous test case of the civil rights movement and the 'war on poverty'.

In 1963, Martin Luther King Jr led a 200,000-person 'March for Jobs and Freedom' to Washington, and delivered his 'I have a dream' speech at the Lincoln Memorial. Neither race relations nor inner-city economies improved significantly in the mid-1960s, and some feared the capital would soon experience the same sort of riots that had already scarred other major cities. On the 1968 assassination of Martin Luther King Jr, Washington and other cities erupted in flames. Twelve people were killed as rioters burned many small businesses in predominantly black sections of the city.

Congress had already made tentative steps toward enfranchising Washington residents. In 1961, a Constitutional amendment gave Washington residents the right to vote in presidential elections, and in 1967, Congress restored the mayor and council system of government, but with all officials appointed by the president. Despite post-1968 fears that Washington would explode again, progress in establishing an elected

We the people

Freedom of assembly, speech and petition were among the very first rights Americans enshrined in the Constitutional amendments collectively known as the Bill of Rights. And where better for people to take their grievances than directly to the national capital?

Most of Washington's public demonstrations have been galvanised by economic hardship and social injustice. The best remembered are Martin Luther King's 1963 ('I have a dream') civil rights rally and the Vietnam war protests. More recently, gays and lesbians have gathered to claim equal rights, Christians have cried out for a return to 'traditional values' and marchers on both sides of the abortion rights question have thronged the streets.

Some of Washington's more unusual and/or forgotten demonstrations include:

Coxey's Army (1894)

Jacob Coxey, a wealthy Midwesterner, leads a band of 500 protesters on a march from Massillon, Ohio, to Washington, DC, to protest the massive unemployment that followed the Panic of 1893. The group includes a six-piece band, a coterie of reporters and Coxey's infant son, Legal Tender Coxey. They arrive at the US Capitol on 1 May, where Capitol police break up the rally, club the demonstrators and haul Coxey off to jail. He returns on the 50th anniversary of the affair to toast FDR's economic policies.

Ku Klux Klan (1925)

Forty-three chartered trains and numerous cars bring 40,000 Klansmen to a parade that proceeds down Pennsylvania Avenue for almost four hours (*pictured*). Many come from the South and Midwest, but most are from Virginia, Pennsylvania and New Jersey. Though the local chapter is poorly supported, Washington serves as national headquarters for the Klan at this time and it remains strong enough during the 1920s to help prevent the 1928 election of Alfred Smith, the first Catholic presidential candidate.

Anti-Vietnam (1967-71)

- 'Mobilisation Against the War' (Oct 1967): first major Washington anti-war rally of the 1960s includes Abbie Hoffman and Jerry Rubin's attempt to exorcise and levitate the Pentagon. Chronicled by Norman Mailer in *Armies of the Night*.
- 'Moratorium/March Against Death' (Oct, Nov 1969): several hundred thousand gather for Vietnam protest rallies. Richard Nixon pointedly lets it be known he's staying in to watch college football on television.
- 'Cambodia Incursion Protests' (May 1970): Nixon makes midnight visit to student encampment at Lincoln Memorial, discusses football and surfing.
- 'Dewey Canyon III' (Apr 1971): named after a series of military campaigns in Laos. Vietnam vets camp on Mall, take guerrilla theatre to Capitol steps, stage mass discard of ribbons and medals.

Resurrection City (May-June 1968)

Last great action of Martin Luther King Jr's unfinished Poor People's Campaign. Plywood shanty town of 2,500 camps out by Washington Monument to protest both poverty and the Vietnam War. Bad weather and internal dissension trouble the gathering, but Congress passes some modest social welfare measures.

local government was slow. Finally, in 1975, Walter Washington become the city's first elected mayor of the twentieth century and its first African-American one.

The 'Free DC' battle for local voting rights was rooted in, and interconnected with, the larger civil-rights movement. Many of the city's first elected officials – notably Marion Barry, who began the first of four terms as mayor in 1979 – were civil-rights veterans. Almost as important, however, was the anti-freeway campaign. An ad hoc citizens' group managed to stop most of the proposed highways through the city. Protests halted a planned freeway bridge across the Potomac River, and the slogan 'white men's roads through black men's homes' stopped an eight-lane thoroughfare through Upper Northeast.

Local activists preferred a mostly underground rapid-rail system, which had already been discussed for half a century. Congress funded the system that would become the Metro, but influential Congressmen held up financing until city residents also accepted the freeway system. They never did, and the Metro finally opened its long-delayed first section in 1976.

In the 1970s, Washington served as a backdrop for several national struggles, notably the one over the Vietnam war. President Richard Nixon, who recognised his local unpopularity, stressed 'law and order' – considered code words for racial fears – and painted the majority-black city as the nation's 'crime capital'. Then five burglars working indirectly for Nixon were arrested during a break-in at the Democratic National Committee campaign headquarters in the Watergate office building, and 'Watergate' gradually became synonymous with Washington.

The city's reputation was supposed to be bolstered by the 1976 celebration of the nation's bicentennial, but most people skipped the party, perhaps frightened by reports of crowds that never materialised. Still, the year saw the opening of the National Air & Space Museum, which soon became the country's most popular museum.

The following year, members of a small black Islamic group, the Hanafi Muslims, seized the District Building, the B'Nai Brith Building and the Washington Islamic Center in a protest against an obscure film depicting the prophet Mohammed. In the attack on the District Building, then the headquarters of the mayor and the city council, a journalist was killed and councilman Marion Barry was wounded.

Faced with pressure from the DC statehood movement, in 1978 Congress passed a constitutional amendment that would have given the District voting representation in both the House and the Senate. The amendment was ratified by only 15 of the necessary 35 states, however, and expired in 1985.

In 1981, Ronald Reagan became president and, that same year, survived an assassination attempt outside the Washington Hilton Hotel. Reagan was ideologically opposed to big government and temperamentally averse to Washington. Nonetheless, after surviving the major recession of Reagan's first term, the region enjoyed a building boom, as new office buildings rose in both the city and its suburbs, especially in Virginia. Tenants of the latter were known as 'Beltway Bandits', after their proximity to the circumferential highway completed in 1964, which has become the main street of Washington's suburbs; many of them were government contractors benefiting from the Reagan administration's large military build-up.

Although the city benefited from the tax revenues flowing from the new developments, Barry spent much of the money on assuring his political invulnerability. Years of rumours about the mayor's nocturnal activities were validated in 1990, when Barry was arrested after being videotaped smoking crack. Many Barry supporters were angered by the FBI sting, however, charging entrapment. When brought to trial, Barry was convicted of only a misdemeanour, making him eligible for office at the end of his jail term.

DC IN THE 1990s

The city's white population has now stabilised, but middle-class blacks have departed in large numbers over the past two decades. The city's population is now estimated at under 550,000 – although that's based on a highly dubious count of the city's illegal immigrants, many of whom fled Central America in the 1980s. Immigrants from many countries have arrived recently, but Latinos are the fastest-growing group. The tension between these new residents and the city's predominantly black police force erupted in 1991, with two days of anti-police rioting in the largely Latino Mount Pleasant, Adams Morgan and Columbia Heights neighbourhoods.

Barry did indeed run again in 1994, winning re-election in a vote polarised along racial and class lines. He showed little interest in the job, however, and Congress had no patience for the notorious mayor. With revenues diminished by the early 1990s real-estate slump, the city was in perilous financial shape. Congress took advantage of the crisis to seize control of the city, putting a financial control board in charge of most municipal business.

When Barry was replaced by the sober, mild-mannered Anthony Williams in 1999, Congressional leaders quickly backed off. Although the city government is still technically supervised by the control board, Williams has as much power as any of the few mayors in the District's 200-year history. Voting representation in Congress, however, remains an unachieved goal.

Washington Today

It has long been a national irony that the seat of government is considered a paradigm for inner-city blight. But DC's image is gradually improving.

Mayors past and present: **Marion Barry** *on his re-election in 1994 after serving time...*

In 1996, DC's deficit-ridden government couldn't find the money to restore its decrepit city hall, so it made a much-criticised deal to have the building renovated by a developer who would cover costs by renting most of the structure to the federal government. In 1999, with a new mayor in office and the municipal budget in surplus, the city council tried in vain to renegotiate the arrangement. The scenario is emblematic of where Washington finds itself today: with new confidence and a fatter purse, but still entangled in many bad bargains that it made during the past 20 years of fledgling and frequently disastrous home rule that saw the population fall by a fifth.

In the early days of Anthony Williams's tenure as the District's fourth-elected twentieth-century mayor, little of substance has changed. Yet the city's image is much improved, and in Washington image sometimes equals substance. Coincident with the departure of controversial former mayor Marion Barry, tax revenues are up, crime is down and the US Congress – which has absolute veto power over the city's laws and budget – is being more indulgent. Tourist visits and hotel-occupancy rates have also climbed, which is vital to an economy that depends on almost $2 billion in annual tourism revenues. Bill Clinton's antics may have embarrassed many Americans, but that hasn't stopped visitors from lining up for the White House tour. Local tourism officials even argued that NATO's mostly behind-closed-doors 50th-anniversary summit was great publicity.

Naming names

Officially, Washington doesn't exist. The city of Washington, part of the jurisdiction laid out by Pierre-Charles L'Enfant in 1791, outgrew its boundaries a century later, and became legally indistinguishable from the District of Columbia. In fact and in popular usage, Washington and the District of Columbia are the same place.

Of course, there are many other ways to refer to the District, or DC, the two most common nicknames used by longtime residents. Accurate but bland is 'the nation's capital', which since the Cold War has sometimes been inflated to 'the capital of the free world'. (On occasion these two phrases have been jumbled into 'the nation's capital of the free world'.) When Metrorail wanted to brag that it had the deepest subway stations and longest escalators outside the Soviet Union, it pronounced them the deepest and longest 'in the free world'.

Such pomposities are usually uttered with a wink by longtime residents. When a local financial institution recently advertised itself as 'the bank to the most important money in the world', the slogan was quickly laughed out of circulation. Some natives prefer deflationary lines such as 'first in war, first in peace, and last in the American League', a florid description of George Washington altered to poke fun at the city's hapless (and long since departed) baseball team.

The United States' ambivalent relationship with its capital – and indeed with the whole idea of a national government – is reflected in such half-serious sobriquets as 'Sodom on the Potomac' and 'Washington Babylon'.

In the 1970s, African-American residents took the demographics that scared some suburbanites and turned them into a positive, dubbing Washington 'Chocolate City'. That tag has fallen from favour, however, as much of the chocolate has flowed to the suburbs.

Should the District ever win statehood, the name selected by a 1981 state constitutional convention is the unexciting 'New Columbia'. Until then, the city may be best described by the slogan of the 1960s Free DC movement: 'America's last colony'.

POST-INDUSTRIAL STRENGTHS

Washington's biggest business remains government, but the federal purse's significance has dramatically decreased. Federal employment has declined throughout the '90s, while the local service and information industries have boomed. Today, 80 per cent of the area's jobs are in the private sector. Most of these are well-paid professional, managerial or technical positions. According to a recent survey, the Washington area contains the fourth-largest supply of office space in the world, after Tokyo, New York and Paris. Washington was once disparaged for not having an industrial economy, but now that white-collar, information-oriented commerce is the new paradigm, such criticisms are obsolete. No major US cities still have significant manufacturing bases – not even nearby Baltimore, long extolled as more 'real' than Washington because it had actual factories.

Of course, many of the high-tech businesses that took root in the DC area did so because of the proximity of federal agencies: biotechnology companies developed near the National Institutes of Health, while satellite and telecommunications enterprises orbit around the Federal Communications Commission and Intelsat. Such industries, however, have grown to the point where they have their own critical mass, as outsiders have noticed. These days the *Washington Post*'s business pages regularly report on new branch offices opened by Silicon Valley law firms and venture-capital funds. A 1999 survey indicates that the area has slightly more computer programmers than lawyers – and approximately twice as many of each per capita than the country at large. Energy, hospitality, defence and media companies may still be the area's largest, but the local stock to own during the late-'90s boom market has been America Online.

Some of the area jobs created by the new information industries are in the District of Columbia, but most of them are not. The divide between the city and its contiguous suburbs in Maryland and Virginia is one of the region's central dilemmas, and no solutions are imminent. As a practical matter, there is little difference between living in Dupont Circle or Takoma Park, Capitol Hill or Arlington, but the political gap is vast. As long as DC continues to have no voting representation in Congress, the residents of 'the capital of the free world' will always be under the thumb of their suburban neighbours.

CITY LIMITS

When they're not politically overpowering the District, the city's suburbs just make it look bad. Although DC does have crime, destitution and dangerous neighbourhoods, its longstanding reputation as an urban pit of despair has been considerably overstated. Though crime remains a serious problem, DC's per capita income and

...and the present incumbent, **Anthony Williams**, *elected at the end of 1998.*

education rates are actually above average for major American cities, while its poverty rate is below. But the city can't compete demographically with its suburbs, which contain some of the country's most affluent, best educated inhabitants.

DC's appeal to a particular kind of resident – usually single people or couples with no stake in the unreliable local schools – is on the increase after several tricky years in the mid-'90s. The market for houses and apartments in the more affluent neighbourhoods caught fire in 1998, and new residences are being renovated or constructed at a rate not seen since the 1970s, when high gasoline prices sparked a fleeting back-to-the-city movement. The beginnings of a new Downtown residential district, Pennsylvania (Penn) Quarter, appeared in the late '80s and the neighbourhood may become a lively place if the mayor and city council can only resist the customary practice of discarding long-term planning goals every time an influential developer wants to erect another office building. There are also signs that the area may again become, as it was for 150 years, Washington's entertainment district. Among the institutions that have relocated here in the past decade are the Shakespeare Theatre and the Washington Wizards basketball team, which plays in the new MCI Center. An eight-screen arthouse cinema is under construction, a 25-screen cinema is planned and Arena Stage, a pioneer in US regional theatre, is considering a move here.

STAYING STABLE

The most sceptical analysis of the encouraging news is that Washington is currently on the up side of an endless – and endlessly frustrating – cycle. Congress giveth and Congress taketh away. The lawmakers can't let the nation's capital fall into chaos, but neither can they be bothered to repair the structural problems that prevent the city from coming into its own.

Seeing black ink in the ledgers, the city council recently voted in tax cuts to make DC more competitive with its neighbours. Yet the city's economy is inherently fragile, and could be as devastated by the next national economic downturn as it was by the late-'80s real-estate slump. Washington's 68-square-mile area is tiny compared with most US cities, and more than half of that land is tax exempt. In addition, DC is forbidden to tax the income of non-residents, who earn 60 per cent of the wages paid in the city.

There are a number of far-fetched models for making DC economically self-sufficient; Monaco and pre-handover Hong Kong come to mind. Eleanor Holmes Norton, the city's non-voting delegate to Congress, has proposed making it a tax haven by exempting residents from federal income tax. That's unlikely, but the Republican-controlled Congress has instituted tax breaks for first-time home-buyers and businesses that locate in certain parts of the city (not all of them 'blighted' by any definition).

The most logical alternative is equally implausible: the whole Washington area needs a local metropolitan government, a concept that's rarely been tested in the United States. As they stand, Washington's political boundaries reflect no useful distinctions. An area-wide authority could deal with such shared problems as suburban sprawl and a transport system that is, outside the central city, heavily weighted in favour of the car. Now the Metrorail system is almost finished, pressure is growing to build more highways, even though the area's air pollution violates federal standards and expanded highways have been proved, both in this region and elsewhere, to create more traffic congestion than they relieve. But regional government won't happen anytime soon, since the sovereign states of Virginia and Maryland resist ceding any of their power to the politically disenfranchised city-state at the region's centre.

WHOSE CITY IS IT ANYWAY?

In the past two decades, Washington has become the new home for Central Americans, Ethiopians, Vietnamese and, most recently, a few Bosnians. (The more affluent foreign immigrants, including Iranians, Koreans and Indians, tend to move directly to the suburbs.) The newcomers who have recently bid up the prices of rowhouses in Mount Pleasant and Logan Circle, however, are mostly white. This in-migration conjures the spectre of 'The Plan', a secret scheme that some black Washingtonians believe is designed to displace the African-American population of all the city's more appealing and convenient neighbourhoods.

Passions sometimes become overheated on this topic, but if there is a Plan, there's no organised resistance to it. Indeed, the city's two-decade demographic shift from over 70 to less than 60 per cent black is mostly the result of middle-class African-American flight to the suburbs, principally Prince George's County. In 1998 the city's majority-black population even elected its first majority-white city council. This may be just a fluke, but it's not exactly a sign that the forces of reaction are reclaiming the city. Two of the council's recently elected white members are openly gay, and several white council members are – on some issues, at least – notably more liberal than their black colleagues. Still, an era has clearly passed: the DC government is no longer rooted in, and vaguely yearning to be a continuation of, the civil rights movement.

Relations between long-time African-American residents and the new immigrants are sometimes strained, but most of the strife in the city's more diverse neighbourhoods seems to be within groups rather than between them. Perhaps because so many of the new immigrants have located in the same areas – mostly Columbia Heights and Mount Pleasant – the newcomers don't have exclusive turf to defend. The gaps of language and culture can be wide, but neighbourhoods like Columbia Heights have little choice but to serve as a melting pot.

Washington has always attracted a different sort of immigrant, of course: ambitious young people hoping to make a career in politics or a related field. The preponderance of these transients is exaggerated, however, and they're becoming even less significant as the area's economy diversifies. Contrary to legend, there are native-born Washingtonians, from the old-money aristocrat whose grandmother used to have tea regularly at the White House to the blue-collar worker whose grandfather used to take the trolley to Griffith Stadium to see Negro League baseball.

CRIMINAL NEGLECT

Since the late 1980s, arguably the second biggest story in the District has been crime. A decade ago, DC had the highest homicide rate in the country, peaking at 489 murders in 1991; the tally has fallen, but it's still running in the vicinity of an unhealthy 300 a year. Only a murder that's particularly sensational or poignant – or involves an affluent or suburban victim – makes the front page. Violent crime, largely drug related, tends to be ghettoised in poor areas, and reducing it seems an intractable problem. With murder presented breathlessly as a ratings booster by local TV news programmes, some local residents simply tune out the issue.

The murder spree started in DC, as elsewhere in the country, with the boom in crack cocaine, which destabilised the existing illegal drug business and offered the sort of profits worth killing your rivals to maintain. The crisis was compounded by the unravelling of the DC police department, which had a good reputation (and an excellent rate for closing murder cases) before it was politicised by Mayor Marion Barry. Under Barry, the force became ineffective and increasingly demoralised. After all, for a few years some police officers apparently had among their duties the task of keeping the mayor from being busted for possession of crack. The murder crime rate also reflects

Washington by numbers

520,000: Approximate population of District 1998
640,000: Approximate population of District 1980
4 million: Population of greater DC area
1 in 1,700: DC residents murdered per year (1 in 21,200: New York City residents murdered per year)
300,000: Approximate number of federal employees
20,000,000: Tourists to DC annually
160: Gallons of liquor distributed to voters of George Washington's district during his first (pre-Revolutionary) run for public office
86: Percentage of Americans who believe George Washington would be disappointed in federal government today
200: Slaves owned by George Washington
2: 'Out' gay Congresspersons: Representatives Barney Frank (Democrat, Massachusetts) and Jim Kolbe (Republican, Arizona)
1: Native Americans in Congress: Senator Ben Nighthorse Campbell, Northern Cheyenne (Republican of Colorado)
4: Republican Congressmen who voted for 1996 Defense of Marriage Act and were later exposed as adulterers
16: *Hustler* subscriptions rejected out of 435 offered to Congress by publisher Larry Flynt
7: Weeks elapsed between DNA tests of President Clinton's and President Jefferson's affairs. Both confirmed
4: Months after Clinton's election that DC legalised heterosexual fellatio
2,446: Estimated dollars per hour candidate must raise to win party presidential nomination
14,442: Dollars per square foot of Lincoln Bedroom donated to Democratic Party by Clinton's overnight guests
71: Percentage of American public that feels Congress spends more time complaining about government that running it
46: Federal agencies whose officers carry arms and have power of arrest
86,442,642: Fingerprints on file with FBI of citizens with no criminal history
1,644: Requests filed daily under federal Freedom of Information Act, as of 1996
22: Protesters who have scaled the White House fence in last ten years
93: Age of Senator Strom Thurmond (Republican of South Carolina) at time of most recent election to Congress
24: Consecutive hours Thurmond filibustered Senate in attempt to block civil rights legislation in 1957. Longest filibuster on record
3,000: Cases appealed to Supreme Court annually
150: Cases accepted by Supreme Court annually
20,000: Silver teaspoons at Washington Hilton
400,000: Dollars spent by World Bank in 1997 to gild ceilings of DC headquarters
4: Terms Marion Barry served as Mayor of the District
6: Months Barry served for cocaine charges
2: Times Barry's mother-in-law ran for president
4: Zip codes in the Pentagon
26,000,000: Books in Library of Congress
1,000,000: Jokes donated to Library of Congress by Bob Hope

the city's proximity to Virginia, whose lax gun control laws make it the prime East Coast source of guns used to commit crimes.

Though the situation is serious, it is in part a demographic anomaly. Washington is far smaller than most US cities, and most of the metro area's residents live outside its borders. The city serves as the region's centre for vice – drugs, prostitution, alcohol and associated offences – but the per capita crime rate is factored against Washington's official population (which even the Census Bureau concedes is understated). Excluded from the calculations are the hundreds of thousands of people who enter the city every day to work and play. (The majority of people arrested in the city for drunk driving, for example, are not DC residents.)

WHICH WAY WASHINGTON?

'Make no little plans,' said Daniel Burnham, one of the architects of the 1902 McMillan Plan that refashioned central Washington. Accordingly, in 1996 the National Capital Planning Commission released a grand 21st-century plan for the city, which would elevate some of its poorer areas by creating new parks and boulevards in emulation of the National Mall.

Although this scheme would be a boon to organisations seeking sites for new memorials, it spectacularly misses the point. As millions of visitors to the capital of the United States discover every year, Washington's monumental core is quite striking. Other aspects of the city, however, still need some work.

Government in Action

How the theory of government behaves in the Washington laboratory.

DEMOCRATS & REPUBLICANS

US politics is based on a two-party system, with neither party possessing a clear-cut ideology. Broadly speaking, the Democratic Party is what passes for the left of the political spectrum, traditionally perceived as the friend of the common man and the advocate of activist government; the Republican Party stands to the right, the representative of social conservatism, big business and small government.

The Democratic Party originated in the earliest days of the republic, when Thomas Jefferson and James Madison rallied agrarian interests and a nascent working class in opposition to the aristocratic tendencies of Alexander Hamilton and the merchant class. The Republican Party traces its roots to Abraham Lincoln's anti-slavery alliance of Northern industrialists and Midwestern farmers.

While party workers and officials may have ideological tendencies, the mass of voters are drawn to one or the other chiefly on the basis of self-interest, single issues or simple family tradition. The need for compromise among the two parties' various internal factions is one reason both groups end up more similar than not. It was George Wallace, Alabama's die-hard segregationist governor, who remarked, in frustration, that 'there ain't a dime's worth of difference between the two'.

Parties are nationwide but their real strength rests in the individual state party organisations. Political candidates usually work their way up the ladder of office from local to national, though individuals with sufficient fame (often military) have leapfrogged the process. The party system arose completely outside governmental regulation, though laws regarding their structure and function were gradually adopted.

Organised party power reached its peak in the period from the Civil War to World War II. That was when big-city political bosses and state party organisations had firm control of the spoils of victory, chiefly jobs on the public payroll and influence over judicial and regulatory decisions. Reform movements gradually put an end to this source of party discipline, however, and party loyalty has shown a steady decline. Most Americans now forego party affiliation entirely and identify themselves as political independents.

Interest groups wield increasing power.

INTEREST GROUPS

The development of modern telecommunications has democratised the possibility of mass organisation, so identity and interest group politics have come to the fore. Ethnic minorities, women's and gay rights' groups, environmentalists and organised labour provide the hardcore of support for the Democratic Party. The Republicans are based around an uneasy alliance of social conservatives and economic libertarians. Rightwing Christian groups, chiefly fundamentalist Protestants, are especially strong in the Republican Party. These groups function both as individual caucuses within the parties and as pressure groups outside them. The demonisation of 'special interests' is a recurring feature of American political rhetoric, but the definition of the common good is an elusive thing in such a complex society. Every significant issue in American life today has advocacy organisations with conflicting public policy solutions.

Interest groups attempt to influence government action through a variety of methods. These include petitions, letters and email from the general membership, advertising and public relations campaigns and, in the judicial arena, lawsuits. Most organisations also maintain Washington offices whose job it is to appeal directly to individual legislators and their staffs, testify at committee hearings and cultivate the press.

Interest groups cover the broadest swathe of policy through the quasi-academic institutions known as think-tanks, which generally reflect an overall ideological orientation. Some occasionally tend to the left – such as the Brookings Institute, which G Gordon Liddy offered to firebomb on behalf of the Nixon administration – but most are on the political right, such as the Heritage Foundation, from which the Reagan administration lifted its policy programme practically in full.

LOBBYISTS

The effort to tilt policy and influence legislation has spawned another peculiarly Washington figure: the lobbyist. These freelance political operatives work on behalf of industry trade groups, individual corporations and foreign nations, in addition to traditional political organisations. As of 1997, an estimated 11,500 lobbyists worked the suites of Washington, DC, spending some $1.26 billion annually – the equivalent of 21 lobbyists and $2.4 million per Congressperson. Over 200 organisations spent at least $1 million each; 41 of those organisations spent at least $5 million and eight spent $10 million or more.

If the cost of lobbying seems high, the potential rewards are enormous. The tobacco industry, for example, spent $38 million on lobbying in 1997, but the payoff was the defeat of legislation that would have cost them billions in court settlements.

Watching the lawmakers

Both houses of Congress have visitors' galleries that are free and open to the public during whatever hours the house meets. Congress is in session 11 months of the year, with a midsummer break in August and recesses at Easter, Christmas, Thanksgiving and election time (early November). For information on obtaining the requisite gallery pass, see the US Capitol listing on page 51. Seating is allocated on a first-come, first-served basis, so arrive early for contentious hearings.

A US flag flies over the building of whatever chamber is in session and a light glows in the Capitol dome when either meets at night. The most floor activity occurs towards the end of legislative sessions and at the approach of holidays, when there's a rush to finish old business.

Each day's session begins at 9 or 10am, with a ringing of bells in the Capitol. Lights and bells throughout the building announce votes and quorum calls. Both houses open with prayers from their respective chaplains, followed by short speeches from the Majority and Minority Leaders in the Senate, and 'One Minute Speeches' by designated representatives in the House.

In both houses, members' remarks must be addressed to the presiding officer of the chamber: the vice president or his replacement in the case of the Senate, the speaker or his replacement in the case of the House. Members sit grouped by party affiliation on the floor of the House and by individually assigned seats in the Senate. Both chambers have a complicated arrangement of desks below their rostrums, where clerks take minutes, parliamentarians advise on procedures and the two parties' secretarial staffs keep members up to date on proceedings. To either side of the rostrum, stand pages, students in the last years of high school who work as legislators' messengers.

If the chambers appear surprisingly empty while measures are debated, it's because most of the work of legislation is accomplished in committee meetings. These are open to the public, too, though it's advisable to show up early for the more contentious hearings. Senate committees meet in the Russell, Dirksen and Hart Senate Office Buildings, which are connected to the Capitol by subway. House committees meet in the House office buildings across Independence Avenue from the Capitol.

For schedule information for both houses and all committees, consult *Washington Post*'s 'Today in Congress' panel. There are also detailed listings on the House of Representatives website (www.house.gov), the Senate website (www.senate.gov) and also at the website http://thomas.loc.gov.

In your face: television has become a crucial part of the political process.

These hired guns have become so critical to the political process that they've been dubbed the 'Kings of K Street' (for the corridor many of their offices occupy). And because so much of the lobbyist's work depends on access to government officials, the most powerful firms are peppered with former officials who have passed through the 'revolving door'. Former Senate Majority Leaders Bob Dole and George Mitchell, who came from opposite sides of the political aisle, now serve the firm of Verner, Llipfert, Bernhard, McPherson & Hand as advocates for the nation of Taiwan. Former Republican Party Chairman Haley Barbour works for Microsoft, as well as an alliance of tobacco companies, at the firm of Barbour, Griffith and Rogers. Former White House Chief of Staff Ken Duberstein runs a firm whose clients include General Motors and the Wall Street house of Goldman, Sachs.

The lobbyist's ability to open doors also stems from his or her involvement in the fundraising process. Many firms have political action committees (PACs; *see page 21* **Campaign finances**) of their own and the principals of most firms make significant financial contributions to individual campaigns. 'Rainmakers' bring their talents to firms such as the Dutko Group, where former top Democratic money man Daniel Dutko serves as DC liaison for several Silicon Valley companies, while legendary fundraiser JD Williams fronts for outfits such as Coca-Cola and JP Morgan through the offices of Williams and Jensen.

Effective lobbying requires political smarts as well as simple access and fundraising prowess. Carefully crafted position statements from full-time propagandists are an easy out for overburdened officials, for whom lobbyists also serve as freelance political strategists and researchers. While groups with mass memberships – such as the National Rifle Association and the American Association of Retired Persons – can stimulate genuine 'grassroots' action, lobbyists have perfected a kind of pseudo-grassroots technique. 'Astroturf' uses databases and phone banks to identify supporters on particular issues and, charging their clients so much per call, patches them through to Congressional offices at critical junctures in the legislative process.

THE MEDIUM IS THE MESSAGE

The ubiquity of mass media has altered the political equation from the top down. It has enabled individuals with deep pockets and political ambitions to buy their way into the public arena, with or without party support. The 1996 campaign for the Republican presidential nomination saw candidate Steve Forbes rise from zero recognition to a national presence behind a flood of advertising dollars. That same year the transplanted California millionaire Michael Huffington nearly defeated a sitting Democratic senator on the strength of a $20-million media barrage. Ross Perot linked his war chest to a vein of populist discontent and created a new party from scratch.

The gradual assimilation of American politics into the morass of electronic media has come to be called the 'National Entertainment State', the bastard offspring of technology and democracy. This process began with Franklin D Roosevelt's weekly radio addresses, the 'fireside chats'. In the post-war years, public opinion relied chiefly on the major TV networks' evening news broadcasts. Dwight Eisenhower initiated regular, televised news conferences, in which he submitted to questioning from the press. John F Kennedy lent the practice a touch of wit and sophistication, but subsequent presidents fared less well.

Later administrations avoided the uncertainties of spontaneous cross-examination and turned from the press conference to the never-never land of the media event, an approximation of reality in which the setting is carefully chosen and the audience throughly screened. Bill Clinton's well-publicised walk on the Normandy beaches on the 50th anniversary of D-Day is a prime example.

An alternative method of dealing with the press is the 'Rose Garden' strategy, in which the candidate simply stays home. The 1984 Reagan re-election effort, for instance, forswore public appearances in favour of the 'Morning In America' TV advertising campaign, which consisted of little more than reassuring tableaux of amber waves of grain and no substantive discussion of issues whatsoever. The Gipper won in a landslide.

The present juncture holds a world of 24-hour TV news channels, round-the-dial (chiefly rightwing) talk radio and factoid rumour-mongering on the Internet. The speed and pervasiveness of electronic news has forced the hand of more traditional sources such as the *New York Times* and the *Washington Post*. The inescapable prominence of even an unconfirmed rumour in tabloids such as Rupert Murdoch's *Star* or Matt Drudge's online gossip mill becomes news in itself. This hall of mirrors reached dizzying proportions during the Lewinsky scandal, when the story became the intensity of the story.

SPIN CYCLE

At this political pole where the media sun never sets, the campaign goes on for ever. The consequence is that every politician of ambition, and the president most of all, counts among his closest consultants the professional media advisers known as 'spin doctors', who practise 'spin control'. It is the duty of these spin doctors to 'frame the issue' and

Campaign finances

Washington's leading political party is the green party – long green. Because of the enormous cost of campaigning, chiefly due to the expense of TV advertising, a typical run for the Senate today can easily require $10 million, while House races, too, often run into the millions. Consequently, the major complaint of Washington's political figures is the amount of time they're forced to spend raising money – and that of Washington observers is that the pursuit has corrupted the political process.

There is extensive federal regulation of contributions, but there is also a continual search for new loopholes in such laws. When post-Watergate restrictions placed a $1,000 limit on individual and corporate donations to congressional campaigns, the result was the creation of political action committees, or PACs, which are essentially fronts for more unrestricted funding of candidates. Corporate, union and other interest groups currently sponsor over 4,000 such committees across the Washington landscape.

Later restrictions on PACs led, in turn, to the latest problem, 'soft money'. This is money given to political party organisations rather than directly to individual candidates. Soft money contributions in the 1997-98 presidential election cycle were estimated at nearly $200 million, twice that of 1993-94. Theoretically, these are for the purpose of 'party building', but the fact is that through a number of routes they end up used in support of individual political campaigns. The reform organisation Common Cause refers to this process as the 'soft money laundromat'.

Interest groups and labour unions play this game, but it is corporations that predominate. Of the major corporate donors, high-tech and financial industry firms give fairly equally to the two major parties, while Big Tobacco, collectively the largest single contributor, goes overwhelmingly for the Republican Party. It was in pursuit of soft money that the Clinton administration sponsored endless fat-cat coffee-klatches in the White House sitting rooms and turned the Lincoln Bedroom into a multi-million-dollar B&B.

A recent Supreme Court decision, *Buckley v Valeo*, created another substantial campaign finance loophole by affirming the argument that political money was the equivalent of free speech and abolishing any restrictions on issues advertising. This allowed groups organised around particular issues – such as abortion rights or gun control – to spend unlimited amounts on advertising in support of like-minded candidates, as long as the groups remain formally unaffiliated with the candidates' parties or campaign organisations.

Among other pernicious effects of the current system is the high burnout rate of those politicians scrupulous enough to be sickened by such pandering. And this very effect contributes to the difficulty of reform, since those are the legislators most likely to vote for change. In the meantime, Washington is trapped in a vicious cycle of dependence: who'll be the first to kill the golden goose?

The sausage factory

How legislation is made.

It has been remarked more than once that legislation is like sausage: you may like the end product but you wouldn't want to watch it being made. Some 6,500 bills were proposed in the Congress of 1995-96, of which less than 400 actually became law. Those few bills that make it through Congress's tortuous path usually come out significantly different to how they went in.

Bills can originate in either house (except for revenue bills, which must start in the House). They are introduced under the signature of individual legislators, though they're often drafted by the executive branch or individuals and organisations completely outside government. Bills are numbered, printed, distributed to members and assigned to whatever committee has appropriate jurisdiction. Committee hearings are a period for public comment and expert testimony on the necessity and possible impact of the legislation. This is also the period where lobbyists exert most of their influence.

If passed by committee, a bill goes to the powerful Rules Committee, which assigns the time and rules of its debate on the chamber floor. Here it may be debated, further amended and voted up or down. Voting is usually along party lines, especially in the current (post-Gingrich) contentious era. Both parties have whips in each house. Bills passed by one house go through a nearly identical series of steps in the other. If the second house passes the legislation with amendments, it's returned to the first for re-approval. If the two houses cannot agree on a bill, a conference committee is formed to attempt some reconciliation. If that doesn't work, the bill is dead, though usually some sort of accommodation is reached.

A bill must be passed by both houses to become law. It is then signed by the Speaker of the House and vice president (acting as President of the Senate) and forwarded to the president for his approval. If the president vetoes a bill, it can nevertheless be passed into law by a two-thirds vote of both houses. If the president withholds his signature while Congress is in session, it becomes law by default after ten days. If he withholds it and Congress adjourns before ten days expire, the bill dies by 'pocket veto'.

'set the terms of debate'. Is abortion about 'the right to life' or 'freedom of choice'? Is trade with China 'constructive engagement' or 'kowtowing to dictators'? The spin doctor's ultimate prescription is the soundbite, the ear-catching phrase that encapsulates an argument with enough force and precision to rise above the din and sway the mind.

This black art is practised with the tools first perfected in the market research divisions of Madison Avenue. Scientific polling methods assess the mood of the target audience. 'Focus groups' of average Americans are formed to determine their reaction to various presentations of public issues. Journalists are courted with promises of access and threats of its denial.

The chief visible administrators of spin are the press spokesmen of the various cabinet agencies and, preeminently, the president's Press Secretary, though it occasionally happens that other figures capture the spotlight, usually as hatchetmen. Nixon's Vice-President Spiro Agnew filled this role with alliterative attacks on anti-war advocates; Clinton aide James Carville with a Louisiana drawl and barbed, down-home witticisms.

The preeminent public forum for Washington spin is the Sunday morning TV talk shows, where Congressional leaders and presidential emissaries go to make their case to the public and submit to questioning from the press. Viewers suffer the conventional wisdom of the shows' panels of journalists, collectively known as the 'punditocracy', but Washington provides no other regular occasion where one can see public officials cross-examined by the press. Long-established major network programmes such as *Meet the Press* and *Face the Nation* take a civilised, restrained approach; cable shows such as *Hardball* and *The McLaughlin Group* tend to devolve into free-swinging shouting matches, or 'food fights'.

The leading lights of the Washington press corps have so much time in the spotlight they've become as famous and powerful as the politicians they cover. If the average American lacks trust in a media that has lost touch with life outside the Beltway, the multi-million dollar contracts of 'celebrity journalists' such as Sam Donaldson and Cokie Roberts may have something to do with it.

The American revulsion with the Washington media circus is symptomatic of a cynicism in the body politic that threatens the whole system. The most revealing fact about American politics today is the steady decline in citizen participation in the political process. And when a smaller percentage of American citizens exercises their right to vote than any other industrial nation's, it's clear that democracy there stands in need of renewal.

Architecture

Washington's birthright as a seat of government is reflected in its grand streetplan and predominantly neoclassical architecture.

Washington's two best-known buildings are the US Capitol and the White House, which symbolise American government and, specifically, Congress and the president. That's not all they represent, however. They also exemplify the city's dedication to a formal, traditional (and low-rise) style that's at odds with the look of most American cities. Despite some forays into modernism, the practice of architecture in Washington is an ongoing debate about neoclassicism.

Although Washington was the first major Western capital to be designed from scratch, it never occurred to its founders to build a city free of classical precedents. Indeed, such self-taught architects as presidents George Washington and Thomas Jefferson believed that a style derived from democratic Athens and republican Rome was the only proper one for a country beginning a bold new experiment in representative government. But there was also another reason for the grand vistas of Pierre-Charles L'Enfant's baroque street plan and the imposing marble structures built for the president and Congress: they were meant to convey a sense of permanence in a city – and a country – that in its early days seemed a bit wobbly. (*See page 8* **The L'Enfant Plan**.)

Ten storeys and counting...

Washington's low-slung skyline isn't accidental. In 1791, President George Washington and Thomas Jefferson formidably teamed to regulate the new federal city's appearance – with scant success. They sought to limit building heights to no lower than 35 feet to the roof on avenues, no higher than 40 feet elsewhere. Nonetheless, the city's first 'skyscraper', an eight-storey sugar refinery on South Capitol Street at the Anacostia River, promptly disrupted the aesthetics.

A century later, the 1894 Cairo Hotel (1615 Q Street, NW), now a collection of condominiums, shocked the city into action. Its 12 storeys dwarfed neighbouring townhouses, exceeded the reach of fire ladders and allowed roof-garden pranksters to toss pebbles on to the street, panicking horses. Congress passed the Building Heights Act in 1899, allowing structures of 90 feet on residential streets, 110 feet on commercial ones, effectively a 'Ten-Storey Limit'.

The skyline inched upwards through a loophole in the 1910 Height Limit Act that permitted an extra 20 feet on wider streets (Pennsylvania Avenue gets 20 more); another loophole allowed set-back rooftop utility housings, thus keeping real-estate attorneys well fed thereafter. In 1992, a newspaper architectural critic could note 'a proliferation of towers, campaniles, colonnades and domes… atop downtown office buildings whose height is otherwise stringently regulated by law'.

Between legislation and odd-shaped lots dictated by the L'Enfant Plan, the capital forces architectural ingenuity. To achieve its signature soaring atrium in this context, the Hyatt hotel chain has had to adapt. No room in the Hyatt Regency (400 New Jersey Avenue, NW; 737 1234) is exactly rectangular – and in order to soar, it plunges underground, with steep escalators from the street descending some three storeys to the lobby. The later Grand Hyatt (1000 H Street, NW; 582 1234) follows suit, even more elaborately.

The building at 1310 G Street, NW, rose to 13 storeys when the developer promised to link it with an existing structure on wider 13th Street – which he promptly tore down. After flirting with demolition of the excess floors, authorities settled for mandating a lower building on the vacant site 'to put a stop to this sort of artifice'.

Congress casts a protective eye on Washington's skyline – even beyond DC. When a 52-storey monolith was proposed for Oxon Hill, Maryland, where I-95 crosses the Potomac River, influential senators snarled and the project wilted, not because the solons had jurisdiction (they didn't), but because their displeasure frightened financiers. Old DC isn't going to look like Manhattan soon – or ever.

FIRST BUILDINGS

The city's oldest buildings were actually built before Washington's founding. The river ports of Georgetown and Alexandria existed prior to their incorporation into the District of Columbia, and they contain most of the area's examples of eighteenth-century architecture. The city's only surviving pre-Revolutionary War structure is Georgetown's **Old Stone House** (3051 M Street, NW; 426 6851) – a modest 1765 cottage with a pleasant garden, it's a National Park Service site. Much of Georgetown has the feel of a colonial-era village, but most of its structures date from the nineteenth and early twentieth centuries. Some are in the Federal style – a common early nineteenth-century American mode that adds such classical elements as columns, pediments and porticoes to vernacular structures usually made of brick or wood – but many are Victorian.

Across the river in the Old Town district of Alexandria, which was once but is no longer part of DC, there are some larger pre-Revolutionary structures, including **Carlyle House** (121 North Fairfax Street; 703 549 2997), **Gadsby's Tavern Museum** (134 North Royal Street; 703 838 4242) and **Christ Church** (118 North Washington Street; 703 549 1450), a Georgian-style edifice where George Washington was a vestryman. Like Georgetown, however, most of Old Town is of nineteenth- and twentieth-century vintage.

Further south is George Washington's plantation, **Mount Vernon** (at the south end of George Washington Memorial Parkway; 703 780 2000), now a museum about Washington and the life of colonial-era gentry. This Georgian estate (including a dozen outbuildings) is one of the finest extant examples of an eighteenth-century American plantation. Next to Arlington National Cemetery is **Arlington House** (also known as the Lee-Custis House; 703 557 0613), a neoclassical mansion that was once the home of another Virginia aristocrat, Confederate general Robert E Lee.

Washington's two most metonymic structures, the White House and the Capitol, were both first occupied in 1800 and have both been substantially remodelled and expanded since. James Hoban was the original architect of the **White House** (1600 Pennsylvania Avenue, NW), but Thomas Jefferson, who lost the competition to design what was originally called simply the President's House, tinkered with the plans while in residence during 1801-09; the most significant additions were new monumental north and south porticoes, designed in 1807 by Benjamin Latrobe but not built until the 1820s. Many additions followed, with some of the more recent ones (for offices and security equipment) out of sight. The structure got its current name after it was whitewashed to cover damage from being burned in 1814 by British troops, although the sandstone façade was first whitewashed in 1797, while still under construction. Inevitably, the White House has become a visual metaphor for Washington and the presidency.

The **US Capitol**, at the centre of the city's grid, has grown even more dramatically from William Thornton's modest original design. Since

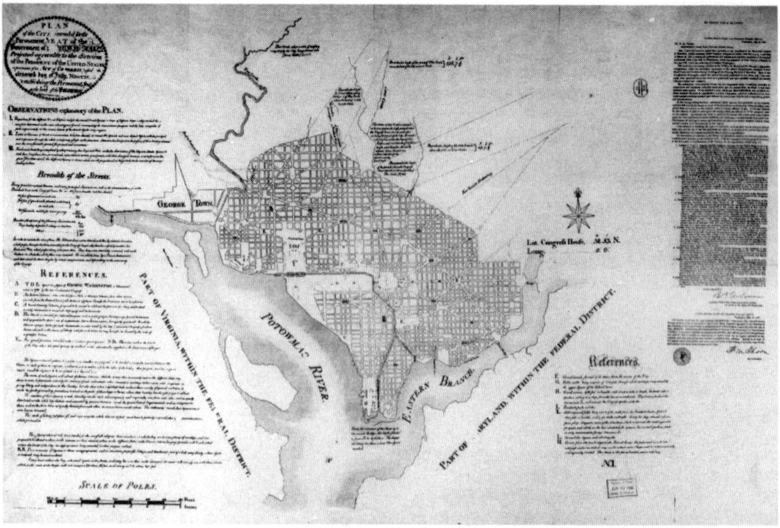

The 1792 **L'Enfant Plan** *determined Washington's distinctive street layout.*

Searching for a memorial style

Compared to many countries, the United States of America hasn't had much history. That, however, hasn't prevented its capital from filling up with monuments and memorials.

Strictly speaking, Washington isn't full of memorials. It's only the most prestigious monumental real estate that's close to being crowded. Every committee raising funds for a new memorial wants a piece of the western half of the Mall, which is defined by such well-known civic shrines as the Washington Monument, the Jefferson Memorial, the Lincoln Memorial and the one that started the latest boom, the Vietnam Veterans Memorial. Currently planned are memorials to World War II veterans and Martin Luther King Jr, which will join recent nearby additions honouring Korean War veterans and Franklin Delano Roosevelt Jr.

Ironically, FDR asked to be remembered only by a modest stone marker, which was dutifully installed outside the National Archives in 1965. The greatest presidents have traditionally been honoured with major structures, frequently in the style of Greco-Roman temples. Lesser figures, often generals and admirals, were usually honoured with straightforward equestrian statues; the monument to Admiral Dupont in his namesake circle is more fanciful, however, with three figures symbolising oceanic exploits clustered around a fountain.

The last of the major traditional war memorials is the United States Marine Corps War Memorial (commonly called the Iwo Jima Memorial), across the river in Arlington. Based on a staged photo of a triumphant World War II flag-raising, the 78-foot-high statue was recently described as 'kitsch' by J Carter Brown, chairman of the city's Commission on Fine Arts. That a taste for such kitsch has not vanished was soon revealed by the outcry over Brown's remark.

A turning point in Washington monument building seemed to come with the dedication of the Vietnam Veterans Memorial in 1982. The memorial (widely known as 'The Wall'), designed by then-21-year-old student Maya Ying Lin, is a simple black marble 'V' engraved with the names of all the country's Vietnam casualties. It was denounced before its opening by both architectural and political conservatives, but was quickly embraced by the war's veterans. Today it is one of the city's most-visited sites.

However, despite the popularity of the Vietnam memorial's widely imitated modern design, pressure for a more traditional approach led to the addition of a statue of three soldiers. This compromise foreshadowed the 1987 US Navy Memorial, whose focus is a plaza engraved with a global map and surrounded by a fountain, but which includes a statue of a sailor. Similarly, the 1997 FDR Memorial features fountains and inscriptions in a series of four outdoor 'rooms', but also includes ten bronze likenesses of Roosevelt. Even more literal is the 1995 Korean War Veterans Memorial, whose sculpture of 19 soldiers on patrol is less heroic than the Iwo Jima Memorial but just as kitschy.

The National Park Service has announced that new territory for national memorials must be found, and the National Capital Planning Commission's highly conjectural scheme for the next century includes extending the city's 'monumental core' by redoing scruffy South Capitol Street as a broad, green boulevard. Wherever the twenty-first century's monuments are constructed, the dispute between traditional and modern forms is sure to continue.

the cornerstone was laid in 1793, virtually every visible part of the structure has been replaced, from the dome to the east and west façades. The last major renovation of the exterior was done in 1987, and new underground office areas were added in 1991. Despite its grander scale, the Capitol remains true to the original neoclassical conception, with Corinthian columns making the case that the building is a temple to democracy.

Other buildings that survive from the Federal period are less august, although one of them takes a singular form. Built in 1800 as the city home of the prosperous Tayloe family, the **Octagon** (1799 New York Avenue, NW; 638 3221) gives a distinctive shape to the Federal style. Actually a hexagon with a semi-circular portico, the house was designed by Capitol architect Thornton.

Both the **Sewall-Belmont House** (144 Constitution Avenue, NE; 546 3989) and **Dumbarton Oaks** (1703 32nd Street, NW; 339 6400) are fine examples of the Federal style, although they've been much altered since they were built in, respectively, 1790 and 1801. (The earliest part of Sewall-Belmont House dates to about 1750.) Dumbarton Oaks is most notable for its elegant gardens and its scenic location on the edge of Rock Creek Park. All three structures are now museums.

Washington's first business district developed around the intersection of Pennsylvania Avenue and Seventh Street, NW, and there are still some examples of pre-Civil War vernacular architecture in this area. The buildings near the intersections of Seventh Street with Indiana Avenue, E Street and H Street in nearby Chinatown all offer examples of the period. Also noteworthy is the 500 block of Tenth Street, NW, whose most imposing structure is **Ford's Theatre** (511 Tenth Street, NW; 426 6924), site of Abraham Lincoln's assassination. Built in 1863, its interior is of historic interest and houses the Lincoln Museum.

The government buildings erected in the first half of the nineteenth century generally adhered to the Greek Revival style, which modelled itself on such Athenian edifices as the Parthenon, rediscovered by European architects in the mid-eighteenth century. Two of these structures, the **Patent Office** and the **Tariff Commission Building**, face each other at Seventh and F Streets, NW. Both are early examples of the city's official style – also known in the US and especially in DC as Neo-Grec – and both were designed at least in part by Robert Mills, who's best known for the Washington Monument. The Patent Office, which has housed the National Portrait Gallery and the National Museum of American Art, is currently closed for renovation, while the Tariff Commission Building is being converted to hotel use.

Mills also designed the **US Treasury Building** (15th Street and Pennsylvania Avenue, NW; 622 0896), with its 466-foot Ionic colonnade along 15th Street. In the first major divergence from the L'Enfant Plan, this edifice was placed directly east of the White House, thus blocking the symbolic vista between the building and the Capitol. Construction began in 1836 and wasn't completed until 1871, but that's speedy compared to the progress of Mills's **Washington Monument**. Started in 1845, it was completed (after a 20-year break due to lack of funds) in 1884. The highest structure in the world at its completion, the 600-foot monument is unusually stark by the standards of nineteenth-century Washington architecture. That's because the colonnaded base of Mills' plan was never built, leaving only a tower modelled on an Egyptian obelisk.

Other notable examples of the pre-Civil War era are **St John's Church** (1525 H Street, NW; 347 8766), designed in 1816 by Benjamin Latrobe, the architect of the Capitol's first expansion, but subsequently much altered; **Judiciary Square** (Fourth and F Streets, NW), which was Washington's original City Hall; and the modest but elegant Georgetown **Custom House & Post Office** (1221 31st Street, NW), derived from Italian Renaissance palazzos and typical of small US government buildings of the period.

The **Metro** *system: successful modernism.*

AFTER THE CIVIL WAR

The more exuberant styles that flourished after the Civil War are presaged by the first Smithsonian Institution building (1000 Jefferson Drive, SW; 357 2700), designed by James Renwick in 1846. Its red sandstone suits the turreted neo-medieval style, which has earned it the nickname **The Castle**. Fifteen years later, Renwick designed the original building of the Corcoran Gallery, now the **Renwick Gallery** (17th Street and Pennsylvania Avenue, NW; 357 2700). Modelled loosely on the Louvre, it is considered the first major French-inspired building in the US. The Renwick is a compatible neighbour to a more extravagant Second Empire structure, the **Old Executive Office Building** (17th Street and Pennsylvania Avenue, NW). The lavish interior of the building, originally the State, War and Navy Building, is open to tours by appointment on Saturdays; call 395 5895.

The Civil War led directly to the construction of the Pension Building, designed by Montgomery Meigs in 1882 to house the agency that paid stipends to veterans and their families. Now the **National Building Museum** (Fifth and F Streets, NW; 272 2448), this structure was based on Rome's Palazzo Farnese, but is twice the size. Outside is a frieze that depicts advancing Union Army troops; inside is a massive courtyard, featuring the world's largest Corinthian columns. The atrium was once essential to one of the building's marvels, its highly efficient passive ventilation system, now supplanted by air-conditioning.

Eero Saarinen's much-copied gull-wing design for **Dulles Airport**, *built in the 1960s.*

The Old Executive Office Building and the Pension Building were disparaged by both classicists and modernists, who often proposed razing them. Equally unpopular was the **Old Post Office** (1100 Pennsylvania Avenue, NW; 289 4224), which now houses shops, restaurants and offices. The 1899 building is an example of the Romanesque Revival, which adapted the rounded arches, dramatic massing and grand vaults of eleventh- and twelfth-century Northern European cathedrals. The structure contrasts with its Federal Triangle neighbours, all built in a more sedate style in the 1920s, and was threatened with demolition in the '20s and again in the 1960s. The battle to save the building from the latter threat led to the founding of a citizens' group, Don't Tear It Down, which evolved into the less confrontational DC Preservation League.

Second Empire, Romanesque Revival and other ornate styles are still well represented in the Logan Circle, Dupont Circle, Sheridan Circle and Kalorama Triangle areas. Many palatial mansions were built in these areas in the late nineteenth and early twentieth centuries, and some survive as embassies, museums and private clubs. Among the ones that are open to the public are the **Heurich Mansion**, now the headquarters of the Historical Society of Washington, DC (1307 New Hampshire Avenue, NW; 785 2068); the **Phillips Collection** (1600 21st Street, NW; 387 2151); and **Anderson House** (2118 Massachusetts Avenue, NW; 785 2040), home to the Society of the Cincinnati, a group founded by Revolutionary War veterans.

One of the city's most remarkable architectural fantasies is the **Scottish Rite Temple** (1733 16th Street, NW; 232 3579), finished in 1915 and modelled on the mausoleum at Halicarnassus, one of the seven wonders of the ancient world. It was designed by John Russell Pope, later the architect of some of the city's most prominent buildings. His work includes the **National Archives** (Pennsylvania Avenue and Seventh Street, NW; 501 5000), the neoclassical temple that holds the country's most fundamental documents.

The Archives is the tallest structure erected during Washington's first massive urban renewal project, which during the 1920s converted one of the city's most notoriously dangerous precincts into the government office district known as the Federal Triangle. The massive structures that made up the Triangle provided the headquarters for most of the executive-branch departments, and reiterated the federal government's preference for classicism. The project, which stretches from Sixth to 15th Streets between Pennsylvania and Constitution Avenues, NW, was interrupted by the Depression, and its completion was then debated for 50 years. Finally the government committed to a design for the final structure, the **Ronald Reagan Building** (14th Street and Pennsylvania Avenue, NW), a hulking mediocrity that opened in 1998. It too is in classical drag, albeit with some tricky angles to show that it's the work of the prominent architectural firm of Pei Cobb Freed.

Pope went on to design several more neoclassical temples, including the 1941 original (now called West) building of the **National Gallery of Art** (Constitution Avenue, between Fourth and Seventh Streets, NW; 737 4125) and the 1943 **Jefferson Memorial** (East Basin Drive, SW; 426 6841). The latter is partially derived from Rome's Pantheon, while its 1922 predecessor, the **Lincoln Memorial** (23rd Street, between Constitution and Independence Avenues, NW; 426 6841), is modelled on Athens' Parthenon.

These contemplative edifices' bustling cousin is **Union Station** (50 Massachusetts Avenue, NE), the 1908 structure whose Daniel Burnham design borrows from two Roman landmarks, the Arch of Constantine and the Baths of Diocletian. Other notable neoclassical structures of the period are the 1928 **Freer Gallery of Art** (Jefferson Drive, at 12th Street, SW; 357 4880) and the 1932 **Folger Shakespeare Library** (201 East Capitol Street, SE; 544 7077), an example of Paul Cret's art deco-influenced 'stripped classicism'.

THE ARRIVAL OF MODERNISM

Modernism arrived in Washington after World War II, but it couldn't get comfortable. Modernist notions of design and planning were applied to another urban-renewal project, the New Southwest, with awkward results. They also produced the nearby **L'Enfant Plaza**, a massive office, hotel and retail complex (bordered by Independence Avenue, Ninth Street and various freeway approaches); its masterplan was the first of several bad Washington designs by IM Pei, later one of the namesakes of Pei Cobb Freed. This ironically named assault on the L'Enfant Plan was followed by many stark, bleak buildings in Southwest, most of which were rented to the federal government.

IM Pei's striking **National Gallery** *wing.*

In the 1960s and 1970s, modernist architects designed some of the city's least popular structures, including the **J Edgar Hoover FBI Building** (935 Pennsylvania Avenue, NW; 324 3447), a brutalist, poured-concrete fortress finished in 1972. Perhaps more damaging to the style's reputation, however, was the profusion of mediocre office buildings in the 'New Downtown' along K Street and Connecticut Avenue, NW. Built with little consideration of Washington's distinctive street plan and without strategies for adapting the Bauhaus-derived American skyscraper style to the city's height limitation, these blank-walled knock-offs look like New York or Chicago office blocks inexplicably stunted at the 12th floor.

Most of these buildings were designed by local architects, but nationally renowned modernists and postmodernists have also done lacklustre work in Washington, including Mies van der Rohe's 1972 black-box **Martin Luther King Jr Memorial Library** (901 G Street, NW; 727 1111) and Marcel Breuer's 1976 precast concrete **Hubert H Humphrey Building** (Second Street and Independence Avenue, SW). Among the major recent disappointments is Michael Graves's 1997 building for the **World Bank's International Finance Corporation** (2121 Pennsylvania Avenue, NW), whose overwhelming size and repetitious façade desperately needs ground-floor shops to break the monotony. As with many institutional buildings erected in Washington since J Edgar Hoover banned retail from the plans for the FBI Building, security concerns precluded any space being open to the unscreened public.

One of modernism's local successes is actually far from the District: **Washington-Dulles International Airport**, designed by Eero Saarinen in 1962 and now being expanded in accord with his widely imitated gull-wing scheme. Others include IM Pei's 1978 **National Gallery of Art East Building** (Fourth Street and Pennsylvania Avenue, NW; 737 4125) and Harry Weese's **Metro** system, which applies the same architectural motifs to all its stations. The latter two designs succeed in part because they're sensitive to their Washington context: the East Building's overlapping triangles play off the trapezoidal plot created by the L'Enfant street plan, while Metro's coffered vaults are simply an extreme example of stripped classicism.

The city's response to modernism is evident in Georgetown, which became a fashionable neighbourhood when it began to be gentrified in the 1930s, and Lafayette Square, which is surrounded

The **National Building Museum** *contains the largest Corinthian columns in the world.*

by Federal-period houses. In the 1960s, when demand for federal office space grew dramatically, it was proposed to replace these houses with new office buildings. The eventual compromise was to erect two large structures just off the square, John Carl Warneke's 1969 **New Executive Office Building** (722 Jackson Place, NW) and **Court of Claims Building** (717 Madison Place, NW), which defer to their older neighbours in form and material, if not in size.

These 'background buildings' set a precedent for design in the city's older districts; several local firms came to specialise in contextual postmodern structures that often incorporated façades of existing buildings. Examples include Shalom Baranes's remake of the **Army-Navy Club** (901 17th Street, NW) and Hartman-Cox's **1001 Pennsylvania Avenue**, NW, both finished in 1987. Such 'façadomys' were widely criticised, especially when the new construction dwarfed the historic component: one conspicuous example of this is **Red Lion Row** (2000 Pennsylvania Avenue, NW), which has been compared to an ocean liner docked behind a string of townhouses.

At first, architects took care to contrast the older structures with modern touches, but in time the style became unabashedly historicist. A prime, if unusually complex, example is Hartman-Cox's **Market Square** (701 and 801 Pennsylvania Avenue, NW), two mirror-image office buildings with apartments on the top floors. From one side, the 1990 structures look like early twentieth-century commercial buildings; on the other, however, a hemicycle of Doric columns faces the Federal Triangle. The nearby area, which was substantially redeveloped in the 1980s, has many other structures in postmodern or historicist styles.

The Downtown building boom imploded around 1990, and when it ended so did the dominance of the Washington historicist school. Money has been flowing into new construction again in the past few years, but no one style now dominates. The 1990s, in fact, have brought a modernist comeback, yielding such striking buildings as Mikko Heikkinen and Markku Komonen's 1994 **Embassy of Finland** (3301 Massachusetts Avenue, NW; 298 5824) and Kohn Pederson Fox's 1997 **World Bank headquarters** (1818 H Street, NW, 202 473 1806). The former is notable for its trellis façade, dramatic atrium and glass-wall overlook of Rock Creek Park; the latter partially disguises its bulk with a white and grey colour scheme, an asymmetrical façade whose detailing suggests heavy machinery and a curved roof that soars 48 feet above the building's 130-foot height limit. (This is legal because the space above the limit is uninhabitable.) Tours of both buildings are by appointment.

Modernism's latest local victory is the June 1999 announcement that Frank Gehry will design a new building for the Corcoran Gallery; early sketches suggest a strong resemblance to the architect's much-discussed Guggenheim Museum in Bilbao, Spain. Still, in Washington classical-revival architecture can never be counted out.

● *Many of the buildings mentioned above feature in more detail in other chapters. Buildings that are listed with phone numbers are open to the public, but not necessarily on a daily basis, so call first.*

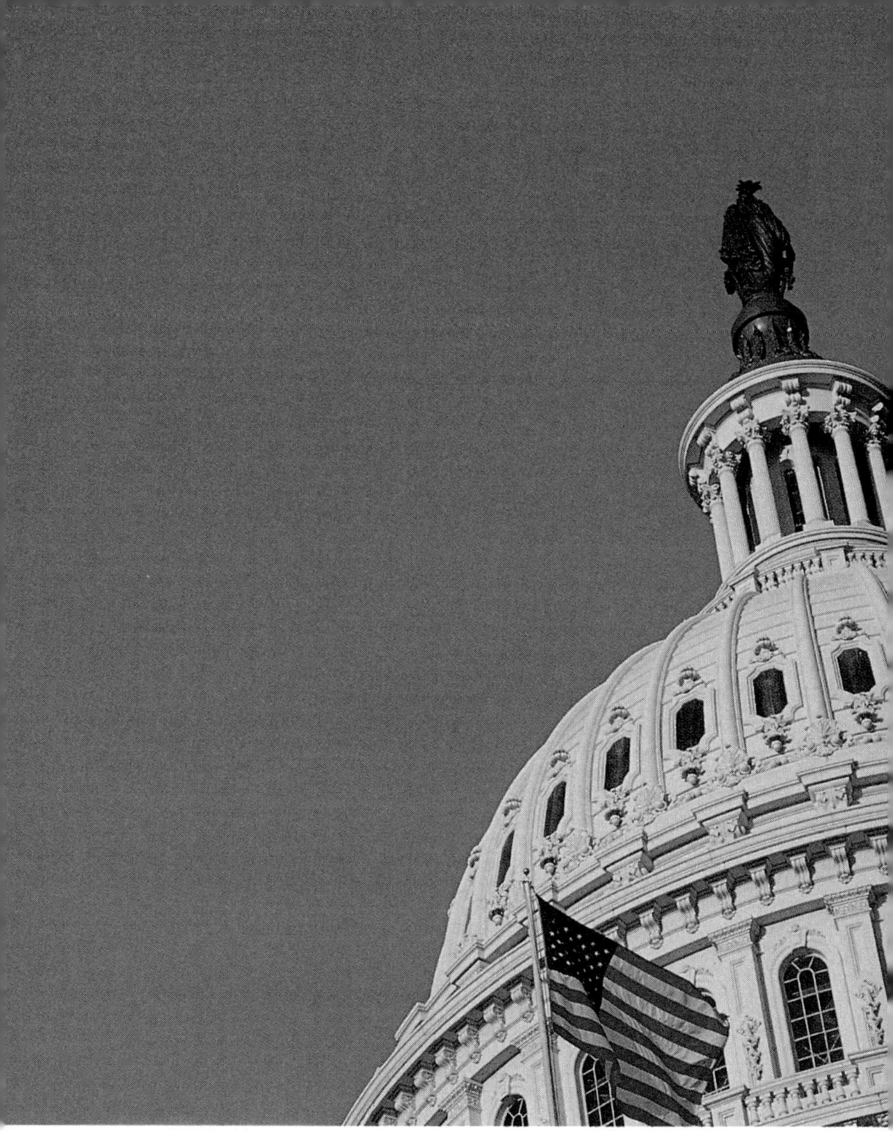

Sightseeing

Tips & Tours

How to get the most out of your visit – and spend the least time waiting in line.

Washington may throw open its arms to around 20 million visitors a year, but its first priority is the business of government. This makes it a distinctly different destination to other tourist towns. On the positive side, they're not in it for the money. Admission is free to the federal institutions, including museums. On the negative side, the exigencies of the local industry are paramount. Visitors experience frequent disruptions, ranging from demonstrations to the temporary closure of parts of the White House and Capitol.

Any terrorist incident affecting the US inspires impetuous restrictions all over town; some solidify into enduring inconveniences, such as the closing of Pennsylvania Avenue near the White House. The demands of simultaneously protecting dozens of heads of state on an occasion such as the recent commemoration of the 50th anniversary of NATO can radically complicate the ordinary visitor's agenda, with streets blocked and Metro stations closed. Prospective visitors are wise to keep up with current events.

Security requirements or limited capacity necessitate reservations, often weeks in advance, for public buildings such as the Treasury and the State Department, and the sheer volume of visitors means that events and exhibitions are often oversubscribed. Ask the **Convention & Visitors Association** (*see page 265*) for a copy of its calendar, which details forthcoming events as far as a year ahead, and book straight away.

The 'book ahead' rule also applies to tours of federal institutions. Though most only issue on-the-day tickets, members of Congress have limited allocations of tickets for 'VIP' guided tours, usually early in the morning, of places such as the White House, the Capitol, the Pentagon and the FBI to constituents who write to them in advance. Visitors on 'Congressionals' may not see much more than those on less-privileged public walk-throughs, but they do get more sleep: lines for the major attractions start to build up at first light at peak times. The ultimate Congressional is an ascent of the Capitol dome, which must be conducted personally by a member of Congress. Aged or portly representatives are unlikely to advertise this little-known perk. Apart from perpetrating a spot of fraud with an American friend, non-US citizens have no way of going VIP (embassies get a small allocation but usually distribute them in-house).

WHERE IT'S AT

DC's planned layout makes taking in the major sights relatively straightforward, with most of the must-see monuments and museums situated on or around the two-mile-long National Mall at the District's heart. These are covered in our **Monumental Centre** chapter, starting on *page 35*. Some institutions overflow into the Downtown area to the north of the Mall, which although lacking the buzz of a more typical city centre, also contains some shops, restaurants and entertainment options. This area is described in **Central DC**, starting on *page 59*.

DC Neighbourhoods, starting on *page 67*, covers the rest of the District, including Dupont Circle (a residential area with an urban feel and buzzing street scene), Adams Morgan (lively and ethnically diverse), the U Street/14th Street corridor (hip, historic and a hub of the African-American community) and, west of the C&O Canal, Georgetown (long on elegance, short on Metro stations). Owing to the ceding of the southwest portion of the original DC diamond, the federal centre extends into Virginia, so Arlington National Cemetery and the Pentagon are included in **Virginia & Maryland**, starting on *page 86*. Our street maps, starting on *page 293*, show these area divisions.

Finding where you need to go is an easy trick to learn once you've mastered a couple of basic rules, owing to DC's logical street-naming system, and getting there is usually a doddle, too. The National Mall and its attendant institutions are on a walkable scale and forays further afield are not a problem given the efficient Metro subway system and relatively low cab fares (driving is not advised). For more information on orientation and transport, *see page 254* **Getting Around**.

Washington is a crime-ridden city, but by and large tourists can ply the monument trail without seeing so much as a jaywalker – the bad stuff goes on in distinct pockets of the neighbourhoods. We have noted any dodgy areas in the relevant chapter, and give general information on crime and personal safety on *page 258*.

For tourist information offices, *see page 265*.

Only in DC: the needle of the Washington Monument viewed from the Lincoln Memorial.

General tours

All About Town
393 3696.
Coach tours with live commentary.

Gold Line/Gray Line Bus Tours
301 386 8300/1-800 862 1400.
Coach-tour circuits with an Arlington link, plus a full roster of in- and out-of-town destinations, including guided interiors tours and an after-dark tour.
Website: www.graylinedc.com

Guide Service of Washington
628 2842.
Call to arrange personal and group tours.

Tourmobile Sightseeing
554 5100.
Narrated tram tours of the major sites around the Mall, as well as Arlington Cemetery, licensed by the National Park service. You can get on at any of the tour stops (marked by blue and white signs), pay on board and hop on and off at will. An all-day ticket costs $16 ($7 3-11s; free under-3s). Tourmobile can accommodate wheelchairs with an hour's notice.
Website: www.tourmobile.com

Washington's Old Town Trolley
832 9800.
Really a bus in twee disguise, offering a similar service to Tourmobile, with some different stops. It's pricier – $24 for adults, $12 ages 4-12, free under-4s – but picks up at more than a dozen hotels. Stops aren't marked, but you can hop on at will. Trolleys run every half-hour and you can only make the circle once. Wheelchair-accessible with 24-hour notice.

Aquatic options

For kayak tours, *see page 224* **Sport & Fitness**.

C&O Canal Barge Rides
1057 Thomas Jefferson Street, at M Street, Georgetown (653 5190).
Leisurely, mule-drawn canal boat rides on the C&O Canal between Georgetown and Great Falls in Maryland. Rides run once a day from April to October and cost $7.50 ($4-$6 concessions).

Dandy Restaurant Cruises
Zero Prince Street, between King & Duke Streets, Alexandria, VA (703 683 6076).
For dinner or lunch cruises ($26-$63 plus taxes) past the monuments, try the *Dandy*, which sails out of Old Town Alexandria year round. Booking advised.

Duck Tours
832 9800/996 3825.
A narrated tour of the monuments in a World War II amphibious vehicle, from the streets to floating the Potomac. The 90-minute tour leaves from the front of Union Station every hour between 10am and 3pm daily (April-Oct only). Tickets cost $24 adults; $12 ages 4-12; free under-4s.

Odyssey Cruises
488 6000.
Lunch and dinner cruises on the Potomac, leaving from Gangplank Marina on Water Street, SW.
Website: www.odyssey-cruises.com

Potomac Riverboat Company
703 684 0580.
DC, Alexandria and Mount Vernon options. From Alexandria Docks, or 31st & K Streets in Georgetown.

Helicopter tours

Capital Helicopters
703 417 2150.
Thirty-mile narrated tours last 20 minutes and take off from the Reagan National Airport. Cost: $95 per person; $60 ages 2-13; free under-2s. You can't fly directly over the Mall for security reasons.

Liberty Helicopter Tours
484 8484/1-800 927 9279.
Breathtaking 15-minute air tour – to RFK stadium, the National Cathedral, plus the monuments – for $84. The heliport is just off Capitol Hill on South Capitol Street, but you can also get on at the Air & Space Museum and Reagan National Airport.

Speciality tours

For bicycle tours, *see page 225* **Sport & Fitness**.

Duke Ellington's DC
636 9203.
Historic half-day coach tours of Shaw, Anacostia, plus the usual monuments and memorials.

Scandal Tour
783 7212.
This 90-minute tour – with costumed performers acting out various scandals – starts at 1pm on Saturdays at the Old Post Office Pavilion (12th Street & Pennsylvania Avenue, NW); tickets are $30.

Walks

Anecdotal History Walks
301 294 9514.
Anthony Pitch, British journalist turned DC historian, gives fascinating, personally narrated walking tours most Sundays from 11am-1pm. Cost: $5-$10.
Website: www.dcsightseeing.com

Discover Historic Downtown DC Tours
639 0908/groups 301 771 5854.
With Discovery Channel, starting at the MCI Center. Tours: 1.30-3pm Sat, Sun. Cost: $7.50; $5 ages 5-18 and seniors; free under-5s. Chinatown vicinity.

Historic Georgetown Tour
301 588 8999.
Ninety-minute tours by happily downshifted attorney Mary Kay Ricks. Cost: $12. Other areas, too.
Website: www.tourdc.com

The Monume
Centre

The civic and cultural heart of the District beats in the august buildings around the National Mall.

The **Washington Monument** *is hidden behind scaffolding until 2000.* *See page 40.*

'New York has total depth in every area. Washington has only politics; after that the second biggest thing is marble.'
Congressman John Lindsay

See **map** page 296.

The Mall & Tidal Basin

Transport

West end: *Foggy Bottom-GWU Metro, then 10-15-minute walk/bus along Constitution or Independence Avenue (many services).*
Central area: *Federal Triangle or Smithsonian Metro.*
East end: *Archives-Navy Memorial, Federal Center or L'Enfant Plaza Metro.*

'If this is the Mall, where are all the stores?' always makes the National Park Service's list of top 10 dumb questions asked by tourists. The term 'Mall' is yet another American steal from Britain: the name adorned the approach to Buckingham Palace in London and was later used to designate any fashionable promenade. The only stores here are the ubiquitous gift shops and snack stands that come with the territory: with more than a dozen

Washington's newest monument, the **Franklin Delano Roosevelt Memorial.**

museums and monuments along its tree-lined expanse, the National Mall is *the* reason for coming to Washington.

The two-mile swathe of green that stretches from 15th Street in the west to the Capitol in the east is the heart – both literally and figuratively – of Washington, DC. Ranged around this proudly public space are the United States' major institutions of government, culture and record and, in its monuments and memorials, the physical manifestations of the identity and experience of a nation. Even locals who wish the term 'tourist season' meant shooting the invaders use the Mall for jogging, picnicking and biking. And the Ellipse, the 54 acres between the White House and the Washington Monument, is marked with rough baseball diamonds, the site of spring and summer softball leagues popular among Congressional staffers and university alumni groups, as well as hockey and football fields. In fact, so sacrosanct is the notion of the US president being able to watch the national game from his balcony that a planned revamp of the area will go out of its way to guarantee the sightlines.

The Mall is also the natural home of national protests and demonstrations, such as the African-Americans' Million Man March in 1995 (*see page 11* **We the people**). And in the summer, the Smithsonian Folklife Festival turns the place into a small-town fair.

The National Mall was an integral part of Washington's original planning blueprint, the L'Enfant Plan (*see chapter* **Architecture**), commissioned by George Washington in 1791 to give the new city an appropriately stately layout. Unfortunately, L'Enfant's designs for the Mall were largely ignored, and wooden office buildings sprang up between the Capitol and the Washington Monument. In 1902, the McMillan Plan reimposed L'Enfant's dictates, and now the National Capital Planning Commission presides over any development – a process that moves with a glacial lack of speed because space on the Mall is so precious.

The Mall from west to east

If you begin at the west end of the Mall, at the imposing, columned **Lincoln Memorial**, to the east is an impressive view of the Reflecting Pool, the needle of the **Washington Monument** and, finally, the Capitol, two miles away. South-east is the circular **Jefferson Memorial**. Washington's newest memorial, the **Franklin Delano Roosevelt Memorial**, is in West Potomac Park, across the cherry tree-rimmed Tidal Basin (paddle-boats for rent; *see chapter* **Sport & Fitness**). In the more immediate vicinity are two war memorials: down the path to the south of the Lincoln Memorial is the slightly neglected but nevertheless powerful **Korean War Veterans Memorial**, and to the north is the V-shaped black wall of the **Vietnam Veterans Memorial**. For more details on all the above monuments, *see below* **Highlights**.

Walking east along Constitution Avenue, the Mall's northern border, there's a closer view of the flag-encircled **Washington Monument**, honouring the Revolutionary War general and first president, who also selected this place as the site of the capital. The small stone building on 17th Street is another reminder of how different the city looks from its early days; it was once a lock-keeper's house on a dirty, disease-ridden canal that ran along the current route of Constitution Avenue.

As you cross 17th Street, to your north rises the **Ellipse**. Formally designated the President's Park South, it was originally swampland that was fenced in and used as corrals during the Civil War. It was the scene of Vietnam protests in the 1960s and early '70s. Today it contains the **Boy Scout Memorial** and the **First Division Monument**, an 80-foot-high memorial to those of the First Division of the US Army who 'gave their lives in the World War'. Atop is a gilded bronze Victory. Two other little-noticed monuments: on the north side of the Ellipse is the **Zero Milestone**, which remains the official marker by which all distances from the capital are measured. The small granite shaft called the **Settlers' Memorial** is a monument to the 18 'original patentees whose land grants embrace the site of the federal city' – in other words, the folks who, however grudgingly, gave their swampland over to a higher cause.

Back on the Mall, past the Washington Monument, and you're into museumland. That turreted red fortress protruding into the park with its carousel is known as the **Smithsonian Castle** (*see page 112* **Museums & Galleries**), which now houses an information centre with maps of the Smithsonian Institution's 16 museums (two are in New York), as well as the crypt for Smithsonian founder James Smithson.

Clustered behind the Castle are the palazzo-like **Freer Gallery** (Asian art), its younger sibling the **Arthur M Sackler Gallery**, the **National Museum of African Art** and the **Arts & Industries Building** (now used as an exhibition space). Between the Sackler and the Museum of African Art is the **Enid Haupt Garden**, which, before the opening of the National Zoo in the nineteenth century, was used as a buffalo pen. Further along are the doughnut-shaped **Hirshhorn** and the modernist marble of the **National Air & Space Museum**, DC's most visited museum, stacked with all manner of returned space hardware. Between here and the Capitol is the site earmarked for the controversial new Museum of the American Indian.

On the north side of the Mall are the plain rectangle of the **National Museum of American History**, the domed **National Museum of Natural History** and the **National Gallery of Art**, also domed and with a fine marble staircase, and finally the geometric lines of the National Gallery's **East Building**, which houses its contemporary collection. Between Seventh and Ninth Streets is the National Gallery's new sculpture garden, which doubles as an ice rink in winter. For more information on all museums, *see chapter* **Museums & Galleries**.

On the far side of the **Capitol Reflecting Pool**, at the foot of Capitol Hill, stands a sprawling sculptural group that includes an equestrian statue of Ulysses S Grant, the Union general who finally won the war for Mr Lincoln. Up the hill is the **US Capitol** itself, whose dome Lincoln insisted be finished during the war as a symbol of the Union's durability (*see below* **The Capitol & around**).

Highlights

Information on all monuments listed below can be found on the National Park Service website at www.nps.gov/nama.

Franklin Delano Roosevelt Memorial

Off West Basin Drive, SW, at the Tidal Basin (426 6841). Smithsonian Metro.

Despite FDR's stated preference for a simple desk-sized memorial slab, which was placed outside the National Archives after his death in 1945, a determined pressure group waged a 42-year campaign – and spent $48 million – for Washington's newest memorial. The consensus is: it's actually worth it.

FDR, who led the country through the Great Depression and World War II and was the only president to serve four terms, is honoured with four spacious outdoor galleries of sculptures, waterfalls and giant stones, engraved with the kind of memorable quotes Bill Clinton is still aiming for. The designer, Lawrence Halprin, sought to use the slabs of red South Dakota granite and water both to symbolise the conflicting grandeur and volatility of FDR's times and to capture his various leadership qualities. For example, the stone wall of the first gallery has the feel of New England fieldstone used at FDR's home in Hyde Park, New York. The second room has, among other things, a waterfall inspired by the Tennessee Valley Authority, part of Roosevelt's New Deal. And look for the statue of Eleanor Roosevelt, the first first lady to be so honoured in a national memorial.

The peaceful monument – open to the sky and dotted with shade trees, it is its own park – belies the controversy behind it. When it was dedicated in March 1997, critics sniped that it didn't show the polio-stricken president as handicapped. Finally, a sculpture of FDR in flowing cloak in a wheelchair – based on one of the only two known photographs of him in the chair – was added. It looks like he's sitting on a throne, and you'll have to look behind him to even see the tiny wheels.

Jefferson Memorial

Southern end of 15th Street, SW, at the Tidal Basin (426 6841). Smithsonian Metro.

Mary Todd Lincoln (Mrs Abe) used to swear she could hear Jefferson's ghost playing the violin in the

The **Korean War Veterans Memorial** *is at its most atmospheric after dark.*

White House's Oval Room. Today, Jefferson is everywhere in Washington, from William Jefferson Clinton to the *Washington Post*, where headlines trumpeted the recent discovery that the Virginian whom America has all but canonised fathered at least one child by his slave mistress. He's in two paintings in the Capitol Rotunda (one presenting the Declaration of Independence, the other witnessing Washington's resignation as Revolutionary commander). There's a dramatic statue of him with pen and parchment in hand by David d'Angers (which was seen in the film *Mr Smith Goes to Washington*). He's in the Library of Congress, where the main building is named after him and contains his private library. His Declaration of Independence is in the National Archives. And he spearheaded the national design contest for the White House in 1792 (his anonymously submitted design lost – no wonder he called the winner's 'a big stone house, big enough for two emperors, one pope and the grand lama in the bargain'). Then there's his memorial, dedicated in 1943, which is a favourite of Washingtonians, particularly in cherry blossom season. Franklin Delano Roosevelt had trees cleared so he could see it from the Oval Office. Like Roosevelt, Jefferson asked for only a small memorial. Instead, John Russell Pope designed an adaptation – sneered at as 'Jefferson's muffin' – of the Roman Pantheon that the architect Jefferson so adored. It also recalls Jefferson's own design for his home, Monticello (*see p239* **Trips Out of Town**), and for the rotunda at what he considered his finest achievement, the University of Virginia.

The white Georgia marble walls surrounding Jefferson's 19-foot likeness – he's addressing the Continental Congress – are inscribed with his enduring writings. For the record, the 92-word quote from the Declaration of Independence contains 11 spelling mistakes and other inaccuracies. Why? Space limitations, a problem Jefferson knew all too well, since his original version was heavily edited and cut by some 500 words.

Korean War Veterans Memorial

West Potomac Park on the Mall, SW, off Independence Avenue (426 6841). Smithsonian Metro.

If the Korean War, lost between the scope of World War II and the upheaval of Vietnam, was the forgotten war, the $18-million Korean War Veterans Memorial was the forgotten monument. Just two years after its 1995 dedication, the fountain had shut down, the pavement was falling and holes replaced the once-green trees. Some repairs have been made, but Park Service rangers only shrug and say the government is still busy pointing fingers when asked about burned-out lights and gaping holes. Which only angers veterans – frequently wearing T-shirts with the monument motto 'Freedom is not Free' – even more. Still, the monument to the 1½ million Americans who fought in this inconclusive, bloody conflict – the first modern war in which the US had to accept a compromise solution in the form of an armistice agreement – is well worth the visit.

It features 19 battle-clad, seven-foot-tall troops slogging across a V-shaped field towards a distant US flag. Fatigue and pain show in the soldiers' finely detailed faces (which are particularly eerie at night); the outlines of full battle packs are visible beneath their ponchos. Why 19 soldiers? Because when they are reflected in the etched granite mural that runs beside them, they become 38 soldiers – in memory of the 38th parallel that separates the two Koreas. To the soldiers' right is a black granite wall, reminiscent of the Vietnam Veterans Memorial, across the Reflecting Pool to the north. But instead of the names of the war dead, the wall at the Korean memorial is a mural sandblasted into rock. Based on real photos of those who served, the mural is a montage of the support troops – drivers and medics, nurses and chaplains – and the equipment they used. Opposite the mural are the names of all the countries that served under the UN command. The field slopes up to a circular 'pool of remembrance'.

Lincoln Memorial

West Potomac Park, 23rd Street, NW, between Constitution & Independence Avenues (426 6841). Smithsonian Metro.

Despite its appearance on the back of the penny and the $5 bill, the Lincoln Memorial is perhaps best known as the site of many public protests and demonstrations. In the 1940s, when the Daughters of the American Revolution barred the African-American singer Marian Anderson from singing in their Constitution Hall, she sang for more than 75,000 people from the steps of the memorial. This was where Martin Luther King Jr gave his 'I have a dream' speech in 1963. And a few months later, President Lyndon Johnson led candle-carrying crowds in ceremonies marking the end of national mourning for John F Kennedy.

After Abraham Lincoln was assassinated in 1865, it took more than 50 years of hot dispute before a decision was made about what kind of memorial should be built in his honour, and where. Finally, in 1911, Henry Bacon's classic design was chosen (over suggestions that included a triumphal arch and even a memorial highway from Washington to Gettysburg).

Statistics don't prepare visitors for the drama of the monument, yet another that's most striking at night. The 'cage' surrounding Lincoln has one Doric column for each of the 36 states in the Union at the time of his death. The man himself – sculpted of Georgia marble on a pedestal of Tennessee marble – sits at the centre of a 19-foot sculpture gazing out over the Reflecting Pool. (A lesser-known but more haunting statue of the gaunt Lincoln, with one hand on the Emancipation Proclamation and the other motioning a newly freed slave to rise from bondage, is in Lincoln Park a mile east of the Capitol at East Capitol and 12th Streets, NE. It was dedicated on the 11th anniversary of his assassination.) Cut into the wall to the left of the entrance is Lincoln's Gettysburg Address, delivered at the dedication of a Civil War cemetery in Gettysburg, Pennsylvania; to the right are words of his second inaugural address. At night, looking toward Arlington, you can catch a glimpse of the eternal flame at John F Kennedy's grave in Arlington Cemetery.

The 'cave under Lincoln', created when construction was underway in 1941 for the memorial, is filled with stalactites and the charcoal drawings of the men who worked on the structure. Occasionally, guides lead special tours – for those physically fit and unafraid of the dark – but the discovery of asbestos has put a temporary stop to that.

Vietnam Veterans Memorial

West Potomac Park, just north of the Reflecting Pool at 23rd Street & Constitution Avenue, NW (462 6841). Smithsonian Metro.

So many people have filed past the sombre black granite walls of this privately funded memorial to touch the more than 58,000 names, make pencil rubbings and leave flowers, letters and flags that the Park Service is cataloguing the mementoes left. There's even a display of wall memorabilia at the

The patrician figure of President Lincoln sits at the centre of the **Lincoln Memorial**.

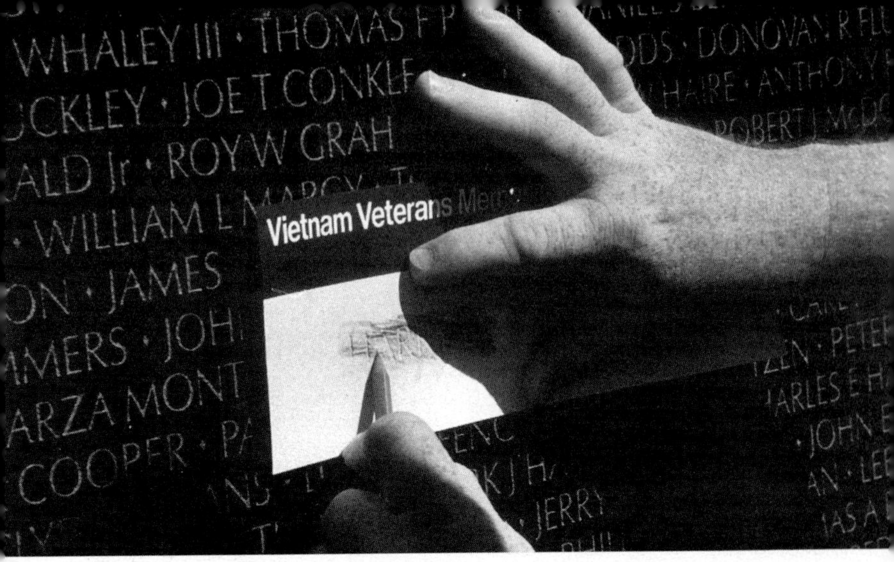

The austere black granite wall of the **Vietnam Veterans Memorial**. *See page 39.*

National Museum of American History. Who could have predicted? When Maya Ying Lin won the nationwide design contest in 1981, she was a 21-year-old Yale University senior whose abstract design – two walls, each 246 feet 8 inches long, angled to enfold the Washington Monument and the Lincoln Memorial in a symbolic embrace – touched off a major debate. Finally, an entirely figurative sculpture by Frederick Hart of three Vietnam GIs was added to mollify critics.

The names on the wall are listed in the chronological order they became casualties, but there's a directory to help locate names. A diamond symbol means the death has been confirmed; a cross means the person has been designated missing. The Vietnam Women's Memorial sculpture – of two uniformed women tending a wounded male soldier, while a third woman kneels in the distance – is based on Michelangelo's *La Pietà*. It was dedicated in 1993, 11 years after the memorial.

Washington Monument

The Mall, between 15th & 17th Streets, and Constitution & Independence Avenues (426 6841). Smithsonian Metro. **Open** *Sept-Mar* 9am-5pm, *Apr-Aug* 8am-midnight, daily.

Yet another monument with a tortured history, the Washington Monument was completed in 1884, 101 years after Congress voted to honour George Washington. It rises in a straight line between the Capitol and the Lincoln Memorial, but is off-centre between the White House and the Jefferson Memorial because the original site was too marshy to build on. Funds for the monument initially came from private groups that solicited $1 apiece from citizens across the nation, and things were fine for seven years – until Pope Pius IX decided to donate a single block of marble, thus infuriating the anti-papist 'Know-Nothing Party'. They stole the Pope's stone and proceeded to stonewall the construction process. Then the Civil War broke out, and the project was abandoned for nearly 20 years. During that time, it was nicknamed the Beef Depot Monument because the grounds were used to graze cattle awaiting slaughter – Walt Whitman, for one, wrote of seeing 10,000 head there. Finally, in 1876, the Army Corps of Engineers took over and continued the building, which is why you can see a slight change in the colour of the marble about a third of the way up. In 1884, the 555-foot monument – the tallest freestanding masonry structure in the world – was capped with a solid aluminum tip, then a rare material.

Until sometime in 2000 – the target date is 4 July – the monument is undergoing restoration and wearing a rather fetching blue mesh straitjacket to conceal the scaffolding (some people find it much improved, especially when lit up at night). However, except during the short period while the scaffolding is removed, elevator trips are running as usual (though the scaffolding hides the usually excellent views), as are the walk-down tours (897 steps) of the obelisk's history and more than 150 ornate and diverse memorial stones embedded in its walls. The ride takes one minute (the restorations have knocked ten seconds off the time).

You'll need a ticket to go up on the elevator. They're free, and available from 7.30am in summer and 8.30am from autumn through to spring. Tickets are timed, and if you're not fussy about when in the day you go you shouldn't have a problem; if you need a specific time during high season, you'll need to get in line early. You can pre-book through Ticketmaster (432 7328) for an admin fee of $1.50 per ticket plus 50¢ per order.

During the restorations, the National Park Service has opened an interpretive centre on the monument grounds with videos, interactive exhibits about the life of George Washington, and virtual views from the top. It's due to close on Labor Day (6 September) 2000 – a shame, since it's a good one.

Also check out the south side of the monument, where there's a Pepco cast iron plate near the light box. In the hole – a Park Service ranger will be on your case faster than you can touch the cover, so don't even bother trying to lift it – is a 162-inch-high miniature of the monument that's used to measure the rate at which the big version is sinking into the ground. (It's about a quarter-inch every 30 years.)

The White House & around

Transport

Farragut North, Farragut West or McPherson Square Metro.

Set above the Ellipse to the north of the Mall, and flanked by various august federal buildings, the **White House** (*see below* **Highlights**) faces south, opening up the rectangular dynamic of the Mall with north-south sightlines to the Washington and Jefferson Memorials. However, though you can peer into the grounds through the hedge on E Street opposite the Zero Milestone (where a tinny loudspeaker planted in the lawn urges respect – an anti-climactic experience), public access is from the north-eastern side, best approached from the White House's downtown hinterland.

Directly to the north is **Lafayette Park**, where, during the building of the White House, labourers camped and bricks were dried. Now the park – named after the Marquis de Lafayette, who aided George Washington in holding off the British at Yorktown – is overrun with protesters, panhandlers pretending to play on the chessboard tables, and, yes, the occasional government worker taking a break on one of the benches. It's best avoided at night, because even though there's a ton of security around, most are undercover – and they're there for the president's protection, not yours.

The stretch of Pennsylvania Avenue separating the park from the White House was closed to traffic in the summer of 1995, after threats from gunmen. The grumbling about the damage to traffic patterns has mostly subsided, and now the barricades and flowerpots have become part of the many rollerblading obstacle courses and hockey games on the street. Though the park is named after Lafayette, the most prominent statue – the guy on the horse in the middle – is Andrew Jackson at the Battle of New Orleans during the War of 1812. The four other statues are of American Revolutionary heroes: General Lafayette (south-east corner), Comte de Rochambeau (south-west corner), General Thaddeus Kosciusko (north-east) and Baron von Steuben (north-west).

The pale yellow **St John's Church**, on H Street to the north of the square, dates back to 1816, and every president since James Madison has attended at least one service there. A brass plate at pew 54 marks the place reserved for the president.

You might recognise the green awning on **Blair House** (1660 Pennsylvania Avenue, NW) across Jackson Place to the west of the square as the place where visiting heads of state bunk while in town. Next door, the **Renwick Gallery** (*see page 105* **Museums & Galleries**), at Pennsylvania and 17th Street - an 1859 building in the French Second Empire mode – is the only museum in Washington to be named after its architect, James Renwick. It's now part of the Smithsonian and houses a collection of twentieth-century crafts. The Renwick was originally home to William Wilson Corcoran's art collection, which at the end of the nineteenth century was moved three blocks south into the purpose-built **Corcoran Gallery** (*see page 102* **Museums & Galleries**), the Beaux Arts building on the north-west corner of 17th and E Streets.

The four-storey townhouse known as **Decatur House** (*see below* **Highlights**) at 748 Jackson Place – built in 1819 as the first private home on Lafayette Square – was home to naval hero Stephen Decatur, French, British and Russian diplomats, nineteenth-century statesman Henry Clay and Martin Van Buren. Today the Federal-style house is a popular – and pricey – wedding spot. On the other side of the square, at H Street and Madison Place, is the **Dolley Madison House** (closed to the public), where the widowed first lady lived until her death.

The two office buildings that 'bookend' Lafayette Square on the west and east are the **New Executive Office Building** and the **US Court of Claims** (which has one of the cheapest, nicest cafeterias around).

Flanking the White House are the **Old Executive Office Building** and the **US Treasury Building** (for both, *see below* **Highlights**), to the west and east, respectively. With 900 Doric columns, the Old Executive Office Building, or OEOB for short, was the world's largest office building when it was finished in 1888. Harry Truman called it 'the greatest monstrosity in America' – yet still didn't want it torn down. The Treasury is the third oldest federal building in Washington. A cluster of banks – mostly neoclassical buildings – surround it, vestiges of the city's old financial district, once known as 'Washington's Wall Street'. The area is now incorporated into the Fifteenth Street Financial Historic District.

Highlights

Decatur House

748 Jackson Place, NW, at H Street (842 0920). Farragut West Metro. **Guided tours** 10am-3pm Tue-Fri; noon-4pm Sat, Sun. **Tours** $4; $2.50 students; free under-5s (free first Tue of the month). **Credit** AmEx, Disc, MC, V.

White House tour details

So high is demand for White House tours that you will need to wait in line for the privilege – sorry, right. In the high season, from mid-March until the first weekend in September (Labor Day), and during December, when the Christmas decorations draw the crowds, the drill is to stand in line for tickets at the Visitors Center, housed in the north end of the Department of Commerce to the east of the Ellipse. Staff will allocate you to a tour later that day (they run from 10am to noon). Each person can get up to four tickets, which are free. To be sure of a place, go as soon as – or before – the centre opens at 7.30am: though capacity seems high at 5,000 a day, tickets can and do run out, and there's no easy way to predict when. It's not uncommon to see a line forming before dawn. From Labor Day through to mid-March, with the exception of December, the advance ticketing system is dropped: just turn up and expect a short wait.

To get on a 'VIP' tour (officially called a Congressional Guided Tour), write and ask your Congressional representative (House or Senate) four to six months in advance. There are 1,600 VIP places each day; tours start between 8.15am and 8.45am. VIPs have a better chance of visiting the China Room and Diplomatic Reception Room, though these will be closed off on busy days and, conversely, on quiet days, will be accessible on the standard tour. VIP tours are effectively unavailable to non-US citizens: though some tickets are issued to embassies, demand far outstrips supply.

The major bonus for VIPs, besides a shorter wait, is that the tours are led by genuine Secret Service-agent-turned-guides, who drop titbits like this: the reason why 'Hail to the Chief' is played when a president makes an entrance is because no one ever noticed when five-foot-six President James Polk walked into a crowded room.

All tours start at the East Visitors Gate of the White House (follow the crowds) and last about 20 minutes. Note that tours are regularly cancelled due to White House events – call before visiting.

White House Visitors Center

Commerce Building, 1450 Pennsylvania Avenue, NW, at 15th Street (208 1631). Federal Triangle Metro. **Open** 7.30am-4pm daily.

The ***White House*** *tour is incredibly popular, so arrive early.*

This elegant Federal-period house was the centre of social life in Washington in the nineteenth century, when it was home to three secretaries of state, several ambassadors, various congressmen and, of course, naval hero Stephen Decatur, its first owner, who was killed in a duel in 1819. The first floor is furnished in the style of his era; upstairs is more eclectic.

Old Executive Office Building

17th Street & Pennsylvania Avenue, NW (395 5895). Farragut West Metro. **Guided tours** 9am-11.30pm Sat. Call one month ahead 9am-noon Tue-Fri for reservations. **Tours** free.

Formerly the home of the old State, War and Navy Departments, the OEOB now houses some offices of the executive staff, not to mention a tunnel connecting it to the White House, which allows the president underground access to a hideaway office and a secret exit for a night on the town.

There's a more rigorous security check here than at the White House, which is why you need to book so far in advance – it gives time for the Secret Service to give you clearance. To even make a reservation, you'll have to provide your date of birth and Social Security number (non-US citizens excepted), and photo ID is required for admission.

US Treasury

1500 Pennsylvania Avenue, NW, at 15th Street (622 0896). Metro Center Metro. **Guided tours** 10-11am Sat, every 20 mins. **Tours** free; reservations required.

In terms of sheer fit-for-a-king surroundings, the Treasury trumps even the White House. The interior of the Greek revival building, designed by Washington Monument architect Robert Mills, is pure Victorian excess: polished stone, cast iron and gilded eagles, great sweeping staircases and ornate offices. And as the only cabinet-level agency whose headquarters have never been moved, most of the Treasury's historic furnishings are the originals. Highlights include the restored Salmon Chase Suite, an 1864 burglar-proof vault, the North Lobby and the Cash Room, scene of President Ulysses S Grant's inaugural ball. The blue and gold Andrew Johnson Suite is so called because Lincoln's successor used it as an executive office for several months while Mary Todd Lincoln, half-mad with grief, clung to the White House. Tours last 90 minutes. Book early.

The White House

1600 Pennsylvania Avenue, NW, between 15th & 17th Streets (456 7041). McPherson Square Metro. **Guided tours** 10am-noon Tue-Sat. **Tours** free.

Part showplace, part workplace, the White House is sometimes referred to as 'the people's house'. Until World War II, the public could walk freely into the house, but not any more. Not only do you have to wait in line to get on a tour, but you only get to peek at a scant eight rooms out of the house's 132 – and that in a shuffly line that allows little time to linger. The public tour is self-guided and there's little in the way of interpretation, although the Secret Service guides posted throughout to answer questions are impressively knowledgeable (and patient). Displays in the visitors' centre (*see opposite*) do fill in on the background, but not in any great depth – it's most useful for its well-stocked bookshop. Even the so-called 'VIP' tour – which Members of Congress can arrange for several thousand of their closest friends – only allows you access to another two rooms. Probably. To see anything really good – the private cinema, the Oval Office, even (notoriously) the Lincoln Bedroom – you'll have to donate something in the neighbourhood of $10,000 to the chief executive's campaign coffers and drop some heavy hints.

Still, despite the problematic access, the White House – inspired by the Duke of Leinster's house in architect James Hoban's native Dublin – remains Washington's most popular tour, and it's not hard to understand why: it's the only head of state's residence that's continuously open to the public. Just don't expect any facetime with the Commander in Chief (or even Socks or Buddy) – green draping prevents any tourist from taking so much as a peek down the hallways that lead to White House offices.

Finished in 1800 and home to every US president except George Washington, the White House got its name in 1815, when it was whitewashed to hide scorch marks left from its burning by British invaders the year before (a fortuitous rainstorm prevented serious damage). The first floor of the original building contained five of the rooms open to the public on the self-guided tour. The second floor served both as the first family's residence and the executive office.

Presidents didn't enjoy their current privacy – or what's passed off as privacy, when you live in the world's biggest fishbowl – until 1902, when Teddy Roosevelt added the East Gallery and the executive office wing, which grew to include today's Oval Office and the first family's quarters on the second floor. Details are a closely guarded secret, though some emerge retrospectively. It's known that each new incumbent (usually the first lady) furnishes them as she pleases: Jacqueline Kennedy, for example, replaced the B Altman department store furniture and frilly florals of her predecessors, the Trumans and Eisenhowers respectively, with plain blues and whites as part of an overall refurbishment of the White House that restored many historic furnishings and artworks to the rooms. The president gets to impose his character on the Oval Office, bringing in favourite furniture and making personal selections from the White House art collection.

There are also, of course, office quarters for around 200 executive branch staffers, and – since presidents have to bring their work home with them – recreational facilities including a 47-seat cinema, tennis courts, a putting green, a bowling alley and, courtesy of George Bush, a horseshoe pitch. The whole caboodle has 32 bathrooms, 413 doors, three elevators, seven staircases and a staff of more than 100, including florists, carpenters and cooks.

The tour starts, after an extensive security check, at the East Wing, which was begun by Theodore Roosevelt and completed, with the addition of wartime offices, by his cousin Franklin Delano

The Oval Office, where the tours won't take you.

Roosevelt. If you're on the self-guided tour, you'll usually be allowed a peek through the roped-off doorways (hard to see when there's a crowd, which there will be) of the **Library**, used to host teas, meetings and press interviews, and the **Vermeil Room**, a yellow room with an extensive collection of gilded silver (vermeil). Next, depending on the crowds, you might get a look in the **China Room**, the showplace for pieces of china used by presidents. Don't miss the once-notorious $952-per-setting red-rimmed china of Nancy Reagan's, which sparked a 1981 controversy about conspicuous consumption.

Up the marble stairs, visitors then enter the cavernous **East Room**, which holds the only item from the original White House: the 1797 portrait of George Washington that Dolley Madison rolled up and rescued for safekeeping just before the British burned the place on 24 August 1814. The East Room is the reception and ceremony room where seven presidents have lain in state – and where Abigail Adams, wife of the second president, John, used to hang her laundry. At 3,200sq ft, the space can hold the average American home.

Next is the **Green Room**, creatively named after its green silk wallcoverings. Once Thomas Jefferson's dining room, it's where James Madison did his politicking after Dolley had liquored up important guests in the **Red Room**, which happens to be the tour's next stop. Named with equal imagination, the Red Room is decorated as an American Empire parlour of 1810-1830. It's where Mary Todd Lincoln held at least one seance to try to contact her dead sons, and where President Ulysses S Grant and his former general refought the Civil War on the carpet using salt shakers and nut dishes as troops.

The colour naming scheme continues in the next room, the **Blue Room** – although it has yellow walls. The furnishings in this room, the traditional home of the White House Christmas tree, were ordered by James Monroe.

Last stop: the cream and gold **State Dining Rooms**, which can seat up to 140. Then you're out the door. Media junkies may want to peer through the fence by the guard shack at the north-west gate: that's where all the TV reporters do their stand-ups.

If you're on a VIP tour, you may also get to see the ground-floor **Map Room**, so called because its panelled walls swing out to reveal layers of maps. It's where President Roosevelt charted the course of World War II. Of course, half the world has probably now seen the Map Room: it's where Clinton gave his infamous televised speech finally admitting to an illicit affair with former intern Monica Lewinsky. VIPs (and sometimes regulars) also see the Diplomatic Reception Room, where visiting heads of state arrive at the White House.

Of course, all the really interesting places in the White House are off-limits to tourists. Thanks to the not-so-divine Ms M (that would be Lewinsky), TV audiences know there's a bathroom and a small kitchen right outside the Oval Office, but no one without an access pass will ever see it. Slightly less scandalous rooms closed to the public include the aforementioned Lincoln Bedroom, originally the Lincoln office, where the huge rosewood bed that dominates the room is thought to have been part of the furniture purchased by Mrs Lincoln in 1861. President Lincoln never slept in the bed, although both Woodrow Wilson and Theodore Roosevelt did. Another off-limits room is the Queen's Room, which served as guest quarters for Queen Elizabeth II of Britain, Queen Wilhelmina and Queen Juliana of the Netherlands, and Queen Frederika of Greece, as well as for other visitors such as Britain's wartime prime minister Winston Churchill and Soviet foreign minister VM Molotov.

Besides the VIP tour, there are a handful of ways to see more of the mansion, or at least be able to pretend that you have. One is to luck into the right April or October weekend, when those on garden tours can wander the grounds. Another is to rent the sappy-sweet Michael Douglas/Annette Bening movie *An American President*, for which filmmakers were allowed unprecedented access to the White House so they could build a replica now referred to in Hollywood as 'White House West'. Or you can stop at the White House Historical Association offices (740 Jackson Place, west side of Lafayette Park; 737 8292) to pick up an extensive guide to the mansion ($5.25-$6), a CD-Rom ($49.95), or the definitive books by official historian William Seale. Finally, you can stroll across Lafayette Square to a restaurant where high-octane hotshots dine: called the Oval Room (800 Connecticut Avenue, NW; 463 8700), it mimics the ceiling (and, of course, the name) of the Oval Office. Then again, you could put the huge sum you could drop on a meal here towards a major donation and get a tour from the president himself.

Disabled: no tickets required for people with mobility disabilities. Free wheelchair-accessible shuttle bus with handicapped drop-offs along Pennsylvania Avenue (15th-17th Street) 8am-4pm Mon-Sat.
Website: www.whitehouse.gov

The Capitol & around

Transport

Capitol South, Federal Center-SW or Union Station Metro.

Standing at the east end of the Mall, the literal centre of the District of Columbia and its highest point, is the US Capitol (*see below* **Highlights**), effortlessly achieving both gravitas and grace wherever it is viewed from (though the walk along the Mall via the Capitol Reflecting Pool and its ducks shouldn't be missed). Around it is bucolic, squirrel-infested parkland, creating the impression that nothing nasty could possibly be going on within.

The **US Botanic Garden** at the foot of the Capitol is closed for renovations until autumn 2000, which is unfortunate, because in it are more than 500 kinds of orchids, along with tropical and

The main reading room in the **Library of Congress**, *the world's largest library.*

subtropical plants, cacti, ferns, palm trees, shrubs and flowers, plus a National Rose Garden. (If you end up in any Hill office building, you may see bits of the garden, which acts as a local flower supplier.) But just across Pennsylvania Avenue is Bartholdi Park, which is operated as a demonstration site for home gardeners. The fountain at the centre of the park was created by Frederic Auguste Bartholdi, sculptor of the Statue of Liberty.

Around the Capitol is a veritable Civic City of Congressional office buildings (the Senate's are to the north on either side of First Street on Constitution Avenue, the House's ranged to the south along Independence). In its eastern lee are the restrained, rectangular **Supreme Court** and the Renaissance-inspired **Library of Congress** with its distinctive dome (for both, *see below* **Highlights**). But in among these monumental greats are a few less imposing buildings. Right outside the Capitol is the **Sewall-Belmont House** (144 Constitution Avenue, NE; 546 3989), saved from being demolished for the Senate parking lot by being entered on the National Register of Historic Places. The three-storey townhouse is characteristic of the Federal period, contains furnishings from Henry Clay and suffragist Susan B Anthony, and celebrates women's struggle to get the vote and pass the Equal Rights Amendment. The **Mountjoy Bayly House** (122 Maryland Avenue) is another Federal-style building on the National Register. Currently, it's the headquarters of the General Commission on Chaplain and Armed Forces Personnel. Books in the **Folger Shakespeare Library** (*see below* **Highlights**) are available only to scholars, but the Elizabethan Garden and the museum are open to the public.

Highlights

Library of Congress

Visitors Center, Jefferson Building, First Street & Independence Avenue, SE (707 8000). Capitol South Metro. **Open** 10am-5.30pm Mon-Sat. **Guided tours** 11.30am, 1pm, 2pm, 4pm, Mon-Sat.

The national library of the US – the world's largest – stuffs some 100 million items, including the papers of 23 US presidents, into three buildings and 535 miles of bookshelves. If you have time, it's best to start with the 20-minute film in the ground-floor visitors' centre; it's excerpted from a TV documentary and provides a clearer picture of the place's scope and size. Another option is to take a guided tour for the overview, then pick an area (say, Matthew Brady's Civil War photos) and have a closer look.

Begun in 1800 with a $5,000 grant from Congress, the original Library was housed in the Capitol. It was burned down by the British in 1814, then begun anew when president-scholar Thomas Jefferson offered his collection of 6,487 books. The Thomas Jefferson Building – the main one – was finished in 1897. Based on the Paris Opera House, the Library has granite walls supporting an octagonal dome, which rises to 160 feet above the spectacular marble and wood reading room.

In the Jefferson Building, a permanent rotating exhibition, 'American Treasures of the Library of Congress', displays more than 240 of the most significant items from America's past, such as a copy of Lincoln's handwritten draft from the Gettysburg Address. A visitors' gallery overlooks the stunning Great Hall – white marble with red and gold roof panels – which is adorned with the illustrations of a childhood's worth of picture books: brass zodiac symbols, neo-Greek mosaics, mermen and nymphs and Muses. And the main reading room, whose rotunda made a bow in the movie *All the President's Men*, has classic marble archways and great plaster figures of disciplines (Philosophy, Religion, Art, History, all women) flanked by bronze images of their mortal instruments (Plato, Moses, Homer, Shakespeare, all men). Even the most strident senator doesn't dare speak above a whisper in this room.

Directly across Independence Avenue is the James Madison Building, opened in 1980, which encloses an area greater than 35 football fields. It houses the copyright office, presidential papers, film and TV reading rooms and the incredible photography collections. Diagonally opposite is the 1939 John Adams Building, which contains the African, Asian, Hebraic, Near East, Science and Social Science reading rooms.

Anyone with photo ID can register for a library card – the process takes about 15 minutes. You can't wander all the shelves yourself: a librarian will dig out your selected text for you. However, now that a new initiative, the American Memory Project, plans to put 80 million of the library's holdings in all media online (http://memory.loc.gov/ammem/amhome.html), you'll be able to do much of your work at home. Eight million items are up already, where appropriate scanned in their original form.
Website: lcweb.loc.gov

Supreme Court

First Street & Maryland Avenue, NW (479 3211). Union Station or Capitol South Metro. **Open** 9am-4.30pm Mon-Fri.

The home of the ultimate judicial and constitutional authority of the United States pays homage in its architecture to the rule of law throughout civilisation. Designed by Cass Gilbert in the early 1930s, its self-consciously awe-inspiring façade incorporates Corinthian columns supporting a pediment decorated with bas-reliefs representing Liberty, Law, Order and a whole crew of historical figures, and in the white marble courtroom itself overhead friezes depict the faces of renowned lawmakers from the pre-Christian and Christian eras.

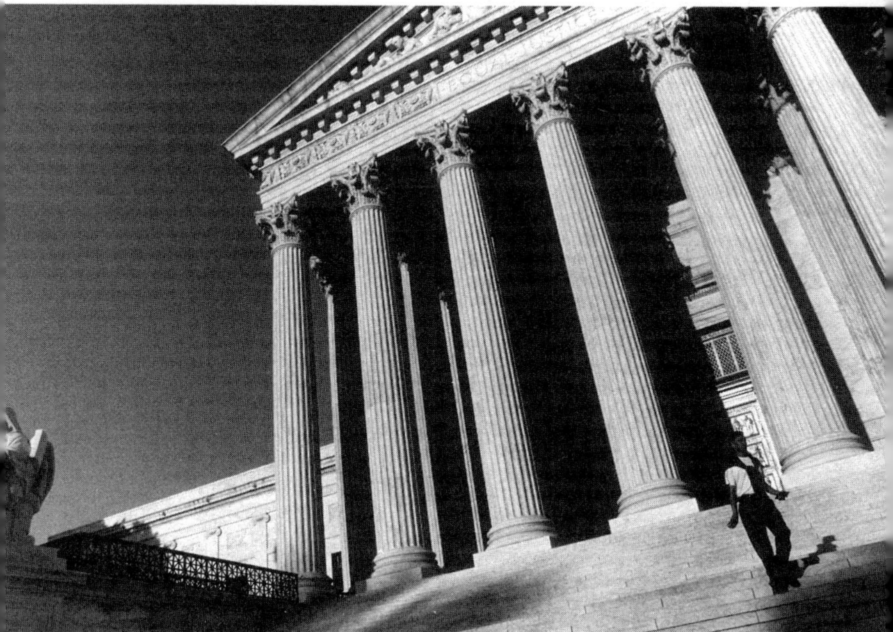

The imposing façade of the **Supreme Court**, *designed by Cass Gilbert in the 1930s.*

Bas reliefs of Shakespeare's plays adorn the **Folger Shakespeare Library**.

Depending on your luck and timing, a visit to the Supreme Court can be the most exciting – or most unbelievably boring – federal tour in town. You enter through the main entrance on First Street, NE, beyond the white marble sculptures of 'Contemplation of Justice' (left) and 'Authority of Law' (right), and pass through airport-style security into a hushed, cathedral-like entrance hall. Straight ahead is the courtroom, with its heavy burgundy velvet draperies and marble pillars, where the nine justices at the bench hear about 120 of the more than 6,500 cases submitted to the court each year. The black-robed figures appear as the Court Marshal announces 'Oyez! Oyez! Oyez!' (French for 'hear!') and sit in seats of varying height, handcarved to their personal preference. As they have been for years, ten-inch-long white goose quill pens are still placed on the lawyers' tables, except now they're purely for souvenirs.

When the court is in session, from October to April, visitors can see cases being argued on Mondays, Tuesdays and Wednesdays from 10am to 3pm. Two lines form in the plaza in front of the building: one for those who want to hear the whole argument (staff advise getting there by 8am), and the other, called the 'three-minute line', for those who just want a peek at the court in session. In May and June, 'opinions' (verdicts, in varying degrees of detail) are handed down on Tuesdays, Wednesdays and some other days. Check the *Washington Post*'s Supreme Court calendar to find out what cases are on the schedule.

When the court is out of session, there's a snoozer of a free lecture in the courtroom every half hour on the hour (9.30am-3.30pm) about court procedure and the building's architecture – it's not even very informative. Better to go to the film and rotating exhibits downstairs.

The levels above the courtroom are closed to the public – there's a gym (where Justice Sandra Day O'Connor requires her female clerks to join her for aerobics) and offices, many of which look like they're furnished with rejects from parents' basements.

Folger Shakespeare Library & Theatre

201 East Capitol Street, SE, between Second & Third Streets (544 7077). Capitol South Metro.

Great Hall open 10am-4pm Mon-Sat. **Tours** 11am Mon-Fri; 11am, 1pm, Sat.

The marble façade of this classical art deco building is riddled with bas reliefs depicting scenes from Shakespearian works. Before going inside, stroll to the west end to see the statue of a playful Puck alighting over a lapping fountain and pool. At the east end is the Elizabethan Garden. And inside is the world's largest collection of Shakespeare's printed works, including the First Folio collection of the Bard's work, published in 1623 and bestowed on Henry VIII by Anne of Cleves as a love token.

The collection was the gift of former Standard Oil chairman Henry Clay Folger, who fell in love with Shakespeare after hearing Ralph Waldo Emerson lecture on him, and also includes musical instruments, costumes and films, as well as 27,000 paintings, drawings and prints. The Tudor-style rooms that house them are worth a look in their own right, especially the oak-panelled Great Hall, with its hand-carved walls, tile floors and recurring motifs.

The reading room, open during the library's annual celebration of Shakespeare's birthday in the spring, has a copy of a bust of the Bard from Stratford's Trinity Church and a stained glass window that portrays the Seven Ages of Man as described in *As You Like It*. And the intimate theatre (*see chapter* **Culture**) is a wooden three-tiered replica of one from the garden of an Elizabethan inn.
Website www.folger.edu

The United States Capitol

Capitol Hill, between Constitution & Independence Avenues (recorded tour information 225 6827). Capitol South or Union Station Metro. **Open** *Sept-Feb* 9am-4.30pm, *March-Aug* 9am-8pm, daily. **Guided tours** usually 9.15am-6pm Mon-Sat.

The US Capitol is at the centre of the original ten square miles of old Washington – not, as some Congressmen might want you to believe, at the centre of the universe. Asked by President George Washington to design a plan for the federal city, French architect Major Pierre Charles L'Enfant chose to put the Capitol in one of two significant locations in the city (the other was the White House). Capitol Hill, then called Jenkins Hill, was, in L'Enfant's estimation, like 'a pedestal waiting for a monument'.

Indeed it was. In 1793, George Washington and an entourage of local masons laid the building's cornerstone – today, nobody knows exactly where it is – and then celebrated by barbecuing a 500-pound ox. Thirty-one years later, despite a fire, a shortage of funds and the War of 1812, the structure was complete. But as the Union grew, so did the number of members, so by 1850, architects projected the Capitol would have to double its size. In 1857, two wings were added, one each for the Senate and the House of Representatives. An iron dome (a 600-gallon paint job each year makes it look like marble) replaced the wooden one in 1865. Abe Lincoln insisted it be finished during the Civil War as a symbol of the durability of the Union. Meanwhile, cattle, sheep, pigs and goats roamed freely on the Capitol grounds.

Today, the Capitol – which has 540 rooms, 658 windows (108 in the dome alone) and 850 doorways – is a small city. Besides the 535 elected lawmakers, an estimated 20,000 workers toil daily among the six buildings (not including the Capitol) that make up the Capitol complex. Within this massive workforce is a 1,200-member police department, doctors, nurses, electricians, carpenters, painters, day-care personnel and more. There are power plants, libraries, shops, restaurants, newspaper offices, pharmacies, gyms, tennis courts and maintenance shops. And nearly every room of the Capitol and the office buildings – few members have offices in the actual Capitol – is a separate fiefdom guarded with the considerable tenacity of a threatened bureaucrat.

A flag flies over the Senate and House wings when either is in session (the House side is to the south, the Senate side to the north); at night a lantern glows in the Capitol dome. (The only time the Capitol was open all night was when John F Kennedy lay in state in the Rotunda.) To enter the galleries of either chamber when in session – and to realise that what C-SPAN doesn't show is that all this posturing and pontificating is often done to a mostly empty house – you will need a pass. Same-day passes for both US citizens and foreign visitors are available from the House and Senate appointments desk on the first floor; alternatively, US citizens can get passes from their representative in advance. You will be asked to check in bags and follow guidelines to avoid disrupting proceedings (no pagers or cameras). For more details on attending congressional sessions, *see p19* **Watching the lawmakers**.

Public access to the Capitol is via the middle steps on the East Front (the opposite side to the Mall), which take you into the Rotunda. You will usually need to wait in line for a ticket, which then gives you immediate access, except on Sundays and at quiet times of year, when you may be allowed in directly. From March to August, the lines are marshalled in the East Front Plaza, at the bottom of the steps. The wait can be as long as two hours. US citizens can bypass the queues and usually get to be in a smaller group by organising a 'VIP' tour in advance through their congressional representative.

The standard tours start every 10-15 minutes from the Rotunda. They last 30-40 minutes and cover the main bases but don't include the House and Senate galleries, to which they will direct you at the end. The red-jacketed guides (sometimes) know their stuff and love to show it off, but, unfortunately, tours tend to be crowded, and hearing can be difficult. The VIP tours from Hill staffers can be equally hit or miss – some are led by folks who have spent years prowling the building and learning bits of trivia, while others are by staffers who freely admit to making things up. Call it revenge for their having to suffer through yet more questions from camera-toting tourists. As for getting a close-up view of the Rotunda ceiling, only 535 people – the 535 members of Congress – can take you up to see it. Blame all the tourists who collapsed while climbing the steps: one account from the nineteenth century says that once a tourist reaches the top 'his collapsed state leaves him in no condition to appreciate' the view.

There are three problems with all the established tours, including the self-guided option. First, they stick to the showpiece areas. Second, they don't point out – much less show you – the rooms where the deals (and laws) get made. Here's a hint: lawmaking rarely happens on either the House or Senate floor but in committee or private conference (aka lunch). Third: they skimp on the art. There are more than 800 pieces in the Capitol's collection, if you include the nineteenth-century gilded frames. It's impossible to point them all out – they're in passageways, on ceilings and along staircases and can take the form of anything from ornamental bronze stair railings to stained glass windows. Although the guides are well informed, if art is your passion, it's best to hit the gift shop on the first floor to pick up *US Art in the Capitol* ($35) or the illustrated guide

An alternative Capitol tour

The Capitol's public entrance takes you into the Rotunda. But, since everything else will seem an anticlimax after this – it's where the most eye-popping (and neck-straining) art is – for now, keep your head down and go straight ahead and down the stairs to the **Crypt** – so called because George Washington was supposed to be buried beneath it – which houses an exhibit, complete with models, on the Capitol's various construction phases. Then head downstairs (and make an immediate U-turn) to see the musty tomb that George Washington's heirs nixed, in favour of Mount Vernon, for his final resting place. You'll see the catafalque on which coffins rest when bodies lie in state (presidents, occasionally members of Congress and, in 1998, the two security officers killed at the Capitol).

Go back upstairs to the Crypt and head north to the **Old Supreme Court Chamber**, where the court met from 1810 to 1860 and handed down a number of historic decisions, including the Dred Scott verdict dramatised in Steven Spielberg's 1997 film *Amistad*, which affirmed that blacks did not have rights of citizenship. The Senate also met here from 1800, when the Capitol opened, to 1807. The senators, who hated the Court, were only too happy to hand the place over, since it was the hottest spot in the building in summer and the coldest in winter. The red-jacketed guide has lots more (of interest) to say on the subject, or ask for a free brochure.

Exit the chamber, heading north, and turn right (east) just before you hit the doors. There you'll see the Senate's **Brumidi corridors**, where every square inch of wall and ceiling is covered with motifs of American birds and flowers and great scenes from American history by Italian refugee artist Constantino Brumidi. He left some of the ovals vacant; in recent years they've been completed with images such as the 1969 moon landing. Follow the corridor around to **S-127** and **S-128**, the office and committee room of the powerful Senate Appropriations Committee. Neither is open to the public, but if you stand outside for a few minutes, a staffer or a senator will come in or out, giving you a peek at the Brumidi-painted ceiling, crystal chandelier and scenes from the Revolutionary War. Originally, the Committee on War met here.

Up a flight of stairs is the **President's Room** (S-216) and the **Senate Reception Room** (S-213), both of which have more of Brumidi's work. The President's Room – so-called because it's the chief executive's only space in the Capitol – is decorated in the style of the 1880s, with red velvet curtains, Moroccan leather sofas with red silk tassels, and a $25,000 gold-plated chandelier. Once used by President Lincoln to confer with Congressmen during the Civil War, it's now the photo op spot after a presidential inauguration.

Take the stairs up one level and then follow the 'Visitors Gallery' arrows – along the way you'll see Tiffany stained glass and William H Powell's 1873 *Battle of Lake Erie* painting – for a view down to the **Senate Chamber**. (If the Senate is in session, you'll need a pass.) The Republicans are on the east side of the aisle; Democrats on the west. Above them is the phrase 'Annuit Coeptis Novus Ordo Seclorum' ('He has looked favourably on the new order of ages'), which is also on the back of the $1 bill. The gold jug-like things on the floor are spittoons, now redundant, like most of the snuff boxes on the desks. And those baby-faced kids sitting on the steps during sessions are high-school kids serving as pages, aka errand runners.

To get to the **Old Senate Chamber,** look for arrows pointing to the House Gallery, and follow the winding corridor, keeping an eye out for a stairwell (there's also an elevator) on your left. Go down a level, turn left to the Rotunda and head north to enter the balcony level of the **Old Senate Rotunda**, whose 16 columns are decorated with tobacco leaf and cotton blossom motifs, signifying the importance of these crops in the young nation's economy. The 44 desks in the chamber are replicas; the originals are still in use in the current Senate Chamber. As for the carpet, it once had to be changed almost every three months because the senators had such poor aim that they missed the spittoons. They used this space from 1810 to 1859, when it became yet another cast-off for the Supreme Court, which then used it until 1935.

Head south through the Rotunda to the **Statuary Hall**, where the House of Representatives met from 1807 to 1857. Every state in the union gave two statues to the display (not all are exhibited here). Brass plaques on the floor commemorate where representatives who became president sat. Also, it was here that John Quincy Adams (the only president to finish his term and then serve in Congress) is said to have sat, pretending to be asleep, but in fact listening to the whispers of his opposing colleagues across the chamber, thanks to some weird acoustics courtesy of the arched ceilings. Every guide will be happy to demonstrate the trick, but how well you can hear depends on the crowds.

The Senate's **Brumidi corridors**.

Unlike those in the Senate, seats in the **House of Representatives' Chamber** (on the third floor) are not assigned. And whereas the Senate votes by roll call, in the House, with four times as many members, that would take forever, so members vote by using a little credit card with a microchip. They insert it into a machine on the back of the chairs and press Yea, Nay, or Present (the last of which is a kind of chickening out).

Around the room are reliefs of great bringers of law: Moses, Hammurabi and more. On the ceiling are seals of the 50 states in the order they entered the union. The four dark blue panels on the second floor of the room – above the 'In God We Trust' motto – are false. During a vote, the panels are lit from the back, and you can see the 435 names and a green light or a red light, depending on how the member voted. Don't expect all the members to be here when the House is in session – you'll be lucky to see 10.

Although you've probably seen more security officers per square foot here than anywhere else – a legacy of the July 1998 shooting of two Capitol police officers that stunned the nation – there are reminders that any security system has its loopholes. In the House, you can still see a bullet hole in the ceiling from a 1940s assassination attempt. There's also a bullet hole in one of the desks.

Now head back downstairs to take in the **Rotunda**, the landmark that divides Washington into quadrants. (It used to double as a flea market, where vendors sold silks, bird cages, even light machinery.) About 95 feet in diameter and 180 feet high, the Rotunda features works of art that glorify the nation's founders and their acts. Eight monumental artworks by John Trumbull depict such historic events: *The Declaration of Independence, The Surrender of Lord Cornwallis* and *Washington Resigning His Commission as General of the Army,* among others. Little wonder that some members of Congress, surrounded by these grandiose paintings, get carried way with a sense of their own importance.

Above your head is the most amazing art of all, the fresco glorifying George Washington. It's called *Apotheosis of Washington,* and was painted by Brumidi in 1865. (Actually, Brumidi designed the painting, but others had to finish it. While working on it, he lost his balance and dangled from the scaffolding 58 feet above the floor for 15 minutes before help arrived. He never recovered from the shock and died five months later. The painting wasn't finished until 1953.) The fresco features a uniformed Washington, flanked by figures representing Victory and Liberty, linked to a circle of 13 cavorting women representing the 13 original states.

The painting that circles the room is a history of the US, from Columbus setting foot on American soil to 1910, when the Wright brothers took flight. The Civil War is conspicuously absent – it's only vaguely suggested by two guys in uniform shaking hands.

Finish your tour by getting on the difficult-to-find Capitol subway (always a good place to spot members who may be dashing across the Capitol for a vote or a meeting). From the Rotunda, walk toward the House side (south), turn left (east) and go down the stairs, heading away from the door. Go left (south) and take the elevator to the sub-basement. Hang a right outside the elevator and you should see the distinctively ugly mustard walls where the subway arrives.

If you want to see more, head to the third floor to the Russell Building's **Senate Caucus Room** (room 325), the site of many famous hearings, such as those surrounding the Teapot Dome and Watergate scandals. At night, it's a favourite party spot of interns and young staffers, who get, well, cheap thrills from bringing cheap beer into the staid chamber, with its gilt-inlaid ceiling and marble Corinthian columns.

Outside the Caucus Room (by the elevators) are two balconies overlooking the Capitol. The glass doors are usually locked, but this is where network correspondents do their stand-ups for the evening news, since the Capitol dome-backdrop is perfectly captured from this spot. The East Lawn is another favourite of TV reporters.

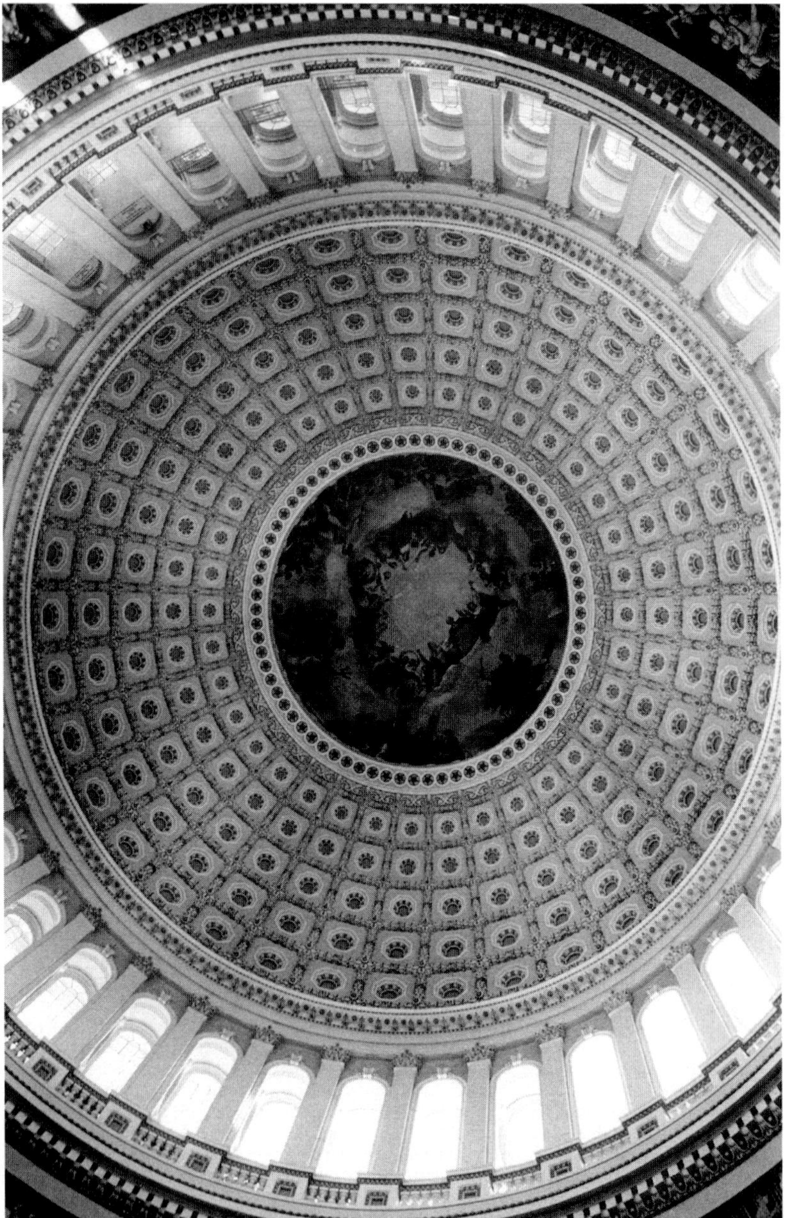

The highlight of the United States Capitol: the 180-foot high ***Rotunda****.*

We the People ($5.95), or to browse www.aoc.gov. Occasionally, the US Capitol Historical Society (543 8919) offers guided tours; check the *Washington Post*'s Friday 'Weekend' section.

However, unlike the White House – and to the astonishment of European visitors used to less openness in government – members of the public can wander more or less at will throughout the entire Capitol complex, including the committee rooms, with the exception of certain areas that will be clearly marked as off-limits. So there's no obligation to go on a tour at all. There's nothing stopping you just going down a corridor, hopping on a lift and seeing where it takes you. Alternatively, you could follow our suggested tour outline (*see p50*), which takes you round both the accepted highlights and some less well-known features.

The only trouble with random explorations is that it is almost impossible not to get lost (though this can be part of the fun). A mere lift ride takes you, Alice-like, from the tourist-friendly epicentre to a warren of functional corridors with impenetrable signage and no one obvious to ask for directions. And even in the ceremonial rooms, the layout can be confusing and areas closed off – if in doubt, ask; there are plenty of guides to help you.

If you're looking for somewhere specific, it helps to know that rooms in the Capitol complex are given a cryptic letter-and-number designation. Inside the Capitol the rooms are labeled H (if on the House or south side) or S (if on the Senate or north side). SROB, SDOB and SHOB refer to the three Senate office buildings on the north side of the Capitol (Russell, Dirksen and Hart); CHOB, LHOB, and RHOB the House buildings on the south side (Cannon, Longworth and Rayburn). The first number following the letters gives the floor; the next two or three are the room number.

Access to the Capitol can be affected by congressional business, so always phone before you visit. Pressing 4 when you get through to the guided tour number given above will take you directly to events information.

The Federal Triangle

Transport

Federal Triangle or Archives-Navy Memorial Metro.

The triangle of monolithic federal buildings contained by the wedge east of the Ellipse where Pennsylvania Avenue angles down to the Mall is known, predictably if unimaginatively, as the Federal Triangle. Once upon a time, this was a residential immigrant area, but when the government faced a building land shortage after World War I, federal officials claimed 'eminent domain' (the right of compulsory purchase) and took over.

The Federal Triangle is now the ballpark for the heavy hitters of the government machine, housing within its 70 acres 28,000 office workers – and counting. The triangle is both a labyrinth and a fortress – security is tight, and visitors usually end up asking about six different people before finally making it to their destination. Wags call it the Bermuda Triangle.

All but one of the buildings in the Triangle were built between 1927 and 1938 as massive Beaux Arts limestone structures, complete with high-minded inscriptions, to house various federal agencies, such as the Departments of Commerce and Justice, the **National Archives** (*see below* **Highlights**) – where visitors wait in line to file past the Declaration of Independence, Constitution and Bill of Rights – and the Internal Revenue Service, which is inscribed with the not-so-comforting words of former chief justice Oliver Wendell Holmes: 'Taxes are what we pay for a civilised society.' North-west is the **Old Post Office Pavilion**. Once sneered at as the 'old tooth' and slated for demolition, the renovated Old Post Office Building now offers a view of Washington's most famous sights from the observatory at the top of its 315-foot tower (*see below* **Highlights**).

The 1990s cuckoo in the Beaux Arts nest is the **Ronald Reagan Building and International Trade Center** (on 14th Street, opposite the Commerce Department), the most expensive federal building ever constructed at over $700 million. It was supposed to be a symbol of Reagan's passion for free enterprise and global trade, but it's really anti-Gipper, an embodiment of big government with one-and-a-half times the floorspace of the Empire State Building.

(More trivia: the Reagan Building sits on a site that was home to brothels and saloons in 1890s. During excavations before construction began, archaeologists found garter hooks and perfume and beer bottles on the site.)

Old Post Office Tower

Old Post Office Building, 1100 Pennsylvania Avenue, between 11th & 12th Streets (606 8691). Federal Triangle Metro. **Open** *Sept-Mar* 10am-6pm, *Apr-Aug* 8am-11pm, daily (closed 7-9pm Thur for bell-ringing practice). **Admission** free.

Washington's best views are probably from the Washington Monument, but from here you get to see the Monument itself as well. It's a 47-second ride to the ninth floor; you then change to another elevator bound for the 12th, and top, floor. The Post Office Pavilion below is a mix of 50 shops, restaurants (useful, as there are otherwise few refreshment stops around bar departmental canteens) and a performing arts centre.

National Archives

Constitution Avenue, NW, between Seventh & Ninth Streets (501 5000). Archives-Navy Memorial Metro. **Open** *mid Oct-mid Apr* 10am-5.30pm, *mid Apr-mid Oct* 10am-9pm, daily). **Admission** free.

Presidential sightings

As recently as the 1920s, the president set aside one day a week for audiences with the public. Now, what with the full diary of the modern-day world leader and ever-increasing security concerns, there are more alien sightings than presidential ones. In fact, there are only two occasions a year when you can pretty much be guaranteed a viewing.

One is the Easter Egg Roll, held the Monday after Easter on the White House lawn, when you and 32,000 other folks should get at least a glimpse; the other is the lighting of the National Christmas Tree in early December on the Ellipse, when the First Couple preside over a hokey but entertaining ceremony. For both, *see chapter* **Washington by Season**.

Each new president is available for public scrutiny at his or her inaugural address, given outside the Capitol in the January following their election. Afterwards, the president and family stroll down Pennsylvania Avenue. You can try to get tickets from your member of Congress, but unless you're a Cabinet secretary, you'll be put so far away you'll need binoculars. Otherwise, join the hopeful throng fringing Pennsylvania Avenue. You're also guaranteed a sighting at the inaugural balls that weekend – if you can score an invite.

Other than that, it's down to happenstance, if only because the president's exact schedule is never released – too much ammunition for assassins. That said, we can give some tips for the Clintons, at least. The habits of the new incumbent are anyone's guess.

The Clinton family likes to eat at Bombay Club (*see p147* **Restaurants**), a tony Indian restaurant across Lafayette Square from the White House. On Sundays, you can often catch them at Foundry United Methodist Church (16th & Q Streets, NW). Look for a gaggle of men with earpieces (some with a hand inside a canvas shoulder bag – their hands rest on Uzi machine guns), plus the tell-tale vans the press follow him in. At about noon, he'll stroll out of church, arm in arm with Hillary, for a photo op (*pictured)*.

Chelsea Clinton is fairly easy to see about town on breaks from Stanford, if only because one of her favourite sports seems to be bucking her blue-jeaned Secret Service agents and hanging out at whatever place is new and hip. She's appeared several times at Xando (*see page 137* **Cafés & Coffeehouses**), where she's said to be a good tipper, and has been spotted in places ranging from Banana Republic in Georgetown to a Sheryl Crow concert.

The president's motorcade – with up to 20 vehicles – usually includes at least two black Cadillac limousines, the War Wagon (containing heavy weaponry) and escorts from city, county, state and federal governments. But since DC is full of dignitaries, it's not always possible to tell whose motorcade is whose. It's also impossible to know if a given plane carries the president (Air Force One isn't a single aircraft but the designation for whatever plane has him on board.) And that blue and white DC-9 jet that reads 'United States of America'? That's just a support plane that accompanies the president's aircraft.

The almost uncountable millions of the National Archive's holdings (from all federal agencies) represent the physical record of the birth and growth of a nation in original documents, maps, photos, recordings, film and a miscellany of objects. The catalogue resonates with national iconography and historic gravitas (and pathos): it includes the Louisiana Purchase, maps of Lewis and Clark's explorations, the Japanese World War II surrender document, the gun that shot JFK, the Watergate tapes and documents of national identity, supreme among them the Declaration of Independence, Constitution and Bill of Rights.

The building that houses them, opened in 1935 and designed to harmonise with existing DC landmarks (ie neoclassical), was designed by John Russell Pope. In a city of monumental architecture where even its 72 columns barely raise an eyebrow, its most distinctive feature is the bronze doors at the Constitution Avenue entrance. Each weighs six and a half tons and is 38 feet high and 11 inches wide. Though security is their main function, they also remind the visitor of the importance of the contents. Cathedral doors spring to mind.

Unless you're a history junkie, skip the dull tour, which basically consists of a guide displaying copies of the various documents held in the stacks. Cut straight to the main attraction. That's the Rotunda, where the original Charters of Freedom are mounted, triptych-like, in a vast glass case at the centre of a roped-off horseshoe of other documentary greats. At night the whole assembly is lowered 20 feet into a bomb- and fire-proof vault. Each sheet of parchment is enclosed in a sealed case containing only helium and water vapour. The documents have a green tinge, thanks to UV filters – as the staffer stationed nearby explains every other minute to the reverential line of visitors shuffling past. For the record, the

A rare sighting of the Clintons.

handwriting on the Declaration of Independence isn't Jefferson's – it was transcribed by Timothy Matlack, an otherwise anonymous clerk. Also in the Rotunda, one for the Brits: a Magna Carta original.

A semi-circular gallery running behind the Rotunda stages temporary exhibitions but nonetheless an infinitessimal fraction of the Archives' holdings are on display. As for the rest, research access (photo ID required) is via the door on Pennsylvania Avenue. Note that all post-World War II records have been transferred to a new Maryland facility at College Park (*see chapter* **Virginia & Maryland**).

On 5 July 2001, the Archives will be closing for renovations, including the re-encasement of the Charters of Freedom using state-of-the-art techniques (goodbye green tinge). They will reopen in 2003. Research access will not be affected.

Website: www.nara.gov

The North-west Rectangle

Transport

Farragut West or Foggy Bottom-GWU Metro/bus L1, 13M.

The North-west Rectangle is not an official appellation, but it's sometimes used to describe the rectangle of federal buildings west of the Ellipse and south of E Street that roughly mirrors the Federal Triangle to the east. It's really a part of Foggy Bottom (*see chapter* **Central DC**), an industrial immigrant area in the nineteenth century, but any original character the area has retained emerges only further north; here it is grandiose federal anonymity all the way, with the only reminder of more plebeian roots in the State Department's occasional nickname (Foggy Bottom).

From west to east, the buildings of interest are the **State Department** (*see below* **Highlights**), whose opulent reception rooms can be toured by arrangement; then, dropping down to Constitution Avenue, the **American Pharmaceutical Association**, the **National Academy of Sciences**, the **Federal Reserve Board** (*see below* **Highlights**) and the **Organization of American States**.

Behind the OAS annexe is the **Department of the Interior** (*see below* **Highlights**), housing in its exhibition space – until the projected opening of the National Museum of the American Indian in 2002 – examples of indigenous arts and crafts.

Highlights

Department of the Interior Museum

1849 C Street, NW, between 18th & 19th Streets (208 4743). Farragut West Metro. **Open** 8.30am-4.30pm Mon-Fri. Photo ID required for admission.

Until the National Museum of the American Indian is built on the Mall's last open space, Washington has no place for the Indians – America's colonised, historically abused, indigenous people – to tell their story. The Department of the Interior's exhibits are no substitute, but they are a hodgepodge of Indian arts and crafts: Pueblo drums, Apache basketwork, Cheyenne arrows that a soldier plucked from dying buffaloes at Fort Sill Indian Territory (Oklahoma) in 1868. You can also see early land bounties and scolding exhibits about endangered species, complete with shoes made from crocodile skins. The gift shop, one of Washington's best, but little known, is over 60 years old and contains wares from 40 Indian tribes, from Navajo folk art to Alaskan ivory.

Federal Reserve Board

20th Street, at C Street, NW (452 3149). Foggy Bottom-GWU Metro. **Tours** 2.30pm Thur. Meet at Eccles Building.

Washington is full of free tours, but this is the only one you'll literally get paid for: four whole bills. No, the tour isn't *that* boring – your payment is just in bits and pieces of shredded cash, a souvenir reminder of one of the Fed's functions, which is the daily disposal of about $240 million worth of worn-out currency (actually done in the Fed's regional banks, not on the premises).

The 45-minute tour is the usual run of historical titbits and a 16-minute video that explains why the Federal Reserve system, the United States' central bank and determiner of monetary policy, was created and how it operates. One warning to visitors: since special sessions of the Fed's governors can be called at any time, tours can be cancelled equally as unexpectedly.

State Department Diplomatic Reception Rooms

C & 22nd Streets, NW (647 3241). Foggy Bottom-GWU Metro. **Tours** 9.30am, 10.30am, 2.45pm, Mon-Fri. Reservations required; call four weeks in advance.

When the State Department was finished in 1961, the wife of the Secretary of State reportedly wept when she looked at the chrome, glass and concrete walls and tasteless furniture. Not any more. The three diplomatic reception rooms, used to receive foreign visitors, are now called Washington's best-kept secret – if your idea of fun is a Sotheby's or Christie's catalogue, because the rooms are nirvana only for serious fine arts and antiques lovers.

They contain one of the finest collections of Americana from 1740 to 1830, valued at some $90 million. Among the collection are Chippendale pieces, the English Sheraton desk on which the Treaty of Paris was signed in 1783, ending the Revolutionary War, and a table-desk used by Thomas Jefferson. There are also some none-too-exciting exhibits in the lobby on the history of the State Department, which is the oldest of the cabinet departments.

Note that tours are by reservation only.

South of the Mall

Transport

Federal Center, L'Enfant Plaza or Smithsonian Metro.

The area south of the Mall is largely stuffed with federal buildings that hold little interest for visitors (Federal Aviation Administration, Transportation Department, etc). The principal exceptions are the acclaimed **Holocaust Memorial Museum** (*see page 107* **Museums & Galleries**) and the **Bureau of Engraving & Printing** (*see below* **Highlights**), where the mighty greenback is printed. Both are to the west near the Tidal Basin. To the east, between Third and Fourth Streets, the relatively distinguished 1930s **Department of Health and Human Services** offers an only moderately interesting tour (10.30am, 1.30pm, 2.30pm, weekdays only; call first to check as times may vary) around the Voice of America radio station (619 3919), which sends out its pro-America (some would say propagandist) broadcasts, in 52 languages, to approximately 86 million listeners around the world from its studios here.

L'Enfant Plaza, ironically, given that it is named in honour of the man whose city plan made Washington so stately, is a modern, grey expanse that's primarily notable for the huge underground shopping mall beneath it (an unremarkable one at that). From the Plaza, L'Enfant Promenade leads across US395 to Benjamin Banneker Memorial Circle (*see chapter* **DC Neighbourhoods: Southwest**).

Tour of shame

Scandal sites in Washington are hardly few, but they certainly can be far between. Still, with the help of a few short hops on the Metro, this one is possible in an afternoon – though it still includes some long walks (or short taxi rides).

Start at the **Watergate Apartment Complex**, Virginia Avenue and 27th Street, NW (Foggy Bottom-GWU Metro). Monica Lewinsky sent pizza to the press who waited outside while she shied away from them in her mother's apartment. More famously, this is the site of the 1972 Watergate break-in to the then-Democratic National Committee Headquarters on the sixth floor. (While you're here, keep an eye out for Bob and Liddy Dole and Supreme Court Justice Ruth Bader Ginsburg, all of whom call this exclusive address home.) Across the street is the one-time Howard Johnson hotel. G Gordon Liddy, general counsel to the Committee to Re-Elect the President, hung out in room 723 here during the break-in.

Take the Metro to the **Tidal Basin** (get off at Smithsonian), where in 1974 it was discovered that Rep Wilbur Mills, chairman of the powerful House Ways & Means Committee, was dating Argentine stripper Fanne Fox. After she and Mills were pulled over for speeding, she panicked and dived in the water. Cameramen caught her rescue on tape, and her identity was revealed. Mills did not seek re-election in 1976.

Walk north to the White House (about 15 minutes). The more things change, the more they stay the same here. For starters, Bill Clinton isn't the only president alleged to have trysted in that closet-sized room near the Oval Office. Besides John F Kennedy's alleged romps, Warren Harding reportedly enjoyed the favours of his mistress Nan Britton there in the 1920s. And Harding makes Clinton look positively virtuous: Britton, 30 years Harding's

Highlights

Bureau of Engraving & Printing

14th Street & C Street, SW (874 3019). Smithsonian Metro. **Tours** 9am-1.40pm (also 5-6.40pm June-Aug), every 20 minutes Mon-Fri. **Admission** free.

As the sign says, 'The Buck Starts Here!'. The printing and engraving of the title refers not to dull federal texts but hard currency: this is where the dollar in your pocket started life (well, here or Fort Worth, anyway). The Bureau produces stamps and other stuff, too (including some White House stationery), and there's a pretty interesting visitors' centre, but make no mistake, it's the prospect of seeing all that cash created that draws huge crowds here.

A 40-minute guided tour (no self-guided) provides a glimpse into the printing, cutting and stacking of the 22,400,000 banknotes produced daily. It's all done behind the thickest plate glass you've ever seen, with enough guards and security cameras to make the White House look positively easy-access. (If you have serious larceny in mind, the tried and tested route is to fill out an employment application, because all the really big scores have been inside

junior, gave birth to a girl presumably fathered by the president and, in 1927, published a steamy tell-all book called *The President's Daughter*.

Next door at the **Old Executive Office Building**, Oliver North, a staffer on the National Security Council, conducted his late-night paper-shredding sessions during the Reagan administration. He was later convicted for obstructing Congress during the investigation into the Iran-Contra affair, although the conviction was later overturned.

Lafayette Square, just across from the White House, sparked some crow-eating from George Bush. In 1989, Bush unveiled his anti-drug and get-tough-on-crime policies on TV. To show just how bad things had gotten, the outraged president hoisted a bag of crack cocaine that undercover DEA agents had purchased in (horrors!) Lafayette Square. Turns out the drug deal had been engineered for the photo op.

Walk about six blocks north up 16th Street to M Street, where the **Jefferson Hotel** sits on the corner. In suite 205, political consultant Dick Morris passed the time telling tales (and sucking toes) with his $200-an-hour call-girl Sherry Rowlands. A night's stay in the room – probably the only way you'll get to see it – will set you back $450. Of course, a view of the balcony, where news photographers captured the twosome, is free from the street.

Two blocks away, at the corner of 14th and M Streets at Thomas Circle, is the **Wyndham Washington** hotel. Better known by its former name, the Vista Hotel, it's where DC Mayor Marion Barry was caught on camera smoking crack in a 1980s FBI drug sting. Barry was stripped of his power – until the obviously forgiving population of DC re-elected him mayor in 1994. Hop back on the Metro at McPherson Square, a two-block walk away, to the **Capitol** (Capitol South Metro) – or, more specifically, the Capitol steps. That's where Rep John Jenrette and his now ex-wife had sex during a late-night session of Congress in 1980. Their liaison was to be exposed by a *Playboy* magazine editor who was looking to do a story on the typical congressional wife. (The congressman was later implicated in the Abscam scandal that nailed several members of Congress.)

Stop by Room 1506 of the **Longworth House Office Building** (Independence and New Jersey Avenues). That's where Rep Wayne Hays's 'secretary' Elizabeth Ray supposedly worked in 1976. Ray, Hays's girlfriend, received $14,000 a year but didn't actually do any office work. When the story broke in 1976, the congressman's days were numbered.

The $500,000 Capitol Hill townhouse where reporters caught 1988 Democratic presidential candidate Gary Hart cavorting with model Donna Rice (Hart's wife was in Denver for the weekend) is six or so blocks away at **517 Sixth Street**, SE. Hart – then the frontrunner for the nomination – withdrew from the race a week later.

Finally, take the Metro to the **Pentagon City Ritz-Carlton** (Pentagon City Metro), which has two claims to fame, er, infamy. Sports broadcaster and bedroom wearer of women's lingerie Marv Albert bit a woman in one of the hotel rooms, leading to a sex scandal and his firing from NBC in 1997. And in the Lobby Lounge, Monica Lewinsky shared a cheeseburger, extra crispy fries and an FBI wire-tapped conversation with one Linda Tripp on 13 January 1997. Three days later, FBI agents sequestered the presidential paramour in room 1012 for questioning.

For an official scandal tour, try the 75-minute guided tour from theatre group Gross National Product (*see page 34* **Tips & Tours**).

jobs.) And when you get to the end of the tour, you can buy a package of $150 for 50¢ – the catch being that the money is shredded because it comes from sheets of bills that didn't pass inspection. Leave it to the government to figure out how to make money on defective merchandise.

In the off-season (September to April) you should be able to go directly in with a minimal wait; in summer, you'll need a ticket on a timed tour. These are given out from 8am to 1.40pm (and also from 3.30-6.40pm from June to August) and you will probably need to stand in line at the ticket booth just outside in Raoul Wallenburg Place. Go at 7.45am to be sure of getting on a tour, or, if you are a US citizen, ask your congressional representative to get you on one of the 'VIP' tours in advance.

Feel the force

You can't get into the office part of the White House and what's going on in the halls of Congress sounds suspiciously unlike actual business. So how can you experience the power buzz in DC?

Power breakfast

One way is to get up early. Really early. Forget power lunches – DC does serious power breakfasting. Try the **Café Promenade** at the Renaissance Mayflower Hotel, where you're apt to hear phrases like 'Are you meeting at the White House?' or 'The Secretary says…'. Primetime is 7.30-8.30am on weekdays; you'll need to book. This is the place to see ABC News talking heads such as Cokie Roberts and Sam Donaldson – their offices are just down the street. The **Jefferson Hotel** is also chock-a-block with lobbyists, lawyers, diplomats and White House staffers chowing down on the hotel's signature breakfast dish, egg 'blossoms' with wild mushrooms and sausage. Other places: the **Hay-Adams Hotel**, just across from the White House, where senators, cabinet members, reporters and ambassadors gather and the **Willard**'s breakfast buffet, which is particularly popular with foreign dignitaries because of all the smoked meat and fish. For details of all hotels, *see chapter* **Accommodation**.

Power lunch

The city that eats together… well, we're sure someone has finished that saying with something pithy. Prime among a quartet of big-hitting Downtown steakhouses (a no-fuss hunk of meat being the traditional accompaniment to delicate political manoeuverings) is the **Palm** (*see p159* **Restaurants**), which, as the *Baltimore Sun* wrote, is not actually located just off the Oval Office, but some days almost seems like it could be. The caricatures of famous regulars are a hoot – George Bush in a loincloth while riding an elephant, Sen Ted Kennedy grinning over a sign to the men's room. The **Oval Room** (800 Connecticut Avenue, NW; 463 8700) really is just across from the White House, and the crowd reflects that. *New York Times* columnist Maureen Dowd and journalists Ted Koppel and Tim Russert are also regulars. For much cheaper lunches: tiny **CF Folks** (1225 19th Street, NW; 293 0515) is down the street from the Palm, and just as packed with lawyers and byline journos. **The Bread Line**, a block from the White House at 1751 Pennsylvania Avenue, NW, 822 8900, is packed with young staffers – and their bosses.

Power socialising

While Congress is in session, **campaign fundraisers** – as many as 20 a night – are held on midweek evenings in hotels and restaurants around the city. You'll need to pay to get in, of course, since that's the whole point, and whatever you do, don't interrupt a lobbyist who has just gotten his or her treasured two minutes with a key congressman. To find out when these are on, try asking your party's campaign office. **Alternatively, pack your tux (and your life savings) and attend a benefit**. All manner of institutions from museums to non-profit outfits hold these, on a scale from drab to dazzling. Museum bashes cost around $100. Check the Benefits page of *Washingtonian* magazine or the 'Style' section of the *Washington Post* for details.

Power ligging

Try to crash the **White House Correspondents Association Dinner**, where a bizarre mix of Hollywood celebrities, politicians, authors and media folk gather. It takes guts – and great party clothes, but it can be done. The dinner – and the pre-dinner cocktail parties, which are really the only part you can crash – is held every year in April at the **Washington Hilton** (*see p133* **Accommodation**), unofficially referred to as the Hinckley Hilton, since it's where John Hinckley attempted to assassinate President Reagan in 1981. The cocktail parties – each media organisation hosts one – are on the hotel's lower level. Invitations are frequently checked at the door, but usually there's more than one entrance to any given party. Once you're in there's almost nowhere you can't go (except, of course, to the actual dinner, which the president attends, and to the very elitist post-dinner *Vanity Fair* soirée).

Central DC

It may be a few skyscrapers short of a skyline, and low on metropolitan buzz, but downtown DC has unique compensations.

See **map** page 296.

Foggy Bottom

Transport

Foggy Bottom-GWU, Farragut West or Farragut North Metro.

Foggy Bottom – the area to the west and northwest of the White House up to the Potomac River, centred around Foggy Bottom-GWU Metro station – owes its name to its original marshy riverside location and its fame to becoming the nickname for the Department of State, which moved into the area in 1950. In the nineteenth century, it was home to German and Irish settlers working in the local gasworks, glass factory and brewery (whose emissions contributed the 'Foggy' part of the name). All three factories and many homes were demolished in the 1950s and 1960s to bring in new apartment buildings and other developments.

Today, this neighbourhood of government offices and expensive apartments is a historic district – it's been on the National Registry since 1987 for the architecture of its row houses – although the real indicators of its immigrant past are the churches where services are still held in German. It's home to a highly transient stream of foreign service workers, federal appointees, college students and performing artists, with the only constants being retirees and empty nesters. And sprawling over more than 20 blocks of the neighbourhood is **George Washington University**, once dubbed 'The Thing That Ate Foggy Bottom' because of its rapid expansion, and still a source of tension among area residents.

Near the dock where the US government first unloaded in its muddy new capital in 1800, the white marble box of the **Kennedy Center** (*see below* **Highlights**) rises above the river. North of the Kennedy Center lie the swirling contours of the **Watergate** office and residential complex (at 26th Street and Virginia Avenue), site of the eponymous 1972 burglary that unravelled Richard Nixon's presidency, later home to ironic next-door neighbours: President Clinton's 1996 election opponent, former senator Bob Dole, and Clinton's

The infamous ***Watergate*** *office and residential complex in Foggy Bottom.*

infamous intern, Monica Lewinsky. Shops and delis line the complex's courtyard. The humble Howard Johnson motel across the street from where Tricky Dicky's 'Plumbers' monitored the break-in is now the Premier Hotel (2601 Virginia Avenue): the Plumbers' room, festooned with Nixon memorabilia, is available at a premium rate. Some guests, discovering that they can't sleep in such a bizarre environment, request transfers.

At Virginia and New Hampshire Avenues, a statue of mid nineteenth-century Mexican President Benito Juarez points symbolically towards the distant monument to George Washington, who inspired him.

Above stately Virginia Avenue, Foggy Bottom seeps from monumental into urban Washington. Although George Washington University bulldozed many of the neighbourhood's characteristic tiny townhouses, some neat pockets – such as the area between New Hampshire Avenue and K Street – survive. The drab George Washington University Hospital at Washington Circle is the school's most noted building – not for any architectural merit, but because its emergency room doctors saved President Reagan's life after John Hinckley's 1981 assassination attempt.

The Octagon (*see below* **Highlights**) sheltered President James Madison for seven months after British invaders torched the executive mansion in 1814. The **Arts Club of Washington** (2017 I Street; 331 7282) was home to his successor, James Monroe – until the charred mansion was rebuilt and dubbed the White House because of the whitewash applied to hide the smoke stains. The Arts Club is open to the public from 10am to 5pm Tuesday to Friday, 10am to 2pm Saturday and 1pm to 5pm Sunday; admission is free.

Around Pennsylvania Avenue, Foggy Bottom frequently succumbs to 'façadeism', token retention of the fronts of historic buildings to comply with preservation rules, with massive modern structures ballooning behind. The blatant Mexican chancery (1911 Pennsylvania Avenue) and slightly subtler Red Lion Row (2000 Pennsylvania Avenue) are prime examples. The Spanish chancery on Washington Circle is subtler still, and stylish.

North of Pennsylvania Avenue, the old West End (aka 'New Downtown', north and west of Farragut Square) is the haunt of the 'K Street Lawyer' lobbyists. Although recent spending limits on entertaining members of Congress have pinched a bit, their expense-account hangouts still aren't cheap. Currently in with the pinstriped smooth-talkers are **The Palm** (1225 19th Street; 293 9091), **Sam & Harry's** (1200 19th Street; 296 4333), **Legal Sea Foods** (2020 K Street; 496 1111), and **McCormick & Schmick's** (1652 K Street; 861 2233). A stroll down the block-long promenade of the **Renaissance Mayflower Hotel** (1127 Connecticut Avenue; 347 3000), renovated to its pristine 1925 chic, may also yield a glimpse of celebrity clientele.

One structure of note is the **Russian Embassy** (1125 16th Street). Built as a wedding gift for the daughter of sleeping-car tycoon George Pullman, the gushy palazzo briefly became the Tsarist Russian embassy in 1917, before relations were severed by the Revolution. With US recognition in 1934, the USSR moved back in, planting hammer-and-sickle motifs amid the gilt cherubs adorning the walls. The red flag came down on 26 December 1991 and the mansion again became the Russian Embassy (although it is now the ceremonial appendage of the larger compound on Wisconsin Avenue).

To keep K Street fit for Guccis to tread, in 1998 property owners formed a self-taxing 38-block Golden Triangle Business Improvement District centred on Farragut Square. Early results have included cleaner pavements, better landscaping and lighting and a corps of uniformed functionaries to give directions and keep an eye on pesky panhandlers.

Highlights

Kennedy Center

2700 F Street, NW, at New Hampshire Avenue (467 4600/1-800 444 1324). Foggy Bottom-GWU Metro.
Open 10am-9pm Mon-Sat; noon-9pm Sun.

Adorned with decorative gifts from many nations, the Ken Cen (officially the John F Kennedy Center for the Performing Arts) is as much a spectacle as the shows it presents, with its five theatres and concert halls, three roof-top restaurants and delightful views from the open-air terrace. Free concerts (6pm daily) are held in the towering Grand Foyer, which astounds with its vast proportions. The Hall of States displays the flags of the states in the order they entered the Union, while the Hall of Nations hangs the banners of nations recognised by the US in alphabetical order – so an event like the fragmentation of the USSR can cause a logistical crisis. Free 45-minute guided tours (10am-4.45pm Mon-Fri; 10am-12.45pm Sat, Sun) leave from Parking Lobby A, opposite the gift shop. Parking is inadequate when several shows are playing at once – better to walk or take the free shuttle bus from the Foggy Bottom-GWU Metro stop. *See also p196* **Culture**.
Website: kennedy-center.org

The Octagon

1799 New York Avenue, NW, between 18th & E Streets (638 3221/recorded information 638 3105). Farragut North or Farragut West Metro.
Open 10am-4pm Tue-Sun. **Admission** $3; $1.50 concessions; free under-6s. **Credit** AmEx, MC, V.

Designed to fit its odd-shaped lot by Dr William Thornton, first architect of the US Capitol, this elegant brick building is the city's oldest private mansion, built between 1798 and 1800. It was home to the Tayloes, aristocratic Virginians, who offered it to the suddenly homeless President James Madison in 1814, after the burning of the White House. Shaped more like a pregnant hexagon than an octagon, the house – reputed to be haunted – is a gem of light and proportion. The related American Institute of Architects' headquarters are next door; hence the Octagon hosts topical architectural exhibits as well as Madison-era furnishings – including the desk where Madison signed the Treaty of Ghent in 1815, ending the last war between the US and UK. *See also p107* **Museums & Galleries**.

Downtown

Transport

McPherson Square, Metro Center, Gallery Place-Chinatown or Mount Vernon Square-UDC Metro.

DC's large downtown area – north of the White House, bordered by Connecticut Avenue to the west, E Street to the south and Sixth Street to the east – is sometimes called 'Old Downtown' to distinguish it from the 'New Downtown' area in Foggy Bottom. Once synonymous with F Street's theatres, restaurants and department stores, it slumped in the 1960s as shoppers fled to suburban malls, and virtually keeled over after the 1968 riots tarnished it as unsafe. Early attempts at revival, such as a half-hearted F Street pedestrian mall that was later torn up, were haphazard. For many years, the area was a ghost town at night.

In 1985, the Hecht Company opened at 12th and G Streets, the first freestanding department store built in an American downtown in four decades. None followed its lead. In 1998, the Washington Opera abandoned plans to turn the vacant, beloved Woodward & Lothrop department store at Tenth and F Streets into an opera house, allegedly because the well-heeled dowagers dominating its board are still wary of venturing Downtown.

But, thanks to a lot of money, effort, and time, Downtown's image is slowly changing. An influx of law firms into new office buildings set the stage for a turnaround. One symptom of this revival is **Franklin Square**, at 14th and I Streets. When progressively sleazier strip clubs gave the vicinity a bad name, landlords united to price them out of business. The longshot plan to spark upscale development worked, with funds contributed to maintain the park itself obliquely returning in higher rents. Even the statue facing 14th Street of Irish-born Commodore John Barry, 'Father of the US Navy', got a polish.

The venerable **National Theatre** (1321 Pennsylvania Avenue; 628 6161) flourishes anew after years as a Ken Cen colony, while the **Warner Theatre** (at 13th & E Streets; 783 4000) enjoyed a thorough restoration after decades of darkness (for details of both, *see chapter* **Culture**). On Tenth Street is **Ford's Theatre** (*see below* **Highlights**), also a functioning theatre but more famous for being the site of Abe Lincoln's assassination. It houses a museum of Lincoln memorabilia.

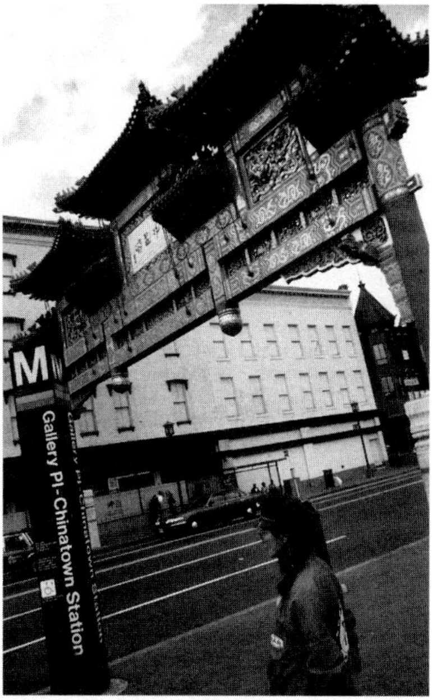

Chinatown *(p62) is experiencing a revival.*

The **National Press Club** (14th and F Streets), opened in 1924, is no longer the media hub it once was, now that major newspapers such as the *New York Times* and *Wall Street Journal* have bureaus elsewhere. Now it's home mainly to the international press and newsletters, although the top floor is still the scene of speeches by national and foreign leaders. The press club is connected to National Place, which opened in 1984 and contains a few unremarkable shops, restaurants and a food court. Downtown is still home to the *Washington Post*, however; its imposing headquarters building, built in 1973 for $25 million, is at 1150 15th Street (at L Street). One block west is the home of the venerable **National Geographic Society** (*see below* **Highlights**).

Until recently the former Greyhound bus terminal at 12th Street and New York Avenue was an abandoned eyesore on the seedy fringe of things. Now its streamlined façade, so treasured by Washington's large community of art deco enthusiasts, fronts a large office building complementing its lines. Street-level tenants include restaurants and the sometimes cacophonous **Capitol City Brewing Company** (*see page 164* **Bars**),

Washington's original brewpub. Another newcomer to the area is the **National Museum of Women in the Arts** (*see page 105* **Museums & Galleries**), or at least the collection, which arrived in 1987 in an airy Renaissance Revival building that predates it by 80 years.

A couple of blocks east, the unlovable concrete fortress that is the **Washington Convention Center** (Ninth Street, at New York Avenue; 789 1600) was pronounced too small almost as soon as it opened in 1983. It appears destined to become an appendage of an even larger successor, controversially approved for Mount Vernon Square, a block to the north-east. For now, it's where the trade, flower and car shows, book fairs and occasional international exhibits happen. One block south is the **Martin Luther King Memorial Library** (*see below* **Highlights**), the main branch in DC's public library system. The National Museum of American Art and the National Portrait Gallery next door are both closed for a three-year renovation from January 2000.

At Seventh and F Streets looms **MCI Center** (*see below* **Highlights**), a pro sports arena and amusement complex opened in 1997 to revive Chinatown, where a score of Chinese and other oriental restaurants struggled under the suburbanite perception that the area was too dangerous. The recovery may be working too well, with upscale replacements driving out some of the older chopstick joints. Gaudy chinoiserie obscures some quite old house façades; **Go-Lo's** restaurant (604 H Street; 347 4656) occupies Mary Surratt's boarding house, where in 1865 John Wilkes Booth met co-conspirators to plot Abe Lincoln's downfall.

Chinatown is not just home to Chinese restaurants. Brazilian, Irish and Texas BBQ establishments now thrive within sight of the world's largest Chinese arch (over H Street, at Seventh Street), given by the People's Republic of China. Although DC's Chinese population has largely dispersed through the suburbs, Chinatown remains the community's spiritual centre and the site of dragon dancing at Chinese New Year.

Besides Chinatown, in the shadow of MCI Center, the churches are among the most tangible reminders of Washington's immigrant past, particularly **St Mary's Mother of God** (727 Fifth Street), a copy of Germany's Ulm Cathedral, that was built in 1890 for German-speaking Catholic immigrants. There's also **St Patrick's Catholic Church** (619 Tenth Street), established in 1794 to serve the Irish immigrants who came to build the White House and Capitol. The current church – the fourth one on the site – dates from 1884.

The Vista International Hotel (now Wyndham Washington DC City Center Hotel) at 1400 M Street got a crack at making history in 1990; this is where flamboyant DC Mayor Marion Barry, muttering, 'the bitch set me up', was arrested in a drug sting concealed as a sexual tryst. He went to prison but ran again for mayor in 1994 and won.

DC has gone some way to achieving its declared goal of a 'living downtown' enlivened after dark by entertainment-seeking residents, but with one conspicuous failure. Its inability to make

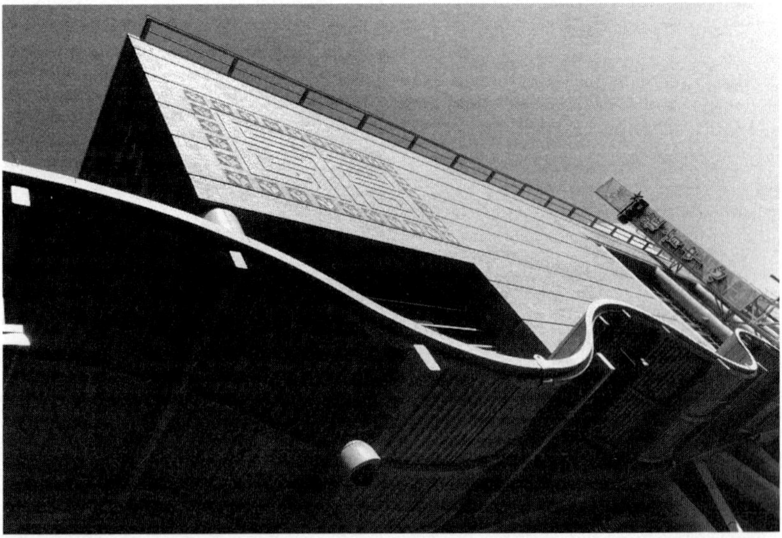

MCI Center: *the new $200-million sports and amusement complex in Downtown.*

developers include less lucrative housing in their office development plans means that, except for the northern fringe and some upscale condos at Pennsylvania Avenue, few call Downtown home.

Highlights

Ford's Theatre & Lincoln Museum

511 Tenth Street, NW, between E & F Streets (box office 347 4833/Park Service 426 6924). Metro Center or Federal Triangle Metro. **Museum open** 9am-5pm daily. **Admission** free.

On Good Friday 1865, Abraham Lincoln sat in a rocking chair in Ford's Theatre watching the comedy *Our American Cousin*, when actor and Southern sympathiser John Wilkes Booth entered the presidential box and shot him. Booth jumped over the balcony, got tangled in the flag draped over the railing and broke his leg on landing. He hobbled to a back alley, where he escaped on horseback and was shot 12 days later.

Today, Ford's Theatre – which serves as a theatre and as a museum of Lincoln and Booth memorabilia – is decorated as it was that 14 April. Later performers did in later presidents here less literally, as when political satirist Mark Russell entertained Ronald Reagan. The slightly macabre exhibits in the basement-level Lincoln Museum include the assassin's Derringer pistol, Lincoln's blood-stained clothes and even the tools used to seal his coffin. Cross the street to Petersen House (516 Tenth Street; 426 6924), then owned by tailor William Petersen, where doctors laid the 6ft 4in president diagonally across the small bed in the back bedroom. Mrs Lincoln and her eldest son, Robert, spent most of the night in the front parlour. Lincoln finally gave up the ghost at 7.22am on 15 April.

Martin Luther King Memorial Library

901 G Street, NW, between Ninth & Tenth Streets (general information 727 1111/ reference 727 1126). Gallery Place-Chinatown Metro. **Open** 10am-9pm Mon-Thur; 10am-5pm Fri, Sat; 1-5pm Sun.

This black Bauhaus box, designed by Mies van der Rohe in 1972, contains the main branch of DC's public library system. Of special interest is the third-floor Washingtoniana Room, where a squad of excellent reference librarians help sort through books, historical directories, maps and more than 13 million newspaper clippings concerning the District of Columbia and vicinity. *See also p261* **Directory**.

MCI Center

601 F Street, NW, at Seventh Street (628 3200). Gallery Place-Chinatown Metro. **Open** 11am-6pm daily; till 9am on event days. **Sports gallery admission** $5; free under-5s.

Opened in December 1997 to the beat of a Barry Manilow concert, this huge, $200-million arena hosts some 200 public events a year, including concerts, family entertainments and local college athletics as well as pro games by the Washington Capitals NHL hockey team and the Washington Wizards NBA basketball team. The women's Washington Mystics basketball team arrived in 1998 and quickly won a devoted following among local females, despite a thoroughly dismal opening season.

The centre involves all the economic excesses now de rigueur in American professional sport: startling admission prices, 110 exorbitant skyboxes for corporate Pooh-Bahs, restaurants restricting admission to top-end ticketholders and other class-based novelties. But it is also well designed, centrally located and set atop a Metro station. The single most important virtue is the seating, which is comfortable and angled to afford even stratospheric spectators a good view. Unless you attend the event, the only way to see the arena itself is on the behind-the-scenes tour ($5), currently held only in summer (though plans are afoot to go year-round), usually at noon and 2pm (call 661 5133 for details).

MCI Center exploits its handy location by operating all week, even if nobody's playing. Concourse attractions include a sporting goods store, a sports and theatre ticket agency and shops such as the **Discovery Channel Store: Destination DC** (639 0908). Opened in 1998, this 25,000-sq ft, three-storey store blurs the distinction between museum and emporium, to the detriment of parental pocketbooks. Here, the self-styled 'world's largest producer of non-fiction entertainment' (taking a cue from Disney) mingles interactive displays about science and nature, from the dinosaurs to the astronauts, with related merchandise. A four-storey high-tech IMAX theatre screens what Discovery Channel modestly proclaims 'the only film to provide an insider's view of the nation's capital'.

MCI National Sports Gallery (661 5133) continues electronic games, with options of virtual-reality competition with stars of various major sports, such as going one-on-one against an image of Wizards basketball favourite Nikki McCray. Sports fans can also try out their gift of the gab as play-by-play broadcasters for some of the great moments in athletics at the American Sportscasters Association Hall of Fame & Museum. All's not gizmos and gimmicks, however. Classic broadcasts can be seen and heard once again, and some of the sports memorabilia is first-rate and well displayed.

National Geographic Society

Gilbert H Grosvenor Auditorium, 1600 M Street, NW, at 16th Street (857 7700).
Explorers Hall, 1145 17th Street, NW, at M Street (857 7588). Farragut North Metro. **Open** 9am-5pm Mon-Sat; 10am-5pm Sun.

Since its founding in 1890 by local patricians, the National Geographic Society has funded more than 5,500 exploration and research projects to destinations from the Himalayas to the Poles. Its dignified flagship *National Geographic Magazine* has always had a slightly stuffy reputation, despite its exquisite photography and the fact that its photos of semi-naked tribespeople provided unintended titillation to generations of smirking schoolboys. The Grosvenor Auditorium still hosts the traditional lecture series by slide-showing adventurers, but now also presents international concerts and videos, even beer tastings. On Tuesdays at noon, you can watch National Geographic TV specials for free.

The adjacent Explorers Hall is a livelier place, a free museum with changing exhibitions on subjects as diverse as the excavations at Petra, Lucy the oldest humanoid and Admiral Peary in the Arctic. Its interactive ecological exhibit, Geographica, invites visitors 'to touch a tornado, play the continent game, explore the solar system…', while Earth Station One simulates an orbital flight 23,000 miles up. Recent special exhibits featured Ch'ing dynasty jade artefacts, the Maya world and the *Whydah* pirate ship.

Penn Quarter

Transport

Archives-Navy Memorial Metro.

On the opposite side of Pennsylvania Avenue from the Federal Triangle, this small, triangular district is bounded by Sixth, 13th and F Streets (though the borders are rather loosely defined and some people consider it spreads further north towards New York Avenue to include Chinatown and MCI Center). In recent years, it has experienced a resurgence, as art galleries, restaurants and new developments have opened; two major new cinemas are also in the works.

In the 1800s, District residents shopped in the area's vast local market and viewed it as the locus of the city. But by the mid-1900s, Penn Quarter had deteriorated. Distressed by the tawdriness of Pennsylvania Avenue as he rode in his 1961 inaugural procession, President Kennedy set a commission to revamping 'America's Main Street'. In 1968, the riots that followed the assassination of Martin Luther King Jr hit the area badly. By 1972, Congress took notice and created the Pennsylvania Avenue Development Corporation, initiating the revitalisation that has come to fruition within the past decade.

The crane perched on the quirky Temperance Fountain at Seventh Street and Pennsylvania Avenue punctuates the Seventh Street arts corridor of galleries and studios blooming behind Victorian cast-iron storefronts (for detailed information on these galleries, *see page 114* **Museums & Galleries**). The former Lansburgh's department store now houses posh apartments above the **Shakespeare Theatre** (450 Seventh Street; *see page 197* **Culture**).

Washington's Hard Rock Café is at 999 E Street, and in the Old Evening Star Building (1201 Pennsylvania Avenue), built in 1898, is Planet Hollywood. The **US Navy Memorial** (*see below* **Highlights**) plaza nicely frames the Eighth Street axis between the National Portrait Gallery and the National Archives. Near the White House, grand old hotels such as the **Washington** (515 15th Street; 638 5900) with its famous roof-top bar and the lavish **Willard** (1401 Pennsylvania Avenue; 628 9100) have recovered their lost lustre, as a stroll down the latter's plush Peacock Alley corridor will confirm. JFK would have been pleased, mostly.

Investigate the investigators at the **FBI Building** *in Penn Quarter.*

However, the **J Edgar Hoover FBI Building** (*see below* **Highlights**) presents a sterile streetscape because Hoover himself vetoed the planned street-level shops and restaurants as potential security threats. The sketchy and inept historical plaques along the blank Pennsylvania Avenue front do little to keep it from being dead space and are universally ignored. Despite the architecture and the rather disappointing tour, it is very a popular tourist attraction.

Highlights

J Edgar Hoover FBI Building

935 Pennsylvania Avenue, NW, between Ninth & Tenth Streets (324 3447). Metro Center Metro.
Open 1-hour tours 8.45am-4.15pm Mon-Fri.
Admission free (from E Street entrance).

After the White House and the US Capitol, the FBI Building is Washington's third most popular tour, though there are few bells and whistles, just some rather dated display boards and the worrying sensation that everything is a lot lower-tech that you thought it would be.

With the agent-guides touting the G-men's triumphs over crime and espionage, the one-hour tour doesn't have time to go close up on Bureau activities, although you'll see a seemingly endless supply of drugs, confiscated guns and gangsters' treasures, along with technicians in glass-enclosed laboratories working up blood samples. But your visit will definitely end with a bang: a real live firearms demonstration. When busy, the feds sometimes rush their guests through so fast that they miss many of the exhibits, but most get the message that crime doesn't pay.

US citizens should write three months in advance to their senator or representative; otherwise, expect to wait at least an hour for tickets.

US Navy Memorial & Heritage Center

701 Pennsylvania Avenue, NW, between Seventh & Ninth Streets (737 2300). Archives-Navy Memorial Metro. **Open** 9.30am-5pm Mon-Sat.
Admission free.

Dedicated on the Navy's 212th birthday in 1987, this memorial features the world's biggest map of itself – a flat granite circular map 100ft across, with Washington, of course, at its centre. At the dedication ceremony, sea water from all the world's oceans was poured into the central fountains. The surrounding sculptured wall has 22 bas-reliefs (of widely varying quality) depicting highlights of naval history, such as the Great White Fleet of 1907, Commodore Perry's 1854 opening to Japan and the 'Silent Service' of submarines.

Off-centre stands a statue of the Lone Sailor, stolid in his pea jacket. The subterranean visitor centre has a cinema with a 52ft-high screen, which shows At Sea ($4), an all-too-authentically noisy depiction of life on an aircraft carrier. A 1,200-seat, open-air amphitheatre presents free summer concerts by military bands.

Judiciary Square area

Transport

Judiciary Square or Gallery Place-Chinatown Metro.

Judiciary Square, anchoring the nondescript central area west of Sixth Street slashed by US 395, has long been the centre of the city's judiciary and local government, but holds little of appeal for visitors beyond a few memorials and a museum.

Two blocks east of Seventh Street, at F Street, the **National Building Museum**, an architectural museum (*see page 106* **Museums & Galleries**), occupies the 1883 Renaissance-palace Pension Building, with its extraordinary frieze of Civil War troops perpetually patrolling the premises. Across F Street, bronze lions flank the 1991 **National Law Enforcement Officers Memorial**, a tribute to the 14,800-plus cops killed in the line of duty since 1794. To help make sense of the memorial, which assigns no chronological or alphabetical order to the names, grab a brochure from the visitors' centre (605 E Street; 737 3400). It will explain the system, and point out lawmen slain by notorious criminals such as Bonnie and Clyde.

Flanking the area is the dwindling domain of bail bondsmen and 'Fifth Street lawyers' (not to be confused with the sleek K Street set): cut-rate but street-savvy barristers hustling in a pinch over to the criminal courts to prevent an incarceration.

Gloriously restored, **Union Station**...

The **Court of Appeals** building (Fifth & D Streets) was once Washington's city hall, a chaste 1820 Greek Revival design by British architect George Hadfield. Lincoln's statue at the front is significant as the first public memorial to the slain president, sculpted by his acquaintance, Lot Flannery, and dedicated on the third anniversary of his death in 1868. Flannery knew how Lincoln looked, and he worked fast, so the oratorical posture is probably quite authentic.

Down the stairs that constitute Fourth Street, beside the statue of Chief Justice John Marshall that once graced the Capitol grounds, the **Canadian Embassy** – awarded its prominent site in honour of close national relations – houses a gallery spotlighting Canadian artists. Protected by statues of Gettysburg's victor, General Meade, and master legal commentator Sir William Blackstone, the **US Court House** opposite the embassy is gradually losing its 'Watergate Courthouse' identity as subsequent scandals, including the trial of former mayor Marion Barry, unfold before interminable grand juries. The **Frances Perkins Department of Labor Building** (*see below* **Highlights**) to the east of the Court House is worth visiting to view its small Labor Hall of Fame.

Highlights

Frances Perkins Department of Labor Building

200 Constitution Avenue, NW, at Third Street (371 6422). Judiciary Square Metro. **Open** 8.15am-4.45pm Mon-Fri. **Admission** free (photo ID required).
Named after FDR's trusty aide, the first female US cabinet minister (1933-45), this building's Labor Hall of Fame displays personal artefacts of leaders ranging from radical activist Mother Jones to unconventional industrialist Henry J Kaiser. Supreme Court Justice Arthur Goldberg's judicial robe is folded back to disclose the garment's union label. Nearby is a presentation about Frances Perkins herself.

Union Station & around

Transport

Union Station Metro.

Uniting the scattered depots of rival railroads, the Beaux Arts-style **Union Station**, built in 1908, grandiosely reflects its inspiration, the Baths of Diocletian in Rome. Determined to make the most splendid railway station in the country, architect Daniel 'Make no small plans' Burnham lavished it with amenities, including a nursery, a swimming pool and even a mortuary for defunct out-of-towners. It is certainly an impressive building; the Main Hall is a huge rectangular space, with a 96-foot-high barrel-vaulted ceiling and a balcony with 36 sculptures of Roman legionnaires.

...is buzzing with shops and restaurants.

But the station languished as rail traffic declined. The President's Room, reserved for chief executives welcoming incoming dignitaries such as King George VI and Emperor Haile Selassie, is now a restaurant. In 1953 a decidedly non-stop express train bound for Ike's inauguration smashed into the crowded concourse, incredibly killing nobody. Two decades later a deliberate but equally disastrous hole was sunk in the Great Hall for the multi-screen video set-up of an ill-conceived visitor centre. Despite its sooty grandeur, the station seemed doomed to the wrecking-ball.

However, painstakingly restored at a cost of $165 million, since 1988 Union Station has thrived with an array of shops, amusements and eateries of all sorts – even a multi-screen cinema downstairs with the buzzing food court – enough to gladden old Burnham's heart. Rents are high and some of the shops have failed, but successors always seem to come along eventually. It is easy to forget that the marble and gilt pleasure palace's main function is still as a railroad station. Some of the streets around Union Station are dodgy after dark, so stick to the main, well-lit thoroughfares.

The Thurgood Marshall Judiciary Building east of Union Station complements the former City Post Office on the west, also built by Burnham – now the **National Postal Museum** (*see page 106* **Museums & Galleries**) – to present an elegant urban vista, lined with the flags of all the US states and territories ranged around the central Columbus Memorial Fountain, built in 1912. The landscaped Union Station Plaza in front of the station stretches all the way to the Capitol.

The neighbourhood around Union Station was once a shanty town of Irish railroad labourers, who christened their marshy abode 'Swampoodle' after its swamps and puddles. The **Phoenix Park Hotel** (*see page 129* **Accommodation**) and bars such as the **Dubliner** and **Kelly's Irish Times** (*see pages 164-5* **Bars**) reflect this Hibernian heritage, but by chance, with Irish newcomers happening to set up here in the early 1970s.

DC Neighbourhoods

Away from the civic anonymity of its monumental core, DC has a unique urban character.

Most people who live in DC could not find their street marked on most tourist maps. This is because anywhere outside the National Mall and the airport does not merit a mention in many guidebooks, save for panicked warnings to steer clear of dark alleys. That oversight is one of the downsides of being the capital city of the United States, where most places north of the White House and east of the Capitol are perceived by outsiders as hazy marginalia. But the Washington Monument, lovely as it may be, has nothing at all to do with the District. It reflects none of the city's richness or personal history. No one feels a cosy sense of hometown pride when they think of a monument.

The reason locals stay in DC is the neighbourhoods – dozens of them, varied, full of stories and devoted residents. For people who stay – or are born here – DC means leafy low-rise blocks, front porches, bustling restaurants and cornerstores, blissfully, but not literally, far away from the stampeding sightseers at the Air & Space Museum.

Northwest

Because the US Capitol, the point used to divide DC into quadrants, is slightly east of the centre, Northwest is far the biggest sector, and also the most affluent, with most of central DC (*see page 59*) falling into it, along with the majority of its residential hinterlands, streetlife and nightlife. It is roughly bisected, north to south, by tiny Rock Creek and the widening wedge of parkland that flanks it. This description begins with the areas to the east of the park, working from the centre outwards, then covers the western area, starting with Georgetown.

Dupont Circle

Transport

Dupont Circle Metro.

See **map** page 294-5.

Dupont Circle is the most metropolitan of all DC's neighbourhoods. Best known for being the largest gay community in the DC area, Dupont Circle's many bars and restored brownstones cater to affluent gay men (although lesbians have a determined, if overshadowed, presence). Although the name technically refers to a traffic circle located in the centre of the neighbourhood, when locals say Dupont Circle they generally mean the entire area radiating off the circle north and south along Connecticut Avenue.

But the circle itself is literally and figuratively the heart of the neighbourhood. The small park achieves what all the other traffic circles in the city were meant to do but don't, serving as a lively green space for neighbours to gather and gawk. It's the premier people-watching location in DC, particularly on weekends, when gangs of bike couriers gather beside homeless people playing chess with businessmen and immaculately dressed guppies walking their pedigree dogs. In the middle of it all, a white marble fountain sprays into the air in honour of Civil War hero Samuel Francis Dupont.

In the nineteenth century, Dupont Circle was the opposite of what it is today – it was a backwater region on the outskirts of Downtown, too underdeveloped and inconvenient to sustain much life.

The eponymous circle in ***Dupont Circle****.*

18th Street *in Adams Morgan: club central.*

But by the turn of the century, mansions began sprouting up along the dirt roads. It experienced a bout of radicalism in the 1960s, when anti-Vietnam War protesters and black-power activists claimed the circle for demonstrations, but by and large, the neighbourhood has remained a relatively well-heeled sector of town.

Although national chainstores have moved with a vengeance into the **Connecticut Avenue** corridor, there are still enough record shops, bookstores, coffeeshops and restaurants to make Dupont Circle worth a stroll – start at the circle and move north.

On warm days, a booming brass band sometimes materialises near the Metro entrances, which are north and south of the circle. Large hotels and apartment buildings start to dominate the landscape about four blocks north. The **Washington Hilton** on the corner of Connecticut Avenue and T Street (*see page 133* **Accommodation**) was the site of John Hinckley Jr's attempted assassination of then-president Ronald Reagan in 1981. Hinckley, who shot Reagan in an ambitious attempt to impress actress Jodie Foster, now lives in Southeast DC at St Elizabeth's mental hospital and is currently lobbying to be allowed out for excursions with his family. The hotel has done its best to make sure no one could get as close to any of its many visiting dignitaries again, installing a bulletproof bunker for cars to pick up VIPs in the driveway where Reagan was shot. The stretch of T Street in front of the hotel is frequently blocked off by frowning Secret Service men in preparation for arriving motorcades.

Aside from the Connecticut Avenue strip, the blocks north of the circle consist largely of well-kept Victorian rowhouses, art galleries and gorgeous mansions now run by embassies or non-profit associations looking to be represented in the nation's capital. If the weather is nice, amble through the blocks west of Connecticut Avenue – known as **Kalorama** – to check out the impressive architecture and exhibitions. The 20 or so galleries include contemporary, experimental and traditional art, from painting to sculpture to photography. At the heart of all the galleries is the **Phillips Collection** (1600 21st Street), which opened in 1921 as the first permanent museum of modern art in America. For more information on all these, *see chapter* **Museums & Galleries**.

West of Kalorama is **Massachusetts Avenue**, also known as 'Embassy Row', running from the circle through Upper Northwest. The extravagance of the diplomatic compounds is directly proportional to the wealth of each country, so the buildings vary tremendously. An eerie hush envelops the embassy areas, particularly after business hours, when no one comes and goes save for guards changing shifts and eyeing passers-by.

All of Dupont Circle is perfect for daytime pursuits such as walking, shopping and lunching. But the movie theatres are downright embarrassing – shoddy little screens and soiled seats, yet full-priced tickets. And it's best to choose your restaurants with care. The main late-night attractions are gay bars. The scene is high-profile and energetic, but small enough to be a bit incestuous. **P Street**, which intersects the circle, is the traditional lifeline of the city's gay community. These days, older men tend to frequent the bars west of the circle on P Street, while the younger party boys stick to the **17th Street** strip east of the circle, parallelling Connecticut Avenue.

Unless you go to a gay bar, drink coffee or hang out at some overly test-marketed chain restaurant, the only mentionable nightspots are a few blocks south of the circle near the intersection of 18th Street and Connecticut Avenue – including the famous **18th Street Lounge** and **Red** clubs (*see chapter* **Nightlife**). Some of the lounge bars are irritatingly pretentious, but compared with other large cities, their cover charges are minimal. And they attract the city's small glam population late into the night.

Adams Morgan

Transport

Dupont Circle Metro, then L2 bus or Woodley Park-Zoo Metro, then 90, 91, 92, 93, 96 bus.

See **map** page 294-5.

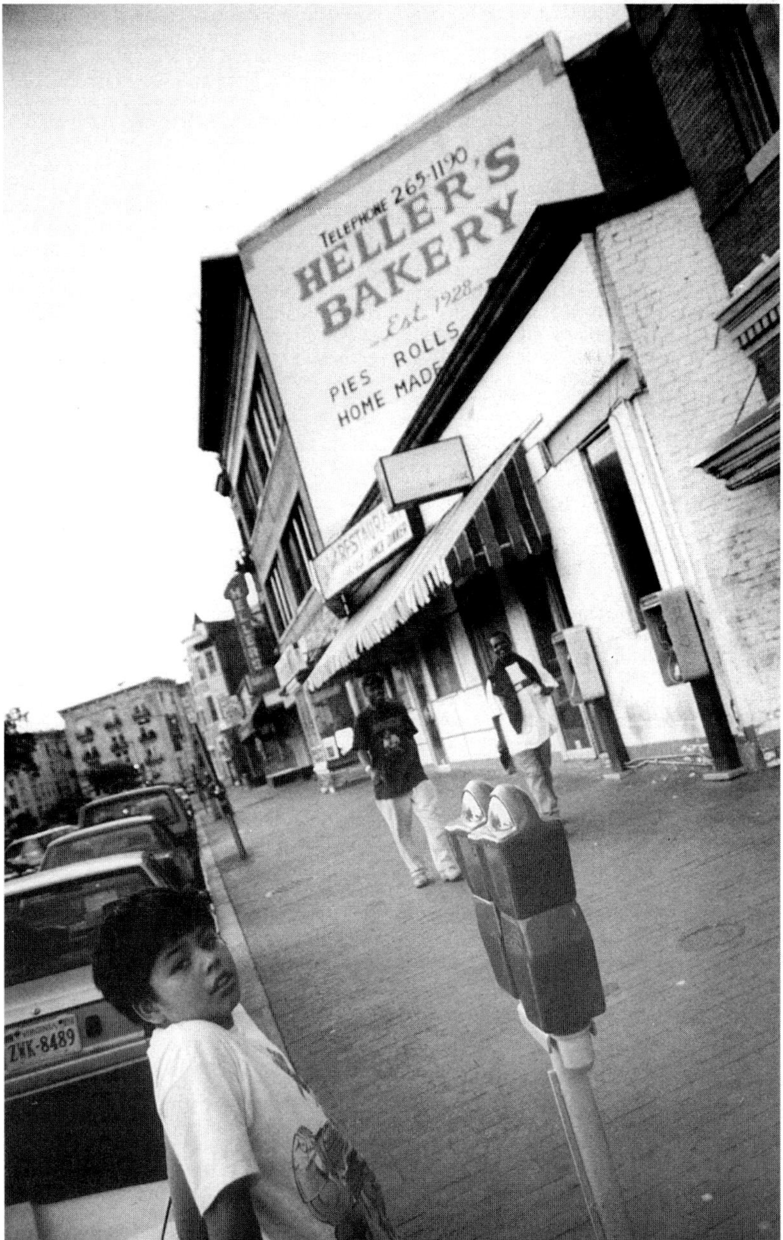

Local stalwart Heller's Bakery on **Mount Pleasant Street**. *See page 74.*

One block east of Dupont Circle is **18th Street**, which becomes the main strip of Adams Morgan about nine walkable blocks north. Adams Morgan is routinely cited for its ethnic restaurants and thriving diversity. And aside from the constant turnover of some of the worse restaurants and bars, it does in fact have an eclectic liveliness reminiscent of many New York neighbourhoods. It also has relatively cheap but safe housing that draws a lot of young, mostly white transplants too sophisticated or too poor for the homogeneity of Georgetown and the suburbs.

But beware: just as it's ill-advised to expect too much out of Dupont Circle at night, it's downright depressing to visit Adams Morgan in the day. Because there are very few offices in Adams Morgan, the restaurants and the streets tend to be barren during the weekday lunch hour. But at night, 18th Street (up to and including the spots along Columbia Road, which intersects 18th Street at the top of the hill) morphs into a jangling bar and dining scene. Parking is a nightmare, and many of the baseball-capped clientele start to look the same after a while, but nowhere else in the city can you hop from one joint to the next with better results. The bars range from flat-out frat-boy hangouts to salsa and reggae clubs. The neighbourhood becomes a happy carnival at night, particularly on warm summer evenings when the strips of outdoor cafés pack in the customers until well after midnight.

In the 1920s and '30s, what is now Adams Morgan was an elite neighbourhood of rowhouses stacked on a hill. The elevation made for precious breezes in the sweltering summers and, for some houses, a charming view of the city. But it wasn't until the 1950s that the neighbourhood got its current name. Progressive-minded residents came up with a plan to integrate blacks and whites in the area by merging the white Adams school with the black Morgan school.

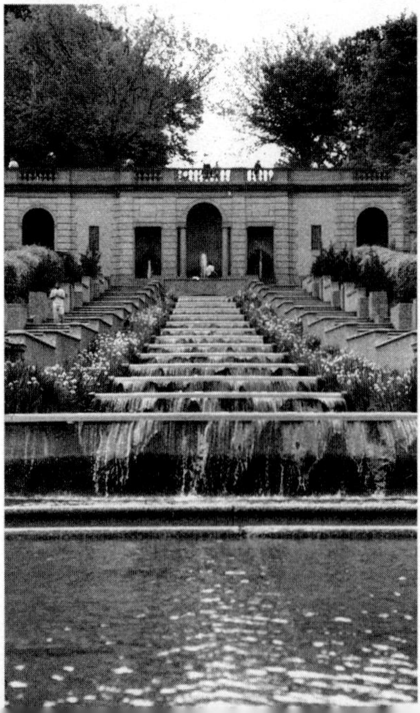

The area continues to attract a wide range of nationalities and races. DC is home to the largest community of Ethiopians outside Ethiopia, and many have opened bars and restaurants in Adams Morgan. Ethiopian food – big bowls of meat and puréed vegetables and starches – makes for a communal and satisfying dining adventure (*see chapter* **Restaurants**). Thai, Vietnamese, Indian and Cajun restaurants also merit visits.

The only exception to the rule about avoiding Adams Morgan during the day is **Malcolm X Park** – which is officially called Meridian Hill Park (*see below* **Highlights**). In fact, unless you're looking for a taste of the local crime scene, you should *only* go to Malcolm X Park during the day. And when you do, you'll experience one of DC's finest secret spots.

Highlights

Malcolm X Park

Bordered by 16th, Euclid, 15th & W Streets.

For some reason – perhaps because it is named after America's most infamous black-power icon – tourists almost never set foot in Malcolm X Park. But it is a 12-acre haven for people who live in the Adams Morgan and Mount Pleasant areas. They come to study, play soccer, walk their dogs, buy pot, whatever. Just before sunset, the park fills with the competing sounds of ad-hoc African, Brazilian and Puerto-Rican percussion groups.

The park's grounds consist of a simple, large rectangle of grass on the northern end and a series of gardens and 13 cascading pools on the south. The park offers a textured view of the whole city, with the Washington Monument in the background. It has a long history as a stage, starting in the middle of the nineteenth century, and when it opened as a park in 1936, it was America's first national park for the performing arts. The fountains were turned off during concerts in favour of light glistening through dry-ice vapour.

After World War II, as both people and federal dollars migrated to the suburbs, the park's artistic importance faded. But in the past decade, as safety has returned to the park, so have the arts. Friends of Meridian Hill have staged over 200 concerts, most aimed at children, since 1990, and the Washington Symphony Orchestra has recently started offering summer concerts.

Visitors rarely venture to ***Malcolm X Park****, a 12-acre oasis of grass, gardens and cascading pools in Adams Morgan.*

The MLK riots

When Martin Luther King Jr toured the country in the spring of 1968, the thousands of people who came to hear him speak had become less and less confident in his message of non-violence. For the past three summers, violence had broken out in cities all over the country, where racial tension met the spark of frustration. Yet rumour had it that DC was riot-proof.

On 4 April, King was assassinated as he stood on the balcony of his hotel in Memphis, Tennessee. Within minutes, crowds had started to gather in DC along U Street and the 14th Street corridor. Already exasperated by the entrenched racist laws and social norms of the nation, African-Americans shared the news of King's death in tones of shocked disgust. For some, the long simmering feelings of defeat turned to anger. Marching through the streets, some militant leaders called for all the white-run stores to close their doors out of respect for King. Within hours, though, the streets turned to chaos. Activist leaders could no longer control the crowds. Late that night, people started looting stores along 14th Street and setting others on fire.

Meanwhile, District officials met with federal operatives at the Pentagon to determine whether to bring troops into the city. Their decision to wait – and their slow-motion response to controlling the riots through other means – was disastrous. Eventually, 14,000 soldiers occupied the streets of Washington, but not before 20,000 rioters had torn through the city.

People continue to define DC's history in two parts: before the riots and after the riots. Economically, politically and socially, the city became even more racially polarised after the uprising. And the evidence of the slow healing – along 14th Street and H Street's empty blocks – is obvious. Fires caused the deaths of 12 people and about $15 million in property damage. Hundreds of businesses burned out by the riots relocated to the suburbs, as did legions of middle-class families, black and white. Most have never returned.

Shaw

Transport

U Street-Cardozo or Shaw-Howard University Metro. See **map** page 294-5.

The large square of the city bounded by North Capitol Street and16th Street on the east and west, and by Florida Avenue and M Street on the north and south, is known as Shaw. It includes dozens of historic neighbourhoods, such as the campus of **Howard University**, the **U Street/14th Street corridor** of bars, clubs and restaurants, and the residential areas of **Logan Circle**. All these areas played vital roles in African-American history in DC, serving as strongholds of black businesses, churches and academic life in the segregated decades of the twentieth century.

These days, most of the blocks that were once shiny monuments to black success have fallen into decline. There are always rumours that one area or another is experiencing a renaissance, but the scars from riots, poverty and crack are deep. Still, there are shining gems in Shaw that prove revival is possible – U Street on a Saturday night, for example – and historic corners not to be missed.

Logan Circle

At the turn of the century, Logan Circle was a fashionable address for the wealthy. Victorian homes built in the 1870s and 1880s still line the neighbourhood, which is bounded by S Street to the north, M Street to the south, Ninth Street to the east and 16th Street to the west. Some houses have been refurbished to show off their glamorous designs; but most are just sad shells of what used to be. Whites gradually moved west into the more segregated neighbourhoods of DC in the 1900s. Then, as in so many areas of the city, the riots of 1968 drove remaining white residents and middle- and upper-income blacks out to the suburbs of Maryland and Virginia. Today, a dedicated group of white 'urban pioneers' has moved into Logan Circle's rowhouses, joining loyal black families who have refused to flee, hoping for a renaissance. But for now, prostitutes are still the defining demographic of the area, particularly after dark.

U Street/14th Street Corridor

U Street has become, in some ways, what the rest of DC would like to be: a thriving commercial strip, surrounded by rowhouses that have become magnets for the city's hipsters; a neighbourhood that remains draped in historical significance; and that most unusual of places where, day and night, blacks and whites actually brush elbows – if not speak to each other.

Running between Dupont Circle on the south and Adams Morgan on the north, the U Street neighbourhood is bisected by 14th Street – which has experienced its own revival, although with less dramatic success. Much like Howard University, the neighbourhood has served as a hub of the African-American community. Poet Langston Hughes and jazz great Duke Ellington both grew up in the U Street area. Along with Ella Fitzgerald, Nat King Cole and Redd Foxx, they made U Street bars world-famous with their performances.

Ben's Chili Bowl, located on U Street between 12th and 13th Streets (*see page 142* **Restaurants**), is an old-school diner frequented by celebs such as Bill Cosby and former DC Mayor Marion Barry, as well as most politicians in the city. It's a greasy dive famous for its chilli dogs and atmosphere, which only gets busier as the night goes on. **Lincoln Theatre** (*see page 192* **Culture**), which was once a grand stage for black performances in the age of segregation, is also on U Street. And at the U Street/Cardozo Metro station, there is an African-American Civil War Memorial.

At night, there is always a line of well-dressed black folks outside the **Republic Gardens** club on U and 13th Streets. Next door is the **State of the Union** nightclub, which is equally popular

Alleyways and avenues

'The alley dwellings… constitute a form of slum housing peculiar to the Capital City,' intoned the 1937 New Deal-sponsored guidebook to Washington, touting legislation to eliminate them by 1944. Happily, lawsuits and war left that goal partially unmet.

The L'Enfant Plan necessitated broad alleys to provide rear access to Washington houses. After the Civil War, freed slaves squatted in these unclaimed spaces. Cut-rate contractors soon threw up more permanent, often dinky, jerry-built alley housing, whose inhabitants worked as domestics for the more affluent householders fronting the streets. Concern about these concealed mini-slums troubled Congress as early as 1870, but it wasn't until the 1930s that a vigorous push by Eleanor Roosevelt sought to bulldoze them in favour of then-promising public housing developments.

Some better-built alley houses survived – longer than enthusiasm for mass public housing would – to be restored into delightful (albeit compact) pads for the imaginative. Capitol Hill conceals a concentration, with adjacent carriage houses often converted into equally smart, discreet apartments. Interesting survivors near tourist routes (invisible on most maps) include **Rumsey Court** behind the Republican Party headquarters (100 block of First Street, SE) and **Terrace Court** behind the Supreme Court (200 block of A Street, NE). Some old structures in **Brown's Court** (100 block of Sixth Street, SE) were modernised early. **Archibald Walk** (600 block of E Street, SE) has a whimsical charm.

A mural in the Metro station reflects the ethnic diversity of the **U Street** *neighbourhood.*

but draws a more mixed black and white crowd. Nearby on 14th Street, aside from a couple of swanky new lounges, the main attraction is the **Black Cat**, which continues to be the vital centre for the city's punk bands. And a few blocks north on V Street at Ninth Street is the **9:30 Club**, DC's premier venue for big-name bands. For more information on the last three, *see chapter* **Nightlife**.

U Street wasn't always a mecca for black artists and club-hopping kids. In fact, it's a wonder it has survived, looking back on some of the neighbourhood's darkest days. In 1968, the riots following Martin Luther King Jr's assassination hit U Street particularly hard (*see page 71* **The MLK riots**). Middle-class blacks, many of whom had already fled to the suburbs, all but vanished. Much of the 14th Street corridor burned to the ground. Even now, it is wise to explore the area in groups, particularly at night, and to stay close to the centres of activity.

Howard University

2400 Sixth Street, NW, at Howard Place (806 6100). Shaw-Howard University Metro.

With a hall of fame that includes authors Zora Neale Hurston and Toni Morrison, alongside former mayors and Supreme Court justices, Howard has a past to brag about. The school was charterd in 1867 as a theological seminary to train black ministers, who could in turn help guide the millions of slaves who had just gained their freedom in the Civil War. Since then, the university has attracted some of the greatest African-American thinkers and leaders of the century. And it was the home base for militant organisers during the civil rights movement and before.

Many famous students, professors and alumni have lived a short walk south of the university in LeDroit Park. This small neighbourhood extends from Florida Avenue on the south, Elm Street on the north, Second Street on the east and Bohrer Street on the west. A long list of black activists, including the Rev Jesse Jackson, owned houses here beside other upper-class black ministers, lawyers, businessmen and Howard professors.

After years of financial trouble, Howard is experiencing a resurgence in popularity and revenue. But the students, like those at most American colleges, share little of the passion of their activist predecessors. Still, the campus houses some of the best collections on African history in the country at the Howard University Museum, on the first floor of the Founders Library, and the Howard University Gallery in the College of Fine Arts.
Website: www.howard.edu

Mount Pleasant & north

Transport

Columbia Heights Metro.
See **map** page 294-5.

Mount Pleasant is aptly named. The streets are lined with trees and row after row of modest homes with front porches. The neighbourhood is bounded on the north by Rock Creek Park, on the south by Harvard Street, on the west by Adams Mill Road and on the east by 16th Street. It is a largely residential area, by far the preferred location for DC's punk rockers and other assorted hipsters. Most live in shared houses, which tend to be on the trashy side, but are homey and cheap.

The neighbourhood also has a strong Salvadorean and Vietnamese population, living in houses and apartments surrounding the main drag, **Mount Pleasant Street**. Must-visits on Mount Pleasant Street include the **Raven** for drinks and **Heller's Bakery**. The Raven is a genuine American dive, built in the 1930s, where old men still meet to catch up and drink weak beer in booths beside groups of hip kids. And Heller's is a neighbourhood landmark right in the centre of things, perfect for morning croissants.

North of Mount Pleasant, unremarkable residential blocks stretch out towards the Maryland line. Some of the streets are more dangerous than others (pockets east of 16th Street are among DC's high-crime areas), but most are just row after row of homes. One historic neighbourhood is the **Gold Coast**, a stretch of 16th Street north of Shepherd Street. The mansions and upscale homes of the Gold Coast have long been status symbols for the city's black upper-middle class.

Georgetown

Transport

Rosslyn Metro/Foggy Bottom-GWU Metro, then 30, 32, 34, 35, 36 bus.
See **map** page 292-3.

Georgetown feels a world away from the rest of the city, with its tranquil mansion-lined streets and haughty boutiques. In fact, Georgetown was an independent city, separate from the rest of the District, until 1871, when it was folded into DC, to the great dismay of its residents.

The area's three obvious boundaries only contribute to its island-unto-itself reputation. On the south, there is the Potomac River; Georgetown University is to the west; and Rock Creek Park is on the east. Georgetown is the oldest neighbourhood in the city. From the mid-1800s until the turn of the century, black Georgetown was located south of P Street between Rock Creek and 31st Street. Some 1,000 black families slept there at night, working by day as cooks, domestics and stable boys for the city's white people.

Although it's hard to fathom now, Georgetown was an unfashionable address until the early part of this century, owing to its distance from Downtown DC. But in recent memory, the area – and its elaborate colonial brownstones – has been the symbol of Washington's upper crust. John F Kennedy lived at 3260 N Street while he was a senator, before his White House days. Elizabeth Taylor lived in Georgetown while married to a Virginia senator. And in addition to the usual clutch of congressmen, Secretary of State Madeleine Albright now calls Georgetown home.

Many of the more than 160 films that have been shot in DC were filmed in Georgetown. Most memorable was *The Exorcist* (1973), in which a 12-year-old girl becomes possessed by the devil and her mother seeks help from a priest at a local college. The 75 steps at Prospect and 36th Streets that lead down to M Street are now known to all as 'the Exorcist steps'.

The stink of all that power and wealth makes Georgetown rather stuffy, day or night. The two main strips are **M Street** and **Wisconsin Avenue**, which intersect one another. The sidewalks are crowded on weekends with people throwing money around at the chic – but often nationally syndicated – clothing stores.

But nestled in the middle of all this madness are a few places that are easily overlooked. The **Old Stone House** (3051 M Street) is the oldest house in DC, and a tiny garden behind it offers repose to the weary consumer. **Dumbarton Oaks** (1703 32nd Street) is home to a first-class collection of Byzantine and pre-Columbian art and also maintains beautiful gardens, a few blocks away from the main drag (*see page 102* **Museums & Galleries**).

Georgetown is also a nice place to just stroll about. Try **Q Street**, between 22nd Street and Wisconsin Avenue: you pass Dumbarton Oaks and some grand old rowhouses, including that of

This long flight of steps at Prospect and 36th Streets in Georgetown featured in the 1970s horror movie The Exorcist.

famous *Washington Post* reporter Bob Woodward. There are red-brick sidewalks, plenty of shady trees and it offers a calm and pretty alternative to the M Street bustle it parallels. The brick-paved **C&O Canal**, perpendicular to M Street, also makes for a lovely, shaded walk.

At night, Georgetown is just as busy, with dozens of bars and restaurants filled with students from **Georgetown University** (*see below* **Highlights**) or international jetsetters from the embassies and the World Bank. In the summer, **Washington Harbour**, located at the southern end of Wisconsin Avenue along the Potomac River, is overrun with people looking to eat, drink and flirt at the waterside. The restaurants are forgettable and the drinks overpriced, but the warm breezes off the Potomac and the drunken ad-hoc parties in boats pulled up beside the boardwalk make it worth a trip.

Highlights

Georgetown University

37th & O Streets, NW (687 0100). Dupont Circle Metro, then G2 bus.

John Carroll, the first Catholic bishop in the United States, founded America's oldest Catholic and Jesuit college in 1789. During the Civil War, Union troops occupied the campus and students fought on both sides. Today the university attracts conservative achievers drawn to its law school and acclaimed department of government. In recent years, the school has struggled to hold on to its religious heritage. Condoms are still not sold at the school store and there has been talk of hanging crosses in the classrooms, but the vast majority of Georgetown students appear relatively aloof, shuffling from bar to bar with baseball hats pulled down low and their eyes on the future.

Website: www.georgetown.edu

Upper Northwest

Transport

Cleveland Park, Woodley Park-Zoo, Van Ness-UDC, Tenleytown-AU or Friendship Heights Metro/Foggy Bottom-GWU Metro, then 30, 32, 34, 35, 36 bus.

See **map** page 292-3

The large swathe of land west of Connecticut Avenue and north of Georgetown and Dupont Circle is often referred to as 'West of the Park', the park being the extensive, tree-filled landscape of **Rock Creek Park** (*see below* **Highlights**). It is home to some of the city's wealthiest residents, including the Rockefellers. Although still within the DC borders, streets such as Foxhall Road and upper Wisconsin Avenue feel more like the suburbs of Hollywood. Massive homes and posh boutiques stack up, one after the other, in stark contrast to other parts of the city.

Washington National Cathedral: *page 77.*

Travelling up **Massachusetts Avenue**, which, along with **Wisconsin Avenue**, is a main thoroughfare in Upper Northwest, are a series of sights. The **British Embassy**, located at 3100 Massachusetts Avenue, became a shrine to Princess Diana after her death in August 1997. The **Naval Observatory** (762 1467) is nearby, also on Mass Ave. Aside from being the home of the vice president, it actually serves as a working observatory with tours available to the public.

Further up Massachusetts Avenue is **Washington National Cathedral** (*see below* **Highlights**) and further still the neighbourhood of Tenleytown. Chelsea Clinton's secondary school, Sidwell Friends, is here, handy for the children of Upper Northwest's affluent residents. There are also a few noteworthy restaurants in Tenleytown, although it is a bit suburban and out of the way.

American University is nearby, but, contrary to the name, is not a national icon. It is a respected school, however, attracting hundreds of budding politicos because of its established internship programmes within the halls of government. Still further north, just before the Maryland border. **Friendship Heights** is another well-heeled residential area with a strip of glitzy shops that attempts to be DC's version of Rodeo Drive (but doesn't quite succeed). Still, if you are desperately in need of a Tiffany vase, this is the place to go.

I, spy

As headquarters for federal intelligence organisations and embassies, Washington has had a long and sordid relationship with espionage. In a city with so many sterile federal buildings and boring government bureaucrats, it's hard to imagine all the secret exchanges and national betrayals that have taken place here. But the remnants are all around.

In Georgetown, there is the famous **mailbox** at R and 37th Streets where Aldrich Ames, the CIA officer caught selling high-level secrets to the Soviets, used to make chalk markings to communicate with his Russian contacts. Six blocks away is **Dumbarton Oaks** museum, where Jonathan Jay Pollard – a Jewish research specialist with the Naval Investigative Service in Maryland – came in 1984 to meet his Israeli handler. The two walked behind the mansion to where the gardens meet the woods and Pollard showed his contact classified documents, including satellite photographs of Iraq's military infrastructure. The photos were noteworthy because they were taken hours after the Israeli handler had commanded an air strike over the very same region.

The exchange of documents flowed a bit too freely, though, as Pollard requested volumes of information on the Middle East – an area outside his expertise. In November 1985, the FBI came to meet with Pollard. Two days later, he tried to seek asylum by entering the Israeli embassy at 3514 International Drive, NW. He got as far as the driveway before he realised the FBI had surrounded the building. Pollard was sent to prison for life, and his contact had to resign from the Israeli airforce.

Also in Georgetown is **Au Pied de Cochon** (1335 Wisconsin Avenue), where you can order a Yurchenko shooter (Stolichnaya vodka and Grand Marnier) in homage to this French dive of cold war infamy. This was the place where key Soviet defector Vitaly Yurchenko gave his CIA escort the slip at dinner by ducking through the back door. He then showed up at the Soviet Embassy and announced he'd been kidnapped.

The **FBI Building** in Downtown (*see chapter* **Central DC**) houses the Freedom of Information Library, which contains former FBI head J Edgar Hoover's confidential files. During Hoover's investigative reign, the FBI acquired files on movie stars and rock bands believed to be affiliated with the Communist party and other nefarious organisations. Some of the most famous subjects investigated include Jimi Hendrix, Janis Joplin, Marilyn Monroe, Martin Luther King Jr, Albert Einstein and Elvis Presley. Many of these files can be viewed by the public (by appointment).

Hotels have also been favourite spots for secret plotting. At Lafayette Square, the **Hay-Adams Hotel** restaurant served as a perfect hideaway in the 1980s for meetings soliciting contributions for the Iran-Contra exchange. On Pennsylvania Avenue, the **Willard Hotel**'s famous lobby has been the site for countless negotiations, going back to the nineteenth century. Lafayette C Baker was recruited there for counter-intelligence missions during the Civil War.

Highlights

Rock Creek Park

282 1063. **Open** sunrise-sunset daily.

Nature Center & Planetarium

5200 Glover Road, NW, at Military Road, Upper Northwest (426 6829). Friendship Heights Metro, then E2, E3 bus. **Open** 9am-5pm Wed-Sun. **Admission** free.

Just where you'd least expect it, wedged between sprawling condominiums and busy commercial strips, lie 1,750 acres of urban forest known as Rock Creek Park. One of the largest forested urban parks in the nation, it begins north of the National Zoo and stretches on – and on – to Nebraska Avenue just south of the Maryland border. It includes 29 miles of hiking trails and more than ten miles of equestrian trails. Running through the centre of it all is **Beach Drive**, a major thoroughfare that is, blissfully, closed to cars on weekends so that bicyclists and skaters can have the paved street all to themselves. The fairly lengthy section of road closed to cars winds along the creek under shady trees and past dozens of picnic sites.

Travelling further into the depths of the park, there are more surprising enclaves: tennis courts, a golf course and two Civil War-era forts. The main visitors' centre is the **Nature Center**, located just off Military Road, which maintains exhibits about the park's wildlife and a library. It also organises daily guided nature walks and other events. Best of all, it houses a planetarium, offering free 45- to 60-minute star-gazing sessions from April through November. *See also chapter* **Children**.

Continue north in the park and there's the 4,200-seat **Carter Barron Amphitheatre** (282 1063), on Colorado Avenue. In summer it stages low-cost concerts and shows – from free Shakespeare in the Park productions to R&B and gospel concerts.

Washington National Cathedral

Massachusetts & Wisconsin Avenues, NW (537 6200). Bus 30, 32, 34, 35, 36. **Open** *Sept-Apr* 10am-4.30pm Mon-Sat; 7.30am-7.30pm Sun; *May-Aug* 10am-9pm Mon-Fri; 10am-4.30pm Sat; 7.30am-7.30pm Sun. **Guided tours** every 15 minutes 10am-11.30am, 12.45pm-3.15pm, Mon, Tue, Thur-Sat; 10am-11.30am, 1.15-3.20pm, Wed; 12.30pm-2.45pm Sun (times may vary).

The National Cathedral is the sixth largest church in the world and the second largest in the US. Although built in fourteenth-century English Gothic style – stone on stone with no structural steel – it was constructed in the 1900s; in fact, it took much of the century to complete, due to its size. It's a bit overbearing, but the design provides a nice change from the Federalist domination of the rest of the city – although it is rather Disneyish, as evidenced by a gargoyle of Darth Vader on its north-west corner. The cathedral also occupies a prime location, on top of a hill overlooking the city. The top of the tower is the highest point in DC.

The cathedral is Episcopalian and holds some 1,200 services a year, but has no membership of its own. Instead, it is meant to be a church for all, particularly celebrities: every president since Theodore Roosevelt has attended services or visited the cathedral at some point, as have Martin Luther King and the Dalai Lama. The peaceful and immaculate grounds are also worth a visit.

Website: www.cathedral.org/cathedral

Woodley Park

Moving east over to Connecticut Avenue before Rock Creek Park, Woodley Park is a small but bustling neighbourhood featuring upscale homes, various restaurants and the **National Zoo** (*see below* **Highlights**). It's easy to find a restaurant just by walking up the short strip by the Metro station on Connecticut Avenue, and the handful of outdoor cafés makes the area a popular spot on summer nights. But there's not much else to do apart from visit the zoo.

Highlights

National Zoo

3001 block of Connecticut Avenue, at Rock Creek Park (357 2700). Woodley Park-Zoo Metro.
Grounds open *mid Sept-Apr* 6am-6pm, *May-mid Sept* 6am-8pm, daily. **Buildings open** *mid Sept-Apr* 10am-4.30pm, *May-mid Sept* 10am-6pm, daily.
Admission free.

The great thing about the National Zoo is that it's free. So it makes an excellent escape, even for just a half-hour. Particularly during the off-season, when the paths are not cluttered by pushchairs, the zoo is a perfect place to go running or walking, away from the smog of Connecticut Avenue. A series of tree-shaded paths wind through the margins past the various animals. It is also a decent zoo. Residents include the giant panda, Hsing-Hsing, a present from China and known by zoo officials as 'the most famous zoo animal in the world'. Hsing-Hsing's 20-year mate, Ling-Ling, died in 1992, and Hsing-Hsing is now elderly and ill. There are also African cheetahs and orangutans, which swing on overhead cables called the Transport System.

Cleveland Park

Further north along Connecticut Avenue is Cleveland Park, home to even wealthier residents than Woodley Park, but similarly organised around a central strip of stores and restaurants on Connecticut. Although the surrounding homes are impressive, the main reason to visit Cleveland Park is for mellow night-time entertainment. There are a couple of excellent restaurants, as well as several coffeehouses and some good, cheap pizza and sandwich places. The **Loewes Cineplex Odeon Uptown**, also on this strip, is possibly the best cinema in the city, with an obscenely large screen, two tiers and comfy seats. Get there early if it's showing a blockbuster: it attracts droves of hardcore moviegoers who want to see their flick on the biggest screen possible.

Northeast

Transport

Union Station or Brookland/CUA Metro.

Although it's principally a residential area, Northeast holds the distinction of being Washington's most industrial quadrant. That's because Union Station's railroad tracks and railyards effectively bisect the area and attract such uses as warehouses and distribution centres. Visitors who arrive from the north-east, whether by train or car, will first see a Washington that bears little resemblance to the city known for green trees and white collars.

The section of Northeast closest to Downtown is the north side of Capitol Hill, which holds fewer attractions than the south side – therefore the bulk of it is dealt with on *page 80* **Southeast**. A few blocks east of the Supreme Court is the **Frederick Douglass Museum** (316 A Street, between Third and Fourth Streets, 547 4273), the first Washington residence of the famous abolitionist. The original site of the Museum of African Art, it's now a house museum. Constantino Brumidi, the Capitol artist, lived at 326 A Street. A crumbling curiosity abutting the Amtrak line just north of Union Station is the former Washington Coliseum (Second and L Streets); it's been reduced to a trash transfer station, but in February 1964 it was the stage for the Beatles' American debut.

The main commercial street on the Hill's north side is **Massachusetts Avenue**, which has many restaurants and bars. The avenue is interrupted by **Stanton Park**, the neighbourhood's principal green area, between Fourth and Sixth Streets. Further north is H Street, whose shops cater to a working-class African-American clientele. On H Street near Union Station is the **Capital Children's Museum** (*see page 189* **Children**).

Off the Hill, Northeast's attractions are few: principally several campuses and Catholic institutions and two nature reserves. The former include **Trinity College** (125 Michigan Avenue), a women's liberal arts school, and **Gallaudet University** (800 Florida Avenue). Set up in 1857, Gallaudet is the world's only accredited liberal arts college for hearing-impaired students. Near Gallaudet is **Florida Avenue Market** (Fifth Street and Florida Avenue), a wholesale food market that includes some stalls for retail customers.

The largest Northeast campus belongs to **Catholic University of America**, founded in 1877 and the only American college under the direct control of the Catholic Church. Aside from the occasional battle between a liberal theologian and the Vatican, the university is known for its schools of architecture and philosophy. Its well-regarded theatre department, however, has produced its most famous alumni, including actors Jon Voight and Susan Sarandon and TV host Ed McMahon. Productions at the university's Hartke Theatre are often first-rate.

On the west side of Catholic's campus is the **Basilica of the National Shrine of the Immaculate Conception** (400 Michigan Avenue, at Fourth Street; 526 8300), claimed to be the largest Catholic church in the western hemisphere and the eighth largest church in the world. The structure, which combines Byzantine and Romanesque styles, was begun in 1914 but not finished until 1959; it's dedicated to the Virgin Mary, who was declared the United States' patroness in an 1847 papal decree. Just south of the university is the converted warehouse that is home to **Dance Place**, the city's leading presenter of avant-garde and African dance (*see page 194* **Culture**).

This area is served by the Brookland/CUA Metro station, named after the neighbourhood to the east side of the rail tracks and the university on the west. Brookland is a diverse, moderate-income section with little of interest to visitors,

Washington's waterways

Water made Washington. A Maryland-Virginia negotiation at Mount Vernon in 1785 about fishing rights on the Potomac, which has the biggest mouth of any American river (12 miles), broadened to include other interstate issues, directly inspiring the Constitutional Convention in 1787. The resulting new government fixed its capital midway between North and South, and as far west as ocean-going vessels could navigate. Abundant streams (now mostly dried up or channelled underground) were also an attractive asset.

The Potomac River also defines the shape of Washington. It cuts a line north-west through the District, forming a 'Y' shape where it merges with the smaller Anacostia River, which flows north-east through DC. The heart of the city sits in the cup of the 'Y', with Arlington on the southern bank.

King Charles I deeded the entire Potomac to Maryland, an act which has inspired perpetual jurisdictional mischief. Downriver, Colonial Beach in Virginia erected casinos on piers when gambling was legal in the latter state. Jones Point in Alexandria, beneath today's Woodrow Wilson Memorial Bridge, provided anchorage for 'arks' – houseboats of ill repute – just beyond the grasp of Virginia authorities, until the late 1950s, when DC police destroyed them by amphibious assault.

By 1965, pollution in the Potomac prompted President Johnson's gigantic clean-up as a model for other rivers. Seventeen years and millions of dollars later, the river was finally declared clean enough to swim in – but it lacks good beach access and is too dangerous. Below Great Falls in Maryland, 14 miles from Georgetown, white water challenges even Olympic-class kayakers, while Little Falls Dam creates a countercurrent that has pulled down many foolhardy swimmers. The river is then forced through a gap at Chain Bridge, and hits a depth of 80 feet. By the time the fresh water broadens into the brackish at Georgetown, it conceals a burden of submerged tree limbs and other debris.

However, the Potomac and Tidal Basin are both popular with fishermen. You can fish from late February to November, but the peak season is mid-March to June. Fishing in DC used to be synonymous with Fletcher's Boat House (4940 Canal Road, NW; 244 0461), a century-old rowboat and bait mecca three miles north-west of Georgetown. It's still an important fishing outlet, but since LBJ's cleansing invited game fish – including the first sturgeon spotted in a century although it does offer some places to grab a snack between the Shrine and the area's other Catholic landmark, the **Franciscan Monastery** (*see below* **Highlights**).

Along the west bank of the Anacostia, DC's neglected river but one that's recently made a significant recovery, is the **National Arboretum**, a 440-acre enclave containing both local and exotic foliage (*see below* **Highlights**). Near the arboretum is **Mount Olivet Cemetery** (1300 Bladensburg Road, between Montana Avenue & Mount Olivet Road; 399 3000), final resting place of White House architect James Hoban, and Mary Suratt, who was hanged for her alleged role in Abraham Lincoln's assassination. On the New York Avenue side of the arboretum, one brick kiln stands as a reminder of the many brickyards that constituted Northeast's first major industry.

Anacostia Park follows the river's east bank and contains **Kenilworth Aquatic Gardens** (Anacostia Avenue and Douglas Street; 426 6905). Although located near a highway that shares its name, the gardens are a quiet retreat full of aquatic plants, including lilies and lotuses. Now that the Anacostia is getting cleaner, this area attracts the sort of reptiles, amphibians and water-loving mammals that lived here before Northeast was industrialised, or even inhabited at all.

The **Franciscan Monastery** *'s catacombs.*

Highlights

Franciscan Monastery of the Holy Land

1400 Quincy Street, NE, between 14th & 17th Streets (526 6800). Brookland-CUA Metro, then H2, H4 bus. **Open** 9am-5pm daily; *tours* on the hour 9am-4pm Mon-Sat; 1-4pm Sun. **Admission** free.

This curious site commemorates the Franciscans' official role as Catholicism's guardians of the Holy Land (encompassing Jordan, Syria, Israel, Egypt,

– back to Downtown, bass boats and guides have provided competition, as President Bush publicised by hauling in a three-pound bass in 1990. Catfish abound, and the world's record carp was snagged in the Tidal Basin in the 1980s.

Several islands within the Potomac are also of interest. Columbia Island, by the Pentagon Lagoon, contains Lady Bird Johnson Park and the LBJ memorial grove, appropriately honouring the first lady dedicated to beautifying America and the president who restored the river. Across the river at Hains Point, *The Awakening*, a cleverly disjointed sculpture of a Titan rising from the muck, commemorates the restoration of the mighty Potomac. No man is an island, but verdant 88-acre Theodore Roosevelt Island (off George Washington Parkway north of its eponymous bridge), comes close, concealing a statue of the proto-environmentalist 'Rough Rider' president amid its nature trails. An aquatic turtle colony patrols its southern extremity. North of the island, the Three Sisters, rock clusters visible north of Key Bridge, confirmed ancient Indian prophecies that the Potomac could not be crossed when repeated proposals for bridges there failed.

The Anacostia – Washington's 'other river' – is often neglected, but it washes a chain of interesting parks, including the wonderful but little-visited Kenilworth Aquatic Gardens in Northeast. Although tobacco cultivation silted the Anacostia so quickly that the colonial seaport at Bladensburg, Maryland, shut down, the river has also been cleaned up and the area's only naturally reproducing trout population now thrives in an upper tributary. Kingman Island in the Anacostia, behind RFK Stadium, is proposed for development as Children's Island, a grandiose conception debated for over a decade.

Other waterways include the Chesapeake & Ohio Canal (begun in 1828), which parallels the Potomac for just over 184 miles to Cumberland, Maryland – as far as it got when its newfangled competitor, the railroad, beat it to the Ohio River. Sluggish commerce dawdled until 1924, when storm damage finally quashed the locks. In 1954, when the *Washington Post* proposed paving the towpath for a highway, Supreme Court Justice William O Douglas led a hike to demonstrate its natural beauty and abundant wildlife. Today, the C&O Canal is a long and very thin National Historical Park, with summertime mule-drawn barge trips a popular attraction in the watered sections above Georgetown.

Rock Creek – the stream that flows through Rock Creek Park – was once navigable to P Street. Its tributaries link a number of 10,000-year-old Native American quarries. Along Soapstone Branch, a schooled eye can spot where Indians scooped the soft rock to make cooking vessels (the trailhead is on Albemarle Street, NW, just east of Connecticut Avenue).

Lebanon, Cyprus and Rhodes). The garden features replicas of key locations from the last days of Jesus, as well as a stations-of-the-cross path. Beneath the church, which is modelled on Istanbul's Hagia Sophia, is a small but nonetheless eerie model of the Roman catacombs, which can be visited but only as part of a tour.

US National Arboretum

Entrance at Bladensburg Road & R Street (245 2726). Stadium-Armory Metro, then B2 bus.
Open *grounds* 8am-5pm, *National Bonsai Collection* 10am-3.30pm, daily. **Admission** free.

Technically a research division of the Agriculture Department, this haven always has many more trees than people, even on its busiest days during the height of the spring azalea season. Highlights include a boxwood collection, dwarf conifers, an Asian collection, a herb garden and 'herbarium' of dried plants and the National Bonsai Collection, which contains more than 200 trees donated by Japan and is worth some $5 million. Also on display, somewhat incongruously, are 22 columns removed from the Capitol's East Front during its 1958 expansion.

Southeast

Southeast is Washington's most notorious quadrant, known to many area residents principally from TV-news reports about decrepit public-housing projects, open-air drug markets and youth-gang skirmishes. Most of that, however, is located far from the central city. The parts of Southeast that visitors are most likely to encounter are Capitol Hill and, to a lesser degree, Anacostia.

Capitol Hill

Transport

Capitol South, Eastern Market, Navy Yard or Stadium-Armory Metro.
See **map** page 292-3.

Bounded on the west by the Capitol and South and North Capitol Streets, to the south by the Southeast Expressway, to the north by H Street, NE, and to the east by 11th Street (though some real-estate agents call everything west of the Anacostia River Capitol Hill), this genteel neighbourhood falls into two quadrants – Southeast and Northeast. Since more of it falls into the former, most of it is dealt with here; the northern extremities are covered in **Union Station & Around** (*page 66*) and **Northeast** (*see above*) and the federal institutions behind the Capitol in **The Capitol & Around** (*see page 47*).

Primarily a residential area of late nineteenth-century stone and brick townhouses, Capitol Hill is a pleasant area for walking and physically resembles Dupont Circle. But the Hill is quieter, less trendy and more family-oriented. The businesses along Pennsylvania Avenue, the main drag on this side of the Hill, include such vintage hangouts as the **Tune Inn** (331½ Pennsylvania Avenue, at Fourth Street; 543 2725) and **Sherrill's Bakery** (233 Pennsylvania Avenue, at Third Street; 544 2480), which show little evidence of change since VJ Day. The neighbourhood's non-federal centrepiece is **Eastern Market** (*see below* **Highlights**), which has been threatened with an update for years but manages to hold on to its ramshackle charm.

Some of the 200 trees in the bonsai collection at the **US National Arboretum**.

The Hill is home to many senators and representatives, but they don't tend to be conspicuous. Among the more scandalous former residents are red-baiting senator Joe McCarthy, who lived at 20 Third Street, and presidential candidate Gary Hart, resident at 517 Sixth Street when he dared the press to prove him an adulterer. (It promptly did.) Several of the first presidents attended **Christ Church** (620 G Street), built in 1806 and probably the oldest surviving church in the city. **St Mark's Episcopal Church** on the corner of Third and A Streets was built in 1888; President Lyndon Johnson was a frequent worshipper. St Mark's is renowned for its stained-glass windows, especially the one designed by Louis Comfort Tiffany (yes, of Tiffany & Co the jeweller's fame). The **Ebenezer United Methodist Church** on Fourth and D Streets was built in 1838 and served as the first schoolhouse for blacks in Washington.

Aside from Pennsylvania Avenue itself, the Hill's principal shopping streets are Seventh Street near Eastern Market, which features speciality food stores, galleries and craft shops, and Eighth Street just south of the Avenue, which has more everyday goods. At the end of that commercial strip is the **US Marine Barracks** (Eighth & I Streets), which was located there in 1801, although none of its extant buildings is that old. On Friday nights from May to September, a Marine parade drill is held (reservations required; call 433 6060).

Capitol Hill's largest open space is **Lincoln Park**, which interrupts East Capitol Street (the road that divides Southeast and Northeast) between 11th and 13th Streets. This haven for kids and dog-walkers has a relaxed neighbourhood feel, but its statues commemorate the major trauma of US history. The Emancipation Monument, sculpted in 1876, depicts Abraham Lincoln and a newly freed slave modelled on the last man seized under the Fugitive Slave Act; nearby is a sculpture of African-American educator Mary McLeod Bethune. A smaller park, **Seward Square**, is bisected by Pennsylvania Avenue between Fourth and Sixth Streets.

East Capitol Street is mostly residential, but it does contain the **Folger Shakespeare Library**, which has the world's largest collection of the bard's plays and poetry (*see page 50* **The Capitol & Around**). Right at the other end of this axis is the **DC Armory** (2001 East Capitol Street; 547 9077), headquarters of the DC National Guard but better known as a site for concerts, circuses and the occasional rave.

Adjacent is **RFK Stadium** (*see page 232* **Sport & Fitness**), which straddles Southeast and Northeast; it was built in 1961 for baseball and football, neither of which is now regularly played there. Instead, it's home to the city's champion soccer team, DC United, and is sometimes used for rock shows, notably the 1998 Tibetan Freedom concert. On Tuesdays, Thursdays and Saturdays,

The 20-foot tall chair in **Anacostia***: page 82.*

from spring to autumn, a farmers' market sets up in stadium parking lot six.

A few blocks south-west of the Stadium-Armory complex is **Congressional Cemetery** (1801 E Street), the resting place of such eminent Washingtonians as photographer Matthew Brady, FBI chief J Edgar Hoover, Choctaw chief Pushmataha and march composer John Philip Sousa, who was also born on Capitol Hill.

South of the Hill – and separated from it by the Southeast Expressway – is an area that's been largely industrial ever since the **Navy Yard** (*see below* **Highlights**) set up there in 1799. Other warehouses grew in the area around what is now Navy Yard Metro station, and in recent years several of these large buildings have found new lives as dance clubs such as **Tracks** (*see page 222* **Nightlife**). Ships are no longer built at the Navy Yard, but guns and weaponry were being manufactured there as recently as the 1991 Gulf War. Today the complex is mostly used for office space, and there are ambitious plans to remake this underused area as a federal employment district.

Highlights

Eastern Market

225 Seventh Street, SE, between C Street & North Carolina Avenue (546 2698). Eastern Market Metro. **Open** dawn-late afternoon Sat, Sun (permanent inside stalls 7am-6pm Tue-Sat; 8am-4pm Sun).

Of the three remaining structures from Washington's nineteenth-century market system, this is the only one still being used for its traditional purpose. Built in 1873 on the site of a previous market established in 1801, the building holds produce, meat and fish stalls, as well as the popular Market Lunch, which serves cuisine that is anything but nouveau. Artists and craftsmen sell their work in the northern part of the market. The spot is liveliest on Saturday, when both food and crafts vendors set up outside.

Washington Navy Yard

Ninth & M Streets. Navy Yard Metro.

The US Navy's oldest shore facility was torched by British forces in 1814. Rebuilt, it produced the big guns for American ships in World War II. Located on the base are the **Navy Museum** (Building 76, 901 M Street, at Ninth Street; 433 4882), which has a permanent exhibition on US naval history from the Revolutionary War to the present, and the **Marine Corps Historical Center** (Building 58; 433 3840), where the top attraction is the flag raised on Mount Suribachi during the battle for the island of Iwo Jima in World War II. You can also tour the USS *Barry*, a decommissioned 1960s-vintage destroyer. The Yard is also the site of Quarters 'A', the official residence of the Chief of Naval Operations, the top uniformed post in the US Navy. But that's off-limits.

Anacostia

Transport

Anacostia Metro.

Across the Anacostia River is a section of Southeast popularly known as 'Anacostia', although its historic name is 'Uniontown' (and, just to confuse things, some people consider Anacostia to mean the whole area of DC south of the river). It is bounded by the Anacostia River to the west, Suitland Parkway to the south, Good Hope Road to the north and Fort Stanton Park to the east.

Anacostia contains the 20-foot-tall 'world's largest chair', erected to publicise a now-defunct furniture outlet (Martin Luther King Avenue and V Street), as well as the campus of **St Elizabeth's Hospital** (2700 Martin Luther King Avenue). The latter is an asylum whose patients have included Ezra Pound and current resident John Hinckley, who in 1981 tried to kill Ronald Reagan in an attempt to impress actress Jodie Foster.

The areas south and east of historic Anacostia contain many of Washington's meanest streets, but also middle-class neighbourhoods of detached homes, mature trees and rolling hills. Atop one of those hills is **Cedar Hill** (*see below* **Highlights**), the home of abolitionist, journalist and diplomat Frederick Douglass. Nearby is the **Anacostia Museum** (*see page 106* **Museums & Galleries**), which sits on a hill in Fort Stanton Park, one of the numerous open spaces east of the river. The largest of the parks are Anacostia, which follows the east bank of the river that bears its name, and Fort Dupont, which in summer is the site of outdoor jazz and R&B concerts.

Cedar Hill: *Frederick Douglass's last home.*

Although these parks don't have a reputation for being crime-ridden, care should be taken in any part of the city east of the Anacostia River. Gang- and drug-related violence is most likely to erupt in the many public housing projects scattered throughout the quadrant, but can spill over into adjacent neighbourhoods. Only self-assured urban explorers should attempt to travel beyond Southeast's best-known attractions.

Highlights

Frederick Douglass National Historic Site (Cedar Hill)

1411 W Street, SE, at 14th Street (426 5961). Anacostia Metro, then B2 bus. **Open** *Oct-mid Apr* 9am-4pm daily; *mid Apr-Sept* 9am-5pm daily. **Admission** $3; $1.50 seniors; free under-7s. **Credit** MC, V.

Built in 1854, this Victorian country house was the final home of abolitionist and author Frederick Douglass, who lived here from 1877 until his death in 1895. Born a slave in Maryland, Douglass taught himself to read, founded an abolitionist newspaper and became an adviser to Abraham Lincoln and other presidents. A small visitor centre at the bottom of the hill provides an introduction to Douglass's life and work. The house itself, open for guided tours on the hour, is preserved largely as Douglass left it, and includes his 1,200-volume library as well as gifts from Mary Todd Lincoln, Harriet Beecher Stowe and others. Cedar Hill also provides an excellent view of central Washington.

Southwest

Transport

Waterfront-SEU Metro.

Hugely truncated when Virginia took its chunk of DC back, and degraded by a large-scale 1950s 'urban renewal project' that bulldozed residential areas in favour of office space, the Southwest quadrant is now merely the western elbow of the National Mall, cradling the Potomac in its curve. Its primary draws are the museums and federal buildings to the south of the Mall, and the Tidal Basin, which are covered – down to the Eisenhower Freeway – in the **Monumental Centre** chapter (starting on *page 35*); otherwise, it clusters its attractions near the riverfront. Banneker Circle, across the promenade from L'Enfant Plaza on Tenth Street, affords a sweeping vista of the quarter.

The 327-acre **East Potomac Park** peninsula sports a tennis bubble and a modest golf course allowing Downtown duffers lunchtime rounds. Army engineers dredged Hains Point from malarial mud flats in the 1880s, thus defining Washington Channel. Below 14th Street Bridge rests the Cuban-American Friendship Urn presented in 1926. In 1982, an Air Florida jet clipped the bridge after taking off from National Airport during a blizzard. The southbound span is dedicated to Arlan Williams, who drowned rescuing another passenger.

Fishing boats have hawked their catch near the Tidal Basin inlet continuously since 1790, before there was a city. You can still get seafood at the **Fish & Seafood Market** (686 1068), just south of the Francis Case Memorial Bridge; some vendors will even cook it up for you for impromptu al fresco picnicking.

The market is now part of the **Waterfront** development, a typical 1960s inner-city regeneration project that has succeeded in bringing some life – largely lunching office staff – to the previously run-down area. It includes the Washington Marina, just south of the 14th Street Bridge, the Capitol Yacht Club and, along Maine Avenue and Water Street, a sprawl of seafood restaurants, all with outdoor seating and views across to East Potomac Park. With the exception of **Le Rivage** (1000 Water Street; 488 8111), a worthy, intimate French seafood room, most of these play to the tourist masses, introducing many to Chesapeake seafood cookery. Past the houseboat colony and the tour-boat docks, the promenade climaxes at the willowy, politically incorrect memorial to the gentlemen who gave ladies their seats on the *Titanic*'s lifeboats.

Inland, **Wheat Row** (1315-21 Fourth Street), is an example of the failure of the 1950s urban renewal programme. Built in 1794, this distinguished residence was incorporated into a modern apartment complex. This theoretical juxtaposition of rich and less well-off populations did not produce the envisioned social harmony.

Law House (1252 Sixth Street), dubbed 'Honeymoon House' in 1796 when its prominent owners moved in, kept the tag despite their messy celebrity divorce a while later. Nearby, though it may soon be moving to Penn Quarter, the pioneering theatre company **Arena Stage** (1101 Sixth Street; 488 3300) continues its vital dramatic presence and in-the-round productions, although the repertory troupe that launched many prominent thespians, such as Robert Prosky, has made its last curtain-less call. *See page 196* **Culture**.

South of the Waterfront is **Fort Leslie J McNair** (*see below* **Highlights**), the US Army's oldest post. Established in 1791, it has no visitor attractions as such bar pleasant waterside walks and a handful of buildings of historic interest.

Highlights

Fort Lesley J McNair

103 Third Avenue, SW, at P Street (685 4645). Waterfront-SEU Metro, then 15-minute walk.
Open 9am-5pm Mon-Fri. **Admission** free.
The gate guard at this active army base distributes historical walking tour pamphlets – unless there's a security alert on; the fort has been known to close abruptly to visitors. Past the Generals' Row homes of the big brass is the National War College, established by Teddy Roosevelt in 1901. The Lincoln assassination conspirators were tried in 1865 at Quarters 20, then publicly hanged at what is now a tennis court. A visitors' quarters was once the clinic of Major Walter Reed, MD, who developed a vaccine for yellow fever. Note that you'll need to show photo ID to gain access.

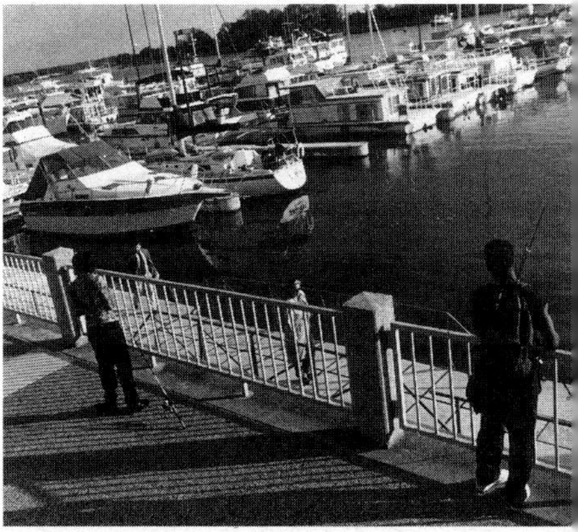

Southwest's *regenerated waterfront.*

X-Files DC

Fans of the television show *The X-Files* know that Washington, DC, is a much stranger place than it appears at first glance. Beyond the gleaming white marble of the federal buildings lie hidden corridors, dark alleys and subterranean offices where FBI agents Mulder and Scully pursue truth, corrupt government operatives and all manner of alien life forms. A savvy tourist can follow in their fictional tracks: although much of the show is filmed on a Los Angeles television lot, there are numerous DC-area attractions that anyone can visit. Just be sure you're not followed...

By closely monitoring the datelines and locations that appear fleetingly at the beginning of every scene, local *X-Files* fans have pinned down many of the locations where the show's important episodes took place. These arcane Washington reference points – and their accuracy – are no coincidence. The show's creator, Chris Carter, has a brother who lives in the Kalorama neighbourhood, which is also where Agent Scully's apartment can be found. Mulder's famous apartment, No.42 (no street name is ever shown), prominently featured in many episodes, can be found across town in the Capitol Hill neighbourhood. You'll have to cross the river to visit assistant director Skinner's nondescript co-op in Crystal City (again, no actual address is given).

The **J Edgar Hoover FBI Building** is the regular haunt for Mulder, Scully, Skinner and,

But what's *really* out there?

Some *X-Files* investigations rather push – nay, explode – the envelope of probability. But some of the real secrets of DC's various government agencies are no less unlikely.

Mulder

Conspiracy-theorist Mulder would probably like to believe the following are true, but in fact they fall into the category of unprovable paranoid fantasies.

Area 51

The Department of Defense won't acknowledge the existence of this facility, a 60sq mile chunk of Nevadan desert at the centre of which is an airbase dedicated to the development of 'black budget' aircraft, from the U2 spy plane of the 1950s to today's Stealth bomber. Conspiracy theorists claim it serves as a holding pen for captured UFOs and a mortuary for alien autopsies.

'Them'

The Federal Reserve System – America's central bank – is unconstitutional, illegal and, along with most other arms of the federal government, a mere front for the machinations of a short-lived eighteenth-century secret society known as the Illuminati, which paranoids hold responsible for everything from the American, French and Russian Revolutions to the demise of the Beatles. The Council on Foreign Relations (*see below*) is the leading – and real – non-governmental arm of this supposed ancient conspiracy.

Fluoridation

Since the 1950s, the federal government has supported the introduction of sodium fluoride into America's drinking water supplies. According to groups like the John Birch Society, fluoridation is a Communist plot to poison the citizenry. Others believe it's a ruse by the aluminum industry to profitably dispose of a toxic waste product. The Wall Street/Moscow axis strikes again.

Christic Institute

This Washington-based think-tank (based at 1324 North Capitol Street) claims there exists a 'Secret Team' of former and current military and intelligence operatives who have operated behind the scenes in everything from the Kennedy assassination to the Iran-Contra affair. Their 1986 lawsuit, brought against former CIA officials, Contra leaders and Colombian cocaine traffickers, was thrown out of court.

occasionally, the Cigarette Smoking Man. 'Every tour I get, there's a question about the *X-Files*,' says one FBI agent, who estimates that half of all real-life agents are *X-Files* fans. Before he was gunned down by shady conspirators, Deep Throat regularly arranged clandestine meetings with Mulder in the parking garage of the **Watergate Hotel** complex (the close-ups are actually filmed on set in LA), which is famous for real scandals from Nixon to Lewinsky.

The province of the Cigarette Smoking Man and other members of the Syndicate, the **Pentagon** of the *X-Files* holds such oddities as frozen alien embryos and computer chip implants from Agent Scully and other alien abductees. The **Vietnam Veterans Memorial** on the Mall, just northeast of the Washington Monument, was the setting for the episode 'Unrequited', which featured an invisible Vietnam veteran with a chilling vendetta.

Other notable *X-Files* locations include:

Lone Gunmen's Hideaway

These three conspiracy theorists, who occasionally assist Mulder and Scully, maintain their headquarters in a nondescript warehouse in Southeast.

Senate Office Building

X-Files sympathiser Senator Matheson occasionally calls Mulder into his office here to offer helpful – if cryptic – advice. Although it's referred to on the show as the 'Senate Office Building', there are in fact four Senate Office Buildings – most senators maintain offices in the Dirksen Building, located at Constitution Avenue and First Street, NE.

Another Universe

3060 M Street, NW, between Wisconsin Avenue & Thomas Jefferson Street, Georgetown (333 8651). Foggy Bottom-GWU Metro, then 30, 32, 34, 35, 36 bus. **Open** 11am-9pm Mon-Thur; 11am-10pm Fri, Sat. **Credit** AmEx, Disc, MC, V.

This sci-fi, comics and games shop in Georgetown doesn't appear on the show, but it's certain to satisfy your *X-Files* merchandising needs.

Scully

Sceptical Scully would not take anything on hearsay, but rational investigation leads to the conviction that the following are hard fact.

Atomic lab rats

At least 4,000 human radiation experiments were sponsored by the federal government – chiefly the Department of Defense, the Atomic Energy Commission and the Department of Health, Education & Welfare – between 1944 and 1974, generally without the subjects' knowledge or consent. At the height of the cold war, nearly 3,000 US military personnel served as atomic guinea pigs at nuclear test sites.

The Council on Foreign Relations

A policy study and advocacy group with an internationalist orientation. It's based in New York, but its roster includes everyone who's anyone in Washington's power elite – present and past presidents, select senators and congressmen, Supreme Court justices, military leaders, international bankers, wealthy industrialists, foundation executives, and so forth – in the words of paranoid preacher Pat Robertson: 'virtually every key national security and foreign policy adviser of this nation for the past 70 years'.

Tuskegee Institute

In a project sponsored by the US Public Health Service, 399 African-American men at an Alabama health clinic were left untreated for syphilis over a period of 40 years. The project was ended when it was finally brought to public attention in 1972. The federal government eventually paid the victims $10 million compensation, and President Clinton offered a public apology in 1997.

'High' intelligence

The Central Intelligence Agency has a long history of collusion with international drug lords, from the Corsican mob in Marseilles in the 1950s to the Hmong opium tribes of Laos in the 1960s and Afghan heroin traffickers in the 1980s. The CIA has frequently stymied the work of drug enforcement officials from other government agencies. The agency's MK Ultra project explored the possibilities of LSD warfare.

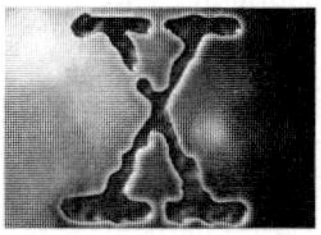

Virginia & Maryland

Much of interest in Washington – notably Arlington Cemetery and the Pentagon – falls outside DC's rough diamond.

Virginia

England's first permanent colony in the present US, Virginia has remained politically more conservative and socially more Southern than its neighbour across the Potomac. A bastion of reaction after Civil War defeat, northern Virginia emerged from the doldrums as Washington's mushrooming suburbs boosted its population after World War II. Today, further-out counties struggle to avoid overdevelopment, even as the close-in communities work to preserve their considerable remaining charm.

Arlington County and 'Old Town' Alexandria were part of the original District of Columbia diamond from 1800 to 1846, when they retroceded to the Old Dominion, claiming federal neglect, but covertly fearing that Congress might ban slavery in the capital. However, governmental boundaries apart, **Arlington** remains effectively part of DC in terms of its character and transport links – as the view of the Pentagon from the Yellow Line bridge over the Potomac, with Arlington Cemetery rising up behind it, can't fail to remind you. A visit to self-consciously quaint **Alexandria**, on the other hand, a restored seaport town with a history that predates the capital's by half a century, can be a welcome break from all that federal gravitas.

Arlington

Transport

Various Orange, Blue and Yellow Line stations.

Arlington has its martial version of DC's ceremonial core along the Potomac, centring on Memorial Bridge (1932), decorously connecting Lincoln's monument to the home of Confederate icon Robert E Lee, in symbolic reconciliation of North and South. As the bridge makes landfall, among the trees of Columbia Island, home of Lady Bird Johnson Park and Lyndon B Johnson's discreet Memorial Grove, the **Pentagon** rises squatly to the south and **Arlington Cemetery** gracefully ahead, with **Fort Myer** army base in its lee (for all, *see below* **Highlights**).

The cemetery is a bucolic and serene place today, but until relatively recently it was virtually in the country: Arlington the neighbourhood, to its north-west, was a semi-rural pocket transformed into modest early suburbia only after World War II. Since then, as further-out neighbourhoods have grown fashionable, many of the original inhabitants have moved upwards and outwards, and immigrants have taken up much of the ageing housing here: first Latinos, then Vietnamese refugees desiring proximity to their former comrades-in-arms at the Pentagon, and later West Asians and others.

The benefit to visitors of this mini-melting pot is a potpourri of inexpensive ethnic restaurants centred on the Metro subway stations. A stroll from Clarendon station (on the Orange Line) eastwards down steep Wilson Boulevard for about a mile towards Rosslyn passes a culinary league of nations. The most curious refreshment stop, however, is a domestic hybrid, **Bardo Rodeo** (2000 Wilson Boulevard; 527 1852), a cavernous brewpub raucously occupying a former quasi-industrial automobile dealership, incongruously accented with Tibetan-inspired food and décor. The first stretch of this walk also takes you through Arlington's thriving nightlife strip, past such venues as **Galaxy Hut** and **Iota Café** (*see chapter* **Nightlife**).

At the far end of Wilson Boulevard, **Rosslyn** used to be just a trolley terminal squatting amid seedy bars and pawnshops exiled here by DC's usury regulations. The arrival of the Metro in the late 1970s unleashed glitzy overdevelopment, typified by the USA Today Buildings, stuck into the land like giant meat cleavers, all too close to the flight path to National Airport. News media museum **Newseum** (*see page 108* **Museums & Galleries**) across the street, and its oddly conceived free-press memorial park, don't quite atone.

Dropping to the south-east of the cemetery, following the Blue Line round, is the Pentagon City development, which contains the ritzy **Fashion**

Arlington National Cemetery *(page 88) contains John F Kennedy's simple grave...*

...the US Marines' Iwo Jima Memorial...

...and long lines of veterans' graves.

Arlington: *great for ethnic restaurants.*

Centre at Pentagon City mall (*see chapter* **Shopping**). Just opposite is the **Drug Enforcement Administration** and its new **Museum and Visitor Center** (*see below* **Highlights**), and a short, two-block walk away (or catch the hotel shuttle bus) is the Doubletree Hotel, where the glassed-in circular **Skydome** lounge bar rotates 360° every hour and provides a fabulous view of the Pentagon, Arlington National Cemetery and the city.

One Metro stop later is **Crystal City**, an office/apartment development. Built in a former railyard, its various buildings are connected by a series of bizarre subterranean tunnels, some filled with fast-food outlets and stores. Fellini would have put it straight on his location list. One of its more interesting components is the idiosyncratic and surprisingly fun **United States Patent & Trademark Museum** (*see below* **Highlights**). Across Jeff Davis Highway, 23rd Street offers a funkier alternative strip of a dozen moderate restaurants, serving almost as many cuisines. On the other side of Crystal City is **Ronald Reagan Washington National Airport** (*see below* **Highlights**).

When planning a visit to Arlington, note that even though some of its attractions are close together, walking between them is usually impracticable. It is not easily possible, for example, to walk between the Pentagon and Arlington National Cemetery, or the cemetery and downtown Arlington. And though the area is well served by Metro stops, you often have to change, so allow plenty of time, especially at weekends.

Highlights

Arlington National Cemetery

Arlington, VA (703 607 8052). Arlington Cemetery Metro. **Open** *Apr-Aug* 8am-7pm, *Sept-March* 8am-5pm, daily (last admission 30 mins earlier).
Admission free.

The serene Valhalla of America's heroes started out in a gesture of vengeance. Union forces seized the estate of Confederate General Robert E Lee in 1861, appreciating its commanding position opposite the capital. Condemning him as an arch-traitor, in 1864 the Feds started burying soldiers so close to Arlington House, the Lee residence, as to render it unsuitable as a home should they regain it, even filling Mrs Lee's rose garden with unknown soldiers. Intending further insult, the US opened Freedman's Village here to resettle liberated slaves, also burying them on the property. By 1866 the despoiled estate's designation as a military cemetery was official, but only time transformed it into a place of honour. Now it is the right of anyone killed in action in any branch of military service, or who served for 20 years, to be buried here, along with their spouse (the criteria used to be more generous but, soberingly, Arlington has a space problem).

Built in 1802-1816 by Martha Washington's grandson, George Washington Parke Custis, Arlington House seeks gravity in the massive pillars of its portico. Lee married Custis's adopted daughter, Mary Custis (who was Martha's great-granddaughter by her first marriage) in the family parlour in 1831 and made his home here thereafter. The house, which is now a museum (open 9.30am-4.30pm daily), has been restored to its appearance when the Lees lived there and features several of Custis's paintings.

Entranced by Arlington House's view of the city across the river, President Kennedy murmured: 'I could stay here forever'. Upon his assassination shortly after, his remark was recalled and literally honoured in his gravesite, just below the house. With the adjacent grave of his brother, Robert – also assassinated, in 1968 – the simple flame and inscription is still a place of pilgrimage for Americans, and reverence hangs in the air.

The other beacon for visitors is the Tomb of the Unknowns, erected after World War I, then expanded to include unidentified casualties of other conflicts. In 1998, DNA identification caused the representative of the Vietnam war to be removed. Now the Pentagon keeps DNA samples of all troops, making future unknowns unlikely. The changing of the guard on the hour (and also the half-hour, from April to September) remains moving in its reverent precision, as are occasional wreath-layings by dignitaries at the Tomb and the processions of ordinary funerals elsewhere, with flag-draped caskets borne on horse-drawn caissons and the haunting bugle strains of 'Taps'.

Tombs range from plain white headstones, such as actor Lee Marvin's, to sculpted personal memorials, such as that to heavyweight champion Joe Louis, next to it. The Tourmobile route naturally targets such celebrity sites, but discovery of more obscure heroes rewards the contemplative stroller. There's ex-slave James Parks, born at Arlington and buried here; John Clem – the youngest US soldier ever, who entered service as a nine-year-old drummer and retired in 1916 a major-general; Vinnie Ream, a 17-year-old sculptress who managed to have President Lincoln sit for her; detective novelist

Dashiell Hammett of *Maltese Falcon* fame and countless others worthy of note. Other memorials include the mast of the battleship *Maine*, whose 1898 explosion sparked the Spanish-American War and the monument to the Navaho Code Talkers, whose language baffled Japanese codebreakers during World War II.

At the north end is the Netherlands Carillon, a Dutch gift thanking the US for liberation from the Nazis. Beyond is the US Marines' Iwo Jima Memorial, a giant recreation of the famous photo of leathernecks raising the flag on Mount Suribachi in the furious 1942 battle. Irritated when the National Gallery of Art director described their statue as kitsch, the Corps got positively angry in 1998 when a US Air Force monument was proposed for a site that they deem too close. That interservice spat still rages.

Opened in 1997, the Women in Military Service to America Memorial (703 533 1155) was brilliantly inset behind the decorous (but deteriorating) Main Gate retaining wall to create a light-flooded arch with eight display niches, only two permanently filled as yet. Honorees include Mary Walker, MD, trouser-clad Civil War surgeon, so far the only female recipient of the Congressional Medal of Honor; Sarah Osborne, Revolutionary army cook who survived to be photographed at the age of 104; and Lieutenant Sharon Lane, the only female trooper killed by enemy fire in Vietnam. The massive female contribution in World War II was fittingly first of the permanent displays.

The cemetery's visitors' centre is just past the entrance on Memorial Avenue. You can enquire about the location of particular graves or pick up maps here if you prefer to wander the cemetery on foot (pleasant, practicable and somehow appropriate, but note that some of the significant gravesites are a mile or more's walk uphill); alternatively, you can buy tickets for the Tourmobile coach circuit ($4.75; $2.25 3-11s). The coach makes brief stops at each major point of interest, but to avoid that cattle-drive feeling, take your time and reboard the subsequent service (tickets are valid).

Drug Enforcement Administration Museum

700 Army Navy Drive, at Hayes Street, Arlington, VA (307 3463). Pentagon City Metro. Call for admission details.

A curious highlight among Virginia museums is this small exhibition tracing the history of illegal drugs in America, primarily relics of twentieth-century drug culture culled from collections of retired agents: drug paraphernalia, narc (cop) disguises, even a surfboard with a hollow hull used in an ingenious albeit unsuccessful 1977 smuggling attempt. Except for a kiosk offering messages from DEA officials, the display isn't particularly preachy. A gift shop (open 10am-3.30pm Tue, Thur) sells DEA caps and sweatshirts; sorry, no contraband.

Website: www.usdoj.gov/dea

Fort Myer: The Old Guard Museum

249 Sheridan Avenue, at Macomb Street, Fort Myer, VA (703 696 6670). Rosslyn Metro, then 4A bus. **Open** 9am-4pm Mon-Sat; 1-4pm Sun. **Admission** free.

The army's oldest active infantry regiment, the Old Guard (Third US Infantry) is a spit-and-polish troop dignifying state occasions and funerals at adjacent Arlington National Cemetery. They're not just tin soldiers, though, having started in 1784 patrolling the nation's bloody western frontiers and later fought in Vietnam. Exhibits at the museum include a video explaining the significance of flags and military ceremony along with displays on the history of both the unit and the fort.

A Civil War bastion, the fort's parade ground was the scene of the world's first fatal aeroplane crash, on 3 September 1908, when a demonstration flight killed Lieutenant Thomas Selfridge and seriously injured inventor Orville Wright. Wright recovered to fly here again in 1909, persuading the brass to buy his 'Wright Flyers'.

By the field is the honoured grave of Black Jack, best known as the riderless horse attending President Kennedy's casket. Soldiers tend today's ceremonial steeds in stables downhill. The base's thrift shop is known for chance bargains.

Access is generous, though you'll have to tell the guard at the gate where you're going.

The Pentagon

I-395 (703 695 1776). Pentagon Metro. **Tours** on the hour 9am-3.30pm Mon-Fri. Photo ID required for over-16s. Under-16s must be accompanied by an adult. **Admission** free.

Thrown up in an incredible 15 months to meet the demands of World War II, the 34-acre, five-sided, five-storey-high pile may seem the work of a mad numerologist, but it has served well for five decades. The headquarters of all the US armed forces is still the world's largest government building, and indeed office building, housing up to 25,000 employees. Now each thread of the giant screw is to be modernised in turn, as the building acquires wiring and plumbing suitable for today's electronic warmaking.

As late as 1967, guidebooks said that 'Visitors are welcome to wander about almost at will' through the 17½ miles of corridors, gazing leisurely at paintings and exhibits'. No more! Get there early because it's very popular. The one-mile, 75-minute tours march regularly from the Metro entrance, guided at double-time by an enlisted-rank trooper walking backwards (the better to stop foreign agents taking off), mouthing rote narrative and tailed by a colleague keen to keep visitors in close formation. You'll be chivvied past ranks of display cases too briskly to examine them, and allowed to view operational areas – such as the *Dr Strangelove* War Room – only on video. Yet you'll get a whiff of martial bustle just by passing through the rush of Very Serious People, uniformed and civilian, bent on military business. The ironic highlight has to be Ground Zero, a structure at the centre of the courtyard that the erstwhile Soviets targeted missiles upon, convinced it concealed some high-tech defensive marvel. In fact, it was, and is, a hot-dog stand.

Ronald Reagan Washington National Airport

703 417 8000. National Airport Metro.

Like Union Station, the airport may well become a destination as well as a transport facility. Its new domed terminal packages up great views of the runways and the city, 60 or so shops and restaurants you'd actually choose to eat at (though some are through security gates, which has been proving a deterrent to custom). Between parking garages are the ruins of Abingdon, a ruined eighteenth-century plantation house now developed as an archaeological exhibit, which, with its gardens, makes a curiously contemplative place amid the chaos of the airport. Some of the artefacts excavated

The other Washington Monument

The Washington area has two massive stone phalli dedicated to the memory of the Father of Our Country. The familiar one is the Washington Monument, 555 feet of gleaming white marble, the tallest structure in the city. The other, the George Washington Masonic National Memorial, which sits on the hill that dominates low-lying Alexandria, is three-fifths as tall and infinitely less well known. Unlike the graceful original, the Masonic Memorial, completed in 1932, has about it an air of foreboding. Of course, this could simply be because of its squat form (inspired by the Pharos of ancient Alexandria) but it's hard to separate perceptions of the tower from perceptions of the organisation that financed its erection.

The Free and Accepted Masons are an international men's fraternal order with about three million members in the United States and five million worldwide. Some claim the group dates back to Solomon's temple, but the modern organisation originated in the UK in the early eighteenth century. The Masons' rituals have a vaguely occult and medieval feel, but today their activities are purely social and charitable. Nevertheless, the group's mysterious ways and the prominence of so many of their members have made them frequent candidates for political scapegoating. Consider the following:

- A good number of the nation's founding fathers were Masons, including Thomas Jefferson, Benjamin Franklin and John Hancock. Among the Masons who have occupied the White House are both Roosevelts, Harry Truman and Lyndon Johnson.
- George Washington was a Master Mason, ordained in a Virginia lodge in 1753. He used a ceremonial Masonic trowel to lay the cornerstone of the Capitol building in 1800. The same trowel was used to lay the cornerstone of the Washington Monument in 1843.
- The US dollar bill is replete with Masonic symbols such as the pyramid and the all-seeing eye. The currency's mottos – *e pluribus unum* (out of many one) and *novus ordo seclorum* (a new order of the ages) – have Masonic origins. That last phrase has special resonance for the current crop of political paranoids, who have a particular fetish about the 'new world order'.
- In the political disarray of the post-Revolutionary years, a political movement dedicated to the elimination of Freemasonry became the nation's first alternative party. The Anti-Masons figured in the presidential campaigns of the 1820s and 1840s, elected numerous members of the House of Representatives and captured the governorships of Pennsylvania and Vermont. Their most serious run for national office, however, did nothing more than assure the election of Andrew Jackson, a brother Mason out of Harmony Lodge No.1 in Nashville, Tennessee.
- The Masons survived their enemies and thrive in DC. Their Georgetown lodge (closed to the public) has occupied the same two-storey brick building since 1810, and the national headquarters are here in Alexandria. They also have a foothold on Dupont Circle, where the spectacular, neoclassical House of the Temple (1733 16th Street, NW) offers a shrine to fellow Mason J Edgar Hoover. Now there's food for (paranoid) thought.

George Washington Masonic National Memorial

101 Callahan Drive, between King & Duke Streets (703 683 2007). King Street Metro. **Open** 9am-5pm daily. **Tours** on the half hour 9.30am-noon, 1-4pm. **Admission** free.

Displaying memorabilia of George Washington's activity as a Freemason, including a reconstruction of the lodge hall he frequented, the museum at the base of the monument also commemorates later presidents involved with the Brotherhood (including Gerald Ford, whose home while in Congress lies just up the street). The view from the top (accessible on tours only) of this landlocked lighthouse is impressive.

are on display in the old Terminal A, itself in the process of being restored to its original 1938 art deco snappiness.

The partisan gesture of the Republican 104th Congress renaming the facility to honour their sainted – but still living – Gipper caused much resentment. Locals still call the airport just 'National'.

United States Patent & Trademark Museum

2121 Crystal Drive, Suite 0100, off 23rd Street (703 305 8341). Crystal City Metro. **Open** 8.30am-5.30pm Mon-Fri. **Admission** free.

This paean to Yankee ingenuity is a small, witty facility delighting in the six million patents granted since Samuel Hopkins received the first one, for a method of making potash, in 1790. The old Patent Office, in what is now the National Portrait Gallery, had been a tourist magnet in antebellum Washington City; its descendant exhumes some charming early samples of everything from folding beds to dental plates. The champion is Thomas Edison, who patented a vote-counting device in 1879 followed by 1,092 other handy gizmos, including the phonograph and the lightbulb.

Surprising patentees include actresses Hedy Lamar (a World War II spy communication system) and campy TV Catwoman Julie Newmar (pantyhose designed for the few women with figures like hers). Here, too, is Walt Disney's trademark application for Mickey Mouse. Sampson Rope, the oldest US trademark still in use, sits by its British equivalent, Bass Ale. Full tours of the agency must be arranged in advance.

Alexandria

Transport

King Street Metro, then 20-minute walk or 28A, 28B or DASH bus AT2, AT5, AT7.

Established in 1749 by Scottish traders, Alexandria marked its 250th anniversary – plus the bicentennial of the death of its prime homie, George Washington (who surveyed its street layout) – in 1999. Snoozing into slumishness after World War II, its Old Town awoke to its colonial charm and maritime heritage (it was briefly the third-largest seaport in Britain's American colonies) in the 1960s, with neglected houses meticulously restored and vacant warehouses at the foot of King Street suddenly sprouting bars, boutiques and dozens of antiques shops. Recently, gentrification has extended to the 16 blocks between the river and the Metro station. It's a great place to hang out, with lots of interest in a small area and tons of local street events.

Revival has had its comic aspects. Cobblestone streets surviving more from lethargy than historical sensibility got re-cobbled at vast expense. When the colonial revival waxed cutesy in the 1970s, a vigilante (never apprehended) took to spray-painting signage touting 'Olde Towne Shoppes' and similar pseudo-historical banalities. Happily, Alexandria took the hint. War smoulders continually between genteel householders bent on parking and zoning limitations and restaurateurs keen to accommodate visitors.

One sport of strollers is trolling for flounders: 'flounder houses', two- or three-storey dwellings with half-gable roofs descending asymmetrically. At least 40 of these Alexandria anomalies from the eighteenth and early nineteenth centuries (possibly designed to evade the wording of some now-forgotten tax rule) mingle with standard Georgian neighbours. Recent housing developments include at least 60 neo-flounders as a local flourish.

The Civil War indelibly marked the swiftly conquered community, including the hard-to-miss (especially for motorists, one of whom actually knocked it down in 1988) Confederate Statue (1888), glowering in the middle of the intersection of South Washington and Prince Streets, its back defiantly turned on the Nation's Capital. It's here to stay. In 1890, the Virginia legislature decreed it should remain in that spot as a 'perpetual and lasting' monument to Southern heroes. A free map of Civil War sites is available at the nearby **Lyceum** museum (*see below* **Highlights**).

Jones Point Park, to the south beneath Wilson Bridge, contains a unique sliver of land where

Old Town Alexandria *is full of restaurants...*

Maryland, DC and Virginia meet, along with a minimalist 1851 lighthouse and a tendentious plaque honouring Margaret Brent, who in colonial Maryland became the first American woman to demand the vote (1648). She didn't get it, so she huffed across to Virginia, buying land here.

Alexandria rewards random wanderings, and you won't find it hard to stumble on places to eat, drink and shop, but if you'd like to pick up a map and events information, make your first stop the Convention & Visitor Association, which the regular and DASH buses pass. Guided walking tours ($8; $5 under-13s) leave the office at noon (Mon-Sat) or 2pm (Sun).

Alexandria Convention & Visitor Association

Ramsey House, 211 King Street, at Fairfax Street (1-800 388 9119/703 838 4200). **Open** 9am-5pm daily.

Highlights

Alexandria Black History Resource Center

638 North Alfred Street, at Wythe Street (703 838 4356). Braddock Road Metro. **Open** 10am-4pm Tue-Sat; 1-5pm Sun. **Admission** free.

Opened in 1983 as a museum of Virginia's African-American heritage, the centre occupies the former Robinson Library, a Jim Crow institution built as a subsitute for racially integrating the Alexandria Public Library. The 1939 demo that called the question was apparently the first civil rights sit-in.

...and old, cobblestone streets.

Carlyle House

121 North Fairfax Street, between King & Cameron Streets (703 549 2997). King Street Metro, then 28A, 28B or DASH bus AT2, AT5, AT7. **Open** 10am-1.30pm Tue-Sat; noon-4.30pm Sun. **Tours** every half-hour. **Admission** $4; $2 students; free under-11s. **No credit cards.**

John Carlyle, a Scots merchant who traded well and married better, built his Scottish-Palladian stone palace on a double lot here in 1751. In 1755, General Edward Braddock convened a council of five British colonial governors in this, his temporary headquarters, to plot a campaign against French forces squeezing the Crown's claims to the Ohio River Valley. Braddock Road follows the path of his march west, toward Pennsylvania and disaster.

Christ Church

Cameron & North Washington Streets (703 549 1450). King Street Metro,then 28A, 28B or DASH bus AT2, AT5, AT7. **Open** 9am-5pm Mon-Fri. **Tours** 9am-4pm Tue-Sat.

On completion in 1773, this dignified Episcopal shrine was dubbed 'The Church in the Woods' by a town still hugging the shoreline. It has been in continuous service since. The ubiquitous General Washington's pew, No.15, is preserved in its original high-backed eminence.

Fort Ward

4301 West Braddock Road (703 838 4848). King Street Metro, then 29K, 29M, 29N bus. **Open** 9am-5pm Tue-Sat; noon-5pm Sun. **Tours** $2; $1 students. **No credit cards.**

With the outbreak of Civil War in 1861, the Union army snatched northern Virginia and threw up a ring of 162 forts and interconnected batteries to defend its capital. Fort Ward was one of the major posts in this belligerent beltway. Its earthwork ramparts survive, with the north-west bastion completely restored. Its museum is patterned after a typical headquarters building.

Friendship Firehouse

107 South Alfred Street, between King & Prince Streets (703 838 4994). King Street Metro. **Open** 10am-4pm Fri, Sat; 1-4pm Sun. **Admission** free.

Formed in 1774, the volunteer fire brigade built this snug station in 1855. Very early hand-drawn engines feature in the displays.

Gadsby's Tavern Museum

134 North Royal Street, between King & Cameron Streets (703 838 4242). King Street Metro. **Open** *Oct-Mar* 11am-4pm Tue-Sat; 1-4pm Sun; *Apr-Sept* 10am-5pm Tue-Sat; 1-5pm Sun. **Admission** $4; $2 11-17s; free under-11s. **Tours** every half hour. **Credit** MC, V.

Englishman John Gadsby joined a 1770 tavern to the 1792 City Hotel, creating Alexandria's social hotspot. In 1798, George Washington graced a ball here, the first public celebration of his birthday; his impersonators still review Alexandria's annual Washington's Birthday parade from its steps. The older building preserves the life of a first-rate hostelry of the eighteenth century. The 'ordinary' next door serves colonial-style food and drink, to the tune of period entertainment. A rare specimen of primitive refrigeration, the ice cellar permitted mint juleps that made steamy summers endurable.

Lee family homes

Boyhood Home of Robert E Lee *607 Oronoco Street, between North Saint Asaph & North Washington Streets (703 548 8454). Braddock Road Metro.* **Open** 10am-4pm Mon-Sat; 1-4pm Sun.
Lee-Fendall House *614 Oronoco Street, at North Washington Street (703 548 1789). Braddock Road Metro.* **Open** 10am-4pm Tue-Sat; 1-4pm Sun.
Both **Admission** $4; $2 11-17s; free under-11s.
No credit cards.

The aristocratic Lees were quintessential 'FFVs' (First Families of Virginia). Among the Revolutionary War generation, Francis Lightfoot Lee and Richard Henry Lee were the only brothers to sign the Declaration of Independence, while kinsman 'Lighthorse' Harry Lee was a celebrated cavalry hero. The daring that sparked Harry in war wrecked him in finance, and he was twice jailed for debt. Losing his magnificent plantation, Stratford Hall, he found his family this more modest house at 607 Oronoco Street, then fled to Barbados, ostensibly for his health. He left behind a classic toast to Washington ('first in war, first in peace, first in the hearts of his countrymen') and a five-year-old son, who would grow up to become Confederate military genius, General Robert E Lee.

Harry sold the lot across the way to Philip Fendall, second husband of his mother-in-law, who in 1785 built the large white home at No.614, later remodelled to its Federal period look. In the twentieth century, fiery United Mine Workers leader John L Lewis bunked here.

Nearby 609 North Washington Street (privately owned) was the home of yet another Lee, Harry's brother Edmund Jennings, Alexandria's mayor in 1814. An overview of Lee's Corners, as this intersection was known, affords a glimpse of the cosy world of Virginia's old ruling class.

The Lyceum, Alexandria's History Museum

201 South Washington Street, at Prince Street (703 838 4994). King Street Metro. **Open** 10am-5pm Mon-Sat; 1-5pm Sun. **Admission** free.

In 1839, local culture vultures built the Greek Revival library-auditorium for debates, concerts and literary soirées. Today, it is Alexandria's history museum, with highlights of its changing displays including locally manufactured stoneware, silverware and furniture.

Seaport Center

Thompsons Alley, at the Potomac River, north of Torpedo Factory (703 549 7078). King Street Metro, then 28A, 28B or DASH bus AT2, AT5, AT7.
Open 9am-4pm daily. **Admission** free.

To recapture Alexandria's maritime heritage, the Alexandria Seaport Foundation formed in 1983, converting the Swedish schooner *Lindo* into the city's flagship. Rechristened the *Alexandria*, she sank off Cape Hatteras in December 1996. In 1999, the foundation rallied with its floating Seaport Center, with demonstrations on boat-building and other exhibits.

The centre's unique pattern for a skiff ideal for construction projects with children has received orders from all over the world.

Stabler-Leadbetter Apothecary Shop

105-107 South Fairfax Street, at King Street (703 836 3713). King Street Metro. **Open** 10am-4pm Mon-Sat; 1-5pm Sun. **Admission** $2.50; $2 11-17s; free under-11s. **Credit** AmEx, Disc, MC, V.

From 1792 until the Depression overwhelmed them, Quaker druggist Edward Stabler's family dosed nostrums for patrons including Washington, Lee and superpol Henry Clay. When the last pharmacist closed shop in 1933, he simply locked the door, creating a time capsule of old-time medications, with modern pharmaceuticals alongside Native American herbals in their original jars. The revival of 'alternative therapies' puts the dated remedies into intriguing perspective. The gift shop vends odd old collectibles.

Torpedo Factory

105 North Union Street, at King Street (703 838 4565/tours 703 683 0693). King Street Metro, then 28A, 28B or DASH bus AT2, AT5, AT7. **Open** 10am-5pm daily. **Tours** $2; free children, students. **Credit** MC, V.

A forbidding World War I munitions plant now spawns arts, not arms, with three storeys of studios and galleries. Exhibits of the old war work line the lobby, including a specimen torpedo. Alexandria Archeology operates a small 'hands-on' museum upstairs, where volunteers and guests help clean and preserve cultural detritus excavated from colonial privies. There are excursion boats and snack vendors on the riverside promenade.

Out to the Beltway

Travelled by over 175,000 cars each day, the Capital Beltway (I-495) makes a wide loop around Washington, DC, encompassing large chunks of Virginia and Maryland, which are considered part of the Washington metropolitan area. 'The Beltway' was the catchier term for 'The Circumferential Highway' that planners mapped in the late 1950s, then built in pieces. When the Woodrow Wilson Bridge across the Potomac River finally closed the circle in 1962, the omens were bad. En route to the span's dedication, President Wilson's widow, Edith, suffered a fatal stroke.

Her de facto memorial also has circulation problems, embodied by the notorious 'Mixing Bowl' at Springfield to the south, a snarl-prone tangle of highways and exit ramps at the intersection of I-395 and the Beltway that's undergoing massive reconstruction. I-95 – which joins the Beltway as it swings east around DC – is the major north-south transport corridor of the eastern US, and its double duty as a commuter route makes it especially congested in the Virginia suburbs.

Arlington and Old Town Alexandria aside, the parts of Virginia ringed by the Beltway, comprised of unmitigated suburbia, are famously uninteresting. The closer-in 'burbs abound with 'Broyhill Boxes', basic houses with two bedrooms and a den upstairs designed to qualify for federal housing loans available to returning veterans after World War II. Elected to Congress, developer Joel T Broyhill got on to the House Committee on the District of Columbia, promoting policies for the city that made moving to his suburbs desirable. Elsewhere, parts are pretty, parts are wealthy, parts are desirable, but the whole is so neverending that the term 'Fairfaxisation' is now used to describe the kind of featureless suburban sprawl that planners and developers try to avoid creating.

There is no real reason for visitors to come here; their trip through the area from Washington Dulles Airport will give them an adequate sample. However, there are a few points of interest. In the northern sector (and an easy detour if you're driving to Dulles) is the chic enclave of **McLean**, with its wooded estates (including Bobby and Ethel Kennedy's 'Hickory Hill') lining Chain Bridge Road.

Also here is the **Claude Moore Colonial Farm** (6310 Georgetown Pike, McLean; 703 442 7557), a reconstructed 'common man's farm' of the Revolutionary War period. McLean's Dolley Madison Highway is so named because it was the first lady's escape route from the Brits in 1814 after they set fire to the White House. On the other side of the Georgetown Pike, is **Langley**, home of the CIA (*see page 250* **All very hush hush**) but little else – and it doesn't exactly welcome visitors.

Further south is the modest early suburb of **Falls Church**, the hub of a huge Asian community, predominantly Vietnamese. The eponymous church was constructed in 1767 at what even then was a major crossroads and served in the Revolutionary War as a recruitment agency and in the Civil War as a stables.

Parts of Alexandria spread far west and south of Old Town, but they don't share its charm, having been annexed by the city a mere handful of decades ago. Instead of historic houses and quaint streets there are the usual residential developments and shopping malls.

Maryland

Maryland inside the Beltway contains historical towns dating to the time when Maryland was still a colony of Great Britain, alongside modern suburban spaces. **Montgomery County** borders the Potomac River across from Virginia on the west and moves eastwards around the DC border to **Prince George's County**, which wraps around DC until it reaches the Potomac River at the bottom. When the capital city was planned in 1791, land was taken from these two counties to form the diamond-shaped city. This part of the metropolitan area is serviced by the Metro and various bus systems, but the best way to explore is by car.

Each of the District's four original corners is marked with a boundary stone, placed by original surveyor Benjamin Banneker, an African-American astronomer, engineer and mathematician. One of those boundary stones was rediscovered in May 1999 by volunteers cleaning up an area overgrown with weeds and strewn with garbage, on the exact eastern corner of DC, at Eastern and Southern Avenues, where the District runs into Prince George's County.

The following description starts in the west of Maryland inside the Beltway at the Potomac River and moves clockwise around the city.

Near the bottom of Montgomery County, right next to the Potomac River, Glen Echo is a unique combination of history and entertainment. An amusement park from 1899 until 1968, **Glen Echo Park** (7300 MacArthur Boulevard; 301 492 6282) had a swimming pool that could hold 3,000 people. The pool and amusement park are now closed, but the site is administered by the National Park Service. A 1921 carousel with 52 hand-carved animals is open from May to September (50¢ a ride). The 1931 art deco **Spanish Ballroom** has been refurbished and is again one of the premier dance venues in the area, hosting popular swing dances every Saturday night. Folk festivals are also held on the ten-acre property and a puppet company and children's theatre operate year round (*see also page 190* **Children**).

The **Clara Barton National Historic Site** (5801 Oxford Road, off MacArthur Boulevard; 301 492 6245) is also in Glen Echo. Barton, founder of the American Red Cross, lived here until her death in 1912. The 1891 Victorian house served as a warehouse for Red Cross supplies and as the American Red Cross headquarters. Furnished as it was during Barton's last years, the house is open to the public daily; admission is free.

North-west from Glen Echo on Wilson Lane lies **Bethesda**. Montgomery County is among the nation's wealthiest counties, and this area is a concentration of distinguished homes with landscaped gardens near exclusive private schools. Downtown Bethesda is a bustling modern

The **Spanish Ballroom** *in Glen Echo.*

commercial centre, known for its many excellent restaurants (*see page 151* **Eating in Bethesda**), sleek office buildings and creative architecture. The centre of Bethesda is the Bethesda Metro Center Plaza at the intersection of Old Georgetown Road and Wisconsin Avenue. Here, in front of the Hyatt Regency hotel, dance concerts are held every Friday evening in summer and, in winter, an ice skating rink is open daily. Bethesda also has a wealth of bookshops, clothing stores and thrift shops. The **Bethesda Theatre Café** (7719 Wisconsin Avenue; 301 656 3337/website www.jwdc.com/movies) serves beer, nachos and pizza, along with second-run movies. The audience (who must be over 21 or accompanied by a parent), sit in swivel chairs at tables.

Bethesda was named after the biblical Pool of Bethesda, which had great healing power. The name seems particularly appropriate today, since Bethesda is home to the **National Institutes of Health**, the principal research branch of the national public health service. More than 16,000 employees work in more than 50 modern buildings on the 305-acre campus. The visitor centre just off Rockville Pike (Building 10, Center Drive; 301 496 1776) offers a slide show and tour of the clinical centre on Monday, Wednesday and Friday. The National Library of Medicine leads an excellent tour at 1pm Monday to Friday. The Naval Medical Center, constructed just before World War II, is also located here.

Chevy Chase is bordered by Bethesda on the west, Kensington on the north, Silver Spring on the east and straddles the DC/Maryland border on the south. Upscale neighbourhoods surround exclusive country clubs and Chevy Chase's own mini 'Fifth Avenue' along a two-block stretch of Wisconsin Avenue just north of the DC border, with stores such as Tiffany & Co and Versace.

Rock Creek Park, one of the most beautiful swathes of land in Montgomery County, follows the meanderings of Rock Creek, which begins in Maryland and stretches south through north-west DC to the Potomac River. The three-mile Maryland section of the park from the Beltway to Boundary Bridge on the DC border has a deep-in-the-woods feeling, far from city noise and pollution. A paved path attracts hikers, bikers and rollerbladers (*see chapter* **Sport**).

On quiet Jones Mill Road, just up a zigzagging path from Rock Creek Park, is the **Audubon Naturalist Society** (8940 Jones Mill Road; 301 652 9188). Founded by famous bird lover John James Audubon, the Society is located in a Georgian mansion on a 40-acre estate of meadows and woodland, traversed by a three-quarter-mile nature trail and scattered with birdhouses and bird feeders. The Society offers free wildlife identification walks, and its bookstore stocks titles on environmental issues and birds.

Forest Glen – a steep ravine with a narrow stream running through it – is just inside the Beltway on the other side of Rock Creek Park. This is the site of the Walter Reed Army Medical Center Annex, where wounded GIs were cared for during World War II. The Army bought the buildings and grounds from the old National Park Seminary, a fancy finishing school for daughters of the very rich around the turn of the century. The girls were housed in whimsical, quirky buildings, including a Japanese pagoda, Dutch windmill and turreted castle along Linden Lane. The buildings are still there, slowly falling apart in their sylvan setting, surrounded by crumbling statues and ancient trees. Walking tours are given on the fourth Saturday of each month at 1pm (details on 301 495 9079).

Looking across the Beltway from Forest Glen, the striking white towers of the **Temple of the Church of Jesus Christ of Latter-Day Saints** are visible through the trees. The $15-million temple is sheathed in 173,000 square feet of Alabama white marble. The highest of six gold-plated steel spires supports a gold-leaf statue of Moroni, the Mormon angel and prophet. Although a Beltway traffic-stopper, the temple is closed to non-Mormons, but a visitor centre (9900 Stoneybrook Drive, off Capitol View Avenue; 301 587 0144) is open daily.

Silver Spring doesn't enjoy the eminence of Bethesda, but still has a number of worthwhile restaurants and shops. It is not an incorporated city and covers a large area both inside and outside the Beltway, but downtown Silver Spring – where Georgia Avenue crosses Colesville Road (State Route 29) and East-West Highway (State Route 410) – has been the subject of much heated controversy over development and revitalisation projects. Second-hand book stores, flea markets, pawn shops, ethnic grocery stores and restaurants abound, notably in the area bordered by Fenton Street, Georgia, Wayne and Silver Spring Avenues. **Blair Mansion Inn** (7711 Eastern Avenue; 301 588 1688) presents murder mysteries with a buffet dinner in a century-old house.

Follow East-West Highway east from Silver Spring and it will turn into Philadelphia Avenue and take you to the heart of **Takoma Park**, a town of regal Victorian houses, ageing hippies and a declared Nuclear Free Zone. **Mark's Kitchen** (7006 Carroll Avenue; 301 270 1884) in the centre of the old town dishes up sushi and burgers, while, across the street, **Chuck & Dave's** independent bookstore (7001 Carroll Avenue; 301 891 2665) invites browsers to look through a good selection of alternative literature and New Age self-help books. The **Takoma Underground** (7000B Carroll Avenue; 301 270 6380) houses an eclectic mix of retro clothing, jewellery and knick-knacks. The **Takoma Park/Silver Spring Food Co-op** (201 Ethan Allen Avenue; 301 891 2667) sells milk in reusable jars, fresh-baked breads, hand-dipped candles and all-natural toothpaste.

Sligo Creek Park runs through Takoma Park, from Silver Spring into Prince George's County. It features miles of scenic hiking and biking on a paved trail along Sligo Creek, criss-crossing the creek on picturesque wooden bridges.

Langley Park is Takoma Park's neighbour, across the county border in Prince George's County, one of the most populous jurisdictions in the Washington area and rapidly growing. The unemployed loiter in 7-Eleven parking lots near cheap clothing stores, and the crime rate is high. Langley Park is a multi-ethnic area with many recent immigrants, mostly Spanish-speaking. Fast-food and strip malls abound, as do good, cheap, ethnic restaurants – such as the popular vegetarian Indian **Udupi Palace** (1329 University Boulevard, Langley Park; 301 434 1531) – the only reason to venture into this area.

University Boulevard runs north-east from Langley Park to **College Park**, home of University of Maryland-College Park, one of the nation's top-ranked state-supported schools, which began as one of America's first agricultural colleges in 1856. It is also the location of the world's oldest continuously operating airport, established in 1909 when Wilbur Wright taught two military officers to fly in the government's first airplane. The **College Park Aviation Museum** (1985 Corporal Frank Scott Drive, between US 1 and Kenilworth Avenue; 301 864 6029) is open daily. **Archives II** (8601 Adelphi Road; 301 713 6800/ free public event listings 501 5000), part of the National Archives, where you can listen to the legendary Watergate tapes, is also in College Park.

University Boulevard continues through the campus, which is bordered by Adelphi Road on the east and Baltimore Avenue (US 1) on the west – the latter runs through the commercial section of town, which has the requisite coffeeshops, bars and funky clothing stores of any college town.

West of College Park is **Greenbelt Regional Park** (6565 Greenbelt Road; 301 344 3948). Only 12 miles from downtown DC, this is a quiet forest haven with four walking trails and numerous camping and picnic facilities.

South of Greenbelt on the Baltimore-Washington Parkway (State Route 295) is the historical town of **Bladensburg**, site in 1784 of the first hot-air balloon launch in the US. The town was also the home of Washington's 'dark and bloody duelling grounds', where duels were fought until the middle of the nineteenth century.

The **Jack Kent Cooke Stadium** in Raljon was built in 1997 and is home to the Washington Redskins, Washington's NFL football team. Raljon was named by Redskins-owner the late Jack Kent Cooke, in honour of his two sons, Ralph and John. It was even given its own zip code by the US Postal Service, much to the chagrin of local Prince Georgians, who point out that the town is really Landover, not Raljon. They say there is no such place, so if you're looking for the stadium, don't ask for directions to Raljon.

Further south, in Suitland, the **Paul E Garber Facility** (3904 Old Silver Hill Road, at Branch Avenue; 301 238 3407) serves as the National Air & Space Museum's preservation, restoration and storage facility. Eighty-five per cent of the aircraft collection is housed here (compared with only ten per cent at the National Mall showpiece museum) in five buildings. Model satellites, kites and astronautical artefacts are also on display, and visitors can sometimes see curators and preservationists working on the planes. Tours are held daily, but reservations are required two weeks in advance.

For those tired of walking long city blocks, country life can be glimpsed at **Oxon Hill Farm** in the town of Oxon Hill (6411 Oxon Hill Road; 301 839 1177). It's a working farm, where visitors can watch cows be milked and fields ploughed by farmhands. There is also a forest, orchard and vegetable garden. Activities are administered by the National Park Service.

By Season

There's lots of pomp in DC's calendar, but some of the local events don't stand on ceremony.

Washington, DC, has all the state ceremonials you would expect of a capital municipality, along with a bursting calendar of events and seasons associated with the big cultural institutions. But beyond the marble, DC's distinct and diverse communities organise local events that give the lie to the idea that the city has no streetlife.

For a more complete events list, check the *Washington Post*'s Friday 'Weekend' section, *Washington City Paper* or www.sidewalk.com. Note that DC's lack of effective local government means that local festivals sometimes fail to get off the ground. For information on DC's various film festivals, *see page 203* **Film**.

NATIONAL HOLIDAYS

New Year's Day (1 Jan); Martin Luther King Jr Day (third Mon in Jan); President's Day (third Mon in Feb); Memorial Day (last Mon in May); Independence Day (4 July); Labor Day (first Mon in Sept); Columbus Day (second Mon in Oct); Election Day (first Tue in Nov); Veteran's Day (11 Nov); Thanksgiving Day (fourth Thur in Nov); Christmas Day (25 Dec).

Rolling Thunder on **Memorial Day** *(page 98).*

Spring

St Patrick's Day Parade

Information 310 879 1717. Constitution Avenue, NW, from Seventh to 17th Streets, Mall & Tidal Basin. **Date** starts at noon Sun before 17 Mar.

Smaller than the celebrations in cities north of DC, St Patrick's Day nevertheless inspires revelry, with a parade of dancers, bands, bagpipes and floats. The partying continues in pubs around the city. Celebrations are also held in Alexandria; details on 703 237 2199.

Smithsonian Annual Kite Festival

Information 357 2700. West side of the Washington Monument Grounds, Mall & Tidal Basin. **Date** 10am-4pm last Sun in Mar.

Hand-made kites are flown in various competitions by kite lovers of all ages, plus demonstrations with novelty and sport kites by 'kite making masters'. Great fun for kids.

Annual White House Easter Egg Roll

Information 456 2200/456 2322. White House South Lawn. **Date** 10am-2pm Mon after Easter Sun.

For children aged three to six. Eggs provided. Start at the Southeast Gate on E Executive Avenue and E Street; it gets very crowded, so arrive early. The night before is best, but make sure the kids are with you come 7-7.30am when the tickets are handed out.

White House Spring Garden & House Tours

Information 456 2200/456 2322. White House. **Date** mid-Apr.

Tour the quirky garden choices of past and present White House residents, including the Rose Garden, South Lawn and Jacqueline Kennedy Garden, as well as the state rooms of the White House. No tickets or reservations, but get in line early at the Southeast Gate, at E Executive Avenue & E Street.

Eastern Market Day

Information 675 9050. Seventh Street, SE, from Pennsylvania Avenue to N Carolina Street, Southeast. **Date** 11am-6pm first Sun in May.

Neighbourhood festival with arts and crafts, games, rides, entertainment and food. All funds raised go to Friendship House, a local social services agency.

Washington National Cathedral Flower Mart

Information 537 6200. Grounds of Washington National Cathedral, Massachusetts & Wisconsin Avenues, NW, Upper Northwest. **Date** first weekend in May.

Flower booths, ethnic foods, entertainment and flower decorating demonstrations.

Annual Georgetown Garden Tour

Information 387 0002. Georgetown. **Admission** $15 pre-booked; $20 day of tour. **Date** second Sat in May.

More than a dozen gardens are on view in this self-guided walking tour, a rare opportunity to see past the gates of some of the most beautiful homes in Washington. Admission includes tea and transport between the gardens.

Annual Goodwill Embassy Tour

Information 636 4225 ext 1255. Meet at Naval Security Station, Massachusetts & Nebraska Avenues, NW, Upper Northwest. **Admission** $30 pre-booked; $35 day of tour. **Date** 10am-5pm second Sat in May.

Self-guided tour of eight to ten embassies.

Memorial Day celebrations

Date Memorial Day weekend.

On Sunday evening, the National Symphony Orchestra performs a free concert on the West Lawn of the US Capitol (details on 619 7222). On Monday, the presidential wreath-laying and memorial services are held at Arlington National Cemetery (685 2851), Vietnam Veterans Memorial (619 7222), and the US Navy Memorial (737 2300). Rolling Thunder, a motorcycle demonstration at the Pentagon on Sunday morning, also honours the dead.

Memorial Day Jazz Festival

Information 703 883 4686/703 838 4844. Jones Point Park, 1 S Lee Street,at the end of the street under the Woodrow Wilson Bridge, Old Town Alexandria, VA. **Date** noon-8pm Memorial Day.

Day-long concert with seven or so jazz artists, plus food stalls, held on the waterfront at Jones Point Park in touristy but quaint Old Town.

Summer

Marine Band's Summer Concert Series

Information 433 4011. East Terrace of the US Capitol, Capitol & Around, and the Ellipse, White House & Around. **Date** 8pm Wed (US Capitol), 8pm Sun (Ellipse), June-Aug.

Free, twice-weekly outdoor concerts, from classical music to brass bands.

Mount Pleasant Festival

Information 588 5272. Mount Pleasant Street, NW, between Irving Street & Park Road, Mount Pleasant. **Date** first Sun in June.

A street fair (Mount Pleasant Street is closed to traffic) that celebrates this economically and ethnically mixed, hip neighbourhood north of Adams Morgan. Food vendors, live music, games for kids, crafts and work by local artists. No alcohol.

Uni-Fest

Information 889 7707/678 8822. Union Temple Baptist Church, W Street & Martin Luther King Avenue, SE, Anacostia. **Date** first weekend in June.

Celebrating the African American community, this festival includes gospel singers, dancers and food.

Capitol Jazz Fest

Information 310 218 0404. Merriwether Post Pavilion, S Entrance Road, off US 29, Columbia, MD. **Admission** free Fri; $26.50-$125 Sat, Sun. **Date** first weekend in June.

A three-day outdoor music festival billed as the 'world's largest showcase of contemporary jazz music'. Indeed, some of the best jazz musicians around take to the stage each year.

Website: www.capitoljazz.com

National Race for the Cure

Information 1-703-556-9402. Starts at Constitution Avenue, between 12th & 15th Streets, Mall & Tidal Basin. **Date** first Sun in June.

The largest 5km run/walk in the world – there were more than 52,000 participants in 1998 – raising money for and awareness of breast cancer.

Website: www.natl-race-for-the-cure.org

Dance Africa-DC

Information 269 1600. Dance Place, 3225 Eighth Street, NE, at Monroe Street, Northeast. **Date** mid-June.

Two-day festival celebrating African and African-American dance and music, with master classes, free outdoor performances and crafts. A gala performance is held at Howard University.

Website: www.danceplace.org

Smithsonian Folklife Festival

Information 357 2700. National Mall, between Seventh & 14th Streets, Mall & Tidal Basin. **Date** last weekend in June and first weekend in July.

One of the highlights of the DC calendar, this festival celebrates the arts, crafts and food of selected US states and other countries (the honorees shift each year). Food and demonstration booths stretch down the National Mall. Past performances have ranged from Bahamian music, quilting and pottery demonstrations. The atmosphere is cheerful, the weather usually hot.

Independence Day

Information 619 7222. Various venues. **Date** 4 July.

The Fourth of July in Washington is all about crowds. Official events begin at 10am at the National Archives, with a dramatic reading of the Declaration of Independence and a demonstration of colonial military manoeuvres. At noon, the Independence Day parade starts to wind its way down Constitution Avenue (from the National Archives to

Very cherry

In 1912, 3,000 cherry trees were donated to the city of Washington by Mayor Yukio Ozaki of Tokyo as a symbol of friendship between Japan and the United States. These original trees were planted along the Tidal Basin; today, the path that rings the basin becomes clogged with ogling tourists – and even normally cynical DC natives – between late March and mid-April each year, when the trees explode into bloom.

Ironically enough, given the World War II fate of the 'friendship' between Japan and the US, the city has become famous for the immigrant blossoms and celebrates with near-pagan worship and a weekend (usually the second in April) of special events – including a parade, golf and rugby tournaments and the Sakuri Matsuri Street Festival, a celebration of Japanese art, food and culture held on the Saturday, on 12th Street between Pennsylvania and Constitution Avenues. Hotels are booked to capacity and the Metro feels like rush hour all day, but it's a congenial atmosphere and the blossoms are truly wonderful to behold.

In 1999, near-panic broke out when nine trees were felled at the height of blossom season. The tree-terrorists turned out to be a little family of well-meaning but misguided beavers living peacefully in the Tidal Basin. True to the blossom-mania, the *Washington Post* dutifully covered the capture of the beavers with diligence worthy of a political scandal.

National Cherry Blossom Festival
Information 547 1500.

17th Street), and later (5-9.15pm), the Washington Monument Grounds hosts entertainment and scads of revellers. The National Symphony Orchestra performs a concert on the steps of the US Capitol building at 8pm and, at 9pm, fireworks (some say the best in the country) are set off over the Washington Monument.

Walk to the festivities if you can; Fourth of July crowds eat up parking spots for miles and test the limits of the public transport system. Check local listings for smaller celebrations around the city.

Latino Festival

Information 301 588 8719. Pennsylvania Avenue, NW, between Ninth & 14th Streets, Penn Quarter. **Date** last weekend in July.

DC is home to a large Latino population, and you can taste the foods and hear the music of that community as hundreds of display booths, food stalls and performers fan out over Pennsylvania Avenue for this two-day festival. On Sunday, there's a parade.

Autumn

Adams Morgan Day

18th Street, between Columbia Road & Florida Avenue, Adams Morgan. **Date** second weekend in Sept.

For 20 years, thousands of DC residents came out to celebrate this NW Washington community, home to large Latino, white, African and African-American populations. Musicians, crafts and ethnic foods were in great supply. But in 1998 political infighting and debts cancelled the 21st annual festival. Angry community residents took over the planning of the festival for 1999 and 2000. If it's on, it will be advertised in the listings mags.

Takoma Park Folk Festival

Information 301 589 3717. Philadelphia & Maple Avenues, Takoma Park, MD. **Date** first Sun after Labor Day.

Traditional and original folk music (including local DC talent) on six stages, plus dance, crafts and foods. *Website: www.pubcom.com/tpff/*

Kalorama House & Embassy Tour

Information 387 4062 ext 18. Various venues. **Admission** $10 pre-booked; $20 day of tour. **Date** noon-5pm second Sun in Sept.

Tour the lovely late nineteenth-century homes and embassies in the 'Kalorama triangle', north of Dupont Circle.

White House Fall Garden & House Tours

Information 456 2200/456 2322. White House. **Date** mid-Oct.

The White House gardens and a few select rooms are on display, and military bands play. No tickets or reservations, just stand in line at the Southeast Gate at E Executive Avenue & E Street.

Halloween Annual High Heel Race

Information 328 0090. 17th Street, NW, between S & P Streets, Dupont Circle. **Date** on or around 31 Oct (check local listings for exact date and time).

Dupont Circle residents swarm to 17th Street to catch a glimpse of the participants in this ultimate drag race. The race itself lasts only minutes, but the atmosphere is festive and the men fabulous.

Veteran's Day ceremonies

Information 685 2851. Arlington National Cemetery, Memorial Drive, Arlington Drive, VA. **Date** 11am Veteran's Day.

A solemn ceremony with military bands, in honour of the country's war dead. Ceremonies are also held

What a drag! The **High Heel Race** *(page 99).*

at 1pm at the Vietnam Veteran's Memorial (details on 619 7222), Mount Vernon (703 780 2000) and the US Navy Memorial (737 2300.)

Winter

National Christmas Tree Lighting

Information 619 7222. The Ellipse, Mall & Tidal Basin. **Date** early Dec.

The president kicks off the holiday season by switching on the lights on the giant National Christmas Tree. For a place in the enclosure, you'll need a ticket: apply at least six weeks in advance as they run out early. The ticketless can usually get glimpses from the other side of the fence. The ceremony begins at 5pm; arrive early. From now until New Year's Day, the Ellipse hosts Christmas performances as part of the annual Pageant of Peace.

Lighting of the Menorah

Information 619 7222. The Ellipse, Mall & Tidal Basin. **Date** mid-Dec.

A huge menorah – the nine-branched candelabra that signifies the Jewish holiday Hanukkah – is lit for all eight nights of the holiday.

White House Christmas Candlelight Tours

Information 456 2200/456 2322. White House. **Date** three days in late Dec.

Free evening tours of the White House Christmas decorations, plus musical performances. Arrive early because lines will be long.

Holidays at Mount Vernon

Information 703 780 2000. Mount Vernon, south end of George Washington Parkway, Mount Vernon, VA. **Admission** $4-$8; free under-6s. **Date** 9am-4pm daily 1 Dec-6 Jan.

Mount Vernon offers a 'colonial holiday experience'. The tour is short but interesting – and makes you glad you live in a century with electric heating. The candlelight programme, held on the first three weekends, is popular (reservations 703 799 8604).

New Year's Eve celebrations

Various venues. **Date** New Year's Eve.

Events range from free celebrations at the Kennedy Center (music in the Grand Foyer) to several-hundred-dollar-a-plate dinners at some of the area's more upscale dining establishments. Restaurants and clubs often offer jazz, dinner and a champagne toast for a fixed price. Most restaurants start taking reservations early. There are also alcohol-free 'first-night' celebrations in the suburbs (such as Alexandria). DC celebrates the millennium with a street fair on Pennsylvania Avenue.

Presidential Inauguration

Date 20 Jan (next inauguration 2001).

Every four years, the city turns upside down to welcome the country's newly elected leader. In addition to free public festivals on the Mall and the actual inauguration itself – ceremonies take place on the west front of the US Capitol – Inaugural Balls are held in venues around the city. If you can secure yourself a ticket (at a price), you'll catch a glimpse of Hollywood stars, Capitol Hill celebrities and maybe even the president himself.

Website: www.whitehouse.gov

Martin Luther King Jr's Birthday Celebrations

Information Lincoln Memorial celebration 727 1111/ WPAS concert 833 9800. **Date** third weekend in Jan.

A birthday celebration is held on the steps of the Lincoln Memorial, where Dr King gave his famous 'I have a dream' speech. The Washington Performing Arts Society (WPAS) hosts an annual children's concert at the Lincoln Theatre in Shaw (tickets $12), with Sweet Honey in the Rock, who combine gospel, African rhythms and rap into a cappella combinations – a tremendous show.

Website: www.wpas.org

Chinese New Year

Information 638 1041. Chinatown, H Street, NW, between Sixth & Ninth Streets, Downtown. **Date** late Jan-mid-Feb, determined by the lunar calendar.

Celebrations for Chinese New Year begin with a bang – dancers, dragons, firecrackers and parades – and continue, a bit muted, for ten days.

Black History Month

Date Feb.

The Smithsonian Institution (357 2700) holds special events, exhibitions and cultural programmes throughout the month. For additional activities, contact the Martin Luther King Library (727 0321).

Famous birthdays

Information Lincoln 619 7222; Washington 703 780 2333; Douglass 426 5961. **Date** 12-15 Feb.

A trio of famous men's birthdays. A celebration of Abe Lincoln's birthday (12 February) is held at the Lincoln Memorial; Lincoln's Gettysburg address is read and a wreath is laid. For hard-core history buffs only. George Washington's birthday celebration, with a patriotic military programme and a George Washington impersonator, is held (on the third Monday in February) at Mount Vernon, Virginia. The Frederick Douglass birthday tribute celebrates this great African-American statesman, orator and freedom advocate. It's held on or near 14 February at the Frederick Douglass National Historic Site, 1411 W Street, SE, at 14th Street, Anacostia.

Museums & Galleries

The mighty Smithsonian heads the field among DC's world-class collection of museums.

Museums

The geography of the District's National Mall – a monumental greensward ringed by the city's biggest museums and crowned by the US Capitol building – exemplifies the tight-knit relationship between arts and government in Washington. DC's museums not only serve a broad constituency of national and international visitors, but many owe their lifeblood to funding from the national government – which is renowned for its conservative tastes. As a result, museum research departments, libraries and collections of acknowledged genius thrive in Washington; cutting-edge visual art does not.

You can't visit Washington's museums without bumping into the Smithsonian Institution – the country's largest museum complex, comprising 14 museums and the National Zoo in DC, plus two museums in New York (the Smithsonian's museums are designated in the listings below by '**S**' in parentheses after their name). For more information on this venerable and unique organisation, *see page 112* **The Smithsonian**.

The Smithsonian's museums exhibit everything from fossilised microbes to Francis Bacon's screaming popes, so visitors will likely find a collection that interests them. Scholars are also attracted to the institution's extensive research facilities: the **Museum of Natural History**'s 500 scientists and scholars do everything from helping the federal government compile its endangered species lists to researching biodiversity, while the **Sackler** and **Freer** galleries house the largest Asian art research library in the US.

The city's visual arts venues offer unparalleled selections of acknowledged masterpieces and important touring exhibitions usually stop at one of Washington's larger art museums. The privately funded **National Gallery of Art** presents a superlative survey of painting and sculpture from the fourteenth century to the present. Although the NGA's twentieth-century collections and one-off exhibitions rarely stride the cutting edge, the latter prove consistent blockbusters with wide appeal. The city's other visual arts behemoth, the Smithsonian's **Hirshhorn Museum & Sculpture Garden**, has a strong nineteenth- and twentieth-century collection, with holdings akin to the Pompidou or the Tate. But art connoisseurs know that the Museum of Modern Art in New York holds the country's pre-eminent twentieth-century art collection.

Asian art at the **Sackler** *(page 102).*

Although sometimes overshadowed by the Mall museums, the District's quirkier venues merit attention. The **National Museum of Health & Medicine** provides a detailed – some might argue, stomach-churning – look at the human body, and the **Octagon** shows are gems of architectural history. Intimate visual arts venues such as the **Phillips Collection** and **Kreeger Museum** boast works by Picasso, Van Gogh and Stella – with considerably smaller crowds.

For museum listings, check the *Washington Post* and the free *City Paper*. On federal holidays, certain museums are closed, so ring first to check. Note that the Smithsonian's National Museum of American Art and the National Portrait Gallery are both closed for a three-year renovation from January 2000. Their collections will circulate in national exhibits and will rotate into available gallery space at the Renwick Gallery.

Fine art

Arthur M Sackler Gallery (S)

1050 Independence Avenue, SW, between 11th & 12th Streets, Mall & Tidal Basin (357 4880). Smithsonian Metro. **Open** 10am-5.30pm daily. **Admission** free.

The Sackler is considered the Smithsonian's younger, hipper Asian art museum because, unlike its neighbour, the Freer Gallery (*see below*), its mandate allows an active roster of international loan exhibits of ancient and contemporary Asian art. Connected to the Freer by an underground passageway and sharing its director and administration, the Sackler was built around a 1,000-piece Asian art gift from Dr Arthur M Sackler, a New York City research physician and medical publisher. The museum opened in 1987.

Visitors enter through Shepley Bullfinch Richardson and Abbott's granite pavilion (its twin, by the same firm, is at the National Museum of African Art) in to a maze of overlapping bridges and long passageways that give the feel of an ancient temple. Artefacts from China – such as lacquered tropical hardwood Ming-style furniture (1368-1644) and a late seventeenth-century Quing dynasty rosewood armchair – and sculpture from South and Southeast Asia – including twelfth-century Hindu temple sculpture and fifth-century BC Jainist religious figures – are on permanent display.

Disabled: access, audio guides to some exhibitions.

Corcoran Gallery of Art

500 17th Street, NW, between New York Avenue & E Street (639 1700). Farragut West Metro. **Open** 10am-5pm Mon, Wed, Fri, Sat; 10am-9pm Thur. **Admission** free.

When District financier William Wilson Corcoran's collection outgrew its original space (now the Renwick Gallery), gallery trustees engaged architect Ernest Flagg to produce its current Beaux Arts building, which opened in 1897. Despite a handful of significant bequests that added the minor Renoirs and Pissarros now gracing the wood-panelled Clark Landing, the Corcoran's strength remains its nineteenth-century American painting collection, featuring landscapes of the American West by Albert Bierstadt, Frederick Church and Winslow Homer. Church's mammoth 1857 oil, 'Niagara', and Bierstadt's 'Mount Corcoran' (1875-77) capture Americans' reverence for the natural world.

The museum's 6,000 pieces include contemporary art, photography, prints, drawings and sculpture. Notable displays include the Evans-Tibbs collection of African-American art and drawings by John Singer Sargent. The eighteenth-century neo-classical Salon Doré –transported from the Hôtel de Clermont in Paris, complete with gilded and mirrored panelling decorated with garlands, Corinthian pilasters and trophy panels – is a feast for the eyes.

Freer Gallery: *Whistler's Peacock Room.*

The Corcoran hosts regular exhibitions by students and faculty from its adjunct school of art, as well as an ongoing programme of contemporary art, showcased in its Biennial.

Disabled: access.

Dumbarton Oaks Research Library & Collections

1703 32nd Street, NW, between R & S Streets, Georgetown (339 6400). Bus 30, 32, 34, 36. **Open** *museum* 2-5pm Tue-Sun; *garden* 2-6pm (*Nov-Mar* 2-5pm) daily. **Admission** *museum* free; *garden* $4; $3 concessions.

After wealthy art connoisseurs Robert and Mildred Bliss purchased the nineteenth-century Federal-style brick mansion Dumbarton Oaks in 1920, they filled a commissioned McKim, Mead and White Beaux Arts addition with their modest-sized collection of Byzantine and pre-Columbian art. The museum's collection of portable, sumptuous Byzantine objects, including rare sixth-century ecclesiastical silver, is one of the world's finest.

Bliss conveyed the property, collections and a newly endowed research library to Harvard University in 1940. The octagonal Philip Johnson-designed wing, completed in 1963, houses the pre-Columbian collection in galleries encircling the central fountain. Don't miss the miraculously preserved Peruvian burial mantle from 400 BC or the fanciful

and grotesque 'Head of a Maize God', originally crafted in 775 AD for a Honduran temple. The 16 acres of flora-filled formal gardens skirting the mansion are also open to the public.
Disabled: partial access.

Freer Gallery of Art (S)

Jefferson Drive, at 12th Street, SW, Mall & Tidal Basin (357 4880). Smithsonian Metro. **Open** 10am-5.30pm daily. **Admission** free.

When Detroit business magnate Charles Lang Freer (1854-1919) began collecting the works of American painter James McNeill Whistler in the 1880s, the artist encouraged Freer to collect Asian art while on his travels to the Middle and Far East. So Freer amassed neolithic Chinese pottery and Hindu temple sculpture along with work by nineteenth-century American painters. In 1904, he offered his collection to the Smithsonian, which commissioned from architect Charles Adam Platt this dignified, grey granite, Renaissance palazzo-style building with a sun-drenched courtyard. It opened in 1923. Its mandate stipulates that it neither lend nor borrow from its 26,500-piece holdings, so selections are rotated semi-annually in its dimly lit, meditative galleries.

Freer purchased the gallery's jewel, Whistler's deep green and gilt Peacock Room, in 1904. The museum's only permanent installation, this 1876-77 dining room was transported wholesale from British shipowner Frederick R Leyland's London townhouse. Whistler covered the ceiling with a gold leaf and peacock feather pattern and gilded shelving and painted wooden shutters with immense plumed peacocks. His Japonais-style canvas, *The Princess from the Land of Porcelain*, presides over the room.

An underground passage connects the Freer to the neighbouring Sackler Gallery (*see above*).
Disabled: access, audio guides.

Hillwood Museum & Gardens

4155 Linnean Avenue, NW, between Tilden & Upton Streets, Upper Northwest (686 8500). Van Ness-UDC Metro. **Open** 9am-5pm Tue-Sat (reservations required). **Admission** suggested donation $10; $5 students; $5 garden with guided tour; $2 garden self-guided tour; under-12s not permitted in museum.

Cereal heir Majorie Merriweather Post purchased Hillwood in 1955 to house her extensive collection of French and Russian decorative art. Seduced by Russian culture after living there for 18 months in the 1930s, Post soon amassed the largest collection of imperial Russian art objects outside that country. Portraits of czars and czarinas, palace furnishings, a porcelain service commissioned by Catherine the Great and a selection of Fabergé eggs are displayed in Hillwood's gilt and wood-panelled rooms. The French collection includes Sèvres porcelain, eighteenth-century furniture and Beauvais tapestries.

You can also roam the 12-acre manicured grounds, including a Japanese-style garden with plunging waterfall. Guided evening tours, when offered, are not to be missed: the waning light makes for romantic strolls in the gardens, and the home's ceremonial rooms are illuminated as if for a party.

Hillwood closes for renovation until spring 2000.
Disabled: access, audio guides.

Hirshhorn Museum & Sculpture Garden (S)

Independence Avenue & Seventh Street, SW, Mall & Tidal Basin (357 1300). L'Enfant Plaza Metro. **Open** 10am-5.30pm daily. **Admission** free.

This spectacular cylinder enlivens the predominantly neo-classical architecture ringing the Mall with an aggressively modern Skidmore, Owings and Merrill building, completed in 1974 to house self-made Wall Street millionaire Joseph Hirshhorn's collection of twentieth-century painting and sculpture. SOM's chief designer Gordon Bunshaft created a three-storey hollow concrete drum supported on four curvilinear piers. Bunshaft's original plan to encase his cylinder in pink travertine became cost-prohibitive, so he settled for sand-blasting the concrete aggregate to clarify and smooth its surface. In keeping with the modernist tradition, there is no ceremonial entrance, only a single utilitarian revolving door issuing on to Independence Avenue.

The upstairs galleries were recently refurbished. The third-floor galleries present a predominantly chronological survey of international modern art, beginning with American realists such as Edward Hopper through Sigmar Polke's capitalist realism. Particular strengths include a significant Giacometti collection, the largest public collection of work by Thomas Eakins outside the artist's native Philadelphia and a pair of Willem de Kooning's rare 'door paintings' (the museum boasts the largest public collection of his work in the world).

A daylit, sculpture-filled ambulatory running alongside the circular painting galleries holds small Henry Moores in wood and a Cubist work by Josef Albers. The basement galleries are reserved for more recent twentieth-century work by such artists as Gerhard Richter, Richard Long and Damian Hirst. The sunken sculpture garden features Rodin's *Burghers of Calais* (1184-89), Marino Marini's rendering of post-war angst in *Horse and Rider* (1952-53), and a number of Giacometti bronzes.

Each year, the Hirshhorn presents three major exhibitions, often single-artist retrospectives. The well-regarded Directions series spotlights cutting-edge artists; past shows have included Tony Ourseler, Juliao Sarmento and Sam Taylor-Wood.
Disabled: access, wheelchairs, touch tours.

Kreeger Museum

2401 Foxhall Road, NW, between Dexter & W Streets, Upper Northwest (337 3050/reservations 338 3552). D4 bus. **Open** 90-minute tours 10.30am, 1.30pm, Tue-Sat (reservations required). **Admission** free.

Security concerns dictate that this intimate museum, housed in a spectacular, 1967, Philip Johnson-designed travertine home nestled in woods, can only be visited on small guided tours. But even those who

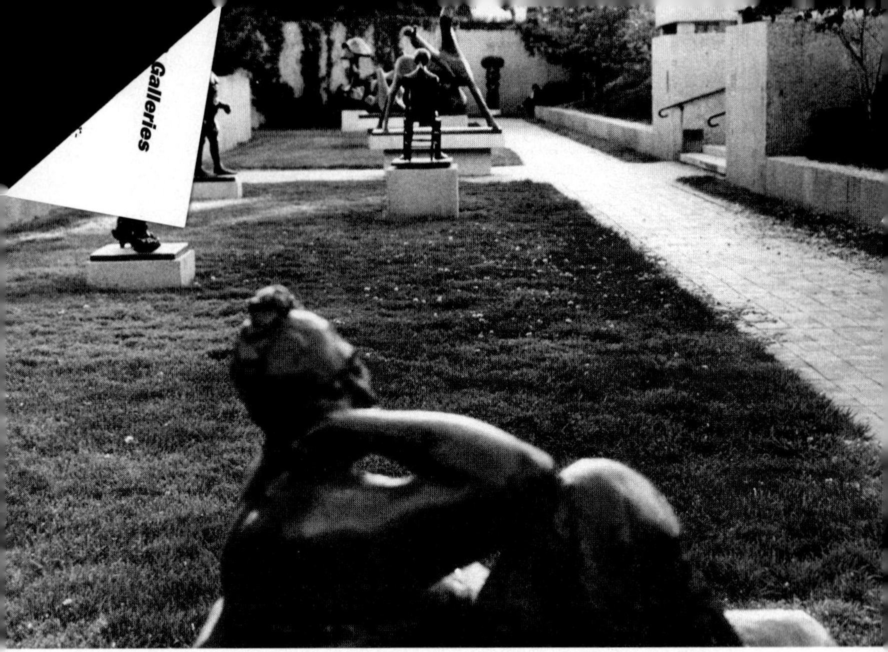

The sunken sculpture garden at the **Hirshhorn Museum**. *See page 103.*

bristle at tour guides should not be put off: the late insurance magnate David Lloyd Kreeger and his wife Carmen amassed a small but striking collection of 180 works by nineteenth- and twentieth-century heavyweights.

The museum's scale allows visitors to savour the details of works by Kandinsky, Chagall and Stella. Braque's *Vase, Pallette, and Skull* is a Cubist update of the traditional *memento mori*. Two rooms showcase Monet cliffside landscapes, with surprisingly thick daubs of sometimes gaudy coloured oils. The Kreegers also collected African ceremonial art, and their outdoor sculpture terrace overlooking a verdant wood has bronzes by Henry Moore, Jean Arp and Aristide Maillol.

Public transport doesn't take you very close to the museum; it's probably easier to take a cab.
Disabled: partial access.

National Gallery of Art

West Building: Constitution Avenue between Fourth & Seventh Streets, NW; East Building: Constitution Avenue & Fourth Street, NW, Mall & Tidal Basin (737 4215). Judiciary Square or Archives-Navy Memorial Metro. **Open** 10am-5pm Mon-Sat; 11am-6pm Sun. **Admission** free.

Pittsburgh investment banker and industrialist Andrew Mellon was born the poor son of an Irish immigrant but went on to serve as US Treasury Secretary from 1921-1932, and presented the National Gallery's West Building as a gift to the nation in 1941. Mellon's son, Paul, created the gallery's East Building in 1978. Mellon *fils*, who had donated over 900 artworks during his lifetime, bequeathed $75 million in cash and 100 paintings – including works by Monet, Renoir, Seurat and Cézanne – on his death in February 1999.

In designing the Tennessee marble West Building, architect John Russell Pope borrowed motifs from the temple architecture of the Roman Pantheon. The white marble stairs at the Constitution Avenue entrance lead to the main-floor rotunda with its impressive green Italian marble floors and columns around a bubbling fountain encircled by fragrant greenery and flora. On this level, galleries issue off the building's 782ft longitudinal spine. The ground-level houses artificially lit galleries as well as a gift shop and garden court café. An underground concourse has a cafeteria, another shop and a moving walkway that connects the West Building to the skylit, IM Pei-designed East Building.

The West Building's skylit main floor reads like an art history text: masterworks from the fourteenth to the nineteenth century pepper practically every gallery. Late medieval Flemish highlights include Jan Van Eyck's *Annunciation*, looking particularly vibrant after a thorough 1994 cleaning, and Rogier van der Weyden's tiny yet finely detailed *St George and the Dragon*. Pre- through high-Renaissance Italian works represent a significant proportion of the collection: Giotto's seminal fourteenth-century *Madonna and Child* hangs in gallery 1, Leonardo da Vinci's almond-eyed portrait of Ginevra de' Benci in gallery 6 and Botticelli's *Adoration of the Magi* in gallery 7. Giovanni Bellini and Titian's *Feast of the Gods* commands gallery 17 north of the West Garden Court.

Snaking westward, galleries 23 and 24, primarily devoted to Titian, hold his luscious *Venus with a*

Mirror and the terrifying *St John the Evangelist on Patmos*. Downstairs, sculpture galleries house Degas' plaster dancer studies and Rodin marbles. Rembrandt's intent gaze in his 1659 self-portrait hangs among seventeenth-century Dutch and Flemish works in galleries 42 to 51, including a solid selection of Van Dyck in galleries 42 and 43.

In the East Building, Alexander Calder's 9m by 23m 1976 aluminum and steel mobile dangles languidly above the triple-height, skylit atrium. The gallery's strong but small collection of twentieth-century art – including Jackson Pollock's drip painting *Number 1 (Lavender Mist)* and Robert Motherwell's expansive *Reconciliation Elegy* – is housed in the concourse-level galleries. The upper galleries are used for touring exhibitions.

The new Micro Gallery, just inside the West Building's main-floor Mall entrance, has 15 individual cubicles with touch-screen colour monitors where you can learn more about individual works, movements and artists, including thorough explanations of conservation techniques. You can assemble up to ten works in a 'personal tour', which can then be printed on to a gallery map showing each selection's exact location.

The gallery opened a sculpture garden in 1998 on a six-acre square across Seventh Street from the West Building. Designed by Philadelphia landscape architect Laurie Olin, its circular fountain bubbles in summer, transforming into an ice-skating rink in winter. Nestled among the Lebanon cedars and linden trees are Louise Bourgeois' 10ft bronze cast *Spider*, whose spindly legs span 24ft, Sol LeWitt's 15ft-high concrete *Four-Sided Pyramid* and Tony Smith's stout *Moondog*.
Disabled: access, audio guides..

National Museum of African Art (S)

950 Independence Avenue, SW, between Seventh & Twelfth Streets, Mall & Tidal Basin (357 4600). Smithsonian Metro. **Open** 10am-5.30pm daily. **Admission** free.
This museum's entrance pavilion, designed by Shepley Bullfinch Richardson and Abbott, lies across the Enid Haupt Garden from its twin, the Sackler. Opened in 1987, the collection's primary focus is ancient and contemporary work from sub-Saharan Africa, although it also collects arts from other African areas. It includes a particularly strong array of royal Benin art. The Point of View gallery is devoted to thematic explorations of objects in the collection, while temporary shows present a wide variety of African visual arts, including sculpture, textiles, ceramics, musical instruments and photos.
Disabled: access.

National Museum of Women in the Arts

1250 New York Avenue, NW, at 13th Street, Downtown (783 5000). Metro Center Metro. **Open** 10am-5pm Mon-Sat; noon-5pm Sun. **Admission** suggested donation $3; $2 concessions.
Founded in 1981 by Wallace and Wilhelmina Holladay to showcase important art by women, the museum didn't occupy its current 70,000sq ft, landmarked Renaissance Revival building, built by Waddy Butler Wood in 1907, until 1987. It provides a survey of art by women from the sixteenth century to the present. Highlights include Renaissance artist Lavinia Fontana's dynamic *Holy Family with St John* and Frida Kahlo's defiant 1937 self-portrait *Between the Curtains*. Artists Helen Frankenthaler, Camille Claudel and Elisabeth Vigee-LeBrun are also represented. Temporary exhibitions, while not always blockbusters, present intelligent examinations of women's art history.

Phillips Collection

1600 21st Street, NW, at Q Street, Dupont Circle (387 2151). Dupont Circle Metro. **Open** 10am-5pm Tue-Wed, Fri, Sat; 10am-8.30pm (*mid July-Sept* 10am-5pm) Thur; noon-7pm (*June-Sept* noon-5pm) Sun. **Admission** Sat, Sun $6.50; $3.25 concessions; free under-12s; Mon-Fri suggested donation same as weekend prices; after 5pm Thur $5.
This Dupont Circle mansion, former home of Marjorie and Duncan Phillips, opened in 1921 and underwent renovation in the late 1980s, when a modern addition extended its space by almost 20,000sq ft. Renoir's cheery *Luncheon of the Boating Party*, one of the Phillips's first purchases, remains the keystone of this cosy gallery where few works predate 1850. Significant Van Gogh oils rub shoulders with Steiglitz prints and a there is a solid selection of lesser-known works by Picasso, Bacon, Vuillard and Rothko.

The luxuriant turn-of-the-century mansion offers a welcome escape from Mall mêlée: note the music room's spectacular oak wainscoting and ceiling coffers. The historical surveys and one-person shows held in the Goh Annex tend to be conservative – Impressionists and twentieth-century photography are recent examples – although a recent Richard Diebenkorn show attracted significant crowds.
Disabled: access.

Renwick Gallery of the National Museum of American Art (S)

17th Street & Pennsylvania Avenue, NW, White House & Around (633 8998/357 2700). Farragut North or Farragut West Metro. **Open** 10am-5.30pm daily. **Admission** free.
Built in 1859 by architect James Renwick to house William Wilson Corcoran's art collection, Corcoran's holdings quickly outgrew this mansarded building modelled on the Louvre, and it changed hands several times before opening in 1972 as the Smithsonian's craft museum. The second-floor exhibition of twentieth-century American craft – defined as objects created from materials associated with trades and industries, such as clay, glass, metal and fibre – often showcases striking work. In the mansion's refurbished Grand Salon picture gallery, paintings that exemplify the taste of wealthy turn-of-the-century collectors hang in gilt frames stacked two and three high. Downstairs, temporary exhibits survey artistic movements or artists.

The Renwick is closed for a three-year renovation from January 2000.
Disabled: access.

Society of the Cincinnati at Anderson House

2118 Massachusetts Avenue, NW, at 21st Street, Dupont Circle (785 2040). Dupont Circle Metro. **Open** 1-4pm Tue-Sat. **Admission** free.

Practically unknown to most DC residents, this museum, the former residence of turn-of-the-century American diplomat Larz Anderson III and his wife Isabel, contains works acquired on the Andersons' many trips to Asia and Europe. Anderson, a direct descendant of a founding member of the Society of the Cincinnati, bequeathed his house to that organisation, which was formed during the American Revolution with the aim of sharing wealth among bereft army men who had fought for independence (the group included Founding Father George Washington).

The Andersons hired Boston firm Arthur Little and Herbert Browne to construct the limestone Beaux Arts mansion, and imported Italian artisans to carve and inlay wood and gilt floors and ceilings. Downstairs, a room devoted to rotating historical exhibitions about the American Revolution, and others hung with Japanese screens and wall frescos, are open to the public.

The upstairs rooms are only accessible on hourly guided tours; they contain numerous bejewelled Chinese semi-precious stone and jade trees and late sixteenth- and early seventeenth-century Flemish Renaissance tapestries.
Disabled: access.

History & culture

Anacostia Museum & Center for African American History & Culture (S)

1901 Fort Place, SE, at Martin Luther King Jr Avenue, Anacostia (287 2061). Anacostia Metro. **Open** 10am-5pm daily. **Admission** free.

Housed in an unprepossessing red brick building atop a hill in the District's historically black Anacostia neighbourhood, this modest museum hosts changing thematic exhibitions spotlighting national and international African-American artists. The Center for African American History & Culture also presents exhibits in the Smithsonian's Arts & Industries Building on the Mall.
Disabled: access.

Arts & Industries Building (S)

900 Jefferson Drive, SW, between Seventh Street & Independence Avenue, Mall & Tidal Basin (357 2627). Smithsonian or L'Enfant Plaza Metro. **Open** 10am-5.30pm daily. **Admission** free.

The Smithsonian's original exhibition hall, this 1881 building showcased the original holdings of the National Museum (as it was then called). These scientific and anthropological specimens, steam engines and works of art were placed in the specialised Smithsonian museums as they were built. Now the building houses changing exhibitions representing varied arms of the Institution.
Disabled: access.

B'nai B'rith Klutznick National Jewish Museum

1640 Rhode Island Avenue, NW, at 17th Street, Dupont Circle (857 6583). Farragut North or Dupont Circle Metro. **Open** 10am-5pm Mon-Fri, Sun; closed Jewish holidays. **Admission** free.

Artefacts and artworks of Jewish culture and history from antiquity to the present day comprise the museum's permanent collection. Highlights include a pair of seventeenth-century Sabbath candlesticks from Danzig and the oldest Torah scroll in the Americas. It also hosts temporary exhibitions of contemporary Jewish art or historical surveys.
Disabled: access.

Jewish Historical Society of Greater Washington

701 Third Street, NW, at G Street, Judiciary Square Area (789 0900). Judiciary Square Metro. **Open** noon-4pm Mon-Thur, Sun; closed Jewish holidays. **Admission** suggested donation $2.

Exhibits of local Jewish history organised by the Jewish Historical Society occupy the ground floor of this now-landmarked former synagogue – the oldest in Washington. Built in 1876 of red brick, the structure was adopted by the society in 1960; its sanctuary was restored in the 1970s, preserving the original ark, pine benches and slender columns that support the women's balcony.

National Building Museum

401 F Street, NW, between Fourth & Fifth Streets, Judiciary Square Area (272 2448). Judiciary Square Metro. **Open** 10am-4pm (*June-Aug* 10am-5pm) Mon-Sat; noon-4pm Sun. **Admission** free.

Although this privately run museum produces smart, noteworthy exhibits focusing on architects and urban design concerns both contemporary and historical, it's the building's Italian Renaissance-style Great Hall, with its central fountain and eight colossal 75ft-high Corinthian columns, that astonishes visitors, who crane their necks for a vertiginous glance of the ceiling hovering 15 storeys above. The red brick building, designed as the US Pension Building, was completed in 1887. One permanent exhibition is on the building's history; another documents changing architectural styles. The museum shop offers the quirkiest gadgets in town.
Disabled: access, audio guides, closed captioned videos, some braille captions, tactile models of monuments.
Website: www.nbm.org

National Postal Museum (S)

2 Massachusetts Avenue, NE, at First Street, Union Station & Around (357 2700). Union Station Metro. **Open** 10am-5.30pm daily. **Admission** free.

Audio-visual and interactive presentations in this family-friendly museum detail the invention and history of stamps and the postal service, as well as the history of stamp collecting; computer kiosks meter, address and send postcards to visitors'

friends and family. The museum's modest collection of rare stamps won't floor serious philatelists.
Disabled: access.

National Museum of American Jewish Military History

1811 R Street, NW, at 18th Street, Dupont Circle (265 6280). Dupont Circle Metro. **Open** 9am-5pm Mon-Fri; 1-5pm Sun; closed Jewish holidays. **Admission** free.
This small museum recognises American Jews' contributions to war efforts; a recent temporary exhibit focused on Jewish women's roles in World War II.
Disabled: access.

National Museum of American History (S)

Constitution Avenue & 14th Street, NW, Mall & Tidal Basin (357 2700). Federal Triangle Metro. **Open** 10am-5.30pm (*June-Aug* 10am-7.30pm) daily. **Admission** free.
Camp dioramas and quirky displays make this a retro-chic haven. The permanent collection, which hasn't changed much in the past 25 years, contains gems reflecting aspects of American culture both venal and endearing: the lunch counter from Greensboro, North Carolina, where black students staged a sit-in in 1960 protesting segregation; Judy Garland's ruby slippers from *The Wizard of Oz*; and a Firearm Study Center. Recent additions, including an IT pavilion, appear to lag about five years behind contemporary technology. Beware the legions of children that descend at weekends and holidays.
Disabled: access, audio guides, closed captioned videos, some braille captions.

The Octagon

1799 New York Avenue, NW, between 18th & E Streets, Foggy Bottom (638 3221/recorded information 638 3105). Farragut North or Farragut West Metro. **Open** 10am-4pm Tue-Sun. **Admission** $3; $1.50 concessions; free under-6s.
This museum of the American Architectural Foundation hosts two to three exhibits of art historical interest annually in its Federal-style house.
Disabled: limited access.

United States Holocaust Memorial Museum

100 Raoul Wallenberg Place, SW, at 14th Street, Mall & Tidal Basin (488 0400). Smithsonian Metro. **Open** 10am-5.30pm daily (*Apr-Aug* 10am-8pm Thur); closed Yom Kippur. **Admission** free.
Since its opening in 1993, the Holocaust Museum has attracted legions of visitors to its permanent exhibit, for which timed passes are required (call ahead to reserve through ProTix; most same-day passes are distributed by 10am). The three-floor exhibit presents a chronological history of the Holocaust from the rise of Hitler and Nazism in the late 1930s, the forced incarceration of Jews in ghettos and death camps in the early 1940s, and the Allied liberation and subsequent war crime trials. Visitors, assigned a Holocaust victim's identity card and biography referred to during their visit, are herded into a dimly lit, steel-clad freight elevator that deposits them into an environment of unparalleled sobriety. Photo- and text-intensive accounts of atrocities unfold dispassionately, but objects and symbols make powerful impressions: thousands of camp victims' shoes piled in a heap personalise the losses.

The building (designed by Pei Cobb Freed) incorporates red brick and slate-grey steel girders and catwalks echoing death camp architecture; within the permanent exhibition, sky-lit zones alternate with claustrophobic darkness. Notable artworks include a Richard Serra sculpture and graceful Elsworth Kelly and Sol LeWitt canvases.
Disabled: access, some braille captions.
Website: www.ushmm.org

Science & nature

National Air & Space Museum (S)

Sixth Street & Independence Avenue, SW, Mall & Tidal Basin (357 2700). L'Enfant Plaza Metro. **Open** 10am-5.30pm (*June-Aug* 9.30am-6pm) daily. **Admission** *museum* free; *planetarium* $3.75.
Opened in 1976, this is the city's most popular museum, with ten million visitors in 1998. HOK's imposing Tennessee marble modernist block incorporates three skylit, double-height galleries, which house the missiles, aircraft and space stations. In the central Milestones of Flight hall, towering US Pershing-II and Soviet SS-20 nuclear missiles stand next to the popular moon rock station, where visitors can stroke a lunar sample acquired on the 1972 Apollo 17 mission. The 1903 *Wright Flyer* – the first piloted craft to maintain controlled, sustained flight (if only for a few seconds) – and Charles Lindbergh's *Spirit of St Louis* are both suspended here.

Permanent exhibitions detail the history of jet aviation and satellite communications. Updates acknowledge contemporary information technology, but most of the collection's low-tech presentation maintains the quaint optimism of the early space age. A bevy of interactive, hands-on exhibits appeal to children who line up to pilot a full-size Cessna aircraft in the How Things Fly exhibit or to walk through the claustrophobic research lab in the Skylab Space Station. The Albert Einstein Planetarium offers half-hour multimedia presentations about stars and outer space; the Langley Theater shows IMAX films on air and space flight.
Disabled: access, audio guides, closed captioned videos.

National Museum of Health & Medicine

6825 16th Street, NW, at Alaska Avenue, Upper Northwest (782 2200). Silver Spring Metro, then KS4 or S5 bus. **Open** 10am-5.30pm daily. **Admission** free.
Founded as the Army Medical Museum in 1862, this anatomical museum's highlights include an assortment of preserved organs, a coal miner's blackened lungs and a pair of live leeches bobbing about in a petri dish. The memorable exhibit on medicine during the Civil War includes the bullet that killed

Abraham Lincoln, as well as a detailed account of Major General Daniel Sickles' annual visits to his formaldehyde-preserved amputated leg. Temporary shows have included AIDS education and images of illness in African art. Although the museum is more informative than stomach-churning, don't head for dinner immediately afterwards.
Disabled: access.

National Museum of Natural History (S)

Tenth Street & Constitution Avenue, NW, Mall & Tidal Basin (357 2700). Smithsonian Metro.
Open 10am-5.30pm (*June-Aug* 10am-7.30pm) daily. **Admission** free.

A major renovation and restoration recently added a new IMAX cinema and an 80,000sq ft brushed steel and granite Discovery Center housing a new cafeteria and exhibition space. But you'll still find 1950s dioramas in faux-wood panelled caverns interspersed among the chrome- and halogen-filled renovated galleries. The gem and mineral collection attracts gawking spectators who ring two-deep the well-guarded 45.52-carat cut blue Hope Diamond.

The museum is a kid magnet: Dinosaur Hall has an assortment of fierce-looking dinosaur skeletons and a 3.4-billion-year-old stromatolite that is one of the earliest records of life; tarantulas and other live arthropods ripe for petting inhabit the Insect Zoo. The museum's signature diorama remains the 8-ton African bush elephant – the earth's largest land animal – looking as lively as the day it died in 1955.
Disabled: access.

Drop in at the **Air & Space Museum** *(p107).*

Newseum

1101 Wilson Boulevard, between Lynn & Nash Streets, Arlington, VA (703 284 3544). Rosslyn Metro. **Open** 10am-5pm Wed-Sun. **Admission** free.

Founded by the Freedom Forum – a foundation promoting free speech backed by publishing giant Gannett, publisher of the popular 'McNewspaper' *USA Today* – the Newseum's decidedly high-tech aluminum and glass interior hosts an Interactive Newsroom, News History Gallery and functioning broadcast studio. A frenetic environment populated by interactive monitors and video screens, the museum (which opened in 1997) attracts spectacle-seekers, including lots of kids and young adults. TV clips of hair-raising news events, such as the Space Shuttle Challenger explosion and the Reagan assassination attempt, walk adults down memory lane. Next to the museum is Freedom Park, a plaza dotted with glazed memorials to slain journalists and free speech advocates.
Disabled: access, audio, braille & large print guides.
Website: www.newseum.org

Specialist & curiosities

Bead Museum & Learning Center

400 Seventh Street, NW, at D Street, Penn Quarter (624 4500). Archives-Navy Memorial Metro. **Open** 11am-4pm Mon, Wed; 1-4pm Sun; otherwise by appointment. **Admission** free.

Not just for bauble zealots, this one-room museum and library dedicated to ornament and beads hosts themed shows of international jewellery and ornament. The bead library and learning centre will appeal to aficionados, not the indifferent.
Disabled: access.

Black Fashion Museum

2007 Vermont Avenue, NW, between U & V Streets, U Street/14th Street Corridor (667 0744). U Street-Cardozo Metro. **Open** by appointment only. **Admission** suggested donation $2; $1 concessions.

Black fashion designer Lois Alexander built this museum in New York's Harlem neighbourhood in 1979; in 1996, ill-health forced her to relocate the collection to Washington where her daughter Joyce Bailey now presides. Rotating exhibits in this tiny museum sheltered in a two-storey townhouse spotlight important black fashion designers, many of whose work is in the museum's 5,500-piece collection. The yellow-flowered dress that civil rights icon and seamstress Rosa Parks sewed the day she refused to cede her seat on an Alabama bus to a white man is on permanent display.

Textile Museum

2320 S Street, NW, at 23rd Street, Dupont Circle (667 0441). Dupont Circle Metro. **Open** 10am-5pm Mon-Sat; 1-5pm Sun. **Admission** suggested donation $5.

They might look like toys, but it's more than just a game at the **US Chess Hall of Fame**.

This modest museum nestled amid regal Embassy Row townhouses has two permanent exhibitions with a multicultural bent: the Textile Learning Center describes the history and procedures of textile production, while the Collections Gallery rotates selections of historic rugs and textiles. Recent changing shows have included Indonesian batik and the indigenous costume of Highland Ecuador.
Disabled: large print captions.

US Chess Hall of Fame & Museum

1501 M Street, NW, at 15th Street, Downtown (857 4922). McPherson Square or Farragut North Metro.
Open 6-9pm Mon-Thur; noon-6pm Sat, Sun and by appointment.
You'll probably encounter chess enthusiasts huddled anxiously over their boards in this basement museum's games room, where a permanent exhibition of US chess history lines the walls, including a Grandmasters' Hall of Fame with photos, posters and informative placards detailing the lives of great American chessmen.
Disabled: access.

World Against Racism Foundation

1824 R Street, NW, between 18th & 19th Streets, Dupont Circle (462 0808). Dupont Circle Metro.
Open by appointment only. **Admission** $5; $2.50 students.
Perhaps the District's first virtual museum – albeit one with a physical site – WARF occupies an office suite dotted with computer terminals. After a brief tour of anti-racism artwork, visitors nestle in comfy chairs to manipulate computer terminals connected to the museum's website – WARF has a dozen high-speed Internet connections that prevent annoying time lapses while loading its graphics- and sound-intensive site. The Foundation's mission is tolerance education, so the text is laden with liberalism and occasionally far-flung notions (WARF encourages visitors not to discriminate against Vulcans).

Galleries

Historically, Washington's proximity to New York drained DC of ambitious and energetic young artists, who emigrated northward in search of international art stardom. But in the late 1990s, the abandonment abated as citywide optimism, economic upturn and a new mayor encouraged a tide of younger artists to invest in the city by creating new exhibition venues and guerrilla arts events. Look out for work by these alternative groups, including **CAVE** (*see page 110*), **Masters of Art** (293 6955/website: www.3dgallery.com/masters) and **Vox Pop Kultur** (voicemail 319 9440/website: www.voxpopkultur.com).

So far, no singular style has emerged in the 1990s to match the stir in DC in the 1960s, when Washington Color School artists (reputedly influenced by New York abstract expressionist Helen Frankenthaler) stained raw canvas with vivid acrylic washes. Although many of that movement's significant players – Morris Louis, Kenneth Noland and Gene Davis among them – left town to pursue the New York limelight, their shadows remain in the District's arts community. A handful of Color School pioneers, including Sam Gilliam and Willem de Looper, maintain studios here and have spawned a league of second- and third-generation imitators.

CAVE *leads DC's alternative art scene.*

Washington collectors' predominantly conservative tastes dictate a commercial gallery scene less avant-garde than New York's. This atmosphere translates into a casual, supportive (some might argue insular) gallery-going community where artists rub shoulders with Capitol Hill aides and lawyers at openings held in the city's three distinct gallery neighbourhoods, which each host monthly evening gallery openings.

There are three main gallery areas. **Dupont Circle** hosts a dense gallery concentration in turn-of-the-century townhouses lining R Street between Connecticut and Florida Avenues. The edgier Seventh Street corridor in Downtown's **Penn Quarter**, once a studio haven offering cheap rents, has recently witnessed soaring property values driven by development and business improvement initiatives that gain galleries wider audiences while making the area prohibitively expensive to resident artists. **Georgetown** serves up a hodgepodge of art: galleries varying from avant-garde to conservative cater to both the blue-haired and the blue-bloods. *City Paper* is the best publication for gallery listings.

While on the gallery crawl, some District artists worth noting are:

Clark and Hogan (Museum of Contemporary Art): Clark and Hogan's signature canvases are Pop Art-inspired George Washington portraits.
Renee Stout (David Adamson Gallery): Her metal and wood constructions addressing African-American themes are included in Smithsonian collections.
Y David Chung (Gallery K): Chung's vibrant screenprints are graphic, with comic-book stylisation.
William Christenberry (Hemphill): A member of the District's photography elite, Christenberry documents rural barns and shacks.

Dupont Circle

Most galleries line R Street between Connecticut and Florida Avenues; a handful are tucked in Hillyer Court, an alley south of R Street between Florida Avenue and 21st Street.

Joint gallery openings are held on the first Friday of the month (6-8pm).

Affrica

2010 R Street, NW, at Connecticut Avenue, Dupont Circle (745 7272). Dupont Circle Metro. **Open** 2-6pm Tue; noon-6pm Wed-Sat.
Founded in 1979, the gallery's collection of traditional African fine art includes statuary, metalwork, textiles and furniture.
Website: www.affrica.com

Anton Gallery

2108 R Street, NW, between Florida & Connecticut Avenues, Dupont Circle (328 0828). Dupont Circle Metro. **Open** noon-5pm Tue-Sat.
Stepping through the Romanesque arch marking the entrance of Gail Enns' gallery, visitors encounter shows that include artists of all stripes: mixed-media artists from nearby Baltimore or contemporary British porcelain makers.
Website: www.antongallery.com

CAVE (Center for Collaborative Art & Visual Education)

Information 483 4655.
In 1998, a handful of twentysomething local artists opened a gallery on Connecticut Avenue offering exhibition space for low-visibility DC artists and a centre for arts outreach. Stepping outside DC gallery establishment norms, CAVE's curatorial regimen rejects traditional commission and curatorship for non-profit shows juried by artist peers. It works with local non-profit groups to mount socially conscious exhibits and offers figure drawing classes and mentorship programmes with District public school students. CAVE lost its lease in summer 1999, but shows continue in borrowed spaces around town (details on their telephone hotline) while the group searches for new digs.

Elis Art Gallery

1615 17th Street, NW, at Corcoran Street, Dupont Circle (232 6025). Dupont Circle Metro. **Open** noon-8pm Tue-Fri; 10am-9pm Sat; 4pm-8pm Sun.
A recent addition to the gallery scene, Elis stocks African furniture, painting, masks and statuary. You'll find a late nineteenth-century royal altarpiece from the Nigerian kingdom of Benin displayed alongside contemporary Senegalese masks.

Gallery 10 Ltd

1519 Connecticut Avenue, NW, at Q Street, Dupont Circle (232 3326). Dupont Circle Metro. **Open** 11am-6pm Wed-Sat.

Projectspace: *pioneering experimental art and performance.* *See page 116.*

Many of the District's most respected artists jump-started nascent careers with shows at Gallery 10. Shows here vary from undisciplined to cohesive, but they're worth a look.
Disabled: access.

Gallery K

2010 R Street, NW, at Connecticut Avenue, Dupont Circle (234 0339). Dupont Circle Metro. **Open** 11am-6pm Tue-Sat; and by appointment.
Owners H Marc Moyens and Komei Wachi's predilection for colourful abstractions means shows here can verge on the gaudy, but Gallery K is relentlessly successful. The gallery's stable includes locals such as Wayne Edson Bryan, who installed three fanciful balustrade panels in Cesar Pelli's National Airport, and lesser-known international artists such as French abstractionist Yves Popet.

Kathleen Ewing Gallery

1609 Connecticut Avenue, NW, between R & Q Streets, Dupont Circle (328 0955). Dupont Circle Metro. **Open** noon-5pm Wed-Sat; otherwise by appointment.
Director Kathleen Ewing's unpretentious approach to art dealing, coupled with her gimlet eye, have earned her a reputation as the city's finest photography dealer. Her laid-back gallery has evolved into a focus point for local photographers who regularly drop in to chat. Since opening in 1976, Ewing's stable of nineteenth- and twentieth-century photographers has grown to include Berenice Abbott, Arnold Newman, Dana Salvo and District photographer Frank DiPerna.

Marsha Mateyka Gallery

2012 R Street, NW, between 21st Street & Connecticut Avenue, Dupont Circle (328 0088). Dupont Circle Metro. **Open** 11am-5pm Wed-Sat; closed Aug.
Marsha Mateyka represents and exhibits painting, sculpture and works on paper by established contemporary American and European artists. Past highlights have included monotypes by Diebenkorn associate Nathan Oliveira and the 'Vital Statistics' series by DC painter Christopher French. The gallery is worth a peek for its architecture, too: the turn-of-the-century brownstone's interior features spectacular cherrywood fireplaces, wainscoting and carved wood transoms.

Robert Brown Gallery

2030 R Street, NW, at 21st Street, Dupont Circle Metro (483 4383). Dupont Circle Metro. **Open** noon-6pm Tue-Sat.
Brown's collection weighs heavy on prints, etchings and lithographs, and the gallery hosts some big names: past shows have included lithographs and woodcuts by German Expressionist Käthe Kollwitz and prints, drawings and videos by William Kentridge.

St Luke's Gallery

1715 Q Street, NW, between 17th & 18th Streets, Dupont Circle (328 2424). Dupont Circle Metro. **Open** 11am-6pm Sat; by appointment Tue-Fri.
Dupont's only Old Master gallery, St Luke's brims with oils, watercolours and etchings by the likes of Domenichino, Whistler and Piranesi. The airy townhouse is a favourite with local curators, who cite the gallery's print collection as the best in the city.

Troyer Gallery

1710 Connecticut Avenue, NW, at R Street, Dupont Circle (328 7189). Dupont Circle Metro. **Open** 11am-5pm Tue-Fri; noon-5pm Sat.
Formerly called the Troyer Fitzpatrick Lassman Gallery and operated by a respected Washington arts triumvirate. Today only Sally Troyer maintains this grey-walled gallery, which promises to maintain its stable of quality local painters, photographers and sculptors.
Disabled: access.

The Smithsonian

The Smithsonian Institution, the world's largest museum complex, dominates the District's museum landscape. It has 14 museums in Washington, nine of which are on the Mall, plus two in New York City; together they drew a grand total of 28.5 million visitors in 1998, while the Smithsonian's National Zoo, also in DC, draws an additional three million visitors a year. It's a unique institution, with nearly 141 million objects, covering everything from ancient Chinese pottery, to dinosaurs, Italian Renaissance painting and moon landings.

The Institution's founding makes for a peculiar yarn. Wealthy British chemist and mineralogist James Smithson (1765-1829) named his nephew beneficiary to his estate in his will, stipulating that should the nephew die without heir (as he did in 1835), Smithson would confer his fortune of $515,169 to the United States government to found 'at Washington, under the name of the Smithsonian Institution, an establishment for the increase and diffusion of knowledge among men', which remains the Institution's mandate today.

The US Congress, befuddled by the unusual bequest, spent ten years after Smithson's nephew's death debating the interpretation of the will. Finally, in 1846, Congress passed an act that created a trust fund and administrators for an institution promoting research and the dispersal of academic knowledge.

Smithson's motivations remain unclear. He had never set foot on American soil (save one posthumous journey: Smithson was disinterred from an Italian cemetery in 1904 and relocated to a crypt below the Smithsonian Castle, where he remains). Some suspect the bequest was revenge against the strict British society that refused to officially recognise Smithson's right to his father's name (he was illegitimate); the less tawdry attribute his generosity to his Enlightenment ideals.

Architect James Renwick designed the first building, known as the Castle (*pictured*) because its combination of late Romanesque and early Gothic styles included signature turrets, on a prime piece of national real estate smack on the verdant Mall. Completed in 1855, the Castle now serves as the Smithsonian Information Center and administrative hub – and should be the first port of call for any visitor.

The Victorian red brick Arts & Industries Building, designed as the Smithsonian's first hall devoted solely to exhibitions, was added in 1881. Over the years, collections shown here became large enough to warrant their own buildings. After the creation of the National Zoo in 1890, Congress began the steady erection of museums lining the Mall, beginning with the Museum of Natural History in 1910. From 1923 to 1993, 11 new museums entered the Smithsonian portfolio, most holding fine art. A National Museum of

Georgetown

Most galleries are located on or near M Street, the main east-west artery. Six galleries in the Canal Square complex (1054 31st Street) host joint openings every third Friday of the month; in warm months, bands perform for gallery-goers nibbling on snacks donated by local restaurants.

Fine Art & Artists

2920 M Street, NW, between 29th & 30th Streets, Georgetown (965 0780). Foggy Bottom-GWU Metro, then 30, 32, 34, 35, 36 bus. **Open** 11am-6pm Tue-Sat.

A selection of Lichtenstein and Warhol prints join other twentieth-century heavies on this townhouse gallery's white walls.

Disabled: access

Website: www.faagallery.com

Fraser Gallery

1054 31st Street, NW, at M Street, Georgetown (298 6450). Foggy Bottom-GWU Metro, then 30, 32, 34, 35, 36 bus. **Open** noon-3pm Tue-Fri; noon-6pm Sat.

British expat Catriona Fraser concentrates on photography, but occasionally shows innovative local sculpture and work in other media.

Disabled: access.

Govinda Gallery

1227 34th Street, NW, at Prospect Street, Georgetown (333 1180). Rosslyn Metro. **Open** 11am-6pm Tue-Sat.

Although the Govinda Gallery is removed from Georgetown's commercial fray, it's worth a trip to see its signature rock 'n' roll-themed photography and painting shows. The gallery represents the estate of artist and former Beatle Stuart Sutcliffe and rock photographers Bob Gruen and Gered Mankowitz, and frequently shows classic Stones and Beatles photos.

Hemphill Fine Arts

1027 33rd Street, NW, at M Street, Georgetown (342 5610). Foggy Bottom-GWU Metro, then 30, 32, 34, 35, 36 bus. **Open** 11am-5pm Tue-Sat and by appointment.

the American Indian, at the Mall's eastern end, and a branch of the National Air & Space Museum, at Virginia's Dulles Airport, are both slated to open in 2002.

From June to August, the Smithsonian's Hirshhorn Museum, Sackler Gallery, Freer Gallery and National Museum of African Art participate in Art Night on the Mall, when they open until 8pm on Thursdays, and host activities such as outdoor music performances, gallery talks and films.

INFORMATION

Conveniently, there is one central phone number – **357 2700** – where you can get information on all the Smithsonian's museums. The Smithsonian's well-designed website – **www.si.edu** – is very useful and has links to the individual museums' homepages. All museums are free, open 10am-5.30pm daily (except the Anacostia, which shuts at 5pm) and closed only on Christmas Day. Some have extended hours in summer. Many museums get very crowded; the best time to visit is usually just after opening time at 10am.

Smithsonian Access, a brochure detailing the disabled facilities at the museums, is available at each museum – or write to Smithsonian Information, SI Building, Room 153, Washington, DC 20560-0010. If you need to arrange special facilities – such as a sign language interpreter – call the museum you wish to visit two weeks in advance.

Smithsonian Information Center

1000 Jefferson Drive, SW, between Seventh & Twelfth Streets, Mall & Tidal Basin (357 2700/ 24-hour recorded information 357 2020 English/ 633 9126 Spanish). Smithsonian Metro. **Open** 9am-5.30pm daily.

The Castle opens one hour before the museums to give you time to plan your visit. Staff are very helpful and well informed.

George Hemphill's six-year-old contemporary art gallery hosts quirky shows with ironic flair: past group exhibitions include Depression-era photographs of men in hats juxtaposed with fashion photos. Its artists are among the Washington' strongest and most established; collectors with avant-garde notions buy painter Steve Cushner's abstract organic canvases and Tara Donovan's tar and paper sculptures. Promising young District artists who secure a show in Hemphill's tiny gabled back room know that, despite its claustrophobia, they've arrived.

Maurine Littleton Gallery

1667 Wisconsin Avenue, NW, at Reservoir Road (333 9307). Foggy Bottom-GWU Metro, then 30, 32, 34, 35, 36 bus. **Open** 11am-6pm Tue-Sat.

This gallery, founded by the daughter of studio glass art pioneer Harvey Littleton, shows glasswork that transcends the obvious goblet or bowl (although these are available) by incorporating photo-images and collage.

Museum of Contemporary Art

1054 31st Street, NW, at M Street, Georgetown (342 6230). Foggy Bottom-GWU Metro, then 30, 32, 34, 35, 36 bus. **Open** 1-6pm Wed-Sat; by appointment Sun.

Artist duo Michael Clark and Felicity Hogan's MOCA is DC's answer to the hip, alternative galleries of New York. The fluorescent lights and low ceilings may not be much to look at, but Clark and Hogan show risky, innovative work. Ponytailed Clark (he prefers to go by his last name) and wife Hogan paint collaboratively as Clark and Hogan, turning out vibrant, Pop Art-inspired studies of oranges and George Washington portraits that have attracted a cult following among DC collectors.

Reality Room

1010 Wisconsin Avenue, NW, between M & K Streets, Georgetown (333 3709). Bus D51. **Open** 1.30-7.30pm Tue-Sun.

This newcomer on the Georgetown circuit showcases work by women, minorities and marginalised cultures. Although slightly New Agey, the gallery has produced quality multimedia shows in

Top 10 museums

Dumbarton Oaks
A treasure trove of Byzantine and pre-Columbian artworks in a Georgetown house.

Hirshhorn Museum & Sculpture Garden
A world-class display of twentieth-century art in a spectacular modernist building.

National Gallery of Art
A lesson in the history of art, from the fourteenth century to the present.

Kreeger Museum
An intimate collection of modern masters, from Monet to Kandinsky.

National Air & Space Museum
This hugely popular museum takes you out of the world – literally.

Holocaust Museum
A sobering and moving account of the Holocaust.

Phillips Collection
Post-1850 paintings in a luxurious Dupont Circle mansion.

Museum of Natural History
Dinosaur skeletons to 1950s dioramas, plus the impressive new Discovery Center.

Freer Gallery of Art
Superlative collection of Asian art and nineteenth-century American paintings.

Corcoran Gallery of Art
Nineteenth-century American masters along with contemporary work in all media.

conjunction with Tibetan refugee organisations and Amnesty International.
Disabled: access (no toilets).

Susan Conway Gallery
1214 30th Street, NW, at M Street, Georgetown (333 6343). Foggy Bottom-GWU Metro, then 30, 32, 34, 35, 36 bus. **Open** 11am-5pm Tue-Sat; otherwise by appointment.
Conway has shown consistently strong twentieth-century painting and sculpture since opening her gallery in 1987. Painters of abstracted landscapes are popular, among them Eric Aho, Will Barnet and Mary Ellen Doyle. Conway also adores caricature and carries a comprehensive selection of Pat Olifant caricatures, cartoons and sculpture.

Washington Studio School & Courtyard Gallery
3232 P Street (courtyard), NW, at Wisconsin Avenue, Georgetown (333 2663). Dupont Circle Metro, then G2 bus. **Open** 11am-4pm Tue-Sat; noon-4pm Sun.
Local artists and studio school students show in this small, skylit gallery tucked in an alley behind P Street rowhouses.

Penn Quarter

Galleries in this burgeoning arts and entertainment district are clustered near the corner of Seventh and E Streets, NW; the 406 Seventh Street complex houses six. Monthly 'Third Thursday' joint openings (6-8pm) feature volunteer-led gallery walks and drinks specials at local bars and restaurants.

David Adamson Gallery/Editions
406 Seventh Street, NW, between D & E Streets, Penn Quarter (628 0257). Archives-Navy Memorial or Gallery Place-Chinatown Metro. **Open** 10am-5pm Wed-Fri; 11am-5pm Sat.
The gallery's adjoining printmaking studio collaborates with contemporary art heavyweights such as Kiki Smith, Roni Horn and the Starn twins to create the digital ink-jet prints frequently on view here. Painting and print exhibitions by prominent local and national artists make this one of the city's most innovative spaces.

DC Unite Sculpture Park
431 Seventh Street, NW, between D & E Streets, Penn Quarter. Archives-Navy Memorial or Gallery Place-Chinatown Metro.
Not a gallery but a government-funded park occupying an outdoor lot between two abandoned government-owned buildings and showing changing group and one-person sculpture shows. Large-scale works in stone and metal, such as Claire McArdle's 7ft-tall marble figure 'Gaia' and Randy Jewart's bronze and limestone 'Crouching Man', enliven this otherwise lonely nook.

Numark Gallery
406 Seventh Street, NW, between D & E Streets, Penn Quarter (628 3810). Archives-Navy Memorial or Gallery Place-Chinatown Metro. **Open** 11am-6pm Tue-Sat.
Cheryl Numark is Washington's power dealer: her gallery openings draw legions of artists and discerning patrons aching to see works by recognised New Yorkers and promising Washingtonians. Tony Feher inserted his imaginative push pin (drawing pin) installations into the same walls that have featured works by Jennifer Bartlett, Sol LeWitt and Frank Stella. Numark's group shows are the sharpest in town.

'The Loge' by American painter Mary Cassatt, at the world-class ***National Gallery of Art****.* *See page 104.*

DC artist duo Clark and Hogan feature at the **Museum of Contemporary Art** *(page 113).*

Projectspace

625 E Street, NW, between Sixth & Seventh Streets, Penn Quarter (783 2185). Gallery Place-Chinatown Metro. **Open** noon-5pm Thur-Sat.

During spring, summer and autumn, Projectspace hosts a variety of exhibitions and performances programmed by WPA/Corcoran, an arts partnership under the Corcoran Gallery of Art umbrella that was created to preserve DC's once pre-eminent alternative arts space, Washington Project for the Arts (WPA), when that organisation declared bankruptcy in 1995.

The décor is the grubby, downmarket chic you'd expect: two giant arthropods – remnants of the space's former incarnation as the Insect Club – flank the interior doorway. Despite some inconsistencies, group shows often include high-quality experimental work, and vibrant evening performances and readings are held on an irregular basis.

At time of writing, Projectspace was about to move to another space, so phone before you visit to check their latest whereabouts.

Website: www.corcoran.org/wpac

Touchstone Gallery

406 Seventh Street, NW, between D & E Streets, Penn Quarter (347 2787). Archives-Navy Memorial or Gallery Place-Chinatown Metro. **Open** 11am-5pm Wed-Fri; noon-5pm Sat, Sun.

Touchstone, an artist-owned co-operative gallery, shows works by area artists and lesser-known internationals. Although quality can be hit or miss, the gallery's ample size increases the chances of finding a gem or two on its walls.

Zenith Gallery

413 Seventh Street, NW, between D & E Streets, Penn Quarter (783 2963). Archives-Navy Memorial or Gallery Place-Chinatown Metro. **Open** 11am-4pm Mon; 11am-6pm Tue-Fri; noon-7pm Sat; noon-5pm Sun.

Owner Margery Goldberg's tireless activism against Downtown developers who advance capitalism before art, combined with her long-standing presence on Seventh Street, have secured her position as a Washington institution; nevertheless, her gallery consistently shows mediocre painting and craft.

Disabled: access.

Elsewhere

DCAC (District of Columbia Arts Center)

2438 18th Street, NW, between Columbia & Belmont Roads, Adams Morgan (462 7833). Woodley Park-Zoo Metro, then 90, 91, 92, 93, 96 bus. **Open** 1-7pm Wed-Fri; closed July, Aug.

This independent gallery programmes its small gallery and 50-seat theatre with innovative avant-garde performances and exhibitions that occasionally border on the incomprehensible.

Arlington Arts Center

3550 Wilson Boulevard, at Monroe Street, Arlington, VA (703 524 1494). Virginia Square-GMU Metro. **Open** 11am-5pm Tue-Fri; 1-5pm Sat, Sun.

This non-profit, non-collecting contemporary visual arts centre housed in a turn-of-the-century schoolhouse is Virginia's principal art node.

Consumer

Accommodation

It's business all the way on the DC hotel scene, but that means some great deals outside the working week.

The lobby of the stylish **Hotel George** *near Union Station.* *See page 129.*

Characterful and budget-priced accommodation is thin on the ground in Washington: given the business nature of most visits it is not surprising most hotels are towards the top end of the scale – and you pay for what you get. However, although you'll see prices displayed in the rooms, in practice there is no such thing as a fixed hotel rate in DC – almost no one pays the figure posted. Rates vary according to the time of year, the day of the week and what discounts you can secure.

In general, prices drop by as much as half over the weekend, when the corporate accounts leave town. In addition, most hotels will usually offer special weekend packages. Rates are also lower during summer and late autumn and rock-bottom around Christmas. They are at their highest in spring, when DC sees a flux of school groups and cherry blossom gazers.

When booking your room, it's worth asking about a corporate rate even if your company has no formal arrangement with the hotel. If it applies, enquire about senior rates, too: some hotels offer as much as 50 per cent off to guests over 65. Also mention any and all associations or frequent-flyer schemes you belong to – or, especially at quiet times, just ask straight out if there are any discounts available.

Some chains will offer reductions for bookings completed online, and Internet wholesalers such as **www.priceline.com** and **www.wdcahotels.com** offer hotel rooms at short notice or for the highest bidder. You can also reserve through **Capitol Reservations** (452 1270) or **Washington, DC Accommodations** (289 2220), which can sometimes track down discounts and find a room even when the city's rammed.

The luxurious indoor pool in the **Four Seasons** *in Georgetown. See page 134.*

There are few low-budget options in the city. DC has no campgrounds or RV sites, although there are a few well within an hour's drive in Maryland and Virginia. And there is only one youth hostel (**Washington International Youth Hostel**; *see page 128*), but thankfully it's a very good one. Student accommodation is seldom available, even during the long vacation.

ABOUT THE HOTELS

DC's internationalism means that just about all hotels boast a multilingual staff. This normally means they will speak Spanish, but can also include Arabic and Ethiopian in even the smallest hotels. All rooms have telephones, cable television and air-conditioning (unless otherwise indicated below) and all hotels have no-smoking rooms and/or floors. Parking garages normally cost extra; you should check with the front desk for daily rates before you hand over your keys. All hotels bar the smallest B&Bs have access for the disabled, but only those with 'disabled-adapted' rooms are specially designed for wheelchair-users. Most rooms have a clock radio and every hotel *Time Out* surveyed has a safe or safety deposit boxes at the front desk.

The Watergate complex, home of the **Swissôtel Washington** *(see page 125).*

The historic **Hotel Washington***: one of the few hotels located near the White House.*

Rates listed below are for single occupancy and do not include DC hotel tax of 13 per cent plus a $1.75 occupancy tax per room.

Be warned that hotels downtown near the Mall are the most expensive (but also the most luxurious). As you would expect, the further away from the centre, the more you get for your money. Hotels change hands – and names – often in Washington, so double-check the address before booking.

The Monumental Centre

The planned architecture of DC's civic centre allows little room for hotels, and those that are there or thereabouts charge for the privilege. However, although the location is central for sightseeing, it offers little else.

Capitol Hill Suites

200 C Street, SE, at Second Street, Capitol & Around, DC 20003 (reservations 1-800 424 9165/ front desk 543 6000/fax 547 2608). Capitol South Metro. **Rates** single suite $125-$219; double suite $179-$239. **Credit** AmEx, DC, Disc, MC, V.
An all-suite hotel comprised of two conjoined apartment buildings on a quiet street. Service is courteous and the neighbourhood is gorgeous. You can walk to the Metro and the Mall.
Hotel services *Breakfast. Fitness facilities (passes to nearby sports club). Parking.*
Room services *Coffee maker. Kitchen.*

Hotel Washington

515 15th Street, NW, at Pennsylvania Avenue, White House & Around, DC 20004 (reservations 1-800 424 9540/front desk 638 5900/fax 638 1595). Metro Center Metro. **Rates** single/double $245. **Credit** AmEx, DC, Disc, JCB, MC, V.
Historically minded hotel with 350 oversized rooms. It suffers slightly in comparison with its posher neighbour, the **Willard** (*see p124*), but offers arguably the best roof-top drinks view from its Sky Terrace (*see p163* **Bars**).
Hotel services *Bar. Beauty salon. Conference facilities. Fitness facilities. Laundry. Parking. Restaurant. Sauna.*
Room services *Coffee maker. Dataport. Hair dryer. Pay movies. Turndown. Voicemail.*
Website: www.hotelwashington.com

JW Marriott

1331 Pennsylvania Avenue, NW, between 14th & E Streets, Federal Triangle, DC 20004 (reservations 1-800 228 9290/front desk 393 2000/ fax 626 6991). Metro Center Metro. **Rates** single/ double $234-$374; suite $700-$1,050. **Credit** AmEx, DC, Disc, JCB, MC, V.
The clinical exterior belies the comfort of the rooms within, while the architecturally awkward bay windows provide great views of Freedom Plaza. The hotel connects to the National Press Building next door, which offers three floors of shopping and food.
Hotel services *Bars (2). Business centre. Conference facilities. Disabled-access rooms. Fitness facilities. Laundry. Parking. Pool & whirlpool. Restaurants (2). Sauna.*
Room services *Coffee maker. Dataport. Hair dryer. Iron & ironing board. Minibar. Pay movies. Room service (24 hours). Turndown. Voicemail.*
Website: www.marriott.com

Loews L'Enfant Plaza

480 L'Enfant Plaza, SW, at Seventh & D Streets, South of the Mall, DC 20024 (reservations 1-800 635 5065/front desk 484 1000/fax 466 4456). L'Enfant Plaza Metro. **Rates** single/double $259-$299; suite $375; 2-bedroom suite $495. **Credit** AmEx, DC, Disc, JCB, MC, V.
Large opulent hotel located near the Mall and the Capitol. The balconies offer great views but the business-heavy area basically shuts down at night. It's also kid-friendly and dogs are allowed (with advance notice). Check out the roof-top swimming pool. The hotel has its own entrance to the Metro.
Hotel services *Bars (2). Disabled-adapted rooms. Fitness facilities. Laundry. Parking. Pool. Restaurants (2).*
Room services *Hair dryer. Fax. Iron & ironing board. Minibar. Safe. VCR.*
Website: www.loewshotel.com

The Oval Suite in the famous **Willard Inter-Continental**.

Willard Inter-Continental

1401 Pennsylvania Avenue, NW, at 14th Street, Federal Triangle, DC 20004 (reservations 1-800 327 0200/front desk 628 9100/fax 637 7326). Metro Center Metro. **Rates** single/double $380-$525; suite $900-$3,500. **Credit** AmEx, DC, Disc, JCB, MC, V.

The best hotel in DC, full stop. Every and any figure of historical note in the life of the country has stayed here, from Lincoln to Martin Luther King, and every president since 1853 has spent the night at the Willard. This many great figures cannot be wrong. All 303 rooms and 38 suites have been recently renovated. It has great bars, a power-filled restaurant and superb staff. Some rooms have partial views of the White House or Capitol building. It's hard to believe it's all owned by the same company that owns Holiday Inn.

Hotel services *Bars (2). Business centre. Conference facilities. Disabled-access rooms. Fitness facilities. Laundry. Parking. Restaurants (2). Shoeshine.*

Room services *Dataport. Hair dryer. Minibar. Pay movies. Room service (24 hours). Turndown. Voicemail.*

Central DC

Foggy Bottom

Most of Central DC's hotels are clustered in the area around Foggy Bottom. Although somewhat characterless, it is, thanks to the presence of George Washington University, extremely safe, since both DC and university police patrol the streets. Though there are few tourist attractions in the immediate area and little nightlife, it's a good place from which to reach Georgetown, Dupont Circle and points north, and the west end of the Mall. Some rooms offer views of the Potomac River or Georgetown.

Allen Lee Hotel

2224 F Street, NW, at 23rd Street, Foggy Bottom, DC 20037 (reservations 1-800 462 0186/front desk 331 1224/fax 296 3518). Foggy Bottom-GWU Metro. **Rates** double (shared bath) $34; double (private bath) $47; triple (shared bath) $55; triple (private bath) $65; quad (shared bath) $65; quad (private bath) $75. **Credit** AmEx, MC, V.

Full of backpackers and students, the Allen Lee has small, spartan rooms with shabby furniture. A step up from a hostel, most rooms have shared bathrooms but TVs and phones. Service is brusque, but at this price, you can't expect white gloves.

George Washington University Inn

824 New Hampshire Avenue, NW, between I & H Streets, Foggy Bottom, DC 20037 (reservations 1-800 426 4455/front desk 337 6620/fax 298 7499). Foggy Bottom-GWU Metro. **Rates** single/double $75-$225; suite $99-$250. **Credit** AmEx, DC, MC, V.

A wonderful 95-room inn located in the heart of Foggy Bottom. Don't be put off by the quoted rate because discounts or weekend stays can quickly bring the price down by a third. Owned by George Washington University but open to all-comers, the Colonial-style inn is tucked in a quiet street lined with townhouses. **Zuki Moon**, the attached restaurant that provides room service, offers highly rated

food and a patio (*see p154* **Restaurants**). Guests get to use the extensive sports facilities at GWU, which put all other hotel workout rooms to shame.
Hotel services *Business centre. Conference facilities. Disabled-adapted rooms. Fitness facilities. Laundromat. Parking. Pool. Restaurant*
Room services *Coffee maker. Dataport. Hair dryer. Iron & ironing board. Kitchenette. Refrigerator. Room service (7am-10pm). Turndown. Voicemail.*
Website: www.gwuinn.com

Hotel Lombardy

2019 I Street, NW, at Pennsylvania Avenue, Foggy Bottom, DC 20006 (reservations 1-800 424 5486/ front desk 828 2600/fax 872 0503). Farragut West Metro. **Rates** single $115-$135; double $135-$175; suite $159-$250. **Credit** AmEx, DC, Disc, MC, V.
Formerly an apartment building, this 127-unit hotel retains some charm with old-fashioned touches such as brass fixtures and crystal doorknobs. The views over Pennsylvania Avenue are good, but try not to get stuck in the back of the building. It also has an attendant-operated lift – when was the last time you saw that in a hotel?
Hotel services *Parking.*
Room services *Coffee maker. Dataport. Hair dryer. Kitchens (suites). Room service (7-10am, 11am-2pm, 5.30-9.30pm). Voicemail.*

Park Hyatt

1201 24th Street, NW, at M Street, Foggy Bottom, DC 20037 (reservations 1-800 233 1234/front desk 789 1234/fax 457 8823). Foggy Bottom-GWU Metro. **Rates** single/double $199-$330; suite $224-$370; park suite $595. **Credit** AmEx, DC, Disc, MC, V.
The Park Hyatt puts the 'state' in stately. It has the kind of lobby that makes you want to whisper and a clientele that seems straight out of the horsey 'dahling' set. Think Scarlett O'Hara, with a European education. Expect to see women in hats here. The restaurant has an outdoor café, so you can gaze across the street at yet another hotel. Some suites have jacuzzi tubs.
Hotel services *Bars (2). Business centre. Conference facilities. Disabled-adapted rooms. Fitness facilities. Laundry. Parking. Pool. Restaurant.*
Room services *Coffee maker. Dataport. Hair dryer. Minibar. Pay movies. Room service. Turndown. Voicemail.*
Website: www.hyatt.com

River Inn

924 25th Street, NW, between I & K Streets, Foggy Bottom, DC 20037 (reservations 1-800 424 2741/ front desk 337 7600/fax 337 6520/email riverinn@ erols.com). Foggy BottomGWU Metro. **Rates** single/double $89-$175; suites $89-$275; under-16s free. **Credit** AmEx, DC, MC, V.
Although normally filled with government and university types, the River Inn is a reasonably priced, extremely comfortable hotel with 98 studio rooms and 28 suites. Some of the upper-floor rooms have amazing views of Georgetown. Staff are welcoming and knowledgeable. Children stay free.
Hotel services *Bar. Business centre. Conference facilities. Disabled-adapted rooms. Laundromat. Shoeshine. Parking. Mobile phone rental. Restaurant.*
Room services *Coffee maker. Dataport. Hair dryer. Iron & ironing board. Kitchenette. Pay movies. Refrigerator. Room service (7.30am-10pm Mon-Fri, 8.30am-10pm Sat, Sun). Turndown. Voicemail.*
Website: www.theriverinn.com

Swissôtel Washington – The Watergate

2650 Virginia Avenue, NW, at New Hampshire Avenue, Foggy Bottom, DC 20037 (reservations 1-800 424 2736/front desk 965 2300/fax 337 7915). Foggy Bottom-GWU Metro. **Rates** single/double $350-$400; suite $475-$575; presidential suite $1,950. **Credit** AmEx, DC, Disc, JCB, MC, V.
Think of the classiest hotel you've ever been in. Now think classier. You've come close to the white-gloved elegance of the Swissôtel in the Watergate. The marble and antiques in the lobby complement the cordial but aloof atmosphere of the front desk staff. Although the building may be infamous for its break-ins and celebrity scandals (this, after all, is the same apartment complex where Monica kept her stained dress), the hotel is popular for its amazing views of the Potomac River and Georgetown, and some rooms have balconies. The hotel was bought in 1998 by a Swiss hotel chain and is undergoing renovation to modernise the rather dated colour schemes in the rooms. There's a private underground entrance to the Kennedy Center so your Ferragamos won't get wet. The health club costs extra (like you care?).
Hotel services *Bar. Beauty salon. Business centre. Conference facilities. Disabled-adapted rooms. Hairdresser. Laundry. Limousine service (Mon-Fri). Masseuse. Mobile phone rental. Parking. Pool. Restaurant. Sauna & jacuzzi in presidential suites.*
Room services *Dataport. Fax. Hair dryer. Kitchenette (suites). Minibar. Pay movies. Room service (24 hours). Turndown.*
Website: www.swissotel.com

W (a bit pricey)

1 Washington Circle, NW, between 23rd Street & New Hampshire Avenue, Foggy Bottom, DC 20037 (reservations 1-800 424 9671/front desk 872 1680/ fax 887 4989). Foggy Bottom-GWU Metro. **Rates** single/double $209; suite $229; deluxe suite $249. **Credit** AmEx, DC, Disc, MC, V.
An immensely elegant, oft-ignored suite-hotel (formerly One Washington Circle) situated steps from Georgetown. Nixon used to stay here. The extremely attentive, friendly staff will offer help before it's asked for (or before you knew you needed it). The West End Café attached to the hotel has a jazz trio on Friday and Saturday evenings. The lobby has a computer concierge service that will recommend restaurants and sights.
Hotel services *Babysitting. Conference facilities. Laundromat. Parking.*
Room services *Coffee maker. Dataport. Hair dryer. Kitchenette. Refrigerator. Room service (7am-10pm Mon, 7am-11pm Tue-Sat, 8am-10pm Sun). Turndown. Voicemail.*

Downtown

Though it's hardly the US's buzziest downtown, at least there are some shops, bars and restaurants, and the transport is good. Most hotels are within walking distance of the Mall.

Capital Hilton

16th & K Streets, NW, Downtown, DC 20036 (reservations 1-800 445 8667/front desk 393 1000/ fax 639 5784). Farragut North or Farragut West Metro. **Rates** single/double $119-$309; suite $239-$369. **Credit** AmEx, DC, Disc, JCB, MC, V.

This is a stodgy block of towers, centrally located and with the normal Hilton service and reliability. The horrid exterior architecture doesn't get much better inside, but at least the amenities are fulsome. For a little bit extra, you can enjoy 'tower' privileges, which include breakfast, in-room fax and use of the tenth-floor bar, where weary businessmen try to forget the day's business with a stiff drink and CNN.

Hotel services *Bars (2). Breakfast. Business centre. Conference facilities. Fitness facilities. Hair salon. Parking. Restaurant.*

Room services *Coffee maker. Dataport. Hair dryer. Minibar. Voicemail.*

Website: www.hilton.com

Center City Travelodge Hotel

1201 13th Street, NW, at M Street, Downtown, DC 20005 (reservations 1-800 578 7878/front desk 682 5300/fax 371 9624). McPherson Square Metro. **Rates** single $79; double $89. **Credit** AmEx, DC, Disc, MC, V.

A cheap, if somewhat lifeless, 100-room hotel close to the iffy section east of Scott Circle. Rooms are clean and well-appointed and complimentary breakfast is served every morning.

Hotel services *Breakfast. Business centre. Parking.*

Room services *Coffee maker. Hair dryer. Minibar. Pay movies. Voicemail.*

Crowne Plaza

14th & K Streets, NW, Downtown, DC 20005 (reservations 1-800 637 3788/front desk 682 0111/ fax 682 9525). McPherson Square Metro. **Rates** single/double $109-$240; suite $199-$269. **Credit** AmEx, DC, Disc, JCB, MC, V.

This Beaux Arts building on Franklin Square dates from the 'Roaring Twenties' and the gorgeous architecture matches the small but elegantly appointed rooms. The hotel has 318 rooms and suites, some with skyline views – but it's the location that really makes this place a winner. 'Club level' guests get a private elevator, in-room fax and turndown service, along with the club lounge and free breakfast.

Hotel services *Bar. Business centre. Conference facilities. Disabled-access rooms. Espresso bar. Fitness facilities. Laundry. Parking. Restaurant.*

Room services *Coffee maker. Dataport. Hair dryer. Iron & ironing board. Pay movies. Room service (6.30am-10.30pm). Voicemail.*

Website: www.basshotels.com/crowneplaza

The Hay-Adams Hotel

800 Lafayette Square, NW, between 16th & H Streets, Downtown, DC 20006 (front desk 638 6600/ fax 638 2716). Farragut North or McPherson Square Metro. **Rates** single/double $189-$465; suite $515-$2500. **Credit** AmEx, DC, Disc, JCB, MC, V.

As soon as you enter the dark wood-panelled lobby, you'll realise why the Hay-Adams is a well-loved and extremely well-maintained building. Its location on Lafayette Square provides great people-watching, as various presidential protests take place in the park. The hotel was also the site of the infamous Iran Contra scandal in the 1980s, when millions of dollars of 'fundraising' changed hands in its leathery lounges. The roof deck has the best view of the White House.

Hotel services *Bar. Business centre. Conference facilities. Fitness facilities. Laundry. Parking. Restaurant.*

Room services *Dataport. Hair dryer. Kitchens (suites). Room service (24 hours). Turndown. Voicemail.*

Hotel Harrington

436 11th Street, NW, at E Street, Downtown, DC 20004 (reservations 1-800 424 8532/front desk 628 8140/fax 347 3924/email reservations@hotel-harrington.com). Metro Center Metro. **Rates** single $84; double $89-$99. **Credit** AmEx, DC, Disc, JCB, MC, V.

A clean but dingy 85-year-old hotel that is near what passes for DC's theatre district but not much else – though there's a great burger joint beneath it. Although the hotel is still family-owned, the rooms have a cookie-cutter feel. The décor is floral on beige: best to keep the lights off and just use it as a crash pad. Harry's Bar downstairs has the air of a tired *Cheers* knock-off.

Hotel services *Bar. Conference facilities. Disabled-adapted rooms. Laundromat. Parking. Restaurant.*

Website: www.hotel-harrington.com

Jefferson Hotel

1200 16th Street, NW, at M Street, Downtown, DC 20036 (reservations 1-800 555 8000/front desk 347 2200/fax 331 7982). Farragut North Metro. **Rates** single/double $219-$329; suite $389-$1,200. **Credit** AmEx, DC, Disc, JCB, MC, V.

This gilt-edged hotel suffers a bit from its sense of self-importance. It trips the line between old-fashioned and fogeyish and the by-the-book staff don't help. If the smugness gets a bit much, just remember that this was where presidential advisor Dick Morris was caught with a hooker's toe in his mouth. Rooms are well appointed but small. Try out the clubby restaurant, which is a hangout for the Beltway's elite and occasionally offers a menu from the era of President Thomas Jefferson.

Hotel services *Bar. Fitness facilities. Laundry. Parking. Pool. Restaurant.*

Room services *Coffee maker. Dataport. Hair dryer. Pay movies. Room service.*

Website: www.camberleyhotels.com

The Beaux Arts **Crowne Plaza** *(page 127).*

Morrison-Clark Inn

1015 L Street, NW, between 11th Street & Massachusetts Avenue, Downtown, DC 20001 (reservations 1-800 332 7898/front desk 898 1200/ fax 289 8576). Metro Center Metro. **Rates** single/double $145-$260. **Credit** AmEx, DC, Disc, MC, V.

This slightly out-of-the-way Victorian manse has 54 uniquely designed and individually decorated rooms and suites. The antique furnishings add to the traditional feel – the inn is listed on the National Register of Historic Places. The hotel restaurant is a favourite romantic spot for locals.

Hotel services *Bar. Breakfast. Fitness facilities. Parking.*

Room services *Hair dryer. Room service (6-9.30pm). Voicemail.*

Renaissance Mayflower Hotel

1127 Connecticut Avenue, NW, between L & M Streets, Downtown, DC 20036 (reservations 1-800 228 9290/front desk 347 3000/fax 776 9182). Farragut North Metro. **Rates** single/double $155-$390; suite $119-$575. **Credit** AmEx, DC, Disc, MC, V.

As big as a city block and right in the centre of town, the Mayflower is elegant and extravagant. The courteous staff even brought cookies to the paparazzi staking out Monica Lewinsky during a stay. For an extra fee, you can have a room with a computer and Internet access. Presidential inaugurations have been held here for the past 60 years.

Hotel services *Bar. Business centre. Conference facilities. Fitness facilities. Laundry. Parking. Restaurant.*

Room services *Coffee maker. Dataport. Hair dryer. Minibar. Pay movies. Room service. Turndown. Voicemail.*

Washington International Youth Hostel

1009 11th Street, NW, at K Street, Downtown, DC 20001 (reservations 1-800 909 4776, then at prompt, dial 04/front desk 737 2333/fax 737 1508/ email dchostel@erols.com). Metro Center Metro.

Rates single $19-$21, including linen.

Credit MC, V.

A top-notch, dirt-cheap hostel close to the Metro, which offers 250 beds divided between single-sex rooms and four-bed 'family' rooms. Kitchens, lockers and a laundromat are at your disposal, and the staff arrange group walking tours and theatre outings. Most importantly, there is no lock-out time. You'll have to book well in advance, because this is the only hostel in town.

Union Station & around

Close both to transport and the US Capitol, this area is well located, if somewhat anonymous (though just a short walk from the more characterful Capitol Hill neighbourhood), and it's hardly jumping at night – to the extent that you should stay alert to your personal safety. Hotels here tend to be empty during the Congressional recesses (July and August, December and January) and pretty full the rest of the time.

Holiday Inn on the Hill

415 New Jersey Avenue, NW, between D & E Streets, Union Station & Around, DC 20001 (reservations 1-800 638 1116/front desk 638 1616/fax 638 0707). Union Station Metro.

Rates single/double $99-$184. **Credit** AmEx, DC, Disc, JCB, MC, V.

The most family-friendly hotel we surveyed. There's a Discovery Zone for kids where they can play games, watch videos and have a snack under supervision. Under-19s (!) stay free in a parent's room and under-12s eat free in the restaurant. The hotel also provides 10,000sq ft of meeting space and plenty of amenities for the business traveller. Rooms and bathrooms are not huge, but you won't bump into the walls. It's also near the Mall and all major attractions, as well as the Metro. You'll be hard pressed to find more amenities for your money.

Hotel services *Babysitting. Bar. Business centre. Conference facilities. Disabled-access rooms. Fitness facilities. Laundry. Parking. Pool. Restaurant. Sauna.*

Room services *Coffee maker. Dataport. Hair dryer. Iron & ironing board. Nintendo. Pay movies. Voicemail.*

Hotel George

15 E Street, NW, at North Capitol Street, Union Station & Around, DC 20009 (reservations 1-800 576 8331/front desk 347 4200/fax 347 4213). Union Station Metro. **Rates** single $149-$205; double $169-$225; suite $575. **Credit** AmEx, DC, Disc, MC, V.

This is probably the closest DC gets to a boutique hotel: it's stylish but by no means frivolous – more Armani than Versace. The communal facilities – a lobby with a grand piano and signature architectural flower arrangement, the acclaimed French-ish **Bis** restaurant (*see p145* **Restaurants**) and a pool room – are small but sharp. Rooms vary, but are quite generously sized and decorated with refreshing restraint and style – not a floral in sight, and the only flourish a Warhol-like wall print of a dollar bill. Staff are crisply uniformed but entirely human.

Hotel services *Bar. Conference facilities. Laundry. Mobile phone rental. Parking. Restaurant. Shoeshine.*
Room services *Coffee maker. Dataport. Disabled-adapted rooms. Hair dryer. Iron & ironing board. Minibar. Pay movies. Room service (6am-11pm). Turndown.*
Website www.hotelgeorge.com

Phoenix Park Hotel

520 North Capitol Street, NW, at Massachusetts Avenue, Union Station & Around, DC 20001 (reservations 1-800 527 8483/front desk 638 6900/ fax 393 3236). Union Station Metro. **Rates** single $159; double $249. **Credit** AmEx, DC, Disc, MC, V.

A couple of blocks from the Capitol and across from Union Station, this hotel has one huge benefit going for it: the massive **Dubliner** pub below it (*see p164* **Bars**) – be wary of the drunken Hill staffers, but enjoy the overarching (and a tad overwhelming) Irish theme.

Hotel services *Fitness facilities. Parking.*
Room services *Dataport. Hair dryer. Minibar. Pay movies.*

Dupont Circle

Dupont Circle has a wide variety of places to stay, from impersonal chains to more characterful B&Bs, plus plenty of restaurants and nightlife – which mean you may be troubled by street noise at some locations (notably P Street). Most of the major sights are within walking distance – just.

Brickskeller Inn

1523 22nd Street, NW, between P & Q Streets, Dupont Circle, DC 20037 (front desk 293 1885/fax 293 0996). Dupont Circle Metro. **Rates** single/ double (shared bath) $46-$66; single/double (private bath) $66-$87. **Credit** AmEx, DC, Disc, MC, V.

Don't be put off by the buzzed entry for the hotel. The 800-beer bar and restaurant below the hotel make it a necessity. Cheap and, well, moderately cheerful, the hotel is near Rock Creek Park and tons of restaurants on P Street. Most rooms have shared baths, none have TVs.

Governor's House Hotel

1615 Rhode Island Avenue, NW, at 17th Street, Dupont Circle, DC 20036 (reservations 1-800 821 4367/front desk 296 2100/fax 331 0227). Dupont Circle or Farragut North Metro. **Rates** single/double $125; suite $145. **Credit** AmEx, DC, Disc, MC, V.

A smaller alternative to the chain hotels, Governor's offers generous sized rooms and a refined Federalist-style lobby (lots of leaves and dark wood). The staff is as warm as the décor. The hotel has 149 rooms, and some of the suites have kitchens. It's convenient for Connecticut Avenue shopping and a short hike from the White House.

Hotel services *Bar. Business services. Conference facilities. Disabled-adapted rooms. Fitness facilities (some YMCA passes on request). Laundry. Parking.*
Room services *Coffee maker. Dataport. Hair dryer. Pay movies. Refrigerator. Room service (7am-10pm). Turndown. Voicemail.*

HH Leonards Mansion

2020 O Street, NW, between 20th & 21st Streets, Dupont Circle, DC 20036 (front desk 496 2000/fax 659 0547). Dupont Circle Metro. **Rates** single/ double $125-$600. **Credit** AmEx, MC, V.

A beautiful 12-room B&B that's hidden on a residential side street with no sign to announce its presence. Every room in the three interconnected townhouses has a different theme; the Log Cabin suite, for example, has huge log beams, cowhide rugs and a Frederic Remington sculpture for sale. President Teddy Roosevelt once played pool in the pool room. The owner is also an antiques dealer, so just about everything you see, from the furniture to wall hangings, is for sale.
Website: www.erols.com/mansion

Radisson Barcelô Hotel

2121 P Street, NW, at 21st Street, Dupont Circle, DC 20036 (reservations 1-800 333 3333/front desk 293 3100/fax 956 6693). Dupont Circle Metro. **Rates** single $225-$245; double $245-$265; suite $199-$525. **Credit** AmEx, DC, Disc, MC, V.

Located plum in the middle of P Street's cruising corridor, the Barcelô is a calm oasis steps from Rock Creek Park and the restaurants and cafés of Dupont Circle. With 301 rooms, 77 suites and conference facilities measuring 7,000sq ft, it's big – but not impersonal. There are shared kitchen facilities for all guests and a decent restaurant, Gabriel. Note that the parking lot is often full.

Hotel services *Babysitting. Bar. Business services. Courtyard pool. Disabled-adapted room. Fitness facilities. Laundry. Parking. Restaurant. Roof-top sundeck. Video rental.*
Room services *Coffee maker. Dataport. Hair dryer. Iron & ironing board. Pay movies. Room service (breakfast & dinner only). Turndown. VCR (on request). Voicemail.*

Swann House

1808 New Hampshire Avenue, NW, at 18th Street, Dupont Circle, DC 20009 (265 4414/fax 265 6755/ stay@swannhouse.com). Dupont Circle Metro. **Rates** $135-$250. **Credit** AmEx, DC, MC, V.

Suburban dreams

DC may not be the most populous of cities, but nevertheless it is still surrounded with plenty of suburbs. If you'd prefer to stay somewhere family-friendly with a neighbourhood feel, and avoid city-centre prices, the Maryland 'burb of Bethesda may suit. An easy and – out of rush hour – stress-free ride north on the Metro's Red Line, it offers decent shopping and a sizeable restaurant enclave (*see page 151* **Eating in Bethesda**). Hotels are mushrooming here; they're slightly cheaper than in the city centre, especially at weekends, since most are geared towards government and corporate accounts. Below are a few that are Metro-accessible.

American Inn of Bethesda

8130 Wisconsin Avenue, between Battery Lane & Cordell Avenue, Bethesda, MD 20814 (reservations 1-800 323 7081/front desk 301 656 9300/fax 301 656 2907/email innkeeper@ american-inn.com). Bethesda Metro. **Rates** single $69-$130; double $79-$140. **Credit** AmEx, DC, Disc, MC, V.

The smallish rooms make the American Inn a good choice for travellers looking to spend more time out of the hotel than in. The outdoor pool is pitifully small, but private. Children stay for free with parents, and rates fall by as much as half on the weekends. The staff are pleasant.

Hotel services *Breakfast. Business centre. Laundry. Pool. Parking. Restaurant.*

The Bethesda Ramada

8400 Wisconsin Avenue, at Woodmont Avenue, Bethesda, MD 20814 (reservations 1-800 272 6232/ front desk 301 654 1000/fax 301 986 1715). Medical Center Metro. **Rates** single/double $79-$139. **Credit** AmEx, DC, Disc, MC, V.

A few blocks from the Metro station and what passes for 'bustle' along Wisconsin Avenue, this large and somewhat anonymous chain hotel has 163 rooms and suites. It's geared more for business than pleasure, but is a great bargain for the money. Avoid the Rockin' Sports Bar in the hotel at all costs.

Hotel services *Business centre. Conference facilities. Disabled-adapted rooms. Fitness facilities. Laundry. Parking. Pool.*
Room services *Coffee maker. Hair dryer. Iron & ironing board. Pay movies. Room service. Voicemail.*

Residence Inn Bethesda-Downtown

7335 Wisconsin Avenue, between Waverly Street & Montgomery Lane, Bethesda, MD 20814 (reservations 1-800 331 3131/front desk 301 718 0200/fax 301 718 0679). Bethesda Metro. **Rates** single/double suite $199. **Credit** AmEx, DC, Disc, MC, V.

They don't call this the Residence Inn for nothing: all of the 187 suites in this hotel are spacious and equipped well enough to live in – although it's mostly business types that stay here, looking for a home away from home while doing work. Enjoy the well-designed space.

Hotel services *Breakfast. Business centre. Conference facilities. Fitness facilities. Laundromat. Parking. Pool. Sauna.*
Room services *Coffee maker. Dataport. Iron & ironing board. Kitchen. Voicemail.*

Unlike DC's other townhouse B&Bs, the Swann House is a freestanding mansion, which means the hallways aren't cramped and the lighting is good throughout. Built in 1883, the house retains many of its original features, such as the multicoloured slate shingle roof and turret windows. The rooms are romantic without being twee and some have working fireplaces. A small swimming pool nestles in a brick courtyard at the back. Although it's a four-block hike to the nearest Metro station, your reward is a beautiful tree-lined neighbourhood within an easy stroll of the trendy bars on U Street and the hip strip of 17th Street. Children are not encouraged, but they are tolerated. The whole place is no-smoking, but there are plenty of decks and porches. Prices include breakfast, afternoon nibbles and a sherry in the evening. Best of all, the owners leave you alone.

Hotel services *Business services. Conference facilities. Breakfast. Garden. Laundry. Parking. Pool.*
Room services *Dataport. Hair dryer. Iron & ironing board. Kitchen (suites). Turndown. Voicemail.*
Website: www.swannhouse.com

Tabard Inn

1739 N Street, NW, at Connecticut Avenue, Dupont Circle, DC 20036 (front desk 785 1277/fax 785 6173). Dupont Circle Metro. **Rates** single/double (shared bath) $65-$95; single/double (private bath) $99-$155. **Credit** AmEx, MC, V.

This is the only hotel where you'll be directed to your room with the instruction: 'Go past the naked mannequin in the bathtub.' The Tabard Inn employs a full-time interior designer – and it shows. Each of the 42 rooms is decorated in brilliant colours with a hodgepodge of slightly chipped antiques. Unique and funky, the Tabard draws locals with its excellent restaurant and offers a garden courtyard in summer months and a roaring drawing-room fire in the winter. It's made up of three nineteenth-century townhouses – making it the oldest continually

operated hotel in the District; the floors and doors squeak and there's no lift or TVs. Don't worry – you won't miss them at all.
Hotel services *Bar. Business services. Continental breakfast. Laundry. Parking. Restaurant. Sports facilities & pool (passes to the nearby YMCA).*
Room services *Dataport.*

Adams Morgan

Adams Morgan is funky, as DC goes, with plenty of ethnic restaurants, bars and nightclubs. But it's also relatively far out – and there's no convenient Metro station. You'll have to hike across the Ellington Bridge or take a bus to get to and from the Woodley Park-Zoo or Dupont Circle Metro stops. Parking is a horror, and the area starts to get sketchy the further north you go.

Best hotel...

To keep your mistress

Swissôtel Watergate (*p125*) in Foggy Bottom, where private 'diplomat' entrances secure you from prying eyes.

To plan for higher office

The Hay-Adams Hotel (*p127*) in Downtown has such a great view of the White House that you can almost see yourself inside it.

To survive an assassination attempt

Washington Hilton & Towers (*p133*) in Adams Morgan, where Reagan was shot by a Jodie Foster-obsessed John Hinckley. Since that infamous occasion the hotel has built an underground passageway to safeguard the limousines of visiting luminaries.

To sell your soul

The **Jefferson Hotel** (*p127*) in Downtown almost invented the concept of lobbying. Listen to the insider gossip at lunchtime in the pricey restaurant.

To be pampered

The **Four Seasons** (*p134*) in Georgetown, which has the best health spa in town and staff who would sell their grandmothers into slavery for you – with a smile.

To drop acid

Joke. But if you did, the **Tabard Inn** (*p131*) in Dupont Circle, with its naked mannequin and multi-coloured décor, would provide the raw materials for a great trip.

Adams Inn

1744 Lanier Place, NW, at 18th Street, Adams Morgan, DC 20009 (reservations 1-800 578 6807/front desk 745 3600/fax 319 7958/email adamsinn@adamsinn.com). Woodley Park-Zoo Metro, then 90, 91, 92, 93, 96 bus. **Rates** single (shared bath) $45; single (private bath) $60; $10 per extra person. **Credit** AmEx, DC, Disc, MC, V.
Simple and clean rooms fill this three-storey B&B in a quiet part of Adams Morgan. The flea-market furnishings and fireplaces make it cosy. Rooms don't have phones or TVs, but there is a common lounge and kitchen.
Hotel services *Laundromat. Parking.*
Website: www.adamsinn.com

Doyle Normandy

2118 Wyoming Avenue, NW, at Connecticut Avenue, Adams Morgan, DC 20008 (front desk 483 1350/fax 387 8241). Dupont Circle Metro, then L1 bus. **Rates** single/double $79-$179. **Credit** AmEx, DC, Disc, MC, V.
This is a mid-size hotel with gracious touches; the garden patio and glass conservatory are just a few of the unexpected pleasures. It's slightly too floral in design, but was newly remodelled in 1998 with all mod cons.
Hotel services *Parking.*
Room services *Coffee maker. Minibar. Refrigerator.*

Hotel Sofitel

1914 Connecticut Avenue, NW, between California Avenue & Leroy Place, Adams Morgan, DC 20036 (reservations 1-800 424 2464/front desk 797 2000/fax 462 0944). Dupont Circle Metro, then 42 bus. **Rates** single/double $149-$299; suite $189-$309. **Credit** AmEx, DC, Disc, MC, V.
A first-class French hotel in a gorgeous building on the highest point in DC. Rooms are generous in size, the staff are superb and it's a short walk to the heart of Dupont Circle and Kalorama. The Pullman bar in the hotel is one of the city's unknown treasures.
Hotel services *Bar. Business centre. Conference facilities. Fitness facilities. Limousine service. Parking. Pool. Restaurant. Room service (5.30am-11pm).*
Room services *Dataport. Hair dryer. Minibar. Pay movies. Turndown. Voicemail.*
Website: www.sofitel.com

Kalorama Guest House

1854 Mintwood Place, at Columbia Road, Adams Morgan, DC 20009 (front desk 667 6369/fax 319 1262). Woodley Park-Zoo Metro or Dupont Circle Metro, then 42 bus. **Rates** single/double (shared bath) $50-$75; single/double (private bath) $75-$105; suite $110-$140. **Credit** AmEx, DC, Disc, MC, V.
A B&B that's trying to become a chain (it also has a location in Woodley Park, *see p135*), this is a successful enterprise because it's such a great deal. This 29-unit location is situated in prime real estate, close enough to Columbia Road for nightlife but far enough to prevent noise. There's a fabulous garden

Tabard Inn: *individual and funky (page 131).*

patio in the back and hors d'oeuvres on Friday and Saturday nights. No TVs or phones in the rooms.
Hotel services *Laundromat. Refrigerator. Parking.*

Washington Hilton & Towers

1919 Connecticut Avenue, NW, at T Street, Adams Morgan, DC 20009 (reservations 1-800 445 8667/ front desk 483 3000/fax 232 0438). Dupont Circle Metro, then 42 bus. **Rates** single/double $204-$229; suite $475-$970; 2-bedroom suite $750-$1,220.
Credit AmEx, DC, Disc, MC, V.

A massive hotel complex that specialises in balls, conventions and any other outlandishly sized occasion. The ballroom is supposedly one of the largest in the eastern US and the place is normally filled with conventioneers – be prepared to see plenty of people wandering the hotel wearing name tags. The two restaurants and two bars should keep you busy, and the upper-level rooms have great city views. There's also a heated pool and lots of tennis courts.
Hotel services *Bars (2). Business centre. Conference facilities. Disabled-adapted rooms. Fitness facilities. Parking. Pool. Restaurants (2).*
Room services *Coffee maker. Dataport. Hair dryer. Iron & ironing board. Minibar. Pay movies. Room service. Turndown. Voicemail.*

Windsor Park Hotel

2116 Kalorama Road, NW, at Connecticut Avenue, Adams Morgan, DC 20008 (reservations 1-800 247 3064/front desk 483 7700/fax 332 4547). Woodley Park-Zoo Metro, then L1 bus. **Rates** single $104; double $112; suite $155. **Credit** AmEx, DC, Disc, MC, V.

A 43-room hotel dating from the 1930s, offering Chippendale-style furniture in small, clean rooms. The street it's on is quiet and lined with pretty, well-maintained houses, while the neighbourhood holds a few cabinet ministers and high-ranking Congressmen. It's close to 18th Street and ground zero of Adams Morgan's nightlife.
Hotel services *Breakfast. Parking.*
Room services *Refrigerator.*

Logan Circle

Logan Circle is not the most interesting area and the Metro is a schlepp away at Dupont Circle, but it's well located for the nightlife of Dupont Circle and the U Street/14th Street corridor.

Doubletree Park Terrace Hotel

1515 Rhode Island Avenue, NW, between 15th & 16th Streets, Logan Circle, DC 20005 (reservations 1-800 222 8733/front desk 232 7000/fax 518 5747). Dupont Circle or McPherson Square Metro.
Rates single/double $96-$189. **Credit** AmEx, DC, Disc, MC, V.

Reasonably priced chain hotel on Scott Circle. Rooms are cookie-cutter in feel, but the staff are friendly and accommodating. Try not to get a room in the back of the hotel, where you overlook rubbish bins. The breakfast buffet offers a nice selection (although it's not free), but avoid at all costs the cheesy hotel restaurant, Chardonnay.
Hotel services *Bar. Business centre. Conference facilities. Fitness facilities. Parking. Restaurants (2).*
Room services *Coffee maker. Dataport. Hair dryer. Pay movies. Room service. Turndown. Voicemail.*

Howard Johnson Plaza Hotel & Suites

1430 Rhode Island Avenue, NW, between 14th & 15th Streets, Logan Circle, DC 20005 (reservations 1-800 368 5690/front desk 462 7777/fax 332 3519). Dupont Circle or McPherson Square Metro. **Rates** single/double $79-$129; suite $139-$159; under-16s free. **Credit** AmEx, DC, Disc, JCB, MC, V.

The best of the Howard Johnson chain in DC, this all-suite hotel offers a roof-top pool and good-sized suites with walk-in closets. Just off Scott Circle and very near the cool clubs of 14th and U Streets, rates are good and there are plenty of amenities. Under-16s stay for free with their parents.
Hotel services *Bar. Business centre. Conference facilities. Disabled-adapted rooms. Laundry. Parking. Pool. Restaurant.*
Room services *Coffee maker. Dataport. Hair dryer. Iron & ironing board. Pay movies. Turndown.*
Website: www.hojodc.com

s largely a residential district, few hotels: a shame, since it's a pleasant place to stay, with a walkable, village feel that contrasts pleasantly with the monolithic centre. As there is no Metro station (Foggy Bottom-GWU is the closest, a 10-15-minute walk away), visitors must brave the tortuous bus routes, take cabs or drive. However, driving is teeth-grinding on the best of days and parking for any length of time is all but impossible.

Four Seasons

2800 Pennsylvania Avenue, NW, between 28th & 29th Streets, Georgetown, DC 20007 (reservations 1-800 332 3442/front desk 342 0444/fax 944 2076/ email seasons@erols.com). Foggy Bottom-GWU Metro, then 30, 32, 34, 35, 36 bus. **Rates** single/double $370-$490; suites $575-$3,500. **Credit** AmEx, DC, Disc, JCB, MC, V.

Far from being just another branch in a chain, this discreetly off-street Four Seasons is one of DC's most individual hotels, with a distinctly buzzy and exceedingly comfortable vibe. It has long attracted guests of serious status and pampers them with every luxury or facility they may desire. It boasts that it is a 'no luggage required' hotel: almost anything you've forgotten can be found for you, and the list of on-demand accessories includes bow ties, hot water bottles and nail polish. A new wing has added 60 rooms and suites, bringing the total to 260. The basement health spa is both serious and sybaritic. If the mind also needs stimulation, art works are dotted around liberally.

Hotel services *Business centre. Conference facilities. Disabled-adapted rooms. Fitness facilities. Hair salon. Laundry. Limo service. Parking. Pool. Sauna. Shoeshine. Shop. Valet. Video & CD library.*
Room services *Dataport. Fax (on request). Hair dryer. Minibar. Room service (24 hours). Turndown. Voicemail.*
Website: www.fourseasons.com

Georgetown Dutch Inn

1075 Thomas Jefferson Street, NW, between M & K Streets, Georgetown, DC 20007 (reservations 1-800 388 2410/front desk 337 0900/fax 333 6526). Foggy Bottom-GWU Metro, then 30, 32, 34, 35, 36 bus. **Rates** single $105-$155, double $105-$175. **Credit** AmEx, DC, MC, V.

This quaint, 47-suite hotel on a side street is due to close for four to five months for renovations from November 1999. Its smallish, dark rooms are crying out for a redesign. The limited services should be boosted once all renovations are complete.

Hotel services *Breakfast. Disabled-adapted rooms. Fitness centre (at Monarch Hotel).*
Room services *Iron & ironing board. Kitchenette. Refrigerator. Room service (6am-10pm).*

Georgetown Suites & Georgetown Suites Harbor Building

1111 30th Street, NW, at M Street, Georgetown, DC 20007 (reservations 1-800 348 7203/front desk 298

The newly renovated **Doyle Normandy** *(p132).*

7800/fax 333 0143). Foggy Bottom-GWU Metro. **Rates** suite $195-$230. **Credit** AmEx, DC, MC, V.

This 217-suite hotel divided into two buildings) is on a quiet street off the main drag of M Street. Well-situated for forays into Georgetown and the C&O Canal, it's become a favourite with visiting musicians. There are no views to speak of (unless you're a big fan of motorways or like staring at the more expensive **Four Seasons** hotel opposite – *see above*), but the rooms are bright and spacious. Formerly condominiums, each suite is well equipped with full kitchens and some first-floor units have patios. The hotel allows small dogs and cats.

Hotel services *Breakfast. Conference facilities. Fitness facilities. Laundry & laundromat. Parking.*
Room services *Coffee maker. Dataport. Hair dryer. Iron & ironing board. Microwave. Pay movies. Refrigerator. Turndown. Voicemail.*

Upper Northwest

The Upper Northwest area is where most of DC's young professionals live. It's pretty suburban and quite far from the centre, but the low prices reflect this, and there are pockets of activity around the Metro stops at Woodley Park and Cleveland Park.

Kalorama Guest House at Woodley Park

2700 Cathedral Avenue, NW, at 27th Street, Woodley Park (reservations 328 0860/fax 328 8730). Woodley Park-Zoo Metro. **Rates** single $45-$80; double $55-$105. **Credit** AmEx, DC, Disc, MC, V.

A twee B&B near the Metro, the Zoo, the park and a variety of cheap, international restaurants. Set in a 90-year-old house, it has 19 rooms filled with doilies and floral patterns. There are no phones or TVs in the guest rooms, but a common area has both. There is also a **Kalorama Guest House** in Adams Morgan (*see p132*).

Marriott Wardman Park

2660 Woodley Road, NW, at Connecticut Avenue, Woodley Park, DC 20008 (reservations 1-800 228 9290/front desk 328 2000/fax 387 5397). Woodley Park-Zoo Metro. **Rates** single/double $214-$244; suite $234-$264. **Credit** AmEx, DC, Disc, MC, V.

A huge (more than 1,300 rooms) and labyrinthine hotel perched on a hill near the Woodley Park Metro stop. If you get lost (as you inevitably will), ask the friendly staff who seem to be everywhere. Although the 1918 building is gorgeous and surrounded by luscious greenery, the rooms lack character, suffering from too many corporate owners. There are extensive conference facilities, and the hotel should be completely renovated by the end of 1999.

Hotel services *Bars (2). Business centre. Conference facilities. Disabled-adapted rooms. Minibar. Parking. Restaurants (3).*
Room services *Coffee maker. Dataport. Hair dryer. Room service (6am-1am). Turndown. Voicemail.*

Arlington

Well served by the Metro, Arlington is not the most exciting of cities, but it does offer easy access to Arlington Cemetery and National Airport and makes a good base for sightseeing ventures to Old Town Alexandria, the Pentagon and Georgetown.

Key Bridge Marriott

1401 Lee Highway, at Wilson Street, Arlington, VA 22209 (reservations 1-800 228 9290/front desk 703 524 6400/fax 703 524 8964). Rosslyn Metro. **Rates** single $199; double $209; suite $235. **Credit** AmEx, DC, Disc, JCB, MC, V.

You will not find a better view of the Washington skyline at night than from the steakhouse restaurant at the top of the Key Bridge Marriott. A large and luxurious hotel built for conventions (it has 16 meeting rooms and 61 rooms specifically designed for the business traveller), it's only a mile from the cemetery and a quick walk across the bridge to Georgetown. The Metro is nearby. Pay the extra $15 for a room with a city view.

Hotel services *Bar. Business centre. Hair salon. Laundry. Parking. Restaurants (2).*
Room services *Coffee maker. Dataport. Hair dryer. Iron & ironing board. Pay movies. Voicemail.*
Website: www.marriott.com

Quality Hotel – Courthouse Plaza

1200 North Courthouse Road, at Wilson Street & US 50, Arlington, VA, 22201 (reservations 1-888 987 2555/front desk 703 524 4000/fax 703 522 6814). Court House Metro. **Rates** single/double $80-$166; suite $100-$200. **Credit** AmEx, DC, Disc, MC, V.

The Quality's rooms are larger than normal and the pool is obscenely big – and it's cheaper than comparable rooms across the Potomac River in Washington. Décor is lacking, but as the name says, you can expect quality. It's close to the Metro and the Iwo Jima memorial.

Hotel services *Bar. Fitness facilities. Kitchens (suites). Parking. Pool. Restaurant. Sauna.*
Room services *Coffee maker. Dataport. Hair dryer. Iron & ironing board. Nintendo. Refrigerator. Voicemail.*
Website: www.qualityhotelarlington.com

Chain hotels

The various national hotel chains have many locations in the Washington area – call the toll-free numbers below for more information. Increasingly, the chains have been gobbling up existing hotels, rather than building new ones, and then slapping their corporate logo on the outside – which, sadly, means there are very few truly independent hotels left in Washington.

First-class

Hilton 1-800 445 8667
Hyatt 1-800 233 1234
Ritz-Carlton 1-800 241 3333
Sheraton 1-800 325 3535
Westin 1-800 937 8461

Mid-range

Doubletree 1-800 222 8733
Holiday Inn 1-800 465 4329
Howard Johnson 1-800 446 4656
Marriott 1-800 228 9290
Radisson 1-800 333 3333

Budget

Best Western 1-800 780 7234
Comfort Inn 1-800 228 5150
Quality Inn 1-800 228 5151
Ramada 1-800 272 6232
Travelodge 1-800 578 7878

Cafés & Coffeehouses

The coffee craze has finally hit DC, so lovers of latte and connoisseurs of chai have plenty of options.

Once upon a time, Washington offered slim pickin's for a good cup of joe. Now, you've got all kinds of caffeinated choices, from cookie-cutter branches of Starbucks to late-night haunts, lounges and bookstore combos. You don't even have to like coffee any more – most places are more like beverage emporia, offering the latest in tea chic (chai, zillions of herbals and infusions, tea/juice drinks), fruit smoothies, alcohol and lassis. Whatever your preference, Washington has finally joined the ranks of other cities, where sipping, slurping and slouching had long been fashionable while we were still working out the enigma of decaff.

Most of the character coffeehouses listed here are in DC's neighbourhoods. Few are in central DC or near the Mall and its showpiece attractions, where there is a dearth of good fill-up stations. For the best of them, *see page 148* **Eating near the Mall**. Some of the coffee chains also have central branches, and these are often the best option: *see page 139* **Fast-food coffee**.

Foggy Bottom

Borders Books, Music & Café

1800 L Street, NW, at 18th Street, Foggy Bottom (466 4999). Farragut North Metro. **Open** 8am-10pm Mon-Fri; 9am-9pm Sat; 11am-7pm Sun. **Credit** AmEx, Disc, MC, V.

Not a destination café in its own right, but its location in the middle of the Downtown Borders bookstore makes it a convenient meeting point. Apart from the usual array of coffee and tea, the menu is nothing to write home about.

The Bread Line

1751 Pennsylvania Avenue, NW, between 17th & 18th Streets, Foggy Bottom (822 8900). Farragut West Metro. **Open** 7am-7pm Mon-Fri. **Credit** AmEx, MC, V.

From empanadas and focaccia to Chinese pork buns and French toast, the Bread Line is a United Nations of bread products. Expect local, organic and often upscale ingredients: the ham and cheese sandwich, for example, is prosciutto and mascarpone with fig jam. It's a block from the White House and the Corcoran Gallery of Art.

Café des Amis du Café

1020 19th Street, NW, between K & L Streets, Foggy Bottom (466 7860). Farragut North or Farragut West Metro. **Open** 7am-6pm Mon-Fri. **No credit cards**.

Open only in the day, this café attracts mainly the Downtown workforce. The sandwiches and salads are fresh and the management is from Ethiopia, so there are also a few dishes from their homeland. A counter-and-stool operation, with strewn newspapers and CNN on the tube, this is a bit like a neighbourhood bar – but without the booze or late hours.

Penn Quarter

Footnotes' a Café

Olsson's Books & Records, 418 Seventh Street, NW, between Fourth & Fifth Streets, Penn Quarter (638 4882). Archives-Navy Memorial or Gallery Place-Chinatown Metro. **Open** 8am-6pm Mon-Fri; 8am-4.30pm Sat, Sun. **Credit** MC, V.

One of the last independent bookstores in the area has caught up with its corporate competition and now houses a café in two of its branches (this and Arlington). It's a small space with a living-room feel, and makes a great pitstop while gallery-hopping. The food is salads and sandwiches (cutely named after literary celebrities).

Dupont Circle

Firehook Bakery & Coffeehouse

1909 Q Street, NW, at Connecticut Avenue, Dupont Circle (588 9296). Dupont Circle Metro. **Open** 7am-8pm Mon-Thur; 7am-10pm Fri; 9am-10pm Sat; 9am-8pm Sun. **Credit** MC, V.

You can't go wrong with pastry chef Kate Jansen's cakes, tarts or cookies, all available for devouring on the spot or to take away – an espresso chew or a slice of the chocolate raspberry cake could send you into orbit. A handful of savoury items, including house-made focaccia and consistently interesting sandwiches on Firehook's signature breads, are also available. The Dupont location has just a few stools; the other two branches are more spacious.

Branches: 912 17th Street, NW, Downtown (429 2253); 3411 Connecticut Avenue, NW, Cleveland Park

(362 2253); 214 N Fayette Street, Alexandria, VA (703 519 8020); 105 S Union Street, Alexandria, VA (703 519 8021).

Java House Coffeeshop

1645 Q Street, NW, at 17th Street, Dupont Circle (387 6622). Dupont Circle Metro. **Open** 7am-midnight daily. **Credit** MC, V.

One of the most pleasant things about this neighbourhood spot is the outdoor patio, where you can linger over a bagel and coffee served in hand-made pottery mugs. They also roast their own beans. One of the most painful things is the service – oh so pleasant, but often as slow as molasses.

Jolt 'N Bolt Coffee & Tea House

1918 18th Street, NW, at M Street, Dupont Circle (232 0077). Dupont Circle Metro. **Open** 7.30am-1am daily. **Credit** MC, V.

The name of this neighbourhood mainstay is misleading: the shady alley patio practically begs people not to bolt, while the tables inside are usually monopolised by caffeine-addled students immersed in textbooks. The bagels are better than average – they're chewy, dense and available with home-made olive cream cheese. The staff can be surly, a characteristic that has perversely become part of Jolt 'N Bolt's charm.

Soho Tea & Coffee

2150 P Street, NW, at 22nd Street, Dupont Circle (463 7646). Dupont Circle Metro. **Open** 7am-3am Mon; 7am-4am Tue-Thur; 7am-5am Fri; 8am-5am Sat; 8am-3am Sun. **No credit cards**.

Known in Dupont Circle for offering a refreshing respite from the Starbucks model, Soho is close to several gay bars, which helps explain its clientele as well as the photos of half-naked men that adorn the walls. The fresh coffee is better than the espresso, and smoking is permitted (hell, it's practically encouraged) after 3pm. But if you're in search of quality baked goods, go elsewhere.

Teaism

2009 R Street, NW, at Connecticut Avenue, Dupont Circle (667 3827). Dupont Circle Metro. **Open** 8am-10pm Mon-Thur; 8am-11pm Fri; 9am-11pm Sat; 9am-10pm Sun. **Credit** AmEx, MC, V.

Freshly baked naan, salty oat cookies and Thai chicken curry are on offer at this cafeteria-style oasis from the bustle of urban living. Whether you stop off for a cup of chai or a bento box, you'll no doubt feel ready to pound the pavement once again.

Branches: 800 Connecticut Avenue, Downtown (835 2233); 400 Eighth Street, NW, Penn Quarter.

Xando

1350 Connecticut Avenue, NW, at 19th Street, Dupont Circle (296 9341). Dupont Circle Metro/42, N2, N4 bus. **Open** 6.30am-1am Mon-Thur, Sun; 6.30-2am Fri, Sat. **Credit** AmEx, MC, V.

A step up from wham-bam-tha Starbucks, this Connecticut-based spreading rapidly throughout the East its coffeebar/lounge concept. In the morning queue to get your java and a pastry (hit or m go, and then, at 4pm, a mural at the bar is raised suddenly alcohol is served. There are lots of sofa dressed in bright fabrics and groovy outdoor seating. Big on coffee cocktails, the menu also features playfood such as S'mores (complete with your own at-table hibachi for proper marshmallow toasting). It's loud, it's young and it's always jammed.

Branches: 1647 20th Street, NW, Dupont Circle (332 6364); 301 Pennsylvania Avenue, SE, Capitol Hill (546 3345).

If you're exploring Arlington, stop at **Palladio's Café**, *a popular haunt for locals and expat North Africans. See page 139.*

Adams Morgan

Churreria Madrid

2505 Champlain Street, NW, at Columbia Road, Adams Morgan (483 4441). Dupont Circle Metro, then L2 bus or Woodley Park-Zoo Metro, then 90, 91, 92, 93, 96 bus. **Open** 11am-10.30pm Tue-Sat; 11am-10pm Sun. **Credit** AmEx, MC, V.

This is a full-service restaurant serving a mixture of Spanish and Latino fare, but let's cut to the chase – this is perhaps the only place in Washington that makes churros: fried dough crescents sprinkled with sugar, which put Dunkin' Donuts to shame. Dunk the churros in a cup of thick, goopy hot chocolate. The Churreria serves them by the dozen, so bring a friend to share in the calorific madness.

Franklyns Coffee House Café

2000 18th Street, NW, at Vernon Street, Adams Morgan (319 1800). Dupont Circle or U Street-Cardozo Metro. **Open** 8am-8pm Mon, Tue; 8am-10pm Wed, Thur; 8am-midnight Fri, Sat; 9am-6pm Sun. **Credit** DC, Disc, MC, V.

ntry home and the food: the English own, and the jams grandma's cup- d the music often olk musicians. ly slow.

...eet, NW, between Belmont Street & Columbia Road, Adams Morgan (232 5500). Dupont Circle Metro, then L2 bus or Woodley Park-Zoo Metro, then 90, 91, 92, 93, 96 bus. **Open** 7am-1am Mon-Thur; 7am-3am Fri; 8am-3am Sat; 8am-midnight Sun. **Credit** MC, V.

Not quite a club, a bar or even a coffeehouse, for that matter, Tryst is the ultimate community living room. Overstuffed chairs, comfy sofas and country-style kitchen tables create a hip, relaxed vibe without feeling collegiate. If you want to drink alcohol, fine. If not, the coffee, served in enormous mugs, is very good. There are also a dozen sandwiches (half of which are vegetarian) and several small plates for nibbling. Chat to a stranger, work from your laptop or just people-watch. *See also p166* **Bars**.

Georgetown

Ching Ching Cha

1063 Wisconsin Avenue, NW, between M & K Streets, Georgetown (333 8288). Foggy Bottom-GWU Metro, then 30, 32, 34, 35, 36 bus. **Open** 11.30am-10pm daily. **Credit** AmEx, Disc, MC, V.

Walking into this traditional Chinese tea house is like walking into a house of worship. It's quiet and peaceful and the space is gorgeous, with a high ceiling and ornate wooden chairs. There's also seating on the floor, with cushions. Try the $10 'Tea Meal': a bento box containing an entrée (from a choice of three), three vegetables, rice and a bowl of inspiring tomato-tofu soup. The staff take time to explain the ritual of tea and the differences between the many varieties. It's not cheap, but it may be one of the best-kept secrets in town for a moment of meditation.

Dean & Deluca

3276 M Street, NW, at Potomac Street, Georgetown (342 2500). Foggy Bottom-GWU Metro, then 30, 32, 34, 35, 36 bus/Rosslyn Metro, then 13M, 38B bus. **Open** 8am-8pm Mon-Thur; 8am-9pm Fri, Sat (later in summer). **Credit** AmEx, MC, V.

The Georgetown branch is kin to the famous Dean & Deluca in New York's SoHo, with its super chi-chi gourmet market as the main attraction. The café, which is off the main market, feels like a greenhouse, long and glass-enclosed. Service is at the counter, where you can order a freshly squeezed orange juice, a macchiato or a pretty, overpriced salad. The Pennsylvania Avenue location is also cafeteria-style and attracts nearby World Bankers for pretentious, pricey sandwiches and espresso.

Branch: 1919 Pennsylvania Avenue, NW, Downtown (296 4327).

Pâtisserie Poupon

1645 Wisconsin Avenue, NW, between Q Street & Reservoir Road, Georgetown (342 3248). Foggy Bottom-GWU Metro, then 30, 32, 34, 35, 36 bus. **Open** 8am-6.30pm Tue-Sat; 8am-4pm Sun. **Credit** AmEx, MC, V.

Light and airy in that LA-chic sort of way, PP gets points for presentation and attitude. The tarts and cakes are just like you'd find in Paris, and the menu is short but oh-so-French: salade niçoise, crudités, quiche and baguette sandwiches. All coffee drinks are made in the back at the espresso bar and hand-delivered by the barista himself.

Senses

3206 Grace Street, NW, at Wisconsin Avenue, Georgetown (342 9083). Foggy Bottom-GWU Metro. **Open** 8am-10pm Tue-Sat; 8am-6pm Sun. **Credit** AmEx, JCB, MC, V.

Tucked away on a cobblestone alley off busy Wisconsin Avenue, this patisserie is a little gem you don't expect as you're walking along the C&O Canal. The traditional French desserts are exquisite (pastry chef Bruno Feldeisen was nominated for a prestigious pastry chef of the year award in 1998), and reason alone to come. But there's more: the food is delightful. Try the menu 'sur le pouce' and get three courses (including one of those fabulous desserts) for about $15 at lunch or $25 at dinner. Seventh heaven.

Experience a taste of café life, French-style, at the elegant **Pâtisserie Poupon** *in Georgetown.*

Woodley Park

Dolce Finale

2653 Connecticut Avenue, NW, at Woodley Road, Woodley Park (667 5350). Woodley Park-Zoo Metro. **Open** 5.30-11.30pm daily. **Credit** AmEx, DC, Disc, MC, V.

It's easy to miss this basement-level grotto: don't, because it's a cool discovery. Strictly an after-sunset operation, Dolce serves only the finishing touches to a meal, from dessert wines and tiramisu to Irish coffee. Dark, cavernous and undoubtedly romantic, it's a great place to extend a date that's going well.

Capitol Hill

Roasters on the Hill

666 Pennsylvania Avenue, SE, at Seventh Street, Capitol Hill (543 8355). Eastern Market Metro. **Open** 7am-7pm Mon-Sat; 8am-5.30pm Sun. **Credit** AmEx, Disc, MC, V.

The locals are lining up to get their first coffee of the day on weekend mornings, when Eastern Market is in full swing. Maybe they're also coming to pick up their weekly supply of house-roasted beans or to catch up on the local gossip. Aside from the handful of seats at the counter (and on the patio, weather permitting), there's a lot of standing room only.

Arlington

Atomic Grounds

1555 Wilson Boulevard, between N Oak & N Pierce Streets, Arlington, VA (703 524 2157). Rosslyn Metro. **Open** 6.30am-6.30pm daily. **Credit** Disc, MC, V.

At first glance, the mod-minimalist industrial look of Atomic Grounds doesn't seem to belong among the surrounding cluster of corporate high-rises. But this funky and friendly cybercafé up the hill from the Newseum is just what cement-heavy Rosslyn needs. Catch up with your email or explore the Internet on the four computers ($2 for 15 minutes, $7 per hour). The best seats in the house are the big, *Alice in Wonderland*-like chairs. The large window facing on to the street has stools and a wide counter. Nosh includes bagels, really tasty, oversized cookies from Uptown Bakery, sandwiches and soup.

Palladio's Café Coffeehouse

2311 Wilson Boulevard, opposite Courthouse Plaza, Arlington, VA (703 516 0003). Court House Metro. **Open** 6.30am-6.30pm Mon-Thur; 6.30am-10.30pm Fri; 8am-10.30pm Sat; 9am-6.30pm Sun (later in summer). **No credit cards**.

A cross between a neighbourhood hangout and a club for expat North Africans, this endearing nook serves espresso drinks and an assortment of paninis and desserts. The few small tables (with very low seats that make you feel like you're in kindergarten) and window seats are usually occupied with pre- or post-moviegoers, 'Afropean' music fans (there's always something good on the CD player) or soccer buffs watching World Cup re-runs.

Fast-food coffee

If you're really pressed for time and just need to grab a quick cup of joe, here's the rundown on the nationally franchised cafés that work more like fast-food operations. These are the most useful locations in the District:

Au Bon Pain

2000 Pennsylvania Avenue, NW, at I Street, Foggy Bottom (887 9215). Foggy Bottom-GWU Metro. **Open** 6am-midnight Mon-Fri; 6am-11pm Sat, Sun.

Union Station, 50 Massachusetts Avenue, NE, at North Capitol Street, Union Station & Around (898 0299). Union Station Metro. **Open** 6am-9pm Mon-Fri; 8am-9pm Sat, Sun.

1701 Pennsylvania Avenue, NW, at 17th Street, White House & Around (887 9331). Farragut West Metro. **Open** 6.30am-6pm Mon-Fri.

All **No credit cards**.

Best for brewed coffee, freshly squeezed orange juice and a not-bad cheese danish.

Corner Bakery Café

Union Station, 50 Massachusetts Avenue, NE, at North Capitol Street, Union Station & Around (371 8811). Union Station Metro. **Open** 7am-8.30pm Mon-Fri; 8am-8.30pm Sat; 9am-5.30pm Sun.

National Press Building, 529 14th Street, NW, at F Street, Downtown (662 7400). Metro Center Metro. **Open** 7am-7pm Mon-Fri; 9am-6pm Sat, Sun.

All **Credit** AmEx, DC, Disc, MC, V.

Better sandwiches and bread than coffee.

Starbucks

800 Seventh Street, NW, at H Street, Downtown (289 1576). Gallery Place-Chinatown Metro. **Open** 6am-7.30pm Mon-Fri; 7am-7.30pm Sat, Sun.

325 Seventh Street, NW, at Indiana Avenue, Penn Quarter (628 5044). Archives-Navy Memorial Metro. **Open** 7am-7pm daily.

1501 Connecticut Avenue, NW, at Dupont Circle, Dupont Circle (588 1280). Dupont Circle Metro. **Open** 6am-11pm Mon-Thur; 6am-midnight Fri; 7am-midnight Sat; 7am-11pm Sun.

All **Credit** AmEx, MC, V.

This ubiquitous chain (29 branches in the DC area alone) is better for people-watching than anything else. The service is often lacking, and food is not why you come to Starbucks, despite the chain's efforts to market lunch in the ever-competitive café business.

Restaurants

From formal to funky, DC's wide-ranging restaurant scene can hold its own with any capital city.

For a long time, defenders of Washington's restaurant scene could always argue that, at the very least, the nation's capital city was the place for ethnic dining. As the hub for international politics, Washington was where you could try the cuisine of more countries than in any other city in the United States, including even New York. But in the past few years, the dining landscape has taken on new and more interesting dimensions. Although ethnic eateries remain a viable staple of Washington's repertoire, it's not the only reason to eat here anymore.

Like other historically food-centric cities such as New York and San Francisco, Washington has become an eating destination. And it's brimming with culinary talent – a growing circle of very committed chefs includes Jeff Buben (**Vidalia**, **Bis**), Ann Cashion (**Cashion's Eat Place**), John Cochran (**Rupperts**), Bob Kinkead (**Kinkead's**), Susan McCreight Lindeborg (**Morrison-Clark Inn**) and Mary Richter (**Zuki Moon**). These tireless souls (and their many colleagues) are primarily responsible not only for educating the palates of Washingtonians but for attracting others from around the country. As a result, the variety and quality of DC restaurants keeps growing and changing faster than a foodie can keep up with.

For listings of restaurants by area, *see page 161*.

American: contemporary

1789 Restaurant

1226 36th Street, NW, at Prospect Street, Georgetown (965 1789). Rosslyn Metro. **Open** 6-10pm Mon-Thur, Sun; 6-11pm Fri; 5.30-11pm Sat. **Credit** AmEx, DC, Disc, MC, V. **Main course** $18-$22.

As many people come to this restaurant for the setting – eighteenth-century federal townhouse, working fireplaces, period furniture and china – as they do for the food, which, under the direction of chef Ris Lacoste, is more contemporary than the furnishings. An alumnus of **Kinkead's** (*see p142*), Lacoste is known for her way with fish, as well as true-blue American favourites, such as roast turkey with all the trimmings (1789 is a terrific Thanksgiving and Christmas Day destination).

Ardeo

3311 Connecticut Avenue, NW, at Macomb Street, Cleveland Park (244 6750). Cleveland Park Metro. **Open** 5.30-10.30pm Mon-Thur, Sun; 5.30-11.30pm Fri, Sat. **Credit** AmEx, DC, MC, V. **Main course** $16-$20.

Ardeo: *fashionable food and superb staff.*

The design of Ardeo is very attractive – sleek, art deco-esque lines and design details – but without feeling pretentious. And maybe that's got something to do with the staff, who are incredibly attentive, savvy and confident. The food consists of primarily updated classics; typical seasonal dishes include lamb chops with asparagus and mashed potatoes, and linguini with pesto made from pumpkin seeds. Bread comes with a wonderfully addictive, garlicky bean purée. This is also a good place to have fun with the wine list.

BET on Jazz

730 11th Street, NW, between G & H Streets, Downtown (393 0975). Metro Center Metro. **Lunch** 11.30am-2.30pm Mon-Fri. **Dinner** 5.30-10pm Mon-Thur; 5.30pm-midnight Fri, Sat; 5.30-9pm Sun. **Credit** AmEx, DC, Disc, MC, V. **Main course** lunch $10-$20; dinner $15-$25.

The second food venture of Washington-based cable TV network Black Entertainment Television (BET), BET on Jazz is unlike anything else in Washington. Although not catering exclusively to African-

Americans, this is where you'll find many of Washington's up-and-coming black professionals listening to live jazz acts, socialising at the bar or lingering in one of the more intimate, supper club-like booths over dinner. Although there are attempts to be Caribbean – conch fritters and katafi-wrapped shrimp – the menu is more of a collection of American classics, including an upscale meatloaf and a 'Caribbean' Caesar salad.

Cashion's Eat Place

1819 Columbia Road, NW, between Biltmore Street & Mintwood Place, Adams Morgan (797 1819). Dupont Circle Metro, then L2 bus or Woodley Park-Zoo Metro, then 90, 91, 92, 93, 96 bus. **Open** 5.30-10pm Tue, Sun; 5.30-11pm Wed-Sat. **Credit** MC, V. **Main course** $15-$21.

Chef/owner Ann Cashion consistently puts on a good show, offering classic style in both her food and the dining room. The menu is seasonal and based on what her local purveyors have on hand – from wild mushrooms to cranberry beans. There's always a balance of heavier meat (pork loin, lamb steak, buffalo) with fish dishes. The food is a little bit Euro, a little bit New Orleans, plus a little bit of Asian thrown in for zest. There's room at the bar for eating, but if you do want a table, you should book. In warm months, the outdoor seating area is one of the most festive in DC.

Clyde's of Georgetown

3236 M Street, NW, between Wisconsin Avenue & Potomac Road, Georgetown (333 9180). Foggy Bottom-GWU Metro, then 30, 32, 34, 35, 36 bus. **Open** 11.30am-midnight Mon-Thur; 11.30am-1am Fri; 9am-1am Sat; 9am-midnight Sun. **Credit** AmEx, DC, Disc, MC, V. **Main course** lunch $11-$16; dinner $13-$18.

This was the first of many Clyde's branches to open in the area, and if there was ever a catch-all restaurant, this is the place. It's dark and woody inside, with lots of Americana hanging on the walls, and a friendly and easygoing atmosphere. On weekdays (4-7pm), you can have a snack at the bar and take advantage of incredible bargains, including a very tasty crabcake sandwich and one of the best burgers in town. Clyde's prides itself on buying produce from local farms and does a nice job on local seafood, too.

DC Coast

1401 K Street, NW, at 14th Street, Downtown (216 5988). McPherson Square Metro. **Lunch** 11.30am-2.30pm Mon-Fri. **Dinner** 5.30-10.30pm Mon-Thur; 5.30-11pm Fri, Sat. **Credit** AmEx, MC, V. **Main course** lunch $13-$18; dinner $16-$25.

DC Coast is one of Washington's hottest restaurants. The interior is spectacular (it was once a bank), with high ceilings, a long sexy bar off to the side and a grand mermaid statue watching over things. DC veteran Jeff Tunks serves mostly seafood with coastal American influences, namely Atlantic, Gulf and Pacific (hence the restaurant's name). Signature dishes include the Chinese-style smoked lobster and chilled Malapeque oysters with iced, vodka-flavoured, Japanese pickled ginger. Be warned: the prices are inflated and the scene is very mobile phone-centric.

Classy seafood for a price at ***DC Coast*****.**

Equinox

818 Connecticut Avenue, NW, between H & I Streets, Downtown (331 8118). Farragut West Metro. **Open** 11.30am-2pm, 5.30-10pm, Mon-Thur; 11.30am-2pm, 5.30-10.30pm, Fri; 5.30-10.30pm Sat. **Credit** AmEx, DC, MC, V. **Main course** lunch $11-$14; dinner $14-$19.

Chef Todd Gray, who last could be found cooking at Roberto Donna's **Galileo** (*see p149*), is now running his own kitchen. Although Gray has imported Italian influences, you'll also see lots of melding on the menu, such as polenta with duck confit. The operative word at Equinox is simplicity: nothing's dripping in puddles of sauce or part of a culinary sculpture. And they've got a great cheese plate, something of a rarity in Washington.

Greenwood at Cleveland Park

3529 Connecticut Avenue, NW, & Porter Street, Cleveland Park (833 6572). Cleveland Park Metro. **Open** 5.30-10pm Tue-Sun. **Credit** AmEx, MC, V. **Main course** $11-$28.

Chef Carole Wagner Greenwood makes pretty pictures with her food – a bouquet of greens atop a soup or a tower of smoked salmon stacked with avocado, for example – and because she's so particular about the use of local and organic ingredients, the results are super-fresh and super-seasonal. Perhaps that's characterised as Californian, into that hearty hunk of locally beef, the West Coast will be far from . The dining room is lovely and muted, you didn't make reservations, the bar is wide ough for supping and sharing.

Kinkead's

2000 Pennsylvania Avenue, NW, between 20th & 21st Streets, Foggy Bottom (296 7700). Foggy Bottom-GWU Metro. **Lunch** 11.30am-2.30pm daily. **Dinner** 5.30-10pm Mon-Thur, Sun; 5.30-10.30pm Fri, Sat. **Credit** AmEx, DC, Disc, MC, V. **Main course** lunch $12-$18; dinner $20-$26.

Billed as an American brasserie, Bob Kinkead's restaurant is more of a hybrid where ambience is concerned. The ground floor is more of a lounge, where you'll find lots of regulars perched at the bar, taking in the tunes of jazz piano/bass duo Hilton Felton and Ephriam Wolfolk. If you haven't booked a table upstairs, the bar is an excellent and more casual alternative, with all the benefits of top-shelf service, the full menu and an earful of fabulous music. With the exception of a few meaty items, the menu offers primarily seafood (cooked and raw) that is fresh, inventive and consistently well prepared.

Kramerbooks & Afterwords Café

1517 Connecticut Avenue, NW, at Q Street, Dupont Circle (387 1462). Dupont Circle Metro/42 bus. **Open** 7am-1am Mon-Thur; 7am Fri-1am Sun. **Credit** AmEx, Disc, MC, V. **Main course** $9-$16.

A Washington staple since the 1970s, Kramer's, as it's affectionately called, is one of the city's great meeting places. The menu at this bookstore-bar-café is, appropriately, a mélange of offerings, from a hangar steak sandwich to the biggest plate of black-bean nachos in town. The two-storey dining room has a sidewalk patio that's very popular, and you can also eat at the bar, though there's not much space. As well as salads, quesadillas and stir fries, chef Pete Barich changes the menu weekly, usually working with a theme, depending on the time of year or the kind of mood he's in. You can always find reliable fish entrées, including sea bass, crab cakes and soft-shell crabs, and prices stay under $20. *See also p213* **Nightlife**.

Morrison-Clark Inn

1015 L Street, NW, at Massachusetts Avenue & 11th Street, Downtown (898 1200). Metro Center Metro. **Lunch** 11am-2pm Mon-Fri. **Dinner** 6-9.30pm Mon-Sat; 6-9pm Sun. **Brunch** 11am-2pm Sun. **Credit** AmEx, DC, Disc, MC, V. **Main course** lunch $13-$20; dinner $16-$30.

The dining room at this historic inn can be a bit off-putting: it's very formal. But if you can get past the décor, you're in for a treat. Chef Susan McCreight Lindeborg, who's passionate about local and seasonal ingredients, seems to meld whatever feels right, from the sweet potato tart with Virginia country ham and pecans to a grilled salmon with Indian spices and macadamia rice. Many items, such as rabbit or catfish, will get a Southern infusion – not to mention the hush puppies that accompany the soft-shell crabs in summer. Whatever you choose, you'll be able to sense the amount of care and detail that goes into Lindeborg's food. One last note: don't leave without tasting some of pastry chef Valerie Hill's lemon chess pie.

Rupperts

1017 Seventh Street, NW, between New York Avenue & L Street, Downtown (783 0699). Mount Vernon Square-UDC Metro. **Lunch** 11.30am-2.30pm Thur. **Dinner** 6-10pm Tue-Thur; 6-11pm Fri, Sat. **Credit** AmEx, DC, MC, V. **Main course** $25.

Chef John Cochran continues to surprise local foodies with his daily-changing menu that's both innovative and sublime. There might be wood pigeon, wild ramps (onions), bison or corbia. One never knows, except for a couple of things: the food is all locally grown or raised and the servers, who are extremely well schooled on the details and nuances of this unconventional menu, make a newcomer feel at ease. All distressed grandeur inside, Rupperts occupies a nondescript storefront in a somewhat shaky neighbourhood, so take a taxi.

Tabard Inn

1739 N Street, NW, between Connecticut Avenue & 17th Street, Dupont Circle (785 1277). Dupont Circle Metro. **Breakfast** 7-10am Mon-Fri; 8-10am Sat; 8-9.30am Sun. **Lunch** 11.30am-2.30pm Mon-Fri. **Dinner** 6-10pm Mon-Thur, Sun; 6-10.30pm Fri, Sat. **Brunch** 11am-2.30pm Sat; 10.30am-2.30pm Sun. **Credit** AmEx, DC, MC, V. **Main course** breakfast $3-$8; lunch $9-$15; dinner $18-$28; brunch $5-$15.

The food can vary in quality here, mainly because the chefs don't seem to stay. That said, the Tabard is still a great restaurant. It owes much of the draw to the cosy, grandma's living room ambience, not to mention the glorious, enclosed outdoor courtyard that opens in spring. It's located in one of the oldest hotels in DC (opened in 1924) and the lounge is popular for cocktails. Much of the produce is grown on the Tabard Farm in the Virginia countryside and the wine list is one of the most diverse in town.

American: regional

Americana

Ben's Chili Bowl

1213 U Street, NW, between 12th & 13th Streets, U Street/14th Street Corridor (667 0909). U Street-Cardozo Metro. **Open** 6am-2am Mon-Thur; 7am-4am Fri, Sat; noon-8pm Sun. **No credit cards. Main course** $2-$5.

This is a family business, serving chilli dogs and chilli half-smokes. Big, greasy heartburns waiting to happen. No matter. This was one of the few places in the area to survive the 1968 civil rights riots. Go and be part of the scenery: Bill Cosby does whenever he strolls into town. With Motown playing on the jukebox and the counter stools swivelling, Ben's is a sure thing.

Sholl's Colonial Cafeteria

1990 K Street, NW, at 20th Street, Foggy Bottom (296 3065). Farragut West Metro. **Breakfast** 7-10am, **lunch** 11am-2.30pm, **dinner** 4-8pm, Mon-Sat. **Brunch** 8am-3pm Sun. **No credit cards. Main course** $3-$6.

Now in its 71st year, Sholl's is the longest operating restaurant in Washington. The food offers traditional, homespun American classics – meatloaf, creamed corn, cherry pie – and you work your tray through the line and make your selections. But with a recent rent increase imposed by their landlord, Sholl's may soon shut down. The community has banded together to form SOS (Save Our Sholl's), but despite the publicity, the future of this local institution looks uncertain.

Cajun/Creole

Bardia's New Orleans Café

2412 18th Street, NW, at Columbia Road, Woodley Park (234 0420). Woodley Park-Zoo Metro. **Open** 11am-10pm Mon-Fri; 10am-10pm Sat, Sun. **Credit** AmEx, MC, V. **Main course** $4-$12.

Weekend 'brunch' – when there is an open menu all day – is the best reason to hang out at this cosy nook. Order a plate of beignets, linger over chicory-flavoured coffee and try one of the Creole-style omelettes. The red beans and rice will make you yearn for Jazz Fest.

Southwestern

Red Sage

605 14th Street, NW, at F Street, Downtown (638 4444). Metro Center Metro. **Open** 11.30am-11.30pm Mon-Sat; 4.30-11pm Sun. **Credit** AmEx, MC, V. **Main course** ground level $7-$16; basement $19-$29.

Originally conceived by Mark Miller, the chef-turned-restaurateur of Coyote Café fame, Red Sage is an East Coast outpost for those still fascinated by Santa Fe and the Southwestern thing. The restaurant's design alone is worth a stop – it's like a set for a play – with lots of regional touches such as checked napkins, colourful dishware and bolo-wearing servers. In the basement dining area, the scene is much more formal (and more expensive); on the ground level, you can choose from a selection of quesadillas, fajitas and the like, all of which beautifully complement a margarita (there's a broad selection of tequila). A good pitstop after a visit to one of the nearby museums.

Southern/Soul/BBQ

Florida Avenue Grill

1100 Florida Avenue, NW, at 11th Street, U Street/14th Street Corridor (265 1586). U Street-Cardozo Metro. **Open** 6am-9pm Tue-Sat. **Credit** AmEx, DC, Disc, MC, V. **Main course** $8-$13.

This is close to a real diner, but with a down-home Southern bent. A bit of a local institution not too far from Howard University, Florida Grill is where you might go if (a) you're homesick for your mama's greens and macaroni and cheese, (b) you want to run into Janet Reno, who's known to come in for breakfast regularly on Saturdays, or (c) you want to see black and white folks connect with each other in an otherwise pretty segregated city. It's worth a spin on one of the counter stools.

Georgia Brown's

950 15th Street, NW, between I & K Streets, Downtown (393 4499). McPherson Square Metro/ L2 bus. **Open** 11.30am-10.30pm Mon-Thur; 11.30am-11.30pm Fri; 5.30-11.30pm Sat; 5.30-10.30pm Sun. **Brunch** 11.30am-2.30pm Sun. **Credit** AmEx, DC, Disc, MC, V. **Main course** $15-$22; prix-fixe brunch $21.95.

Georgia Brown's offers low-country cuisine with modern twists. The fried chicken comes as a traditional platter with greens, cornbread and mashed potatoes, but also in a salad with pecans, blue cheese, lots of greens and a buttermilk dressing. There are biscuits, sweet tea and grits with shrimp, but gussied up in very downtown digs. Power lunchers, including local sports celebs and politicos, often dominate during the day. The bar, where a bourbon might be nice, often buzzes after work. The brunch, with all the Southern trimmings, works well for big eaters.

Rocklands

2418 Wisconsin Avenue, NW, at Calvert Street, Upper Northwest (333 2558). Foggy Bottom-GWU Metro, then 30, 32, 34, 35, 36 bus. **Open** 11.30am-10pm Mon-Fri; 11am-10pm Sat; 11am-9pm Sun. **Credit** AmEx. **Main course** $4-$6.

A polished version of a barbecue shack, Rocklands offers a bit of everything, from pulled pork and ribs to whole chickens. At the Glover Park branch, the seating is at a long communal table, where there are peanuts to shell and various hot sauces to share. Side dishes include baked beans, corn pudding, slaw, potato salad and all the stuff of a good picnic. The Arlington branch has a bar, but no alcohol is served at Glover Park.

Branch: 4000 North Fairfax Drive, Arlington, VA (703 528 9663).

Vidalia

1990 M Street, NW, between 19th & 20th Streets, Dupont Circle (659 1990). Dupont Circle Metro. **Lunch** 11.30am-2.30pm Mon-Fri. **Dinner** 5.30-10pm Mon-Fri; 5.30-10.30pm Sat; 5-9pm Sun (closed Sun July-Aug). **Credit** AmEx, DC, Disc, MC, V. **Main course** lunch $12-$18; dinner $18-$29.

Jeffrey Buben's Southern-infused menu has long attracted power-lunching Washingtonians to this underground dining room. Buben, who also runs French bistro **Bis** (*see p145*) across town, has become something of a culinary staple in town. There's Southern and local specialities, including grits, biscuits, crab cakes and Shenandoah trout. By the way, Vidalia is named after Vidalia onions, a very sweet variety grown in Georgia.

Tex-Mex

Austin Grill

2404 Wisconsin Avenue, NW, at Calvert Street, Upper Northwest (337 8080). Foggy Bottom-GWU Metro, then 30, 32, 34, 35, 36 bus. **Open** 11.30am-10pm Mon; 11.30am-11pm Tue-Thur; 11am-midnight Fri, Sat; 11am-10pm Sun. **Credit** AmEx, DC, Disc, MC, V. **Main course** $7-$14.

The Tex-Mex cousin of **Jaleo** (*see p152*), Austin Grill fills the gap between upscale dining and fast-food scarfing. Festive in that roadhouse-dancing armadillo sort of way, it's good for families who don't want to deal with high-maintenance restaurants and for singles who are looking for chow that doesn't interrupt meeting potential suitors. There are plenty of tequilas to try and everything comes with chips and salsa, of course.

Branches: 750 E Street, NW, Penn Quarter (393 3776); 7278 Woodmont Avenue, Bethesda, MD (301 656 1366); 801 King Street, Alexandria, VA (703 684 8969).

The Burro

1621 Connecticut Avenue, NW, at R Street, Dupont Circle (483 6861). Dupont Circle Metro. **Open** 11am-10pm Mon-Thur, Sun; 11am-11pm Fri, Sat. **Credit** MC, V. **Main course** $4-$6.

One of the best in the cheap-and-good category, the Burro consistently puts out fresh and healthy-tasting Tex-Mex. Far from serving the greasy stereotype of larded-up refried beans, owner Tony Brown has gone to great lengths to bring out simple flavours in his tacos, burritos and fajitas. It's counter service, with plasticware and a far from elegant ambience, but what do you expect for less than seven bucks?

Branch: 2000 Pennsylvania Avenue, NW, Foggy Bottom (293 9449).

Chinese

City Lights of China

1731 Connecticut Avenue, NW, between R & S Streets, Dupont Circle (265 6688). Dupont Circle Metro. **Open** 11.30am-10.30pm Mon-Thur; 11.30am-11pm Fri; noon-11pm Sat; noon-10.30pm Sun. **Credit** AmEx, DC, Disc, MC, V. **Main course** $9-$40.

For years, this restaurant was a local favourite and always jammed, known for its consistency and variety (although not particularly adventurous), as well as its proximity to neighbourhood cinemas and shopping. When the management changed, the locals complained, but City Lights remains a decent choice to get quick westernised Chinese and a beer, before or after the movies.

Full Kee

509 H Street, NW, between Fifth & Sixth Streets, Judiciary Square Area (371 2233). Gallery Place-Chinatown Metro. **Open** 11am-1am Mon-Thur, Sun; 11am-3am Fri, Sat. **No credit cards. Main course** lunch $5-$6; dinner $8-$16.

Full Kee is a throwback to pre-MCI Center Chinatown, to the days before the landlords squeezed out the Chinese business owners to make way for sleek chains trying to capitalise on the sports-fan traffic. The restaurant is rather dank, but the food, especially the soups and stews, is good, cheap and unapologetically authentic. (Yes, dear, that man *is* eating intestine.) Full Key has no alcohol licence, but you can bring your own beer or wine. It stays open late, so it's also popular with local chefs just getting off work.

Hope Key

3131 Wilson Boulevard, at Highland Street, Arlington, VA (243 8388). Clarendon Metro. **Open** 11am-1am Mon-Thur, Sun; 11am-2am Fri, Sat. **Credit** AmEx, DC, Disc, MC, V. **Main course** $5-$25.

A no-nonsense place with red leatherette booths, a smattering of round tables and crispy ducks hanging in the front window. Always busy and open late for those after-midnight cravings, there's something here for the culinarily meek as well as for the more adventurous. If you call ahead, the staff can even prepare a banquet of your choice – a little dim sum, some of the heavenly, shrimp dumpling soup, some sautéed watercress, whatever you like.

Ethiopian

There are more Ethiopian restaurants in DC than in any other US city. Most seem to be concentrated on Adams Morgan's 18th Street, which could easily be called 'Little Ethiopia'. The menus don't vary much between restaurants, so what you'll be choosing is atmosphere and experience.

You'll be eating with your hands, with the help of the sour, spongy, scoopable bread called injera. Food is served family-style on a big silver platter rather than on individual plates, and this acts as both serving dish and launch pad for injera-scooping. You'll find regular, Western-style seating at a few places, including Meskerem; also the option of sitting at a traditional table that looks like a basket, with cushions for chairs. Dishes are meat-oriented, but there's always something for meatless eaters, often curried.

Many of these restaurants also function as bars and clubs, so if extracurricular dining is not your thing, head for quieter **Meskerem**. But if you want to hang out with the local Ethiopian community, catch a soccer game on the tube or listen to live reggae while chowing down, head for **Addis Ababa**, **Fasika's**, **Awash** or **Red Sea**.

Addis Ababa

2106 18th Street, NW, between Wyoming Avenue & California Street, Adams Morgan (232 6092). Dupont Circle Metro, then L2 bus or Woodley Park-Zoo Metro, then 90, 91, 92, 93, 96 bus. **Open** 11am-midnight Mon-Thur; 11am-3am Fri-Sun. **Credit** AmEx, DC, Disc, MC, V. **Main course** $7-$12.

Bis: *famed for its fabulous zinc bar and classic French bistro food.*

Awash
2218 18th Street, NW, between Kalorama Road & Wyoming Avenue, Adams Morgan (588 8181). Dupont Circle Metro, then L2 bus or Woodley Park-Zoo Metro, then 90, 91, 92, 93, 96 bus. **Open** 11am-2am daily. **Credit** DC, Disc, MC, V. **Main course** $8-$10.

Fasika's
2447 18th Street, NW, between Columbia & Belmont Roads, Adams Morgan (797 7673). Dupont Circle Metro, then L2 bus or Woodley Park-Zoo Metro, then 90, 91, 92, 93, 96 bus. **Open** 5-11.30pm Mon-Thur; 5pm-1am Fri; noon-1am Sat; noon-11.30pm Sun. **Credit** AmEx, DC, MC, V. **Main course** $8-$22.

Harambe
1771 U Street, NW, at 18th Street, Adams Morgan (332 6435). Dupont Circle Metro, then L2 bus or Woodley Park-Zoo Metro, then 90, 91, 92, 93, 96 bus. **Open** noon-1am Mon-Thur, Sun; noon-2am Fri, Sat. **Credit** AmEx, DC, Disc, MC, V. **Main course** $5-$10.

Lion's Den
2427 18th Street, NW, between Columbia & Belmont Roads, Adams Morgan (265 6088). Dupont Circle Metro, then L2 bus or Woodley Park-Zoo Metro, then 90, 91, 92, 93, 96 bus. **Open** 7pm-2am daily. **No credit cards. Main course** $6-$13.

Meskerem
2434 18th Street, NW, between Columbia & Belmont Roads, Adams Morgan (462 4100). Dupont Circle Metro, then L2 bus or Woodley Park-Zoo Metro, then 90, 91, 92, 93, 96 bus. **Open** noon-midnight Mon-Thur, Sun; noon-1am Fri, Sat. **Credit** AmEx, DC, MC, V. **Main course** $9-$12.

Red Sea Restaurant
2463 18th Street, NW, between Columbia & Belmont Roads, Adams Morgan (483 5000). Dupont Circle Metro, then L2 bus or Woodley Park-Zoo Metro, then 90, 91, 92, 93, 96 bus. **Open** 11.30am-11.30pm daily. **Credit** AmEx, DC, Disc, MC, V. **Main course** $7-$11.

Fish

Pesce
2016 P Street, NW, between 20th & 21st Streets, Dupont Circle (466 3474). Dupont Circle Metro. **Lunch** 11.30am-2.30pm Mon-Fri; 12-2.30pm Sat. **Dinner** 5.30-10pm Mon-Thur; 5.30-10.30pm Fri, Sat; 5-9.30pm Sun. **Credit** AmEx, DC, Disc, MC, V. **Main course** $14-$19.

Using fish as the medium, the menu can go in many and any direction, from Italian to Scandinavian. Pesce is a blackboard, daily-changing menu operation, reflecting market availability and freshness. The choices are many; the simpler dishes are best. It's often crowded and noisy, the tables are close together and it's not the most relaxing place to dine, but if you only want fish, it's a good catch. You can also buy fresh fish here.

French

Bis
Hotel George, 15 E Street, NW, between North Capitol Street & New Jersey Avenue, Union Station & Around (661 2700). Union Station Metro. **Breakfast** 7am-10am daily. **Lunch** 11am-2.30pm Mon-Fri. **Dinner** 5.30-10.30pm daily. **Brunch** 11am-2.30pm Sat, Sun. **Credit** AmEx, DC, Disc, MC, V. **Main course** lunch $13-$15; dinner $17-$22; brunch $7-$18.

Sit at the zinc bar and drink up the atmosphere. Chef Jeffrey Buben (of Southern-style Vidalia; *see p143*) serves up classic bistro fare, including steak frites, frisée and lardons, foie gras terrine and an outstanding rotisserie chicken, which comes out crispy and redolent of garlic and thyme, served with watercress and more of those wonderful frites. A hop from Union Station and within earshot of the Capitol building, Bis is ideal for a special occasion dinner, a power lunch or simply taking it all in – martini in hand – at that gorgeous bar.

Bistro Français

3128 M Street, between Wisconsin Avenue & 31st Street, Georgetown (338 3830). Foggy Bottom-GWU Metro, then 30, 32, 34, 35, 36 bus. **Open** 11am-3am Mon-Thur, Sun; 11am-4am Fri, Sat. **Credit** AmEx, DC, JCB, MC, V. **Main course** $13-$20.

Aside from its classic steak frites and rotisserie chicken, which have kept the locals happy for years, Bistro Français stays up later than almost any other place in town. In fact, it's known as a late-night pitstop for local chefs after they close their own kitchens. It's also very popular with young Latin and European expats and at weekends you often have to wait until 2am for a table.

Café La Ruche

1039 31st Street, NW, between M & K Streets, Georgetown (965 2684). Foggy Bottom-GWU Metro, then 30, 32, 34, 35, 36 bus. **Open** 11.30am-11.30pm Mon-Thur; 11.30am-midnight Fri; 10am-midnight Sat; 10am-11.30pm Sun. **Brunch** 10am-3pm Sat, Sun. **Credit** AmEx, MC, V. **Main course** $7-$15; prix-fixe brunch $9.95.

Quaint from the outside, a little more hip on the inside, La Ruche is a comfort zone for Francophiles who don't want to drop a big wad of cash. The food is café-style, with choices in the quiche/sandwich/salad range, plus a smattering of daily entrée specials that might include moules or canard a l'orange. Desserts, which include a variety of traditional tarts, are made in-house. Brunch is popular, especially in the garden when the weather co-operates.

Gerard's Place

915 15th Street, NW, between I & K Streets, Downtown (737 4445). McPherson Square Metro. **Lunch** 11.30am-2pm Mon-Fri. **Dinner** 5.30-10pm Mon-Sat. **Credit** AmEx, DC, Disc, MC, V. **Main course** lunch $20-$24; dinner $25-$30.

Frenchman Gerard Pangaud is one of only two Michelin-starred chefs in town. The staff at his flagship restaurant often have their own ideas, but Pangaud's cooking is generally refined without being off-putting or kookily intellectual. He allows seasonal ingredients to speak for themselves, and his best dishes are expressions of one of the States' finer French culinary technicians. If the weather is mild, ask for a seat on the sidewalk patio.

La Fourchette

2429 18th Street, NW, between Belmont & Columbia Roads, Adams Morgan (332 3077). Dupont Circle Metro, then L2 bus or Woodley Park-Zoo Metro, then 90, 91, 92, 93, 96. **Open** 11.30am-10.30pm Mon-Thur; 11.30am-11pm Fri; 4-11pm Sat; 4-10pm Sun. **Credit** AmEx, DC, MC, V. **Main course** $11-$23.

It's French but without the fuss and pretentiousness. Bistro-style dishes, including pâté maison, onion tart, house-smoked salmon, entrecôte and vol-au-vents, are predictable but done right and priced moderately. This is a more casual alternative to some of the fancier French restaurants in town, and a popular neighbourhood haunt.

Lespinasse

St Regis Hotel, 923 16th Street, NW, at K Street, Downtown (879 6900). McPherson Square Metro. **Breakfast** 7-10.30am Mon-Fri; 7-11am Sat, Sun. **Lunch** noon-2pm Tue-Fri. **Dinner** 6-10pm Tue-Sat. **Credit** AmEx, DC, Disc, MC, V. **Main course** breakfast $9-$19; lunch $17-$20; dinner $24-$33; prix-fixe 3-course lunch $36; 4-course dinner $48, 6-course dinner $85.

Lespinasse isn't just a fancy hotel restaurant, it's a special-occasion destination. The dining room alone, decorated in velvet and with hand-painted ceilings, is reason to visit, even if it's just for afternoon tea (served Thursday to Sunday). Chef Sandro Gamba, who was making heads turn in New York City, has continued the tradition of the elaborate prix-fixe menu. Complete with an in-house sommelier, this is the kind of restaurant where you'll drop gobs of cash but will remember your fancy experience for some time to come.

Marcel's

2401 Pennsylvania Avenue, NW, at 24th Street, Foggy Bottom (296 1166). Foggy Bottom-GWU Metro. **Open** 11.30am-2.30pm, 5.30-10pm, Mon-Thur; 11.30am-2.30pm, 5.30-11pm, Fri, Sat; 5.30-10pm Sun. **Credit** AmEx, DC, MC, V. **Main course** lunch $13-$21; dinner $15-$28.

Chef Robert Wiedmaier (who named his new restaurant after his baby boy) calls his food 'French with a Belgian flair'. Subtle influences are evident on the extensive menu: the mussels are à gratin with gruyère, for example, and the entrecôte is paired with a shallot tart rather than with the traditional frites. The dining room is open and spacious, with an all-male waiting staff in formal attire. With one of the few in-house sommeliers in town, Marcel's is a very fitting special-occasion restaurant.

Michel Richard Citronelle

Latham Hotel, 3000 M Street, NW, at 30th Street, Georgetown (625 2150). Foggy Bottom-GWU Metro. **Breakfast** 6.30-10.30am daily. **Lunch** noon-2pm Mon-Fri. **Dinner** 6.30-10pm Mon-Thur, Sun; 6.30-10.30pm Sat. **Credit** AmEx, DC, Disc, MC, V. **Main course** breakfast $8-$13; lunch $16-$20; dinner $27-$35.

Michel Richard helped set the pace for Southern Cali cuisine in the early 1980s with Citrus, in Los Angeles. After a $2-million makeover of Citronelle in 1998, complete with a 'mood wall' and 5,300-bottle wine collection, the former pastry chef has been making a similar impression in DC. Richard's affection for crisp textures – try his shrimp wrapped in shredded filo, or a 'chocolate bar' that's like a KitKat made with really good ingredients – has earned him the nickname Captain Crunch. The food is serious (many of the dishes begin life as sketches), but it's the wit that Richard projects on to the plate that ultimately make his meals worthy of their high prices. Décor and ambience are sleek, formal and spendy.

Fusion

New Heights

2317 Calvert Street, NW, at Connecticut Avenue, Woodley Park (234 4110). Woodley Park-Zoo Metro. **Open** 5.30-10pm Mon-Thur; 5.30-11pm Fri, Sat; 11am-2.30pm, 5.30-10pm, Sun. **Credit** AmEx, DC, Disc, MC, V. **Main course** $17-$28.

You eat upstairs at New Heights, and the tables are spaced far apart enough for it to feel intimate and exclusive; it's a great place for a date. Service is extremely accommodating and knowledgeable. Chef John Wabeck continues the restaurant's fusion tradition, most of which works; typical dishes include risotto with Virginia Smithfield ham and wild mushrooms, and seared wahoo served over a lentil dhal and aubergines in a lemongrass broth. The menu changes seasonally, so there's always something interesting to look forward to.

Indian

Bombay Club

815 Connecticut Avenue, NW, between H & I Streets, Downtown (659 3727). Farragut West Metro. **Open** 11.30am-2.30pm, 6-10.30pm, Mon-Thur; 11.30am-2.30pm, 6-11pm, Fri; 6-11pm Sat; 11.30am-2.30pm, 5.30-9pm, Sun. **Credit** AmEx, DC, MC, V. **Main course** $13-$19; prix-fixe Sunday champagne brunch $18.50.

By far the swankiest Indian restaurant in town, Bombay Club is as known for its elite setting as it is for its food. Located a block from the White House, it attracts Washington's money-makers and decision-makers. There's no sense of home-grown ethnic dining here; the aesthetic is British colonial, and you can have a Pimm's Cup at the bar to prove it.

Delhi Dhaba

2424 Wilson Boulevard, at Barton Street, Arlington, VA (703 524 0008). Court House Metro. **Open** 11am-10pm Mon-Thur, Sun; 11am-11pm Fri, Sat. **Credit** AmEx, Disc, MC, V. **Main course** $7.

This no-frills, cafeteria-style eatery presents consistently tasty Indian fare at budget prices. From chicken tandoori to goat biriani, entrées top out at $8 and always come with a choice of two hearty side dishes. Vegetarians are more than welcome here.

Branch: 7236 Woodmont Avenue, Bethesda (301 718 0008).

Heritage India

2400 Wisconsin Avenue, NW, at Calvert Street, Upper Northwest (333 3120). Foggy Bottom-GWU Metro, then 30, 32, 34, 35, 36 bus. **Lunch** 11.30am-2.30pm Mon-Fri, Sun. **Dinner** 5.30-10.30pm Mon-Fri, Sun; 5.30-11pm Sat. **Credit** AmEx, Disc, MC, V. **Main course** lunch $8-$11; dinner $7-$22.

Until Heritage opened in early 1999, the choices for Indian restaurants were either very high-end (Bombay Club) or very low-end, local holes in the wall (Delhi Dhaba). Now you can have the best of both worlds: very high-quality, complex-flavoured Indian food (the chef is a Bombay Club alumnus) and an interesting wine list, but without the worry of getting dressed up. Vegetarians will love this place, where meatless dishes make up about a third of the menu, including the fabulous begumi khazana (the queen's meal), a feast served on a silver platter. Try the gargantuan, succulent tandoori prawns.

Taste of DC

Food lovers rejoice. 'Taste of DC', the largest annual outdoor food and music festival on the East Coast takes place in Washington. It runs for three days over the Columbus Day weekend and takes place on the six-block stretch of Pennsylvania Avenue between Ninth and 14th Streets, which is blocked off for pedestrians, sampling the fare of more than 40 restaurants from around town. You buy tickets which are traded for portions of food from the restaurants' booths – the downside is that it's pricey ($1-$4.50 per item) and you'll be eating out of a paper cup. But there's also live music, kids' activities and good vibes – and the proceeds benefit various charities.

For more information, call 724 4093 or, as the event approaches, check the website www.washington.org.

Italian & pizza

Coppi's

1414 U Street, NW, between 14th & 15th Streets, U Street/14th Street Corridor (319 7773). U Street-Cardozo Metro. **Open** 5-11pm Mon-Thur; 4pm-midnight Fri, Sat; 4-11pm Sun. **Credit** AmEx, Disc, MC, V. **Main course** $9-$16.

Historically black U Street has been through some rough times but in the early 1990s began to experience some gentrification. This pizza joint was one of the first pioneers to do business here and so became known as a yuppie enclave. It's small and cramped but packs in the crowds. Cycling paraphernalia and photos are everywhere, reflecting the passion of owner Pierre Mattia. The pizza is expensive and a bit pretentious but very tasty, with liberal sprinklings of fresh herbs. Pierre and his wife, chef Elizabeth Bright, have also opened a much larger space in Cleveland Park, to accommodate even more yuppies.

Branch: **Coppi's Vigorelli** 3421 Connecticut Avenue, NW, Cleveland Park (244 6437).

Eating near the Mall

Traipsing around the attractions on the National Mall certainly does a number on your appetite, but, unfortunately, the choice of places to eat within the area is paltry, limited principally to museum cafeterias and departmental canteens in federal buildings, many of which are open to the public at least some of the time.

Starting at the east end of the Mall, the **US Capitol** has 14 eating places, which are open during the week. Some of these are closed to the public at various times (depending on how busy Congress is – or how hungry it is, we suppose). The two most likely to be open most often are the Senate Chef, between the Dirksen and Hart Office Buildings, which serves burgers and sandwiches until at least 5pm, and the public/press dining room in the main building, whose hours change daily. The House dining room is mainly for members of Congress but is also open to the public from 8 to 11am and 1.30 to 2.30pm.

The **Library of Congress**, which is a city unto itself with three buildings, has a cafeteria on the sixth floor of the Madison Building. It's open Monday to Friday, from 12.30 to 3pm. The **US Supreme Court** cafeteria is open for breakfast (7.30-10.30am) and lunch (11.30am-2pm) on weekdays; the snack bar from 10.30am-3.30pm.

Further west along the Mall, the Cascade Café (open 10am-4.30pm daily) on the concourse-level of the **National Gallery of Art** (Constitution Avenue, between Fourth and Seventh Streets, is a relatively new addition, offering lovely salads and sandwiches. Nearby is the Cascade Buffet (open 10am-3pm Monday-Saturday, 11am-4pm Sunday) and, on the ground level of the West Building, at the Sixth Street entrance, is the Garden Café restaurant (open 11.30am-3pm Monday-Saturday, noon-4pm Sunday; details of all three on 215 5966). There's also a snack bar in the basement of the **National Archives**.

The airy new Atrium Café on the ground floor of the **National Museum of Natural History** (Tenth Street and Constitution Avenue; 357 2700), open 10am-4pm daily, until 7pm in June and August, is worth a visit. Opposite, the Commons Restaurant in the **Smithsonian Castle** (1000 Jefferson Drive; 786 1229) is open to the public for buffet lunch on Saturdays (11am-2pm) and brunch on Sundays (11am-3pm); it's best to book in advance.

At the west end of the Mall, options are very limited: apart from refreshment kiosks at the **Lincoln Memorial** and **Jefferson Memorial**, which are open from about 8am-6pm and serve soft drinks, hot dogs and suchlike, you can try the Interior Cafeteria in the basement of the **Department of the Interior Museum** (1849 C Street), one block north of the Mall. It's open 7am-2.45pm Monday to Friday.

For less institutional options, you'll need to get off the Mall itself. Back at the east end, head north up Seventh Street. At the corner of Seventh and Indiana Avenue is a **Starbucks** (628 5044, open 7am-7pm daily) – they've got a cold case of prepared salads and sandwiches. One block north, at D Street, is **The Mark** (783 3133), chef Alison Swope's latest nouveau American venture, plus the adjoining **Markette**, the restaurant's takeaway extension that whips up sandwiches, cookies, fresh juices and prepared dinners. **Footnotes' a Café**, at Olsson's Books & Records (418 Seventh Street; 638 4882) is good for a java recharge.

At the corner of E Street is **Jaleo** (*see page 152*) for tapas, sangria and good energy; its Tex-Mex cousin **Austin Grill** (750 E Street; 393 3776) is just next door. Or pop into nuevo Latino **Café Atlantico** (*see page 151*) on Eighth Street, between D and E Streets, for upmarket nibbles and cocktails.

Further west on Pennsylvania Avenue you'll find **The Capital Grille** steakhouse (*see page 157*); **701 Restaurant** (at No.701; 393 0701) for caviar and attitude; and **Les Halles** (No.1201; 347 6848) for Parisian-style onglet frites and other French seasonal treats. And if you've had it up to here with fine dining and just want to shovel something down your gullet, hit **TGI Friday's** (628 8443), which is right next door, for burgers and sundry fried items.

Faccia Luna

2400 Wisconsin Avenue, NW, at Calvert Street, Upper Northwest (337 3132). Foggy Bottom-GWU Metro, then 30, 32, 34, 35, 36 bus. **Open** 11.30am-11pm Mon-Thur, Sun; 11.30am-midnight Fri, Sat. **Credit** AmEx, MC, V. **Main course** $8-$14.

Brick-oven pizzas with 20 different toppings, pastas made on the premises (dinner only) and rather simple sauces make up the menu at this Glover Park outpost. Dinner comes with a salad, and the prices are budget-oriented. There are booths for larger parties and plenty of beer on tap. Faccia Luna is nothing fabulous, just decent family fare in a neighbourhood setting.

Branch: 2909 Wilson Boulevard, Arlington, VA (703 276 3099).

Galileo

1110 21st Street, NW, between L & M Streets, Foggy Bottom (293 7191). Farragut North or Foggy Bottom-GWU Metro. **Open** 11.30am-2pm, 5.30-10pm, Mon-Thur; 11.30am-2pm, 5.30-10.30pm, Fri; 5.30-10.30pm Sat; 5.30-10pm Sun. **Credit** AmEx, DC, Disc, MC, V. **Main course** lunch $15-$20; dinner $20-$30.

In DC's haute-cuisine conscious circles, Galileo's name still gets dropped more frequently than it probably should. Yes, the restaurant was established by celebrity chef Roberto Donna and, yes, the menu relies on Mediterranean stalwarts for traditionally based offerings. However, reputation seems to have replaced effort recently as the overpriced meals no longer live up to their past splendour. The chef's fixed menu is your best bet in terms of price.

Il Radicchio

223 Pennsylvania Avenue, SE, between Second & Third Streets, Capitol Hill (547 5114). Capitol South Metro. **Open** 11.30am-10pm Mon-Thur; 11.30am-11pm Fri, Sat; 5-10pm Sun. **Credit** AmEx, DC, MC, V. **Main course** $10-$15.

The bargain basement of chef Roberto Donna (known more for his very pricey flagship **Galileo**; *see p149*), Il Radicchio is where to get fed rather than enlightened. Pasta here is a matching game: you pick a sauce (which is brought to table in a sort of gravy boat) and you pick a pasta, which comes under separate cover. Apply sauce to pasta. There's also roasted pork panini and a variety of trattoria-style pizzas, which are delicious.

Branches: 1211 Wisconsin Avenue, NW, Georgetown (337 2627); 1509 17th Street, NW, Dupont Circle (986 2627); 1801 Clarendon Boulevard, Arlington, VA (703 276 2627).

Pearl

2228 18th Street, NW, at Kalorama Road, Adams Morgan (328 0846). Dupont Circle Metro, then L2 bus or Woodley Park-Zoo Metro, then 90, 91, 92, 93, 96 bus. **Open** 6.30-9pm Mon, Sun; 6.30-10.30pm Tue-Thur; 6.30-11pm Fri, Sat. **Credit** AmEx, MC, V. **Main course** $12-$20.

Upon entering, you'll think 'bar'. But the small café tables are there for chowing down and if you like dining in a cosy, loungy atmosphere, Pearl is a good bet. The menu is an eclectic mix: Italian seems to be the main influence, with lots of olive-oil spritzes, pancetta and asiago (an Italian cheese), but it's fused with a mélange of items, including cranberries, oyster mushrooms and roasted pears.

Millie & Al's

2440 18th Street, NW, between U & V Streets, Adams Morgan (387 8131). Dupont Circle Metro, then L2 bus or Woodley Park-Zoo Metro, then 90, 91, 92, 93, 96 bus. **Open** 4pm-1am Mon-Thur; 4pm-3am Fri, Sat. **Credit** MC, V. **Main course** about $5.

Locals know that when they're in the mood for a good old-fashioned pizza with nothing fancy on top, they should head for this no-frills neighbourhood bar. The dough is their own make, the price is right and what could be better than oozing cheese over a couple of Rolling Rocks? *See also p166* **Bars**.

Obelisk

2029 P Street, NW, between 20th & 21st Streets, Dupont Circle (872 1180). Dupont Circle Metro. **Open** 6-10pm Tue-Sat. **Credit** DC, MC, V. **Main course** prix-fixe five-course dinner $47-$49.

Chef Peter Pastan owns this prix-fixe-only trattoria as well as next door's Pizzeria Paradiso, but it's here where Pastan's purist sensibilities really shine. With just 12 tables (reservations are essential), the kitchen is really able to focus on each table's four-course meal. Pastan, who makes his own butter, vinegar and breadsticks, highlights various regions of Italy, depending on the seasonal availability of ingredients. Preparation is generally simple and authentic to its place of origin. A very special treat.

Pasta Mia

1790 Columbia Road, NW, at 18th Street, Adams Morgan (328 9114). Dupont Circle Metro, then L2 bus or Woodley Park-Zoo Metro, then 90, 91, 92, 93, 96 bus. **Open** 6-10.30pm Mon-Sat. **Credit** MC, V. **Main course** $7-$10.

Red checked tablecloths and Frank Sinatra or Tony Bennett from the speakers sets you up for an inexpensive, homegrown Italian dinner, complete with a carafe of house red and a basket of crusty bread. If you don't like pasta, you're out of luck. They do it 29 different ways here, just like mamma. And don't get wise and suggest a substitution to the kitchen. The menu is set – capisce?

Pizzeria Paradiso

2029 P Street, NW, between 20th & 21st Streets, Dupont Circle (223 1245). Dupont Circle Metro. **Open** 11.30am-11pm Mon-Thur; 11.30am-midnight Fri; 11am-midnight Sat; noon-10pm Sun. **Credit** DC, MC, V. **Main course** $7-$16.

A nice restaurant that sells mostly pizza – but please, it's wood-burning pizza. Peter Pastan of Obelisk also owns this one-roomed eatery, and in true Pastan form, the pizza is made with great care and detail. Toppings include pancetta, gorgonzola, potatoes and buffalo mozzarella.

Japanese

Atami

3155 Wilson Boulevard, at Henderson Road, Arlington, VA (703 522 4787). Clarendon Metro. **Open** 11am-10pm Tue-Thur; 11am-10.30pm Sat; 5-10pm Sun. **Credit** AmEx, MC, V. **Main course** $8-$14.

With red booths lined up against the far wall, this feels a bit like a neighbourhood diner. Atami is pretty easygoing, and most folks know it for its 'all you can eat' sushi for $25 (it's not on the menu; you have to ask). You can just keep ordering from the bar while taking your time in one of those booths, kicking back with some house sake. If you just can't eat $25 worth, they'll forgive you and charge you the per-piece price instead. Non-sushi fans can expect some Vietnamese influences, including rice vermicelli with grilled meats, peanut sauce and curries. It's very convenient for the Clarendon Metro stop.

Kaz Sushi Bistro

1915 I Street, NW, between 19th & 20th Streets, Foggy Bottom (530 5500). Farragut West Metro. **Open** 11.30am-2.30pm, 6-10pm, Mon-Fri; 6-10pm Sat. **Credit** AmEx, MC, V. **Main course** lunch $10-$16; dinner $12-$20.

Sushi king Kazuhiro Okochi, who made his mark at Sushi-Ko successfully melding Asian and Western ingredients, now has his own place in which to shine. The sushi is top-notch – the fish is consistently gorgeous and glistening, the rice has a bit of sweetness unlike anywhere else – and prepared by *atami* (sushi chefs) that will soon become your new best friends. There's also a bounty of wonderful cooked items, including Asian-style short ribs, ginger-cured duck confit and barbecued eel.

Makoto

4822 MacArthur Boulevard, NW, at Reservoir Road, Georgetown (298 6866). Dupont Circle Metro, then D4 bus. **Lunch** noon-2pm, **dinner** 6-10pm, Tue-Sun. **Credit** MC, V. **Main course** $40.

When you make a reservation (highly recommended for this very small space), you should be getting prepared for a very special experience. Entering Makoto is like entering a private home, where you must trade your shoes for slippers at the front door. Dinner is prix-fixe, a seemingly never-ending feast of delicate bites. The food is beautiful, clean and a great lesson in Japanese cuisine, from egg custards and seaweed to sashimi and aubergine.

Sushi-Ko

2309 Wisconsin Avenue, NW, between Calvert & W Streets, Upper Northwest (333 4187). Foggy Bottom-GWU Metro, then 30, 32, 34, 35, 36 bus. **Lunch** noon-2.30pm Tue-Fri. **Dinner** 6-10.30pm Mon-Thur; 6-11pm Fri; 5.30-11pm Sat; 5.30-10pm Sun. **Credit** AmEx, MC, V. **Main course** $10-$19.

Owner Daisuke Utagawa is committed to the fusion of Japanese and Western ingredients and techniques, as well as matching dishes with wines and premium sakes. His team in the kitchen also reflects this bicultural focus, led by chef Tetsuro Takanashi (who returned to Sushi-Ko in 1998) and locally based chef de cuisine Duncan Boyd. The recently renovated westernised décor is stylish, with simple lines and pastels. Known to have one of the best-quality sushi bars in town, this Sushi-Ko has been a mainstay in Washington for more than 20 years.

Sushi Taro

1503 17th Street, NW, at P Street, Dupont Circle (462 8999). Dupont Circle Metro. **Lunch** 11.30am-2pm Mon-Fri; noon-2.30pm Sat. **Dinner** 5.30-10pm Mon-Thur, Sun; 5.30-10.30pm Fri, Sat. **Credit** AmEx, DC, Disc, MC, V. **Main course** lunch $7-$15; dinner $13-$45.

With its open sushi bar and kitchen located almost as you enter, Sushi Taro is a hub of activity. It's always busy and a favourite with visiting Japanese journalists. Kimono-clad servers are sometimes so busy with larger groups that they forget the single diner. Perks include a hot towel as you're seated and a small dish of edamame (boiled, salted soybeans) to snack on while you wait for dinner to arrive. The menu, which is quite extensive, includes specialities such as live lobster sashimi, a prix-fixe dinner designed by the chef and ginger, green tea or sweet bean ice-cream made in-house.

Tono Sushi

2605 Connecticut Avenue, NW, at Calvert Street, Woodley Park (332 7300). Woodley Park-Zoo Metro. **Lunch** 11.30am-2.30pm Mon-Fri; noon-3pm Sat, Sun. **Dinner** 5-10.30pm Mon-Sat; 5.30-10pm Sun. **Credit** AmEx, MC, V. **Main course** lunch $7-$9; dinner $10-$20.

This is a small, cosy and dressed-in-red space, anchored by the sushi bar in the middle, with

Wine events

Although Washington is near northern Virginia, the centre of the state's thriving wine-growing region, Virginia wines have not yet achieved enough recognition to propel them into DC restaurants. A few vineyards, such as Barboursville (in Orange County), are producing more consistent wines every year, but even these are not yet widely available in shops or restaurants, so your best bet is to get in the car and go straight to the source (for wineries near DC, *see page 245* **Trips Out of Town**). For a list of vineyards and wine-related events, call Virginia Wine Marketing Program at 1-800 828 4637.

That's not to say that Washingtonians aren't wine savvy. In fact, there's a thriving tasting and events scene organised by two wine-tasting organisations – Tasting Society International and the Wine Tasting Association. Membership is not necessary; just call in advance to see what is coming up.

Tasting Society International

333 5588.

Hosts a combination of tastings with *Washington Post* columnist Michael Franz, wine dinners and social, theme-oriented events.

Website: www.tastedc.com

Wine Tasting Association

703 765 8229.

Events tend to be themed and very social, often held at various embassies and private social clubs, for a flat fee. You may also want to check with the Henley Park Hotel (638 5200), which hosts wine dinners year-round.

Website: www.winetasting.org

Western bar stools rather than the traditional Japanese low-seaters. The staff are friendly and eager to please, so the neighbours are becoming regulars. If you're not hankering for raw fish (which is reasonably priced and glistening), there's plenty of non-sushi items, from tempura and noodle soups to negimaki. Good for a quiet, low-key meal and very close to the National Zoo.

Latin/Caribbean

Café Atlantico

405 Eighth Street, NW, between D & E Streets, Penn Quarter (393 0812). Archives-Navy Memorial Metro. **Lunch** 11.30am-2.30pm Mon-Sat. **Dinner** 5.30-10pm Mon-Thur, Sun; 5.30-11pm Fri, Sat. **Credit** AmEx, DC, Disc, MC, V. **Main course** lunch $6-$14; dinner $7-$22.

The food here is fashionable pan-Latin, drawing from both South and Central American influences. The décor is self-consciously chi-chi. If you're a purist, then have a caipirihna and move on. If you like trends and fusion experimentation, then take off your coat and stay awhile. Or come for lunch on Saturday, when chef Jose Andres (also of **Jaleo**; *see p152*) offers 'Latino dim sum', a prix-fixe sampling of the menu.

Chi Cha Lounge

1624 U Street, NW, at 17th Street, U Street/14th Street Corridor (234 8400). U Street-Cardozo Metro/ 90, 91, 92, 93, L2 bus. **Open** 6pm-2am Mon-Thur, Sun; 6pm-3am Fri, Sat. **Credit** AmEx, DC, Disc, MC, V. **Tapas** $3.75-$7.50 each.

Don't let the ambience fool ya. Just as you're getting comfortable on one of the low-riding, 1970s-style couches, sipping on a cocktail and groovin' to the Latin/Cuban/Brazilian jazz mix, there's the menu to consider. In fact, Chi Cha may be the only place in town to sample tapas from the Andes. So we can learn a little something too, as we nibble on ceviche, tostados and llapingacho (potato pancake stuffed with cheese and yucca), and watch under-35 Washington at play. *See also p166* **Bars**.

Havana Breeze

1401 K Street, NW, at 14th Street, Downtown (789 1470). McPherson Square Metro. **Open** 11am-7pm Mon-Wed; 11am-midnight Thur, Fri; 5pm-midnight Sat. **Credit** AmEx, MC, V. **Main course** $5-$8.

Lunchtimers are drawn to the bright ground level, where you can order cubano sandwiches, frijoles negros, ropa vieja, croquetas, fried yucca and other Cuban snacks at the counter. Upstairs, the seating is more café-style, with a bar, in case you're craving a mojito, a cigarette and Spanish-dubbed TV.

Hibiscus Café

3401 K Street, NW, under Key Bridge, Georgetown (965 7170). Foggy Bottom-GWU Metro. **Open** 6-10.30pm Tue-Thur; 6pm-midnight Fri, Sat, 5.30-10pm Sun. **Credit** AmEx, DC, MC, V. **Main course** $11-$28.

You won't find this place from the address alone – it's tucked away under the K Street thruway, in the direction of the Potomac. But what you'll find is truly a Caribbean oasis, chockful of funky colours, furniture and island tunes. Chef Sharon Banks jerks all kinds of things, from quail to shark fish, which regulars know as 'shark and bake'.

Julia's Empañadas

2452 18th Street, NW, at Columbia Road, Adams Morgan (328 6232). Dupont Circle Metro, then L2 bus or Woodley Park-Zoo Metro, then 90, 91, 92, 93, 96 bus. **Open** 10am-10.30pm Mon-Thur, Sun; 10am-3am Fri, Sat. **No credit cards. Main course** $3-$4.

Big enough to warm your hands on a cold day, empanadas are the main attraction here. With at least eight varieties, including one for vegetarians and one for dessert, these mostly baked, warm, pie-like wonders are, as the sign says, 'made by hand… baked with love'. The Adams Morgan branch is open very late on weekends to nourish after-bar crowds. The two newer locations cater more to the lunchtime office market and have more table seating, particularly the Vermont Avenue branch.

Eating in Bethesda

If you head north on Wisconsin Avenue into the state of Maryland, you'll eventually end up in Bethesda. Unlike any other suburban enclave in the Washington area, Bethesda is a dining mecca. In the past few years, it has exploded with restaurants, and there are now more than 120, from Thai and Persian to Indian and Italian.

Parking is a nightmare, even with 17 parking lots and garages, so your best bet is to take the Metro to the Bethesda stop on the Red line (30 minutes from Downtown Washington) and then head east or west – it's an easily walkable area. Remember that the Metro shuts down at midnight.

The following restaurants are recommended: **Persimmon** (7003 Wisconsin Avenue; 301 654 9860) for eclectic American; **Matuba** (4918 Cordell Avenue; 301 652 7449) for sushi; **Tara Thai** (4828 Bethesda Avenue; 301 657 0488) for Thai curries; **Louisiana Express** (4921 Bethesda Avenue; 301 652 6945) for po-boys and étouffée; **Bacchus** (7945 Norfolk Avenue; 301 6571722) for Lebanese; and **The Pines of Rome** (4709 Hampden Lane, at Wisconsin Avenue; 301 657 8775) for unpretentious pasta.

For more information on Bethesda, call 301 215 6660 or visit website www.bethesda.org.

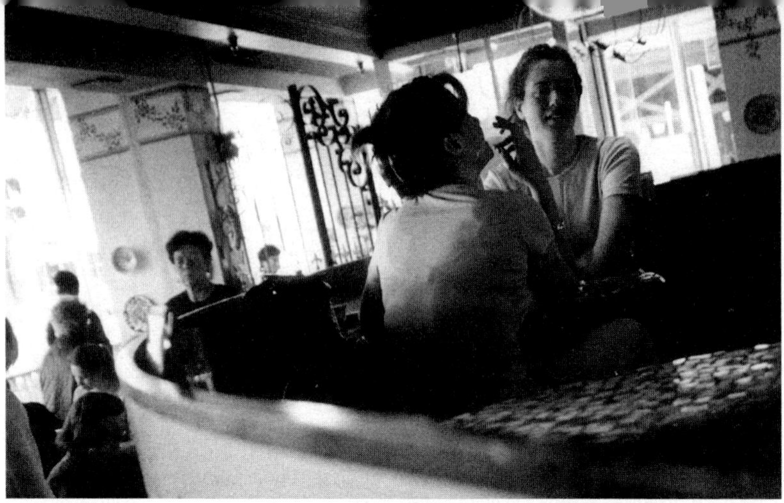

Visit **Jaleo** *for Spanish tapas, flamenco dancing and an upbeat atmosphere.*

Branches: 1000 Vermont Avenue, NW, Logan Circle (789 1878); 1221 Connecticut Avenue, NW, Dupont Circle (861 8828).

Lauriol Plaza

1801 18th Street, NW, at S Street, Dupont Circle (387 0035). Dupont Circle Metro. **Open** 11.30am-11pm daily. **Credit** AmEx, DC, Disc, MC, V. **Main course** $6-$17.

Lauriol Plaza has been the anchor of this neighbourhood corner for years, and its outdoor tables are particularly popular in warm weather. In fact, that's one of the best reasons to visit: to take in the sidewalk ambience over a margarita, chips and salsa or some ceviche. Because it's always crowded (you might think they were giving out prizes), the owners are planning an extra, larger establishment (with seating for 350) just a block away at 18th and T Streets, which should open in early summer 1999.

Mexicali Blues

2033 Wilson Boulevard, at Garfield Street, Arlington, VA (703 812 9352). Clarendon Metro. **Open** 11am-10pm Mon-Thur; 11am-midnight Fri, Sat; 4-10pm Sun. **Credit** MC, V. **Main course** $7-$11.

They pack 'em into this friendly corner spot dotted with Christmas lights, bright colours and festive Latino tunes. The food is as authentic as you're going to get in this part of the world – all prepared by an intent group of señoras milling about in the semi-open kitchen. A little bit Mexican (flautas, enchiladas, sopes), a little bit Salvadorean (pupusas, tamales), the menu has plenty of starters that work well as bar snacks or as an ad hoc dinner.

Mediterranean

Catalan

1319 F Street, NW, between 13th & 14th Streets, Downtown (628 2299). Metro Center Metro. **Lunch** 11.30am-2.30pm Mon-Fri. **Dinner** 5.30-10pm Mon-Thur; 5.30-11pm Fri, Sat. **Credit** AmEx, DC, MC, V. **Main course** lunch $18-$22; dinner $18-$32.

Catalan's red drapes, dark wood and curvy bar with enormous tiled mirrors make for a very romantic spot. Stop here before having dinner reservations elsewhere and enjoy a glass of big Rioja and some tapas. The plates are small enough for a snack and not seasoned well enough to make you want to stay, so keep it short. If you've got a hot date or a secret to share, the bar may be just the place.

Jaleo

480 Seventh Street, NW, at E Street, Penn Quarter (628 7949). Gallery Place-Chinatown Metro. **Open** 11.30am-10pm Mon, Sun; 11.30am-11.30pm Tue-Thur; 11.30am-midnight Fri, Sat. **Credit** AmEx, DC, Disc, MC, V. **Tapas** $3-$8 each.

Young Spaniard Jose Andres is running the show here and the kitchen at neighbouring Latino-centric **Café Atlantico** (*see p151*). Jaleo focuses on tapas – garlic shrimp, chorizo with garlic mashed potatoes and a Spanish-style Caesar salad with manchego cheese, to name a few – which it has been doing quite well for years. The bar area is often filled with a pre-theatre and after-work crowd enjoying a zesty sangria or a little nibble. Always a reliable place for fun and upbeat energy, Jaleo also features flamenco dancers on Wednesday nights.

Lebanese Taverna

2641 Connecticut Avenue, NW, at Woodley Road, Woodley Park (265 8681). Woodley Park-Zoo Metro. **Lunch** 11.30am-2.30pm Mon-Fri; 11.30am-3.30pm Sat. **Dinner** 5.30-10.30pm Mon-Thur; 5.30-11.30pm Fri, Sat; 5-10pm Sun. **Credit** AmEx, DC, Disc, MC, V. **Main course** $9-$15.

This family-owned operation, a reliable favourite for almost two decades, starts filling up early for dinner. The crowds are a mix of families, singles out on a date and more formal business groups. Make a meal of appetisers, which are quite substantial, fun to share and a bit more of a bargain. There's the familiar tabouleh and falafel as well as more interesting variations, such as houmous bel shawarma, shankleesh (herbed and spiced feta with a tomato

Superior Mediterranean food at the classy **Mezza 9** *in Arlington.*

salad) and manakish b'sbanigh, a Lebanese-style pie topped with a spinach, pine nut and kashkaval cheese mixture. Try the baklava, topped off with a demi-tasse of Arabic coffee scented with cardamom.
Branch: 5900 Washington Boulevard, Arlington (703 241 8681).

Levantes

1320 19th Street, NW, at Dupont Circle (293 3244). Dupont Circle Metro. **Open** 11am-midnight Mon-Thur; 11am-2am Fri, Sat; 11am-11pm Sun. **Credit** AmEx, DC, MC, V. **Main course** $12-$19.

In 1998, Dr Fuat Mehmetoglu and his wife, Dr Anita Fuertes (he's Turkish, she's Austrian), brought their restaurant concept, which had been doing so well in Austria and Germany, to Bethesda, and then, in spring 1999, to Dupont Circle. Focusing on the dishes of the now-defunct Levant empire, the menu leans toward the eastern part of the Mediterranean, so you'll see fried Greek cheese, dolmas and grilled anana kebab (ground lamb with their own spice blend) among standard regional dishes, such as baba ganoush, houmous and falafel. The Dupont Circle branch has a wide outdoor terrace that spills on to the street and seats about 100. It's a smartly designed, light-filled space, working just as well for after-work cocktails and appetisers as for a quick, well-priced lunch.
Branch: 7262 Woodmont Avenue, Bethesda, MD (301 657 2441).

Mezza 9

Hyatt Arlington, 1325 Wilson Boulevard, at Nash Street, Arlington, VA (703 276 8999). Rosslyn Metro. **Breakfast** 6.30-10.30am Mon-Fri; 7am-noon Sat, Sun. **Lunch** 11.30am-2pm Mon-Fri. **Dinner** 5.30-10pm daily. **Credit** AmEx, DC, Disc, MC, V. **Main course** $11-$26.

From the glassware and table decorations to the wine list and the tasty bread baskets, the folks at Mezza 9 have gone to great lengths to make you feel like you're not in a typically faceless hotel restaurant. Best of all, the menu is interesting enough to be a draw even if you're not spending the night. Aside from its namesake meze (there are always nine to choose from), the menu is heavy on fish, which is a consistent winner, and has a good assortment of panini and entrée-sized salads plus many vegetarian choices. A popular business lunch spot.

Beyond the Beltway

Some of the best – and most expensive – restaurants in the Washington area are outside the city limits in Virginia. The most famous of these is **The Inn at Little Washington** (1-540 675 3800), 67 miles west of DC, where Michelin-starred chef Patrick O'Connell has a devoted following for his predominantly French cuisine. The prix-fixe seven-course dinner costs between $98 and $128.

The **Willow Grove Inn** (1-540 672 5982/1-800 949 1778) is a ten-bedroom estate set on 37 acres that dates back to 1778, about 25 miles north of Richmond. The kitchen is run by Eliza Abbey, the inn by Angela Mulloy. Much attention is paid to seasonal and local ingredients, infused with a Southern touch, and there's a good choice of Virginia wines.

Clifton – The Country Inn (1-804 971 1800/1-888 971 1800) in Charlottesville, dates back to 1799. Prix-fixe dinner features five or six courses, and emphasises the bounty of local, farm-raised veal and beef. This is another place to try Virginia wine.

Best for…

Foodies

Makoto (*p150*), where the fixed-price meals are dissertations on Japanese cooking; **Rupperts** (*p142*), for fresh local ingredients treated like gems; **Lespinasse** (*p146*), which boasts a young Michelin-starred chef who's taking French cuisine into uncharted territory.

Fashion victims

DC Coast (*p141*). Your best clothes won't be wasted in this sexy, high-ceilinged room; **Chi Cha Lounge** (*p151*), for lively people-watching and food from the Andes; **Café Atlantico** (*p151*), with its Latin-fusion cuisine and sleek tri-level space; as downtown as DC gets.

Late-night

Kramerbooks & Afterwords Café (*p142*), which is open 24 hours on the weekend; **Bistro Français** (*p146*) in Georgetown, for steak frites or moules; **Quick Pita** (*p154*) in Georgetown, for a kebab or falafel sandwich; and **Hope Key** (*p144*) in Arlington, for after-hours crispy duck and shrimp dumplings.

A view

Sky Terrace atop the Hotel Washington (15th & Pennsylvania Avenue, NW; 638 5900). The food's not much to write home about but if it's clear, you can see all the way to Mount Vernon. Only open during the summer. *See p163* **Bars**.

Politico-sightings

The Palm (*p158*). From Donna Shalala to James Carville (and partner Mary Matalin), your chances are good at this celeb hangout; also **The Capital Grille** (*p157*), the steakhouse of choice for DC's power brokers.

Moby Dick House of Kabob

1070 31st Street, NW, at M Street, Georgetown (333 4400). Foggy Bottom-GWU Metro, then 30, 32, 34, 35, 36 bus. **Open** 11am-10pm Mon-Thur, Sun; 11am-3am Fri, Sat. **No credit cards.** **Main course** $4-$11.

There's not much to this place, just the counter to place your order and two tables to the right – all the action is going on behind the scenes. Take in the aromas of grilled meat and the clay oven-baked pita; the food is earnest, tasty and authentic. Middle East expats from all over the region are always queuing up for kubideh (ground beef), halal lamb or one of the daily specials. The servings are enormous – even the souvlaki sandwiches are big enough to share. Don't fret about the lack of seating: take your goodies home, eat in the car or walk down to the C&O Canal.

Branches: 7027 Wisconsin Avenue, Bethesda (301 654 1838).

Quick Pita

1210 Potomac Street, NW, between M & Prospect Streets, Georgetown (338 7482). Foggy Bottom-GWU Metro, then 30, 32, 34, 35, 36 bus. **Open** 11.30am-3.30am Mon-Wed, Sun; 11.30am-4.30am Thur-Sat. **Credit** AmEx, MC, V. **Main course** $3-$10.

There are just seven seats in this tiny storefront restaurant, which offers authentic Lebanese staples including baba ganoush, falafel, tabbouleh and sandwiches such as shawarma, gyro and kebab combinations. The Quick Pita Special ($3.95) is an oddly delicious mixture of grilled cubes of chicken, garlic paste, tomatoes and french fries, rolled into a warm pita. Despite the limited seating, Quick Pita is good for a quick bite while shopping or a late-night snack – it's open until a very ripe 4.30am on weekends.

Pan-Asian

Raku: An Asian Diner

1900 Q Street, NW, at 19th Street, Dupont Circle (265 7258). Dupont Circle Metro. **Open** 11.30am-10pm Mon-Thur, Sun; 11.30am-midnight Fri, Sat. **Credit** AmEx, MC, V. **Main course** $7-$13.

Conceived by Mark Miller, the chef/restaurateur known for his signature Coyote Café in Santa Fe, as well as DC's Red Sage, Raku is an odd combination of noodle house, bar and warm-weather-patio hipster hangout. The more upscale Bethesda location boasts a sushi bar, while the DC branch is smack in the middle of the Dupont Circle scene, so it attracts a young, single set enjoying the ritual of parading themselves on the patio. The food can be uneven, so order appetisers on an as-you-go basis. A good place for meeting friends for a drink and a snack before moving on.

Branch: 7240 Woodmont Avenue, Bethesda (301 718 8680).

Zuki Moon

824 New Hampshire Avenue, NW, between H & I Streets, Foggy Bottom (333 3312). Foggy Bottom-GWU Metro. **Breakfast** 7-10am Mon-Fri; 8-10.30am Sat, Sun. **Lunch** 11.30am-2.50pm Mon-Fri. **Dinner** 5-10.30pm Mon-Thur; 5-11pm Fri, Sat; 5-10pm Sun. **Credit** AmEx, DC, Disc, MC, V. **Main course** breakfast $7; lunch & dinner $9-$17.

Chef/owner Mary Richter is a 11-year veteran of the DC restaurant scene and this is her best effort yet. She is committed to healthy fare with clean Asian flavours that challenge and inspire. The

Zuki Moon: *top DC chef Mary Richter's Asian noodle house in Foggy Bottom.*

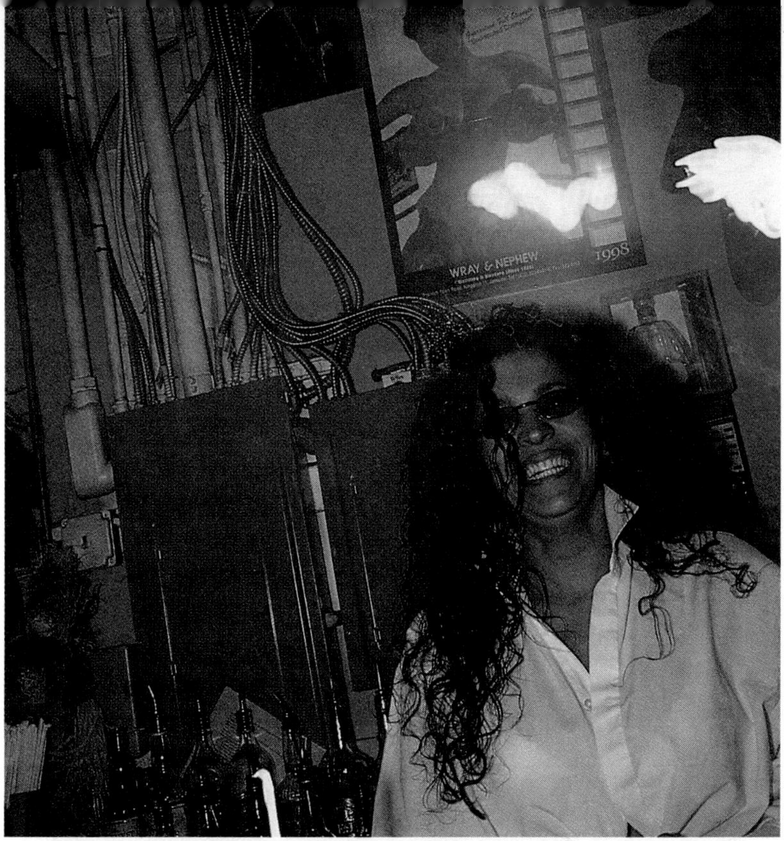

Caribbean colours and cuisine at Georgetown's **Hibiscus Café**. *See page 151.*

menu features several kinds of noodle soups (all noodles are made in-house, as are the stocks) as well as yam cellophane noodles, green tea noodles with smoked salmon, yummy pork gyoza, grilled squid stir-fry and an interesting wine list. The dining room colours are more Caribbean than Asian and conjure warmth even in winter, and its proximity to the Kennedy Center makes it a great pre- or post-concert haven.

Steakhouses

What is it about politicians and red meat? In this town, they can't seem to stay away from each other. The choices here are seemingly endless, and from the end of 1999, power steakhouse chain Smith & Wollensky will be gracing Washington with its cattle. Dry-aged slabs of beef hang in the front windows at **The Capital Grille**, which, because of its proximity to the action, attracts political power brokers. For one of the best martinis in town, head for **The Palm**. Within earshot of the White House, **Max's of Washington** has a Franco-American angle, and **Morton's** – well, there are Morton's all around the country, but the big draw here is the larger-than-life 48-ounce double porterhouse, enough meat for a small village of children to gnaw on.

The Capital Grille

601 Pennsylvania Avenue, NW, at Sixth Street, Federal Triangle (737 6200). Archives-Navy Memorial Metro. **Open** 11.30am-3pm, 5-10pm, Mon-Thur; 11.30am-3pm, 5-11pm, Fri, Sat; 5-10pm Sun. **Credit** AmEx, MC, V. **Main course** $20-$30.

Max's of Washington

1725 F Street, NW, between 17th & 18th Streets, White House & Around (842 0070). Farragut West Metro. **Open** 11.45am-2.30pm, 6-10pm, Mon-Fri; 6-10pm Sat. **Credit** AmEx, DC, Disc, MC, V. **Main course** lunch $9-$22; dinner $22-$32.

Morton's of Chicago,

1050 Connecticut Avenue, NW, at L Street, Downtown (955 5997). Farragut North Metro. **Open** 11.30am-2.30pm, 5.30-11pm, Mon-Fri; 5.30-11pm Sat; 5-10pm Sun. **Credit** AmEx, DC, MC, V. **Main course** lunch $9-$22; dinner $19-$31. **Branch**: 3251 Prospect Street, NW, Georgetown (342 6258).

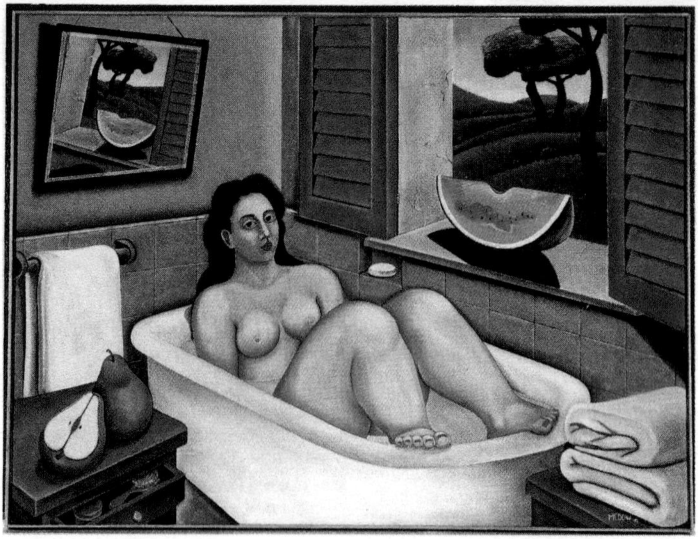

Ben's Chili Bowl: *classic chili dogs at this family-run diner on U Street.* *See page 142.*

The Palm

1225 19th Street, NW, between M & N Streets, Dupont Circle (293 9091). Dupont Circle Metro. **Open** 11.45am-2.30pm Mon-Fri; 5.30-10.30pm Sat; 6.30-10.30pm Sun. **Main course** lunch $15-$20; dinner $25-$45.

Thai

Basil Thai

1608 Wisconsin Avenue, NW, at Q Street, Georgetown (944 8660). Foggy Bottom-GWU Metro, then 30. 32, 34, 35, 36 bus. **Open** 11am-10.30pm Mon-Sat; 4-10pm Sun. **Credit** AmEx, DC, MC, V. **Main course** lunch $8-$11; dinner $9-$13.

Pale orange walls greet you in this charming, one-room storefront. To start, try a plate of fishcakes, fried and served with tangy/spicy cucumbers and peanut sauce. The chef's specials tend to be fun, such as a crispy duck in a spicy basil sauce jazzed up with lemon grass. Desserts include sweet sticky rice with mango and coconut-battered fritters with honey. Its location (upper Georgetown) means that parking is a pain.

Jandara

2606 Connecticut Avenue, NW, at Calvert Street, Woodley Park (387 8876). Woodley Park-Zoo Metro.

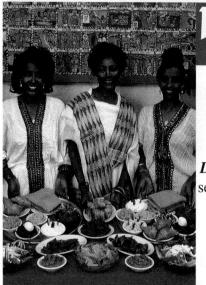

Open 11.30am-10.30pm Mon-Thur, Sun; 11.30am-11pm Fri, Sat. **Credit** AmEx, DC, Disc, MC, V. **Main course** $8-$25.
Ethnic dining in a rather outdated, 1980s setting, with shades of purple and moody blues. The menu features the standards, which could use some zip from time to time, but if you want quick, relatively reliable curry, Jandara is just fine. Staff tend to push you out of the door, so don't plan for a leisurely, well-paced dinner.
Branch: 4237 Wisconsin Avenue, NW, Georgetown (237 1570).

Sawatdee

2250 Clarendon Boulevard, at Courthouse Road, Courthouse Plaza, Arlington, VA (703 243 8181). Court House Metro. **Open** 11.30am-10pm Mon-Thur; 11.30am-10.45pm Fri; noon-10.45pm Sat; 4.30-9.30pm Sun. **Credit** AmEx, DC, Disc, MC, V. **Main course** lunch $6-$19; dinner $7-$22.
Hidden amid a concrete jungle of office and apartment towers, Sawatdee is a bit of a surprise. The décor, reminiscent of Chinese restaurants still stuck in the 1970s, with its oversized booths, crystal chandeliers and stiff linen, throws you as well. But the food is right on target. Flavours are sharp, pungent when necessary and wake up the sinuses if you ask. Sawatdee is reliable, relatively kid-friendly and, despite the fussy décor, very casual. It's also a good flick pitstop – the AMC Courthouse cinema is a few hundred feet away.

Vietnamese

Little Viet Garden

3012 Wilson Boulevard, between Highland & Garfield Streets, Arlington, VA (703 522 9686). Clarendon Metro. **Lunch** 11am-2.30pm, **dinner** 5-10pm, Mon-Fri. **Open** noon-10pm Sat, Sun. **Credit** AmEx, DC, Disc, MC, V. **Main course** lunch $5-$7; dinner $6-$12.
There are plenty of Vietnamese restaurants in this area of Arlington, but Little Viet Garden gets points for ambience. It's an exotic hideaway, with white Christmas lights, tables pushed closely together to give that cosy café feel and when the weather's warm, lovely garden seating. If it's busy (as it often is), consider eating at the bar, where service seems to be a tad more attentive than tableside. The menu runs the gamut, from noodles to shrimp toast; one dish worth a look is the spicy fried tofu cooked in a clay pot, incredibly flavourful and un-tofu-like in texture.

Restaurants by area

Bars

As you might expect, swanky hotel bars and political hangouts abound, but there are hip lounges and neighbourhood dives, too.

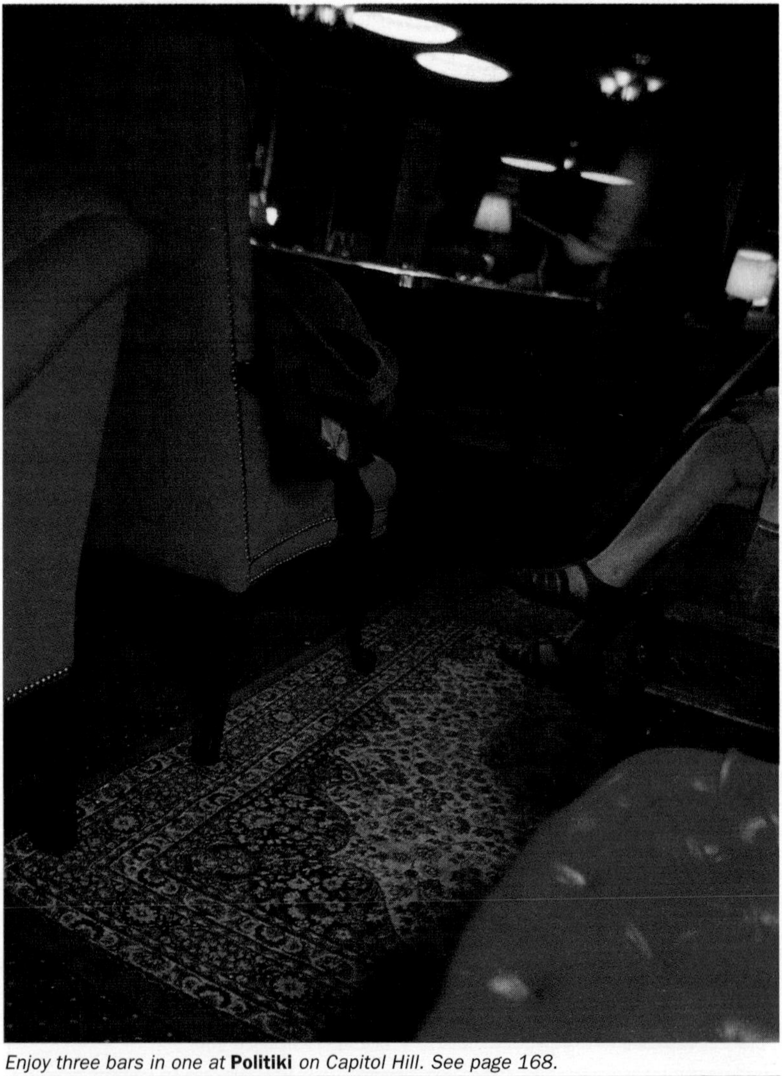

Enjoy three bars in one at **Politiki** *on Capitol Hill.* *See page 168.*

Bars are usually open until 3am on Fridays and Saturdays, until 2am the rest of the week, although some select establishments, particularly those that double as dance clubs, stay open until at least 4am at weekends. The legal drinking age in the US is 21 and, for the most part, it's strictly enforced in DC, especially in Adams Morgan and Georgetown, both of which get a lot of college-age traffic. So bring photo ID with you – even if you're just going to have a glass of wine with your food.

The Metro closes at midnight but most buses run until about 2am; however, if you're partying late, it's often easier to take a cab home. For specifically lesbian and gay bars, *see chapter* **Nightlife**.

The Monumental Centre

Old Ebbitt Grill

675 15th Street, NW, between F & G Streets, White House & Around (347 4800). Metro Center Metro/30, 32, 34 bus. **Open** 7.30am-2am Mon-Thur; 7.30am-3am Fri; 8am-3am Sat; 9.30am-2am Sun. **Credit** AmEx, DC, Disc, MC, V.

This restaurant/bar's first incarnation was in 1856, when it opened as a boarding house near Chinatown; guests included Presidents Grant, Johnson, Cleveland and Teddy Roosevelt. Its current location, a block from the White House, makes it a popular place for the power lunch (in the main dining room, not in the atrium). Patrons' ages edge up into the 40s and 50s, probably because of Old Ebbitt's reputation for oysters and wine. The two bars – one at the back, one at the front – are always packed, usually with older men who ensure that no nubile young thing pays for her own drinks.

Round Robin Bar

Willard Inter-Continental Hotel, 1401 Pennsylvania Avenue, NW, at 14th Street, Federal Triangle (637 7348). Metro Center Metro/30, 32, 34 bus. **Open** 11am-1am Mon-Sat; 11am-midnight Sun. **Credit** AmEx, DC, Disc, JCB, MC, V.

A clubby, dark green bar with the feel of a gentleman's study – if you added some books and subtracted those outrageously priced drinks (the bill can top $15 for two). It's a dressy, cocktails kind of place – there's no beer on tap – and it's lobbyist central; in fact, the term 'lobbying' was invented here, because influence-seekers used to hang out in the lobby waiting to bend a Congressman's ear. Portraits depict some of the Willard's most prominent guests: Walt Whitman (who immortalised the bar in his appeal to Union troops during the Civil War), Mark Twain, Nathaniel Hawthorne and Abraham Lincoln, who lived at the hotel for two weeks before his inauguration.

Sky Terrace

Hotel Washington, 515 15th Street , NW, at Pennsylvania Avenue, White House & Around (638 5900). Metro Center Metro/30, 32, 34 bus. **Open** May-Sept 11.30am-1am daily. **Credit** AmEx, DC, Disc, MC, V.

A tourist-heavy outdoor bar, open only in summer, which is worth a visit mainly for the spectacular views it offers of the monuments. It's very popular as a place to watch the Fourth of July fireworks, but you can't book until exactly two weeks before.

Central DC

Foggy Bottom

Ozio

1835 K Street, NW, between 18th & 19th Streets, Foggy Bottom (822 6000). Farragut West Metro/D4, D5, L2 bus. **Open** 10am-2am Mon-Thur; 10am-3am Fri; 5.30pm-3am Sat. **Admission** *men only* $20 plus two-drink minimum Fri, Sat. **Credit** AmEx, DC, Disc, MC, V.

Ozio opened as a cigar and martini lounge at the height of the craze in the mid-1990s, and some say its lustre has faded since. These days, the ochre-walled lounge with columns decorated with silk-screened images of Bogey and Bacall attracts a slightly less Euro clientele than other lounges like it. Perhaps it's the K Street address, but the crowd here is more traders and lawyers. At happy hour, cocktails cost less than $3. Dress up.

Downtown

Fadó Irish Pub

808 Seventh Street, NW, between H & I Streets, Downtown (789 0066). Gallery Place-Chinatown Metro/70, 71, 73 bus. **Open** 11.30am-2am Mon-Thur, Sun; 11.30-3am Fri, Sat. **Credit** AmEx, DC, Disc, MC, V.

If Disneyworld included an Irish bar, Fadó (Gaelic for 'long ago') would be it, with its rooms decorated to reflect different Irish themes: Victorian, library, cottage and Celtic. Mercifully, the patrons – Downtown professionals at happy hour and fans headed to or coming from games at the MCI Center at other times – don't seem to mind the kitsch. *See also p213* **Nightlife**.

Grand Slam

Grand Hyatt Hotel, 1000 H Street, NW, between Tenth & 11th Streets, Downtown (637 4789). Metro Center Metro/42, 80, G8 bus. **Open** 11am-2am daily. **Credit** AmEx, DC, Disc, MC, V.

This lower-level bar is home to 25 TVs, video games, a basketball hoop, a computer with free Internet access and the requisite sports bar memorabilia. Keep an eye out for Washington Wizards players, who have been known to show up and even shoot hoops with the patrons.

Library Lounge

St Regis Hotel, 923 16th Street, NW, at K Street, Downtown (638 2626). McPherson Square or Farragut North Metro/L2, S1, S2 bus. **Open** noon-midnight daily. **Credit** AmEx, DC, Disc, JCB, MC, V.

A replica of an English gentlemen's club, with a green marble bar, tons of mahogany, a cigar humidor, a fireplace and rows and rows of leather fake

Tradition abounds at the Willard Hotel's clubby **Round Robin Bar** *(page 163).*

books, not to mention sherries and ports. The celebrity quotient is high here – Billy Joel and the Rolling Stones (who took up 60 rooms of the hotel) were recent guests. You'll need to dress smartly.

McCormick & Schmick's

1652 K Street, NW, at 16th Street, Downtown (861 2233). Farragut North Metro/L2, S1, S2 bus. **Open** 11.30am-11pm Mon-Thur; 11.30am-midnight Fri; 5pm-midnight Sat; 5-10pm Sun. **Credit** AmEx, DC, Disc, MC, V.

If you're single and hungry, this may be your place. At happy hour (3-6.30pm weekdays), the bar menu, which includes shrimp cocktail and half-pound hamburgers, is $1.95, though the drinks will cost you. Then there's the scene: K Street lawyers and lobbyists, journalists and other Downtowners. Anything less formal than work clothes will stand out; for women, think ageing Southern sorority sisters: pearls and ash blonde hair are practically mandatory.

Judiciary Square area

My Brother's Place Bar & Grill

237 Second Street, NW, at Constitution Avenue, Judiciary Square Area (347 1350). Judiciary Square Metro/A12, J11, X1 bus. **Open** 11am-2.30am Mon-Sat. **Credit** AmEx, MC, V.

This bar's almost-hidden location (Second Street is a tiny one-way road) keeps tourists away and safeguards its reputation as a hangout for locals and assorted rugby players. The bartenders – who have 30 beers on tap – know the regulars by name.

Union Station & around

B Smith's

Union Station, 50 Massachusetts Avenue, NE, at North Capitol Street, Union Station & Around (289 6188). Union Station Metro/97, D8, X8 bus. **Open** 11.30am-11pm Mon-Fri; 11.30am-midnight Sat; 11.30am-9pm Sun. **Credit** AmEx, DC, Disc, MC, V.

Owned by former cover girl and Oil of Olay model Barbara Smith and located in what used to the presidential waiting room in Union Station, this bar claims 'Southern comfort and New York style' (it's an offshoot of a fairly prominent NYC restaurant). It attracts a largely upscale and black clientele, with a sprinkling of Hill types (maybe a senator or two) and tourists. The bar isn't really for hanging out; it's best for a drink or two before dinner.

Capitol City Brewing Company

2 Massachusetts Avenue, NE, at North Capitol Street, Union Station & Around (842 2337). Union Station Metro/91, 96 bus. **Open** 11am-midnight Mon, Tue, Sun; 11am-1.30am Wed-Sat. **Credit** AmEx, DC, Disc, MC, V.

There are two Cap City branches: this one opposite Union Station and another in Downtown. Both have a slick, prefabricated feel, but no one seems to mind the décor since both are packed, particularly at lunchtime and happy hour. The Downtown branch is in a converted Greyhound bus station, while this larger one – which draws both a Hill and tourist crowd – is in what used to be the Postmaster General's office. About six brewed-on-the-premises beers are available at any given time; Cap City brews primarily top-fermented ales and produces pilsners only about four times a year. A much-loved gimmick is the substitution of soft pretzels for rolls for patrons ordering food.

Branch: 1100 New York Avenue, NW, Downtown (628 2222).

Dubliner

Phoenix Park Hotel, 520 North Capitol Street, NW, at Massachusetts Avenue, Union Station & Around (737 3773). Union Station Metro/91, 96 bus. **Open** 7am-1.30am Mon-Thur; 7am-2.30am Fri; 11am-2.30am Sat; 11am-1.30am Sun. **Credit** AmEx, DC, MC, V.

A clubby Irish pub in a hotel, which is largely full of suited men in their 40s and 50s, mainly politicians and lobbyists. Later at night, the crowd gets a little younger and a little more mixed, but not enough to keep some young single women from feeling uncomfortable. Live Irish music every night.

Kelly's Irish Times

14 F Street, NW, between North Capitol Street & New Jersey Avenue, Union Station & Around (543 5433). Union Station Metro/96 bus. **Open** 10.30am-1.30am Mon-Thur, Sun; 10.30am-2.30am Fri, Sat. **Credit** AmEx, DC, Disc, MC, V.

The Irish Times has the same theme (the Emerald Isle) as the Dubliner next door, but it might as well be a world away. It's relatively quiet in the day, but at night, when it's filled with young Hill staffers and American & Catholic University students, this is one of the places in DC known for its hook-up factor: as in, if you want to, you can't fail to. Live Irish music on Thursdays, Fridays and Saturdays.

Dupont Circle

18th Street Lounge

1212 18th Street, NW, between Jefferson Place & M Street, Dupont Circle (466 3922). Farragut North Metro. **Open** 9.30pm-2am Tue, Wed; 5.30pm-2am Thur; 3pm-3am Fri; 9.30pm-3am Sat. **Credit** AmEx, MC, V.

There used to be no affirmative action for the terminally unhip at this of-the-moment lounge. The plain wooden door with a gold handle – right next to Candey Hardware, and unmarked – was always locked and you couldn't see in, though the bouncers could see out. Nowadays, the occasional jeans-wearer will actually be let in to the only nightspot that hip magazine *Details* deemed worthy of visiting in Washington. *See also p217* **Nightlife**.

The Big Hunt

1345 Connecticut Avenue, NW, between Dupont Circle & N Street, Dupont Circle (785 2333). Dupont Circle Metro/42, N2, N4 bus. **Open** 4pm-2am Mon-Thur; 4pm-3am Fri; 5pm-3am Sat; 5pm-2am Sun. **Credit** AmEx, MC, V.

Once upon a time, this was an über-hip hangout for DC's underground. Now the *Jurassic Park*-ish bar (it has leopard booths and canvas tents lodged in the jaws of prehistoric prey) is almost as yuppified as Dupont Circle. The beer list is long and respectable, and new lures include the opening of a patio and some live music in the basement.

Brickskeller

1523 22nd Street, NW, between O & P Streets, Dupont Circle (293 1885). Dupont Circle Metro/G2 bus. **Open** 11.30am-2am Mon-Thur; 11.30am-3am Fri; 6pm-3am Sat; 6pm-2am Sun. **Credit** AmEx, DC, Disc, MC, V.

This labyrinthine saloon claims to have the world's largest selection of beers: 800 brands from all over the world, from America to Zaire. Not, of course, that all 800 of these often-expensive bottles are available at the same time. Brickskeller is a place to come with friends; there's little mixing between groups.

Buffalo Billiards

1330 19th Street, NW, at Dupont Circle, Dupont Circle (331 7665). Dupont Circle Metro/42, N2, N4 bus. **Open** 4pm-2am Mon-Thur; 1pm-3am Fri, Sat (1-4pm under-21s permitted); 1pm-1am Sun. **Credit** AmEx, MC, V.

A subterranean pool hall with what feels like acres of tables, as well as darts, boardgames and a cigar counter. This is a huge happy hour spot, though at night the suits morph into gangs of pals in jeans.

Dragonfly

1215 Connecticut Avenue, NW, between M & N Streets, Dupont Circle (331 1775). Farragut North or Dupont Circle Metro/42, N2, N4 bus. **Open** 5.30pm-1am Mon-Wed; 5.30pm-2am; 6pm-1am Sun. **Credit** AmEx, MC, V.

Behind the frosted glass windows lies an all-white sushi restaurant-turned-bar that looks like *2001: A Space Odyssey* meets the Frankie Avalon scene in *Grease*. Movies – frequently Japanese porn – play on the walls and music pulses until late in the night. Wearing anything but black may brand you too colourful (read: unhip) to be allowed in.

Fox & Hounds

1533 17th Street, NW, at Q Street, Dupont Circle (232 6307). Dupont Circle Metro/S1, S2, S4 bus. **Open** 11am-2am Mon-Thur; 11am-3am Fri; 10am-3am Sat; 10am-2am Sun. **Credit** AmEx, Disc, MC, V.

A scrappy neighbourhood pub that's dim and cave-like, with hardcore drinkers hunched over the bar. It's a true biergarten in warm weather, when crowds pack the patio and swarm the great jukebox. The Fox & Hounds is a place for lingering, a reputation that the sometimes painfully slow waiting staff take a little too seriously.

Adams Morgan

Bedrock Billiards

1841 Columbia Road, NW, between 18th Street & Belmont Road, Adams Morgan (667 7665). Dupont Circle Metro, then 42 bus. **Open** 4pm-2am Mon-Thur; 4pm-3am Fri; 1pm-3am Sat; 1pm-2am Sun. **Credit** AmEx, MC, V.

Unpretentious pool hall/games room (with 30 pool tables, Scrabble, Uno, Connect Four and other childhood favourites), which aims for a prehistoric look with caveman drawings on the green walls. Don't worry – the décor isn't a reflection of the clientele, which mainly consists of under-30 folks from the neighbourhood.

The Common Share

2003 18th Street, NW, at U Street, Adams Morgan (588 7180). Dupont Circle Metro, then L2 bus or Woodley Park-Zoo Metro, then 90, 91, 92, 93, 96 bus. **Open** 5.30pm-2am Mon-Thur; 5.30pm-3am Fri, Sat. **Credit** Disc, MC, V.

There are two ways to find Common Share: look for the mass of bikes outside (it's bike courier central), or for the long line that snakes several doors down. Interns, students and underpaid twentysomethings love the cheap drinks: $2, all the time. Don't expect to get a seat (on the garage sale-reject furniture) unless you arrive when the doors open.

Crush

2323 18th Street, NW, at Kalorama Street, Adams Morgan (319 1111). Dupont Circle Metro, then L2 bus or Woodley Park-Zoo Metro, then 90, 91, 92, 93, 96 bus. **Open** 7pm-2am Tue-Thur; 7pm-3am Fri, Sat. **Credit** AmEx, MC, V.

Get crushed in a twentysomething crowd that you won't mind looking at on the long, narrow dance-floor. This super-popular place is hot – literally – so dress accordingly.

Habana Village

1834 Columbia Road, NW, between Biltmore Road & Mintwood Place, Adams Morgan (462 6310). Dupont Circle Metro, then 42 bus. **Open** 6.30pm-2am Wed, Thur; 6.30pm-3am Fri, Sat. **Credit** AmEx, DC, MC, V.

This multi-level salsa palace caters to most whims, with a couple of lounges, multiple dancefloors and live music. The Latin flavour includes the music, clientele and décor, making this a popular alternative for those who've grown tired of the largely Anglo-focused clubs in Adams Morgan. Naturally, cigar smoking is permitted. For details of dance classes, *see p226* **Sport & Fitness**.

Madam's Organ Restaurant & Bar

2461 18th Street, NW, at Columbia Road, Adams Morgan (667 5370). Dupont Circle Metro, then L2 bus or Woodley Park-Zoo Metro, then 90, 91, 92, 93, 96 bus. **Open** 5pm-2am Mon-Thur, Sun; 5pm-3am Fri, Sat. **Admission** $2-$5. **Credit** AmEx, Disc, MC, V.

The 'Sorry We're Open' sign used to mock Madam's Organ's old neighbours, who finally succeeded in pushing this we-love-to-thumb-our-nose-at-everyone establishment several blocks north to get rid of the noise. (Its new neighbours have tried to force the bar to wipe the huge mural of a huge-breasted, red-headed woman off the side of the building.) As the bar's motto goes, this is 'where the beautiful people go to get ugly' – and ugly it gets: the crowds dance (or attempt to, in the tiny space) to the live music, play pool on the second floor and hook up shamelessly. Redheads – make that red-headed women – get in half-price. *See also p209* **Nightlife**.

Millie & Al's

2440 18th Street, NW, between U & V Streets, Adams Morgan (387 8131). Dupont Circle Metro, then L2 bus or Woodley Park-Zoo Metro, then 90, 91, 92, 93, 96 bus. **Open** 4pm-1am Mon-Thur; 4pm-3am Fri, Sat. **Credit** MC, V.

One of Washington's great dives, Millie & Al's (named after the owner and his girlfriend-waitress) has been around since the 1960s, long before Adams Morgan was chic. It's a no-frills, two-floor place that celebrates group-guzzling, where the friendly bartenders will send over shot glasses filled with jelly beans to patrons looking a little too morose. Keep an eye on the lightbulb over the bar; when it lights up, college students belly up to the bar for jello shooter specials. *See also p149* **Restaurants**.

Pharmacy Bar

2337 18th Street, NW, at Belmont Road, Adams Morgan (483 1200). Dupont Circle Metro, then L2 bus or Woodley Park-Zoo Metro, then 90, 91, 92, 93, 96 bus. **Open** 5pm-2am Mon-Thur, Sun; 5pm-3am Fri, Sat. **Credit** AmEx, MC, V.

New on the scene, Pharmacy – pills are suspended in liquid glass on the table tops, in honour of the owner's pharmacist grandfather – is becoming known as a late-night hangout for neighbourhood types. One draw is the good beer selection, which ranges from basic Budweiser upwards.

Toledo Lounge

2435 18th Street, NW, between Columbia & Belmont Roads, Adams Morgan (986 5416). Dupont Circle Metro, then L2 bus or Woodley Park-Zoo Metro, then 90, 91, 92, 93, 96 bus. **Open** 6pm-2am Mon-Thur, Sun; 6pm-3am Fri, Sat. **Credit** AmEx, MC, V.

The native Toledo (Ohio) owners opened their 1950s-themed bar for, as they put it, 'smoking, drinking and eating red meat'. You won't find any trendy rosemary or coriander in the food or bizarre chocolate martini concoctions at the bar – though the (classic) martinis and margaritas are first-rate. Expect a line of attractive under-35s if you arrive after 10pm at the weekend.

Tryst

2459 18th Street, NW, between Columbia & Belmont Roads, Adams Morgan (232 5500). Dupont Circle Metro, then L2 bus or Woodley Park-Zoo Metro, then 90, 91, 92, 93, 96 bus. **Open** 7am-1am Mon, Tue; 7am-2am Wed, Thur; 7am-3am Fri, Sat; 8am-midnight Sun. **Credit** MC, V.

For all the hanging out done in Adams Morgan, the area was missing a true hangout, the kind of place where the cast from *Friends* would come to sip their lattes if the show was set in DC. This coffeehouse-cum-bar fills that void during the day; at night, it becomes just as much of a packed scene as almost all the other bars that line 18th Street. Don't miss the retro menu, which includes Nutella, peanut butter and jelly sandwiches and animal crackers, along with the requisite designer espresso drinks.

U Street/14th Street corridor

Chi Cha Lounge

1624 U Street, NW, at 17th Street, U Street/14th Street Corridor (234 8400). U Street-Cardozo Metro/ 90, 91, 92, 93, L2 bus. **Open** 6pm-2am Mon-Thur, Sun; 6pm-3am Fri, Sat. **Credit** AmEx, DC, Disc, MC, V. **Tapas** $3.75-$7.50 each.

Ecuadorian owner Mauricio Fraga-Rosenfeld has just one rule: no suits and ties. Still, the clothes can get pretty chic and chi-chi at Chi Cha, a candle-lit meet-market/living room with comfy sofas for the under-40 crowd. Don't miss the Andean tapas, but skip the sickly sweet house-special drinks. *See also p151* **Restaurants**.

The dress code is casual and the rhythms Latin at the **Chi Cha Lounge**.

Polly's Café

1342 U Street, at 14th Street, NW, U Street/14th Street Corridor (265 8385). U Street-Cardozo Metro/ 52, 90, 91, 92, 93 bus. **Open** 6pm-1.30am Mon-Thur; 6pm-2.30am Fri; 10am-2.30am Sat; 10am-12.30am Sun. **Credit** MC, V.

Polly's lives up to its café name, with a cosy atmosphere, a fireplace and terrific home-made cookies. As the patio sculpture of two people sharing a drink suggests, couples abound, though things get a little rowdier late at night, at around 11pm, when the late-night happy hour gets rolling.

Republic Gardens

1355 U Street, NW, between 13th & 14th Streets, U Street/14th Street Corridor (232 2710). U Street-Cardozo Metro/90, 91, 92, 93, L2 bus. **Open** 5pm-2.30am Wed, Thur; 5pm-4am Fri; 8.30pm-4am Sat. **Admission** $5-$10. **Credit** AmEx, DC, Disc, MC, V.

The name pays homage to a jazz club that operated in this space from the 1920s to the 1960s and, like the U Street of yore, this bar is an African-American oasis. Now the patrons are mostly buppies in dapper suits who have driven in from the suburbs. Rap impresario Sean 'Puffy' Combs has thrown parties here, as has comedian Chris Rock. The bar – well, it's five bars with rivers of hammered steel and semi-abstract sculptures – is a post-game hangout for Washington's pro basketball team.

State of the Union

1357 U Street, NW, at 14th Street, U Street/14th Street Corridor (588 8810/588 8926). U Street-Cardozo Metro. **Open** 6pm-2am Mon-Thur; 6pm-3am Fri-Sun. **Admission** $5 Tue-Thur, Sun; $7 Fri, Sat. **Credit** MC, V.

Communism is nothing but ironic fun now at this seven-year-old club, which offers 36 vodkas and is decorated in Commie Dearest style: sickle-shaped sconces and murals of Lenin and Mother Russia. It's frequented by the well-pierced (and, often, some folks old enough to be their parents), who seem to be undeterred by a floor so mistreated that your feet will stick to it. *See also p212* and *p218* **Nightlife**.

Stetson's

1610 U Street, NW, between 16th & 17th Streets, U Street/14th Street Corridor (667 6295). U Street-Cardozo Metro/90, 91, 92, 93 bus. **Open** 4.30pm-2am Mon-Thur, Sun; 4.30pm-3am Fri, Sat. **Credit** AmEx, MC, V.

U Street's neighbourhood bar long before anyone was calling U Street a neighbourhood, Stetson's is just a shade too bright to be a true corner saloon. There are a couple of pool tables and darts, as well as what the place claims is 'the best deal on U Street' on Thursdays: $3.95 for 64oz pitchers of Coors and Rolling Rock. Free pool on Sundays from 7.30pm until closing time.

Velvet Lounge

915 U Street, NW, between Ninth & Vermont Streets, U Street/14th Street Corridor (462 3213). U Street-Cardozo Metro/90, 91, 92, 93 bus. **Open** 8pm-2am Mon-Thur, Sun; 8pm-3am Fri, Sat. **Admission** $3 Mon-Thur, Sun; $5 Fri, Sat. **Credit** AmEx, Disc, MC, V.

This tiny, two-storey lounge has decent bordering on really good live music, fraternity house furniture, an ancient pinball machine and a pool table. Exposed brick walls hung with the requisite local artists' work complete the bohemian décor. *See also p211* **Nightlife**.

Georgetown

Billy Martin's Tavern

1264 Wisconsin Avenue, NW, at N Street, Georgetown (333 7370). Foggy Bottom-GWU Metro, then 30, 32, 34, 35, 36, 13M bus. **Open** 10am-midnight Mon-Thur; 10am-2am Fri; 8am-2am Sat; 8am-midnight Sun. **Credit** AmEx, DC, Disc, MC, V.

Opened in 1933, the dark wood, Irish-inspired Martin's is an institution. It's not a kiss-kiss kind of place, but movie stars routinely opt for the safety and relative sanctity of the booths or the tiny back-room called the 'Dugout'. VIPs today include Madeleine Albright, Willard Scott and Eunice Shriver. The martinis are among the best in town.

Café Milano

3251 Prospect Street, NW, at Wisconsin Avenue, Georgetown (333 6183). Foggy Bottom-GWU Metro, then 30, 32, 34, 35, 36, D5 bus. **Open** 11.30-1am daily. **Credit** AmEx, DC, Disc, V.

'You have to be a celebrity to get a table there,' Candace Bergen once sighed about Café Milano on the hit TV show *Murphy Brown*. Well, not quite, although looking good helps if you'd like to sit by the window. Though it's a fairly staid Italian restaurant by day, as the night gets later (around 10pm or 11pm), the skirts get much, much shorter. Moneyed and Euro describes most of the late-night patrons; earlier you'll find a mix of tourists, businessmen and Georgetown old guard.

The Guards

2915 M Street, NW, between 29th & 30th Streets, Georgetown (965 2350). Foggy Bottom-GWU Metro, then 30, 32, 34, 35, 36 bus. **Open** 11.30am-2am Mon-Thur, Sun; 11.30am-3am Fri, Sat. **Credit** AmEx, DC, Disc, MC, V.

The Guards is a popular choice any time of year. In winter, a fireplace warms the middle room; in warmer weather, the windows are opened and the atrium becomes the spot of choice. The elegant, burnished brown interior is probably better suited to the bar's usual briefcase clientele, though college students take over after 10pm.

J Paul's

3218 M Street, NW, at Wisconsin Avenue, Georgetown (333 3450). Foggy Bottom-GWU Metro, then 30, 32, 34, 35, 36 bus. **Open** 11.30am-1.30am Mon-Thur; 11.30am-2.30am Fri, Sat; 10.30am-1.30am Sun. **Credit** AmEx, DC, Disc, MC, V.

In good weather, young professionals fight for the seats of choice along the open windows facing M Street. They're also drawn to the good raw shellfish and the 55 varieties of Scotch. Like almost every other drinking hole in Georgetown, this bar also gets its share of students.

Nathan's

3150 M Street, NW, at Wisconsin Avenue, Georgetown (338 2000). Foggy Bottom-GWU Metro, then 30, 32, 34, 35, 36 bus. **Open** noon-2am Mon-Thur; noon-3am Fri; 11am-3am Sat; 11am-2am Sun. **Credit** AmEx, DC, Disc, MC, V.

Located in one of Georgetown's most happening spots, on one of the corners of Wisconsin and M, Nathan's nautical-themed bar is often standing-room only. An older, pinstriped crowd predominates and suburbanites often take over on Saturday nights.

Capitol Hill

Bullfeathers

410 First Street, SE, between D & E Streets, Capitol Hill (543 5005). Capitol South Metro/P6 bus. **Open** 11am-10.30pm Mon-Sat; 10.30am-9pm Sun. **Credit** AmEx, DC, Disc, MC, V.

'Bullfeathers', President Teddy Roosevelt used to snort every time he wanted people to know they were full of it. It's an all-too-appropriate name for this place, which is full of trash-talking Hill types drinking up a storm Thursday nights are popular, and shoptalk is so prevalent that TV crews have to check their cameras at the door.

Branch: 112 King Street, Alexandria, VA (703 836 8088).

Capitol Lounge

231 Pennsylvania Avenue, SE, between Second & Third Streets, Capitol Hill (547 2098). Capitol South Metro/30, 32, 34 bus. **Open** 3pm-2am Mon-Thur; 3pm-3am Fri; 11am-3am Sat; 11am-2am Sun. **Credit** AmEx, MC, V.

A cigar and martini bar that's mostly the province of young Hill staffers and interns. There's no shortage of entertainment here, what with the drunken antics of the crowd, the 14 TVs and the handful of pool tables. The bar shows mostly football games, plus a healthy dollop of soccer.

Hawk & Dove

329 Pennsylvania Avenue, SE, between Third & Fourth Streets, Capitol Hill (543 3300). Capitol South or Eastern Market Metro/30, 32, 34 bus. **Open** 10am-2am Mon-Thur, Sun; 10am-3am Fri, Sat. **Credit** AmEx, DC, Disc, MC, V.

Political memorabilia competes with game trophies (aka dead animals) at this hunting lodge-esque relic from the Vietnam War. Hence the name, which recalls the heated debates from those days. Today, the bar attracts a slightly older and wealthier Hill crowd than the Tune Inn (*see below*) next door – in other words, plenty of thirtyish types in suits – though the free food at happy hour is a big draw for the young and hungry.

Politiki

319 Pennsylvania Avenue, SE, between Third & Fourth Streets, Capitol Hill (546 1001). Capitol South Metro/30, 32, 34 bus. **Open** 4pm-2am Mon-Thur; 4pm-3am Fri, Sat. **Credit** AmEx, MC, V.

Three bars in one: a tiki bar in the basement, a Polynesian-accented bar on the ground floor, and a floor above that of lipstick-red banquettes and World War II posters that looks like a 1940s-era dance hall. The latter bar, frequently used for swing dancing, also doubles as a gathering spot for college football and basketball fans, who watch the games on the handful of TVs. Don't worry – you can sample the drinks, including cocktails served in kitschy bowls, from any floor.

Tune Inn

3332 Pennsylvania Avenue, SE, at Fourth Street, Capitol Hill (543 2725). Capitol South Metro/30, 32, 34 bus. **Open** 8am-2am Mon-Thur, Sun; 8am-3am Fri, Sat. **Credit** AmEx, DC, Disc, MC, V.

The Tune Inn is one of the few places in DC that starts serving beer at 8am – and you'll probably need a pint to deal with the rowdy blue-collar crowd and the surly staff. No microbrews here – this place regularly wins awards for being Washington's best dive, with prices to match.

Shopping

No one comes to DC to shop, but in-the-know shopaholics can still find their fix.

In the nation's capital, where politicians can spend millions of dollars on smart bombs that aren't so smart and get away with it, shopping has its own two-party system: bargain-hunters and big spenders. The city caters to both types in good measure. The heavy dose of diplomats and expats with expendable incomes has led to a growth in designer stores and upscale boutiques. On the other hand, that same international influx shows up in the form of myriad small, accessible shops offering art, clothing, trinkets and jewellery from around the world. Nonetheless, it must be admitted that for the leisure shopper, Washington is a disappointment, with no thriving central shopping area, a stifling amount of chains and generally conservative tastes.

DC sales tax is 5.75 per cent on top of the marked price of all merchandise and services.

SHOPPING DISTRICTS

For the best of Washington's shopping, be prepared to travel from the monumental centre. **Downtown** has a few large department stores, chains such as Ann Taylor, Nine West and the Gap, and some discount shops near Metro Center, but the area tends to cater to working professionals and many stores close shortly after the workday ends at 5pm. Buzzy it ain't.

Dupont Circle is a booklover's paradise, and has the requisite sidewalk cafés as well. Souvenir shops here tend to be more interesting than on the Mall, and unique gifts and small luxuries abound. Shops here line Connecticut Avenue.

In artsy, ethnic **Adams Morgan**, you can get a henna tattoo or a real one; pick up a new indie CD, an African dress, some platform shoes and a vintage guitar – all within a three-block walk (on 18th Street around the junction with Columbia Road). Unlike Downtown areas, merchants here often keep odd hours, so it's best to call first.

Georgetown is where the posh and powerful live, and is also walking distance from two major universities, so shopping here caters to both old and new money and tastes. The city's finest antique stores are also here, as is the best central mall, Shops at Georgetown Park. The main drags are M Street and Wisconsin Avenue.

Fashion Centre at Pentagon City: *a glamorous shopping experience. See page 170.*

Capitol Hill's main attraction is Eastern Market, an extensive indoor and outdoor market with food vendors, fine art and, at weekends, antiques and the work of local artisans.

Chevy Chase/Upper Wisconsin Avenue on the DC/Maryland border is where the ladies who lunch do their shopping. Saks Fifth Avenue, Gianfranco Ferre and Neiman Marcus are among the many upscale clothiers located here in a clutch of posh but characterless malls. On the opposite side of the DC diamond's northern tip, 'Nuclear Free Zone' **Takoma Park**, long a haven for activists, hippies, artists and other left-leaning types, redresses the balance with speciality shops that sell Tibetan artefacts, rare musical instruments and funky vintage clothes.

One-stop shopping

Malls

Chevy Chase Pavilion

5335 Wisconsin Avenue, NW, at Western Avenue, Chevy Chase, Upper Northwest (686 5335). Friendship Heights Metro. **Open** 10am-8pm Mon-Fri; 10am-6pm Sat; noon-5pm Sun.

This small, self-contained shopping mall in Chevy Chase across the street from Mazza Gallerie (*see below*) has an elegant sensibility. Most of the stores, such as the Pottery Barn, Joan & David shoes and Country Road Australia, offer fashions and housewares. The food court has a good selection of international fare.

Fashion Centre at Pentagon City

1100 South Hayes Street, between Army Navy Drive & 15th Street, Arlington, VA (703 415 2400). Pentagon City Metro. **Open** 10am-9.30pm Mon-Fri; 11am-6pm Sun.

Just walking among the golden escalators and glass sculptures of this Arlington mall will make you feel rich and glamorous. It's a pleasure to shop at department store Nordstrom, which prides itself on its emphasis on customer service. There's also a Macy's. The four levels of shops range from mid-scale to upscale, including outposts of the Disney Store, Talbot's, the Limited, Liz Claiborne and Kenneth Cole.

Mazza Gallerie

5300 Wisconsin Avenue, NW, at Western Avenue, Chevy Chase, Upper Northwest (966 6114). Friendship Heights Metro. **Open** 10am-8pm Mon-Fri; 10am-6pm Sat; noon-5 Sun.

Construction efforts have dampened some of the glamour of this mall's interior looks, but there's still great shopping to be found. Posh Neiman Marcus anchors the mall at one end, while the dependable upscale bargain source, Filene's Basement (*see p179*), holds down the other. Other stores include Williams-Sonoma, with kitchen furnishings for the gourmet cook, athletic shoes from Foot Locker and Pampillonia Jewelers.

Shops at Georgetown Park

3222 M Street, NW, at Wisconsin Avenue, Georgetown (298 5577). Foggy Bottom-GWU Metro, then 30, 32, 34, 35, 36 bus. **Open** 10am-9pm Mon-Sat; noon-6pm Sun.

If walking through Georgetown in overly humid weather gets too much, this well-heeled, climate-controlled mall can be a welcome relief. From undergarments to outerwear, everything one could need is here – lingerie from Victoria's Secret, fashion from Ann Taylor and J Crew, raincoats and streetwise basics from Abercrombie & Fitch. There is a food court, but better food is available outside the mall.

Shops at National Place

13th & F Streets, NW, Downtown (662 1250). Metro Center Metro. **Open** 10am-7pm Mon-Sat; noon-5pm Sun.

Located in the middle of the Downtown theatre/museum/sightseeing scene, the Shops have a bit of a tourist trap aura and little you'd actually want to buy. Serious fashionistas would be better off in some of the city's more elegant or larger malls. Still, it's a convenient place to pick up something on the run and has a good selection of souvenir T-shirts and casual wear.

Union Station

50 Massachusetts Avenue, NE, at North Capitol Street, Union Station & Around (371 9441). Union Station Metro. **Open** 10am-9pm Mon-Sat; noon-6pm Sun.

One of the country's loveliest train stations now does double duty as a shopping mall, whose marble floors and wide staircases recall another era. The 100 or so shops are thoroughly modern, however, and include fine toiletries from Crabtree & Evelyn, wool goods at Pendleton, upscale toys at The Great Train Store and American-made decorative housewares at Appalachian Spring. The East Hall has Covent Garden-style vendors, selling jewellery and pretty gift items from all over the world. Good for gifts, souvenirs (there's a political ephemera concession) and leisure but less so for practical shopping, though there's a small liquor store and a decent-sized Olsson's bookshop, and a shoe repairer and film developer down the Metro escalators.

Watergate Shops

2650 Virginia Avenue, NW, at 26th Street, Foggy Bottom. Foggy Bottom-GWU Metro. **Open** 10am-6pm Mon-Sat.

As if the Watergate hotel's history of political intrigue and sexual dalliances weren't enough, the prices at the boutiques here are positively scandalous. You'll find Vera Wang Bridal Boutique, where dresses are priced from $3,000 to $20,000, as well as Louis Feraud, Gucci, Valentino, Saks Jandel and Yves St Laurent.

Department stores

These are freestanding department stores; many of the malls listed above also contain stores such as

Nordstrom (the best one's at the Fashion Centre at Pentagon City), Neiman Marcus (Mazza Galerie) and Macy's (also at Pentagon City).

Hecht's

12th & G Streets, NW, Downtown (628 6661). Metro Center Metro. **Open** 10am-8pm Mon-Sat; noon-6pm Sun. **Credit** AmEx, Disc, MC, V.

Hecht's should get an award for longevity: it's the only true freestanding department store left in Downtown where once there were many. An exit in the Metro station takes you directly into the store. Once inside you'll find mid-priced contemporary men's, women's and children's clothing from a range of well-known brands, as well as jewellery, cosmetics and home furnishings.

Lord & Taylor

5255 Western Avenue, NW, at Wisconsin Avenue, Chevy Chase, Upper Northwest (362 9600). Friendship Heights Metro. **Open** 10am-9pm Mon-Fri; 10am-7pm Sat; 11am-7pm Sun. **Credit** AmEx, Disc, MC, V.

Understated elegance describes this store, which specialises in classic American clothing for men, women and children. In addition to jewellery and cosmetics, it also has a department for larger-sized women. Typical labels found here include Jones New York, Liz Claiborne and Ralph Lauren.

Saks Fifth Avenue

5555 Wisconsin Avenue, NW, at South Park Avenue, Chevy Chase, MD (301 657 9000). Friendship Heights Metro. **Open** 10am-6pm Mon-Wed, Fri, Sat; 10am-9pm Thur; noon-6pm Sun. **Credit** AmEx, DC, Disc, MC, V.

Diamonds, furs, silk, lingerie… Sak's is the place for high-priced luxuries, from couture evening gowns to tailored designer suits.

Discount & factory outlets

Ames

514 Rhode Island Avenue, NE, at Fourth Street, Northeast (635 6022). Rhode Island Avenue Metro. **Open** 9am-9.30pm Mon, Wed-Sat; 8am-9.30pm Tue; 9am-8pm Sun. **Credit** AmEx, DC, Disc, MC, V.

'Bargains by the bagful' is Ames's motto – and it's true. It's just too bad the DC location is so short on customer service. Self-sufficient shoppers will find ridiculously low-priced casual clothing, shoes, housewares, furnishings and electronics.

City Place Mall

8661 Colesville Road, at Fenton Street, Silver Spring, MD (301 589 1091). Silver Spring Metro. **Open** 10am-9pm Mon-Sat; noon-6pm Sun.

Bargain behemoths Nordstrom Rack, Marshall's, Ross Dress for Less and Burlington Coat Factory are joined by an array of cheap shops in this basic mall.

Potomac Mills Discount Mall

2700 Potomac Mills Circle, Woodbridge, VA (1-703 490 5948). **Open** 10am-9.30pm Mon-Sat; 11am-7pm Sun.

Floral heaven at **Eastern Market** *(page 181).*

You definitely need a car to reach this outlet oasis, one of the Washington area's biggest tourist draws. Not only to make the trip from DC to the suburban hinterlands, but to travel from store to store in the mile-long mall. The 230 stores include Ikea, Linens N Things, Ann Taylor, Eddie Bauer, Calvin Klein and many many more.

Antiques & flea markets

Antique stores tend to be clustered in neighbourhoods. Georgetown has the most; you can pick up a free guide in stores. Capitol Hill, Dupont Circle and Adams Morgan have a few, and there is also a cluster of antique and vintage stores in the U Street corridor and on 14th Street, branching off U Street towards Q Street.

Eastern Market Flea Market

Seventh Street, between Pennsylvania & North Carolina Avenues, SE, Capitol Hill (703 534 7612). Eastern Market Metro. **Open** 10am-5pm Sun.

The beauty of flea markets is that you can haggle with stallholders over prices of everything from walnut wardrobes to jazz 78s. This market has the most democratic vibe of all the antique centres.

Georgetown Flea Market

Parking lot of the Hardy Middle School, Wisconsin Avenue, between S & T Streets, NW, Georgetown

(296 4989). Foggy Bottom-GWU Metro, then 30, 32, 34, 35, 36 bus. **Open** 9am-5pm Sun.
This flea market has a reputation for being slightly overpriced. Still, devotees say early risers can get some great finds.

Millennium Decorative Arts

1528 U Street, NW, between 15th & 16th Streets, U Street/14th Street Corridor (483 1218). U Street-Cardozo Metro. **Open** 3.30-7pm Mon; noon-7pm Thur-Sun. **Credit** AmEx, MC, V.
Traditional antiquers might quibble with Millennium's claim to be a dealer of '20th-century antiques', but lovers of furniture, clothes, books and knick-knacks from the 1940s to the 1970s will find shopping here completely satisfying.

Miss Pixie's

1810 Adams Mill Road, NW, between 18th Street & Columbia Road, Adams Morgan (232 8171). Woodley Park-Zoo Metro, then 90, 91, 92, 93, 96 bus. **Open** noon-9pm Thur; noon-7pm Fri-Sun. **Credit** MC, V.
A pleasant hodgepodge of tableware, bed frames, books, furniture, clothes and accessories. They even provide free miniature chocolate-chip cookies, but you have to bring your own milk.

Arts & entertainment

Books

The national book chains are, of course, present in town. **Barnes & Noble** has a large store in Georgetown (3040 M Street, NW; 965 9880), and there's a **Borders** in Foggy Bottom (1800 L Street; 466 4999). Both have an extensive selection of books and pleasant cafés, as does the local alternative, **Olsson's Books & Records** (418 Seventh Street, NW; 638 4882). But more interesting are the smaller, independent shops:

ADC Map & Travel Store

1636 I Street, NW, between Connecticut Avenue & 17th Street, Downtown (628 2608/1-800 544 2659). Farragut West Metro. **Open** 9am-6.30pm Mon-Thur; 9am-5.30pm Fri; 11am-5pm Sat. **Credit** MC, V.
You'll find street maps and a comprehensive Metro system map that shows all the bus and train routes, as well as atlases, nautical charts and other items for geography buffs. ADC also has an excellent selection of guidebooks to plan day trips to Virginia and Maryland, many centred around a specific sport such as biking or white water rafting.

Bird-In-Hand Bookstore & Gallery

323 Seventh Street, SE, at Pennsylvania Avenue, Capitol Hill (543 0744). Eastern Market Metro. **Open** 10am-5pm Tue-Sat. **Credit** AmEx, DC, MC, V.
If you missed a major museum exhibition, you're likely to find the catalogue here, along with dozens of books on art, architecture and design.

Chapters

1512 K Street, NW, between 15th & 16th Streets, Downtown (347 5495). McPherson Square Metro. **Open** 10am-6.30pm Mon-Fri; 11am-5pm Sat. **Credit** AmEx, MC, V.
This store prides itself on its literary inclinations. Staff recommendations point browsers to worthwhile selections, while benches around the store allow patrons to read a few pages before buying.

A café, a restaurant and plenty of things to read at **Kramerbooks** *(page 175).*

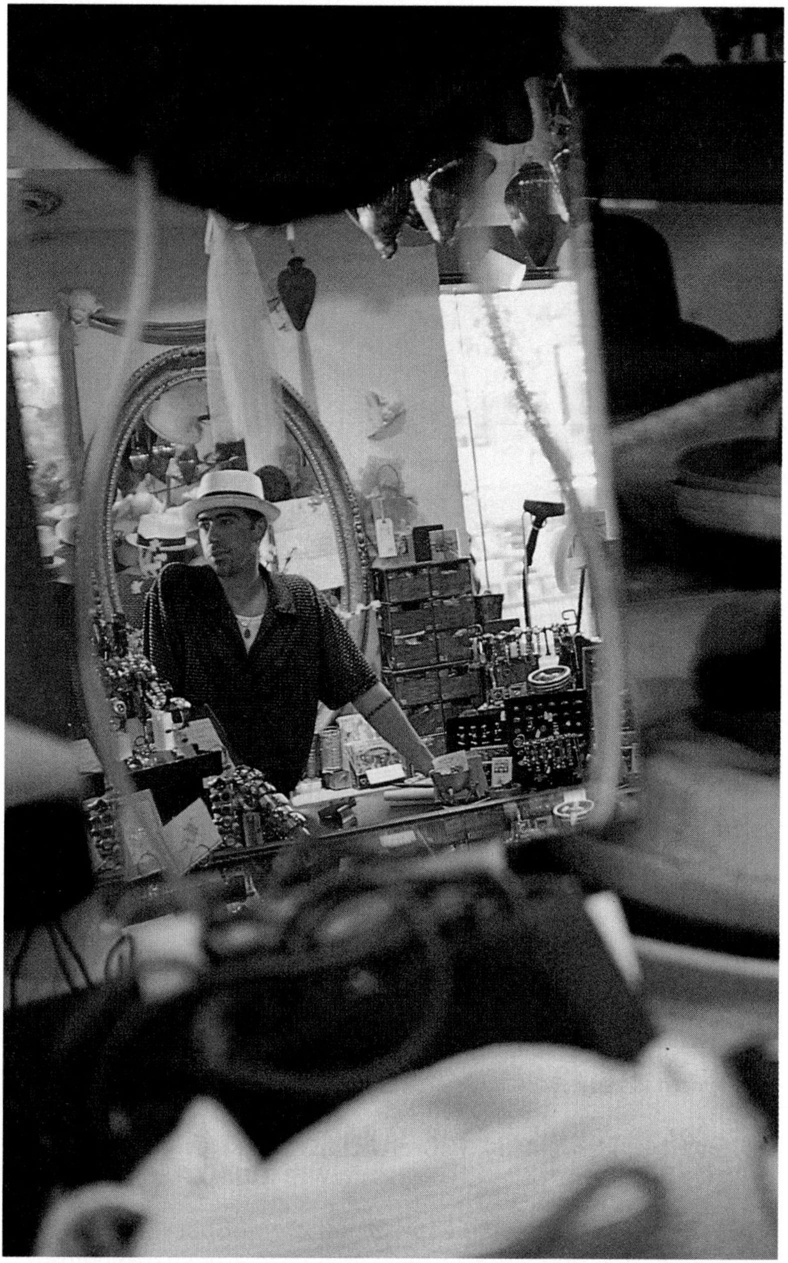

Vintage accessories at **Proper Topper** *in Dupont Circle (page 178).*

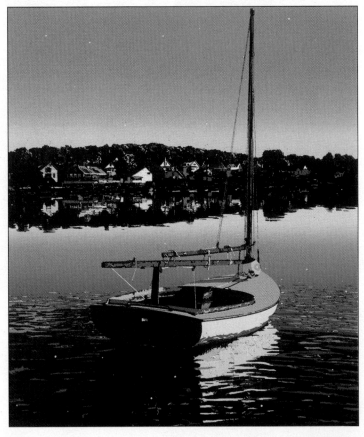

Kramerbooks

1517 Connecticut Avenue, NW, at Q Street, Dupont Circle (387 1400). Dupont Circle Metro. **Open** 7am-1am Mon-Thur; 7am Fri-1am Sun. **Credit** AmEx, Disc, MC, V.

The window display offers bestselling fiction such as Frank McCourt's *Angela's Ashes* and funny Japanese books on the intricacies of farting. Afterwords Café is on the same premises.

Lammas Women's Books & More

1607 17th Street, NW, at Q Street, Dupont Circle (775 8218). Dupont Circle Metro. **Open** 11am-9.30pm Mon-Thur; 11am-10.30pm Fri; noon-10.30pm Sat; noon-9.30pm Sun. **Credit** AmEx, MC, V.

The bra-burning 1960s may have gone, but Lammas keeps the torch going by selling female-penned books and music with feminist and lesbian slants.

Mysterybooks

1715 Connecticut Avenue, NW, at R Street, Dupont Circle (483 1600/1-800 955 2279). Dupont Circle Metro. **Open** 11am-7pm Mon-Fri; 10am-6pm Sat; noon-5pm Sun. **Credit** MC, V.

As its name suggests, you can find all manner of mystery and suspense books here, from Agatha Christie to Patricia Cornwell, Michael Connelly to Mary Higgins Clark.

Politics & Prose

5015 Connecticut Avenue, NW, between Fessenden Street & Nebraska Avenue, Upper Northwest (364 1919/1-800 722 0790). Van Ness-UDC Metro, then L1, L2 bus. **Open** 9am-10.30pm Mon-Thur, Sun; 9am-midnight Fri, Sat. **Credit** AmEx, MC, V.

Despite the name, this bookstore isn't the least bit stuffy. Author readings take place several times a week, a children's play section is surrounded by books for young people and a cosy café allows for thoughtful adult conversation.

Website: www.politics-prose.com

Second Story Books

2000 P Street, NW, at 20th Street, Dupont Circle (659 8884). Dupont Circle Metro. **Open** 10am-10pm daily. **Credit** AmEx, Disc, MC, V.

One of the best second-hand bookstores in the city. It also has a solid collection of records, posters and memorabilia.

Sisterspace & Books

1515 U Street, NW, between 15th & 16th Streets, U Street/14th Street Corridor (332 3433). U Street-Cardozo Metro. **Open** 10am-7pm Mon-Sat; noon-5pm Sun. **Credit** AmEx, MC, V.

With its regular readings, workshops and discussion groups, this bookshop has become a focus centre for the area's black womanist community.

Vertigo Books

1337 Connecticut Avenue, NW, between Dupont Circle & N Street, Dupont Circle (429 9272). Dupont Circle Metro. **Open** 10am-7pm Mon-Fri; 11am-7pm Sat; noon-5pm Sun. **Credit** AmEx, MC, V.

This shop has one of the best calendars of literary events in the city, with an emphasis on African-American writers, ranging from novelist Walter Mosley to poet Rita Dove. The Noam Chomsky book group also meets here.

Yawa Books & Gifts

2206 18th Street, NW, between Wyoming Avenue & Kalorama Road, Adams Morgan (483 6805). Woodley Park-Zoo Metro, then 90, 91, 92, 93, 96 bus. **Open** 11am-8pm Mon-Fri; 11am-9pm Sat; noon-6pm Sun. **Credit** AmEx, MC, V.

Books, incense, gifts and cards from the African motherland fill this friendly store.

Cameras & electronics

Circuit City Express

Georgetown Park, 3222 M Street, NW, at Wisconsin Avenue, Georgetown (944 1870). Foggy Bottom-GWU Metro, then 30, 32, 34, 35, 36 bus. **Open** 10am-9pm Mon-Sat; noon-6pm Sun. **Credit** AmEx, Disc, MC, V.

One-stop shop for all your basic electronic needs.

CVS

6-7 Dupont Circle, NW, between Massachusetts & New Hampshire Avenues, Dupont Circle (833 5704). Dupont Circle Metro. **Open** 24 hours daily. **Credit** AmEx, DC, Disc, MC, V.

With more than 30 branches around the city, this 24-hour drugstore is a reliable source for one-hour photo developing and general supplies. Call 1-800 746 7287 to find your nearest location.

Motophoto

1105 19th Street, NW, at L Street, Foggy Bottom (293 5484). Farragut North Metro. **Open** 8am-7pm Mon-Fri; 9am-5pm Sat. **Credit** AmEx, MC, V.

Known for its one-hour film processing service, Motophoto also does passport and visa photos at its eight DC locations.

RadioShack

1100 15th Street, NW, at L Street, Downtown (296 2311). McPherson Square Metro. **Open** 9am-7pm Mon-Fri; 10am-5pm Sat. **Credit** AmEx, Disc, MC, V.

Once synonymous with disposable equipment, the RadioShack chain has successfully improved the quality of its store-brand products while keeping low prices. It also sells brand-name goods.

Ritz Camera

1750 L Street, NW, at 18th Street, Downtown (861 7710). Farragut North Metro. **Open** 8.30am-6pm Mon-Fri. **Credit** AmEx, Disc, MC, V.

Ritz sells cameras and film at five locations around the city, as well as providing film developing.

Music & video

DC CD

2423 18th Street, NW, between Biltmore Street & Columbia Road, Adams Morgan (588 1810). Woodley Park-Zoo Metro, then 90, 91, 92, 93, 96 bus. **Open** 11am-midnight Mon-Thur; 11am-2am Fri, Sat; noon-10pm Sun. **Credit** AmEx, Disc, MC, V.

Get an earful of your favourite electonica at **Musicnow**.

This Adams Morgan store stocks plenty of good indie rock, as well as alternative, hip hop and general rock. The staff will usually open packaging so that customers can listen before buying. There are also occasional in-store performances by local bands and flyers for local music events.

Musicnow

3209 M Street, NW, at Wisconsin Avenue, Georgetown (338 5638). Foggy Bottom-GWU Metro, then 30, 32, 34, 35, 36 bus. **Open** noon-9.30pm Mon-Thur; noon-10.30pm Fri, Sat; noon-7pm Sun. **Credit** AmEx, DC, Disc, MC, V.

The best source for electronic dance music, from early techno to the latest drum 'n' bass. It is also a good source for information on upcoming parties and raves.

Sankofa Video

2714 Georgia Avenue, NW, between Girard & Fairmont Streets, Shaw (234 4755). Columbia Heights Metro. **Open** 10am-8pm daily. **Credit** AmEx, DC, Disc, MC, V.

Owned by acclaimed film maker Haile Gerima, this film production centre also has a video store with a wide selection of African, international and African-American films for sale and rental.

Tower Records

2000 Pennsylvania Avenue, NW, between 21st & I Streets, Foggy Bottom (331 2400). Foggy Bottom-GWU Metro. **Open** 9am-midnight daily. **Credit** AmEx, Disc, MC, V.

This multimedia giant has CDs and cassettes of every genre of music, as well as music-related books and magazines.

Twelve Inches Dance Records

2010 P Street, NW, at 20th Street, Dupont Circle (659 2010). Dupont Circle Metro. **Open** noon-9pm Mon-Sat; 1-6pm Sun. **Credit** AmEx, Disc, MC, V.

The name says it all. You can buy CDs and cassettes here, but they specialise in 12in remix singles on vinyl. Many of the city's DJs consider this store a second home.

Washington Video

2012 S Street, NW, at Connecticut Avenue, Dupont Circle (265 1141). Dupont Circle Metro. **Open** 10am-11pm Mon-Sat; 11am-10pm Sun. **Credit** AmEx, MC, V.

This local chain, with four outposts around the city, has an excellent selection of old movies, foreign films and camp classics, for sale or rent.

Toys & games

Another Universe

3060 M Street, NW, between Wisconsin Avenue & Thomas Jefferson Street, Georgetown (333 8651). Foggy Bottom-GWU Metro, then 30, 32, 34, 35, 36 bus. **Open** 11am-9pm Mon-Thur; 11am-10pm Fri, Sat. **Credit** AmEx, Disc, MC, V.

This is the shop to satisfy your jones for science fiction, underground comics and graphic novels, as well the place to find obscure action figures and brainteaser games.

FAO Schwarz

Shops at Georgetown Park, 3222 M Street, NW, at Wisconsin Avenue, Georgetown (965 7000). Foggy Bottom-GWU Metro, then 30, 32, 34, 35, 36 bus.

Open 10am-9pm Mon-Sat; noon-6pm Sun. **Credit** AmEx, DC, Disc, MC, V.
Giant stuffed animals at this upscale toy chainstore can go for as much as $300, but it also offers books, games, music and hand-crafted gifts.

Sullivan's Toy Store

3412 Wisconsin Avenue, NW, between Idaho Avenue & Newark Street, Upper Northwest (362 1343). Tenleytown-AU Metro, then 30, 32, 34, 35, 36 bus. **Open** 10am-6pm Mon, Tue, Sat; 10am-7pm Wed-Fri; noon-5pm Sun. **Credit** AmEx, Disc, MC, V.
A classic toy store with *Star Wars* action figures, Teletubbies, Barbie dolls, board games, kites and puzzles as well as hundreds of hands-on crafts kits for ages five to 12 – make-your-own keychain, bead-your-own necklace, build-your-own model airplane. (Not, sadly, pay-your-own credit account.)

Décor & home supplies

Little Caledonia

1419 Wisconsin Avenue, NW, at P Street, Georgetown (333 4700). Foggy Bottom-GWU Metro, then 30, 32, 34, 35, 36 bus. **Open** 10am-6pm Mon-Sat; noon-5pm Sun. **Credit** AmEx, Disc, MC, V.
Beautiful plates for the dining table or display case, vases, candleholders, lamps and lots of other decorative housewares fill this converted nine-room townhouse.

Restoration Hardware

1222 Wisconsin Avenue, NW, at Prospect Street, Georgetown (625 2771). Foggy Bottom-GWU Metro, then 30, 32, 34, 35, 36 bus. **Open** 10am-9pm Mon-Thur; 10am-10pm Fri, Sat; noon-6pm Sun. **Credit** AmEx, MC, V.
A bit like Banana Republic for the home, this chain offers appealing displays of kitchenware, bedding and bathroom accessories, much of it retro-style.

Skynear & Co

2122 18th Street, NW, at Wyoming Avenue, Adams Morgan (797 7160). Woodley Park-Zoo Metro, then 90, 91, 92, 93, 96 bus. **Open** 11am-7pm Mon-Sat; noon-6pm Sun. **Credit** AmEx, Disc, MC, V.
From stylised champagne flutes to boldly painted plateware, this store sells sleek, modern, artsy housewares from around the world.

Fashion

DC has all the usual clothing chains. Stores such as the Gap, Ann Taylor and Limited Express are clustered in Downtown along Connecticut Avenue. Georgetown is where you'll find the trendier stores, such as Urban Outfitters, Benetton and Betsy Johnson, as well as pricier shops such as Emporio Armani and Diesel. True designer boutiques tend to be located in the upper Wisconsin Avenue area, and in the Watergate Shops (*see p170*).

What follows is a sampling of the city's more unique fashion spots.

Amano

7030 Carroll Avenue, between Westmoreland & Tulip Avenues, Takoma Park, MD (301 270 1140). Takoma Metro. **Open** 10.30am-7.30pm Mon-Thur; 10.30am-8pm Fri; 10.30pm-6pm Sun; 10am-5pm Sun. **Credit** AmEx, MC, V.
Women who like to look both relaxed and sophisticated will appreciate Amano's mix of clean lines, comfortable loose tunics and wide-leg pants in linens and knits.

Betty

2439 18th Street, NW, between Belmont & Columbia Roads, Adams Morgan (234 2389). Woodley Park-Zoo Metro, then 90, 91, 92, 93, 96 bus. **Open** noon-8pm Mon, Wed, Thur; noon-9pm Fri, Sat; 1pm-6pm Sun. **Credit** Disc, MC, V.
Fun, sexy, young, fashion-conscious clothes that seem of the moment without being silly or too trendy. Many of the clothes are made by small independent designers locally and from New York.

Betsy Fisher

1224 Connecticut Avenue, NW, between N Street & Jefferson Place, Dupont Circle (785 1975). Dupont Circle Metro. **Open** 10am-7pm Mon-Wed, Fri; 10am-8pm Thur; 10am-6pm Sat. **Credit** AmEx, DC, Disc, MC, V.
Betsy Fisher sells stylish, contemporary suits and dresses by designers such as Anna Sui, Tahari and Vivienne Tam for Washington's slightly more daring women.

Brooks Brothers

1201 Connecticut Avenue, NW, at Rhode Island Avenue, Dupont Circle (659 4650). Farragut North Metro. **Open** 9.30am-7pm Mon-Fri; 9.30am-6pm Sat; noon-5pm Sun. **Credit** AmEx, DC, Disc, MC, V.
The place to go if you want to look like a DC lawyer or high-powered lobbyist. Yes, it's a chain, but in a conservative town like Washington, longevity sometimes passes for distinctiveness.

Commander Salamander

1420 Wisconsin Avenue, NW, between O & P Streets, Georgetown (337 2265). Foggy Bottom-GWU Metro, then 30, 32, 34, 35, 36 bus. **Open** 10am-9pm Mon-Thur; 10am-10pm Fri, Sat; noon-7pm Sun. **Credit** AmEx, Disc, MC, V.
Head here if you need to update the streak of blue Manic Panic dye in your hair, buy some bondage pants or a clear plastic backpack made in Japan.

Khismet Showroom

1800 Belmont Road, NW, at 18th Street, Adams Morgan (234 7778). Woodley Park-Zoo Metro, then 90, 91, 92, 93, 96 bus. **Open** 1-8pm Sat; 1-6pm Sun; and by appointment. **Credit** AmEx, DC, Disc, MC, V.
Designer Millée Spears puts a new twist on traditional African patterns and designs in her design studio/boutique.

Peace Frogs

1073 Wisconsin Avenue, NW, between K & M Streets, Georgetown (298 7663). Foggy Bottom-GWU Metro, then 30, 32, 34, 35, 36 bus.

Contemporary African-inspired clothing and more at **Trade Secrets**.

Open 11am-9pm Mon-Thur; 11am-10pm Fri, Sat; noon-6pm Sun. **Credit** MC, V.
Good vibes emanate from the colourful, eco-friendly T-shirts and casual gear in this tiny store which takes frog appreciation to new levels.

Rizik's

1100 Connecticut Avenue, NW, at L Street, Downtown (223 4050). Farragut North Metro. **Open** 9am-6pm Mon-Wed, Fri, Sat; 9am-8pm Thur. **Credit** AmEx, MC, V.
Hosiery starts at $30, but prices for the beautiful designer dresses and suits tend to be more to scale.

Trade Secrets

1515 U Street, NW, between 15th & 16th Streets, U Street/14th Street Corridor (667 0634). U Street-Cardozo Metro. **Open** 11am-7pm Tue-Sat; noon-5pm Sun. **Credit** AmEx, DC, Disc, MC, V.
These contemporary, African-influenced designs, combining raw silk, velvet and knobby wool fabrics, just beg to be touched.

Up Against the Wall

3219 M Street, NW, at Wisconsin Avenue, Georgetown (337 9316). Foggy Bottom-GWU Metro, then 30, 32, 34, 35, 36 bus. **Open** 10am-9.30pm Mon-Thur; 10am-10pm Fri, Sat; 1am-7pm Sun. **Credit** AmEx, Disc, MC, V.
Streetwear and club gear appealing to musical youth, featuring labels such as Mossimo and Porn Star. A DJ plays in the main Georgetown store. The Wearhouse outlet in Adams Morgan (1749 Columbia Road; 328 8627) has great clearance bargains.

Accessories

Proper Topper

1350 Connecticut Avenue, NW, between Dupont Circle & N Street, Dupont Circle (842 3055). Dupont Circle Metro. **Open** 10am-7pm Mon-Wed, Fri, Sat; 10am-8pm Thur; noon-6pm Sun. **Credit** AmEx, MC, V.
Audrey Hepburn-style hats, handmade hair clips, 1920s-style rings and necklaces, velvet scarves, striking sunglasses – this store has accessories for every season, every occasion.

Tiny Jewel Box

1147 Connecticut Avenue, NW, between L & M Streets, Downtown (393 2747). Farragut North Metro. **Open** 9.30am-5pm Mon-Sat; *July-Aug* closed Sat. **Credit** AmEx, MC, V.
Three slim floors filled with more than 9,000 pieces of jewellery, ranging from estate-sale antiques to moderately priced costume pieces to high-end contemporary designs. It's a bit like a small Harvey Nichols, sans clothing, with scarves, gloves, handbags and gift items.

Tip Tops

1140 19th Street, NW, between L & M Streets, Foggy Bottom (822 9334). Farragut North or

Farragut West Metro. **Open** 10am-7pm Mon-Fri; 11am-5pm Sat. **Credit** AmEx, Disc, MC, V.
Fab hats and cool sunglasses at great prices.

Discount fashion

See also page 171 **Discount & factory outlets**.

Filene's Basement

Mazza Gallerie, 5300 Wisconsin Avenue, NW, at Jenifer Street, Chevy Chase, Upper Northwest (966 0208), Friendship Heights Metro. **Open** 10am-9pm Mon-Sat; noon-6pm Sun. **Credit** AmEx, Disc, MC, V.
Glamour at a fraction of the cost. Filene's has low prices on designer clothing from casual to upscale. The clearance sales can often yield great prizes.
Branch: 1133 Connecticut Avenue, NW, Downtown (872 8430).

Sunny's the Affordable Outdoor Store

912 F Street, NW, at Ninth Street, Downtown (737 2032). Gallery Place-Chinatown Metro. **Open** 9am-6.30pm Mon-Sat; 11am-5pm Sun. **Credit** Disc, MC, V.
In addition to military surplus clothing, Sunny's also sells workwear by brands such as Ben Davis and Carhartt, combat and construction boots and camping equipment.

TJ Maxx

4350 Jenifer Street, NW, at Wisconsin Avenue, Upper Northwest (237 7616). Friendship Heights Metro. **Open** 10am-9pm Mon-Sat; noon-6pm Sun. **Credit** AmEx, Disc, MC, V.
Not as glam as its neighbour, Filene's, TJ Maxx offers tremendous savings on clothing for men, women and children, as well as housewares and accessories.

Drycleaning & laundry

Georgetown Cleaners

1070 31st Street, NW, at M Street, Georgetown (965 9655). Foggy Bottom-GWU Metro, then 30, 32, 34, 35, 36 bus. **Open** 7.30am-7pm Mon-Fri; 8.30am-6pm Sat. **Credit** MC, V.
Residents of this posh neighbourhood appreciate this cleaner's high-quality services: drycleaning, laundry, fur storage, alterations and repairs.

Imperial Valet

1331 Connecticut Avenue, NW, between Dupont Circle & N Street, Dupont Circle (785 1444). Dupont Circle Metro. **Open** 7.30am-6.30pm Mon-Fri; 9am-3pm Sat. **Credit** AmEx, MC, V.
Imperial offers one-hour drycleaning and same-day laundry services. All work is done on the premises and includes alterations, reweaving, garment and shoe dying, and fur and fine garment cleaning.

Mom's Laundry

686 1300. **Open** 6.30am-9pm Mon-Fri; 10am-6pm Sat; noon-6pm Sun. **Credit** AmEx, Disc, MC, V.
Mom will pick up your laundry and return it the following day, washed and folded. They also have a drycleaning service.

Eyewear

For Eyes

2021 L Street, NW, between 20th & [illegible], Foggy Bottom (659 0077). Farragut West Metro. **Open** 9.30am-6pm Mon-Fri; 10am-5pm Sat. **Credit** AmEx, Disc, MC, V.
This national chain, with four locations in DC, offers quality eye examinations and stylish eyewear at inexpensive prices.

Hour Eyes

1915 M Street, NW, at 19th Street, Dupont Circle (463 6364). Dupont Circle or Farragut West Metro. **Open** 8.30am-5.30pm Mon-Thur; 8.30am-4.30pm Fri; 9am-3pm Sat. **Credit** AmEx, Disc, MC, V.
A good place for emergencies or if you're short of time: you can get new glasses in an hour at three locations in the city.

Embassy Opticians

1325 Connecticut Avenue, NW, between Dupont Circle & N Street, Dupont Circle (785 5700). Dupont Circle Metro. **Open** 9am-6pm Mon, Tue, Thur, Fri; 9am-7pm Wed; 9.30am-5pm Sat. **Credit** AmEx, DC, Disc, MC, V.
This full-service shop features seriously stylish eyewear by top designers (Oliver Peoples, Kata, Kenneth Cole) for those who don't mind spending lots of cash for hip specs.

Shoes

Bootlegger

1420 Wisconsin Avenue, NW, between O & P Streets, Georgetown (333 0373). Foggy Bottom-GWU Metro, then 30, 32, 34, 35, 36 bus. **Open** 10am-7pm Mon-Wed; 10am-9pm Thur, Fri; 10am-8pm Sat. **Credit** AmEx, Disc, MC, V.
This is the place for heavy-soled, pavement-stomping, urban dweller shoes, from colourful Doc Martens to fashionable Birkenstocks.

Comfort One

1630 Connecticut Avenue, NW, between Q & R Streets, Dupont Circle (328 3141). Dupont Circle Metro. **Open** 10am-9pm Mon-Thur; 10am-10pm Fri, Sat; 11am-7pm Sun. **Credit** AmEx, Disc, MC, V.
Stylish shoes that promise not to pinch or bite, by designers such as Arcopedia, Ecco and Bastad.

Parade of Shoes

1020 Connecticut Avenue, NW, between K & L Streets, Downtown (872 8581). Farragut North Metro. **Open** 9am-7pm Mon-Fri; 10am-6pm Sat. **Credit** AmEx, Disc, MC, V.
It seems like there's always a sale at this shop offering fabulous leather knock-offs of popular designer styles, from professional pumps to strappy evening shoes.

Shake Your Booty

2324 18th Street, NW, at Belmont Road, Adams Morgan (518 8205). Woodley Park-Zoo Metro, then 90, 91, 92, 93, 96 bus. **Open** noon-8pm Mon, Wed-Fri; noon-9pm Sat; noon-6pm Sun. **Credit** AmEx, MC, V.

Depending on how you look at it, this store is a shoe fetishist's worst nightmare or best friend. The two branches offer stylish, youthful platforms, pumps and sandals by the likes of Steve Madden and Fornarina, as well as distinctive accessories. **Branch**: 3225 M Street, NW, Georgetown (333 6524).

Shoe Scene

1330 Connecticut Avenue, NW, between Dupont Circle & N Street, Dupont Circle (659 2194). Dupont Circle Metro. **Open** 10am-6.30pm Mon-Fri; 10am-6pm Sat. **Credit** AmEx, Disc, MC, V.
Popular with busy Washington women, Shoe Scene offers a surprisingly wide selection of contemporary styles at moderate prices.

Shoe & luggage repair

Georgetown Shoe Hospital

3147 Dumbarton Street, NW, between Wisconsin Avenue & 31st Street, Georgetown (965 2478). Foggy Bottom-GWU Metro, then 30, 32, 34, 35, 36 bus. **Open** 10am-7pm daily. **Credit** V.
If it can be fixed at all, the staff here will do it right. In addition to the usual refitting of soles and shoes, they can transform any pair of regular shoes into customised platforms.

Lane's

1146 Connecticut Avenue, NW, at M Street, Downtown (452 1146). Farragut North Metro. **Open** 9.30am-6pm Mon-Fri; 9.30am-5pm Sat. **Credit** AmEx, MC, V.
Handily located, Lane's does luggage repairs and specialises in business travellers' needs, from briefcases to personal planners to fine pens and gifts.

Specialist

Backstage

2101 P Street, NW, at 21st Street, Dupont Circle (775 1488). Dupont Circle Metro. **Open** 10am-6pm Mon-Sat; 10am-7pm Thur. **Credit** AmEx, MC, V.
This performing arts store has costumes to rent or buy, plus wigs, make-up, masks and anything else you might possibly need for a theatrical production or party.

Dream Dresser

1042 Wisconsin Avenue, NW, between K & M Streets, Georgetown (625 0373). Foggy Bottom-GWU Metro, then 30, 32, 34, 35, 36 bus. **Open** 11am-8pm Mon-Sat. **Credit** AmEx, MC, V.
From latex dresses to strappy, 6in spike-heeled boots, this store offers an array of fetish fashions for professionals, or those who just like to experience something different on the side.

Georgetown Formal Wear & Custom Tailor

1251 Wisconsin Avenue, NW, between M & N Streets (625 2247). Foggy Bottom-GWU Metro. **Open** 10am-7pm Mon-Sat. **Credit** AmEx, Disc, MC, V.
Free pick-up and delivery to Downtown hotels.

Scogna Formal Wear

1908 L Street, NW, between 19th & 20th Streets, Foggy Bottom (296 4555). Farragut North or Farragut West Metro. **Open** 9am-5.45pm Mon-Fri; 9am-2pm Sat. **Credit** AmEx, Disc, MC, V.
Since 1920 the proprietors of this shop have rented, sold and tailored many a tuxedo to Washington men.

Vintage & second-hand

Glad Rags

7306 Carroll Avenue, at Ethan Allen Avenue (State Route 410), Takoma Park, MD (301 891 6870). Takoma Metro, then 12, 13, 18 Ride-On bus. **Open** 10am-6pm Mon, Tue, Thur-Sat; 10am-7pm Wed; noon-5pm Sun. **Credit** MC, V.
You'll find brightly coloured clothing, happily gaudy accessories and bargains galore in this vintage second-hand shop.

Meeps & Aunt Neensie's

1520 U Street, NW, between 15th & 16th Streets, U Street/14th Street Corridor (265 6546). U Street-Cardozo Metro. **Open** 3-7pm Thur, Fri; noon-7pm Sat; 2-6pm Sun. **Credit** MC, V.
With plenty of old clothes for men and women, especially from the 1950s and 1960s, rummaging through this store located in a classic townhouse feels like going through an old relative's closet.

Mood Indigo

1214 U Street, NW, at 13th Street, U Street/14th Street Corridor (265 6366). U Street-Cardozo Metro. **Open** 6-8pm Tue-Fri; noon-8pm Sat; 2-5pm Sun. **Credit** AmEx, Disc, MC, V.
This store, located in an old drycleaner's complete with motorised clothing rack, provides old-movie glamour with many well-kept pieces from the 1940s as well as more recent decades.

Secondi

1702 Connecticut Avenue, NW, at R Street, Dupont Circle (667 1122). Dupont Circle Metro. **Open** 11am-6pm Mon, Tue, Sat; 11am-7pm Wed-Fri; 1-5pm Sun. **Credit** AmEx, MC, V.
Style-conscious Washingtonians swear by this wallet-friendly second-hand shop, which offers everything from designer suits and dresses to casual wear and accessories. It also has a small men's section.

Florists

Baumgarten Krueger Florists

1-800 377 7080. **Credit** AmEx, Disc, MC, V.
This established FTD (Florists' Transworld Delivery) florist offers same-day and worldwide delivery services and takes orders 24 hours a day from its free catalogue.

Johnson's Flower & Garden Center

4200 Wisconsin Avenue, NW, at Van Ness Street, Upper Northwest (244 6100). Tenleytown-AU Metro. **Open** 8.30am-6.30pm Mon-Thur, Sat; 7.30am-7.30pm Fri; 9am-5.30pm Sun. **Credit** AmEx, Disc, MC, V.

From beautiful, freshly cut flowers to potted plants for the home and garden, Johnson's has the best selection in the city, as well as friendly and knowledgable staff who don't mind explaining how best to make your garden grow.

Food & drink

Bakeries

Firehook Bakery & Coffeehouse
1909 Q Street, NW, at Connecticut Avenue, Dupont Circle (588 9296). Dupont Circle Metro. **Open** 7am-8pm Mon-Thur; 7am-10pm Fri; 9am-10pm Sat; 9am-8pm Sun. **Credit** MC, V.
All the many wonderful breads here are made with unbleached, organic flour and are naturally leavened, giving them a rich, sourdough taste.

Heller's
3221 Mount Pleasant Street, NW, between Park Road & Lamont Street, Mount Pleasant & North (265 1190). Columbia Heights Metro. **Open** 6.30am-6.30pm Mon-Sat; 6.30am-2pm Sun. **Credit** AmEx, Disc, MC, V.
Until a few years ago, Heller's décor hadn't changed much since its beginnings in 1928. Fortunately, the café-style renovation hasn't affected its output of great cakes, croissants and pastries.

Uptown Bakers
3313 Connecticut Avenue, NW, between Newark & Macomb Streets, Cleveland Park (362 6262). Cleveland Park Metro. **Open** 7am-7.30pm Mon-Sat; 7.30am-7pm Sun. **No credit cards.**
Considered by many to make the best bread in the city, Uptown ships its crusty loaves to stores all over the region daily. At the premises, you can also get delicious soups and sandwiches to take away.

Beer & wine

Georgetown Wine & Spirits
2701 P Street, NW, at 27th Street, Georgetown (338 5500). Dupont Circle Metro, then G2 bus. **Open** 10am-9pm Mon-Sat. **Credit** AmEx, Disc, MC, V.
This reliable shop offers a solid range of wine, beer and spirits, augmented by cigars and Saturday afternoon wine tastings.

The Wine Specialists
2115 M Street, NW, between 21st Street & New Hampshire Avenue, Dupont Circle (833 0707). Dupont Circle Metro. **Open** 10am-8pm Mon, Tue, Sat; 10am-9pm Wed, Thur, Fri. **Credit** AmEx, MC, V.
In addition to a good selection of wine, this conveniently located shop specialises in single malt whiskies and fine brandies.

Ethnic

Addisu Gebeya
2202 18th Street, NW, between Wyoming Avenue & Kalorama Road, Adams Morgan (986 6013). Woodley Park-Zoo Metro, then 90, 91, 92, 93, 96 bus. **Open** 9am-10pm Mon-Sat; 9am-9pm Sun. **Credit** AmEx, MC, V.
This Ethiopian market sells an array of spices, lentils, spongy injera bread and the special teff flour used to make it, as well as Ethiopian cookbooks.

Da Hua Market
623 H Street, NW, at Seventh Street, Downtown (371 8888). Gallery Place-Chinatown Metro. **Open** 10am-8pm daily. **Credit** Disc, MC, V.
One of the increasingly few authentic Asian shops in Chinatown, offering fresh produce, packaged goods, seasonings and a broad selection of teas and imported confectionery.

Manuel's Grocery
1813 Columbia Road, NW, at 18th Street, Adams Morgan (986 5680). Woodley Park-Zoo Metro, then 90, 91, 92, 93, 96 bus. **Open** 8.30am-10pm Mon-Thur, Sun; 8am-11pm Fri, Sat. **Credit** AmEx, Disc, MC, V.
You'll find all the ingredients you need to make authentic Latin American and Caribbean foods at low prices. And you can't beat the home-made tamales sold at the store's lunch counter.

Vace
3315 Connecticut Avenue, NW, at Macomb Street, Cleveland Park (363 1999). Cleveland Park Metro. **Open** 9am-9pm Mon-Sat; 10am-5pm Sun. **Credit** AmEx, MC, V.
This Italian deli stocks fresh pastas and sauces as well as the packaged kind, good cheeses, olive oil, and imported condiments. It also has perfect pizza by the slice.

Farmers' markets

In the warmer months, and sometimes year-round in warehouse spaces, local farmers gather at spots around the city to sell the fruits of their labour. The produce is usually better quality and cheaper than that found in supermarkets.

Adams Morgan Farmers' Market
18th Street & Columbia Road, NW, Adams Morgan (1-814 448 3904). Woodley Park-Zoo Metro, then 90, 91, 92, 93, 96 bus. **Open** *June-Dec* 8am-1pm Sat.

Eastern Market
225 Seventh Street, SE, between C Street & North Carolina Avenue, Capitol Hill (546 2698). Eastern Market Metro. **Open** dawn-late afternoon Sat, Sun; permanent inside stands 7am-6pm Tue-Sat; 8am-4pm Sun.

Freshfarm Market
Riggs Bank parking lot, 20th & Q Streets, NW, Dupont Circle (331 7300). Dupont Circle Metro. **Open** *May-mid Dec* 9am-1pm Sun.

Takoma Park Farmers' Market
Laurel Avenue, between Eastern & Carroll Avenues, Takoma Park, MD (301 422 0097). Takoma Metro. **Open** *mid April-mid Dec* 10am-2am Sun.

Gourmet

Dean & Deluca

3276 M Street, NW, at Potomac Street, Georgetown (342 2500). Foggy Bottom-GWU Metro, then 30, 32, 34, 35, 36 bus/Rosslyn Metro, then 13M, 38B bus. **Open** 8am-8pm Mon-Thur; 8am-9pm Fri, Sat (later in summer). **Credit** AmEx, MC, V.

The Washington outpost of this New York staple offers the same exquisite, though ridiculously overpriced, fancy food items, espresso and pastries.

Marvelous Market

1511 Connecticut Avenue, NW, between Fessenden Street & Nebraska Avenue, Upper Northwest (686 4040). Van Ness-UDC Metro, then L1, L2 bus. **Open** 7.30am-8pm Mon-Fri; 8am-7pm Sun. **Credit** AmEx, MC, V.

Most of this small store consists of a fresh bakery, but it also sells fresh pasta, produce, unusual condiments and lunch items, such as sandwiches, soups and topped focaccia. There are several other branches around town.

Rodman's

5100 Wisconsin Avenue, NW, between Harrison & Garrison Streets, Upper Northwest (363 3466). Friendship Heights Metro. **Open** 8am-10pm Mon-Sat; 9am-7pm Sun. **Credit** AmEx, Disc, MC, V.

This eclectic supermarket sells appliances and housewares on its basement level and discount-priced produce, groceries and wine on its main floor. It also has a great selection of imported teas, cookies, cheese and crackers.

Natural foods

Fresh Fields

4530 40th Street, NW, at Wisconsin Avenue, Upper Northwest (237 5800). Tenleytown-AU Metro. **Open** 8am-10pm Mon-Sat; 8am-9pm Sun. **Credit** AmEx, DC, Disc, MC, V.

This regional chain of full-service grocery stores has earned its fans by offering top-quality produce, much of it organic. It also has a full-service bakery, gourmet deli and complementary medicine section, in addition to the usual array of products. Prices are higher than at other supermarkets.

Good Food Store

2104 18th Street, NW, between Wyoming Avenue & California Street, Adams Morgan (628 8725). Dupont Circle Metro, then L2 bus. **Open** 11am-9pm daily. **No credit cards**.

This cosy, independently owned health food store sells Uptown Bakers bread and a good assortment of packaged food items. Note that their opening hours can be irregular.

Naturally Yours

2029 P Street, NW, between 20th & 21st Streets, Dupont Circle (429 1718). Dupont Circle Metro. **Open** 10am-8pm Mon-Sat; 11am-6pm Sun. **Credit** MC, V.

This store offers a good selection of complementary medicines, organic groceries and a juice bar.

Yes! Natural Gourmet

1825 Columbia Road, NW, at 18th Street, Adams Morgan (462 5150). Woodley Park-Zoo Metro, then 90, 91, 92, 93, 96 bus. **Open** 9am-8pm Mon-Fri; 9am-7pm Sat; 11am-6pm Sun. **Credit** AmEx, Disc, MC, V.

A nice range of organic goods, plus health-conscious groceries, a juice bar and an extensive selection of complementary medicines and beauty aids.

Branch: 3425 Connecticut Avenue, NW, Cleveland Park (363 1559).

Health & beauty

Beauty supplies

EFX Store

1745 Connecticut Avenue, NW, between R & S Streets, Dupont Circle (462 1300). Dupont Circle Metro. **Open** 10am-8pm Mon-Sat; noon-6pm Sun. **Credit** AmEx, DC, Disc, MC, V.

A sister to the Georgetown spa of the same name (*see p185*), this shop offers upscale beautifiers such as Kiehl's skincare and nail colours by Hard Candy.

Judy's Beauty Supply

520 Rhode Island Avenue, NE, at Fourth Street, Northeast (832 1300). Rhode Island Avenue Metro. **Open** 9am-9pm Mon-Sat; 10am-7pm Sun. **Credit** AmEx, Disc, MC, V.

Hair weaves in a rainbow of colours, perm kits, bulk beauty aids and deliciously tacky hair accessories at low prices.

Complementary medicine

All the natural food stores listed above sell herbal and homeopathic remedies, but the practitioners and shops below offer a more specialised service.

Acupuncture Health Center

5225 Wisconsin Avenue, NW, suite 305, at Jenifer Street, Chevy Chase, Upper Northwest (363 5664). Friendship Heights Metro. **Open** 1-6pm Mon; 9am-6pm Tue-Fri; 8am-noon Sat. **Credit** MC, V.

Dr Shahin Nasseri uses disposable needles to cure everything from allergies to injuries. The centre also offers nutritional counselling and specialises in women's health.

Clover Horn Co

2543 14th Street, NW, at Euclid Street, Shaw (483 5112). Columbia Heights Metro. **Open** 10am-5pm Mon-Sat. **No credit cards**.

This nondescript herbalist shop barely looks like it's in business from the outside, but inside it takes on a magical quality, with its shelves overflowing with potions and powders, from simple camomile and echinacea to exotic sandalwood and frankincense.

Tschiffely Pharmacy

1330 Connecticut Avenue, NW, between Dupont Circle & N Street, Dupont Circle (331 7176). Dupont Circle Metro. **Open** 8.30am-6.30pm Mon-Fri; 10am-4pm Sat. **Credit** AmEx, DC, MC, V.

In addition to filling prescriptions for conventional

Power cuts

In a city where a sense of community can be hard to find, DC barber shops are a world of their own, a place where guys can be guys, where history sometimes seems to stand still. Visiting a barber shop is an experience, it's about more than just getting your ends trimmed. It's the smell of Aqua Velva and baby powder, the feel of a straight razor gliding expertly over the jaw. It's listening to the old timers tell stories about the good old days and knowing that those good old days aren't all gone.

Camillo Barber Shop
3921 Windom Place, NW, between Wisconsin & Nebraska Avenues, Upper Northwest (966 7994). Tenleytown-AU Metro. **Open** 8.30am-6pm Mon-Fri; 8am-4.45pm Sat. **No credit cards.**
Owner Camillo Damiano perfected the art of the straight razor shave in his home town of Abruzzi, Italy, more than 30 years ago. His Old World charm and skill aren't lost on the locals here.

Carroll's Barbershop
1363 H Street, NE, between Maryland & Florida Avenues, Northeast (396 9662). Union Station Metro. **Open** 7.30am-5pm Tue-Sat. **No credit cards.**
Stanley Carroll is a third-generation barber and a native Washingtonian with a rich history to tell. His father, Raymond, started the business in 1931, making it the oldest shop on H Street and one of the oldest still operating in Washington.

Eddie's Hair Creations
1718 Florida Avenue, NW, at Kalorama Road, Adams Morgan (232 8180). U Street-Cardozo Metro. **Open** 8am-7.30pm Tue-Fri; 8am-5.30pm Sat; 9am-3.30pm Sun. **No credit cards.**
With its red-and-white chequered floor, stylish red barber chairs, reggae music in the background and kente-clad barbers, walk-ins don't mind the wait for a shape-up.

Hillman's Barber Shop
1106 H Street, NE, between 11th & 12th Streets, Northeast (396 9640). Union Station Metro. **Open** 9am-6pm Mon-Sat. **No credit cards.**
Another classic H Street spot, Albert C Hillman's grandfather first opened a barber shop a couple of blocks away in 1948. He has run the family business from its current location since 1983, where he trains young barbers in the art of the Philly-style fade.

Joe's Barber Shop
2300 Wisconsin Avenue, NW, at Hall Place, Upper Northwest (338 8533). Foggy Bottom-GWU Metro, then 30, 32, 34, 35, 36 bus. **Open** 9am-5pm Tue-Sat. **No credit cards.**
It's a man's world inside Joe's Barber Shop, where girlie mags lie atop the table and there's usually a game of checkers happening. Proprietor Joe Maggi used to cut Bill Clinton's hair in this shop when Bill was still a student in Georgetown who didn't inhale.

medicines, this small chain sells herbal and homeopathic medicines and aromatherapy beauty aids.

Washington Institute of Natural Medicine
3402 Connecticut Avenue, NW, between Porter & Newark Streets, Cleveland Park (237 7681). Cleveland Park Metro. **Open** 9.30am-5pm Fri; 10am-5pm Sat. **Credit** AmEx, MC, V.
The eyes are windows to the soul, or at least one's health, when certified naturopath Victoria Goldstein uses the ancient art of iridology to diagnose health according to specific patterns in the irises. She also offers nutritional counselling and prescribes homeopathic remedies.

Day spas & hair salons

Andre Chreky
1604 K Street, NW, at 16th Street, Downtown (293 9393). Farragut North Metro. **Open** 8am-8pm Mon-Sat; 9am-5pm Sun. **Credit** AmEx, Disc, MC, V.
Housed in a beautiful, light-filled, four-storey townhouse, this full-service spa and salon – hairstyling, facials, make-up, massage, waxing, manicure and pedicure – fulfils its promise of glamour at comparatively low prices.

Cristophe
1125 18th Street, NW, between L & M Streets, Downtown (785 2222). Farragut North Metro. **Open** 9am-7pm Tue, Wed, Fri; 9am-8pm Thur; 9am-5pm Sat. **Credit** AmEx, MC, V.
The Beverly Hills stylist gave President Clinton a $50 discount when he cut his hair at LAX airport – usually, it's $250 for a first styling. But you can get an indirect experience at this DC outlet from a stylist trained in his method for a mere $60.

Cornrows & Co
5401 14th Street, NW, at Jefferson Street, Upper Northwest (723 1827). Bus 52, 54. **Open** 9am-6pm Wed-Sat. **Credit** AmEx, MC, V.
Owner Pamela Ferrell designed all the elaborate braid hairstyles in the indie film *Daughters of the Dust*. No chemical hair straighteners to be found here; this popular natural hair care salon specialises in braids, twists, dreadlocks and extensions.

Harlow
1607 Connecticut Avenue, NW, at Q Street, Dupont Circle (332 1800). Dupont Circle Metro.
Open 10am-7.30pm Mon, Tue; 10am-8pm Wed-Fri; 9am-6.30pm Sat; 10am-5pm Sun.
No credit cards.
If you don't mind passers-by seeing you, this Dupont Circle shop with windows overlooking the street and a bevy of hip stylists gives great cuts at affordable prices.

Jolie
7200 Wisconsin Avenue, at Bethesda Avenue, Bethesda, MD (301 986 9293). Bethesda Metro.
Open 9am-6pm Mon, Tue, Fri, Sat; 9am-8pm Wed, Thur; 10am-5pm Sun. **Credit** AmEx, MC, V.
This day spa in the Maryland suburb of Bethesda doesn't do hairstyling, they do 'hair design'. The best way to take advantage of their many treatments is to buy a spa package, which range from the two-hour 'Executive Escape' to the seven-hour 'Pure Pampering Day'.

Roche
Washington Harbour, 3050 K Street, NW, at 31st Street, Georgetown (775 0775). Foggy Bottom-GWU Metro. **Open** 10am-8pm Tue-Thur; 10am-7pm Fri; 9am-5pm Sat. **Credit** AmEx, MC, V.
This salon has featured in *Vogue, Harper's Bazaar* and *Glamour*. With its blue-sky-and-cloud-painted walls and funky furniture in Crayola-crayon hues, it's no surprise that it specialises in hair colouring.

Massage

All the day spas listed above offer massages, but if you're in a hurry, the **Healthy Back Store** (1341 G Street, NW; 393 2225) offers ten-minute ($12.95) and 15-minute ($17.95) chair massages from 11am-5pm Mon-Fri.

Shopping with Monica

No one comes to Washington to shop, unless their idea of high fashion is wing tips and bad haircuts. But Monica Lewinsky, accustomed to shopping in New York City and on Rodeo Drive, managed to find a few things to buy.

Start your Monicamania tour at Georgetown's upscale **Toka** hair salon (3251 Prospect Street, Georgetown Court), where you can get the same $60 haircut that Monica got from Ismail Demir. Next stop: **Watergate** apartment complex in Foggy Bottom (Virginia Avenue and 27th Street). Monica shared an apartment with her mother here, and while she was in hiding when being chased by the press, she still managed to hit the stores: eyebrow wax from the Watergate Salon and chocolate mousse cake from the Watergate Pastry shop. She also ducked into the Safeway for groceries – no doubt you can pick up some Altoids here. And she took her drycleaning – though obviously not *that* blue dress – to the Watergate Valet.

You're on your own when it comes to guessing where she bought the thong underwear she snapped at the president – though if we had to guess, we'd go for **Victoria's Secret**. The one closest to the White House is at 1050 Connecticut Avenue, NW. It's also just a block from midnight-blue-dress purveyor the **Gap** (1120 Connecticut Avenue) – which, alas, no longer stocks that $50 belted frock.

You can look for a suitable imitation, along with a knock-off of the $38 DKNY black beret she bought in 1992 and wore on the news clip beamed round the world, at **Filene's Basement** (1133 Connecticut Avenue, NW). Word is Monica stopped in there for some discount shopping while she was cooped up at the Mayflower Hotel being quizzed by senators. Also in the neighbourhood: the upmarket **Morton's of Chicago** (1050 Connecticut Avenue) where Monica put away a 14-ounce filet mignon with lawyer William Ginsburg.

The **Brooks Brothers** Monica actually shopped at – and possibly bought the blue patterned Ermenegildo Zegna tie she gave the president (he bought the hatpin he gave her at Union Station) – was at 18th and L Streets; it's since moved to 1201 Connecticut Avenue, a block north of Filene's. While the scandal (and reporters) swirled around her, Monica came browsing at Brooks Brothers with Ginsburg for gifts for her dad. At Dupont Circle's **Kramerbooks** (1517 Connecticut Avenue, NW), where Monica bought Nicholson Baker's steamy novel *Vox*, employees still wear black 'Subpoenaed for Book Selling' T-shirts. That's because Ken Starr tried to seize records of Lewinsky purchases; the shop went to court and he eventually backed off.

Around the White House are a couple of other restaurants where Monica chowed down. There's the **Hay-Adams Hotel** on Lafayette Square opposite the White House, where she lunched with Betty Currie. A couple of blocks south at the **Bombay Club** (815 Connecticut Avenue, NW) – where the Clintons have eaten several times – she confronted *New York Times* columnist Maureen Dowd with: 'Why do

Skin & body care

EFX Spa

3059 M Street, NW, between 30th & 31st Streets, Georgetown (965 1300). Foggy Bottom-GWU Metro, then 30, 32, 34, 35, 36 bus. **Open** 10am-8pm Mon-Sat; noon-6pm Sun. **Credit** AmEx, MC, V.

The front of this store has an array of high-priced, seductively packaged beauty products. Behind the sliding door, the spa's aestheticians slough off dead skin and massage tired bodies.

Georgette Klinger

5345 Wisconsin Avenue, NW, at Military Road, Upper Northwest (686 8880). Friendship Heights Metro. **Open** 9am-6pm Mon, Fri, Sat; 9am-8pm Tue-Thur; 10am-5pm Sun. **Credit** AmEx, Disc, MC, V.

Klinger's reputation precedes her. Washington women (and, increasingly, men) swear by this upscale, discreet national chain.

Victoria's Day Spa

1926 I Street, NW, at 20th Street, Foggy Bottom (254 0442). Farragut West Metro. **Open** 11am-7pm Mon-Fri; 9am-7pm Sat. **No credit cards**.

Charming and accessible, Victoria's offers traditional spa services as well as linen herbal or seaweed body wraps, and a 'salt glow' body scrub. There are discounts for students.

Tattoos & body piercing

Fatty's Custom Tattooz

1333 Connecticut Avenue, NW, third floor, between Dupont Circle & 18th Street, Dupont Circle (452 0999). Dupont Circle Metro. **Open** noon-8pm daily. **Credit** MC, V.

If you're anxious about getting a permanent tattoo or piercing, this shop also does henna tattoos and body paint. A small gallery features 'alternative art'.

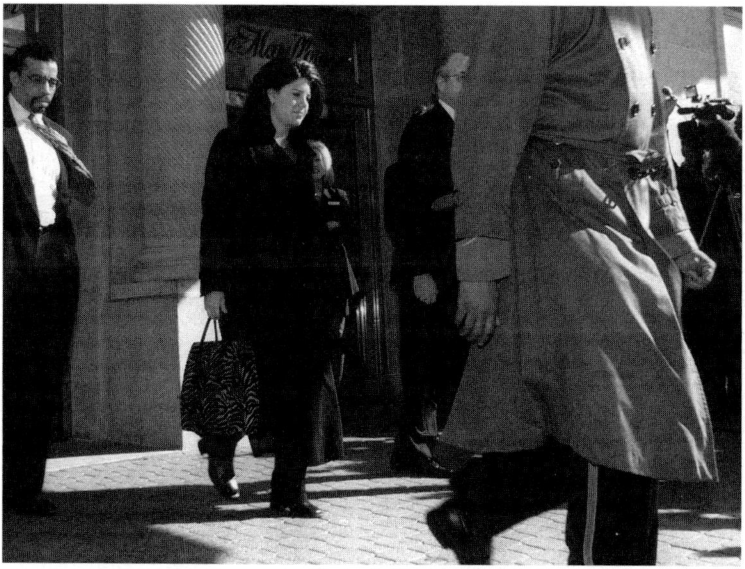

Monica hits the streets for yet another shopping expedition…

you write such scathing articles about me?' Dowd was at a rare loss for words: 'I don't know,' she answered.

Last stop on the tour: **Pentagon City** mall (1100 South Hayes Street, Arlington), which has a slew of stores, including a Gap, a Victoria's Secret and a Joan & David, a favourite of Monica's – and where prosecutor Michael Emmick took the girl who would become the world's most famous ex-intern window-shopping the day that she was lured to a meeting with Starr's investigators.

Jinx Proof
3306 M Street, NW, between 33rd & 34th Streets, Georgetown (337 5469). Rosslyn Metro, then 13M, 38B bus. **Open** noon-9pm daily. **Credit** Disc, MC, V.
The first tattoo and piercing studio to open in Washington, DC (most were located in suburban borders before moving into town), Jinx Proof has more than 10,000 designs to choose from.

Speciality & gift shops

Appalachian Spring
1415 Wisconsin Avenue, NW, at P Street, Georgetown (337 5780). Foggy Bottom-GWU Metro, then 30, 32, 34, 35, 36 bus. **Open** 10am-8pm Mon-Fri; 10am-6pm Sat; noon-6pm Sun. **Credit** AmEx, MC, V.
It doesn't get more American than this array of fine housewares, many hand-made, including traditional quilts, carved wood and blown-glass items.

Counter Spy Shop
1027 Connecticut Avenue, NW, between K & L Streets, Downtown (887 1717). Farragut North Metro. **Open** 9am-6pm Mon, Fri; 9am-6.30pm Tue-Thur; 11am-4pm Sat. **Credit** AmEx, MC, V.
Afraid the CIA is after you? You can get anti-wire tap devices, bug detectors and bullet-proof vests here. Or for your own spy campaign, pick up a pair of video sunglasses, some night-vision goggles, an encryption system that fits into a briefcase or a lie detector telephone. Call for an appointment.

dZi Tibet Collection
117 Carroll Street, NW, at Maple Street, Upper Northwest (882 0008). Takoma Metro. **Open** 11am-7pm Tue-Sat; noon-5pm Sun. **Credit** AmEx, MC, V.
Richard Gere would have a field day in this tiny store filled with all things Tibetan – clothing, singing meditation bowls, incense, books and music. It's right on the DC/Maryland border.

Georgetown Tobacco
3144 M Street, NW, at Wisconsin Avenue, Georgetown (338 5100). Foggy Bottom-GWU Metro, then 30, 32, 34, 35, 36 bus. **Open** 10am-9pm Mon-Sat; noon-8pm Sun. **Credit** AmEx, Disc, MC, V.
Whether you need a pack of Nat Shermans, a hand-rolled cigar or Indian beedies, most nicotine cravings can be satisfied easily here.

Ginza
1721 Connecticut Avenue, NW, between R & S Streets, Dupont Circle (331 7991). Dupont Circle Metro. **Open** 11am-7pm Mon-Sat; noon-6pm Sun. **Open** AmEx, Disc, MC, V.
This store focuses on the more refined elements of Japanese culture, with its exquisite tea sets and books on Zen meditation, but you can also get Japanese T-shirts and plastic knick-knacks.

National Organization for Women Store
1615 K Street, NW, between 16th & 17th Streets, Downtown (467 6980). Farragut North or Farragut West Metro. **Open** 10am-6pm Mon-Fri. **Credit** AmEx, MC, V.
Eliminate doubt with a NOW-endorsed T-shirt that reads 'This is what a Radical Feminist looks like' and other in-yer-face quotations. You can also stock up on Goddess jewellery, 'Grrrls Rule' T-shirts, political badges and, for the supportive man, a bumper sticker saying 'Another Man Against Violence Against Women'.

Silk Road
311 Seventh Street, SE, between Pennsylvania & North Carolina Avenues, Capitol Hill (543 1758). Eastern Market Metro. **Open** 10am-6pm Tue-Sun. **Credit** AmEx, MC, V.
This store sells the kind of South American and Asian decorative pieces that appeal to armchair travellers willing to pay a significant mark-up for rustic, hand-made wares.

Treasures
1608 17th Street, NW, between Q & R Streets, Dupont Circle (332 4221). Dupont Circle Metro. **Open** 11am-7pm Mon-Thur; 11am-9pm Fri, Sat; 11am-6pm Sun. **Credit** AmEx, MC, V.
Candy-coloured scented candles, balloon bouquets, hand-made greeting cards, palm-size gift books and lots of other charming un-necessities.

WH Smith
Grand Hyatt Hotel, 1000 H Street, NW, at 11th Street, Downtown (393 6177). Metro Center Metro. **Open** 7am-11pm daily. **Credit** AmEx, DC, Disc, MC, V.
Die-hard Republicans can show their political affinity with a T-shirt that says 'Friends don't let friends vote Democrat' or a 'WeePublican' shirt for the kids. Plus American flag keychains and erasers.

Sporting goods

For shops that rent and sell bicycles, *see page 225* **Sport & Fitness**.

A&A Athletic
212 Seventh Street, SE, Capitol Hill (543 0556). Eastern Market Metro. **Open** 11am-6pm Tue-Fri; 10am-5pm Sat. **Credit** AmEx, MC, V.
Equipment for pretty much every team sport – soft-ball bats, baseballs, basketballs, soccer balls, tennis racquets – as well as shoes and some clothing.

Fleet Feet
1841 Columbia Road, NW, between Biltmore Street & Mintwood Place, Adams Morgan (387 3888). Dupont Circle Metro, then 42 bus. **Open** 10am-8pm Mon-Fri; 10am-7pm Sat; noon-4pm Sun. **Credit** AmEx, DC, Disc, MC, V.
Run, jog or walk here if you're looking for shoes, clothing and accessories for cross-training, tennis, cycling, swimming, aerobics or running.

Hudson Trail Outfitters
4530 Wisconsin Avenue, NW, at Brandywine Street, Upper Northwest (363 9810). Tenleytown-AU Metro. **Open** 9am-10pm Mon-Sat; 11am-6pm Sun. **Credit** AmEx, Disc, MC, V.
Goods for camping and hiking, from clothes to tents.

Arts & Entertainment

Children

Washington's attractions may be grown-up, but it's a surprisingly child-friendly city.

Washington is a great city for kids. Paradoxically, although it is perhaps the most elegant of American cities, it is as accommodating to families as any destination in the US. The scale of the city – low-rise buildings, tourist attractions centred in a compact area and plenty of open space – is unintimidating, and children are present – and welcome – everywhere. The main tourist attractions – the monuments, the Smithsonian museums, the White House, the Supreme Court and the Capitol – are all free, which makes a family trip to Washington an affordable rite of passage for American families as well as a relatively low-budget US destination for foreign visitors.

It's a good idea to start your visit with a tour around the monuments and the Mall, which will both impress your children and give them an overview of the scope of what Washington has to offer (to avoid transport hassles, take one of the day-long tours offered by Old Town Trolley Tours or Tourmobile; *see page 34* **Tips & Tours**). Especially if you are travelling with younger children, you may want to break the somewhat daunting length of the Mall with a stop at the carousel in front of the Smithsonian Castle or with a pedal boat ride on the Tidal Basin.

If you have time, consider taking a day trip to Baltimore, an hour's drive north of Washington. It's full of good things for kids, including the National Aquarium, Maryland Science Center and Port Discovery 'The Kid-Powered Museum' – all of which are in the Inner Harbor. For more details, *see chapter* **Trips Out of Town**.

Practicalities

Babysitting

They're not cheap, but the following services will send a babysitter to your hotel or other lodgings.

Mothers' Aides Inc (703 250 0700/Maryland office 301 424 6000/1-800 526 2669) charges $35 agency fee a day plus $10-$15 per hour paid directly to the carer (four-hour minimum). **WeeSIT** (703 764 1542) charges $12 transport fee and $10 per hour for one child plus an extra 50¢ per hour for each additional child (four-hour minimum). **White House Nannies** (301 652 8088/1-800 270 6266) uses independent carers at a typical rate of $10-$12 per hour plus a small agency fee.

Scrambling on the **FDR Memorial**.

Eating out

Children are welcome at all but the fanciest Downtown expense-account restaurants (which you're unlikely to want to take them to anyway). For budget meals, fast-food restaurants are plentiful and easy to find, but if your kids aren't fussy eaters, you can spend a little more and introduce them to new cuisines, such as Afghan, Ethiopian or Caribbean, at one of the many moderately priced ethnic restaurants in Washington (*see chapter* **Restaurants**).

For lunch, the food court in **Union Station** near Capitol Hill is convenient for the Capitol and the Supreme Court, while the food court in the Pavilion at the **Old Post Office** (1100 Pennsylvania Avenue, NW, between 11th and 12th Streets), is near the Museums of Natural History and American History. There are also Downtown branches of the **Hard Rock Café** (999 E Street, NW, at 10th Street – next to Ford's Theatre – 737 7625) and **Planet Hollywood** (1101 Pennsylvania Avenue, NW, at 11th Street; 783 7827).

Shopping

The **CVS** pharmacy chain (1-800 746 7287), which has branches in virtually every neighbourhood in the city, stocks baby supplies and snack foods, in addition to a full range of toiletries and other essentials. Clothing and shoes for children (and adults) are available at the Downtown branch of **Hechts** department store at 12th and G Streets, NW (628 6661). Museum gift shops typically stock unusual toys and souvenirs. For toys and children's books, *see chapter* **Shopping**.

Entertainment

The listings below focus on attractions in or near Downtown DC. For places further afield and in the suburbs, consult *Going Places With Children in Washington, DC* ($14.95), published by the Green Acres School and now in its 15th edition, the best of the specialised guides to Washington for children. It's available in all good bookstores.

Museums

Three of the Smithsonian museums offer exhibits geared to children and are consistently rated as tops with kids: the **National Air & Space Museum,** the **National Museum of American History** and the **National Museum of Natural History**. The **Newseum,** the **National Postal Museum** and the **National Building Museum** are also very popular. For details of all, *see chapter* **Museums**. Museums designed primarily for children include:

Capital Children's Museum

800 Third Street, NE, at H Street, Union Station & Around (675 4120). Union Station Metro. **Open** 10am-5pm (June-Aug 10am-6pm) daily. **Admission** $6; $4 seniors; free under-3s. **Credit** AmEx, Disc, MC, V.

This museum used to compare poorly with the Smithsonian's museums, but has improved greatly in recent years. The emphasis is on interactive exhibits such as a science laboratory where children can perform their own simple experiments.

MCI National Sports Gallery

MCI Center, 601 F Street, NW, at Seventh Street, Downtown (661 5133). Gallery Place-Chinatown Metro. **Open** 11am-6pm daily; 11am-9pm on event nights. **Admission** $5. **Credit** AmEx, MC, V.

Inside the new Downtown sports arena, this gallery combines sporting history with 35 high-tech interactive games that allow kids (and adults) to engage in simulated play against sports stars. Babe Ruth's bat features in an extensive sports memorabilia collection. The Discovery Channel Store also here shows short child-friendly nature films for a dollar.

National Geographic Society Explorers Hall

1145 17th Street, NW, at M Street, Downtown (857 7000/ recorded information 857 7588). Farragut North Metro. **Open** 9am-5pm Mon-Sat; 10am-5pm Sun. **Admission** free.

One end of the hall contains a permanent exhibition on ecology, oceanography, weather and other aspects of the earth, with interactive and multimedia exhibits. The other end is used for special shows; recent exhibits include 'Petra: Jordan's City in the Rocks' and 'Maya: Portrait of a People'.

Washington Dolls' House & Toy Museum

5326 44th Street, NW, between Harrison & Jenifer Streets, Upper Northwest (244 0024). Friendship Heights Metro. **Open** 10am-5pm Tue-Sat; noon-5pm Sun. **Admission** $4; $3 seniors; $2 under-12s. **Credit** AmEx, Disc, MC, V.

This small and slightly out-of-the-way museum is worth a trip for its unusual collection of antique doll's houses from various countries, including an 1890 Mexican mansion and a Bauhaus-style house from Germany. Miniature toys, including several versions of Noah's Ark, also feature.

Animals & the outdoors

Within the District, the best outdoor activity for children bar none is a trip to the **National Zoo** (*see page 77* **DC Neighbourhoods**). Particularly popular with children are Hsing-Hsing, the famous but now elderly and ailing giant panda from China, and the prairie dogs opposite Monkey Island. Survival tip: the zoo slopes steeply downhill to Rock Creek from the entrance on Connecticut Avenue, so to avoid a long, hot climb at the end of your visit, plan a circular route that gets you back to the entrance before your kids run out of energy.

For information on the many wonderful parks and outdoor recreational facilities in the suburbs around Washington, check *Going Places With Children in Washington, DC.*

National Aquarium in Washington

US Department of Commerce Building, 14th Street & Constitution Avenue, NW, Federal Triangle (482 2826/recorded information 482 2825). Federal Triangle Metro. **Open** 9am-5pm daily. **Admission** $2; 75¢ 2-10s; free under-2s. **No credit cards.**

If you don't have time for a trip to Baltimore to see the infinitely superior (but also much more crowded and expensive) National Aquarium, this place is worth a visit. Special features are a 'touch tank' containing hermit crabs, sea urchins and horseshoe crabs, and the shark and piranha feedings, which happen on alternate days – check before you go.

Rock Creek Nature Center & Planetarium

5200 Glover Road, NW, at Military Road, Upper Northwest (426 6829). Friendship Heights Metro, then E2, E3 bus. **Open** 9am-5pm Wed-Sun. **Admission** free.

Located on the western edge of Rock Creek Park, the planetarium hosts two shows on Saturday and Sunday, one at 1pm for ages 4-plus, the other at 4pm for ages 7-plus. The nature centre offers guided hikes and hands-on activities. More limited programmes are offered from Wednesday to Friday.

Theatre & the arts

The 'Carousel' listings in the 'Saturday's Child' column of the 'Weekend' section of Friday's *Washington Post* cover performances and other activities for children in and around DC.

Other institutions that sometimes offer children's art and theatre programmes include the **National Gallery of Art,** the **Corcoran**

Take a break at the **carousel** *in front of the Smithsonian Castle on the Mall.*

Gallery of Art, the **Hirshhorn Museum & Sculpture Garden** and the **National Building Museum** (for all, *see chapter* **Museums**).

Arthur M Sackler Gallery

1050 Independence Avenue, SW, between 11th & 12th Streets, Mall & Tidal Basin (357 4880). Smithsonian Metro. **Open** *gallery* 10am-5.30pm daily; *Imaginasia* times vary. **Admission** free.

The Sackler Gallery, one of the Smithsonian's two museums of Asian art, offers Imaginasia several days a week (call for the schedule, which varies during the year). Children aged 6-12, who must be accompanied by an adult, are given a special art tour of the museum and then take part in an art workshop inspired by the tour.

Glen Echo Park

7300 MacArthur Boulevard, at Goldsboro Road, Glen Echo, MD (301 492 6282). Ride-On Bus 29.

Until 1968, Glen Echo was a popular amusement park just a trolley ride from Downtown. Today, it is preserved by the National Park Service as a site for theatre, art and dance. It also has a playground, picnic tables and an old-fashioned carousel (open May-Sept). Glen Echo offers the following child-friendly activities:

- **Puppet Company Playhouse** (301 320 6668) presents plays for all ages, most of them adaptations of classic stories for children (10am, 11.30am Wed-Fri; 11.30am ,1pm Sat, Sun). **Admission** $5; free under-2s. Reservations recommended.
- **Adventure Theatre** (301 320 5331) presents plays based on fables, fairytales, musicals and children's classics, using live actors and puppets (1.30pm, 3.30pm Sat, Sun). **Admission** $5.
- **Discovery Creek Children's Museum** (364 3111) offers interactive events designed to teach children about nature and geography (10am-3pm Sat, noon-3pm Sun). **Admission** $4; $3 members; free under-3s, over-11s.

Kennedy Center

2700 F Street, NW, at New Hampshire Avenue, Foggy Bottom (467 4600/1-800 444 1324). Foggy Bottom-GWU Metro.

On most weekends from October to May (7pm Fri; 1pm, 3pm Sat; 1pm Sun), the Kennedy Center offers a variety of plays for kids, such as *Alexander and the Terrible, Horrible, No Good, Very Bad Day*. The National Symphony also presents occasional family concerts here.

Saturday Morning at the National

National Theatre, 1321 Pennsylvania Avenue, NW, between 13th & 14th Streets, Downtown (783 3372). Metro Center or Federal Triangle Metro.

On Saturdays at 9.30am and 11am, from September to April, the National Theatre offers an eclectic mix of free entertainment for children and adults. The one-hour events include theatre, music, dance, clowning, juggling, story-telling, magic and instructional nature and science shows.

Smithsonian Discovery Theater

Arts & Industries Building, West Entrance, 900 Jefferson Drive, SW, between Seventh & Ninth Streets, Mall & Tidal Basin (357 1500). Smithsonian or L'Enfant Plaza Metro. **Admission** $5; $4 members. **Credit** Disc, MC, V.

At 10am and 11.30am Monday to Friday (and occasional Saturdays) year round, Discovery Theater presents plays covering a wide range of subjects and ages – from a production of the *Wizard of Oz*, aimed at ages 3-7, to *The Escape*, the story of an African-American slave, for ages 13-18.

Culture

The word 'innovative' hardly leaps to the lips, but DC's cultural scene is nonetheless a serious one – in more ways than one.

Washington is big on culture in the same way that it's big on monuments. The performing arts tend to be impressive, accessible and serious, but not too daring or unusual. However, culture vultures can enjoy a life of genteel poverty, thanks to the free museums, discounted tickets, pay-what-you-can previews and city-sponsored festivals. Galleries, libraries and cultural/historical centres often host free lunchtime performances, films, lectures and readings. Except for getting tickets for the Washington Opera, savvy trumps money every time as far as taking in culture goes.

INFORMATION & TICKETS

For event listings, try the free weekly *Washington City Paper* or the *Washington Times*' 'Weekend' section, both of which come out on Thursday. The *Washington Post* has a small 'Lively Arts' section every day, but its 'Weekend' section (out on Friday) is more extensive. *Making Impressions* (265 3443), a free monthly newsletter distributed

The mulitcultural **Liz Lerman Dance Exchange** *is DC's only nationally touring dance company. See page 194.*

All the jazz legends have played at the **Lincoln Theatre** *on U Street.*

in bookstores, libraries and black cultural centres, details African-American cultural events.

Tickets for most performances can be obtained direct from the venue. Ticket agencies such as **Ticketmaster** (432 7328/1-800 551 7328) and **ProTix** (703 218 6500) allow you to order by credit card over the phone, but add high surcharges. Theatregoers can also try **Ticketplace** (1-800 842 5387), which sells day-of-show tickets for half price, plus a ten per cent surcharge. **Top Centre** (452 9040/1-800 673 8422) is a last resort for a must-see show: it sells tickets to sold-out events at a very high premium.

General venues

Very few venues in DC are dedicated to showcasing only one artform. This is especially true of the larger venues where music, dance, theatre and performance art can be scheduled in the same month.

George Mason University Center for the Arts

Roanoke Lane, at Mason Drive, Fairfax, VA (703 993 8888). Vienna Metro, then CUE bus. **Tickets** $20-$50. **Credit** AmEx, DC, Disc, MC, V.

High glass windows create a jewel-box effect at this modern complex, which houses three theatres. The 1,900-seat concert hall and the 500-seat proscenium Harris Theatre host ballet, modern dance, theatre and music, while in the smaller black box the Theatre of the First Amendment company presents daring new dramas and performance art pieces. Best reached by car, it's a good 30-minute drive from DC.

Lincoln Theatre

1215 U Street, NW, between 12th & 13th Streets, U Street/14th Street Corridor (328 6000). U Street-Cardozo Metro. **Tickets** $5-$70. **Credit** AmEx, Disc, MC, V.

From the 1920s to the 1940s, U Street was DC's answer to Sugar Hill in Harlem, and the Lincoln Theatre was twin to the Apollo. Every jazz great of the era played here. Restored in recent years, it continues to feature terrific jazz as well as gospel choirs, international dance, small-scale musicals and special, one-off events.

Lisner Auditorium

730 21st Street, NW, at H Street, Foggy Bottom (994 6800/concert line 994 1500). Foggy Bottom-GWU Metro. **Tickets** $5-$75. **No credit cards**.

Located on the campus of George Washington University, the 1,500-seat Lisner presents all types of music, dance and theatre. Performers often include rare international acts such as the Japanese dance-theatre troupe Buto-Sha-Tenkei, *Umabatha* (the Zulu version of Macbeth) and Cape Verdean singer Cesaria Evora.

Warner Theatre

13th & E Streets, NW, Downtown (783 4000). Metro Center Metro. **Tickets** $30-$60. **Credit** AmEx, Disc, MC, V.

Built in 1924, the Warner Theatre, located a few blocks east of the White House, still retains some of its art deco charm and has a gorgeous, gold-leafed domed ceiling. Performances here run the gamut from Mikhail Baryshnikov's White Oak Dance Project and comedian Chris Rock to

European-style circuses and the uplifting vocals of Washington's own Sweet Honey in the Rock.
Website: www.warnertheatre.com

Classical music & opera

Classical music in Washington tends to be very high quality, but not very adventurous. Name recognition ensures sell-out crowds at the larger venues, while many concerts take place in galleries, museums and churches, providing intimate and often free or inexpensive performances. Some of the embassies also host visiting performers from their respective countries.

Companies

Capitol City Opera

Information 703 683 1220. **Tickets** $20-$46. **Credit** AmEx, V.

This fledgling opera company, which performs at various venues in the DC area including the Kennedy Center, has added some dynamism to a scene long dominated by the Washington Opera. In recent seasons it has performed works by Puccini and featured singers from New York's Met.

Choral Arts Society

Information 244 3669/Kennedy Center for tickets 467 4600. **Tickets** $13-$42. **Credit** MC, V.

This highly regarded chorus – made up of volunteers – has performed at Carnegie Hall and regularly takes the stage at the Kennedy Center with the National Symphony Orchestra, with which they performed a world premiere of a new John Corigliano composition in March 1999. It also presents popular holiday concerts in December and an annual concert in January honouring civil rights activist Martin Luther King Jr.
Website: www.choralarts.org

National Symphony Orchestra

Information 416 8100/box office 467 4600. **Tickets** $15-$65. **Credit** AmEx, Disc, MC, V.

Under the direction of the highly regarded Leonard Slatkin, the NSO features contemporary American composers and classical European works during its Kennedy Center season (September to June). 'Meet the Performers' and 'Conversations with Conductors' discussions give patrons glimpses into artists' lives, while the 'Kinderkonzerts' appeal to smaller children. The NSO also gives free concerts at the Carter Barron Amphitheater and, on Memorial, Independence and Labor Day weekends, at the US Capitol (*see chapter* **By Season**).
Website: http://kennedy-center.org

Washington Chamber Symphony

Information 452 1321. **Tickets** $9-$32. **Credit** MC, V.

Best known for its popular family and children's concerts, this symphony performs at the Corcoran Gallery and in the Kennedy Center's Terrace Theater and Concert Hall. The Holiday Singalong in December, which features a 300-voice choir, full orchestra, bell choir and children's chorus, sells out months in advance. The regular series ranges from baroque to twentieth-century work.

Washington Opera

Information 295 2400/1-800 876 7372. **Tickets** $61-$140. **Credit** MC, V.

Under the direction of Placido Domingo, the Washington Opera performs eight lavish productions a year at the Kennedy Center – in their original language with English subtitles. Shows are often sold out to subscribers well in advance, but those with a few hundred dollars to spare can pick up returns at the Ken Cen box office or buy standing room tickets in the week before a performance.
Website: www.dc-opera.org

Main venues

Folger Shakespeare Library

201 East Capitol Street, SE, between Second & Third Streets, Capitol & Around (544 7077). Capitol South Metro. **Tickets** $22-$38. **Credit** AmEx, MC,V.

The Folger Consort presents medieval, Renaissance and baroque chamber recitals, along with guest early music ensembles, in the intimate Elizabethan Theatre, which is designed much like theatres in Shakespeare's time with a three-tiered gallery and carved oak columns.
Website: www.folger.edu

Library of Congress

First Street & Independence Avenue, SE, Capitol & Around (707 5502). Capitol South Metro. **Tickets** free, but small service charge. **Credit** AmEx, Disc, MC, V.

The Coolidge Auditorium in the Library of Congress's Jefferson Building is an acoustic marvel. For the past 75 years the Library has commissioned work by the best composers of each generation, such as Bartók and Stravinsky. Aaron Copland's *Appalachian Spring* premiered here in 1944 in a collaborative performance with Martha Graham and her dancers. After a long hiatus, the renovated auditorium reopened in 1998 and has since hosted strong classical and avant-garde jazz performers – recent players include the Julliard String Quartet, the Arcado String Trio, Cecil Taylor and the Arditti String Quartet. All shows are free, but tickets are required – call Ticketmaster.
Website: www.loc.gov

National Academy of Sciences

2100 C Street, NW, between 21st & 22nd Streets, Northwest Rectangle (334 2436). Foggy Bottom-GWU Metro. **Tickets** free.

The National Academy hosts performances by its resident company the National Musical Arts Chamber Ensemble, and the US Marines Chamber Orchestra. All performances are free and seated on a first come, first served basis. The season runs from autumn to spring.

Smithsonian

Information 357 2700. **Tickets** free-$70. **Credit** Disc, MC, V.

While the Smithsonian focuses primarily on American music forms, particularly jazz, it does have occasional classical offerings. In the National Museum of American History, musicians sometimes play historical instruments from the collection. The Meyer Auditorium in the Freer Gallery presents chamber concerts, often tied in with an exhibit of Asian art. Past performers include the Shanghai String Quartet with pipa player Wu Man.

Website: www.si.edu

Churches & galleries

Basilica of the National Shrine of the Immaculate Conception

400 Michigan Avenue, NE, at Michigan Avenue, Northeast (526 8300). Brookland-CUA Metro. **Open** 7am-7pm Mon-Sun. **Tickets** vary.

Dedicated to the Virgin Mary, this is the largest Catholic church in the US. The stunning mosaics and frescoes add an awe-inspiring quality to the occasional choral performances held here.

Website: www.nationalshrine.com

Corcoran Gallery of Art

500 17th Street, NW, between New York Avenue & E Street, White House & Around (639 1770). Farragut West Metro. **Tickets** $15-$30. **Credit** AmEx, MC, V.

The highlight of the year-round season is the Musical Evening Series, eight Friday evening concerts (from October to May) featuring a range of ensembles from the Brentano String Quartet to Hungary's Takacs String Quartet. However, the series often sells out in advance.

Website: www.corcoran.org

Mount Vernon College

2100 Foxhall Road, NW, at W Street, Upper Northwest (625 4655). Dupont Circle Metro, then D4 bus. **Tickets** $16-$25. **Credit** MC, V.

The 'In Series' programme presents new or rarely produced chamber operas and operettas twice a year in the small, beautiful and intimate space of the Hand Chapel on the campus of this women's liberal arts college. Past performances include Mozart's *Idomeneo* and *The Little Barber of Lavapies* by Francisco A Barbieri. It's awkward taking public transport to the college; better to drive or take a cab.

Phillips Collection

1600 21st Street, NW, at Q Street, Dupont Circle (387 2151). Dupont Circle Metro. **Tickets** free with museum admission. **Credit** AmEx, MC, V.

This mansion, situated near the embassies, hosts a series of Sunday afternoon chamber music concerts, often solos or duets, from September to May.

Washington National Cathedral

Wisconsin & Massachusetts Avenues, NW, Upper Northwest (537 6200). Tenleytown-AU Metro, then 30, 32, 34, 35, 36 bus. **Tickets** free.

The Cathedral Choral Society presents regular performances with well-known guest artists inside the soaring space of this English Gothic-style cathedral – the sixth largest cathedral in the world. Free organ music, evensong, choral groups and solo recitals also take place regularly.

Website: www.cathedral.org/cathedral

Dance

While there are many small local dance companies – offering everything from modern to African to tap – the dance scene in Washington tends to be focused largely on touring companies. The only nationally touring dance company based in the DC area is the **Liz Lerman Dance Exchange** (301 270 6700), which, ironically, has bigger audiences outside the Washington region than it does at home. Liz Lerman founded this multicultural, multigenerational company in 1976, before such adjectives had become overused. She still creates some of the most innovative work in the area and several of the company members are impressive choreographers in their own right. The company's studio in Takoma Park, Maryland, offers modern, ballet and a host of other dance classes.

The **Maru Montero Company** (244 7281) represents DC's vibrant Latin American community with its award-winning folkloric and contemporary dance. **Kankouran West African Dance Company** (737 4941) is one of the strongest of the area's many African troupes.

Each June, **Dance Place** (*see below*) hosts the DanceAfrica-DC festival, a lively mix of local and international dancers, drummers and artisans. The **George Washington University** dance department (994 0739) hosts an international festival of improvisational dance every December, as well as occasional workshops and masterclasses by visiting artists. The Hand Chapel at **Mount Vernon College** (*see above*) also showcases dance events, as well as music, theatre and performance art.

For details of places offering dance classes, *see page 226* **Sport & Fitness**.

Dance Place

3225 Eighth Street, NE, at Monroe Street, Northeast (269 1600). Brookland-CUA Metro. **Tickets** $5-$15. **Credit** AmEx, MC, V.

This studio, which offers morning and evening classes in modern and African dance, doubles as a performance space, often featuring emerging artists. A recent season included modern auteur BeBe Miller, hip hop innovators Rennie Harris/Pure Movement and Canadian alternative dance outfit the Holy Body Tattoo. It is also the home for several modern companies – Carla & Co, Carla's Kids, Deborah Riley Dance Projects, Lesa McLaughlin & Dancers, Images of Cultural Artistry – and African-based Coyaba Dance Theatre.

Website: www.danceplace.org

Reasons to rhyme

The politicians aren't the only ones who get to blow hot air in Washington. There are a surprising number of open mics around the city where poets convene in gatherings somewhat more democratic than Senate committee hearings. Just show up early, sign your name on a list and wait for your turn to wield the microphone. Olympic competition-style poetry slams, which were popular several years ago, happen only sporadically now, but you can find readings most nights of the week.

The Monday night reading at **Bar Nun** (*see page 217* **Nightlife**) hosted by the Movement Collective could easily give you the impression that you had suddenly stumbled on to the set of the movie *Love Jones*. Talented live jazz/funk band the Sound Poets provide spontaneous back-up to an eclectic array of poets. Hip-hop rhythms abound as do Gil Scott Heron-style political poems and sexual healing verse.

The Tuesday night reading at **Mango's Restaurant** (2017 14th Street, NW; 332 2104) is one of the oldest and most established events in the city. Started in 1993 by 'jazz diva poet' Toni Asante Lightfoot at a café in Georgetown, it moved to this Caribbean restaurant off U Street when the café closed. The audience tends to be good listeners and first-timers are affectionately called 'virgins'.

On Wednesday night **Cup of Dreams** (3629 12th Street, NE; 526 6562) in the Brookland neighbourhood hosts an intimate reading with a supportive and friendly vibe. The café has a good selection of tea, espresso drinks and veggie snacks. On the same night, in Dupont Circle, **Soho Tea & Coffee** (2150 P Street, NW; 463 7646) has an eclectic open mic with poets sharing space with folksingers.

Face, easily the most insane MC in the city, hosts readings at **Kaffa House** (1212 U Street, NW; 462 1212) on Thursday nights. The club, a haven for Ethiopian Rastafari and DC hip-hop heads, has a cave-like atmosphere with its dim lighting, tree-like sculptures and incense-filled air. Add Face's restless pacing and gravelly voice and you've got the literary equivalent of a Tricky concert.

On Sunday nights at 8.30pm there's **Poetry in Hell** at Club Hell in Dupont Circle (2327 18th Street, NW; 667 4355), hosted by Dee Snyder. It's a dark place, though not as warm as the name would suggest. Drinks are pretty cheap and you never know what to expect. Could be fratboys, could be sailors, could be a drunk local reading from a paper napkin.

Not every event is a weekly affair; some really good readings happen only once a month. **Groove Gumbo** (1526 14th Street, NW; 424 0867) is more performance-oriented than other open mics. Hosted by poet/actor W Ellington Felton, it features a live band, DJ Munch on the wheels of steel, singers, MCs, poets and special events such as a fashion show of local designs or funk-filled tap dancing.

Joy of Motion

5207 Wisconsin Avenue, NW, at Harrison Street, Upper Northwest (362 3042). Friendship Heights Metro. **Tickets** $10-$12. **No credit cards**.

This studio has two locations and specialises in jazz dance. Resident companies – including the youthful Jazzdanz.dc, modern-based City Dance Ensemble, Ziva's Spanish Dance Ensemble and TAPestry – perform at the Wisconsin Avenue studio's Jack Guidone Theatre.

Washington Ballet

Information 362 3606. **Tickets** $20-$45.

The Washington Ballet presents a solid season of contemporary and classic ballets by the likes of Nils Christie, Krzysztof Pastor and George Balanchine every year from September to May, as well as an annual production of *The Nutcracker* for two weeks in December. Performances are usually held at the George Mason University in Virginia or the Warner Theatre in Downtown.

Website: www.washingtonballet.org

Theatre

In the past ten years, DC's theatre scene has grown phenomenally. In 1997, the weekly showbiz rag *Variety* inexplicably ranked Washington as the number two theatre town in the country (second only to New York), but even conservative estimates would place it in the top five. Large productions often use Washington as a testing ground before heading to Broadway, and smaller theatres offer new work by as-yet-unknown playwrights.

Performance art experienced a heyday in the 1980s when venues such as the now-defunct dc space might present avant-garde jazz group Sun Ra, punk rockers Minor Threat and performance artist Laurie Anderson. It now seems to be experiencing a resurgence but recent Downtown development and a lack of affordable warehouse space means stable venues are hard to come by.

Several theatres offer pay-what-you-can preview nights or special rates for under-26s.

The Kennedy Center

Kennedy Center

2700 F Street, NW, at New Hampshire Avenue, Foggy Bottom (467 4600/1-800 444 1324). Foggy Bottom-GWU Metro, then free shuttle bus. Website: http://kennedy-center.org

Washington is big on honouring past chiefs of staff – not always in ways that are architecturally appealing or useful. Ronald Reagan is barely retired and already they've renamed the airport after him and constructed a hulking monstrosity of a building in his honour. That the John F Kennedy Center for the Performing Arts (to give it its full title), a 'living memorial' to the 35th prez, was ever built is a small miracle, considering that the US government continually cuts funding for public broadcasting and the arts. Or a very large miracle, depending on how you look at it. The Washington Monument would easily fit sideways inside the centre's Grand Foyer, with 75 feet to spare. The building itself was made with 3,700 tons of Carrera marble from Italy and takes up eight acres.

An act to establish a national culture centre was signed into law by President Eisenhower in 1958. After JFK's assassination in November 1963, Congress designated the centre as a memorial to him. Construction began two years later and the building opened in 1971. Before its arrival, Washington was a cultural desert. Now the Kennedy Center stands as the crown jewel in a thriving arts scene.

In the Grand Foyer, visitors can view Robert Berks' massive brass bust of JFK and enjoy free daily performances on the Millennium Stage. There are five theatres within the centre: the Concert Hall, the Opera House, the Eisenhower Theater and the much smaller Terrace Theater and Theatre Lab. The American Film Institute screens foreign, independent and classic films daily. Three roof-top restaurants – the Roof Terrace, the Hors D'Oeuvrerie and the Encore Café – offer a range of dining options, from formal to casual, while the centre's 'back porch', an open-air terrace, offers a beautiful view of the Potomac River.

A free shuttle transports patrons to and from the Foggy Bottom-GWU Metro station.

Concert Hall

This underwent a million-dollar facelift in 1997, which tremendously improved the acoustics and rearranged seating so that every seat has a clear sightline to the stage. The National Symphony Orchestra and the Washington Chamber Symphony call the Concert Hall home. The Choral Arts Society and venerable artists such as flautist James Galway and cellist Yo-Yo Ma perform here, as well as more contemporary artists such as the Kronos Quartet and Bobby McFerrin, who guest-conducted the National Symphony Orchestra in Gershwin's *Porgy & Bess*.

Opera House

As its name suggests, this is where the Washington Opera performs. It is also the site for many ballet and modern dance performances by the likes of the Stanislavsky Ballet, Dance Theater of Harlem and Mark Morris Dance Group. Big Broadway musicals, such as *Titanic*, also set up shop here.

Major venues

Arena Stage

1101 Sixth Street, SW, at Maine Avenue, Southwest (488 3300). Waterfront Metro. **Tickets** $30-$45. **Credit cards** AmEx, Disc, MC, V.

Despite being in a fairly desolate part of the city, where the only other attraction is the fish market, this is the most highly regarded theatre in DC. It has three stages – the 800-seat round-house Fichlander, the 500-seat proscenium Kreeger and the small, cabaret-style Old Vat Room – and was the first theatre outside New York to win a Tony award. Pulitzer Prize winner Paula Vogel is currently playwright-in-residence. Note: a move to Downtown's Penn Quarter may be on the cards.

Carter Barron Amphitheater

16th Street & Colorado Avenue, NW, Rock Creek Park, Upper Northwest (282 1063). Bus S1. **Tickets** free-$16. **No credit cards**.

The lush trees of Rock Creek Park canopy this large outdoor venue, which presents classical, jazz, pop music and theatre (May-Sept. In June the Shakespeare Theatre presents two weeks of free performances.

Ford's Theatre

511 Tenth Street, NW, between E & F Streets, Downtown (347 4833). Metro Center Metro. **Tickets** $27-$43. **Credit** AmEx, DC, Disc, MC, V.

This is where President Lincoln was shot while watching *Our American Cousin*. For the most part, Ford's presents apple-pie-American, family-oriented fare, although there are occasional surprises such as the Steve Martin-penned comedy *Picasso at the Lapin Agile*. Every December, it stages Dickens' *A Christmas Carol*.
Website: www.fordstheatre.org

National Theatre

1321 Pennsylvania Avenue, NW, between 13th & 14th Streets, Downtown (628 6161). Metro Center

Eisenhower Theater

This stage usually offers dramatic plays, such as Wendy Wasserstein's *The Heidi Chronicles* and Tony Kushner's *Angels in America*. Popular modern dance companies such as Bill T Jones/ Arnie Zane Dance Company and Pilobolus sometimes perform, and works developed by the Kennedy Center's Fund for New American Plays also début here.

Terrace Theater

Designed by architect Philip Johnson, this space presents chamber recitals, dramatic plays and experimental theatre. Athol Fugard's most recent work, *The Captain's Tiger*, was staged here in 1998. In addition to jazz concerts by big-name groups (Mingus Big Band, Art Blakey's Jazz Messengers), Dr Billy Taylor hosts regular jazz lecture/performances with renowned guest artists.

Theatre Lab

For more than a decade, this intimate space has been the home for the audience-participation suspense comedy *Shear Madness*, but it focuses primarily on programmes for young people – recent subjects include vocalist Marian Anderson and inventor Thomas Edison – as well as original works such as *Alexander and the Terrible, Horrible, No Good, Very Bad Day*, adapted from Judith Viorst's kids' book.

or Federal Triangle Metro. **Tickets** $15-$75. **Credit** AmEx, DC, Disc, MC, V.

To call the National a phoenix rising from the flames would be true on several levels. One of the city's oldest theatres, it was built in 1835 and then rebuilt four more times after being destroyed by fires over the years. The theatre has struggled to stay in the black financially, but in recent years extended runs of Broadway hits such as *Rent, Chicago* and *Ragtime* have boosted its budget. It offers an eclectic calendar of free performances by local artists on Monday evenings and free shows for children on Saturday afternoons.

Website: www.nationaltheatre.org

Shakespeare Theatre

450 Seventh Street, NW, between D & E Streets, Penn Quarter (547 1122). Gallery Place-Chinatown Metro. **Tickets** $14-$56. **Credit** AmEx, MC, V.

Under the artistic direction of Michael Kahn, this company performs five plays a year, often bringing in film and television actors (such as Dixie Carter, Harry Hamlin, Elizabeth Ashley, Patrick Stewart) to guest star in its productions. Housed for many years at the Elizabethan-style Folger Shakespeare Library near the Library of Congress, it now presents classical work in an intimate and thoroughly modern Downtown venue.

Website: www.shakespearedc.org

Smaller venues & performance art

Church Street Theater

1742 Church Street, NW, between 17th & 18th Streets, Dupont Circle (265 3748). **Tickets** $15-$25. **No credit cards**.

Run as a commercial theatre renting itself out to various local companies, Church Street has no general ethos or overriding style to speak of, but a few jewels turn up every season.

DCAC (District of Columbia Arts Center)
2438 18th Street, NW, between Columbia & Belmont Roads, Adams Morgan (462 7833). Woodley Park-Zoo Metro, then 90, 91, 92, 93, 96, L2 bus. **Tickets** $8-$15. **Credit** AmEx, MC, V. **Closed** July, Aug.
This tiny black box theatre consistently presents innovative experimental plays and performance art, as well as outside-the-mainstream visual artists in its adjacent gallery space. Since 1990, Playback Theatre, an improvisational theatre company that turns audience stories into instant plays, performs here on the third Sunday of every month.
Website: www.dcartscenter.org

GALA Hispanic Theatre
1625 Park Road, NW, between 16th & Mount Pleasant Streets, Mount Pleasant (234 7174). Bus 42. **Tickets** $12-$20. **Credit** AmEx, MC, V.
Located in the heart of DC's Salvadorean community, GALA presents plays in Spanish and English, as well as music, dance, spoken word and performance art centred around Latin American culture.

DCAC: *avant-garde art and performance.*

Signature Theatre
3806 South Four Mile Run Drive, between Shirlington Road & Walter Reed Drive, Arlington, VA (703 820 9771). Pentagon Metro, then 22A, 22B, 22C bus.
Tickets $21-$30. **Credit** AmEx, MC, V.
Don't expect glitz or big bucks, but this theatre manages to consistently turn out award-winning plays. Each season always includes at least one work by Stephen Sondheim.
Website: www.sig-online.org

Source Theatre Company
1835 14th Street, NW, between S & T Streets, Logan Circle (462 1073). U Street-Cardozo Metro.
Tickets $23-$25. **Credit** AmEx, MC,V.
Recently remodelled, the Source focuses on 'new American classics' by the likes of David Mamet, Steven Dietz and Nicky Silver. For four weeks in July and August, it hosts a theatre festival with readings and productions of more than 30 new scripts, a junior festival for young playwrights and a competition for the best ten-minute play.

Studio Theatre
1333 P Street, NW, at 14th Street, Logan Circle (332 3300). Dupont Circle or U Street-Cardozo Metro. **Tickets** $20-$40. **Credit** AmEx, Disc, MC, V.
In 1998, Studio received kudos in the *New York Times* for director Joy Zinoman's version of *Waiting for Godot*, which featured African-American leading men. With two mid-sized stages and the 50-seat Secondstage, popular productions are easily extended. Past highlights include a revival of the musical *Hair* and poet Eve Ensler's solo performance of *The Vagina Monologues*.
Website: www.studiotheatre.org

Washington Stage Guild
924 G Street, NW, between Ninth & Tenth Streets, Downtown (529 2084). Gallery Place-Chinatown Metro. **Tickets** $20-$22. **No credit cards**.
Four plays a year, ranging from classic works by playwrights such as George Bernard Shaw to contemporary unknowns, are performed in the environs of St Patrick's parochial school.

Woolly Mammoth Theatre Company
1401 Church Street, NW, at 14th Street, Logan Circle (393 3939). Dupont Circle Metro. **Tickets** $16-$29. **Credit** AmEx, MC, V.
Woolly has a reputation for going as far outside the mainstream as a theatre can go and still be considered a traditional theatre. In the past it has presented performance artist Brian Freeman's *Civil Sex*, the solo tour de force *A Huey P Newton Story* by Roger Guenvere Smith and British farce *Dead Funny*.

WPA/Corcoran
Information 639 1714.
Funding cutbacks have led the once-independent Washington Project for the Arts to join forces with the Corcoran Gallery. In its new incarnation, the WPA presents a spring series of performance art, installations, poetry readings and visual arts exhibits at Downtown warehouse spaces.

Film

Excellent repertory at DC's institutions more than compensates for a dearth of quality mainstream venues.

Many Hollywood films are set in Washington, which provides instantly recognisable symbols of power as well as locations unique among major US cities. DC is also home to a significant film making industry, which claims to be the third largest in the country, after those in Los Angeles and New York. These two things have almost nothing to do with each other.

Washington has long been a useful location for Hollywood movies, but the crews usually spend just a few days in town, filming at conspicuous landmarks before heading back to LA or continuing the shoot in cheaper locales, such as Toronto, Vancouver or even Baltimore. Anyone who's been in DC even a short time will recognise some of the more obvious signs that a 'Washington' scene wasn't actually shot here: palm trees, skyscrapers, mountains. The Metro doesn't allow violent acts to be staged on its property, so subway scenes in Washington-based thrillers are usually shot in Baltimore's underground system.

Most of the movies made by filmmakers who live in Washington full-time are documentaries on, not surprisingly, political or historical subjects. Georgetown-based director Charles Guggenheim won his fourth Oscar for such films in 1999. More surprisingly, this is also the base for many nature filmmakers: Washington is the home of Discovery and National Geographic, two of the largest producers of such films.

Most Washingtonians see these films the way everyone else does: on television or video. Still, there are an increasing number of showcases for local filmmakers. The annual Rosebud awards are for Washington-area filmmakers, with the winning films showcased during Filmfest DC, Washington's international film festival, held in spring. A monthly series of screenings of local work is held at one of the largest local production houses, Atlantic Video; the event is called Studio 650 after the facility's address: 650 Massachusetts Avenue, NW, at Seventh Street, Downtown (408 3432/408 0900).

The cinemas

All the city's commercial cinemas are run by the Loews Cineplex Odeon chain (except for AMC Union Station) – although that will soon change. After a decade in which DC's cinemas did nothing but disappear, there's a flurry of plans for new multiplexes: an eight-screen General Cinema is set to open at the Mazza Gallerie shopping mall in Friendship Heights in late 1999, and deals have been made to bring cinemas to several other locations, including Georgetown and a site directly north of the MCI Center. The latter will have 20-25 screens, making it by far the city's biggest. It will also fill a geographical gap: currently the only cinema in Downtown DC is the AMC at Union Station. Visitors will find this most convenient, along with the Loews at Dupont Circle and Foggy Bottom, unless they're prepared to make a Metro trip to better screens further out.

Perhaps more significant is the Biograph, a new eight-screen cinema that is scheduled to open at 11th and E Streets in Penn Quarter, in late 2000. This will be operated by Landmark, an LA-based art-house chain, and promises to show independent and foreign films of the sort that have become rarer locally since the closing of the city's last two independent art cinemas, the Key and the original Biograph, in 1996 and 1997. Loews Cineplex Odeon does programme such films, but the company's booking policies are less adventurous than those of the old Biograph, whose co-owner is a consultant to the new theatre.

Mainstream films

AMC Union Station

Union Station, 50 Massachusetts Avenue, NE, at N Capitol Street, Union Station & Around (703 998 4262). Union Station Metro. **Admission** $3.75-$7.50.

Located in a cavern-like space under Union Station's waiting room, this nine-screen cinema is the city's largest multiplex. Each screen is named after a vanished Washington moviehouse. The largest auditorium is fine; the others are acceptable.

Loews Cineplex Odeon Avalon

5612 Connecticut Avenue, NW, between Northampton & McKinley Streets, Upper Northwest (966 2600). Friendship Heights Metro or Van Ness-UDC Metro, then L1, L2 bus. **Admission** $5-$7.75.

A neighbourhood cinema that has become glamorous by default, this is notable for its steeply raked seats, large screen and an elaborate ceiling mural that melds classical and cinematic motifs. The second screen upstairs is definitely an afterthought.

Loews Cineplex Odeon Cinema
5100 Wisconsin Avenue, NW, between Harrison & Garrison Streets, Upper Northwest (966 7248). Friendship Heights Metro.
Admission $5-$7.75.
This movie theatre is without architectural charm, but it's almost as large as the Uptown, with the biggest flat screen in town. A drawback is that, like many of this chain's cinemas, it's located in Upper Northwest (near Friendship Heights), a good trek from the centre of town.

Loews Cineplex Odeon Uptown
3426 Connecticut Avenue, NW, between Porter & Ordway Streets, Cleveland Park (966 5400). Cleveland Park Metro.
Admission $5-$7.75.
With the destruction of the last of the Downtown movie palaces in the 1980s, what was once just an average neighbourhood theatre has become the city's premier cinema. Blockbusters (and would-be blockbusters) are the normal fare at this 1936 art deco theatre, whose 1,500 seats make it the city's

The popcorn presidents

Since silver-haired heart-throb Bill Clinton replaced the somewhat less dishy George Bush in 1992, Hollywood's perception of America's president has become more leading man than world leader. But how would the celluloid candidates actually perform on the campaign trail?

James Marshall

Screen persona Harrison Ford
Celluloid CV *Air Force One* (1997, dir Wolfgang Petersen)
Personal style Indiana Jones goes into politics.
Campaign credentials Fending off terrorist attack on the presidential plane – and guess who gets to land it…?
Greatest moment in politics Dialling the White House from a mobile phone while 30,000 feet in the air *and getting through to an operator first time.*
Electability rating Politics take a back seat when Marshall's in the cockpit – but let's face it, it's all about personalities: 8/10

Thomas J Whitmore

Screen persona Bill Pullman
Celluloid CV *Independence Day* (1996, dir Roland Emmerich)
Personal style Clinton meets a young Reagan.
Campaign credentials The President takes it upon himself to save the world from certain destruction by aliens.
Greatest moment in politics The only person in America to say that Area 51 does not exist – and believe it.
Electability rating Good in a crisis: 8/10

Jack Stanton

Screen persona John Travolta
Celluloid CV *Primary Colors* (1998, Mike Nichols)
Personal style Clinton but nicer on the record; Clinton but nastier off it.

Campaign credentials Survives well-founded accusations of draft-dodging, adultery and moral bankruptcy on the campaign trail.
Greatest moment in politics Managing to look like a crap dancer at his birthday party.
Electability rating The end justifies the means: 7/10

Bill Mitchell

Screen persona Kevin Kline
Celluloid CV *Dave* (1993, dir Ivan Reitman)
Personal style Jeez, what a *nice guy.*
Campaign credentials Presidential impersonator Dave Kovic is asked to stand in as US president while the man himself recovers from a stroke.
Greatest moment in politics Managing to pull the wool over everyone's eyes and avoid awkward questions regarding moles on embarrassing parts of the presidential anatomy.
Electability rating Dishonest, fraudulent, excellent liar: 10/10

Andy Shepherd

Screen persona Michael Douglas
Celluloid CV *The American President* (1995, dir Rob Reiner)
Personal style So squeaky clean that he's obviously hiding something…
Campaign credentials Commits the ultimate sin by falling in love during an election campaign at a time when the opposition candidates are willing to dish the dirt.
Greatest moment in politics Introducing a bill into Congress – which the US Constitution does not allow the president to do.
Electability rating Housewives' choice: 5/10

DC's premier cinema: the **Loews Cineplex Odeon Uptown**, *in Cleveland Park.*

largest auditorium. Don't sit too too near the front: it still has a curved Cinerama screen.

Loews Cineplex Odeon Wisconsin Avenue

4000 Wisconsin Avenue, NW, at Upton Street, Upper Northwest (244 0880). Tenleytown-AU Metro. **Admission** $5-$7.75.

This well-designed six-plex is the city's newest cinema. It offers good sightlines, and the two largest auditoriums are excellent.

Foreign & independent films

Loews Cineplex Odeon Dupont Circle

1350 19th Street, NW, at M Street, Dupont Circle (333 3456). Dupont Circle Metro. **Admission** $5-$7.75. Five screens.

Loews Cineplex Odeon Janus

1660 Connecticut Avenue, NW, at R Street, Dupont Circle (265 9545). Dupont Circle Metro. **Admission** $5-$7.75. Three screens.

Loews Cineplex Odeon Inner Circle

2301 M Street, NW, at 23rd Street, Foggy Bottom (333 3456). Foggy Bottom-GWU Metro. **Admission** $5-$7.75. Three screens.

Loews Cineplex Odeon Outer Circle

4849 Wisconsin Avenue, NW, at Ellicott Street, Upper Northwest (244 3116). Tenleytown Metro. **Admission** $5-$7.75. Two screens.

These four cinemas usually show foreign and independent films. None of them is great, but if you want to see a non-Hollywood feature you probably won't have a choice. The Outer Circle has the biggest screen and the best sightlines, while the Dupont is the newest. The Janus is the worst of the lot, and its third screen (entrance around the corner) should be avoided if at all possible.

Repertory

As in most US cities, there are no longer any commercial repertory cinemas in Washington. The city does, however, have, one of the country's most extensive non-commercial rep film scenes. Keeping abreast of the programmes at these venues is a major undertaking, but not an expensive one: most of them are free.

Among many other local institutions that sometimes screen films are the **National Archives** (mainly US documentaries from its own collection; 501 5000); the **DC Jewish Community Center** (Jewish films; tickets 1-800 494 8497/information 518 9400 ext 229); the **National Museum of Women in the Arts** (films by and about women; 783 7370); and the **French Embassy** (monthly French-language films; 944 6091). See *Washington City Paper* for listings.

American Film Institute

Kennedy Center, 2700 F Street, NW, at New Hampshire Avenue, Foggy Bottom (785 4600). Foggy Bottom-GWU Metro (free shuttle bus from station). **Admission** $6.50.

Unpleasantville?

There have been so many movies made recently about politics and presidents (as action hero or anti-hero) that Washington seems ready for a special Oscar category of its own. The Hollywood connection has grown so intimate that the realms of the screen and the soapbox have overlapped and their borders blurred. Bill Clinton bombs Iraq at the height of his impeachment problems and pundits endlessly cite the *Wag the Dog* scenario.

Hollywood used Washington for material in the past too, of course. In a more innocent age, Frank Capra's populist manifestos, *Meet John Doe* and *Mr Smith Goes to Washington*, showed manipulative plutocrats brought low by noble commoners like Gary Cooper and James Stewart. In the early post-war years, affectionate satires such as Capra's *State of the Union* and George S Kaufman's *The Senator Was Indiscreet* showed a system more silly than venal.

But the most interesting and entertaining Hollywood Washingtons emerged in the 1960s, when paranoia and black humour came in for their close-ups. Here are some bizarro classics of silver-screen DC:

The Manchurian Candidate (1962)

Director John Frankenheimer's adaptation of Richard Condon's novel featured a brainwashed former POW (a poshly glib Laurence Harvey) programmed to kill at the command of his handler, his own Machiavellian dowager mother (a horrifying Angela Lansbury). *The Manchurian Candidate* was so weirdly prescient that, although the studio kept the film out of general circulation for almost 30 years after the Kennedy assassination, its premise became fodder for popular speculation and its title phrase entered the language.

Dr Strangelove: or, How I Learned to Stop Worrying and Love the Bomb (1963)

The machinery of government appeared as hilarious as it was malevolent in Stanley Kubrick's 1963 film. Among many brilliant touches: Peter Sellers' triple play as US President Merkin Muffley, British exchange officer Group Captain Mandrake and semi-rehabilitated Nazi war scientist Dr Strangelove; George C Scott's enthusiastically warmongering General Buck Turgidson; and Sterling Hayden's airbase commander Jack D Ripper ('I can no longer sit back and allow Communist infiltration, Communist indoctrination, Communist subversion and the international Communist conspiracy to sap and impurify all of our precious bodily fluids…').

The President's Analyst (1967) & Wild in the Streets (1968)

Two slighter Washington films, but among the kookiest of a kooky era. In *The President's Analyst*, James Coburn, as the First Shrink, finds himself the target of a comically crazed manhunt whose ultimate mastermind proves to be none other than 'The Phone Company'. In *Wild in the Streets*, a Roger Corman-esque drive-in cheapie, a Constitutional amendment puts the Great Seal in the hands of a 14-year-old pop star.

Secret Honor (1984)

A more recent film, and a more straightforward one, but brilliantly made and scandalously unappreciated, this Robert Altman tour de force opened to great critical acclaim, sank like a stone and disappeared without a trace.

A one-character drama with actor Philip Baker Hall playing Richard Nixon, in retirement, alone at night with a tape recorder (which he can barely manage to operate) and a bottle of Pinch (the real-life Nixon's favourite Scotch), unburdening himself of the truth behind Watergate. In the course of one long and increasingly drunken rant, he takes us through the whole of Nixon's personal and political history and, veering from laughter to tears, illuminates the story of America's post-war years.

Recent budget cutbacks mean this excellent theatre is dark about half the month and longer runs have partially supplanted more complicated (and expensive) multi-film programmes. Still, there's usually something interesting happening here when the projector is flickering. Revivals of classic or recently restored movies and first runs of new foreign films mix with retrospectives of directors and overviews of national cinema. DC filmmakers commonly introduce and discuss their work here.

Freer Gallery of Art

Meyer Auditorium, Jefferson Drive, SW, at 12th Street, Mall & Tidal Basin (357 2700). Smithsonian Metro. **Screenings** usually 7pm Fri, Sat; 2pm Sun. **Admission** free.

The films shown here come from the countries represented in the gallery's collection, which emphasises Asia and the Middle East. This is one of the best places in town to see movies from India and Iran, but arrive early – the theatre soon fills up with emigrés from those countries. Recently, the Freer has shared Mizoguchi and Imamura retrospectives with the National Gallery of Art (*see below*). There's also an annual survey of kinetic action films and raucous comedies from Hong Kong.

Hirshhorn Museum & Sculpture Garden

Seventh Street & Independence Avenue, SW, Mall & Tidal Basin (357 2700). L'Enfant Plaza Metro. **Screenings** usually 8pm Thur, Fri. **Admission** free.

Showcases work by upcoming and experimental directors, often fresh from success on the international film festival circuit. Highlights from several alternative festivals are shown annually and filmmakers sometimes show works in progress. Programmer Kelly Gordon was one of the first Americans to champion such directors as Derek Jarman and Peter Greenaway, leading to exclusive US premieres of such films as *The Baby of Mâcon.*

Library of Congress

Mary Pickford Theater, Madison Building, First Street & Pennsylvania Avenue, SE, Capitol & Around (707 5677). Capitol South Metro. **Screenings** usually 7pm several weeknights. **Admission** free; reservations recommended.

The Library draws on its own extensive holdings to programme its small cinema. Recent series have explored such themes as 'Religion and the Founding of the American Republic' and 'Native Americans in Silent Film'. The Library may have the only copies of some of the early films it shows, although it screens better-known fare in its ongoing series of movies that have been appointed to the National Film Registry of cinematic treasures.

National Gallery of Art

East Building Auditorium, Fourth Street & Constitution Avenue, NW, Mall & Tidal Basin (842 6799). Judiciary Square or Archives-Navy Memorial Metro. **Screenings** afternoon Sat, Sun, some weekdays. **Admission** free.

This auditorium has one of the biggest screens and some of the most interesting programming in the city, as well as the most leg room. Film series are sometimes linked to major exhibitions, such as the films about Edo-period Japan co-ordinated with the Gallery's 1998-99 show of Edo art. It also hosts major retrospectives. Documentaries about art and related topics are shown on weekdays.

Website: www.nga.gov

Film festivals

The largest local annual festival is **Filmfest DC** (628 3456), which shows about 75 films, most of them international, during a two-week period beginning in late April. Its organisers also sponsor an overview of Arab films, usually in January. In October and November, the American Film Institute (785 4600) presents the **European Film Showcase**, introducing new films (and frequently new directors) from Europe.

Other festivals of note are the **Environmental Film Festival** (342 2564) in March; **Reel Affirmations** (986 1119), the gay and lesbian film fest in October; and the **Jewish Film Festival** (518 9400 ext 248) in December. Check *Washington City Paper* listings for details.

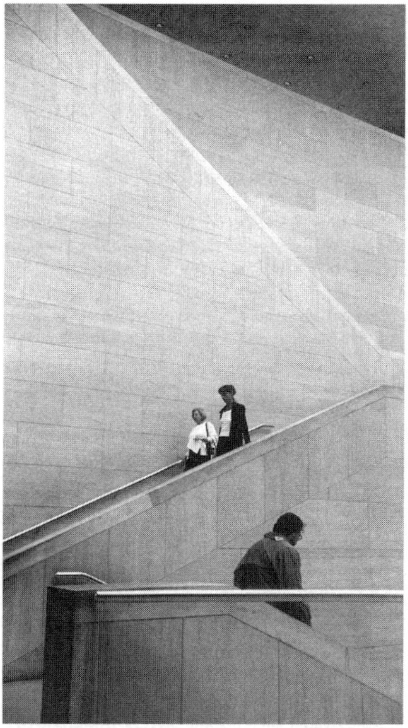

National Gallery of Art: *art-house movies.*

Media

As the place where a free press meets an 'open' government, Washington generates nearly as much newsprint as it does bureaucracy.

Washington produces news, but it also consumes it. This is the one US city where many people actually watch those political chat (and, increasingly, shout) shows that the TV networks run every Sunday to prove they're really interested in policy. Some DC political junkies try to keep up with the burgeoning public affairs programming of such new 'news' cable channels as MSNBC and Fox News, and even listen to the local radio station that carries an audio version of the C-SPAN cable channel's Congressional coverage. Taxi drivers atually know what they're talking about. In exchange for this touching dedication, some news organisations go to financially unjustifiable lengths to reach the DC audience. The *Los Angeles Times*, for example, prints a special edition just for a thousand or so Washington readers.

With all the major American news organisations and many foreign ones in residence, news crews are a common sight in Washington. Reporters can be spied doing 'stand-ups' in front of many official buildings, although the most common ones are, of course, the White House and the Capitol. Newsmakers frequently appear at the National Press Club, although few of these events are open to the public. For mainstream US journalism's hymn to itself, visit the country's only press museum, the **Newseum** (*see page 108* **Museums & Galleries**).

Newspapers & magazines

Dailies

The Godzilla of local print journalism is the *Washington Post*, whose clout is the object of some awe and much resentment. The *Post* has the highest market penetration of any major-city US daily, although its executives fret, with reason, that its power is waning with younger Washingtonians. The *Post*'s coverage exemplifies the inside-the-Beltway mentality, with heavy emphasis on politics and policy and a poorly concealed scepticism that anything else really matters. By the standards of US newspapers, international coverage is strong, and as the local high-tech sector has grown the paper has expanded its coverage of business and technology. Local news and the arts are often treated with indifference. On Fridays, the *Post* publishes its 'Weekend' section, with extensive arts and entertainment listings. The much-syndicated 'Doonesbury' strip, renowned for its beyond-cynical attitude, appears daily. Creator Gary Trudeau frequently uses it to lampoon the unholy alliance between politics and the press (*see below*).

Owned by cronies of the Rev Sun Myung Moon, the *Washington Times* offers an extreme-right view of the day's events, with front-page stories that are often amusingly partisan. It's read only by paleo-conservatives and people who really, really hate the *Post*.

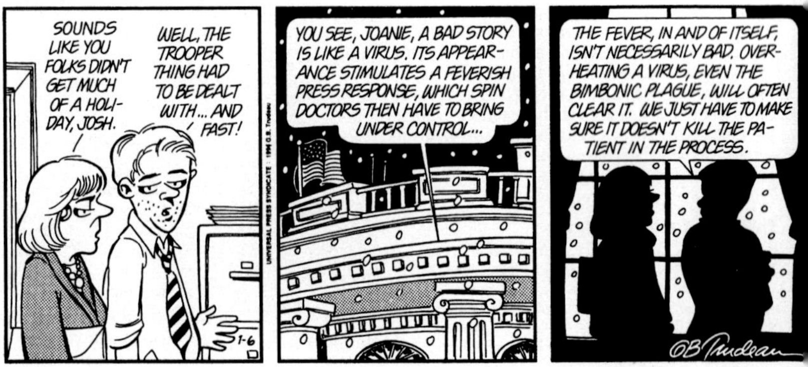

The *New York Times* has a significant local readership, especially on Sundays, when its arts and feature writing trounces the *Post*'s. (Sunday's *Times* comes in a Washington 'edition' whose only local features are a weather forecast and TV listings.) Most large US newspapers are available in local street boxes, although only the *Los Angeles Times* prints a special daily edition for DC. *USA Today*, the country's only national general-interest daily, is produced across the river in Rosslyn, but its terse stories, graphics-heavy presentation and middle-American sensibility are not much to Washington's taste.

Weeklies

Geographical or cultural subdivisions of the metropolitan area are served by many weekly tabloids, including some suburban ones owned by the *Post*, but the only such weekly of regional significance is *Washington City Paper*. Founded in 1981 and owned by the *Chicago Reader*, this 'alternative' free weekly publishes sprawling features on topics both urgent and whimsical. It's read mostly, however, for its arts coverage, listings and adverts.

The recently redesigned *New Republic*, once the voice of neo-liberalism – or is it neo-conservatism? – has been damaged by its affiliation with two briefly hot young writers, one a plagiarist, the other a fabulist. Its diminished authority also stems from the boom in new political journals (*The Weekly Standard*, *The American Prospect*, *Slate*) that have claimed some of the weekly's old turf.

Roll Call and *The Hill* compete for the small but influential readership that makes national policy in the Capitol and its adjacent office buildings. These tabloids occasionally break major stories, but to outsiders most of the coverage will seem arcane.

Although it still looks like a daily, the venerable *Washington Afro-American* has been reduced to weekly publication, and most of its readership has been claimed by an assortment of small freesheets.

Garry Trudeau's deflationary 'Doonesbury' strip, in the Post.

Monthlies

The *Washingtonian* was once rated among the best US city magazines, but it has retreated from serious reporting and now favours a mix of service journalism and tepid profiles. Its readership is overwhelmingly suburban. *Capital Style*, a new monthly owned by *Roll Call*, focuses narrowly on the glamorous side (such as it is) of federal Washington. It attempts to be hipper than the *Washingtonian*, but the difference is marginal.

The right-wing *American Spectator* may have started 'Monicagate' by printing the first account of Clinton's alleged dropped-trousers overture to a woman identified only as 'Paula'. The author of that piece went on to write a sympathetic book about Hillary Clinton, and the *Spectator* has been short on bombshells recently.

George magazine, although based in New York, focuses on Washington. John F Kennedy Jr's glossy initially attracted lots of advertisers by wrapping political coverage in the sort of upscale celebrity gush associated with *Vanity Fair*. Following the death of its founder, its future is uncertain.

Published mostly for its members but available on some newsstands, *Smithsonian*'s coverage of science, history and other subjects of enduring importance exemplifies the side of Washington that is not consumed by the latest poll numbers.

A pioneering 'neo-liberal' policy journal, the *Washington Monthly* was once known as much for grooming young journalists as for anticipating Washington policy shifts. The magazine is tired these days, and its graduates rarely become stars.

Outlets

Outdoor newsstands (along with sidewalk cafés) were illegal in Washington for much of the twentieth century, and since the ban was lifted in the 1960s most attempts to establish them have failed – which explains why the sidewalks at major intersections are overwhelmed by newspaper vending machines. Still, the city has more newspaper and magazine outlets than meet the eye. Many large office buildings have newsstands, often concealed in their lobbies so that only workers and regular visitors are aware of them.

Among the larger newsstands – and the ones with the best selection of foreign publications – are **Newsroom** (1753 Connecticut Avenue, NW, Dupont Circle; 332 1489), **News World** (1001 Connecticut Avenue, NW, Foggy Bottom; 872 0190) and **Metro Center News** (620 G Street, NW, Downtown; 393 1644). Best of the book 'superstores' for papers and magazines are **Barnes & Noble** (3040 M Street, NW, Georgetown; 965 9880) and **Borders** (1800 L Street, NW, Foggy Bottom; 466 4999). **Tower Records** (2000 Pennsylvania Avenue, NW, Foggy Bottom; 331 2400) has the best choice of music and youth-culture titles.

Television

Washington's airwaves carry all the usual suspects: NBC (WRC, channel 4), Fox (WTTG, channel 5), ABC (WJLA, channel 7), CBS (WUSA, channel 9), UPN (WDCA, channel 20) and WB (WBDC, channel 50). These offer the familiar sitcoms, cop and hospital dramas and growing numbers (because they're cheap to produce) of news magazine shows. There are also three local public TV stations featuring the customary line up of *Sesame Street*, British drawing-room dramas and highlights from *Riverdance*: WMPT (channel 22), WETA (channel 26) and WHUT (channel 32); the latter runs some Spanish-language shows. Washington's local TV news programmes are supposedly less lurid than in most American cities, although that's hard to imagine.

On cable, the fare is also commonplace, although it varies sightly among local jurisdictions. Among the national channels that are based in Washington are BET (Black Entertainment Television) and Discovery Channel, Animal Planet, the Learning Channel and the History Channel (all of them owned by Discovery). Washingtonians watch more C-SPAN and C-SPAN II (with live coverage of Congress and other public affairs programming) than most Americans; channels seen locally only include NewsChannel 8 and Home Team Sports.

Columnists who count

A generation ago, there were columnists whose writings shaped the American political debate. Today, a syndicated column or other political-commentary job is just a launchpad for a TV career. Virtually all the *Washington Post*'s op-ed columnists – and their counterparts from the *New York Times*, the *Wall Street Journal* and other publications – appear regularly on such established TV vehicles as *This Week with Sam Donaldson & Cokie Roberts*, *Crossfire* and *The Capital Gang*, as well as such new ones as *The Beltway Boys*. There is nobody today with the clout of columnists such as Walter Lippman or Joseph Alsop.

Despite this profusion of punditry, the range of opinion comes dressed in shades of grey – from conservative to neo-conservative to moderate. This was particularly obvious during the early days of the Clinton-Lewinsky controversy, when virtually every prominent Washington commentator not only demanded the president's departure from office, but forecast that it was imminent. (Such predictions are a major feature of most TV commentary programmes, which only emphasises their sport-betting approach to current events.)

The dean of conservative columnists is **George F Will**, whose work is widely syndicated by the *Washington Post* and who also appears on television in *This Week with Sam Donaldson & Cokie Roberts*. Will has cut back on the learned quotations that eventually become an object of fun in the 'Doonesbury' comic strip, but he's still expected to provide an intellectual basis for the current positions of mainstream conservatism. A would-be Victorian, Will has difficulty reconciling his reverence for the free market with his distaste for almost everything American capitalism has wrought since 1960.

Although **Cokie Roberts** is a veteran reporter for National Public Radio, she's better known for her appearances on ABC-TV, notably on the show that bears her name. A liberal by the standards of mainstream US journalism, she's the scion of a political dynasty and a steadfast voice for the Washington establishment.

The *Post*'s **David Broder** is both a reporter and a commentator. An earnest moderate who is intensely reverent of the political process, he's most concerned when it appears that either the voting public or a prominent politician (most recently Clinton) is being disrespectful to the American system.

Paleo-conservative **Robert Novak** appears on *The Capital Gang* and writes a column that appears in the *Washington Post*. He's one of the more entertaining right-wing columnists because his focus is often on intramural battles among his conservative brethren.

When not running for president, Washington native **Patrick Buchanan** bellows on *The McLaughlin Group*. He's known for advocating economic protectionism (unusual among conservatives) and an empathy with white racists and former Nazis (unusual among people who want to occupy the White House).

British-born **Christopher Hitchens**, who writes a column for leftist weekly *The Nation*, is considered too radical for a regular gig on a TV talk show. He is occasionally invited to appear, usually when a producer decides to inflame the show's viewers with one of Hitchens's denunciations of Princess Di or Mother Teresa. He recently outraged many on the left by testifying in a court deposition that a former friend, a journalist who became a Clinton aide, had spread disinformation about Monica Lewinsky.

Radio

Because Washington is upscale, urban and has a large African-American population, local radio stations play more classical and hip hop and less country music than in most of parts of the US. However, since the Federal Communication Commission recently weakened regulations restricting the number of stations that could be owned by large corporations, regional diversity in US radio programming is rapidly dwindling. Increasingly, stations are tightly formatted to please a chosen demographic, often with a carefully test-marketed subset of 'oldies': Classic Rock (WKIK, 1560 AM; WARW, 94.7 FM), Golden Oldies (WINX, 1600 AM; WBIG, 100.3 FM) and the new Urban Contemporary Oldies (WMMJ, 102.3 FM).

Long a pioneering 'underground' and then 'alternative' rock outlet, WHFS (99.1 FM) is now as tightly (and unadventurously) programmed as the 'album rock' of WWDC (101.1 FM). College radio, a free-form catalyst in many markets, is insignificant here; the University of Maryland's WMUC (88.1 FM) can be received only in the north-eastern suburbs. 'Urban contemporary' (hip hop and soul) is heard on WKYS (93.9 FM) and WPGC (95.5 FM); WHUR (96.3 FM) offers 'adult urban contemporary' (aka 'Quiet Storm'). WGMS (103.5 FM) is Washington's commercial classical station.

The two public radio stations, WETA (90.9 FM) and WAMU (88.5 FM), broadcast much of the news and arts programming of Washington-based National Public Radio. The former also plays classical music; the latter offers public-affairs talk shows and folk and bluegrass music. The once-radical WPFW (89.3 FM) still mixes jazz and politics, but both have got tamer recently.

Websites

Washington Post

www.washingtonpost.com

The *Post* makes every word it prints available online, although stories are moved after two weeks to the archives, access to which requires a fee. The 'Style Live' section features web-only content, mostly about arts and entertainment.

Washington City Paper

www.washingtoncitypaper.com

Most of this paper's content is not online, but its listings and classifieds are. The 'In DC' section has web-only features, principally about music.

Sidewalk

www.washington.sidewalk.com

In the face of disappointing revenues, Microsoft's city listings service has been trimming features and emphasising national content. This site still has local arts and entertainment listings, however, and extensive restaurant coverage.

The **Newseum** *(p204) headlines the press.*

Slate

www.slate.com

This webzine is based at Microsoft's suburban-Seattle headquarters, but is staffed largely by alumni of several Washington publications. Although Slate is attractively designed and makes good use of the web's interactive and archiving possibilities, it has attracted relatively few readers, perhaps because its voice is staler than its format; Slate's sensibility often mirrors that of the *New Republic*, editor Michael Kinsley's alma mater.

Salon

www.salon.com

Perhaps the best of the country's webzines, this San Francisco site boosted its DC profile dramatically when it began running articles critical of Clinton prosecutor Kenneth Starr and his allies. It now has a Washington bureau.

Drudge Report

www.drudgereport.com

This right-wing LA site also benefited from the Clinton scandal, airing controversial rumours about the president and his intimates before anyone else, some of which actually proved to be true (and one of which spawned an ongoing libel suit).

Progressive Review

www.prorev.com

Veteran DC statehood activist and commentator Sam Smith posts the highlights of his subscription-only journal (and his several books) here. He also provides links to a wide range of Washington progressive (and libertarian) organisations.

Mid-Atlantic Anarchists

www.inshop.com

For those who find the *Progressive Review*'s links too tame, this page's links lead to the sorts of groups whose very existence would surprise Washington's political (and journalistic) mainstream.

Nightlife

You work hard, you play hard: Washington's lights-out scene is surprisingly bright.

Local jazz hero **Duke Ellington** *is celebrated in this U Street mural.*

Music

It's strange that Washington is not thought of as more of an adventurous arts hub, especially considering the diversity of its population and the palpable presence of different cultures. Larger venues such as the **Kennedy Center** (*see page 196* **Culture**) routinely host the crème de la crème for the classical crowd, while small, hip spots such as the **Black Cat** and **State of the Union** book acts for a more eclectic and urbane audience. Arenas such as the relatively new **MCI Center** host the Rolling Stones and other mega groups, while the **RFK Stadium** has been the site of music festivals such as the Tibetan Freedom Concert and the annual WHFStival (for details of both, *see chapter* **Sport & Fitness**). Truth is, sooner or later, everyone who is anyone plays in town. Generally included on the touring route of most big names, Washington is also visited by scores of new and buzz-worthy acts.

The diversity of the population is only one reason why the District attracts notable acts. In terms of music history, DC has secured its place in the books. Jazz greats such as Duke Ellington honed their crafts while building their legends here, and rebellious hardcore and post-punk acts – Minor Threat, Fugazi and Jawbox – forged a sound that is uniquely DC. In the 1980s, go-go emerged in the capable hands of Trouble Funk and Experience Unlimited with a beat-crazy, answer-and-call chorus style that rivalled early rap for its influence (*see page 211* **Have a go-go**).

In the 1990s, locally grown DJ talents such as Scott Henry and electronic and production teams such as Deep Dish, playing in lounges and dance clubs, have created more than just a ripple in the surface of the local music scene, but there are still plenty of venues and artists continuing the tradition of live performance.

Rock

On any given night, the chance of hearing and seeing a meaty slice of rock is pretty high. Scores of clubs turn over their stages to local and/or national acts, and the venues are as unique as the acts that play them. DC shows can sell out quickly, so get tickets in advance.

9:30 Club

815 V Street, NW, at Ninth Street, Shaw (393 0930/ Ticketmaster 1-800 432 7328). U Street-Cardozo Metro. **Open** (if show is on) from 7.30pm Mon-Thur, Sun; 9pm Fri, Sat. **Admission** $1-$50. **Credit** Disc.

In the annals of DC's modern music history, the 9:30's position is legendary. Starting in more humble digs on F Street in the late 1970s, the club was the premier showcase of the new music scene and featured performances by the Lounge Lizards, Bauhaus, Minor Threat and the Bush Tetras. In 1996, the club moved into the renovated WUST Radio Music Hall, a former staple of the city's gospel scene. With a state-of-the-art face-lift, the new 9:30 is thriving and still booking eclectic acts. In the course of a week, you could see the likes of Patti Smith, Bob Dylan, Johnny Cash, Tricky, Underworld or the Mekons. Go early, as the main floor and balconies get crowded. Those who are vertically challenged might hear more than they see.

Website: www.930.com

Black Cat

1831 14th Street, NW, between S & T Streets, U Street/14th Street Corridor (667 7960/ Ticketmaster 432 7328). U Street-Cardozo Metro. **Open** 8pm-2am Mon-Thur, Sun; 7pm-3am Fri, Sat. **Admission** $5-$20. **No credit cards**.

This large, cavernous space – co-owned by Dave Grohl, former Nirvana drummer and current Foo Fighter – boasts some of the best indie rock talent around. Acts such as Sleater-Kinney are booked along with home-grown poster boys Girls Against Boys and the soulful The Make-Up. Unfortunately, the sound system does not live up to the needs of the artists, and the staff can exhibit an annoying hipper-than-thou attitude. The adjoining bar has one of the best-stocked jukeboxes in the District.

Galaxy Hut

2711 Wilson Boulevard, between Danville & Edgewood Streets, Arlington, VA (703 525 8646). Court House or Clarendon Metro. **Open** 5pm-2am Mon-Fri; 7pm-2am Sat, Sun (live music 10pm-midnight Mon, Sat, Sun). **Credit** AmEx, MC, V.

Success hasn't spoiled this Arlington gem, and it's unlikely that it ever will – the club's quarters are so cramped that most curiosity-seekers are forced to leave rather than squeeze in alongside the faithful. It offers everything hipsters want in a haunt, from the interesting art adorning the walls to a vegetarian kitchen (which serves tasty and aptly named items such as the Sputnik Burger) to the whimsical yet provocative local talent that takes its stage.

Grog & Tankard

2408 Wisconsin Avenue, NW, at Calvert Street, Upper Northwest (333 3114). Tenleytown-AU Metro, then 30, 32, 34, 35, 36 bus. **Open** 6pm-1.30am Mon-Thur, Sun; 6pm-2.30am Fri, Sat. **Admission** $5. **Credit** AmEx, MC, V.

If it's a challenge you're looking for, better look elsewhere. However, if you want to re-live some of your college glory days, the Grog & Tankard will deliver. A favourite with DC's university students, baseball hats, Abercrombie & Fitch clothes and cover bands are the currency of choice here. The bands occasionally play originals, but tend to shy away from material to which the crowds can't sing along.

Iota Café

2832 Wilson Boulevard, at Filmore Street, Arlington, VA (703 522 8340). Clarendon Metro. **Open** 5pm-2am Mon-Sat; 11am-2pm Sun. **Admission** free-$15. **Credit** AmEx, DC, Disc, MC, V.

Along with its neighbour **Galaxy Hut** (*see above*), Iota is a great reason to cross the Potomac River. Its friendly atmosphere and wealth of talented performers have made it a favourite. Some complain that the shift in clientele to a more polished professional audience has hurt the place, but that hasn't kept people away. It's a good venue for local folky acts as well as national singer/songwriter types such as Freedy Johnson and Kevin Salem. The Sunday Poetry series has become legendary in local literary circles – all are welcome, and encouraged, to read.

Jaxx

6355 Rolling Road, at Old Keene Mill Road, Springfield, VA (703 569 5940). Franconia-Springfield Metro, then cab. **Open** 4pm-midnight Mon-Wed, Sun; 6pm-2am Thur-Sat. **Admission** $5-$25. **Credit** AmEx, MC, V.

Old hair bands never die, they just keep playing Jaxx. This rock club books ageing, road-tested bands such as Nazareth as well as guitar-geek heroes such as Robin Trower and Robert Fripp, and its patrons and décor reflect the scene. It's outside the District proper, but essential for fans of what seems to be a dying era.

Website: www.jaxroxx.com

Madam's Organ Restaurant & Bar

2461 18th Street, NW, at Columbia Road, Adams Morgan (667 5370). Dupont Circle Metro, then L2 bus or Woodley Park-Zoo Metro, then 90, 91, 92, 93, 96 bus. **Open** 5pm-2am Mon-Thur, Sun; 5pm-3am Fri, Sat. **Admission** $2-$5. **Credit** AmEx, Disc, MC, V.

Hunting trophies line the walls of this infamous saloon-style bar whose stage has been graced by bluegrass, rock and blues acts. An open jam breaks out from time to time on stage, and if you live by the motto 'have guitar (or banjo or harmonica), will travel', then you're bound to be invited to join the festivities. In a city that at times takes itself way too seriously, Madam's Organ is a refreshingly unpretentious zone. *See also p166* **Bars**.

Metro Café

1522 14th Street, NW, at Church Street, Logan Circle (518 7900/588 9118/box office 1-800 494 8497). Dupont Circle Metro. **Open** 7pm-2am Mon-Thur, Sun; 7pm-3am Fri, Sat. **Admission** $5-$10 after 9pm. **Credit** AmEx, Disc, MC, V.

Have a go-go

It's hard to imagine there was ever a time when a rival form thumped it out with rap for the crown of urban music, but in the 1980s, at least in DC, go-go ruled – and rocked – the proverbial house.

A party-ready mix that relied on big beats, role 'shouts' and call-and-response audience participation, the go-go scene funked its way into the mainstream on the grooves of Experience Unlimited's (that's EU to those in the know) hit 'Doin' The Butt'. Sadly, go-go lost its steam due to the hard-edged appeal of gangsta rap, and with it its chance for wider acceptance. But you can still occasionally hear the old school gangs go-go-ing; if you're lucky, you might catch one of the genre's reunion shows, which always bring down the house.

Go-go acts such as the Backyard Band sometimes play **Capital City Pavilion** (3401 Georgia Avenue, NW) although a crime-riddled area and bad vibes have taken their toll on this once-mighty club. **Deno's** (2335 Bladensburg Road, NE) is the new reigning club for go-go-ers and has played host to the Backyard Band, as well as current quintessential torch-carriers Rare Essence. Be warned that the club only accepts cash and heading out to this area loaded with a wad of bills might not be the best idea. For both venues, you'll need to check local papers to see if a show is on.

This small club has had trouble catching on, but it will be a loss if it doesn't survive. Rich red accents decorate the space, walking a strange line between the kitsch and the sophisticated. There's an air of grandeur to the tiny space that turns every performance into an event, whether it's local post-punks such as Burning Airlines or international provocateurs such as Kinney Starr. A few tables are squeezed on to the pavement out front for warm-weather hanging between sets.

Velvet Lounge

915 U Street, NW, between Ninth & Vermont Streets, U Street/14th Street Corridor (462 3213). U Street-Cardozo Metro/90, 91, 92, 93 bus.
Open 8pm-2am Mon-Thur, Sun; 8pm-3am Fri, Sat. **Admission** $3 Mon-Thur, Sun; $5 Fri, Sat. **Credit** AmEx, Disc, MC, V.

With its martini glass neon sign, the Velvet Lounge lets you know what to expect before you enter. It's reminiscent of what its neighbour, the **9:30 Club** (*see p209*), used to be – a small space that encouraged big ideas on its stage. Acts tend to be of the local, edgier type, plus some touring bands, while the atmosphere tends to be hip and artsy without the scenester-ish snarl present at similar DC venues. It can get crowded late in the evening as the overflow from the 9:30 exits a show. *See also p167* **Bars**.

Jazz

The lively Shaw neighbourhood gave birth to some of the jazz greats – DC local Duke Ellington and Ella Fitzgerald regularly performed in the area – and the Lincoln Theatre is still a draw. With such a rich history as its foundation, Washington's jazz scene still thrives, although there aren't as many venues as there once were.

Blues Alley

1073 Wisconsin Avenue, NW, between M & K Streets, Georgetown (337 4141) Foggy Bottom-GWU Metro, then 30, 32, 34, 35, 36 bus. **Open** 6pm-midnight daily. **Admission** $14-$50. **Credit** AmEx, DC, MC, V.

Considered by many to be *the* jazz club in the District, Blues Alley has set a standard that attracts artists such as Wynton Marsalis, who recorded a live set here in 1988, and Eartha Kitt, whose two-week run in 1999 caused a sensation. Unfortunately, premium talent means premium prices: don't be surprised if on top of the cover charge (sometimes near $50) you also have to meet a table minimum during the set. Fortunately, the club is intimate and you're unlikely to find better acoustics.

Capitol City Blues

2651 Connecticut Avenue, NW, between 24th Street & Woodley Road, Woodley Park (232 2300). Woodley Park-Zoo Metro. **Open** 11am-2am Mon-Thur, Sun; 11am-3am Fri, Sat. **Admission** $5 Thur-Sat. **Credit** AmEx, MC, V.

A great place to catch local jazz and blues talent, as well as the occasional big-name act. It's an understatement to say it's a tight squeeze, especially when the music starts. Fine acoustics make every act perfectly audible, even if they're not visible, but you can always occupy yourself with the murals of Muddy Waters and Aretha Franklin.

Columbia Station

2325 18th Street, NW, between Columbia & Kalorama Roads, Adams Morgan (462 6040). Dupont Circle Metro, then L2 bus or Woodley Park-Zoo Metro, then 90, 91, 92, 93, 96 bus. **Open** 4pm-2am Mon-Thur; 4pm-3am Fri; 11am-3am Sat; 11am-2am Sun. **Credit** AmEx, MC, V.

Don't let the facade of this Adams Morgan favourite fool you: it may look rundown, but inside it's a class act. A cross between a New Orleans theme bar (brass instruments on the wall) and a 1950s European railway station, it attracts a crowd that ranges from under-age to the over-40s. The emphasis is on ambience as much as the music, and the artwork alone could entertain for hours. A fine, upscale spot to relax and enjoy local and upcoming jazz talent.

Mr Henry's

601 Pennsylvania Avenue, SE, at Sixth Street, Southeast (546 8412). Eastern Market Metro. **Open** 11.15am-1.30am Mon-Thur, Sun; 10am-1.30am Fri, Sat. **Admission** two-drink minimum Fri, Sat. **Credit** AmEx, MC, V.

Part of Mr Henry's legend is that this is where soul stylist Roberta Flack got her start. There's always plenty of activity here, both upstairs where the bands play – usually first-rate local talent – and on the ground floor, where the cocktails alone are brassy enough. The curtain drops rather early for a jazz club, so if you want to glide on a sax solo till dawn, you'll have to glide somewhere else.

State of the Union

1357 U Street, NW, at 14th Street, U Street/14th Street Corridor (588 8810/588 8926). U Street-Cardozo Metro. **Open** 6pm-2am Mon-Thur; 6pm-3am Fri-Sun. **Admission** $5 Tue-Thur, Sun; $7 Fri, Sat. **Credit** MC, V.

While State of the Union may rely on Trotsky and Stalin figures for its décor, there's nothing retro about this U Street hotspot – it's so hip it hurts. Up to the second with the latest jazz, acid jazz and jazz-influenced blasts, State of the Union turns its stage over to new sonic pioneers several nights a week. Mondays and Wednesdays are your best bet as the weekend is usually reserved for the deepest house beats imaginable. Two things: yes, that is an image of Rasputin behind the stage, and, yes, the snarled traffic two blocks away is trying to unload itself here. Best to take a cab to 14th & U Streets and walk the 50 feet to the front door. *See also p218* **Dance clubs** and *p167* **Bars**.

U-topia

1418 U Street, NW, between 14th & 15th Streets, U Street/14th Street Corridor (483 7669). U Street-Cardozo Metro. **Open** 11am-2am Mon-Thur; 11am-3am Fri; 5pm-3am Sat; 11am-4pm, 5-11.30pm, Sun. **Credit** AmEx, DC, Disc, MC, V.

A few doors down from State of the Union, U-topia continues the U Street tradition of great music in the Shaw area. The schedule changes regularly: you might find a poetry reading rather than the next Miles Davis, so call ahead. The emphasis here is on celebrating creativity, no matter what the medium. Interesting art, challenging reading material (books are readily found by sticking your hand into the exposed brick portions of the wall) and great jazz all co-exist perfectly in this beautiful space. Sound utopian? Well, it's close.

Country & folk

A country capital, DC ain't. Some venues book the occasional country-influenced act, but one Willie Nelson cover does not a country bar make. Country's Appalachian cousin, bluegrass, can be heard at clubs that book a variety of other acts – such as the **Birchmere** (*see below*) or **Madam's Organ** (*see page 209*). Your best bet for folk is to catch an act at the **Galaxy Hut** or **Iota Café** (for both, *see page 209*), although there is also a smattering of folk-tinged spots.

Birchmere

3701 Mount Vernon Avenue, between Glebe & South Glebe Roads, Alexandria, VA (703 549 7500). Braddock Road Metro, then 10A, 10B, 10C bus. **Open** box office 5-9pm on show nights. **Admission** free-$30. **Credit** AmEx, DC, Disc, MC, V.

The Birchmere occupies that strange ground between club and concert hall. While it can handle crowds as large as 500, the staff are still able to service each table during a show, eliminating scrambling for the bar before each set. The club typically caters to folk, blues and bluegrass acts and was the home stage for local heroes the Seldom Scene. Legendary rockers such as surf-king Dick Dale perform regularly, as do acoustic acts. Make sure you sample the fruits of the Birchmere's own brewery.

Blackie's

6710 Commerce Street, at Franconia Road, Springfield, VA (703 971 4200). Franconia-Springfield Metro, then 110, 111, 401 bus. **Open** 4pm-midnight Tue-Thur, Sun; 4pm-3am Fri, Sat. **Admission** $2-$3. **Credit** AmEx, Disc, MC, V.

Sure, it's a bit off the Beltway's typical club route, but when it comes to sheer numbers, few places can compete with the 1,000-plus crowds that stampede here on Saturday nights to hear local country bands such as Wild At Heart and Southern Wind. The mix of live music and Ladies Night specials on Tuesdays pulls in the 25-and-up on-the-make types. Dance lessons are offered several nights a week, so you can learn to 'Roll The Rug' and 'Tush Push' like a pro.

Cowboy Café North

4792 Lee Highway, between North Glebe Road & Columbus Street, Arlington, VA (703 243 8010). Ballston-MU Metro, then 22F, 23A, 23B, 23C, 23T bus. **Open** 11am-midnight Mon-Fri; 9am-2am Sat, Sun. **Credit** AmEx, DC, Disc, MC, V.

Along with its counterpart, Cowboy Café (2421 Columbia Pike, at Adams Square, Arlington, VA; 703 486 3467), this comfortable little hangout is a great hideaway if you're in need of a relaxing night of acoustic-driven folk or blues. If you're looking for a rowdy time reminiscent of the Wild West, don't be fooled by the name: the pace is slow, the atmosphere inviting – and the food's not bad either.

St Elmo's Coffee Pub

2300 Mount Vernon Avenue, at East Del Ray Avenue, Alexandria, VA (703 739 9268). Braddock Road Metro, then 10E bus. **Open** 6am-10pm daily. **Credit** AmEx, Disc, MC, V.

Even more laidback than the Cowboy Cafés, St Elmo's has the feel of a 1990s enterprise with 1960s sensibilities. Desserts are first-rate, as is the talent that graces the stage. It has a calm, bohemian appeal and the pace is slow, inviting you to linger and enjoy the moment for as long as you want it to last. Live bands play mostly folk and jazz.

Look back in anger

DC has a stake in jazz history thanks to Duke Ellington. The go-go scene of the 1980s also made a substantial, if not truly lasting mark. But it's the angry (and guilt-ridden) white boy scene that erupted into hardcore punk that truly sealed Washington's place in the books.

Somewhere around 1981, young Ian MacKaye took his wrath, his energy and his DIY ethic and formed the paradigm of hardcore bands, Minor Threat. Releasing the band's material on his own label, Dischord Records, MacKaye laid the groundwork for a movement, and quite possibly an industry, that would evolve into something bigger than anything he may have envisioned.

Built on the philosophy of a 'straight edge' abstinence from anything that might diminish the spirit (drugs, nicotine, alcohol), MacKaye and Minor Threat railed against their lives of privilege and the burden that wracked their consciences. Their innocence only added to their sincerity, but by the time their ethic was catching on, the band was not only turning their critical eye on themselves, they were ready to call it quits.

MacKaye, always one to speak out about 'the system', insisted on doing things his way, releasing his own music and the music of his friends as a way of avoiding the 'corrupt' record industry and its star-obsessed machinery. Ironically, by the time MacKaye had built his new engine, Fugazi, his fans had made him into the type of legendary, adored figure he obviously seemed to hate. Even as his own story became the stuff of myth, MacKaye and Fugazi continued to release their own brand of brilliant noise, defining a city's scene in the process. Sharp, rhythmic and intense, the stuff of the DC music scene was hard on intolerance and long on influence.

Through his label Dischord, MacKaye has released some of the most interesting and influential music of the last quarter of the century. Bands such as the highly revered Jawbox, angular art glamsters Shudder To Think and Soulside all got their start thanks to Dischord. Fiercely independent – he refuses any type of corporate help – MacKaye still denies the major press access: any publication that accepts alcohol or nicotine advertising essentially doesn't exist in his world.

But it's not as if he or his bands need the exposure. Fugazi and their label mates have garnered legions of fervent fans who faithfully buy the CDs and flock to the shows. Even if they didn't, odds are that MacKaye would keep at it.

Hardcore: **Ian MacKaye** *of Fugazi.*

World

With the diversity of the District's population you might expect a plethora of world music venues. But, like so many other genres, the representation is sparse. Larger acts tend to appear at university auditoria or the Kennedy Center, but there are a few spots worth venturing out to, depending on your international flavour of choice. Start by trying the following:

Fadó Irish Pub

808 Seventh Street, NW, between H & I Streets, Downtown (789 0066). Gallery Place-Chinatown Metro/70, 71, 73 bus. **Open** 11.30am-2am Mon-Thur, Sun; 11.30am-3am Fri, Sat. **Credit** AmEx, DC, Disc, MC, V.

The proprietors might not want to have this Irish-themed pub deemed 'lovely', but between the pleasing aesthetics of the surroundings and the live Irish music on Sundays, it fits. *See also p163* **Bars**.

Kramerbooks & Afterwords Café

1517 Connecticut Avenue, NW, at Q Street, Dupont Circle (387 1462). Dupont Circle Metro/42 bus. **Open** 7am-1am Mon-Thur; 7am Fri-1am Sun. **Credit** AmEx, Disc, MC, V.

The joy of Afterwords, the café and restaurant part of Kramer's bookshop, is that you truly never know what to expect. Anything from African drumming acts to flamenco to Irish lilts can be heard, along with quartets doing jazz improvs – but call first to check. It's probably best to browse the bookstore and listen for as long as you want; you don't have to take a table. Open late, it provides an interesting chance for some celeb spottings. *See also p142* **Restaurants**.

Rumba Café

2443 18th Street, NW, at Columbia Road, Adams Morgan (588 5501). Woodley Park-Zoo Metro.
Open 5.30pm-2am Mon-Thur, Sun; 5.30pm-3am Fri, Sat. **Admission** $4. **Credit** AmEx, MC, V.
Located near the city's highest concentration of Latins and Hispanics, Rumba Café offers live salsa and Latin-inspired music six nights a week. The digs are modest, but do not diminish the lively atmosphere. While other clubs merely spin their salsa, Rumba Café serves it live with a mix of Cuban and Caribbean bands. As authentic an experience as you're going to get north of Miami.

Songhai

1211 U Street, NW, between 12th & 13th Streets, U Street/14th Street Corridor (232 1965 Fri, Sat/ 341 5050 Mon-Thur, Sun). U Street-Cardozo Metro.
Open 3-11pm Mon-Thur, Sun; noon-3am Fri, Sat. **Admission** $6 after 7pm Fri, after 10pm Sat. **Credit** AmEx, DC, Disc, MC, V.
The U Street corridor between 11th and 14th Streets is the hotspot for Washington's African-American cultural nightlife. Songhai specialises in African (primarily West African) music, mixed with more generic world beats and reggae, while the kitchen turns out dishes as authentic as the beats. The space is so small that it's almost impossible not to get swept up in the activities. While the neighbourhood is not dangerous, things can get sketchy after dark.

Dance clubs

The most common assessment you're bound to hear (or read) about DC nightlife is that 'it's not New York'. That's right, it's not. So does that mean the District's denizens spend their nights sitting on their booty, rather than shaking it? Not at all.

In some ways, DC is more akin to New York than you might think. Like the Big Apple, clubs in Washington pop up like seedlings in the spring, with just as little chance of survival. Few events, parties or even locales seem to have much longevity here. Maybe it's because of the city's transient population: everyone comes to DC, but it's hard to find anyone who was actually born and bred here – and without a real sense of background, there's nothing to build on. On the plus side, the influx of energy from DC's diverse inhabitants galvanises the city's nightlife scene, making for some not-to-miss parties.

Like their live music counterparts, Washington's dance club scenesters have made their mark on the national and international beat route. House divas Crystal Waters and Ultra Nate hail from the area, as do production superstars Deep Dish and 18th Street Lounge mix-masters Thievery Corporation (*see opposite* **A Corporation town**). The DJ culture also has its celebrities with Scott Henry, Angelo Kortez and spinning star at large, Michelle Miruski.

The famous **18th Street Lounge***: DC's most happening dance club. See page 217.*

A Corporation town

Eric Hilton *(left) and* **Rob Garza** *of sampling duo Thievery Corporation.*

If you want proof that DC is indeed a multi-cultural centre, look no further than its nightlife. A snapshot of most dance club floors in the city could serve as a public service announcement for diversity. So it only makes sense that the people providing the grooves are products of their environment. Thievery Corporation, the sonic tag team sampling duo, are a perfect example. Known individually as Rob Garza and Eric Hilton, the pair have set the dance world on its ear.

When Thievery Corporation's beats first started infecting clubs around the world, their dub-heavy mix of break beats, laid-back lounge and saucy bossa nova had scenesters stumped: where did these kids come from? Most agreed this poly-international vibe was honed somewhere in Europe. In fact, Europe so embraced Thievery Corporation that their debut Sounds From The Thievery Hi Fi was London's Rough Trade shop's highest-selling album in 1996. So imagine the gasps when it was discovered that the duo hailed not only from the US, but from DC. The District had a long history on the front lines of the punk scene, but nothing like this had ever emerged from inside the Beltway.

Savvy and sophisticated, Garza and Hilton draw upon their own tastes and the rhythmic frames of reference that DC's multi-culturalism places at their disposal. Add to that the air of international intrigue that comes from Garza's stint as a counter-terrorism PI, and you've got a mysterious mélange that has garnered praise from the likes of Gus Gus, Pizzicato Five and Kruder & Dorfmeister.

Thievery Corporation are no doubt extremely busy and always in demand. However, it's not uncommon to catch one or both of them at the helm of the **18th Street Lounge** (*see page 217*), or another club, spinning their faves and casting their sonic spell.

Keeping up with the latest in DC nightlife is relatively easy: *City Paper* and *Bar Stool* (both free) have listings, and radio station WHFS (99.1FM) provides a daily concert calendar. It's also worth checking record shop DC CD (2423 18th Street, NW, between Biltmore Street & Columbia Road, Adams Morgan; 588 1810). Sometimes a well-placed ear is the best detector. When turntable wunderkind DJ Cam played the 18th Street Lounge last year, the event was so hush-hush that promoters forbid the publishing of his name in any of the city's periodicals. Exclusive? You bet. But it's one of the drawbacks of the appeal versus space problem.

18th Street Lounge

1212 18th Street, NW, between Jefferson Place & M Street, Dupont Circle (466 3922). Farragut North or Dupont Circle Metro. **Open** 9.30pm-2am Tue, Wed; 5.30pm-2am Thur; 3pm-3am Fri; 9.30pm-3am Sat. **Credit** AmEx, MC, V.

If you want a club to have an assemblage of arty sorts, fashion-forward types, great music and an allegedly discriminating door policy, well, you've found your spot. The lounge's top tier offers live jazz on most weekend nights, while dub, house, lounge and the latest electronic cut-and-pastes are spun on the second floor. Dancefloor space is relatively limited, but there's a roomy deck to handle the overflow and plenty of lounging space where hipsters can dangle cigarettes and sip expensive cocktails. The Lounge also doubles as the headquarters of sample and beat bandits Thievery Corporation, and the possibility of their guest DJ-ing at their own club only adds to the place's allure. *See p215* **A Corporation town**.

Bar Nun/Club 2000

1326 U Street, NW, between 13th & 14th Streets, U Street/14th Street Corridor (667 6680). U Street-Cardozo Metro. **Open** 7pm-2am Mon-Thur, Sun; 8pm-3am Fri, Sat. **Admission** $5-$10. **Credit** AmEx, DC, MC, V.

If you're looking for a reprieve from the super-disco scene, tidy Bar Nun (and its new sister club, Club 2000) will do nicely. No real special effects are employed here, the emphasis is on the beats – and heavy is as heavy does. Those who remember getting lost in a trance from hypnotic house grooves will find the experience transcendental. The crowd is serious about its music, but not so serious about itself – a refreshing attitude for a club of this calibre. Bar Nun occasionally books other events into the space, so call ahead.

Bravo! Bravo!

1001 Connecticut Avenue, NW, between K & L Streets, Downtown (223 5330). Farragut North Metro. **Open** 11am-9pm Mon, Tue, Thur, Sun; 11am-4am Wed, Fri, Sat. **Admission** $10. **Credit** AmEx, DC, Disc, MC, V.

Latin music was never steamier than it is at Bravo! Bravo!. It is the spot of choice for the young Latin and Euro set (over-30s will feel over the hill), as the line outside attests. An interesting interior, which some describe as industrial baroque, sets the stage for Latin nights (Wednesday, Saturday) and International Night (Friday). There's no exclusivity at the door, but it's best to get there early.

Club Zei

1415 Zei Alley, NW, between 14th, 15th, H & I Streets, Downtown (842 2445). McPherson Square Metro. **Open** 10pm-2am Thur, Sun; 10pm-3am Fri, Sat. **Admission** $10. **Credit** AmEx, MC, V.

Over the years, Club Zei, which is housed in a former electrical power station, has been the site of some of DC's more interesting dance parties. Its alley location only adds to its appeal, and blinding white lights and clouds of smoke heighten the effect. The kids love it and the lines can be long at weekends. The music is mainly a mix of house and techno and, even though under-21s predominate, the dress code is adhered to faithfully: no athletic gear, no ripped, torn or frayed clothing.

Earth

DC Live, 932 F Street, NW, between Ninth & Tenth Streets, Downtown (301 215 7575). Gallery Place-Chinatown Metro. **Open** 10pm-2.30am Thur. **Admission** $10. **Credit** AmEx, Disc, MC, V.

Earth is grounded on Thursday nights inside converted department store DC Live. The troubled past of the space hasn't discouraged scores of the faithful from lining up for this ultra party. With five DJs and as many dancefloors, the urban and international sets line up to dance to everything from Euro-house, middle eastern mix, salsa and merengue to techno. The décor is a bit cheesy, but the emphasis is on the dancefloor and the people who inhabit it. The vibe inside is peace-loving, but the surrounding neighbourhood has witnessed its fair share of violence, so be cautious.

Heaven & Hell

2327 18th Street, NW, at Florida Avenue, Dupont Circle (667 4355). Dupont Circle Metro, then L2 bus.

It's retro heaven at **Heaven & Hell.**

Open *Heaven* 9.30pm-2am Mon-Thur, Sun; 9.30pm-3am Fri, Sat; *Hell* 7pm-2am Mon-Thur, Sun; 7pm-3am Fri, Sat. **Admission** $5. **Credit** AmEx, MC, V.
When it comes to retro nights, Heaven probably does it better than anywhere else. The 80s Dance Party (Thursdays) is the real deal, and celebrity DJ Jon handles the helm nicely. Tuesdays sees the Gothic-Industrial Dance Party, while Fridays and Saturdays offer the latest 'popular' – but not the most current – dance beats. There's also a busy roof-top deck and downstairs bar – called Hell, of course.

Polly Esther's

605 12th Street, NW, between F & G Streets, Downtown (737 1970). Metro Center Metro.
Open 9pm-2am Thur; 8pm-3am Fri, Sat.
Admission $5 Thur; $8 Fri; $10 Sat. **Credit** AmEx, MC, V.
As the name implies, Polly Esther's is devoted to most things retro. The music draws upon the best of the best from the 1970s and 1980s and never disappoints. But if you're looking for atmosphere, it might be wiser to steer clear. Kitsch is never a crime when it's blissfully unaware, but Polly Esther's blatant sensory overload of retro memorabilia is too much of a good thing. Best to keep your eyes closed and your feet on the dancefloor.

Red

1802 Jefferson Place, NW, at 18th Street, Dupont Circle (466 3475). Dupont Circle or Farragut North Metro. **Open** 10pm-3am Thur; 10pm-6am Fri, Sat.
Admission $5-$10. **Credit** AmEx, MC, V.
This small, basement-like club is white hot. Given a nod by *Harpers* 'Bizarre', it's probably the best place in town to hear the latest and greatest beats, sometimes courtesy of the mix-masters who created them. Red serves as the unofficial sister club for the younger half – average age is around 25 – of the **18th Street Lounge** set (*see p217*). What the club lacks in ambience – its subterranean digs give it the atmosphere of a dark, smoky jazz club – it makes up for in sheer energy. Local celebs such as Deep Dish and Teddy Douglass (of Basement Boys fame), as well as house regular 95 North routinely rock the floorboards Thursday through Saturday. A new, state-of-the-art sound system should keep things rocking here for a while.

State of the Union

1357 U Street, NW, at 14th Street, U Street/14th Street Corridor (588 8810/588 8926). U Street-Cardozo Metro. **Open** 6pm-2am Mon-Thur; 6pm-3am Fri-Sun. **Admission** $5 Tue-Thur, Sun; $7 Fri, Sat. **Credit** MC, V.
If you like your beats deep and hard, State of the Union's got your bass covered. Relying on a stable of groove-savvy DJs, the club offers the best mix of house, jungle, drum 'n' bass and hip hop you're likely to find in the District. The dancefloor is adequate if a little cramped. The constant stream of cars outside brings traffic to a standstill on weekend nights. While popularity is not always the best barometer for a club's appeal, in this case you can believe the hype. Cab door to club door is advised – the surrounding neighbourhood can be a bit dodgy. *See also p212* **Jazz** and *p167* **Bars**.

Comedy & cabaret

For a city that provides so much fodder for one-liners and lampoons, you might expect comedy and cabaret clubs by the dozen. Thus, the noticeable lack of them might lead you to believe Washingtonians take themselves far too seriously. In some cases that may be true, but in general denizens of the District enjoy – and need – a good laugh, and they know where to get it. The offerings are limited but worth checking out.

Comedy

Chelsea's

Foundry Mall, 1055 Thomas Jefferson Street, NW, between K & M Streets, Georgetown (298 8222). Foggy Bottom-GWU Metro, then 30, 32, 34, 35, 36 bus. **Open** 10pm-2am Mon-Thur, Sun; 10pm-4am Fri, Sat. **Admission** $10 Mon-Sat; $8 Sun. **Credit** Disc, MC, V.
Chelsea's splits its reputation: it's a haven for those who want to dance the night away to sultry salsa and merengue beats, and is also the home of the notorious and uproarious Capitol Steps comedy troupe, which takes the stage on Fridays (8pm) and Saturdays (7.30pm) and rarely fails to entertain. Capitol Steps has been skewering the antics of politicians and pundits for several years, and insiders still say the city's power elite actually boast about being roasted. The only drawback is that, if laughter is the best medicine, it's best to have a healthy bankroll: show tickets cost $34, $50 with dinner.

Improv

1140 Connecticut Avenue, NW, between L & M Streets, Downtown (296 7008). Farragut North Metro. **Open** shows 8.30pm Mon-Thur, Sun; 8pm, 10.30pm Fri, Sat. **Admission** $12 Mon-Thur, Sun; $15 Fri, Sat. **Credit** AmEx, MC, V.
The Improv delivers exactly what you would expect of a comedy club: a slew of tables crammed on to the floor and a brick wall behind the stage. The no-frills décor places the spotlight on the acts – usually big-name stars (road-tested up-and-comers are occasionally allowed to take their turn at the mike). Tickets can be hard to come by for more popular shows; it's best to book well in advance.

Cabaret

Black Cat

1831 14th Street, NW, between S & T Streets, U Street/14th Street Corridor (667 7960/ Ticketmaster 432 7328). U Street-Cardozo Metro.
Open 8pm-2am Mon-Thur, Sun; 7pm-3am Fri, Sat
Admission $5-$20. **No credit cards**.
An indie rock hangout most nights, this dark club

occasionally books performance artists as well as open-mike 'anything goes' events. Cabaret fans should be warned, however – the acts lean towards the avant-garde and can be rather, well, adventurous in presentation. Those expecting clichéd, Liza Minelli fare would do best to seek their entertainment elsewhere. *See also p209* **Rock**.

Cabaret at Windows

1637 17th Street, NW, at R Street, Dupont Circle (reservations 301 229 8664). Dupont Circle Metro. **Open** shows 7pm, 7.30pm, 8.30pm, 9pm, Mon; 8pm Sat. **Admission** $15 (reservations required). **No credit cards.**

A traditional cabaret packs them into this small upstairs club on Monday nights. Wildly popular, it attracts bigger crowds every week, all craving the intimacy afforded by the close quarters and the first-rate acts. Fans of torch singers will not be disappointed as the performers here work the room in every sense. If you're shy, it's best to hide in the back as regulars such as Wendy Lane Bailey make a point of locking eyes with every soul in the house.

Paris Bisou

1338 Wisconsin Avenue, NW, at O Street, Georgetown (333 5886). Foggy Bottom-GWU Metro, then 30, 32, 34, 35, 36 bus. **Open** 5pm-2am Mon-Thur, Sun; 5pm-5am Fri, Sat (shows 7.15pm-2am Thur-Sat). **Credit** AmEx, DC, Disc, JCB, MC, V.

Dramatic and touching one minute, campy and bawdy the next, the Bisou offers everything from traditional sets of standards (such as Duane Myers' aptly titled 'Standards') to audience participation activities (such as pre-show tango lessons). Shows are held from Thursday to Saturday, with no cover charge. Cabaret in its more classic sense, at least by American standards.

Gay & lesbian

The gay and lesbian communities of the major cities in the States each have their own identity. In DC, that identity is defined by the power of the political. The promise of 'a place at the table' from the early Clinton administration galvanised gay DC like never before. Already a city of activists and marches, gay and lesbian DC became even more powerful and more politically charged in the 1990s. Gay issues were raised in the city's and the nation's consciousness, and with that, gay visibility increased. Once ghettoised into the Dupont Circle area, gays and lesbians have spread out across the city to neighbourhoods such as Adams Morgan and Capitol Hill.

While Dupont Circle proper is still a hub for the homosexual community, 17th Street, a few blocks east, now challenges Connecticut Avenue (one of the Circle's spokes) as the city's premier Queer Corridor. Although there are only a handful of bars on 17th, the fashionably footed traffic along the street is predominantly gay.

The annual High Heel Race turns 17th Street into a Mardi Gras-like scenario each year on a day near Halloween. The street is barricaded from R to P Streets as a mélange of drag queens and other costumed contestants make a mad dash for the finish line in a race that rivals June's Gay Pride Parade (second weekend) for its colour and exuberance. The event has attracted a mixed mob in the past few years as appreciation for the gay sensibility grows in the District. 1998's race saw mayoral candidates doing the 'grin and grip' with the crowd, further testament to the clout of DC's gay community.

Anchored by Results The Gym at U Street and capped by the intersection of P Street, 17th Street can give first-timers what might be a false sense of security as the area is *sooo* gay and gay-friendly. Couples who feel comfortable displaying their affection publicly would do best to behave otherwise in other parts of the city. But gay-bashers beware: you have no power here.

The political and party elements of DC come together for a variety of events, including the annual Whitman Walker gala and the Miss Adams Morgan Pageant, held the weekend closest to Halloween. Named by *Harpers* as one of the city's top five events on the social calendar, it raises thousands of dollars for local AIDS groups. The city's second national Gay and Lesbian March on Washington in ten years takes place in 2000.

Nightlife in the gay 1990s can be tricky in DC. While it's definitely a living, breathing, booty-shaking – and sometimes groping – animal, it can be rather mercurial. Parties, and venues, come and go, so it's always a good idea to call ahead. For listings, check one of the city's two gay publications. The *Washington Blade* chronicles the city's gay issues from recent community meetings to the latest on Capitol Hill, and the essential *MW Weekly*, a hip, backpack-sized publication, concentrates on the District's people, places and things that go bump in the night. Both are available at many shops, cafés and bars.

Accommodation

DC's hotels and B&Bs are, for the most part, like any other metropolitan lodgings and are used to a wide variety of guests. Same-sex couples should have no problem finding gay-friendly lodgings. If you have any trepidations, book in to one of the many hotels in the Dupont Circle area (*see chapter* **Accommodation**).

Bars & clubs

Atlas/Lizard Lounge

Eleventh Hour, 1520 14th Street, NW, at Church Street, Dupont Circle (331 4422). Dupont Circle Metro. **Open** 8pm-2am Sun. **Credit** AmEx, MC, V.

Sponsor Atlas continues its tradition of Sunday-night soirées with Lizard Lounge, housed in the swank surroundings of the Eleventh Hour club. A great way to wind down the weekend and gear up for the week ahead, it's a relaxed, sophisticated event with just enough of an edge to keep you on your toes. A nice mix of men and women, with the biggest complaints regarding the music (too loud or not loud enough – can't please 'em all) and lack of room to groove. But for those who prefer hip over hype, it's the perfect way to while away the evening.

Badlands

1415 22nd Street, NW, at P Street, Dupont Circle (296 0505). Dupont Circle Metro. **Open** 9pm-3am Tue, Thur; 9pm-4am Fri, Sat. **Admission** $3 Thur; $3 before 10pm, $7 after 10pm, Fri, Sat. **No credit cards**.

There was a time when the A-list flocked to Badlands for its Friday night parties; although the crowds haven't diminished, the bar is not as in with the in-crowd as it once was. Still, it has received Best Dance Club laurels from the readership of *MW* in recent years. The music definitely takes a back seat to the cruising, so don't expect the remixes to have the latest pump in their pulse. There's a line at peak hours (around midnight) and a good deal of 'last-minute shopper' traffic at closing time.

Club Chaos

1603 17th Street, NW, at Q Street, Dupont Circle (232 4141). Dupont Circle Metro. **Open** 4pm-2am Tue-Thur, Sun; 4pm-3am Fri, Sat. **Credit** AmEx, DC, Disc, MC, V.

Housed in the former home of famous lesbian club Trumpets, Club Chaos has given itself a number of makeovers in the hopes of attracting a larger clientele. It seems to be working. The design might never be called swank, but that hasn't stopped a diverse crowd of men and women from filling the tables in the restaurant or bellying up to the bar. The food is consistent if modest, and the cabaret-style drag shows keep folks there well past dessert. An adequate dancefloor provides room to move, even though the music seems to be a secondary draw. Wednesday nights belong to the ladies, Thursday nights feature Latin music and the weekends are an eclectic grab bag of entertainment.

Cobalt

1639 R Street, NW, at 17th Street, Dupont Circle (232 6969). Dupont Circle Metro. **Open** 5pm-2am Mon-Thur, Sun; 5pm-3am Fri, Sat. **No credit cards**.

When this popular bar closed due to fire damage in late 1998, you could practically hear the gasps of the displaced. When it reopened in summer 1999 with an airy, more dramatic redesign, the young hip-boy set once again had a spot to sport their Dolce & Gabbana. Cobalt attracts the well-coiffed, well-dressed, well-informed clubster crowd, rounding out the experience with cheap drinks, great music and just enough of a dancefloor should you feel the urge. A nice mix of drag queens, gym bunnies, students and club scenesters, there's lots of cruising, but of the more subtle variety.

Élan

1129 Pennsylvania Avenue (above Café Italiano), SE, at 12th Street, Southeast (544 6406). Eastern Market Metro. **Open** 9pm-2am Mon, Tue, Thur; 9pm-3am Fri, Sat; 6-10pm Sun. **Admission** $5-$8. **Credit** AmEx, MC, V.

One of the worst offences on the DC gay bar scene is the lack of spots for women. When Élan opened in 1998, many lipstick lesbians had finally found a place to call their own. It caters to an over-30, more sophisticated lesbian clientele (although a small percentage is usually male and/or straight). The décor – antique mirrors, comfortable chairs and big sofas in a candle-lit space – is understated, cosy or rustic, depending on your take. The monthly Women's Bisexual Social (second Friday of the month) is a big draw.

DC Eagle

639 New York Avenue, NW, between Sixth & Seventh Streets, Downtown (347 6025). Mount Vernon Square-UDC Metro. **Open** 6pm-2am Mon-Thur; noon-3am Fri, Sat; noon-2am Sun. **No credit cards**.

The District's only true leather bar. A surprisingly amiable setting, although a bit dim, the Eagle is a great place to meet the man – or the bear – of your dreams. Downstairs, pinball and pool are popular, while upstairs the music tends to lean towards darker beats, favouring industrial, goth and harder-edged techno. The Beer Blasts on Sunday afternoons are popular and drink discounts are often given to those wearing the colours of their motorcycle clubs.

Green Lantern

1335 Green Court, NW, between 13th & 14th Streets, Downtown (638 5133). McPherson Square Metro. **Open** noon-2am Mon-Thur, Sun; noon-3am Fri, Sat. **No credit cards.**

Affectionately known as the 'Green Latrine' by those who frequent it, this is one of the city's most predatory cruising spots. The street level houses a restaurant and bar, while upstairs is rather seedy. Dimly lit and generally packed, this is the type of club where groping is as good an introduction as you're likely to get. Commonly viewed as a 'last hope' destination after an evening of clubbing.

Hung Jury

1819 H Street, NW, at Pennsylvania Avenue, Foggy Bottom (785 8181). Farragut West Metro/ 42, G8, S2 bus. **Open** 10pm-4am Thur, Fri; 9pm-4am Sat. **Admission** $4 women; $7 men. **Credit** AmEx, MC, V.

Open primarily at the weekend, the Hung Jury has been the blossoming spot of choice for budding lesbians for the past ten years or so. A decidedly younger (under-25) crowd hangs here and it's the enthusiasm of their discovery that gives the place its energy. Well, that and the music. A relatively hassle-free zone for women: a strict door policy requires men to be accompanied by a female escort.

JR's

1519 17th Street, NW, at Church Street, Dupont Circle (328 0090). Dupont Circle Metro. **Open** 11am-

Desperately seeking...

DC draws a transient crowd of work-motivated wannabes who lack the time and the social background (and sometimes skills) to attend to their nonetheless pressing romantic needs. Hence it has developed a thriving mainstream singles scene. The stereotypical view is that it's full of egotistical men and unapproachable women. All we can say is... stereotypes don't become stereotypes without at least *some* truth behind them.

Stories abound about male TV reporters or pundits inviting dates to watch tapes of their appearances or of White House aides glued to C-SPAN in a frantic attempt to catch a glimpse of themselves on camera. Then there are the one-sided conversations and the bad dressers and the strings of broken meetings because of votes on the House floor. Securities & Exchange commissioners used to boast that their parking lot was as full on Saturday as it was on Friday, while anyone leaving a congressional office before 8pm apologises for cutting out early. And the law firms? Many offer drycleaning, so that associates who spend the night in the office can have a fresh shirt for the next day.

Meeting a mate in Washington is so difficult it's inspired a 16-page cover section in *Washingtonian* magazine, a book called *Finding Fun and Friends in Washington* and a legendary *City Paper* cover story – tellingly titled 'Bitch Hunt'. Many Washingtonians approach the singles scene with the kind of fervour that once applied only to an associate trying to make partner. When the *Washington Business Journal* profiled an unmarried real-estate broker, it was besieged with calls from women who wanted to contact him. And when a 30-year-old journalist wrote a story for the *Washington Post* food section about her first dinner party – where she mentioned her problems finding enough single men for a proper ratio – several men called her to volunteer.

Where to start the hunt for Mr or Ms Maybe? There are dozens of dating services (some, such as It's Just Lunch, cost almost $1,000 to sign on) and singles nights (hosted everywhere from the Jewish Community Center to the venerable Smithsonian Institution). A drycleaner in Georgetown even posts Polaroids of lovelorn clients on the walls.

The *Washingtonian* has a regular 'Singles' column, and the March 1997 edition (296 3600 for back issues) has an exhaustive list of organisations and events, as does *Finding Fun and Friends in Washington.* There are also two singles party newsletters: the *Monthly Buzz* (send your name and email address to thebuzz@erols.com for a free email) and the *Party Digest*, a $40 annual newsletter of private parties, wine tastings, balls and embassy receptions; a free sampling is available at www.partydigest.com. Many singles are suspicious of both, sneering at the *Party Digest* in particular as the 'Party Crasher', but they have their devotees.

The most tried-and-true option is, of course, a bar or club. Some notables where the hooking up is easy: **The Big Hunt** (*see chapter* **Bars**), **Heaven & Hell** (*see page 217*) and **Polly Esther's** (*page 218*) if you're under 30. If not, try **Nathan's** or **Old Ebbitt Grill** (for both *see chapter* **Bars**).

2am Mon-Thur, Sun; 11am-3am Fri, Sat. **Credit** AmEx, DC, Disc, MC, V.

Generally considered the watering hole of choice for the over-30 professional crowd, JR's' narrow space is usually packed five deep on weekends. Getting from one end of the bar to the other can be a harrowing experience, but it might also conveniently put you face to face with the handsome J Crew type you've been eyeing all night long. There is an upstairs loft with pool tables that is a bit roomier, but the action and fun tends to happen downstairs.

La Cage Aux Follies

18 O Street, SE, at South Capitol Street, Southeast (554 3615). Navy Yard Metro. **Open** 8pm-2am Mon-Thur; 8pm-3am Fri, Sat; 6pm-2am Sun. **Admission** $6-$10. **Credit** MC, V.

If dancing boys wearing nothing but their socks and a smile are your thing, then you've come to the right spot. A variety of dancers display their wares throughout the night in this tight, cramped space. Next door is the Follies proper, a gay adult playground with a theatre (with 'convenient' shower stalls behind it), dancers, private rooms and an interesting (and almost terrifying) pitch-black labyrinth that winds its way through the back of the club. Lockers are on hand to store any belongings that might impede your fun.

Omega DC

2122 P Street, NW, between 21st & 22nd Streets, Dupont Circle (223 4917). Dupont Circle Metro. **Open** 4pm-2am Mon-Thur, Sun; 4pm-3am Fri; 8pm-3am Sat. **No credit cards.**

There is a dancefloor but the main source of Omega's energy seems to be defined by the video room. Signs on the walls warn against 'sexual' groping or fondling, but it makes you wonder what the management expects when that many gay men are squeezed into a dark room and presented with pornographic images. There are also pool tables for men looking for other kinds of pockets.

Phase One

525 Eighth Street, SE, between E & G Streets, Capitol Hill (544 6831). Eastern Market Metro. **Open** 7pm-2am Wed, Thur, Sun; 7pm-3am Fri, Sat. **Admission** $5 Fri, Sat. **No credit cards**.

Phase One is one of the country's longest-running lesbian establishments. It resembles the 'saloon'-style bars of the mid-1970s and, true to form, has lived up to that reputation in the past. Plagued by notorious tales of fist fights and brawls, the proprietors have taken measures to soften the club's edge without alienating its more butch clientele. Fast-acting door persons usually manage to weed out the undesirable element.

Remingtons

639 Pennsylvania Avenue, SE, between Sixth & Seventh Streets, Capitol Hill (543 3113). Eastern Market Metro. **Open** 4pm-2am Mon-Thur, Sun; 4pm-3am Fri, Sat. **Admission** $4 Fri, Sat. **No credit cards**.

For those who prefer their beats with a twang, this is DC's only full-time two-stepping club. The comfortable interior offers warmth rather than cutting edge, making for an inviting atmosphere that's perfect for meeting people; in fact, the patrons are some of the more affable you'll find on the DC bar circuit. The street-level dancefloor is literally centrestage, while upstairs there is a relaxed lounge with pool tables. Dancing lessons are offered before the club's 'rush hour' to lessen performance anxiety.

Tracks

1111 First Street, SE, at M Street, Southeast (488 3320). Navy Yard Metro. **Open** 9pm-6am Thur-Sun. **Admission** $3-$15. **No credit cards**.

There was a time when Tracks' massive main dancefloor was the see-and-be-seen spot of choice among shirtless dancing types. It has lost some of its thunder, but the club's outdoor dancefloor, late-night barbecue and overall cavernous space still manage to attract a consistent clientele. The scene outside the venue can be dodgy, so the shorter your walk from cab door to club door, the better off you'll be.
Website: www.tracks2000.com

Velvet Nation

Nation, 1015 Half Street, SE, between K & L Streets, Southeast (554 1500). **Open** 9pm-5am Sat. **Admission** $12. **Credit** V.

The latest and greatest in a string of Saturday-night parties for the buff and the beautiful. Housed in the newly renovated Nation (formerly the Capitol Ballroom), Velvet capitalises on its stadium-like surroundings and invites a mélange of ultra-hip superstar DJs, carnival antics (fire-eaters, stilt walkers) and the best developed pecs this side of Muscle Beach. Not the best of neighbourhoods: on-site parking is available, but cabbing is advised.
Website: www.velvetnation.com

Wet & The Edge

52 L Street, SE, at Half Street, Southeast (488 1200). Navy Yard Metro. **Open** *Wet* 8pm-2am Mon-Thur, Sun; 8pm-3am Fri, Sat; *The Edge* 9pm-3am Mon-Thur, Sun; 9pm-4am Fri, Sat. **Admission** *Wet* $3-$10; *The Edge* before 9pm $3 men, $10 women; after 9pm $6 men, $10 women. **No credit cards.**

While the Edge is your typical gay disco, its companion, Wet, is not. Modelled after New York bars like Splash, Wet brings new meaning to the term 'steamy' as dancers perform under showers. Whether this is your idea of good clean fun is up to you. The bar also seems to be a favourite hang of porn stars. Wet further upped its reputation when alleged Versace gunman Andrew Cunann was supposedly spotted here mid-spree.

Bookstores

Lambda Rising

1625 Connecticut Avenue, NW, between Q & R Streets, Dupont Circle (462 6969). Dupont Circle Metro. **Open** 9am-midnight daily. **Credit** AmEx, Disc, MC, V.

This narrow shop claims to be the 'only bookstore in the world' that stocks 'virtually every gay, lesbian, bisexual and transgender book in print'. The staff know their product and are extremely helpful when it comes to ordering or locating out-of-print materials. You'll also find videos, calendars, jewellery and novelties. A great place to buy 'adult' necessities without feeling embarrassed.

Lammas Women's Books & More

1607 17th Street, NW, at Q Street, Dupont Circle (775 8218). Dupont Circle Metro. **Open** 11am-9.30pm Mon-Thur; 11am-10.30pm Fri; noon-10.30pm Sat; noon-9.30pm Sun. **Credit** AmEx, MC, V.

Celebrating the feminine experience, Lammas 'gives voice' to women in art, music, history, literature and politics, with a thorough selection of books and work by women artists on the walls. In the warmer months, the roof-top deck hosts female musicians, and a cardio boxing class on Monday nights.

Gyms

Practically every gym in DC has its share of gay members, but there are a few gyms that cater more directly to this clientele:

Results The Gym

1612 U Street, NW, between 16th & 17th Streets, U Street/14th Street Corridor (518 0001). U Street-Cardozo Metro. **Rates** day membership $15. **Open** 5.30am-11pm Mon-Fri; 8am-10pm Sat; 8am-9pm Sun.

Having won awards for its design, Results The Gym truly is a spectacular facility. Clean, spacious, well-lit and well-stocked, the gym is the workout spot of choice for the buff and the beautiful. Evenings are when things hit full-tilt – it practically turns into a nightclub after 6pm as house remixes throb as much as the patrons' muscles. There are 80 pieces

Stake it out: longtime gay hangout **Annie's Paramount Steak House.**

of cardiovascular equipment as well as yoga, kick-boxing and aerobics classes.

Crew Club

1321 14th Street, NW, between N Street & Rhode Island Avenue, Logan Circle (319 1333). McPherson Square Metro. **Rates** day membership $10-$25. **Open** 24 hours daily.

Yes, there are weights and exercise equipment on the premises, but the purpose of this 'gym' is more 'scope out' than 'workout.' A licensed nudist facility, clothes are *not* optional. Guests are given a locker and a towel at the door and encouraged to leave their clothing in the former and wrap themselves in the latter. TV lounges and private rooms are on the premises, as is a masseuse. Day membership is valid for eight hours – if you can't get your heart rate up in that time, you shouldn't be here in the first place.

Restaurants

Annie's Paramount Steak House

1609 17th Street, NW, between Q & Corcoran Streets, Dupont Circle (232 0395). Dupont Circle Metro. **Open** 11.30am-11.30pm Mon-Wed; 11.30am-1.30 am Thur; 11.30am Fri-1.30am Sun. **Credit** AmEx, DC, Disc, MC, V. **Main course** $10-$22.

One look at the menu (standard steak, seafood and fries) and you'll realise it's not the food that keeps this place open. To call it a stalwart of the DC gay scene would be an understatement – it's practically a foundation, and recently celebrated its 50th anniversary. Annie's serves a midnight brunch on weekends and holidays and stays open round the clock from Friday night until Sunday lunchtime.

Banana Café

500 Eighth Street, SE, at E Street, Capitol Hill (543 5906). Eastern Market Metro. **Open** 11.30am-10.30pm Mon-Thur; 11.30am-12.30am Fri; noon-12.30am Sat; 11am-3pm, 5-10pm, Sun. **Credit** AmEx, DC, Disc, MC, V. **Main course** $11-$17.

Slightly off the hub of Dupont Circle, this energetic little café serves a lively mix of Puerto Rican, Cuban and Mexican cuisines. The adjacent piano bar sees a fair amount of happy-hour action, but the Sunday brunch is the real draw. Live mariachi bands have been known to roam the floor, creating an atmosphere that's authentically quaint, if nothing else. Free tapas hors d'oeuvres are served at the bar and the drink specials can be hard to resist.

Du Pont Italian Kitchen

1637 17th Street, NW, at R Street, Dupont Circle (328 3222). Dupont Circle Metro. **Open** 11.30am-11.30pm Mon-Fri; 10.30am-midnight Sat; 10.30am-11pm Sun. **Credit** AmEx, Disc, MC, V. **Main course** $6-$13.

Very casual dining and fine, well-priced, traditional Italian food aren't what make this restaurant the hotspot that it is – it's the spacious wraparound café, which provides a great view of the comings and goings on 17th Street.

Mercury Grill

1602 17th Street, NW, between Q & R Streets, Dupont Circle (667 5937). Dupont Circle Metro. **Open** 5-10.30pm Mon-Thur; 5-11pm Fri, Sat; 5-10pm Sun. **Credit** AmEx, MC, V. **Main course** $10-$23.

This renovated rowhouse can get busy at a moment's notice and stay that way all night. The fine nouveau American menu changes nightly; the fish selections are particularly fresh and the appetisers are true winners, especially the Beggar's Purse, stuffed with whatever the kitchen decides upon that night. Add the excellent, attentive staff and one of DC's best martinis and you've got a pleasant spot to watch the traffic up and down 17th Street.

Sport & Fitness

From kayaking on the Potomac River to cheering the Redskins, sports fans are well catered for in DC.

Rowing, kayaking and fishing: there's plenty of activity on DC's rivers.

The weather is hardly ever truly perfect in DC, but there are plenty of sports to do and watch in the area. You'll find world-class kayaking just up the Potomac River and horse riding right near Downtown. Cycling or boating can add a different dimension to a city-centre tour, and (most) big-league sports have a home team to root for.

Participation Sports

Boating, kayaking & rafting

The Potomac and Anacostia rivers and, yes, the touristy Tidal Basin offer city-centre boating opportunities. Great Falls, just a few miles up the Potomac from Downtown, offers top-notch whitewater kayaking. A popular launch is Old Angler's Inn, below the falls on the Maryland side; there are also put-in sites in Virginia. This is a challenging area, not a place to try kayaking for the first time.

Out of town, there's good white water rafting in west Virginia; **Cheat River Outfitters** (1-800 555 8966) runs day trips for $40-$80. And it's an hour's drive to the yachts of Annapolis and the edge of the Chesapeake Bay, with its extensive fishing, endless inlets and terrific bird watching (*see chapter* **Trips Out of Town**).

Atlantic Canoe & Kayak

1201 North Royal Street, between Third Street & Bashford Lane, Alexandria, VA (703 838 9072). Braddock Road Metro.

Sea kayak tours on local rivers, including Old Town Alexandria and to Mount Vernon, with a historical, cultural or natural history theme. Local tours last 2½-4 hours and cost $40-$55. No experience is needed.

Website: www.atlantickayak.com

Belle Haven Marina

1 Belle Haven Road, off George Washington Parkway, Alexandria, VA (703 768 0018). Drive or take a taxi.

Runs classes and rents a range of boats and windsurfing boards for a minimum of two hours on the Potomac River. No test here – you just have to sign that you know what you're doing.

Website: www.saildc.com

Fletcher's Boat House

4940 Canal Road, NW, at Reservoir Road, Upper Northwest (244 0461). Bus D4.

Three miles along the C&O Towpath, Fletcher's Boat House has rowboats and canoes for use on the canal and the Potomac River and often runs one-evening canoe classes.

Jack's Boats

3500 K Street, NW, under the Key Bridge, Georgetown (337 9642). Rosslyn Metro.
In the same neighbourhood as Thompson's (*see below*), this outfit offers rowboats, canoes and kayaks for use on the Potomac River.

Springriver

5606 Randolph Road, off Rockville Pike, Rockville, MD (301 881 5694). White Flint Metro.
The best kayaking resource in the Great Falls area, Springriver rents boats by the day, weekend or longer. Do not even think about trying to go over the falls. It has three other branches: in Annapolis and Baltimore in Maryland and Falls Church in Virginia.

Thompson Boat Center

2900 Virginia Avenue, NW, at Rock Creek Parkway, Foggy Bottom (333 4861). Foggy Bottom-GWU Metro.
Just off Rock Creek Parkway across from the Kennedy Center, you can rent canoes, sea kayaks and sculling shells – if you are certified – for paddling the Potomac River from April to November.

Tidal Basin Boathouse

1501 Maine Avenue, SW, at Jefferson Memorial, Mall & Tidal Basin (479 2426). Smithsonian Metro.
You can rent paddleboats year round (10am-6pm daily) near the Jefferson Memorial. Take a two-seater ($7 a hour) or four-seater ($14) and paddle around the Tidal Basin; particularly enjoyable, of course, in cherry blossom season.

Washington Sailing Marina

1 Marina Drive, off George Washington Memorial Parkway, Alexandria, VA (703 548 9027). Drive or take a taxi.
Sailboats are available by the hour ($10-$19) for sailing on the Potomac River. You must be certified or have enough experience to pass a written exam. The Marina also offers a weekend sailing school for $170.

Cycling

Washington's streets are a potholed lot, full of double-parking drivers and not recommended for cyclists. However, there is a network of paved bike trails – signposted by green signs with a picture of a bike – that makes cruising this mostly flat region on two wheels a breeze.

ADC produces a map showing all bike trails and on-street bike routes within the Beltway; it costs just under $10 and is available at most bike shops or the ADC Map & Travel Store (*see page 172* **Shopping**). The **Washington Area Bicyclists Association** (628 2500) also has maps and trail brochures.

You can take your bike on the Metro 10am-2pm and after 7pm during the week and all day on weekends and holidays.

Bike trails

C&O Canal Towpath

In Georgetown, just north of the Thompson Boat Center, there's a turn-off from Rock Creek Trail west along the C&O Canal Towpath, a packed gravel path that runs 184 miles to Cumberland, Maryland. There are frequent campsites along the way. Skinny tyres are not recommended.

Capital Crescent Trail

DC's newest trail, this 11-mile path runs through north-west Washington and is the first half of a new 'bicycle beltway'. Start at the Thompson Boat Center in Foggy Bottom, then take the Georgetown Branch Trail (crushed rock, not paved) to join up with the Rock Creek Trail between Georgetown and the suburb of Silver Spring in Maryland.

Mount Vernon Trail

A popular ride is to George Washington's family home, Mount Vernon, 19 miles south-west of DC. From the Lincoln Memorial, take the south (downstream) side of the Arlington Memorial Bridge and head south along the Potomac. En route, it runs through charming Old Town Alexandria. If you want to cut the trip in half, you can rent bikes from **Big Wheel Bikes** in Alexandria (2 Prince Street, at Strand Street; 703 739 2300).

Rock Creek Trail

This trail runs from Hains Point – the southernmost point of the District – up the east bank of the Potomac, taking in the National Mall and Rock Creek Park, to Lake Needwood in the Maryland suburbs, 25 miles from the Mall. In the park, Beach Drive north of Blagden Avenue is closed to cars at weekends and on holidays.

W & OD Trail

This trail heads due west from the Mount Vernon Trail for nearly 50 miles along a former railway track (the Washington & Old Dominion Railroad) through parks and past old train stations. The intersection is just past National Airport, but it's confusing, so it's best to have a map.

Bike rental

One-speed cruiser bikes can be rented by the hour or the day at Fletcher's Boat House, while Thompson Boat Center (for both, *see above*) has cruisers and 21-speeds. Or try the shops listed below. For the best mountain biking, you'll need to get out of town – look for Scott Adams' *Washington Mountain Bike Book* at any bike shop. Some good rides are accessible by bike path, many are best reached by car.

Bike the Sites

Tour starts at Jefferson Drive & 12th Street, NW, Mall & Tidal Basin (966 8662). Smithsonian Metro.
This outfit offers three-hour, eight-mile city bike tours daily for $35 a person, as well as specialised

trips. Price includes bike rental, helmet, water, a snack and a guide. Reservations are required. *Website: www.bikethesites.com*

City Bikes

2501 Champlain Street, NW, at Euclid Street, Adams Morgan (265 1564). Woodley Park-Zoo Metro, then 90, 91, 92, 93, 96 bus.
As well as renting and selling bikes and rollerblades for kids and adults, City Bikes has a full-service repair shop with free 24-hour access to an air pump. Bikes cost $10 per hour to rent, $25 for 24 hours.

Metropolis Bikes

709 Eighth Street, SE, at G Street, Capitol Hill (543 8900). Eastern Market Metro.
Mountain bikes and hybrids cost $25 (11am-7pm).

Fishing

You can fly fish in beautiful, rural rivers within a few hours drive of the city, or take charter fishing excursions on the Chesapeake Bay out of Annapolis; trips run from the end of April to the end of November. It's best to call at least a day or two in advance. But right in DC, plenty of people drop a line into the Potomac River. A popular fishing spot is Hains Point, where the Anacostia flows into the Potomac. It's not advised to eat the bottom feeders such as catfish or carp. You will need a DC fishing licence and/or a Virginia or Maryland one, depending on exactly where you're fishing. A one-year DC licence costs $7.50. They're sold, among other places, at **Fletcher's Boat House** (*see page 224*).

Byrd's Sport Fishing Charters

1-301 927 5594.
Located at the Rod & Reel shop in Chesapeake Beach, this company offers six- to eight-hour trips (including night fishing) for six to 23 people on a 42ft boat. Cost: from $50 per person.

Chesapeake Bay Fishing Charters

1-301 855 4655.
Located 30 miles south of Annapolis, this outfit organises trips for four to 36 people. For four people, the cost is $240 for five hours, $320 for seven.

Fitness

Dance

African Heritage Dance Center

4018 Minnesota Avenue, NE, at Benning Road, Northeast (399 5252). Minnesota Avenue Metro.
$10 drop-in evening classes in traditional African dance with live music.

Habana Village

1834 Columbia Road, NW, between Biltmore Road & Mintwood Place, Adams Morgan (462 6310). Dupont Circle, then 42 bus.
Lessons in salsa, merengue and tango are held from 7-9pm Wed-Sat.

Liz Lerman Dance Exchange

7117 Maple Avenue, at Carroll Avenue, Takoma Park, MD (301 270 6700). Takoma Metro.
In addition to professional-level modern and ballet classes, this studio offers technique classes for teens and seniors and special short-term theme classes, such as Bountiful Bodies (for larger women). You can drop in for a single class.

Joy of Motion

1643 Connecticut Avenue, NW, at R Street, Dupont Circle (387 0911). Dupont Circle Metro.
Drop-in classes for about $10 each in jazz, ballet, modern, tap, flamenco and belly dancing, plus conditioning workouts.

Gyms

DC Jewish Community Center

1529 16th Street, NW, at Q Street, Dupont Circle (518 9400). Dupont Circle Metro. **Rate** $15 per day.
Day membership gives you access to the swimming pool and fitness machines; water aerobics, yoga and aerobics classes are extra.

Gold's Gym

408 Fourth Street, SW, between D & E Streets, Southwest (554 4653). Federal Center SW Metro. **Rate** $10 per day; $30 per week.
Members from other Gold's Gyms can get a two-week pass to those in the Washington area. There are branches in DC, Arlington and the suburbs.

National Capital YMCA

1711 Rhode Island Avenue, at 17th Street, Dupont Circle (862 9622). Farragut North Metro. **Rate** *YMCA members* $7-$10 per day.
This trendy YMCA is affiliated with some area hotels, but otherwise only allows members of other YMCAs to use its facilities, such as the 25m pool and seven floors of weights and fitness machines. Aerobic classes and basketball, racquetball, and squash courts are also available.

Washington Sports Clubs

1990 M Street, NW, at 20th Street, Georgetown (785 4900). Dupont Circle Metro. **Rate** $25 per day.
This club has weights, machines, a sauna and squash courts. There are branches in Capitol Hill, Kalorama and Downtown.

YWCA

624 Ninth Street, NW, at G Street, Downtown (626 0710). Gallery Place-Chinatown Metro. **Rate** *YWCA members* $8 per day; *non-members* $12 per day.
Swimming pool, plus fitness and aerobics classes.

Yoga

St Marks Yoga Center

St Marks Church, Third & A Streets, SE, Capitol Hill (546 4964). Capitol South Metro.
This church basement hosts yoga classes most

evenings and on Saturday mornings and Wednesday lunchtimes. The first class is free.

SpiralFlight-A Center for Yoga & the Arts
1726 Wisconsin Avenue, NW, between R & S Streets, Georgetown (965 1645). Bus 30, 32, 34, 35, 36.
Classes (about $13) in just about every type of yoga, as well as tai chi. Drop-ins are welcome.

Golf

Don't expect to see the pols and power brokers on them, but there are three public courses in the District. All are open from dawn to dusk daily, and you can rent clubs.

East Potomac Golf Course
972 Ohio Drive, SW, between 15th Street & I-395 (554 7660). Smithsonian Metro. **Rates** *9 holes* $11 Mon-Fri; $14 Sat, Sun; *18 holes* $16.50 Mon-Fri; $22 Sat, Sun.
South of the FDR memorial, this has an 18-hole course, a driving range and miniature golf. Prices are a bit higher than at the other public courses, but you get great monument views from the green.

Langston Golf Course
2600 Benning Road, NE, at 26th Street, Northeast (397 8638). Stadium Armory Metro. **Rates** *9 holes* $9 Mon-Fri; $12.25 Sat, Sun; *18 holes* $15 Mon-Fri; $19 Sat, Sun.
Near RFK Stadium, this 18-hole course along the Anacostia River is DC's only public course with water holes. It also has a driving range.

Rock Creek Golf Course
1600 Rittenhouse Street, NW, at 16th Street, Upper Northwest (882 7332). Bus D31. **Rates** *9 holes* $9 Mon-Fri; $12.25 Sat, Sun; *18 holes* $15 Mon-Fri; $19 Sat, Sun.
An 18-hole course in woody, hilly terrain in the middle of Rock Creek Park.

Hiking

Try **Theodore Roosevelt Island** across from the Kennedy Center for easy walks in a wooded setting. The island's tidal freshwater marsh is home to beavers, foxes and a variety of birds. Access, by road or bike path, is from the Virginia side of the Potomac River

In **Rock Creek Park,** the Valley Trail begins off Park Road past the tennis courts east of Pierce Mill and runs over rolling hills up the east side of the creek for six miles. There are many access points along Beach Drive. On the west side of Rock Creek, the Western Ridge Trail offers a more strenuous, nearly five-mile hike. Follow the bike path north past Pierce Mill; the dirt trail picks up after the small parking lot and across the intersection.

The **National Arboretum** on the bank of the Anacostia River has three miles of walking trails and is a peaceful oasis, except in spring, when crowds turn out to 'oooh' and 'aaah' over azalea blooms. Near Georgetown, a three-mile trail runs through **Glover Archibold Park**.

Out of DC at **Great Falls Park** there are trails on both the Maryland and Virginia sides, with great views of the white water of the Potomac.

The name game

What's in a name – and how much morals or money can you make from it? In 1997 the Washington Wizards basketball team switched from being the Washington Bullets because the team owner, Abe Pollin, felt the name promoted an image of violence that was particularly undesirable in what was for a while the 'murder capital of the world'. The name was challenged legally by the Harlem Wizards, a travelling comedy basketball team, but the Bullets won.

Some Washingtonians felt the name change was a basically useless gesture that did nothing to stem the gun violence in the city, which particularly hurt young African-American men. The murder rate has gone down since the change, however. Coincidence? More likely irrelevant.

And on the football field, the Washington Redskins have faced litigation over a trademark challenge brought by a group of native American Indians. US trademark law says 'disparaging' words can't be patented – and the plaintiffs say 'redskin' has always been that, and worse. The football team says they take the name as a tribute to native Americans' endurance and strength on the battlefield.

In March 1999, a three-judge panel in the US Patent Office ruled against the Redskins. If the decision is upheld, the NFL won't be able to keep exclusive control over the making and marketing of Redskin T-shirts, caps and suchlike, although local patent law might help the Redskins multi-millionaire owners. No name change, despite years of pressure, appears to be in the cards.

Horse riding

Real horse country is just beyond the suburban sprawl of Virginia, but there are also stables in DC:

Rock Creek Park Horse Center
5100 Glover Road, NW, at Military Road, Upper Northwest (362 0117). Friendship Heights Metro, then E2, E4 bus. **Open** by appointment only. **Rates** approx $21 1-hour guided ride (12s and up); $7.50 15-minute pony ride.

Guided trail rides and pony rides in the corral. Take a cab (less than $10 from the Dupont or Mall areas) or cycle there.

Ice skating

During DC's short cold season, a tiny temporary ice skating rink is set up at **Pershing Park** (737 6938) on Pennsylvania Avenue, between 14th and 15th Streets, near the White House. The National Gallery of Art's **Sculpture Garden** rink on the Mall (at Seventh Street and Constitution Avenue) opens in winter 1999. Call the gallery on 737 4215 for more details.

Fort Dupont Ice Arena

3779 Ely Place, SE, off Minnesota Avenue, Southeast (584 5007). Bus U6. **Open** noon-2pm Fri; 2.30-4.30pm Sat, Sun (other times vary; call for details).

Fort Dupont used to be run by the Park Service. When it got on the budget death list, parents pulled together and turned it into a non-profit organisation to bring ice skating to inner-city youth. Skate rental costs $1.50.

In-line skating

DC's best in-line skating venue is probably **Beach Drive**, north of Blagden Road in Rock Creek Park, which is closed to traffic on weekends. **City Bikes** in Adams Morgan (*see page 226*) is the closest place to Beach Drive to rent skates.

Since traffic was blocked from **Pennsylvania Avenue** in front of the White House (after the Oklahoma City bombing – to discourage truck-bomber wannabes), skaters, particularly those practising hockey, use the block regularly. Or try the **Pentagon parking lot** on weekends. Washington's **bike paths** (*see page 225*) are also popular, although they are often too narrow to accommodate a real workout what with cyclists, joggers and strollers coming from all directions.

Skater's Paradise

1602 Belleview Boulevard, at Fort Hunt Road, Alexandria, VA (703 660 6525). Huntington Metro, then 101, 102 bus. **Open** noon-8pm Mon, Wed, Thur; 10am-6pm Fri, Sat; 11am-5pm Sun.

Sells – but does not rent – in-line skating equipment.

Pick-up games

Washington is teaming (pun intended) with amateur sports clubs and pick-up games of everything from baseball to frisbee to rugby to field hockey. The sand pits along the **Rock Creek Parkway** between the Kennedy Center and the Lincoln Memorial are the place for volleyball matches, while practically the entire **Mall** turns into a mass of softball fields on summer evenings. Other likely spots for games include the **Ellipse**, just south of the White House, and the fields around the **Lincoln Memorial**. For event listings – races, festivals and local club contacts – pick up a copy of *MetroSports Magazine* (free in street boxes) or check its website at www.metrosports.com.

Rock climbing

The best rock climbing in this part of the world is way out in West Virginia, notably **New River Gorge**, a five-hour drive from the city. Closer in, there are cliffs to be scaled at **Great Falls**, on both the Virginia and Maryland sides.

There is an indoor climbing wall at **Sportrock**, and a much smaller one at **Gold's Gym** in Arlington (703 527 4653). Don't try the monuments – the park police will get you!

Sportrock II Climbing Center

5308 Eisenhower Avenue, at Van Dorn Street, Alexandria, VA (703 212 7625). Van Dorn Street Metro. **Open** noon-11pm Mon-Fri; 11am-8pm Sat; noon-8pm Sun. **Rate** $13 a day.

Sportrock has an 11,000sq ft climbing wall and provides gear and detailed area information.

Swimming

Avoid the Potomac and the Anacostia Rivers. There are nearly three dozen (highly chlorinated) indoor public swimming pools in DC; look in the government listings (blue-edged) in the *Yellow Pages* under 'District of Columbia, Parks and Recreation', or call Aquatic Services at 576 6436. The outdoor pools are usually open from Memorial Day to Labor Day. Some health and fitness clubs (*see page 226* **Gyms**) have pools that are open to the public for a daily fee.

Outdoor pools

Capitol Natorium

635 North Carolina Avenue, SE, at Pennsylvania Avenue, Capitol Hill (724 4495). Eastern Market Metro. **Open** 6.30am-9am, noon-5pm, 6-7pm, Mon-Fri; 1-5pm Sat; 10am-5pm Sun. **Admission** free.

Francis Pool

25th & N Streets, NW, Dupont Circle (727 3285). Dupont Circle Metro. **Open** *June-Aug* 7-9am, 1-8pm, Mon-Fri; noon-7pm Sat, Sun. **Admission** $3; $1 seniors, 5-18s; free under-5s.

Popular with families during the day and lap swimmers before and after work.

Tennis

There are plenty of first-come, first-served courts at various parks and schools around the area; to find the closest court to you, call 645 33944. If other people are waiting, playing time is limited to 30 minutes or an hour.

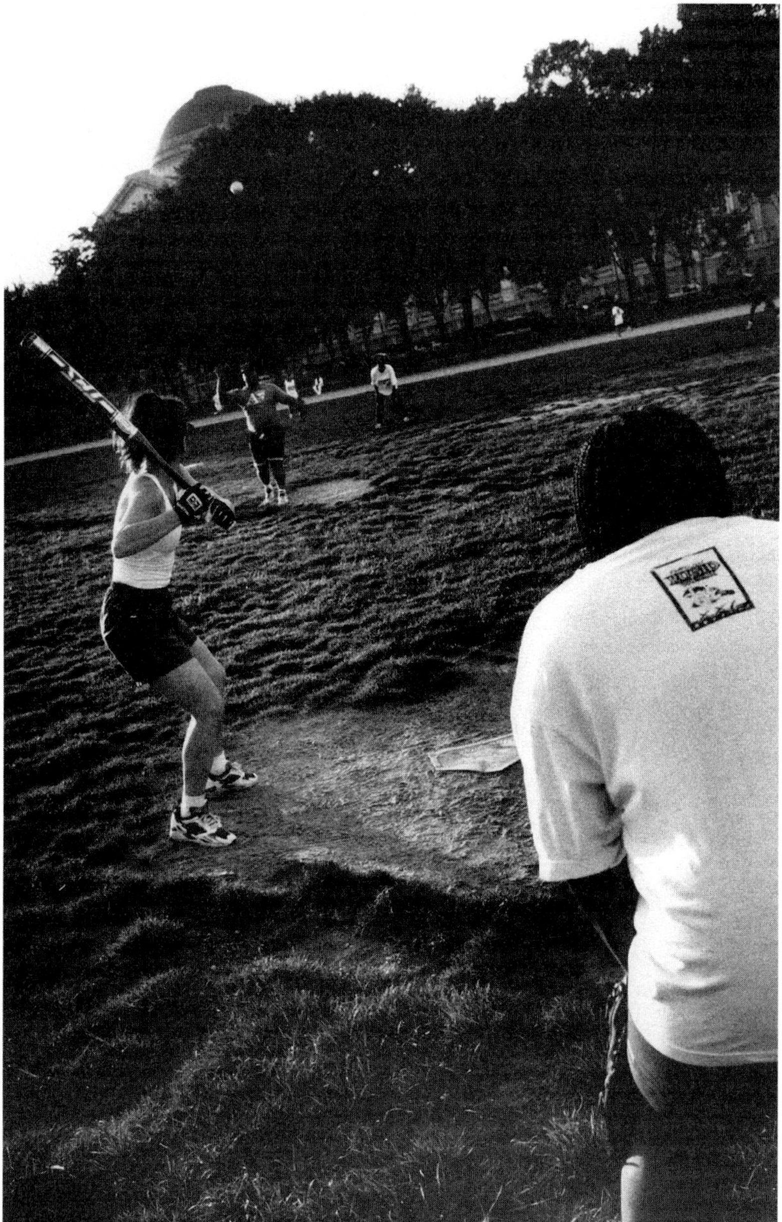

In summer, pick-up softball games take over the National Mall .

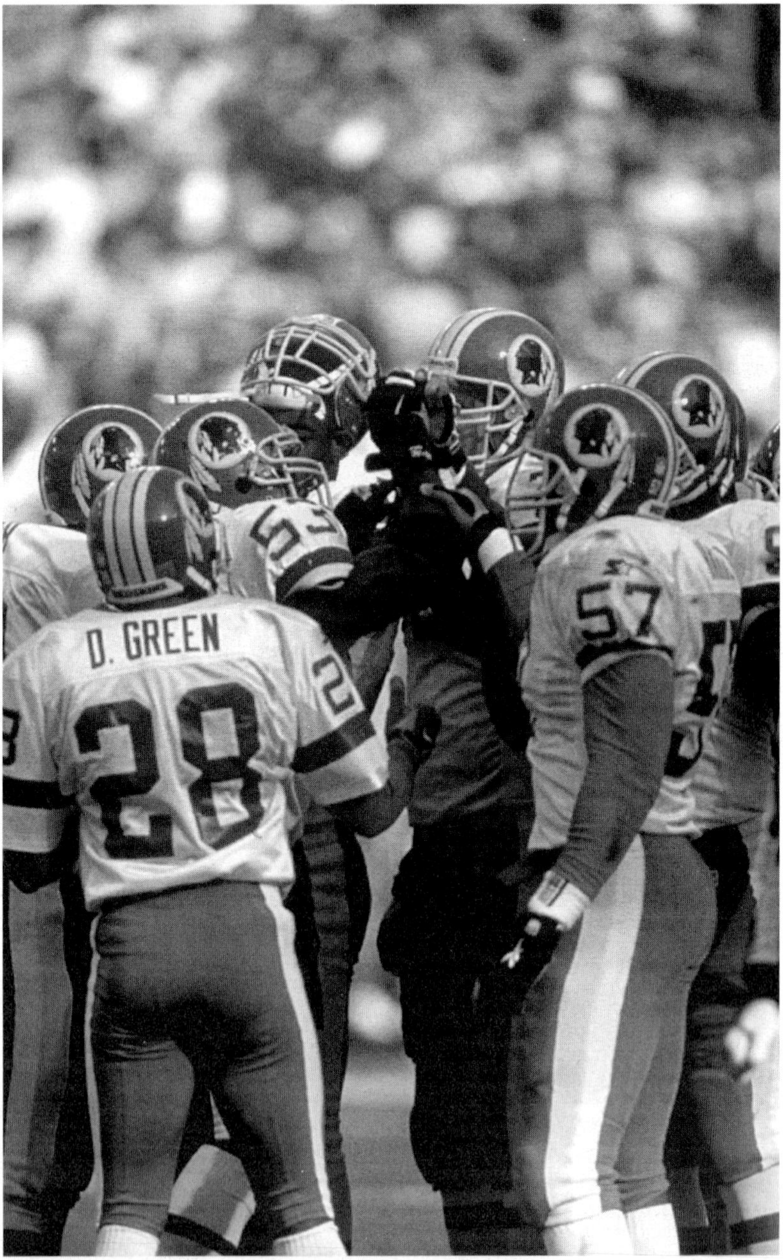

The ever-popular **Washington Redskins**, *three-time winners of the Superbowl.*

East Potomac Tennis Center at Hains Point

1090 Ohio Drive, SW, Southwest (554 5962). Smithsonian Metro. **Open** 7am-10pm Mon-Fri; 7am-8pm Sat, Sun. **Rates** $3.25-$28 per hour.
Next to the Potomac River, with five indoor hard courts and clay and hard courts outdoors.

Washington Tennis Center

16th & Kennedy Streets, NW, Upper Northwest (722 5949). Bus S1, S2, S3, S4, S5. **Open** 7am-11pm daily. **Rates** $3.25-$28 per hour.
This public centre just east of Rock Creek Park has ten hard courts and 15 clay courts. A bubble covers half the hard courts during winter. Reservations are recommended. There's a decent pro shop.

Spectator Sports

For better or worse, it seems that tickets for practically all professional sporting events in Washington are distributed by **Ticketmaster** (432 7328/1-800 551 7328). There is a service charge for all purchases.

American football

You want to see the Washington Redskins, three-time Superbowl champs and the most valuable team in all professional sport? Plan to pay. There's a 20-year waiting list for season tickets – and all seats are season tickets. That leaves the rest of the world to shop the *Washington Post* classified ads or deal with scalpers at the gate.

You have a slightly better chance of seeing a game if you travel to Baltimore, to watch the Baltimore Ravens (ex-Cleveland Browns). Despite having moved to the area only in 1996, the team is popular enough for season tickets to sell out, but not as fast, and 6,000 tickets a game are reserved for individual sales. They go on sale for the whole season in August. Call 1-410 261 7283 for the latest information. The football season runs from August to January.

Jack Kent Cooke Stadium

Landover, MD. Landover, Addison Road or Cheverly Metro, then shuttle bus (on game days).
The new home of the Redskins and named after the longtime team owner, this 80,116-seat bowl is in a nearby Maryland suburb.

Ravens Stadium

Near Camden Yards & the Inner Harbor, Baltimore.
Take a Marc or Amtrak train from Union Station to Camden Yards; the journey is about 45 minutes.

Basketball

The Washington Wizards (formerly known as the Bullets – *see page 227* **The name game**) of the NBA and the Washington Mystics of the hot new WNBA (women's professional basketball) play at the MCI Center in Downtown. Tickets are usually easy to get and cost $30-$77 for the Wizards, less than $20 for the Mystics.

The men play from November to May; the women from June through August.

MCI Center

601 F Street, NW, at Seventh Street, Downtown (628 3200). Gallery Place-Chinatown Metro.
This swanky, $200-million, 20,000-seat stadium was built at the end of 1997. As well as being first-class place to watch games, it has shops and sports memorabilia – *see p63* **Central DC**.

Baseball

Washington has a proud baseball history. But at this point, it's all that – just history.

The Homestead Grays, who played in the Negro League in the 1930s and 1940s, were extremely popular and successful, winning nine out of ten Negro League championships between 1937 and 1947. After Jackie Robinson broke the colour barrier in 1947, the best black players joined other clubs and black fans started going to major league games; the Negro League had pretty much disappeared by the early 1950s. The once all-white club, the Senators, lost so often that Washington was referred to as 'first in war, first in peace and last in the American league'. That team was moved to Minnesota in 1960. A revived Washington Senators left DC for Texas 11 years later. But the dream of a DC baseball team lives on – and there may well be a team to cheer in RFK Stadium (or a new arena) before this guide is out of date.

Meanwhile, the Baltimore Orioles pack fans from DC into Camden Yards in Baltimore. You can get there by car, by Amtrak rail service (by Marc on weekdays) or by $9 round-trip buses from the Greenbelt Metro station on game days. The season runs from April to September; tickets are available from Ticketmaster.

A peculiarly DC phenomenon are the softball games played by various Congressional offices' aides during summer. Competition is very fierce; in fact, it is rumoured that some congressional aides get hired just for their softball abilities.

Hockey

The Washington Capitals, 1998 Eastern conference NHL champs – Go Caps! – play in the MCI Center from October until April. The ever-promising Caps don't usually sell out and tickets cost $20-$60. Call the MCI Center (628 3200) for match information; tickets are available from Ticketmaster (432 7328/1-800 551 7328).

Girl power: the **Washington Mystics**.

Horse racing

It's Pimlico, it's Laurel, it's Rosecroft! These are the three main race tracks in the Washington area.

Laurel Park

Racetrack Road, off State Route 198, Laurel, MD (301 725 0400). You'll need a car to get there.
Halfway between Baltimore and DC, this is where ponies and thoroughbreds race much of the year.

Pimlico Race Course

Winner & Hayward Avenues, Baltimore, MD (1-410 542 9400).
The Preakness Stakes are held at this track on the third Saturday in May. Other thoroughbred races are held – not every day – from April to June and July to September. You'll have to drive or take a train to Baltimore's Penn Station and catch a cab.
Website: www.pimlico.com

Rosecroft Raceway

6336 Rosecroft Drive, off Brinkley Road, Fort Washington, MD (301 567 4000).
Just outside the Beltway, this is the place for year-round harness racing. There's no public transport to the track, but Young Star Tours runs buses from the Convention Center in Downtown to Rosecroft on Thur, Fri and Sat ($10 round trip); call 301 449 1615 for details.
Website: www.rosecroft.com

Soccer

The fans go crazy for DC United, Washington's very good pro team, which plays major league soccer from March to November at the RFK Stadium – they won the MLS Cup in the first two years of the league's existence.

There's also an incredibly dynamic Latino League that fills suburban fields every weekend. Rivalries rooted in Central American villages and coaches with names like 'The Tractor' add to the excitement and emotion. The Taca Cup is this league's championship, a multi-day tournament held at the RFK Stadium soccer fields in late July/early August. Contact the Cup sponsor, Taca Airline (833 2076), for details.

RFK Stadium

22nd & East Capitol Street, NE, Northeast. Stadium-Armory Metro (office 547 9077). **Tickets** *individual* Ticketmaster 432 7328/1-800 551 7328; *group* DC United office 1-703 478 6600.

Duck pins

It was a tough fight, but jousting beat duck pins in the great race to become Maryland's official state sport. Duck pin bowling is a Baltimore-born variation on the familiar ten-pin version. It was invented around the beginning of the twentieth century by two Baltimore Oriole baseball players who owned a bowling alley on the side. According to the duck pin experts (and there are still a few out there, it was a gimmick to bring in business.

Duck pins are shorter and fatter than the standard bowling pins, while the ball is about five inches across, weighs just under four pounds and is rolled from one hand. The meeting of the two apparently makes the pins fly around like wild ducks taking off from a marsh – hence the name. Easy to play, tough to score high. There are a few duck pin houses left in the area.

Meanwhile, jousting lives on. Check out the annual August jousting tournament in Cordova on Maryland's Eastern Shore, held as a benefit for St Joseph's, the oldest Catholic church in the area. Unfortunately for the gory-minded, the lances are too dull to impale.

Trips Out of Town

Trips Out of Town

Reminders of America's struggle towards nationhood dot Washington's otherwise peaceful and varied hinterland.

The so-called Capital Region sprawls far beyond Washington, DC itself, deep into the neighbouring states of Maryland and Virginia – and, at a real stretch, also Delaware – with a population that is many times the capital city's bare half-million. The landscape is widely – and sometimes wildly – varied, from the beaches of Chesapeake Bay to (almost) the Blue Ridge Mountains of Virginia. For visitors who want to take a brief break from the majestic monuments that governments and men build for themselves, there's something out there beyond the infamous Beltway for almost everyone.

Check out another city? There's a considerable one – Baltimore – just up I-95. Water? There's plenty – the Atlantic Ocean, for instance – only an hour or so away. Mountains? They're not exactly the Alps, but the Blue Ridge Mountains are in reasonably easy reach and West Virginia's more rugged peaks not much more distant. History? Most of the region wallows in it – battlefields, grand houses – take your pick. The great outdoors? Parks and wilderness areas invite hiking, biking, horse riding and fishing. And should an oenophilic mood strike, there are several vineyards to tempt.

We've divided the chapter into themed sections, which in some cases overlap geographically: Richmond, for example, is near some Civil War battlefields and the James River plantation houses. See the map on page 286 to help plan your excursions – references for each location are given in the text.

Phone numbers are given as dialled from DC.

Transport

By car

This being the US of A, the preferred way of getting almost anywhere is by car. That should be no problem in most cases as the regional road network is excellent. Visitors should be forewarned, however, that in the immediate vicinity of Washington – and well beyond it, on some major routes, such as I-66 – traffic is extremely heavy in weekday commuting hours. The national car rental companies all have Washington facilities, and there are several local outfits (*see page 254* **Getting Around**).

By rail

Washington has a much better rail network than is the national norm for major cities in the States. Union Station is the arrival and departure point for trains both suburban and long-distance.

Union Station

50 Massachusetts Avenue, NE, at North Capitol Street, Union Station & Around. Union Station Metro/97, D8, X8 bus.

Amtrak

Information & reservations 1-800 872 7245.

Amtrak provides excellent connections to northeastern cities, including the hourly Metroliner express trains to Baltimore (45 minutes) and New York City (three hours 15 minutes), and to points south. For journeys to destinations in this chapter, you seldom need to buy or book ahead.

Marc

Information 1-800 325 7245.

Marc, a primarily commuter rail service operated by the Maryland Depart of Transportation, connects Washington to Baltimore. However, the one-hour trip takes longer than Amtrak and trains are most frequent during the weekday commuter rush, much less so at midday and weekends.

Virginia Railway Express

703 684 0400.

A limited Virginia commuter service on two lines, linking Washington to Fredericksburg and Manassas respectively. But the service is almost entirely inbound during the morning and outbound in the afternoon.

By bus

Greyhound Bus Lines

1005 First Street, NE, at L Street, Northeast (289 5154/1-800 231 2222). Bus 96.

Buses exist, but are a less satisfactory means of getting around the region. Greyhound, the sole-surviving nationwide bus carrier, has services to Baltimore, Richmond, Fredericksburg and Williamsburg, as well as an express service to New York City. The terminal is located in a not particularly appetising area north of Union Station. Note that you cannot book in advance.

By boat

Boats are an option for some destinations, including Mount Vernon and the Chesapeake Bay islands – for details of the latter, *see p249* **Chesapeake Bay & the Maryland Shore**.

Baltimore's nightlife is centred on the funky portside neighbourhood of **Fells Point**.

Spirit Cruises

Pier 4, Water Street, SW, at Sixth Street, Southwest (554 8000). Waterfront Metro.
Service to and from Mount Vernon from Pier 4 on Washington's Southwest Waterfront. The trip takes about four hours. Fare ($26.50; $25 seniors; $17 6-11s; free under-6s) includes admission to the mansion and grounds.

Information

Automobile Association of America (AAA)

701 15th Street, NW, at New York & Pennsylvania Avenues, White House & Around (331 3000). McPherson Square Metro.
Open 9am-6pm Mon-Fri.
The Triple A provides excellent maps, guidebooks (with accommodation and restaurant listings) and campground guides – and they won't cost you a penny if you're a member or belong to an affiliated organisation, such as the British AA. Some hotels offer discounts to AAA members.

Delaware Tourism Office

99 Kings Highway, Dover, DE 19901 (1-302 739 4271/1-800 441 8846). **Open** 8am-4.30pm Mon-Fri.

Maryland Office of Tourism Development

217 East Redwood Street, Baltimore, MD 21202 (office 1-410 767 3400/call centre 1-800 394 5725).
Open 8am-5pm Mon-Fri.

Virginia Tourism Authority

1629 K Street, between 16th & 17th Streets, NW, Washington, DC 20006 (872 0523). Farragut West Metro. **Open** 8.30am-5pm Mon-Fri.
901 East Byrd Street, Richmond, VA 23219 (office 1-804 786 4484/call centre 1-800 932 5827).
Open 8.30am-5pm Mon-Fri.
Website: www.virginia.org

Urban Escapes

Baltimore

To tell the truth, Baltimore (map A3), which dates back to 1729, has a bit of an inferiority complex in respect to its semi-sister city 60 miles to the south. Maryland's metropolis (pronounced 'Bah-mer' by the true native) was one of the half-dozen largest cities in the country and an important port back in the days when the new capital of the new United States was mostly marshland. But Washington (pronounced 'Warshington' by the real old-timers, of whom there aren't that many left) has become the big deal regionally. Baltimore's population is still larger than Washington's and it's still a very busy port, but where Washington's image nowadays is glamour, Baltimore's is grit. It is seen, even by many Bahmerians, as a hangover from an earlier and messier industrial era.

However, that is unfair. In recent decades, the city – at least the historic core – has experienced a stunning renaissance. Nowadays Baltimore is a popular day or weekend break for Washingtonians. If you want to stay overnight, contact the **Baltimore Visitors Center** (*see page 237*) for information on hotels.

The old port area on the Inner Harbor, which had deteriorated into a depressing urban jungle of rundown factories and warehouses, has been transformed into **Harborplace**, a lively civic centre of shops, restaurants and attractions – including the world-class **National Aquarium** (501 E Pratt Street; 1-410 576 3800) and the US frigate **Constellation** (Pier 1, Pratt Street; 1-410 539 1797), the 1854-built namesake of the renowned original which thumped British warships during the Anglo-American tussle of 1812-15.

Glass-walled offices in the new high-rise business district form a glittering backdrop. Along nearby streets, typical Baltimore row houses with marble front stoops have been restored to something approaching their former charm. Next door are **Little Italy**, which has managed to hang on to its ethnic identity in the shadow of downtown's burgeoning skyscrapers, and funky **Fells Point**, a portside neighbourhood dating back to the city's beginnings, where the streets, some cobbled, carry names – Albemarle, Exeter, Lancaster, Shakespeare, Thames ('Thaymes' in Bahmerese) – that may make British visitors think of home.

It doesn't look anything like home, however. The Point is very much a US inner city and familiar as such to Americans nationwide as the setting of TV's *Homicide: Life on the Street*, a long-running and now-defunct cop show. It is also home to the **Broadway Market** (Broadway, between Fleet and Aliceanna Streets), which dates back to the eighteenth century and is a pungent maze of stalls selling virtually every comestible imaginable. Otherwise, the Point is noted for two specialities: antique stores and drinking establishments. There are dozens of the former, selling everything from conventional old stuff to marine artefacts to hip rags with a past. The watering holes are almost as numerous and make the Point the heart of the city's nightlife.

There's also culture in Baltimore. The **Walters Art Gallery** (600 North Charles Street; 1-410 547 9000) is one of the best fine art museums in the US. The **Baltimore Museum of Art** (10 Art Museum Drive, between Charles and 31st Streets; 1-410 396 7100) has a notable collection of modern paintings and sculpture from Van Gogh to Warhol and Rodin to Nevelson. At the **American Visionary Art Museum** (800 Key Highway; 1-410 244 1900), across the harbour in South Baltimore, the focus is on untrained but inspired artists working outside accepted norms. Some viewers may see the results as junk, others as the future of artistic expression.

One way to see Baltimore is on an organised tour. **Zippy Larson's Shoe Leather Safaris** (1-410 817 4141) will lead the way around Little Italy, Fells Point and other nearby neighbourhoods of interest. Other possibilities include **About Town Tours** (1-410 592 7770) and **Harbor City Tours** (1-410 254 8687). **Hollywood on the Harbor** (1-410 547 0479) covers the Fells Point sites featured on TV and in film, and Little Italy.

And then there are boats. It's not quite Venice, but water taxis (1-410 563 3901/1-800 658 8947) make several stops around the Inner Harbor. Tours of the harbour and beyond last several hours aboard the **Bay Lady** and **Lady Baltimore** (301 Light Street; 1-410 727 3113/1-800 695 2628), the schooner **Clipper City** (Fingers Piers; 1-410 539 6277), and **Minnie V** (Harborplace Ampitheater, Pratt and Light Streets; 1-410 685 0295), a sailing boat that was once in the oyster business.

Eating & drinking

Visionary Art's third-floor restaurant **Joy America Café** (800 Key Highway; 1-410 244 6500) has a creative organic menu that complements the museum's eclectic art collection. Otherwise, there's no need to stray far from Harborplace for a satisfactory bite. It offers a wide range of eating options, from fast-food counters to full-service restaurants – such as **Phillips** (301 Light Street; 1-410 685 6600), which has a great harbour view and terrace dining in season.

There's also Little Italy, where the bias in many of the better spots is toward northern Italy, and Fells Point, which offers just about everything. But face it: this is Baltimore on the Bay, where seafood is king and crabcakes are a virtual cult. If you want your delights from the deep served with more than a touch of class, try the **Pierpoint Restaurant** (1822 Aliceanna Street; 1-410 675 2080). **Bertha's** (734 South Broadway; 1-410 327 5795) is touristy but good, with a pub-like bar serving English beer as well as local brews. **Mo's Crab & Pasta Factory** (502 Albemarle Street; 1-410 837 1600) makes the most of two culinary worlds.

Other fishy options include **Fishery Continental Seafood Restaurant** (1717 Eastern Avenue; 1-410 327 9340), just east of the Broadway Market, which mixes Mediterranean dishes with Bay specialities, and **Henninger's Tavern** (1812 Bank Street; 1-410 342 2172). Purely pub possibilities include **Wharf Rat** (803 South Ann Street; 1-410 276 9034) and **Cat's Eye Pub** (1730 Thames Street; 1-410 276 9085), the latter heavily into things Irish.

Getting there

By car

Baltimore is about an hour's drive from Washington. Take I-95 north to I-395, exit 53, which quickly becomes Howard Street (take care not to shoot off to the left on to Martin Luther King Jr Boulevard). Continue north on Howard a short distance (Camden Yards baseball stadium will be on your left) to Pratt Street. Turn right and continue past Charles and Light Streets to Harborplace, on the right.

By train

Amtrak (1-800 872 7245) and **Marc** (1-800 325 7245) trains from Washington arrive at Penn Station (1500 North Charles Street). Amtrak's regular service ($19 one-way) takes about 45 minutes, while its Metroliner service is faster – 36 minutes – and dearer (one-way $28 Mon-Fri, $23 Sat, Sun). Both leave about every hour; the last train from DC is at 10.30pm, the last from Baltimore about an hour later. Marc trains ($5.75 one-way, $10.25 round trip) run Mon-Fri only from 6.30am to about 10pm, leaving about every half-hour during rush hour and every hour otherwise.

Useful information

Baltimore Visitors Center
451 Light Street, Baltimore, MD 21202 (1-410 837 4636/1-800 282 6632). **Open** 9am-5pm Mon-Sat; 10am-5pm Sun.
Information on hotels, dining and sightseeing.

Richmond & around

Can we speak frankly? No one goes to **Richmond** (map E2) in search of excitement. This former capital of the Confederate States of America and ongoing (since 1779) capital of the Commonwealth of Virginia, takes its past and its present very seriously. A scant two-hour drive south from Washington, it is a very different city – and proud of it.

This is the South, as is apparent in the soft accents, the less frenetic pace and the architecture. The stately homes lining **Monument Avenue**, although many have been converted to apartments, call to mind distant New Orleans rather than DC. Time has not passed Richmond by, however. The modern city is a thriving business centre, home to much of the beleaguered but still muscular American tobacco industry, with a high-rise skyline of gleaming new office buildings. But as Richmond looks to the future, it has no intention of letting the past slip away.

This is apparent as you drive into the city along Monument Avenue with its line of heroic statues of Robert E Lee, 'Stonewall' Jackson, JEB Stuart and other captains of the Confederacy. Then you come to the newest local hero to be placed on a pedestal – the late tennis great Arthur Ashe, an African-American and native Richmond son. It was a controversial addition: traditionalists were not happy and even some in the African-American community, while keen to honour Ashe, thought another location would have been preferable. But there he stands, waving a tennis racket in the line-up of soldiers with swords.

Monument Avenue is the east-west axis of the city, becoming Franklin Street once you're past the statues and dead-ending at Capitol Square with its pillared **Virginia State Capitol**. Designed by Thomas Jefferson in his architect mode, the building has served as a seat of government for Virginia since 1788 as well as for the Confederacy from 1862-65. Also on Capitol Square is the 'White House of the Confederacy', the wartime residence of the South's president, Jefferson Davis. Richmond is packed with other historic structures and landmarks, mostly relating to the Civil War; contact the **Metro Richmond Convention & Visitors Bureau** (*see page 238*) for information and directions. *See also page 242* **War Sites**.

Not part of the Civil War context is the **Edgar Allan Poe Museum** (1914 E Main Street; 1-804 648 5523). Although he was born and died elsewhere, America's master of the macabre was a longtime resident of Richmond, first gaining recognition among the literati as editor of the local *Southern Literary Messenger*. The museum's main building is the oldest (1737) house in the city.

Richmond may not be bright lights, big city, but it is not without its livelier side. Head for **Shockoe Slip**, a three-block strip of Cary Street sloping down from the financial district to the banks of the James River. In the nineteenth century, the area was a bustling centre of the tobacco and milling industries. Ornate warehouses along the narrow cobblestone streets have been renovated and now house restaurants, clubs, boutiques and galleries. Along with adjacent **Shockoe Bottom**, this is the centre of the city's cultural life and nightlife. The **Farmer's Market** (Main and 17th Streets) in the Bottom dates back to the seventeenth century. You can tour the historic areas by bus.

One reason for visiting the Richmond area lies an hour's drive to the east – **Williamsburg** (map E3), Virginia's renowned colonial capital. With lavish funding from the Rockefeller family beginning in the 1930s, the town's core has been restored as accurately as possible to its appearance in the late eighteenth century. The half-square-mile historic area contains several hundred restored or reconstructed buildings, from the elegant brick Capitol and Governor's Palace to taverns and private homes. With costumed 'interpreters' strolling about pretending to be gentlemen, housewives, tradesmen and whatever, the effort at bringing a bygone era to life can get a bit thick, but all in all it makes for a diverting show. There's a **Busch Gardens** amusement park nearby, themed – strangely, given all the local history – around seventeenth-century Europe.

Also worth a look are nearby **Yorktown** (map E3), where the defeat of besieged British General Cornwallis by a combined American-French force ended the American Revolution (*see also page 242* **War Sites**), and **Jamestown** (map E3), location of the first (1607) permanent British settlement in North America. And there's still more. Winding along the James River between Richmond and Williamsburg is a string of imposing pre-Civil War plantation homes, some dating back to the early 1700s. Still largely privately owned, a half-dozen of the finest are open to the public (*see page 241* **James River plantations**).

You could also make a stop at **Fredericksburg** (map C2), the halfway point between Washington and Richmond. Also dating from the colonial era, it was George Washington's boyhood home. The historic town centre is surrounded by tacky urban sprawl, but contains some locations of interest. Notable are the **Mary Washington House** (1200 Charles Street; 1-540 373 1569), home of Washington's mother, and **Kenmore** (201

Washington Avenue; 1-504 373 3381), the rather small but elegant home of his sister. You could combine a trip to Fredericksburg with a visit to various Civil War battlefields just to the west of town (*see page 242* **War Sites**).

Eating & drinking

Richmond

The most interesting places to eat are in the Shockoe Slip area. The **Tobacco Company Restaurant** (1201 East Cary Street; 1-804 782 9431) was once what its name says. Restored with a funkily elegant touch, it has plenty of gleaming old wood panelling and leafy plants suspended above a three-storey atrium. The eclectic menu strives for creativity, and sometimes achieves it. Directly across the street, the more upscale and pricier **Berkeley Hotel Dining Room** (1200 East Cary Street; 1-804 225 5105) has a more traditional menu stressing fresh local fare. More raffish possibilities are **The Frog & the Redneck** (1423 East Cary Street; 1-804 648 3764) a bistro-style place where French cuisine acquires a Southern accent, and **Havana '59** (16 North 17th Street; 1-840 649 2822) in Shockoe Bottom, a lively local hangout where the beat is Caribbean.

Williamsburg

The determinedly colonial atmosphere in the restored eateries can be a bit much, but it's all part of the Williamsburg experience. Notable are **Chowning's Tavern** (109 East Duke of Gloucester Street; 1-757 229 1000) and **Shield's Tavern** (422 East Duke of Gloucester Street; 1-757 220 7677). Better (much) are the **Dining Room at Ford's Colony** (240 Ford's Colony Drive; 1-757 258 4107), several miles west of the historic area off US 60, and also a historic setting, and the **Regency Dining Room** (136 Francis Street; 1-757 565 8875) in the very elegant Williamsburg Inn.

Getting there

By car

From Washington, take I-95 south (be warned that this is one of the most heavily travelled highways along the East Coast). For Fredericksburg, take exit 130; the historic town centre is a little more than a mile to the east on State Route 3. For Richmond, continue south on I-95 to exit 78. For Williamsburg, take I-64 from downtown Richmond to exit 238, following the green and white Colonial Williamsburg signs to the visitor centre. Or, if time permits, take the more leisurely State Route 5, which winds along the James River and the historic plantation homes.

By train

Amtrak serves Fredericksburg, Richmond and Williamsburg. From Washington, it takes about 2 hours to Richmond; there are 7 trains daily each way (6 on Sat). Round-trip fare is about $50. There are a couple of trains a day between Richmond and Williamsburg (3 on Fridays); the journey is 75-90 mins and the round-trip fare is $28.

Useful information

Fredericksburg Visitors Center

706 Caroline Street, Fredericksburg, VA 22401 (1-800 678 4748). **Open** *winter* 9am-5pm, *summer* 9am-7pm, daily.
Website: www.fredericksburgva.com

Metro Richmond Convention & Visitors Bureau

550 East Marshall Street, Richmond, VA 23219 (1-800 370 9004). **Open** 8.30am-5pm Mon-Fri.
Website: www.richmondva.org

Williamsburg Area Convention & Visitors Bureau

201 Penniman Road, Williamsburg, VA 23185 (1-757 253 0192/1-800 368 6511). **Open** 8.30am-5pm Mon-Fri.
Website: www.visitwilliamsburg.com

Historic Homes

The Washington area has arguably the greatest concentration of historic homes in the US, most being in Virginia. Many are associated with early presidents. Four of the first five presidents (the 'Virginia dynasty') were from the state, as were several later occupants of the White House. Maryland, a considerably smaller and, some might say, less self-absorbed state, also has some notable residences. The sites mentioned below are merely the tip of an exceedingly large iceberg. Some – such as Mount Vernon, Gunston Hall Plantation and Woodlawn Plantation – are less than an hour's drive south from Downtown DC and could be easily visited in a day; others, such as Monticello and Montpelier, are further away and might involve an overnight stay.

Mount Vernon

George Washington Memorial Parkway, Mount Vernon, VA (703 780 2000). **Open** *spring, summer* 8am-5pm, *autumn* 9am-5pm, *winter* 9am-4pm, daily. **Admission** $9; $4.50-$8.50 concessions. **Map C3**
Website: www.mountvernon.org

Mount Vernon, the graceful plantation home of the first president, is the most celebrated and visited historic home in the country. It's jammed with tour groups during the spring and summer; if you are visiting at this time, go in the afternoon when the crowds thin out. Autumn, when the weather is mostly glorious, is much better.

George Washington has gone down in history as a soldier and statesman, but he thought of himself as first and foremost a farmer, and he devoted the greater part of his life to improving the estate he had inherited from an older half-brother. He sought to recreate on the banks of the Potomac River an English country manor house, complete with bowling green and formal gardens. The house, beautifully restored to its appearance in 1799, the last year

The main dining room at **Mount Vernon**.

of Washington's life, contains original furniture and many of his belongings.

Nearby are other interesting sites with Washington associations, such as George Washington's Grist Mill (Mount Vernon Memorial Highway), built to grind his own grain and that of his neighbour's (no altruist, Washington took an eighth share of all flour produced).

Getting there From Downtown DC, take US 1 south across the 14th Street bridge to the George Washington Memorial Parkway. Continue 14 miles, through Alexandria, to Mount Vernon, where the Parkway ends at the visitors' gate.

Gunston Hall Plantation & Woodlawn Plantation

Gunston Hall, Gunston Road, Mason Neck, VA (1-703 550 9220). **Open** 9.30am-5pm daily. **Admission** $5; $1.50-$4 concessions. **Map C2/3**
Website: www.gunstonhall.org
Woodlawn Plantation, 9000 Richmond Highway, Alexandria, VA (1-703 780 4000). **Open** *Mar-Dec* 10am-4pm daily. **Admission** $6; $4 concessions.
Website: www.nthp.org/main/sites/woodlawn.htm

Not far from Mount Vernon is Gunston Hall, the home of Washington's friend George Mason, a drafter of the US Constitution, but so principled that he refused to sign the document because it did not contain specific guarantees of individual liberties. These were later added as the Bill of Rights. Compared with Mount Vernon, this two-storey brick house is distinctly modest. It is also oddly modern. With a few additions, notably indoor plumbing, it could be very comfortable by today's standards. The restored ground-level rooms are considered outstanding examples of late colonial interior design.

Nearby is **Woodlawn Plantation**, the elegant brick mansion built by Washington as a wedding present for his adopted daughter, Nelly Parkes Custis, and his favourite nephew. In the grounds is another showplace house, but with no connection to Washington and of a very different time. The **Pope-Leighey House** is a small gem by modern master Frank Lloyd Wright. The house was designed to order in the 1930s for a lowly journalist earning $50 a week to demonstrate that Wright's brand of visionary architecture could be adapted to the lifestyles of ordinary people as well as the very wealthy. Encompassing all of 1,200sq ft, the house was moved to its present location when the original site was overrun by highway construction.

Getting there From Mount Vernon, take the Mount Vernon Memorial Highway to Richmond Highway (US 1) and the entrance to Woodlawn Plantation. From Woodlawn, take US 1 south about 5 miles to Gunston Road, which leads to Gunston Hall Plantation.

Monticello

State Route 53, Charlottesville, VA (1-804 984 9822). **Open** 8am-5pm daily. **Admission** $9; $5 concessions. **Map D1**
Website: www.monticello.org

Monticello is almost as celebrated as Mount Vernon. This domed hill-top mansion just outside Charlottesville, about 130 miles south-west of Washington, was the home of the third president, Thomas Jefferson, a largely self-taught but talented architect who also designed it. Construction continued off and on from 1769 to 1809. The house and its contents reflect Jefferson's interests in books, science and other intellectual pursuits. Jefferson, who died 50 years to the day after the adoption of the Declaration of Independence he authored, is buried in the adjacent family cemetery.

Charlottesville itself is a town of more than passing interest, with a history going back to colonial times. It is home to the University of Virginia, which ranks among the top public universities in the US and was founded by Jefferson, who also designed its original buildings. The old town, although engulfed by urban sprawl, contains many handsome old homes and public buildings, many reflecting Jefferson's architectural influence.

Getting there From Washington, take I-66 west to exit 43, then US 29 south through Warrenton and Culpeper to Charlottesville (about 2½ hours). Continue on US 29 around Charlottesville to I-64. Take I-64 east 3½ miles to exit 121, take State Route 20 south and then State Route 53 east, following signs, 2 miles to the mansion.

Montpelier

11407 Constitution Highway (State Route 20), Montpelier Station, VA (1-540 672 2728). **Open** 9.30am-4pm daily. **Admission** $7.50; $3.50-$6.50 concessions. **Map D1**
Website: www.montpelier.org

Montpelier, the home of James Madison, the fourth president, is about 25 miles north of Monticello. It was also designed by Jefferson and originally embodied his classical vision. Later owners, including the Du Pont family, expanded and significantly altered the original structure. Now maintained by the National Trust for Historic Preservation, Montpelier exemplifies American architecture during both the Federal period at the beginning of the nineteenth century and the Gilded Age of great wealth at the close.

Getting there From Washington, follow directions for Charlottesville as far as Culpeper (*see above*), then take US 15 for 20 miles to Orange.

Montpelier is four miles south on State Route 20 (Constitution Highway).

Morven Park & Oatlands

Morven Park, 17263 Southern Planter Lane, Leesburg, VA, (1-703 777 2414). **Open** noon-5pm Tue-Fri; 10am-5pm Sat; 1-5pm Sun. **Admission** $6; $3-$5 concessions. **Map B2**
Website: www.morvenpark.com
Oatlands, 20850 Oatlands Plantation Lane, Leesburg, VA (1-703 777 3174). **Open** 10am-5.30pm Mon-Sat; *April-Jan* 1-4.30pm Sun. **Admission** $8; $1-$7 concessions. **Map B2**
Website: www.oatlands.org

Morven Park, located in Leesburg in northern Virginia's wine and hunt country (*see below*), dates from 1781, but the original modest stone house was greatly enlarged during the nineteenth century. The present lavishly furnished Greek Revival mansion includes a Museum of Hounds and Hunting and a collection of horse-drawn carriages. Oatlands, also near Leesburg, was built in 1803 as the plantation house of the Carter family. Extensively renovated in the Greek Revival style during the 1840s, the property passed through several hands before being purchased and restored by the Eustis family in 1903. In 1965 the land was given to the National Trust for Historic Preservation.

Getting there From Washington, the most direct route is US 7 to Leesburg, but traffic congestion and many traffic lights en route make for slow going. Usually faster and much more pleasant – no lights and lovely rolling countryside – is via I-66 to the Dulles Toll Road and its continuation, the Dulles Greenway. Continue east on the bypass to US 7, then west to Old Waterford Road, turning right and continuing for a short distance. Morven is on the right. For Oatlands, backtrack to the US 15 bypass and head west, then take US 15 south for 6 miles. The Oatlands entrance is on the left.

Belair

12207 Tulip Grove Drive, Bowie, MD (301 809 3089). **Open** *office* 8.30am-5pm Mon-Fri/*tours* 1-4pm Thur-Sun. **Admission** $3; $1-$2 concessions.

Belair, located in otherwise forgettable Bowie (map B3) in Washington's Maryland suburbs, about 20 miles from Downtown DC, dates in its oldest parts from 1740. Known as the 'house of governors' because it was home to two provincial and state governors, the 34-room mansion has been restored and furnished with period antiques. Belair has a long association with racing: the first thoroughbreds in America were brought here from England and the stables later produced several Triple Crown winners. The Stable Museum (open Apr-Oct, 1-4pm Sun) is located in the grounds.

Getting there From DC, take New York Avenue (US 50) east toward Annapolis to exit 11A North, Collington Road (State Route 197). Head north 1 mile to Tulip Grove Drive. Turn right at the sign 'Stables'.

Darnall's Chance

14800 Governor Oden Bowie Drive, Upper Marlboro, MD (301 952 8010). **Open** *office* 8.30am-2.30pm Mon-Fri/*tours* noon-4pm Sun. **Admission** $3; $1-$2 concessions.

Darnall's Chance was built in 1704 by a relative of the Calvert family, Maryland's titled English founders. Then surrounded by an estate of more than 100 acres, the house is now in the centre of the town of Upper Marlboro (map B3). It was the birthplace of several members of Maryland's illustrious Carroll family, including a signatory of the Constitution and America's first Roman Catholic bishop. The original red-brick mansion was extensively remodelled during the nineteenth century in the Greek Revival style. In private hands until the 1970s, it is now a state historical site.

Getting there From Washington, take Pennsylvania Avenue east (which becomes Maryland State Route 4) and head 9 miles beyond the Beltway to the Upper Marlboro exit. Turn left at the bottom of the ramp on to Water Street. Continue to Main Street, where Water becomes Elm Street, then bends to the right and becomes Governor Oden Bowie Drive.

Winterthur

State Route 52, Winterthur, DE 19735 (1-302 888 4600/1-800 448 3883). **Open** 9am-5pm Mon-Sat; noon-5pm Sun. **Admission** $8; $4-$6 concessions; *guided tours* $13; $9-$11 concessions. **Map A4**
Website: www.winterthur.org

Located about 116 miles north-east of Washington, in the beautiful Brandywine Valley north of Wilmington, Winterthur is best combined with a visit to Baltimore (it's about an hour and a half further along I-95). Antiquity is not the big thing about Winterthur. Art is. The original three-storey Greek Revival mansion was built in 1838 for an heiress of the Du Pont family, which remains in possession and has filled it with American decorative arts from 1640-1860. Winterthur, greatly expanded over the years, was opened to the public as a house museum in 1951. Tours of the buildings and 60-acre naturalistic garden are by appointment.

Getting there From DC, take I-95 north to exit 7 in Wilmington (about 110 miles). Exit at Pennsylvania Avenue, which becomes Kennett Pike and then State Route 52. Winterthur is 6 miles from the exit.

Useful information

Charlottesville/Albemarle Convention & Visitors Bureau

PO Box 178, 600 College Drive, Charlottesville, VA 22902 (1-804 977 1783). **Open** *summer* 9am-5.30pm, *winter* 9am-5pm, daily.
Hotel information is also available.
Website: www.charlottesvilletourism.org

Association for the Preservation of Virginia Antiquities

204 West Franklin Street, Richmond, VA 23220 (1-804 648 1889). **Open** 9am-5pm Mon-Fri.
Information on 24 historic houses statewide.
Website: www.apva.org

James River plantations

On a 20-mile stretch of scenic State Route 5 between Richmond and Williamsburg is a string of historic plantation houses, set like jewels in a necklace along the James River (map E2/3). All are still privately owned (some occupied by descendants of the original owners) and open to the public – although in some cases only at specific times or by appointment. While it is theoretically possible to take a (very) quick look at one or two on a day visit to Richmond, anything more requires an overnight stay. Admission to each house averages $8.50, less for children and seniors.

The *Annabel Lee* (1-804 644 5700) offers cruises on the James River with stops – on Tuesdays only – at several of these houses; departures are from the Intermediate Terminal on Dock Street in Richmond. You can also view the homes and nearby Civil War battlefields from the air with Historic Air Tours (1-800 822 9247) in Williamsburg.

Driving from Richmond toward Williamsburg, the first house you come to is **Shirley Plantation** (501 Shirley Plantation Road; 1-804 829 5121), the oldest plantation in Virginia, dating from 1613, although work on the present house did not begin until 1713. Open 9am to 5pm daily, it is noted for its unusual 'flying' staircase, which rises three storeys from the centre hall without visible means of support. The family (tenth and 11th generations) is still in residence.

Next comes **Berkeley Plantation** (12602 Harrison Landing Road; 1-804 829 6018), said to be the site of America's first Thanksgiving observance in 1619. The present 1726 house (open 9am to 5pm daily) is the ancestral home of the Harrison family, which produced two US presidents and a signatory of the Declaration of Independence. The terraced boxwood gardens are of special note.

Nearby is **Westover** (*pictured below*) (7000 Westover Road; 1-804 829 2882), built in the 1730s by William Byrd II, and known for its elegant proportions and sweeping view of the James River. The house is open during Historic Garden Week in April and for group tours by appointment, but the grounds and gardens are open 9am to 6pm daily. Originally part of Byrd's own holdings, **Evelynton** (6701 John Tyler Highway; 1-804 829 5075/website www.evelyntonplantation.org). Open 9am to 5pm daily, this Georgian Revival house has been the home since the1840s of the Ruffin family, one of whose members is reputed to have fired the first shot in the American Civil War.

A relatively modest mansion compared with its neighbours, **Belle Air Plantation** (11800 John Tyler Highway; 1-804 829 2431) dates from the 1670s and contains what is said to be the finest Jacobean stairway in the US. It is open only for group tours by appointment. At the end of the line is **Sherwood Forest Plantation** (14501 John Tyler Highway; 1-804 829 5377/website www.sherwoodforest.org), the home of John Tyler, the tenth president. The restored 1730s frame house, furnished with his possessions, is still occupied by a descendant and is open 9am to 5pm daily.

Getting there From Washington, head south on I-95 to Richmond (120 miles), then take State Route 5 east. The plantations are clustered a few miles to the west and east of Charles City. Entrances are marked.

The climactic battle of the Revolution took place at **Yorktown** *and is re-enacted yearly.*

War Sites

The peaceful countryside outside the urban concentrations belies the Washington area's blood-drenched history. Key battles in all three wars that have taken place on American soil happened within relatively short distances of DC. This is especially true of the Civil War (1861-65), in which more Americans perished on both sides than in all other conflicts in which the country has been engaged combined. Sites associated with the two 'English' wars, the American Revolution and what Americans know as the War of 1812, are less numerous but still historically significant. The battlefields described below are in roughly chronological order, according to the dates of the conflicts. Most have visitor centres and helpful explanatory signs.

Yorktown Colonial National Historical Park

PO Box 210, Colonial Parkway & State Route 238, Yorktown, VA 23690 (1-757 898 3400). **Open** *winter* 8.30am-5pm, *summer* 8.30am-5.30pm, daily. **Admission** $4; free under-17s.

Yorktown (map E3), on the York River 12 miles south-east of Williamsburg, was the location of the climactic land and sea battle of the American Revolution. British General Charles Cornwallis, besieged by a combined American and French army under General George Washington and cut off from reinforcement by the victory of French ships over a British flotilla at the entrance to Chesapeake Bay, was compelled to surrender on 19 October 1781. Siege works and the house where the surrender terms were negotiated can be seen on self-guided tours.

Getting there From Washington, take I-95 south to Richmond, then I-64 east to Williamsburg exit 242B (about 140 miles). Take State Route 199 east to Colonial Parkway and follow signs to Yorktown.

Fort McHenry

End of East Fort Avenue, Baltimore, MD 21230 (1-410 962 4290). **Open** *winter* 8am-5pm, *summer* 8am-8pm, daily. **Admission** $5; free under-17s. *Website: www.nps.gov/fomc*

Fort McHenry, at the entrance to Baltimore's Inner Harbor (map B3), was not the decisive battle of the next British-American dust-up, but it has its place in history. In this engagement, the Americans were the defenders against a British naval force attempting to take the city. Bombarded throughout the day and night of 14 September 1814, the fort held out and the British ships withdrew. Not only was Baltimore saved, but the Americans gained a national anthem. Francis Scott Key, a young lawyer who happened to be aboard one of the British ships to negotiate the release of a captured friend, was inspired by the sight of his country's badly torn flag still flying at dawn on the 14th to write the lyrics of 'The Star Spangled Banner'. Restored to its appearance at the time of the siege, Fort McHenry is now a National Monument and Historic Shrine.

Getting there Follow directions from Washington to Baltimore's Harborplace (*see p236*). From Harborplace, take Light Street south to Key Highway, following the blue and green signs for the fort to Lawrence Street. Turn south on Lawrence, then east on East Fort Avenue to the National Monument park. There is also a shuttle-boat service (every half-hour, 8am-8pm summer, 8am-5pm winter) from Light Street on the Inner Harbor. The voyage takes about an hour.

Fort Washington Park

13551 Fort Washington Road, Fort Washington, MD 20744 (301 763 4600). **Open** sunrise-sunset daily. **Admission** $4 per vehicle. *Website: www.nps.gov/fowa*

Fort Washington, on the Maryland side of the Potomac River between Washington and Mount Vernon, is notable for what didn't happen. Built to protect the city from attack by sea, the fort proved useless in 1814 when British forces captured and burned Washington. The problem was not the fort but the location. The British cleverly decided to sail up an undefended parallel river, the Patuxent, and march overland a few miles to Washington. So much for preparedness. The present fort on the site, replacing the original, dates from 1824 and is considered a choice example of early nineteenth-century coastal fortifications.

Getting there From Downtown Washington, take South Capitol Street, which becomes State Route 210 in Maryland. Continue on State Route 210 to Fort Washington Road. The fort is 3½ miles west.

Manassas National Battlefield Park

6511 Sudley Road, Manassas, VA 22110 (1-703 361 1339). **Open** 8.30am-5pm daily. **Admission** $2; free under-17s. **Map B2**
Website: www.nps.gov/mana

Manassas/Bull Run is one of several Civil War engagements given different names by the opposing sides. In the South, the preference was the nearest community – in this case, Manassas, a railroad junction 25 miles south-west of Washington. In the North, it was the nearest significant stream – hence, Bull Run. There were two battles here.

At the very beginning of the war, in July 1861, a Union force moved on rebel-held Manassas. So confident of victory was the Washington elite that gentlemen and their ladies, packing picnic lunches, rode out in carriages to watch the spectacle. The Northerners were routed in a ten-hour battle by a spirited Confederate counterattack, sending the excursionists racing back to the city in panic. It was déjà vu when larger and more experienced armies clashed in August of the following year – without spectators this time. The convincing Southern victory set the stage for an invasion of the North.

Getting there From Downtown Washington, take I-66 west 25 miles to exit 47 and head north on State Route 234 a half-mile to the battlefield visitor centre.

Antietam/Sharpsburg

PO Box 158, State Route 65, Sharpsburg, MD 21782 (1-301 432 5124). **Open** *winter* 8.30am-5pm, *summer* 8.30am-6pm, daily. **Admission** $2 individual; $4 family; free under-17s. **Map A2**
Website: www.nps.gov/anti

This conflict is known in the North by the first name – a creek that was the focus of much of the fighting. In the South, the nearby town of Sharpsburg gets the nod. The battle here in mountainous western Maryland was the first Confederate attempt to invade the North and saw the bloodiest single day of the entire war on 17 September 1862, when the dead, wounded and missing of both sides exceeded 23,000.

Emboldened by his victory at Second Manasses, General Robert E Lee had moved north but was met by a superior Union force. Neither side could claim a clear victory, but Lee's losses were so severe that he was forced to withdraw to Virginia. There was a crucial diplomatic consequence. The British government, poised to recognise the Confederacy, decided to wait a bit. It also gave President Lincoln the opportunity to issue the Emancipation Proclamation, freeing all slaves in states in rebellion against the Union.

Getting there There are several possible routes from Washington, but the simplest is to take I-270 north to Frederick, join I-70 and continue north to exit 29 (about 75 miles). Head south for 10 miles on State Route 65 to the battlefield.

Fredericksburg National Military Park

1013 Lafayette Boulevard, Fredericksburg, VA 22401 (1-540 373 6122). **Open** *winter* 9am-5pm Mon-Fri; 9am-6pm Sat, Sun; *summer* 8.30am-6.30pm daily. **Admission** $3; free under-17s. **Map C2**
Website: www.nps.gov/frsp

Fredericksburg, located roughly halfway between Washington and Richmond, was the setting of the next confrontation between the two armies. Seeing an opportunity to launch a general offensive against a weakened Lee, Union commanders struck at the strategically situated town on the Rappahannock River in mid-December. Delayed in crossing the river, the Union forces were repulsed by the Confederate defenders. Although casualties were relatively light by Civil War standards, the three-day battle allowed Lee to recoup and prepare to resume the offensive.

The site is part of the Fredericksburg & Spotsylvania National Military Park, which also includes the nearby Chancellorsville, Wilderness and Spotsylvania Court House battlefields.

Getting there From Washington, take I-95 south to Fredericksburg, exit 130 (about 55 miles), then State Route 3 east 1½ miles to Lafayette Boulevard. Turn left and continue for about half a mile to the visitor centre.

Chancellorsville National Military Park

9001 Plank Road, Chancellorsville, VA 22407 (1-540 786 2880). **Open** *winter* 9am-5pm Mon-Fri; 9am-6pm Sat, Sun; *summer* 8.30am-6.30pm daily. **Admission** $3; free under-17s. **Map C2**
Website: www.nps.gov/frsp

Chancellorsville took place south of Fredericksburg in late April and early May of the following year. The ten-day engagement was a stunning Confederate victory over a Union army more than twice as large, thwarting the Northern drive on the Confederate capital and emboldening General Robert E Lee to launch his second invasion of the North two months later. It was also a grievous loss for the South, with the accidental fatal shooting by his own men of General 'Stonewall' Jackson, Lee's most effective commander. There is a visitor centre at the battlefield.

Getting there From Washington, take I-95 south to Fredericksburg, exit 130 (about 55 miles), then State Route 3 west 7 miles to Chancellorsville.

Gettysburg National Military Park

97 Taneytown Road, Gettysburg, PA 17325 (1-717 334 1124 ext 422). **Open** 8am-5pm daily. **Admission** free. **Map A2**
Website: www.nps.gov/gett

Gettysburg was the consequence of Chancellorsville and, in retrospect, the turning point of the war. The battle broke out by accident at a time and site (a small town in southern Pennsylvania) chosen by neither side. Hoping to deliver a devastating blow to Northern morale by defeating the Union army on its own ground, General Lee had moved north with a large force. Always short of supplies and hearing that there was a large supply of shoes in Gettysburg, the Confederates sent a scouting party into the town on the morning of 1 July 1863. They encountered an advance patrol of Union General George Meade's Army of the Potomac and the battle was on.

The struggle continued for four days, with the Southerners driving Meade's men back. But Union lines held and on 4 July, Lee, having suffered heavy losses, was forced to withdraw. It was the bloodiest battle of the war, claiming more than 50,000 casualties. After Gettysburg, Lee was in constant retreat, scoring successes that proved to be only delaying actions. Britain, along with France, lost all enthusiasm for recognising the Confederacy. In November, President Abraham Lincoln journeyed to the battlefield to dedicate a National Cemetery and deliver his Gettysburg Address, a brief but eloquent oration considered the greatest ever delivered by an American.

Getting there Gettysburg is a two-hour drive from Washington. From the Beltway, take I-270 north to Frederick, Maryland (47 miles), then US 15 north to Gettysburg (36 miles).

Wilderness & Spotsylvania Court House

Wilderness Battlefield National Military Park, State Route 20, Wilderness, VA 22407 **Map C2***; Spotsylvania Court House Battlefield, State Route 613, Spotsylvania, VA 22553* (*1-540 786 2880/373 6122).* **Map D2**
Both **Open** *winter* 9am-5pm Mon-Fri; 9am-6pm Sat, Sun; *summer* 8.30am-6.30pm daily. **Admission** $3; free under-17s.
Website: www.nps.gov/frsp

Wilderness, an aptly named tangle of jungle-like overgrowth a few miles west of Chancellorsville, was the beginning of the end for the Confederacy. Abraham Lincoln had at long last found his winning general in Ulysses S Grant, who battled General Lee's depleted army for two days at the beginning of May 1864. Shelling set fire to the woods, incinerating many of the wounded. Neither side gained the advantage but Grant launched the battle plan he followed to the end, continuing to move forward toward Richmond whether he could claim victory or not.

Spotsylvania Court House battle, beginning just two days after Wilderness, continued for two weeks, claiming some 30,000 casualties. Again, neither side gained the edge, but Grant ground forward.

Before visiting the sites, it's a good idea to drop into the visitor centre at nearby Chancellorsville battlefield (*see p243*) or the main visitor centre in the town of Fredericksburg (1013 Lafayette Boulevard; 1-540 373 6122).

Getting there For Wilderness, follow directions to Chancellorsville (*see p243*), then continue west on State Route 3 for another 6 miles. To reach Spotsylvania from Wilderness, head back (east) on State Route 3 and turn right (south) on State Route 613 (Brock Road). It's 10 miles to the battlefield.

Petersburg National Battlefield

1539 Hickory Hill Road, Petersburg, VA 23803 (1-804 732 3531). **Open** 8am-5pm daily. **Admission** *winter* $3 person; $5 vehicle; *summer* $5 individual; $10 vehicle. **Map E2**
Website: www.nps.gov/pete

Petersburg, a railroad hub through which supplies moved to Richmond, 23 miles to the north, was Union General Grant's next target. He began a ten-month siege in June 1864. At one point, Union volunteers from Pennsylvania's coal mines dug a 500-foot shaft beneath the Confederate lines and packed it with powder. The resulting explosion killed hundreds of Southern soldiers. Only the failure of Union troops to follow through quickly saved the city. The crater left by the blast can be seen today. Robert E Lee was finally forced to withdraw on the night of 2 April 1865. Casualties on both sides totalled some 70,000.

Getting there From Washington, take I-95 south for about 135 miles to the Wythe Street exit in Petersburg (State Route 36). Head east 2 miles to the battlefield entrance.

Richmond National Battlefield Park

3215 East Broad Street, Richmond, VA 23223 (1-804 226 1981). **Open** 9am-5pm daily. **Admission** free.
Website: www.nps.gov/rich

Richmond (map E2), the primary Union goal, was a continuing battle for more than three years. It was launched early in May 1862 with the Peninsular Campaign when the Union used its naval superiority to land troops via Chesapeake Bay on the peninsula between the James and York rivers below Richmond. Overcoming strong Confederate resistance at Yorktown and Williamsburg, the drive was within six miles of the Confederate capital when General Lee, taking over as commander, counter-attacked. He relieved pressure on the city in a series of engagements called the Seven Days Battles, but was unable to dislodge Northern forces from the peninsula. The campaign is particularly notable for the first battle between iron-clad warships, the Union *Monitor* and the Confederate *Virginia* (originally a captured Union wooden ship, the *Merrimac*, which had been fitted with armour plate). It was a draw, but changed naval history.

All told, the Union made six attempts to take Richmond before Ulysses S Grant's Overland campaign, launched in 1864, succeeded. With the fall of Petersburg the following year, the capital

became indefensible and was evacuated. General Lee surrendered to Grant one week later.
Getting there From Washington, take I-95 south to Richmond (110 miles). Take Broad Street (US 60) east for just under 2 miles to the park's visitor's centre.

Wine & Hunt Country

Middleburg (map B2) is a pretty little town with a long history, nestled into the rolling, wooded Virginia countryside an easy hour's drive west of Downtown DC. It is also the heart of the state's (actually, as the locals see it, the nation's) horse and hunt country and in the centre of Virginia's most bountiful wine-producing area. There are vineyards throughout the state – by current count more than 50 – but most are in the area of northern and central Virginia in which Middleburg lies.

Both US 50 – in colonial days a stagecoach road from Virginia's settled coast to the frontier west and now the quick connection to DC – and the meandering side roads off it are lined with the white-painted fences that identify horse farms. Many are estates called home by people who belong to the upper reaches of the American elite. This is where Jackie O partied and rode to hounds with assorted bluebloods, as remembered by a gazebo on a downtown street with a plaque that reads: 'This pavilion is dedicated to the memory of Jacqueline Kennedy Onassis and her happy years in the village. October 1995.' Hang around long enough and you're sure to see a pick-up truck or two with horse trailer in tow.

As for the town itself, it doesn't look like much at first – essentially one street with one stoplight. But check out the shops lining that street and it's quickly clear that this isn't your average, every-day village of some 600 souls. The concentration of pricey boutiques may not exactly rival Beverly Hills' Rodeo Drive, but if you don't keep the impulse to buy under firm control your cheque-book may not know the difference.

Tully Rector (13 East Washington Street; 1-540 687 5858) is the standout among several apparel shops that will be delighted, for a price, to dress you as if you were to the hunt country born. Everything is terribly tasteful, tweed and cashmere in muted shades of brown, grey and – for the truly daring – burgundy. At **Estates of Middleburg** (105B West Washington Street; 1-540 687 8027), you can get a glimpse of how some of the better houses in the area are – or were – furnished. Proprietor Saundra Rose-Lasley, who says she's been doing business in Middleburg 'forever', is the dealer of choice when the gentry wants to clear out some clutter. At **Devonshire** (17 East Washington Street; 1-540 687 5990), also known as 'the English garden shop', which has outlets in other enclaves of affluence such as New York's Hamptons and Florida's Palm Beach, they know about clutter. The two upper floors and a basement are an obstacle course of outdoor furniture and decorative *objets*.

Horse-focused events, as might be expected, dominate the local calendar. Connections, not to mention proper togs, are necessary to get in on the hunt action, but anyone can watch the morning workouts of thoroughbred race horses. The best place to do so is **Middleburg Training Center** (1-540 687 3041), which has a mile-long dirt track and barns with large turn-out paddocks. On the last weekend in May, a **Hunt Country Stable Tour** of a dozen choice horse farms is sponsored by Upperville Trinity Church (1-540 592 3711).

The public is also welcome at the spring and autumn steeplechasing meets at **Glenwood Park** in Middleburg. In summer, there are polo matches every Friday night at **Great Meadow** (1-540 253 5001) in nearby The Plains (map B2), and frequent horse shows throughout the area. Other equestrian events are held year round at nearby Leesburg (map B2), Warrenton (map C2) and, considering the social status of most of the locals, the very appropriately named Upperville (map B2), which claims to be home to the oldest horse show in America. For information on horse farms and what's coming up where, contact the visitor bureaus and organisations listed below.

If you want to go riding yourself, there are many bridle trails, but most are of the bring-your-own-horse variety. The notable exception is **Marriott Ranch** (*see page 248*) in Hume (map B1), which also has an inn and historic manor house on 4,200 scenic acres.

Back to wine – Virginia is the number six wine producer in the US and three wineries offering tastings are on the outskirts of Middleburg or just beyond. **Swedenburg Estate Vineyard** (23595 Winery Lane; 1-540 687 5219) is just off US 50 as you approach Middleburg from the east. **Piedmont Vineyards & Winery** (2546C Halfway Road; 1-540 687 5528/website www.piedmontwines.com) is three miles south of town on State Route 626. **Meredyth Vineyards** (2814 Logans Mill Road; 1-540 687 6277) is a bit more of a challenge. The entrance is off State Route 679, a gravel road some three miles from State Route 626. Both Piedmont and Meredyth have picnic facilities and the latter has an especially fine view of distant hills and woods.

Further afield is **Louden Valley Vineyards** (38638 Old Wheatland Road, Waterford, VA; 1-540 882 3375), north of Leesburg, which also has basic picnic-makings available – warm French bread and a small wheel of Brie or Camembert – to go with a bottle of whatever strikes a taster's fancy. All to be consumed, when the weather is right, on

Swanky shops and elegant eateries fill the tree-lined streets of **Middleburg**.

a sunny terrace overlooking the vineyards and nearby hills and vales.

South is **Prince Michel & Rapidan River Vineyards** (Leon, VA, 1-800 869 8242/website www.princemichel.com), off US 29 nine miles south of Culpeper (map C1), which is a bit more than halfway between Washington and Charlottesville. Picnics are not Prince Michel's thing (*horreur*!) – a noted French restaurant is. There is also a small hotel.

Eating & drinking

Middleburg has several more-than-just-adequate restaurants. The best known is the historic **Red Fox Inn** (2 East Washington Street; 1-540 687 6301), which claims to be the 'oldest original inn in America'. Think Jackie O if you dine in the charming restaurant with beamed ceiling and adjacent tack room bar – the place was a particular favourite of hers. However, the talk is that the food – upscale American with Continental flourishes – has since slipped a bit.

Many locals now prefer the **Hidden Horse Tavern** (7 West Washington Street; 1-540 687 3828). It's less elegant but serves a similar cuisine and has a pleasant bar. The Fox still gets the nod for the wine list, however. There's much more to the **Black Coffee Bistro** (101 South Madison Street; 1-540 687 3632) than the name suggests. A newcomer to town, it serves lunch and dinner from a kitchen that strives to be different, frequently to good effect. Even newer is the **Railstop** (647B Main Street; 1-540 253 5644) in The Plains, seven miles south of Middleburg via State Route 626. The proprietor is Robert Duvall, the Oscar-winning actor and a noted tango aficionado. Seriously. He dances publicly (for instance, at a White House state dinner for the visiting president of Argentina), if not exactly professionally. No surprise, then, that the beef-dominated menu has an Argentine flavour.

If your only interest is staving off starvation until you get back to DC, try the basic American diner fare at the **Coach Stop** (9 East Washington Street; 1-540 687 5515) or **Mosby's Tavern** (2 West Marshall Street; 1-540 687 5282), both in Middleburg. The latter is an adjunct operation of the Red Fox.

Getting there

By car

From Downtown Washington, take I-66 west to US 50, exit 57B. Continue on US 50 for another 22 miles to Middleburg.

Useful information

Loudoun Tourism Council

108D South Street SE, Leesburg, VA 20175 (1-703 771 2170/1-800 752 6118). **Open** 9am-5pm daily. *Website: www.visitloudoun.org*

Pink Box Visitor's Center

PO Box 187, 12 North Madison Street, Middleburg, VA 20118 (1-540 687 8888). **Open** 11am-3pm Mon-Fri; 11am-4pm Sat, Sun.
Website: www.middleburgonline.com

Warrenton-Fauquier County Visitor Center

183A Keith Street, Warrenton, VA 20186 (1-540 347 4414/1-800 820 1021). **Open** 9am-5pm daily.

Virginia Thoroughbred Association

38 Garrett Street, Warrenton, VA 20198 (1-540 347 4313).

The Great Outdoors

You might think that the greater Washington-Baltimore metropolitan area, the fourth largest population concentration in the entire US, with more than seven million inhabitants, might be a bit short on mountain greenery and other bucolic delights. You would be wrong. Within easy reach of the area's urban centres are some truly wondrous natural settings – and we're not just talking wine and hunt country. Nor Maryland's fabulous Chesapeake Bay and shore areas – that's a separate topic (*see page 249*).

Virginia

Great Falls & Riverbend Parks

Located ten miles north-west of Downtown DC, across the Potomac River, is the relaxed recreational area of **Great Falls Park** (map B2; 703 285 2966). Set at the point where the foaming river races through an obstacle course of massive boulders, the park has hiking and bridle trails, picnic facilities and a visitor's centre with historical and geological exhibits. Adjoining **Riverbend Park** (703 759 9018) is less developed. Aside from a visitor's centre with minimal exhibits on local wildlife, there's not much there except a boat ramp and some ten miles of trails, but it's a great place for nature walks and bird-watching. There are guided walks on a random schedule; call for details.

Getting there From Downtown, take either the 14th Street Bridge or Theodore Roosevelt Memorial Bridge across the Potomac to the George Washington Memorial Parkway. Take the Parkway north to the intersection with State Route 123. Exit on to 123 west and continue to Georgetown Pike (State Route 193). Continue on the Pike another 12 miles to the entrances to Great Falls and Riverbend parks, on the right.

Shenandoah National Park & around

The undisputed jewel among the Capital Area's easily accessible outdoor attractions is **Shenandoah National Park** (map C1; 1-540 999 3500). Straddling Virginia's Blue Ridge Mountains for more than 100 miles, the park takes its name from the valley and river to the immediate west of the craggy range. Shenandoah, in the language of the native Americans occupying the area when the first European interlopers arrived, translates roughly as 'daughter of the stars'. The park's visual delights include sweeping views, swift mountain streams, waterfalls and mountain valleys shadowed by forested peaks, some of which rise to more than 4,000 feet.

Skyline Drive follows the crest of the range for the entire length of the park. There are 75 overlooks along the route where motorists may pull off to take in the views. In the autumn, changing foliage puts on a spectacularly colourful show, usually peaking during the last weeks of October. Traffic at that time can bring to mind rush hour in DC, and there is a lesser visitor peak in the spring when the azaleas and dogwoods bloom. But for most of the year, the park is a refuge from urban stress, laced with more than 500 miles of trails. Some permit horses, which can be rented at **Skyland Stables** (Skyland Lodge; 1-540 999 2210). Fishing is allowed in some streams.

Dining and overnight facilities (except in winter) are available at **Skyland Lodge** and the more rustic **Great Meadows Lodge** (Shenandoah National Park Lodges, PO Box 727, Luray, VA 22835; 1-800 999 4714). There are also cabins to rent and campgrounds. Current accessible areas and other information can be obtained at park entrances and several visitor centres along Skyline Drive. Or visit the park's website at www.nps.gov/shen. Park admission is $10 per vehicle.

Nearby **Massanutten Mountain** (1-540 289 9441) in the George Washington National Forest (map B1) has great scenery and several hundred miles of trails for hiking as well as riding and biking. Also in the area are several underground caverns accessible to the public. The most developed is **Luray Caverns** (map C1; 1-540 743 6551/website www.luraycaverns.com), a mile south of the town of Luray, with hour-long guided tours through the stalactites and stalagmites. Other options are **Endless Caverns** (map C1; 1-540 896 2283/website www.endlesscavern.com) for which, to date, no end has been located, and **Shenandoah Caverns** (map C1; 1-540 477 3115/website www.svta.org), both off I-81 in the vicinity of nearby New Market.

The Shenandoah, as well as the Tidewater area east of Fredericksburg, are also big on river sport. Take your pick – canoe, kayak, raft or tube – numerous outfitters are ready to to set you up for a whitewater adventure or a leisurely float. In Bentonville, try **Shenandoah River Outfitters** (6502 South Page Valley Road; 1-540 743 4159/website www.shenandoahriver.com) or **Downriver Canoe Company** (884 Indian Hollow Road; 1-540 635 5526/ website www.downriver.com). In Fredericksburg, **Friends of the Rappahannock** (1-540 373 3448/ website www. crrl.org/for) offers canoe river tours. **Front Royal Canoe Co** in Front Royal (PO Box 473; 1-540 635 5440/website www.frontroyalcanoe.com) rents kayaks.

Getting there Of the several entrances to Shenandoah National Park, the most convenient from Washington is at the park's northern tip, 90 minutes or less via I-66 to exit 6, then south 3 miles on US 340 to Front Royal.

Maryland

Catoctin Mountain Park

Maryland has its own back-to-nature retreat, although on a much smaller scale than Shenandoah, in **Catoctin Mountain Park** (map A2). Located near the small town of Thurmont (about 90 minutes by car from Washington or Baltimore), it is not so much nature preserved as restored. Farmers, loggers and others scratching a living from the land had pretty much denuded the area before the National Park Service acquired it in 1935. Since then, the park – now about 5,700 acres – has been returned to something like its original wooded state.

Some of the park's neighbours, and their frequent visitors, give it a cachet that even Shenandoah might envy. The park wraps around **Camp David**, the rustic retreat of American presidents. This is where Jimmy Carter cajoled Menachem Begin and Anwar Sadat into concluding a peace (of sorts) between Israel and Egypt. But trust us, you won't find the exact location pinpointed on any map of the area. What you will find at Catoctin are trees and more trees, hiking and bridle trails, fishing creeks, picnic areas and, in winter, skiing and snowshoeing.

Once the haunt of moonshiners during America's spectacularly unsuccessful attempt to swear off the bottle (1919-33), the park has preserved the Blue Blazes Still as an artefact of the so-called 'Noble Experiment'. Park rangers conduct demonstrations (no samples) on weekends during spring and autumn. Maps, trail guides and information on current park events can be obtained at the visitor's centre (6602 Foxville Road, Thurmont; 1-301 663 9388) off State Route 77.

Should hunger strike and you aren't prepared to picnic, you might want to check out the **Cozy Country Inn** (103 Frederick Road, Thurmont; 1-301 271 4301/website www.cozyvillage.com). You can also stay overnight, in rooms named after Winston Churchill and other world figures who have dropped in at Camp David over the years.

Getting there From Washington's Beltway, take I-270 north to Frederick. Continue north on US 15 for 17 miles, exiting on to State Route 77 just south of Thurmont. The park entrance and visitor's centre are 2 miles to the west.

Little Bennett Regional Park

Closer in to Washington, **Little Bennett Regional Park** has almost the acreage (3,500) of Catoctin but is much less developed. Other than 14 miles of tree-shaded trails and a scattering of playgrounds, there is not much in the way of facilities. But it's a great place to relax in the shade, catch a few rays in the open areas, toss a ball or a frisbee around or even pitch a tent for the night.

Getting there From the Beltway, take I-270 north 16 miles to the Boyds exit at Clarksburg. Bear right at the bottom of the ramp and continue to the stoplight, turning left on to State Route 355. Continue ¼ mile to the park entrance.

Useful information

Luray-Page County Chamber of Commerce

46 E Main Street, Luray, VA 22835 (1-540 743 3915). **Open** 9am-5pm daily.
Website: www.luraypage.com

Marriott Ranch

5305 Marriott Lane, Hume, VA 22639 (1-540 364 2627/1-877 278 4574). **Open** *office* 8am-4.30pm daily; *trail rides* 10am, noon, 2pm, Tue-Sun.
If you're heading towards Shenandoah National Park, you can detour to this ranch for guided horseback trail rides.
Website: www.marriottranch.com

Crab culture

Crabs are the Washington area's quirky culinary delight, an experience as much as a foodstuff. What the pub is to the English village, the marketplace to the Arab town, the crab house is to the Chesapeake Bay region, most particularly the southern reaches of Maryland – a place to hang out, meet and greet, and dawdle over the local cuisine. Steamed crabs enforce leisurely communal meals, since diners work a lot to get a little of the savoury crustaceans. Fast food they are not.

Blue crabs spawn in the southern Chesapeake Bay once the brackish water starts to warm in June, moving up the bay and its 150 tributaries, periodically shedding their shells as they grow. A crab caught during the few hours between shedding its old shell and growing a new one is a 'softshell', capable of being cooked and devoured in toto. 'Hardshells' over legal minimum size are a decidedly different dish. The cycle ends late in autumn, although some crab houses extend their seasons with imports from down South.

Steamed in spicy 'crab boil' (Old Bay is the standard brand) and water or beer, hardshells turn bright red. Served with hush puppies (sweet fried dough balls), corn on the cob and beer or iced tea, the crustaceans come heaped by the dozen on trays set on tables covered with utilitarian brown paper, with cups of vinegar or melted butter for dipping. Knives and mallets are standard tableware.

Then the fun begins, as diners smash and pry

Maryland Department of Natural Resources

580 Taylor Avenue, Annapolis, MD 21401 (Parks Service 1-410 260 8186; Forest Service 1-410 260 8531; Wildlife 1-410 260 8540; Fisheries 1-410 260 8250). **Open** 8.30am-4.30pm Mon-Fri.
Hiking, camping and fishing information.

Shenandoah Valley Visitors Center & Travel Association

PO Box 1040, 277 West Old Cross Road, New Market, VA 22844 (1-540 740 3132).
Open 9am-5pm daily.
Website: www.shenandoah.org

Virginia State Parks, Department of Conservation & Recreation

PO Box 1895, 217 Governor Street, room 212, Richmond, VA 23218 (1-800 933 7275).
Open 8am-8pm Mon-Fri; 10am-4pm Sat.
Hiking and camping information.
Website: www.state.va.us

the crusty shells open, discard the poisonous dendrae, suck meat from the spindly legs, rend the meaty claws, then break the membrane to expose the breast meat. Much labour yields only a little meat, but that's the idea. People hack and crack and joke and take forever to consume their crabs, always pondering whether there's room for a dozen more. It's great fun and incredibly messy. Some crab shacks offer all-you-can-eat fixed-price feasts, but with cruel time limitations.

If the mechanics seem daunting, neophytes don't lack help. Crab-cracking instructions adorn placemats and menus, even coffee mugs. Better, the staff and friendly habitués of genuine crab houses commonly delight in initiating clueless newcomers. Crab gab may be harder to master. For instance, serving 'sooks' (egg-bearing females) is frowned upon; one eats 'jimmies', inevitably expendable males. These terms are important, since they are often used to distinguish men's and women's restrooms.

Baltimore boasts many great crab houses, Washington some, but the quintessential crabberies adorn the little waterside towns, where the crabs are brought fresh off the boat. On the Bay, **Abner's** (1-410 257 3689) in Chesapeake Beach, Maryland, is one of the closer classic specimens to DC, about 25 minutes by car. Pope's Creek, Maryland, a 45-minute drive down the Potomac, consists of an abandoned power plant and three crab houses: **The Original Robertson's Crabhouse** (1-301 934 3300), **Captain Billy's** (1-301 932 4323) and, across the creek, **Pier III** (1-301 259 4514). The latter is the zippiest, with an outdoor band stage, beach volleyball and palm trees trucked in annually to the ersatz-tropical sand beach for a party mood.

Yet traditional arrangements prevail even here. Several generations of a family may swarm a table, all lustily pounding hardshells. The next table may seat demurely jolly nuns from this heavily Catholic region, while the next throbs with brash, bikini-clad teenyboppers. It gets hard to hear the music over the clatter and chatter, but the leisurely exuberance is contagious.

Chesapeake Bay & the Maryland Shore

When the talk turns to the great outdoors, Maryland's Chesapeake Bay and shore areas are in a category of their own. Most of Maryland is defined by water, especially the Bay. Geographically, it divides the state east and west, but in all other respects it is the focus of Maryland's identity. The long finger of water reaching northward from the Atlantic makes Baltimore a world port. It also yields year after year an abundant harvest of seafood, notably the famous blue crab (*see above* **Crab culture**). More than a score of rivers emptying into it and many inlets create ideal sites for recreation facilities and nature reserves. And it's all within an hour or so of fast-paced Washington.

Annapolis & the west shore

Queen city of the Bay area is **Annapolis** (map B3), capital of Maryland since 1695 and briefly (1783) of the fledgling United States. A modern city has grown up around the colonial core, but the historic city is for the most part beautifully preserved. The narrow streets around the old harbour are lined with what is claimed to be the largest concentration of Georgian houses in the country. Annapolis is no longer the major port it was when it did a brisk trade with Britain and the West Indies, but the sea remains very much a part of its identity. Marinas, sailing schools and charter services make it a recreational centre. It is also the site of the US Naval Academy. Several tours, self-guided and otherwise, of the historic area are available. Check at the City Dock information booth for details.

As might be expected in a city on the Bay that produces all those crabs and fish, Annapolis has numerous sea-oriented restaurants – some on the

Soak up the spectactular scenery of Virginia's ***Shenandoah Valley****.* *See page 247.*

All very hush hush

Given that government is by far the biggest business in the Washington area, it is no surprise that the military forms a very large component. Apart from uniformed personnel, tens of thousands of civilian employees draw their paychecks from the Department of Defense. What may be more surprising is that some of these key facilities are open – at least to some degree – to the public, and not just those in showpiece city Washington, DC.

Fort Belvoir

9820 Flagler Road, suite 201, Fort Belvoir, VA 22060 (703 545 6700). **Open** 7am-5pm daily.
Map C2

Overlooking the Potomac River near Mount Vernon, Fort Belvoir is home to the Army Intelligence and Security Command, the Defense Mapping School and the Defense Logistics Agency, among other specialised operations. For all that, it is an open post accessible to visitors – with the exception of a restricted mine-warfare training area on the river. The officers' golf club is open to visitors at lunchtime.
Website: www.belvoir.army.mil
Getting there: From Downtown DC, take I-95 south 16 miles to Pence Gate. Maps of the base are available at the visitor's centre.

Quantico

Quantico (map C2) is a largely open facility where US Marines and FBI agents are trained on 60,000 acres of wooded Virginia countryside (this is where Jodie Foster supposedly prepped for her chilling mission in *Silence of the Lambs*). You won't see any of the actual training, which takes place in restricted areas well away from the main roads (among them a full-scale reconstruction of a typical US town centre where live moves are practised) and the scruffy on-base town of Quantico. But you can visit the Marine Corps Air-Ground Museum (1-703 784 2606) – three early aircraft hangars stuffed with hardware used by the Corps in conflicts during its more than two centuries of existence.

rough-and-ready side, others upscale. For the former, check out **McGarvey's** (8 Market Space; 1-410 263 5700) and **O'Brien's** (113 Main Street; 1-410 268 6288), both saloon-type establishments where you're likely to run into off-duty Academy midshipmen. For smarter restaurants, try **Café Normandie** (185 Main Street; 1-410 263 3382), **Middleton Tavern** (2 Market Place; 1-410 263 3323) in a historic building a few paces from City Dock, and **The Treaty of Paris** (16 Church Circle; 1-410 263 6340), also historically housed.

South of Annapolis, the Chesapeake's less publicised west shore stretches more than 100 miles to Point Lookout, where the Potomac River flows into the Bay. Along the way are pleasant beaches at Bay Ridge, Mayo, North Beach, Chesapeake Beach and other points. They may lack the cachet and action of Eastern Shore sun 'n' surf meccas, but are more appealing to many visitors for that very reason.

Towards the end of the peninsula and a few miles inland, lies **St Mary's City** (map D3), fourth-oldest permanent English settlement and first capital of Maryland. **Point Lookout State Park** (map D4; 310 872 5688), located on the site of a pre-Civil War resort, is a popular recreation area with beaches, fishing pier, nature trails and picnic facilities.

If you'd prefer less informal dining, the town of **Ridge**, midway between St Mary's City and Point Lookout, offers a number of options. **Courtney's** (42890 Wynne Road; 1-301 872 4403), **Scheible's Crab Pot** (48342 Wynne Road; 1-301 872 5185) and **Spinnakers** (Miller's Wharf Road; 1-301 872 4340) are all big on local seafood, especially crab cakes in high season (June-August).

Getting there From Downtown DC to Annapolis, take US 50 (decrepit New York Avenue to the city limits) east 30 miles. It's a 45-minute drive out of rush hour. To continue down the west shore from Annapolis, take State Route 2 south, merging with State Route 4 at Sunderland. After crossing the Patuxent River at Town Point, turn south on to State Route 235 and continue to Ridge and Point Lookout. Signs along the way will indicate exits to beaches and St Mary's City.

Eastern Shore

Across the Chesapeake Bay Bridge (map B3/4) from Annapolis is **Eastern Shore**, similar in some respects but also very different from its western counterpart. It is also much better known and more visited. The Eastern Shore occupies the central and largest portion of the Delmarva Peninsula between Chesapeake Bay and the Atlantic Ocean, the peninsula's name derived by combining letters from the three states sharing it. Residents fancy themselves as somewhat apart from the rest of the state, as expressed in a chant usually heard from students after a few beers: 'I don't give a damn for the whole state of Maryland, because I'm from the Eastern Shore.' Whatever, it is a choice piece of real estate. Short but broad rivers empty into the Bay from the east and the shore is fringed with islands, many barely rising above water level, and deeply indented mini-peninsulas.

Getting there From Downtown DC, take either US 1 or I-95 (much faster) south to Quantico (exit 150), then State Route 619 to the base main gate. It's a 45-minute drive (longer in rush hour).

Central Intelligence Agency

The location of the US's foreign intelligence agency, six miles north-west from Downtown Washington in Virginia's suburban Fairfax County, is plainly marked on maps and by a sign at the entrance turn-off from State Route 123.

It wasn't always that way. Back in the most frigid days of the cold war, the sign read 'Bureau of Public Roads' (in fact, the Federal Highway Research Administration, of which said bureau was a part, was, and is, the CIA's next-door neighbour). Of course, that it was also home to the CIA was one of the worst-kept secrets of the long East-West stand-off. Everyone in Washington knew, including the Soviet embassy. Times have changed.

But even in these more open days, the sign and a guardhouse are all you're going to see of the agency. The headquarters building, recently rechristened in honour of former CIA Director and President George HW Bush, is still very much off-limits. It's set back from the road and thickly screened by trees, so not visible from the road.

Getting there From Downtown DC, cross the Potomac River by either the 14th Street or Theodore Roosevelt Memorial Bridges to the George Washington Memorial Parkway. Take the Parkway north to the intersection with State Route 123 (Chain Bridge Road). Take 123 west and after about 1 mile you will pass the CIA sign and entrance. What a thrill!

National Security Agency

This operation, which snoops on electronic communications worldwide, is so secretive it makes the CIA look like an Internet chat room. But, surprisingly, the NSA also operates a **National Cryptologic Museum** (1-301 688 5849) that is open to the public (9am-3pm Mon-Fri; 10am-2pm Sat). Located, along with the NSA, at **Fort George Meade**, halfway between Washington and Baltimore, it has exhibits and equipment tracing the coding craft back to the early seventeenth century, with heavy emphasis on the World War II exploits of both sides.

Getting there From Washington, take the Baltimore-Washington Parkway (Beltway exit 22) 11 miles north to the State Route 32 east exit. At Colony 7 Road turn right and follow signs to the museum.

Wye & Tilghman Islands

Taking some of the more interesting points from north to south, the first reached after crossing the bridge is **Wye Island** (map B4; 1-410 827 7577), site of a state natural resources facility open to the public for hiking, fishing and picnicking. **Tilghman Island** (map C3; 1-410 822 4606), one of the most picturesque points on the Bay, is a few miles to the south. An old fishing community, it is far from having become a mere museum piece. 'Watermen' still set out daily to dredge for oysters, a few in the old, tall-masted sailboats known as skipjacks.

Getting there From Annapolis, follow US 50/301 across the Chesapeake Bay Bridge, remaining on US 50 after US 301 diverges to the north. For **Wye Island**, continue nearly 3 miles, then turn right on to Carmichael Road and continue just over 5 miles to the bridge across Wye Narrows to Wye Island.

For **Tilghman Island**, At the US 50 and US 301 split, continue 16.4 miles on US 50 to the intersection with State Route 322 north of the town of Easton, bearing right and continuing another 2 miles to State Route 33. Continue for 22 miles, through the village of St Michaels and across the Kapps Narrows drawbridge to the island. The road continues another 3 miles to Blackwalnut Point.

Blackwater National Wildlife Refuge & Deal Island

Next stop is **Blackwater National Wildlife Refuge** (map C4; 1-410 228 2677) on a peninsula south of the town of Cambridge (map C4) and east of the adjoining Hooper Islands. The 20,000-acre refuge is considered one of the best areas in the mid-Atlantic region for migratory waterfowl, eagles and a variety of other birds. There are paved roads and two hiking trails. The roads continue into a marshy area recalling the Florida Everglades and two of the three-island Hooper chain.

Further south is **Deal Island** (map D4; Somerset County Tourism 1-800 521 9189), like Tilghman still a commercial fishing centre. Adjoining the community is **Dames Quarter Marsh**, another wildlife preserve especially attractive to bird-watchers.

Getting there From Annapolis, cross the Chesapeake Bay Bridge. For **Blackwater**, at the US 50/301 split, continue south 34 miles to Cambridge, crossing the Choptank River. Take State Route 16 for 7 miles to the intersection of State Route 335. Turn left; it's 5 miles to the visitor centre.

For **Deal Island**, at the US 50/301 split, head south 66 miles to Salisbury. From Salisbury, take US 13 south 12 miles to the intersection of State Route 363 (Deal Island Road) at the town of Princess Anne. Take 363 east 17 miles to Deal Island.

Smith & Tangier Islands

Smith Island (map D4), ten miles offshore, can be reached only by boat, from Crisfield on the mainland. The island is a cluster of islets lying so low that the thought of high tide can make a visitor uneasy. There are three small communities and a rudimentary road system. But it's more fun to get around by foot or bicycle. Several operators provide passenger ship service from Crisfield to Smith Island year-round except during storms or, rarely, when there is ice in the Bay. **Smith Island Cruises** (1-410 425 2771) operates from nearby Somers Cove Marina. There are several restaurants, some open only in warm weather. Accommodations are also available, likewise seasonally. For details, contact the **Smith Island Center** (1-410 425 3351).

At the end of the line – and in waters claimed by the state of Virginia – is **Tangier Island** (map D4; 1-800 863 2338), almost a legend in the Washington area. It claims to be the crab capital not merely of the Bay, but the world. The few hundred inhabitants speak with an accent that linguists have traced to seventeenth-century Cornwall. Also requiring a short cruise, either from Eastern Shore points or the Virginia mainland, Tangier is another still-thriving community of watermen. The town sprawls across three of Tangier's five islets, and as well as the colourful harbour, there is a long sandy beach.

Tangier Island Cruises in Crisfield (1-410 968 2338/1-800 863 2338) sails daily at 12.30pm; tickets are $20, under-12s travel free. The round-trip can be made in a day, but sailing times will give you only a few hours at best on the island. If you can, stay overnight. Eating options include the **Islander** (1-757 891 2249) and Hilda Crockett's **Chesapeake House** (1-757 891 2331), which is also a B&B ($40 a night). You can also stay at **Shirley's Bay View Inn** (1-757 891 2396).

History footnote: Tangier was a base for British operations in Chesapeake Bay during the War of 1812, including the 1814 assault on Fort McHenry and Baltimore. According to local lore, a clergyman warned the departing troops that many 'in all likelihood would die soon', and the mission would fail. He was right.

Getting there From Annapolis, cross the Chesapeake Bay Bridge. For **Smith Island**, follow directions to Princess Anne (*see above*) and continue on US 13 another 5 miles to the Westover exit. Take State Route 413 south to the Crisfield dock.

Excursion boats for **Tangier Island** depart daily from Crisfield Municipal Dock. There is also the 'mail boat', preferred by locals, which is cheaper but more spartan and one-way daily, meaning an overnight stay. Both islands can also be reached by boat from Reedville on the Virginia shoreline.

Useful information

Annapolis & Anne Arundel County Conference & Visitors Bureau

26 West Street, Annapolis, MD (1-410 280 0445). **Open** 9am-5pm Mon-Fri.
Website: www.visit-annapolis.org

Tangier & Chesapeake Cruises

468 Buzzard Point Road, Reedville, VA 22539 (1-804 453 2628). **Open** 8.30am-4.30pm Mon-Sat; 10am-noon Sun.
Website: www.eaglesnest.net/tangier/

METRO CENTER
4 BLOCKS
RED ORANGE & BLUE LINES
M
metro
GALLERY PLACE - CHINATOWN
ELEVATOR
RED YELLOW & GREEN LINES
M
metro

Resources

Resources

The definitive database for travellers to Washington, DC.

For information on abbreviations used in this guide, *see page vi* **About the Guide**. All phone numbers are given as dialled from Washington, DC. If calling from outside the area, dial 1 and the area code 202. All 1-800, 1-888 and 1-877 numbers are free of charge within the USA, though note that your hotel may still bill you a flat fee. Most are also accessible from outside DC and – at the usual international rates – from outside the US.

Getting Around

Orientation

The District of Columbia used to be a perfect ten- by ten-mile diamond, until Virginia took back its land contribution. Now DC's jagged western border is the Potomac River. The District is surrounded by Maryland on all other sides. The DC border is more significant for administrative reasons than geographical: the metro area spreads into the neighbouring states.

The city is divided into four quadrants – NW, NE, SE and SW – which meet at the US Capitol, the geographical centre of Washington. North, South and East Capitol Streets, and the National Mall to the west, radiate out from the Capitol and serve as quadrant dividing lines.

On one level, the District is completely rational in its layout. Numbered streets run north and south on both sides of the Capitol, intersecting lettered streets, with some named streets tossed in, running east to west, for about 50 square blocks. (Note that I Street is also written Eye Street.) The higher the number, and the further on in the alphabet the letter, the further away the street is from the Capitol. This grid system fades when the alphabet ends (when words beginning with A through Z replace the lone letters). But straightforward as this seems, there is a crucial nuance.

Because the naming system radiates from a central point, there are two First Streets (and Second, etc), one on either side of North/South Capitol Street – and ditto for A Street and so on, one north and one south of the mall. This means that there can therefore be four different places, one in each quadrant, where, say, a Fourth Street and a G Street intersect – so it's crucial to know which you're aiming for. This is why we've given the quadrant after every address in our listings, and this is also how you should give directions to a taxi driver (say 'Northwest' not 'NW').

Street numbers correspond to cross streets; thus 800 C Street will be at Eighth Street and, though it's a less exact science, you can figure out that 400 Eighth Street will be at D Street, D being the fourth letter of the alphabet.

And now for the real complication: on top of the grid of lettered and numbered streets are a mess of diagonal avenues, all named after American states – Pennsylvania Avenue, Massachusetts Avenue, etc – that can easily cause drivers and walkers severe disorientation. Some diagonals can be a fast way across town, but most hit confusing traffic circles designed more for horse-and-buggy contraptions than modern travel, or run into parks or important buildings (such as the White House) that cause them to dogleg disconcertingly.

Most hotels provide adequate tourist maps, but much better is the 'ADC Washington DC Visitor's Map' ($2.95), which helpfully shows the shapes of the buildings on the Mall and subway entrances. It's very good for central DC, but shows almost nothing of the NE or SE quadrants and does not include Arlington. Most bookstores stock maps and gas stations have large-scale driving maps. Or visit the terrific **ADC Map & Travel Store** in Downtown (*see page 172* **Shopping**).

You don't need a car in DC. It's a pedestrian-friendly city and most of the main monuments and museums are well served by public transport. Taxis are reasonably priced and easily flagged down in the city centre. Parking in Downtown DC and hot nightspots is often a hassle. A car can be the best way to get out of town though – but beware: this area rivals Los Angeles in its rush-hour hell.

The airports

Three airports serve Washington. **Ronald Reagan National Washington Airport** (the presidential prefix was added recently and is either uttered proudly or dropped deliberately, depending, like much in this town, on politics) is the closest, located just across the Potomac River from Downtown, and gives you a great view of the monuments as you fly in; it's used for short- and medium-haul flights. **Washington Dulles International Airport**, 25 miles out in the suburbs of Virginia, handles the longer flights into the region, including most international flights. **Baltimore-Washington International Airport** (or BWI) is a heck of a lot closer to the first half of its name but easily accessible from Washington by public transport, and often the port of entry with the cheapest fares.

For airport information, including ground transportation, shops and services, hotels and maps, check the website **www.quickaid.com**.

National Airport

Information 703 417 8000.
National Airport is served by the Metro subway system (Yellow and Blue Lines). Follow signs in the terminal to find the station; it's about a 20-minute ride to Downtown.

Signs outside each baggage claim will direct you to the taxi stand. The taxi stand operator will point you to a particular cab depending on whether you're going to DC, Virginia or Maryland. Virginia-licensed cabs can take you anywhere; DC- and Maryland-licensed cabs can't serve Virginia. The fare is determined by meter in Maryland and Virginia cabs, by mileage in DC cabs. All pick-ups from National Airport add a $1.25 surcharge. A cab to Downtown Washington costs about $12 plus tip.

Dulles Airport

Information 703 572 2700.
The best way from Dulles to Downtown DC is the **Washington Flyer Bus** (1-888 927 4359). This runs every half hour Mon-Fri from 5.20am until about 11pm (and every hour at weekends) between Dulles and the Washington Convention Center, New York Avenue & 11th Street, Downtown ($16 one-way, $26 return; buy tickets on the bus). The departure point is clearly signed and the journey takes around 45-50 minutes. From the Convention Center, a free shuttle runs to certain Downtown hotels. Taxis also hover, and you're a block's walk from Metro Center station. For destinations on the east side of town, there's a Flyer to Union Station (same price, hourly, no service on Sundays).

The Flyer also operates between Dulles and the West Falls Church Metro stop ($8 one-way, $14 round trip), at the western end of the Orange Line, from where you can continue your journey on the subway. There is a regularly scheduled service between Dulles Airport and National Airport ($16 one-way, $26 round trip).

The **Washington Flyer Taxi** company has the sole concession to operate out of Dulles (unless incoming passengers have a prearranged pick-up with another cab company). A ride from Dulles to Downtown DC costs about $50 including tip. Most Washington Flyer cabs take credit cards.

To & from BWI

Information 1-410 859 7111/1-800 435 9294.
Flying into BWI may be cheaper than other area airports, but getting to Washington is frequently more expensive, more of a hassle, or both.

A cheap combination (best if you have little to haul) to Downtown DC is the shuttle-train-Metro option. Take the free shuttle bus (marked 'BWI Rail') from the BWI terminal one mile to the train station, then catch a Marc ($5.75 one-way) or Amtrak (from $12) train south 25 minutes to Union Station, from where you can get on the subway.

BWI is also served by cabs, private car companies and the Super Shuttle (*see below*), but beware long waits to leave the airport on Super Shuttle. You can get complete BWI ground transport information from the booth in Pier C or by calling 1-800 435 9294.

A cab from BWI to Downtown Washington costs $40-$50 plus tip.

Super Shuttle

Information 1-800 258 3826.
Offers door-to-door shared van service between all three airports and anywhere in the area. Prices run from $15-$30 for the first passenger and as little as $5 for the second or more going to the same place. It's helpful to know the zip code of your destination.

Airlines

Air Canada *1-800 776 3000*
Air France *1-800 995 5555*
All Nippon Airways *1-800 235 9262*
American Airlines *1-800 433 7300*
British Airways *1-800 247 9297*
Continental *domestic 1-800 525 0280; international 1-800 231 0856*
Delta *1-800 221 1212*
Lufthansa *1-800 645 3880*
Northwest *domestic 1-800 225 2525; international 1-800 447 4747*
Southwest *1-800 435 9792*
Swiss Air *1-800 221 4750*
TWA *domestic 1-800 221 2000; international 1-800 892 4141*
USAirways *1-800 428 4322*
United Airlines *1-800 241 6522*
Virgin Atlantic *1-800 862 8621*

Public transport

The Washington Metropolitan Area Transit Authority runs the entire DC-area public transport network: for information on the Metrorail subway system and buses, call **637 7000** (6am-10.30pm Mon-Fri, 8am-10.30pm Sat, Sun) or try its website at **www.wmata.com**.

Metro

Started in 1976, the Metrorail subway system is slated to be finished in 2001 when the southern stations on the Green Line open. Trains run from 5.30am from Monday to Friday and from 8am on Saturday and Sunday. The system closes at midnight daily, but the last trains from the 'burbs may depart well before that.

At busy times, trains come as often as a minute apart. But even if everything is running on time, the scheduled waits at nights and weekends can be up to 20 minutes. Most signs and operator announcements use the line's final station as the identifier for platforms and trains (for example, on the Red Line, you're always heading towards either Wheaton or Shady Grove – though note that not all trains go as far as the last station), so you need to know which direction you're heading. You'll find a **Metrorail map** on *page 298*.

Metro publishes several good get-around brochures: you can pick up 'Getting There by Metro' and 'A Metro Guide to the Nation's Capital' in any station. The 'Metro Pocket Guide' usefully lists the nearest Metro station to the monuments and other points of interest. Station entrances are marked on the street by square columns with a big white 'M' on top.

Metro lines run deep and the escalators can be very long. It is, however, wheelchair-accessible via elevators. If the elevators are broken at a particular station, Metro runs a bus from a nearby station. Check at the information kiosk before boarding for the latest on elevator breakdowns.

Resources

Fares & passes

The minimum price of a trip is $1.10 but fares depend on when and how far you travel – and can almost double for some rides during rush hours. Fares are printed on a big board on the information kiosk in each station. Under-5s travel free.

Payment is by Farecard: you put up to $20 into a machine that pops out a flimsy card rectangle with a magnetic stripe on the front. Use the card to enter and exit the Metro turnstiles. The price of each trip is subtracted and the remaining amount printed on the card until there's not enough value left to go anywhere. You can then transfer the remaining amount to a new card using the same machines you buy cards from. You can't get into the Metro without at least $1.10 on your card. If you don't have enough to get out where you want, use the machines just before the exit turnstiles, which take only $1 or $5 bills. If you buy a $20 farecard, you get $22 worth of riding.

A good Metro bargain is the $5 one-day pass for unlimited trips (valid after 9.30am Mon-Fri; all day Sat, Sun). They are sold at some hotels, major grocery stores, most Metro stations and at the Metro Center.

The lines

Red Line: serves the Maryland suburbs north of DC and runs through the Downtown business district. The Zoo, Union Station and UDC (University of the District of Columbia) are on this line.

Green Line: serves Anacostia, the U-Street district, Howard University and the eastern Mall area.

Blue Line: serves Arlington, Alexandria, National Airport, the RFK Stadium and most Downtown memorials and museums. It parallels much of the Orange Line and some of the Yellow.

Yellow Line: serves Alexandria to the Mall. Includes National Airport.

Orange Line: serves the suburbs from eastern Virginia to western Maryland. Parallels the Blue Line through most major tourist sights.

Buses

The bus system, also run by Metro, covers the city well and is heavily used by locals, especially for commuting. Metrobuses cost $1.10, or 25¢ with a subway transfer (get one *after* you enter the Metro but *before* you get on the train – look for a machine near the top of the escalators to the platform). You need exact change; dollar bills are accepted. Bus stops are marked by three horizontal stripes in blue, white and red. Metrorail passes are not valid on the bus, with the exception of certain weekly deals. If you are staying a bus-ride from a Metro stop, enquire about the Short Trip or Fast Pass.

The greater Washington area has different bus systems serving different regions. Alexandria and Fairfax Counties in Virginia and Montgomery, Prince George's and Prince William Counties in Maryland each run their own public transport or ride-share systems. To reach these services, call Metro (637 7000) for phone numbers and more information.

Useful bus routes

One popular area served better by bus than Metro is **Georgetown**: catch a **30**, **32**, **34**, **35** or **36** bus marked 'Friendship Heights' running west on Pennsylvania Avenue. The same buses serve the Upper Northwest area along Wisconsin Avenue, which is far from any Metro station. For **Adams Morgan**, including busy 18th Street, take the **90**, **91**, **92**, **93** or **96** buses from Woodley Park-Zoo Metro.

Trains

Amtrak & Marc

Union Station, 50 Massachusetts Avenue, NE, at North Capitol Street, Union Station & Around (Amtrak 484 7540/1-800 872 7245/ Marc 1-800 325 7245). **Open** 5.15am-11pm daily; *waiting room* 24 hours daily.

Both Amtrak and Marc operate out of DC's Union Station. **Amtrak** connects with cities all over the US, including Baltimore, and also has stops at Alexandria in Virginia and at Rockville and New Carrollton in Maryland. There are multiple trains daily to New York.

Marc is a commuter train running between Union Station and Baltimore. The Penn line goes to Baltimore's northern suburbs and runs all day from 6.22am-10.05pm Mon-Fri (every 30 minutes during rush hour, every hour otherwise). It does not run at weekends. The Camden line stops at Camden Yards (Baltimore's baseball stadium) and runs only during morning and evening rush hours (6.47-8.05am and 4.18-6.25pm). Marc stops at some Metro stations in Maryland. Fares between DC and Baltimore are $5.75 one-way, $10.25 round trip.

Both Amtrak and Marc serve the BWI Airport station, from where you take a free shuttle bus a few minutes to the terminal. *See also chapter* **Trips Out of Town**.

Taxis

As elsewhere in the States, driving a taxi is a typical job for recent immigrants, so it's not uncommon to get a driver who needs directions, especially if you're going somewhere slightly off the beaten track.

There are no taxi ranks, but you can usually find cabs outside hotels and it's easy to flag down a DC-licensed cab around most central parts of the city. Cabs have a light on top and the company name painted on the door. To call a cab in the District, try **Diamond** (387 6200) or **Yellow Cab** (544 1212).

In the District, a zone system for taxi fares is scheduled to switch by the end of 1999 to a metered system based on distance travelled and waiting times. Until then, fares are based on how many zones you travel through (maps should be displayed in every cab), plus extra charges for additional passengers, rush-hour travel, calling for a cab and travelling during designated snow emergencies.

Baggage charges are 50¢ for each largeish, grocery-sized hand bag after the first one and $2 for each big bag – officially defined as 3 cubic feet. In reality, some cabbies charge, some don't, depending it seems, on their mood.

The minimum fare possible under the zone system (for one person, flagging the cab, no bags, not at rush hour or in the snow) is $4 plus tip. That will get you all the way from Capitol Hill to Dupont Circle – and it seems to be this trip that brings the smouldering resentment about the zone system into the open. Most cabbies can't wait to see the congressionally mandated zones disappear.

In Maryland and Virginia, cabs run on meters. Cabs licensed for these areas can legally only pick up passengers in DC on a pre-arranged basis – and only take them to the jurisdiction in which they are licensed. That might be why, no matter how hard you're waving on a DC street, that empty cab went right on by.

Driving

The Washington area is not a great place to drive. Rush-hour driving, especially between DC and Virginia, is reputedly second only to Los Angeles for congestion. In Downtown, signs beg drivers not to crowd the intersections and threaten strict red-light-running enforcement. The traffic circles are confusing and some streets, notably Rock Creek Parkway, change direction in rush hours. Read carefully the times posted in the middle of 'Do Not Enter' signs; at other times, entrance is allowed. You can turn right when the traffic lights are red.

There are plenty of off-street pay parking lots: Monument Parking (833 9357) has 22 locations throughout the city,while QuikPark (393 3650) has a garage at 1301 Pennsylvania Avenue, NW. Street parking ranges from difficult to impossible, especially near the Mall, Downtown and in popular nightlife areas such as Georgetown and Adams Morgan. And the parking police are notoriously nasty. Add to all this regular street shutdowns for presidential and visiting diplomat motorcades and 'diplomatic' drivers (*see page 266* **Diplo driving**) and you'll understand why nearly a third of District residents simply don't own a car.

For up-to-the-minute information on road and traffic conditions, call 863 1313.

Car rental

For getting out of town, driving is often the best option. Most major car rental companies have offices in DC, with pick-ups at airports and various places around the area. National and Budget serve Union Station as well.

British visitors could try booking their car before they leave the UK through **Americars** (0171 355 3995), which works with US rental companies Budget and Dollar. They charge a flat rate which includes CDW, liability insurance and all taxes, and starts at £159 per week (£179 1 July-mid September) for a two-door economy-size car.

Almost every rental agency will require a credit card and matching driving licence, and few will rent to anyone under 25. The price quoted will not include tax, liability insurance or collision damage waiver (CDW), which could double the daily rental rate. If you already have an insured car in the US, your own liability insurance may cover the rental. Ask about discounts, available to members of the AAA (which extend to British AA members), AARP (American Association of Retired Persons) and other corporations and organisations.

National car rental companies

Alamo 1-800 327 9633/ www.freeways.com
Avis 1-800 831 2847/www.avis.com
Budget 1-800 527 0700/ www.budgetrentacar.com
Dollar 1-800 800 4000/ www.dollarcar.com
Enterprise 1-800 736 8222/ www.pickenterprise.com
Hertz 1-800 654 3131/ www.hertz.com
National 1-800 227 7368/ www.nationalcar.com
Thrifty 1-800 367 2277/ www.thrifty.com

Local car rental companies

Bargain Buggies (683 7283). **Open** 8am-7pm Mon-Fri; 9am-3pm Sat; 9am-noon Sun.
Rents to under-25s, who have to pay a $10-a-day young driver fee. US visitors can pay in cash, but need to leave a $300 deposit, provide proof of residency and proof of income. Foreign visitors will need a credit card. Has offices at National and Dulles Airports.

Cycling

DC is great for easy cycling: it's mostly flat. A web of bike paths can take you to out-of-centre spots and riding from museum to monument can save your feet hours of ache (you'll have to lock your bike to a signpost or railings). Beware potholes and drivers when cycling in the street. For more information on bike paths and where to rent bikes, *see page 225* **Sport & Fitness**.

Walking

Wanderers beware, Washington has its fair share of aggressive walkers. Drivers can also be aggressive, cutting up pedestrians even when the traffic lights are in their favour. Walking is a great way to get around within a neighbourhood, but remember that the summers are hot and muggy, and although the Mall might like look like a nice stroll, it is two miles long, with a hill at the Capitol end.

Directory

Emergencies

Ambulance, Fire, Police, Emergency
911 (free from public phones)

Non-emergency Metropolitan Police
727 1010

US Capitol Police
228 2800

US Park Police
619 7300

Auto Impound
727 5000

FBI
324 3000

US Secret Service
406 8000

Mental Health Crisis Hotline
561 7000

Poison Center
625 3333

Suicide Prevention Center
301 864 7130

Rape Crisis Center
333 7273

Attitude & attire

Washington is unquestionably a major tourist destination, so if you wear jeans, trainers and a small rucksack, you should feel right at home. It is also, of course, a major business centre, and in Downtown, on K Street and Connecticut Avenue, you'll see lawyers in suits and other members of a well-dressed workforce. If you dress up just a little, you'll look more like a native.

DC residents are usually very preoccupied with their own little niche. They read the *Washington Post* on the Metro, mind their own business on the sidewalk and get upset when tourists stand on the left side of the escalator instead of the right. But if you do stop someone on the street to ask for directions, they will generally be happy to oblige.

Business hours

In general, business hours are 9am to 5pm Monday to Friday. Most shops are open 10am to 5 or 6pm Monday to Saturday and noon to 6pm on Sunday, though shops in the Downtown business district are not usually open at the weekend. From Monday to Saturday, mall stores usually stay open until 9pm. Most post offices are open 8am to 5pm Monday to Friday; some open for limited hours on Saturdays. Banks open at 9am and close at about 3pm on weekdays only (although hours can vary greatly). Restaurants are usually open for lunch from 11am to 2pm and for dinner from 5 to 10pm, but many are open all day.

Consumer rights

Whenever possible, pay with a major credit card so you can cancel payment or get reimbursed if there is a problem, provided you have documentation. Consider travel insurance that includes default coverage to protect yourself against financial loss.

Better Business Bureau
393 8000
File complaints, receive information and business and consumer alerts.
Website: www.bbb.org

DC Department of Consumer Protection
442 8475
Regulates certain businesses in DC, such as tour guides.

Crime

The areas of DC that are notorious for crime are parts of the Southeast and Northeast quadrants plus pockets of the Northwest, mostly east of 16th Street and north of Columbia Road, far from the main, and even most of the secondary, tourist sights. Where we have included a destination that falls into a crime-affected area, we have noted it in the text.

The threat of crime near the major visitor destinations is minuscule. The area around the Capitol is very heavily patrolled, and Metro trains and stations are also well-patrolled and nearly crime-free.

The Adams Morgan and the U Street/14th Street corridor are much too heavy with traffic to be considered dangerous (the panhandlers are mostly harmless; feel free to ignore them), but the sidestreets surrounding them can be dodgy after dark, as can some streets near Union Station and around Capitol Hill. Stick to the heavily populated, well-lit thoroughfares when walking in these areas at night.

Generally, as in any big city, you should take the usual security precautions. Be wary of pickpockets, especially in crowds. Look like you know what you're doing and where you're going – even if you don't. Use common sense and follow your intuition about people and situations.

If someone does approach you threateningly, don't resist. Hand over your money, then dial 911 or hail a cab and ask the driver to take you to the nearest police station where you can report the theft and get a reference number to claim insurance and travellers' cheque refunds.

Disabled & elderly

Washington is good at providing facilities for all

types of tourists, including the disabled and elderly. Most museums, monuments and memorials are accessible to visitors using wheelchairs and many have other facilities to help disabled visitors. Nearly all Downtown streets have wide sidewalks with kerb cuts for greater accessibility.

The Metro has excellent facilities for visitors with vision and hearing impairments or mobility problems. All stations are theoretically wheelchair-accessible, although elevators are not always in service. A Metro Disability ID Card (available free at Metro sales offices), gives you discounts on the Metro system.

Accessibility to Transportation Services for Persons with Disabilities

366 4070

Tour operators

Outfits organising holidays for disabled travellers include **Access Adventures** in Rochester, New York (1-716 889 9096) and **Sprout** in New York City (1-212 222 9575/1-888 222 9575).

Society for the Advancement of Travelers with Handicaps

1-212 447 7284
New York-based organisation offering advice for disabled travellers in all parts of the States.

Washington Convention & Visitors Association

789 7000
Information and free brochure on city accessibility.

Electricity & appliances

The US electricity supply is 110-120 volt, 60-cycle AC, rather than the 220-240 volt, 50-cycle AC used in Europe. Plugs are standard two-pins. An adaptor and, in some cases, a voltage converter (available at airport shops and hardware stores) are necessary to use foreign electrical appliances. Most US videos and TVs use a different frequency from those in Europe, so you will not be able to play back camcorder footage during your trip. However, you can buy and use blank tapes.

Embassies

Note that most visa services keep shorter hours than the business hours listed. For other embassies/consulates, consult *Yellow Pages*.

Australia

1601 Massachusetts Avenue, NW, at 16th Street, Dupont Circle (797 3000). Dupont Circle Metro.
Open 8am-4.30pm Mon-Fri.
Website: www.austemb.org

Canada

501 Pennsylvania Avenue, NW, at Sixth Street, Penn Quarter (682 1740). Archives-Navy Memorial Metro. **Open** 8am-6pm Mon-Fri.

Ireland

2234 Massachusetts Avenue, NW, at Sheridan Circle, Dupont Circle (462 3939). Dupont Circle Metro.
Open 9am-1pm, 2-4pm, Mon-Fri.

New Zealand

37 Observatory Circle, NW, at Massachusetts Avenue, Georgetown (328 4800). Dupont Circle Metro.
Open 9am-5pm Mon-Fri.

United Kingdom

3100 Massachusetts Avenue, NW, at Whitehaven Street, Georgetown (462 1340). Dupont Circle Metro.
Open 9am-5.30pm Mon-Fri.

Health & medical

Dental Emergency

301 770 0123

Doctors Referral

362 8677

DC Dental Society

Referrals. *547 7613*

24-hour CVS Pharmacy

1-800 746 7287 (for nearby location)

Planned Parenthood

1108 16th Street, NW, between L & M Streets (347 8512). Farragut North Metro. **Open** 9am-7pm Mon, Wed; 9am-6pm Tue, Thur; 9am-5pm Fri.
Contraceptive and medical services, and advice.

Helplines & agencies

All are open 24 hours unless stated. For other helplines, see the front of a local phonebook.

Alcoholics Anonymous

966 9115. **Open** 10am-10pm daily.

National HIV/AIDS Hotline

1-800 342 2437

Sexually Transmitted Diseases Information Line

832 7000

Substance Abuse Hotline

1-877 612 4357

Hospitals

The following all have 24-hour emergency rooms.

Children's National Medical Center

111 Michigan Avenue, NW, between North Capitol Street & Georgia Avenue, Shaw (884 5000). Brookland-Catholic University Metro, then H2, H4 bus.

Georgetown University Medical Center

3800 Reservoir Road, NW, at Wisconsin Avenue, Georgetown (687 2000). Dupont Circle Metro, then D4 bus.

Howard University Hospital

2041 Georgia Avenue, NW, at Florida Avenue, Shaw (865 6100). Shaw-Howard University Metro.

Immigration & visas/Customs

If you are a citizen of the UK, Ireland, New Zealand or most western European countries (check with your local US embassy or consulate to be sure), have proof of intent to leave (such as a return plane ticket) and are visiting the US for less than 90 days, you need only a valid passport and visa waiver form (I-94W) to enter the country. The visa waiver form is generally provided by the airline during check-in or on the plane and must be presented to Immigration at the airport of entry in the US. Canadians and Mexicans do not need visas but must have legal proof of their residency and valid identification. International visitors should allow extra time (about an hour at busy times) in the airport to clear Immigration.

For other types of visas, such as work or study visas that are valid for longer than 90 days, contact your nearest US consulate or embassy a minimum of three weeks before you want to travel.

A customs declaration form is also provided on international flights into the US; this must be filled out and handed to a customs official after Immigration (keep it handy). Current US regulations allow foreign visitors to import the following duty-free: 200 cigarettes or 50 cigars (over-18s only) or 2kg of smoking tobacco, 1 litre of wine or spirits (over-21s only), and up to $100 in gifts. You can take up to $10,000 in cash, travellers' cheques or endorsed bank drafts in or out of the country. Anything above that you must declare on a customs form, or risk seizure. It is illegal to transport most perishable foods and plants across international borders.

US Customs Service

1301 Constitution Avenue, NW, at Pennsylvania Avenue, Penn Quarter (927 6724). Archives-Navy Memorial Metro.
Website: www.customs.ustreas.gov

US Immigration & Naturalization Service

425 I Street, NW, between Third & Fourth Streets, Judiciary Square Area (514 2607). Judiciary Square Metro.
Website www.usdoj.gov/ins

Insurance

Non-nationals should arrange baggage, trip-cancellation and medical insurance before they leave home (but first check what your existing home and medical insurance covers). Medical centres will ask for details of your insurance company and policy number if you require treatment; keep this information with you.

Internet

If you left your laptop at home, and are looking for a place to get online, check out the nearest library (*see below* **Libraries**) for Internet access – particularly college and university libraries. There are also many Internet cafés – Kramerbooks has free access – (*see chapter* **Cafés & Coffeehouses**) and some shops with Internet access. **Cybercafé Guide** (www.cyberiacafe.net/cyberia/guide/ccafe.htm) is useful for finding cybercafés worldwide.

If you are travelling with your own computer/modem, find out in advance if your Internet Service Provider has any local POPs, and, if so, ask about roam rates and dial-in numbers. If it is more practical to set up a temporary account locally, major ISPs include **America Online** (AOL; 1-800 827 6364); **Compuserve** (1-800 848 8990); **Erols** (1-888 463 7657); and **Mindspring** (1-800 719 4332).

For a list of useful and informative DC websites, *see page 265* **Websites**.

Myth.com

3243 M Street, NW, between 31st & 32nd Streets, Georgetown (625 6984). Rosslyn Metro. **Open** 11am-1am Mon-Thur, Sun; 11am-3am Fri, Sat.
Georgetown's first cybercafé, serving good food but no alcohol.

News Byte Café at the Newseum

1101 Wilson Boulevard, at Moore Street, Arlington, VA (703 284 3544). Rosslyn Metro. **Open** 10am-5pm Wed-Sun.
Free access to the Internet at a high, bright bar, serving muffins and other bakery items.

Late

There are some 24-hour convenience stores (such as the CVS chain), supermarkets and gas stations in the metro area. Although many people complain that it's hard to find somewhere to eat after 10pm, in Georgetown, Dupont Circle and Adams Morgan many restaurants and bars are open until 2 or 3am – *see chapters* **Bars** and **Restaurants** for more details.

CVS

6-7 Dupont Circle, NW, between Massachusetts & New Hampshire Avenues, Dupont Circle (833 5704/other locations 1-800 746 7287). Dupont Circle Metro.
Open 24 hours daily. **Credit** AmEx, DC, Disc, MC, V.

Left luggage lockers

Baltimore-Washington International Airport

Located behind security checkpoint. **Rates** $1 per half hour-$7.25 for 24 hours. **Open** 24 hours.

Dulles International Airport

Located near gate T after security checkpoint. **Rates** $2 per half hour-$13.50 for 48 hours. **Open** 24 hours. Storage room for larger luggage.

Ronald Reagan National Washington Airport

Located in terminals B and C. **Rates** $1 per half hour-$7.50 for 24 hours. **Open** 24 hours.
Storage for larger items at Thomas Cook Customer Service Center.

Union Station

Located between gates A-G. **Rates** $1 per hour-$7.50 for 24 hours. **Open** 24 hours.
Storage room available for larger luggage is open 6am-10pm daily.

Libraries

Washington is a good town for library lovers, from the Library of Congress to specialised libraries in each Smithsonian museum. Many national and international organisations also have their headquarters in DC, complete with archive. The universities all have excellent libraries and, of course, DC has its own extensive public library system.

Library of Congress

First Street & Independence Avenue, SE, Capitol & Around (operator 707

Resources

5000/public information 707 8000/ reference 707 5522) Capitol South Metro. **Open** hours vary for different parts of the library.
As the central library for the US, the Library of Congress makes it its business to have everything. However, it may take a very long time to find one small book among nearly 100 million items on 535 miles of shelves. The library is open to the public, but you must first wait in line for a library card. Take photo ID.
Website: lcweb.loc.gov

Martin Luther King Memorial Library

901 G Street, NW, between Ninth & Tenth Streets, Penn Quarter (general information 727 1111/ reference 727 1126). Gallery Place-Chinatown Metro. **Open** 10am-9pm Mon-Thur; 10am-5pm Fri, Sat; 1-5pm Sun.
This is DC's central public library, with five floors of books, periodicals and other reference materials. Check the *Blue Pages* (the governmental version of *Yellow Pages*) under 'Libraries' for details of more than two dozen branches around town.

National Library of Medicine

8600 Rockville Pike, at Center Drive, Bethesda, MD (1-888 346 3656). Medical Center Metro. **Open** 8.30am-5pm Mon-Fri; 8.30am-12.30pm Sat.
Over four million books, specialising in bio-medicine, healthcare, medical technology, public health and toxicology. You can access the library's database via its website.
Website: www.nlm.nih.gov

University libraries

American University Bender Library

4400 Massachusetts Avenue, NW, at Nebraska Avenue, Upper Northwest (885 3200). Tenleytown-AU Metro, then M4 bus. **Open** 8am-2am Mon-Wed; 8am-midnight Thur; 8am-10pm Fri; 9am-9pm Sat; 9am-2am Sun.
Full-service university library, good for international affairs, social sciences, art, science and technology, among other subjects.

Catholic University of America Law Library

3600 John McCormick Road, NE, at Michigan Avenue, Northeast (319 5155). Brookland-Catholic University Metro. **Open** 7am-11.45pm Mon-Fri; 9am-11.45pm Sat, Sun.
Outstanding legal research library.

Georgetown University Lauinger Memorial Library

1421 37th Street, NW, at L Street, Georgetown (687 7687). Rosslyn Metro. **Open** 8.30am-midnight Mon-Thur; 8.30am-10pm Fri; 10am-10pm Sat; 11am-midnight Sun.
Comprehensive collections include colonial and American Catholic history, and intelligence and covert activities. A medical library and law library are also on the campus. Photo ID is required.

University of Maryland-College Park Libraries

College Park Campus, off Baltimore Avenue, College Park, MD (301 314 9428). Bus C2, C8. **Open** hours vary; call for information.
Six libraries (McKeldin Library is the largest) and special collections, including historic preservation, National Public Broadcasting archives and East Asia collection.

Lost property

If you leave something on the bus or subway, chances are you won't see it again, but first call Washington Metro Transit Authority Lost & Found on **962 1195**. Also check the nearest police station in case items have been turned in.

Money & costs

Credit cards are almost a necessity. If you want to rent a car or book a ticket over the phone, you will need a major credit card. They are accepted almost universally in hotels, restaurants and shops, though occasionally you will find a gas station, small store or cinema that only takes cash. Visa and Mastercard are the most widely accepted cards, with American Express a distant third.

Credit cards are also useful for extracting instantaneous cash advances from ATMs and banks. However, where US account holders pay a flat service charge for getting cash this way, UK companies charges vary – and you pay interest, of course.

Dollar travellers' cheques from the major companies are also widely accepted.

The cost of a holiday in DC compares favourably with other US destinations because there are few admission charges to pay. Out of season, accommodation can be cheap, too (but sky-high in summer). Other costs are comparable with other US cities.

Currency

The United States' monetary system is decimal-based: the US dollar ($) is divided into 100 cents (¢). Coins and dollars are stamped with the faces of US presidents and statesmen. Coin denominations are the penny (1¢ – Abraham Lincoln on the only copper-coloured coin); the nickel (5¢ – Thomas Jefferson); dime (10¢ – Franklin D. Roosevelt); quarter (25¢ – George Washington); and the less common half-dollar (50¢ –John F Kennedy). Bills, or notes, are all the same size and come in $1 (George Washington); $5 (Abraham Lincoln); $10 (Alexander Hamilton); $20 (Andrew Jackson); $50 (Ulysses S Grant); and $100 (Benjamin Franklin) denominations.

Changing money & travellers' cheques

Most banks will exchange cash or travellers' cheques in major foreign currencies. The most convenient place to exchange money is the airport when you first arrive – but banks will often give better rates. Thomas Cook and American Express offices are also set up to exchange currency, sell travellers' cheques and generally help to ensure you have money when you travel. Most hotel desks will do the same thing – if you're stuck late at night, they're the best place to try. You can of course use travellers' cheques as payment in shops and restaurants, which seldom ask for ID (though banks and exchange offices do).

American Express

1150 Connecticut Avenue, NW, between L & M Streets, Downtown (457 1300). Farragut North Metro. **Open** 9am-6pm Mon-Fri.
Call 1-800 221 7282 for purchase or refund of travellers' cheques.

Capitol Foreign Exchange

825 14th Street, NW, between I & H Streets, White House Area (1-888 842 0880). McPherson Square Metro. **Open** 9am-5.30 Mon-Fri.
May have the best rates in town.

Thomas Cook Travel

1800 K Street, NW, at 18th Street, Downtown (872 1428). Farragut North Metro. **Open** 9am-5pm Mon-Fri.

Security check

Security in Washington, DC, has grown tighter over the years, as more and more sophisticated weapons technology has developed and the perceived terrorist threat has grown. The most heavily guarded areas are, of course, the White House, US Capitol and other government and embassy buildings, where you can expect to walk through a metal detector and have your bag X-rayed. Don't make any cracks about that plastic explosive you've got on you – the guys in black will take you seriously.

The security measures around Capitol Hill were found wanting when Russell Weston Jr blasted his way past security into the US Capitol building in July 1998, killing two security guards and wounding a bystander. However, lawmakers are determined that the Capitol must remain 'the people's house', open for anyone to visit. An appropriations bill passed in early 1999 included $20 million for improved Capitol perimeter security. Technology will be updated, but visible changes in security are yet to be determined.

Most current Capitol security measures – including sweeps by bomb-sniffing dogs, metal-detecting magnetometers at the entrances, security cameras, sniper posts and required passes for employees and reporters – have only been in place since 1983 when a bomb went off on the Senate side.

Another security issue that has received a lot of media attention of late is biological weapons, believed to be stockpiled by terrorists and potentially more of a threat than any other weapon. But countermeasures are still shockingly inadequate – as was made evident in early 1999 when a leading expert on biological warfare carried 7.5g of powdered anthrax in a small plastic bottle through all DC's major airports, the security systems of the State Department, the Pentagon, the CIA and finally into the Rayburn House Office Building, where he made a report to a House committee and displayed his deadly sample.

Call 872 1233 or 1-800 287 7362 for nearest branch. Has a branch in Union Station, open 9am-5pm Mon-Sat; noon-6pm Sun.
Website www.us.thomascook.com.

ATMs

Automated Teller Machines are located outside nearly all banks, inside all malls and major shopping areas and are fairly easy to find wherever you happen to be. Best of all, they are accessible 24 hours a day (though there is often a daily withdrawal limit of $300). They are the most convenient and often most cost-effective way of obtaining cash – but remember that most charge at least a $1 service fee on top of any charges incurred by your home bank, so don't withdraw small increments throughout the day.

All you need is an ATM card linked with a major national/international network – such as **Cirrus** or **Plus** – and your usual PIN (Personal Identification Number). Check with your bank before leaving home to find out if they are linked to any DC banks and what the fees will be.

Cirrus *1-800 424 7787* to locate nearest Cirrus ATM machine
Plus *1-800 843 7587* to locate nearest Plus ATM machine

International networks

Cirrus and Plus are also linked to **Maestro** (Cirrus) and **Delta** (Plus), which let the card function as a debit card to pay for goods and services, withdrawing the money directly from your bank account, instead of giving you credit as credit cards do. They can also be used to get cash back when making a purchase.

Banks

The following are nationwide banks with centrally located branches.

Century National Bank

1875 I Street, NW, at 19th Street, Downtown (496 4000). Farragut West Metro. **Open** 9am-5pm Mon-Fri.

NationsBank Banking Center

1501 Pennsylvania Avenue, NW, at 15th Street, White House Area (624 4253). McPherson Square Metro. **Open** 9am-3pm Mon-Thur; 9am-5pm Fri.

Riggs National Bank

1503 Pennsylvania Avenue, NW, at 15th Street, White House Area (301 887 6000 for all locations). McPherson Square Metro. **Open** 9am-3pm Mon-Fri.

Cash crisis

Fees for money transfer can be quite expensive. There are Western Union offices around the city and in Safeway supermarkets, but a better idea might be to have someone add funds to your credit card (from which you can request a cash advance) or your bank account (from which you can withdraw money via ATM).

Western Union

516 23rd Street, NW, between E Street & Virginia Avenue, Foggy Bottom (833 1600). Foggy Bottom-GWU Metro. **Open** 7am-7pm Mon-Fri; 7am-5pm Sat; 7am-3pm Sun. Call 1-800 325 4176 for general information and list of Western Union locations.

Lost & stolen

In the event of a lost or stolen card, call the company immediately to deactivate it and request a replacement. Travellers' cheques can be replaced via a local office.

American Express cards *1-800 528 4800*
American Express travellers' cheques *1-800 221 7282*
Diners Club *1-800 234 6377*
Discover *1-800 347 2683*
Mastercard *1-800 307 7309*

JCB *1-800 366 4522*
Thomas Cook travellers' cheques *1-800 223 7373*
Visa *1-800 336 8472*

Places of worship

Adas Israel Congregation
2850 Quebec Street, NW, at Porter Street & Connecticut Avenue, Cleveland Park (362 4433). Cleveland Park Metro.
Conservative Jewish.

Basilica of the National Shrine of the Immaculate Conception
Michigan Avenue & Fourth Street, NW, Shaw (526 8300). Brookland-Catholic University Metro.
Claimed to be the largest Catholic church in the western hemisphere and the eighth largest in the world.
Website www.nationalshrine.com

Foundry Methodist Church
1500 16th Street, NW, at P Street, Dupont Circle (332 4010). Dupont Circle Metro.
On Sundays you might see the Clintons in the congregation.

Islamic Center
2551 Massachusetts Avenue, NW, at Belmont Road, Adams Morgan (332 8343). Dupont Circle Metro.

National Presbyterian Church & Center
4101 Nebraska Avenue, NW, at Van Ness Street, Upper Northwest (537 0800). Tenleytown-AU Metro.

New York Avenue Presbyterian Church
313 New York Avenue, NW, between 13th & 14th Streets, Downtown (393 3700). McPherson Square Metro.

St John's Episcopal Church
1525 H Street, NW, opposite Lafayette Square, White House Area (347 8766). McPherson Square Metro.

St Matthew's Cathedral
1725 Rhode Island Avenue, NW, between Connecticut Avenue & 17th Street, Dupont Circle (347 3215). Farragut North Metro.
Roman Catholic.

Temple of the Church of Jesus Christ of Latter-day Saints
9900 Stoneybrook Road, off Capitol View Avenue, Kensington, MD (587 0144). Silver Spring Metro, then Ride-On 4 bus.
This 16-storey marble temple is not open to non-Mormons, but the visitors' centre is open to all.

Washington Hebrew Congregation
3935 Macomb Street, NW, at Massachusetts Avenue, Cleveland Park (362 7100). Cleveland Park Metro.
Reformed Jewish.

Washington National Cathedral
Massachusetts & Wisconsin Avenues, NW, Upper Northwest (537 6200). Bus 30, 32, 34, 35, 36.
Episcopal. The sixth largest church in the world.
Website: www.cathedral.org/cathedral

Postal services

Post offices are found throughout the city; call **635 5300** or check the phone book to find your nearest. They are usually open 8am-5pm Mon-Fri. Mail can be sent from any of the big blue mailboxes on street corners, but if you are sending a package overseas that is heavier than 16oz, it must be mailed directly from a post office and accompanied by a customs form.

National Capitol Station Post Office
City Post Office Building, North Capitol Street & Massachusetts Avenue, NE, Union Station & Around (523 2628) Union Station Metro. **Open** 7am-midnight Mon-Fri; 7am-8pm Sat, Sun.
The postal museum is also here.

General Mail Facility
900 Brentwood Road, NE, at New York Avenue, Northeast (635 5300). Rhode Island Avenue Metro.
Open 8am-3.30pm.
The main postal facility for DC. A letter sent to General Delivery (Poste Restante) will end up here, but it is miles away from Downtown; better to have mail sent to a specific post office (you'll need to know the zip code). Mail will be held for 30 days. Alternatively, Thomas Cook and American Express provide a postal service for their clients.

Smoking

Fewer and fewer people in the US smoke, and DC is no exception. It is illegal to smoke on public transport, in public buildings, theatres, cinemas, restaurants (except in designated smoking areas) and most shops. If you want to smoke, best to smoke outside.

Montgomery County Council in Maryland recently followed California's example and voted to ban all smoking in bars and restaurants, to take effect in 2002. This may be a harbinger of similar laws in the area.

Study

While not a full-blown university town like Boston, Washington, DC does have its share of colleges and universities. The major ones are listed below, but there are many smaller institutions, branch universities and schools in suburban Virginia and Maryland. Most of these schools conduct summer courses in politics, international relations and other programmes directly relating to DC's weighty political scene.

American University
4400 Massachusetts Avenue, NW, at Nebraska Avenue, Upper Northwest (885 1000). Tenleytown-AU Metro, then M4 bus.
Over 11,000 graduate and undergraduate students attend this university in residential northwest Washington. American has a strong arts and sciences programme and a law library on campus.
Website: www.american.edu

Catholic University of America
620 Michigan Avenue, NE, at North Capitol Street, Northeast (319 5000). Brookland-Catholic University Metro.
Catholic University received a papal charter in 1887. Its diverse programmes include architecture, engineering and law.
Website: www.cua.edu

Georgetown University
37th & O Streets, NW, Georgetown (687 0100). Dupont Circle Metro, then G2 bus.
Georgetown attracts students from all over the world to its prestigious international relations, business, medical and law schools. Only 2.8 per cent of medical school applicants

Back to your roots

As the centre of national record, Washington, DC, is the starting point for many people looking to trace their roots. In fact, the city holds so much genealogical information, from the most recent census data to the National Archives, that it can be overwhelming. Where should you start?

- Talk to relatives before you come. OK, it seems painfully obvious, but most people skip this step. The more information you have, the more you can get.
- Take a class. Usually once a month in the autumn, the **National Archives** (219 2316) offers various workshops on researching family history. Classes usually last three hours and cost $15.
- Hit the stacks. Below are the local places to pan for genealogical gold. You could also try the **Library of Congress** (*see page 260* **Libraries**).

National Archives

Room 400, Seventh Street & Pennsylvania Avenue, NW, Federal Triangle (501 5400). Archives-Navy Memorial Metro. **Open** 8.45am-5pm Mon, Wed; 8.45am-9pm Tue, Thur, Fri; 8.45am-4.45pm Sat.
Holds federal records since the formation of the Union, including census, military and land data, as well as passenger arrival lists. Its useful *Guide to Genealogical Research* ($25) is available in the gift shop or by calling 1-800 234 8861. Also check out the Archives' website, where you can access some records online and email questions to genealogists. Note: research access is via the Pennsylvania Avenue entrance.
Website: www.nara.gov

Family History Center of the Church of Jesus Christ of Latter-day Saints

10,000 Stonybrook Drive, off Beach Drive, Kensington, MD (301 587 0042). Silver Spring Metro, then Ride-On 4 bus. **Open** 9am-5pm Mon, Fri, Sat; 9am-5pm, 7-10pm, Tue-Thur.
Extensive collections of previous research done by church members as well as original records.

National Genealogical Society Library

4527 17th Street North, at Wakefield Street, Arlington, VA (703 525 0050).Ballston-MU Metro. **Open** 10am-9pm Mon, Wed; 10am-4pm Fri, Sat.
Sponsors annual conferences and has reference materials as well as local histories from across the US. Non-members pay a $5 fee.
Website: www.ngsgenealogy.org

Daughters of the American Revolution Library

1776 D Street, NW, between 17th & 18th Streets, Mall & Tidal Basin (879 3229). Farragut West Metro. **Open** 8am-4.45pm Mon-Fri; 1-5pm Sun.
Holds more than 123,000 books and court, church, census and bible records, as well as family and county histories. Non-members pay $5 a day ($3 at lunchtime).

(167 out of 11,000) were accepted in 1998. Prerequisites for attending include an ability to pay the steep tuition and contribute to the country-club atmosphere.
Website: www.georgetown.edu

George Washington University

I & 23rd Street, NW, Foggy Bottom (994 1000). Foggy Bottom-GWU Metro.
GWU houses law and medical schools and has strong programmes in politics and international affairs. The campus starts only four blocks from the White House
Website: www.gwu.edu

Howard University

2400 Sixth Street, NW, Shaw (806 610). Shaw-Howard University Metro.
About 10,000 students attend this predominantly African-American university, studying medicine, engineering, dentistry, social work and communication. Former students include such luminaries as authors Zora Neale Hurston and Toni Morrison and former Supreme Court Justice Thurgood Marshall.
Website: www.howard.edu

University of the District of Columbia

4200 Connecticut Avenue, NW, at Van Ness Street, Upper Northwest (274 5000). Van Ness-UDC Metro.
UDC was formed in 1976 when several district colleges were combined. Not as prestigious as most of its neighbours, it nevertheless has a variety of programmes, including arts, sciences and law.
Website: www.udc.edu

University of Maryland at College Park

Baltimore Avenue, College Park, MD (301 405 1000). Bus C2, C8.
Though not technically in DC, this is the area's largest university with an enrolment of over 32,000. A major public research facility, Maryland is top-ranked in journalism, engineering, computer science, physics and agricultural economics.
Website: www.maryland.edu

Telephones

The Washington, DC metro area can be a confusing place to use the telephone. With so many large businesses and organisations as well as a proliferation of mobile phones, faxes and modems, there are five area codes in the metro area, though most are not long distance from each other.

Area codes

The area code for DC is 202. To make a call within the District, you need only dial the seven-digit local number, not the 202 area code.

Maryland and Virginia are more complicated. The area codes for the city of Alexandria and the counties of Arlington and Fairfax in Virginia is 703. (From April 2000, a new 571 area code will also be used in this area.) In Maryland, Prince George's County and Montgomery County both use 301 and 240 area codes.

Calls from any of these area codes to another area code as well as within one area code are treated as local, but all ten digits must be dialled – the three-digit area code plus the seven-digit local number. Only within DC do you not have to use the area code. Remember, however, if you are calling outside these codes, the call will be long-distance (and charged as such) and you will need to prefix the ten-digit number with a 1. The same goes for further-out parts of the 703 area.

Numbers prefaced by 1-800, 1-888 and 1-877 are toll-free.

Using phones

To use a public phone, pick up the receiver, listen for a dial tone and feed it change (35¢ for a local call). The operator is free, as is directory assistance on a Bell Atlantic phone (other companies may charge 35¢). If you use a payphone for long distance or international calls, use a phonecard (available in various denominations at supermarkets, drugstores and convenience stores everywhere – shop around for the longest talk-time for the lowest price) or calling card. Otherwise, you will need a lot of change (a quarter is the highest denomination a payphone will accept) – after you dial the number a recorded voice will tell you how much you need to put in. Some payphones, especially at airports and big hotels, accept credit cards.

Most hotels charge a flat fee of 50¢-$1 for telephone calls – including local and toll-free calls – which can quickly add up. You can get round this at some hotels by using a house phone and asking the operator to connect you to your number. Alternatively, look for payphones, usually located in the lobby or near the restrooms. If you need to make a long-distance or international call, you will often have to leave a cash deposit or credit card at the hotel desk. The rates will be high, however, so you are better off using a phonecard.

AT&T (1-800 225 5288) allows you to make calls on a Visa credit card, while **MCI WorldCom** (1-800 265 5328) lets you use Mastercard or Discover. Britons will find it is cheaper to do this to call home than to use their own domestic phone chargecard (eg BT Chargecard).

For local directory assistance within the DC metro area, dial 411. For national long-distance enquiries, dial 1 + [area code] + 555 1212 (if you don't know the area code, dial 0 for the operator). For international calls, dial 011 then the country code (UK 44; New Zealand 64; Australia 61; Germany 49 – see the phone book for others). For collect (reverse charge) calls, dial 0 for the operator.

If you encounter voicemail, note that the pound key is the one marked # and the star key is *. On automated answering systems, 0 often gets you to a real-live operator.

Time

Washington, DC, operates on **Eastern Standard Time** (the same time zone as New York and Miami), which is five hours behind Greenwich Mean Time (London) and three hours ahead of Pacific Standard Time (Los Angeles). Clocks go forward one hour on the first Sunday in April to daylight saving time and back one hour on the last Sunday in October.

To find out the exact time, call 844 2525.

Tipping

Cab drivers and waiters in restaurants are generally tipped 15 per cent – 20 per cent if you are feeling generous or for exceptionally good service. Bartenders expect 50¢-$1 per drink. Hairdressers get 10 per cent, bellhops $1 per bag and hotel maids $1-$2 per day.

Visitor information

Brits planning trips can call the DC Convention & Visitors Association's London outpost on 020 8877 4521 for an info pack, or the Capital Region USA Brochure Line on 01234 767928.

Washington DC Convention & Visitors Association

1212 New York Avenue, NW, between 12th & 13th Streets, Downtown (789 7000). Metro Center Metro. **Open** 9am-5pm Mon-Fri.
The city's official tourist centre, but if you phone, expect to be kept on hold for a while.
Website: www.washington.org

DC Chamber of Commerce Visitor Information Center

Ronald Reagan Building & International Trade Center, 1300 Pennsylvania Avenue, NW, between 13th & 14th Streets, Federal Triangle (328 4748).
Open 8am-6pm Mon-Sat; noon-5pm Sun.
Brand-new facility with bags of info to hand out in the form of leaflets and personal advice.

Dial-a-Museum

357 2020
Extensive recorded museum info.

InfoTips

628 0202
Free recorded information on more than 100 topics, from Bell Atlantic, the local telephone company.

International Visitors Information Service

Meridian International Center, 1630 Crescent Place, NW, at 16th Street, Adams Morgan (939 5552). U Street-Cardozo Metro.
Open 9am-5pm Mon-Fri.
Brochures, maps, and resources for international visitors, including a 'language bank' (for translations) with 42 languages (939 5538).

Local weather

936 1212

National Mall monuments information

National Park Service 426 6841
Website: www.nps.gov/nama

Smithsonian information

357 2700
Information on all the Smithsonian's museums.

Travelers Aid Society

Union Station, 50 Massachusetts Avenue, NE, at North Capitol Street, Union Station & Around (371 1937). Union Station Metro. **Open** 9.30am-5.30pm Mon-Fri.
Tourist information and referrals.
Branches: Dulles International Airport, Ronald Reagan National Airport.

Websites

Listed below are stand-alone websites. Of course, many tourist information services, museums and attractions have their own websites, which are given at the end of their respective entry elsewhere in this guide. For newspaper and magazine-related websites, *see chapter* **Media**.

sc94.ameslab.gov

This computer conference website has a detailed map of the capital's major attractions.

thomas.loc.gov

Link to all useful congressional information, including days-in-session for the House and Senate, full-text of bills being considered and a listing of how congressmen and women voted on specific issues.

Diplo driving

Diplomats stationed in DC get special car licence plates – they're red, white and blue, with a 'D' on the left. The code on the plate tells the State Department what country the car is licensed to, but that sensitive information is not for public consumption (probably because then you could tell which diplomats are doing all that double parking and angered non-diplo drivers might call the relevant embassy to complain).

Resentment towards the perceived perks of diplo drivers runs high. In fact, diplomats get an overly bad rap for flaunting traffic and parking laws. They are officially required to pay all traffic fines and parking tickets, and supposedly can lose their State Department-issued licence after running too many red lights. At least one diplomat lost immunity and was sent to jail after killing a teenager in a drunk-driving accident.

Visiting heads of state create more real driving headaches. Most take advantage of the secret-service provided motorcade – which stops traffic for blocks around so the long black cars and screaming siren cars can whizz wherever, undelayed and secure. The US presidential convoy does the same thing – the vice president's entourage, say secret service sources, usually only when they are leaving town.

www.ci.washington.dc.us
DC local government page, with links and facts and figures.

www.dcpages.com
All sorts of local information.

www.dcregistry.com/art.html
Use this diverse (but not definitive) links page to skip the middleman and go directly to the websites for local museums, galleries, bands, theatres (and individuals).

www.fedgate.org
Washington's principal product is information, and the web has made that product more accessible. This Federal Gateway site offers a one-stop-shopping approach to federal agency websites, as well as some state and local ones.

www.washington.sidewalk.com
Local version of the online guide to absolutely everything.

When to visit

The best times to visit Washington, DC, are spring and autumn, avoiding the humidity and heat of summer and the bleakness of winter. In early April, the cherry blossoms are in flower at the Tidal Basin. In autumn, the trees turn brilliant shades of orange, red and yellow and the weather is pleasant. Perhaps most important, the massive crowds of tourists are scarcer during these seasons than in mid-summer – though spring can be busy with school groups and there is never a season without tourists.

If you do visit in summer, be sure to drink plenty of water to avoid dehydration, and start sightseeing early in the day to avoid long lines in the heat. Daytime summer temperatures average 84°F (30°C) but feel hotter because of the high humidity; aim to be inside an air-conditioned building at midday. Winters are fairly mild (37°F/3°C), but even a light snow can bring the city to a standstill. Don't be surprised if there are long periods of bitter weather and occasionally heavy snow. Otherwise, winter days can be bright and clear, even warm in the direct sun.

If you want to see government in action, note that in addition to Christmas and Easter breaks, Congress is in recess for August and the Supreme Court from May to September.

Women

Women travelling alone inevitably face more safety concerns than men or women travelling in groups. Washington is no different from any other big city, so take the usual precautions. Some women carry mace or pepper spray – but note that it is a felony to carry it on an aeroplane, so arm yourself after you reach DC. Many men interpret a woman sitting alone in a bar as a woman wanting to be picked up. If you'd rather be alone, answer any advances with a firm, but polite 'no'.

Local contacts

Center for Women Policy Studies
1211 Connecticut Avenue, suite 312, NW, at Rhode Island Avenue, Dupont Circle (872 1770). Farragut North Metro. **Open** 8.3am-5pm Mon-Fri.
Feminist policy research centre promoting justice and equality for women.
Website: www.centerwomenpolicy.org

National Organization for Women
1000 16th Street, suite 700, NW, at K Street, Downtown (331 0066). McPherson Square Metro.
Open 9am-6pm Mon-Fri.
Plenty of basic information for women on a variety of issues. Can refer women travellers to rape crisis centres and counselling services and provides lists of feminist events. Very active liberals in politics.
Website: www.now.org

Business

There was a time, not that long ago, when the business scene in Washington could pretty much be covered in one word: government. Not only was the federal presence far and away the dominant industry, dealing with it was the primary purpose of most private sector activity.

Government is still the 800lb gorilla of the DC jungle, but in recent years, a number of A-list corporations, such as Mobil Oil and US Airways, have relocated their headquarters to the Capital Region, and a whole new high-tech industry has sprung up along the so-called Dulles Corridor, turning the expressway linking the city with Dulles International Airport in the Virginia countryside into something of a Silicon Valley East. Ground zero is Downtown K Street, lined with glassy office buildings. Citywide, DC now claims to have more office space than any other US city save the big three – New York, Los Angeles and Chicago.

That said, while Washington may have made the big time, standard operating procedures are lower-key than in comparable cities, especially New York. There are similarities, such as the ubiquitous power lunch, but the overall style is less frenetic. In fact, as viewed from New York, Washingtonians have no style. The idea is to dress down: dark (preferably blue) suits, ties with a touch of red (but not so much as to be garish). In summer, when the heat and humidity threaten to reach meltdown levels, light-hued poplin and seersucker suits are almost a uniform. Year-round, by far the preferred accessory is a neck chain from which dangles a photo-ID card – it's virtually a badge of belonging.

Organisations

For details of the **Washington DC Convention & Visitors Association**, *see page 265.* For the **US Customs Service**, *see page 260.*

District of Columbia Chamber of Commerce

1301 Pennsylvania Avenue, NW, suite 309, at 13th Street, Federal Triangle (347 7201). Federal Triangle Metro. **Open** 8.30am-5.30pm Mon-Fri.

Export-Import Bank of the United States

811 Vermont Avenue, NW, between H & I Streets, Downtown (565 3946). McPherson Square Metro. **Open** 8.30am-5pm Mon-Fri. *Website: www.exim.gov*

Greater Washington Board of Trade

1129 20th Street, NW, between L & M Streets, Foggy Bottom (857 5900). Foggy Bottom-GWU Metro. **Open** 8.15am-5.15pm Mon-Fri.

The Board of Trade functions as a regional co-ordinating organisation for DC, northern Virginia and suburban Maryland.

US Department of Commerce

14th Street & Constitution Avenue, NW, Federal Triangle (482 2000). Federal Triangle Metro. **Open** 8am-5.30pm Mon-Fri.

Also contains the Trade Information Center (482 0543/1-800 872 8723).

Conference venues

Washington Convention Center

900 Ninth Street, NW, between New York Avenue & H Street, Downtown (789 1600). Gallery Place-Chinatown Metro. **Open** 8am-5.30pm Mon-Fri; varies Sat.

The premier venue in the Capital Region, the centre was state-of-the-art when it opened in 1982, but has become small and cramped compared to newer facilities in other cities. So a replacement is on the way. Ground was broken in late 1998, with completion set for early 2003.

Hotels

Washington is well stocked with conveniently located hotels catering to business travellers. Those listed below have full business centres with computer and fax facilities, as well as phones with dataports in all rooms. Many are also equipped to handle conferences and large meetings. *See also chapter* **Accommodation**.

Hilton of Alexandria at Mark Center

5000 Seminary Road, at Nottingham Drive, Alexandria, VA (703 845 1010). Pentagon City Metro.
Rates $89-$259.

Hyatt Regency Washington

400 New Jersey Avenue, NW, between D & E Streets, Judiciary Square Area (737 1234). Judiciary Square or Union Station Metro.
Rates $125-$290.

JW Marriott

1331 Pennsylvania Avenue, NW, between 14th & E Streets, Federal Triangle (393 2000). Federal Triangle Metro. **Rates** $234-$1,050.

Marriott Wardman Park

2660 Woodley Road, NW, at Connecticut Avenue, Woodley Park (328 2000). Woodley Park-Zoo Metro. **Rates** $99-$284.

Renaissance Mayflower

1127 Connecticut Avenue, NW, between L & M Streets, Downtown (347 3000). Farragut North Metro.
Rates $155-$575.

Washington Hilton & Towers

1919 Connecticut Avenue, NW, at T Street, Adams Morgan (483 3000). Dupont Circle Metro, then 42 bus.
Rates $204-$1,220.

Willard Inter-Continental

1401 Pennsylvania Avenue, NW, at 14th Street, Federal Triangle (628 9100). Federal Triangle Metro.
Rates $380-$3,500.

Libraries

The **US Department of Commerce Library** (482 5511), has an extensive collection dealing with corporations, export-import activities and other business topics, and is open to the public 1-4pm Mon-Fri. For other libraries, *see page 260.*

Publications

The top domestic business journals are readily available, while foreign publications can be found at larger newsstands. Local journals worth a look include the weekly *Washington Business Journal,* which covers area firms, personalities, developments and trends, and contains a small but useful 'Resource Directory' section.

Business services

Air couriers

All the major international couriers plus several locally based enterprises are active in DC. For other outfits, check *Yellow Pages* under 'Air Cargo & Package Express Service' or 'Delivery Service'. Rates given below are for sending a 4oz package (including pick-up).

Airborne Express
1-800 247 2676. **No credit cards. Rates** approx $14 to Los Angeles, $35 to London.
No deliveries before noon. Call by 7pm for same-day pick-up.

Federal Express
1-800 463 3339. **Credit** AmEx, DC, Disc, MC, V. **Rates** approx $19.25 to Los Angeles by 10.30am, $25.50 to London by second business day.
Call by 6.30pm for same-day pick-up.

Skynet Worldwide Courier
703 548 6022. **Credit** MC, V. **Rates** approx $28 to Los Angeles by noon, $28 to London by second business day.
Based in Alexandria, Virginia. Call before 6pm for same-day pick-up.

United Parcel Service
1-800 742 5877. **Credit** AmEx, DC, MC, V. **Rates** approx $17.25 to Los Angeles by 10.30am, $27.50 to London by second business day.
Call before 7pm for same-day pick-up.

Mobile phone rental

For other providers, check *Yellow Pages* under 'Cellular Telephone Equipment & Supplies'. Most will deliver, for a charge.

Cellular Rental
1008 Sixth Street, NW, at K Street, Downtown (986 2355). Gallery Place-Chinatown Metro. **Open** 8.30am-5pm Mon-Fri. **Credit** AmEx, Disc, MC, V.

Quintex
4425 Wisconsin Avenue, NW, at Nebraska Avenue, Upper Northwest (686 2355). Tenleytown-AU Metro. **Open** 9am-7pm Mon-Fri; 11am-3pm Sat. **Credit** MC, V.

Computer rental & repair

Providers below handle both Mac and IBM-compatible equipment.

Associated Rentals
3610 14th Street, NW, at Spring Road, North of Shaw (462 3222). Georgia Avenue-Petworth Metro. **Open** 9am-6pm Mon-Sat. **Credit** MC, V.
Same-day pick-up and delivery.

Computer Clinic Center
4433 Wisconsin Avenue, NW, between Albemarle Street & Grant Road, Upper Northwest (362 9702). Tenleytown-AU Metro. **Open** 9am-6pm Mon-Fri; 10am-5pm Sat. **Credit** AmEx, Disc, MC, V.
Support and repair.

Messengers

Look in the *Yellow Pages* under 'Delivery' or 'Messenger Service', or try this local company:

Best Messenger
986 0100. **Credit** AmEx, MC, V.
Pick-ups and deliveries within the metro area by bicycle, motorbike or van. You don't need an account; pay by credit card or cash. Rates run from $6.50 to $14.50.

Office space rental

These outfits provide office space, plus services such as telephone answering, net access, receptionists, fax and photocopying, conference facilities – and, in a few cases, free coffee.

Advantis Officing Solutions Worldwide
1215 17th Street, NW, at M Street, Downtown (785 1700/1-800 356 9543). Farragut North Metro. **Open** 8.30am-5.30pm Mon-Fri. **Credit** MC, V.
Branches: 2000 L Street, NW (463 7171); 2300 M Street, NW (973 2800).

International Trade Center
1300 Pennsylvania Avenue, NW, between 13th & 14th Streets, Downtown (312 1300). Federal Triangle or Metro Center Metro. **Open** 8am-6pm Mon-Fri. **Credit** call for details.
Located three blocks from the White House, the Trade Center occupies the Ronald Reagan Building – the newest, second-largest (after the Pentagon) and very very costly federal office building.

Printing & copying

Rates given below are for 50 8 by 11in photocopies.

Kinko's Copies
2000 Pennsylvania Avenue, NW, at I Street, Foggy Bottom (331 9572), Foggy Bottom-GWU Metro. **Open** 24 hours daily. **Credit** AmEx, DC, Disc, MC, V. **Rate** $3.50.
This 24-hour office services chain has plenty of branches in the DC area; call 1-800 254 6567 for your nearest.

Kwik Kopy Printing
1275 K Street, NW, at 13th Street, Downtown (408 1110). McPherson Square Metro. **Open** 8.30am-5.30pm Mon-Fri. **Credit** AmEx, DC, Disc, MC, V. **Rates** $2.50.

Secretarial services

Court House Executive Secretarial Services
910 17th Street, NW, between K & I Streets, Downtown (331 0085). Farragut North or Farragut West Metro. **Open** 9am-5pm Mon-Fri. **No credit cards.**

Manpower
1130 Connecticut Avenue, NW, between L & M Streets, Downtown (331 8300). Farragut North Metro. **Open** 9am-5pm Mon-Fri. **Credit** AmEx, MC, V.
DC outlet of nationwide temp service. Numerous part-timers of varying skill on call.

Translators & interpreters

Diplomatic Language Services
703 243 4856. **Open** 8.30am-5pm Mon-Fri. **Credit** MC, V.
Based in Arlington, Virginia.

TransPerfect Translations
347 2300. **Open** 9am-5.30pm Mon-Fri. **Credit** AmEx, DC, Disc, MC, V.

The US System of Government

ROOTS OF THE SYSTEM

The US system of government follows the broad outlines of a single, 200-year-old document, the United States **Constitution**. The Constitution is the first instance of national government by formal design, rather than happenstance and improvisation, and it has proved flexible enough to accommodate the nation's evolution from a string of coastal settlements to a global power. The Constitution has been appended with 27 Amendments (the first ten, a set of guarantees of personal liberties instituted in the first few years of the republic, are known as the **Bill of Rights**), but its underlying structure is essentially unchanged.

The original 13 states had first experimented with a loose affiliation called the Articles of Confederation, but that arrangement proved inadequate in both foreign affairs and interstate relations. They went back to the drawing board in 1787, when a meeting of mid-Atlantic states over trade and navigation led to a general convention in Philadelphia for the purpose of redrafting the articles. Nationalist leaders such as Alexander Hamilton and James Madison gained the upper hand, however, and the whole system was revamped. The Constitution was the result.

The Founding Fathers (as the conventioneers are called) created a system that rests on two fundamental, related principles: separation of powers, and checks and balances. It is a federal system, with rights and responsibilities apportioned between the various state governments and the national government in Washington, DC. Power at the federal level is further divided among three branches: legislative – **Congress** – to write the laws; judiciary – the **Supreme Court** – to interpret them; and executive – the **Presidency** – to administer them. The underlying theory is that the countervailing functions will cancel out the attempt of any one branch to predominate.

The integrity of individual states was the chief source of dispute at Philadelphia. The resulting Great Compromise called for a bicameral Congress, with equal representation of every state in the upper chamber, the **Senate**, and proportional representation in the lower chamber, the **House of Representatives**.

CONGRESS

The House of Representatives (or, simply, the House) has 435 members, each representing an electoral district of roughly 600,000 voters, though every state is constitutionally guaranteed at least one representative. House members have always been chosen by popular election and stand for office every two years (the next election is in 2000). All House terms run concurrently, so the whole House stands for office simultaneously. Representatives must be aged at least 25, reside in the state in which they run and have been a US citizen for at least seven years.

There are 100 members of the Senate, two from each state, whatever its population. Senatorial terms run for six years. Senators run in 'classes', one-third of the Senate standing for re-election every two years (the next election is also in 2000). Senators must be aged at least 30 and have been a citizen for at least nine years. Senators were originally chosen by individual state legislatures, but in 1913 the Constitution was amended to provide for direct, popular election to the upper chamber.

The House and the Senate meet in separate chambers in the US Capitol.

Because members of the House stand for office so frequently, it is the more populist of the two bodies. House members are by definition more parochial, since the smaller constituencies they represent are more likely to be homogeneous. To compensate for its unruly size, House procedures are very formal and tightly directed. House leadership determines what bills are assigned to what committee, time and length of debate and admissibility of amendments.

The Senate is the more aristocratic body, so overwhelmingly white, male and wealthy it is sometimes called the Millionaires' Club. Because of the length of their terms and because membership elections are staggered, the Senate tends to be more collegial than the House and more resistant to direction. Senators can bypass the committee system and bring legislation directly to the floor. They work with minimal limitation on debate and can amend bills without restriction.

The presiding officer and single most powerful member of the House of Representatives is the **Speaker of the House**, the leader of that body's majority party. Newt Gingrich exemplified the power of that role until the Clinton impeachment fiasco proved his undoing. (Further, the speaker stands second in line of succession to the president, after the VP. If Clinton and Gore had gone down in a plane crash, America would have had President Newt.)

The **Vice President** serves as the presiding officer in the Senate, but his function is more symbolic than real. Actual power in the Senate rests in the hands of the **Majority Leader** (the leader of whichever party has most seats), the best recent example being Lyndon Johnson, in his legislative, arm-twisting heyday. Senators tend to be patrician types, however, so they are not easily led.

The legislative powers of the national government extend to areas of taxation, commerce and foreign relations. Congress is authorised to tax and borrow, to coin money, establish a postal system, regulate patents and raise armed forces. The Senate has exclusive power over the ratification of treaties, so it has more influence than the House in foreign affairs. Two-thirds of the Senate must concur for a treaty to become law. The Senate also has right of approval over presidential nominees to the cabinet, as ambassadors and to the federal judiciary. The House has more control of the federal purse, however, since the Constitution specifies that all revenue bills must originate there.

Both houses are organised in a system of committees and sub-committees with specific areas of legislative concern. Committee assignments are determined in the separate caucuses of the two major political parties, which also draft competing legislative programmes. Committee chairmanships are extremely powerful positions and are usually assigned to the senior member of the majority party on each committee.

Because the Constitution's language includes the accordion-like directive that Congress shall 'make all laws necessary and proper for carrying into execution' the enumerated powers, its legislative reach has grown enormously over the years.

Investigation has become almost as significant a part of Congressional activity as legislation, and decidedly more high profile, particularly with the televising of hearings. Investigative committees have become one of Congress's chief tools for enforcing executive branch accountability – from the Teapot Dome oil reserve scandal of the Harding administration to the Iran-Contra hearings of the Reagan era. The investigative function came into ill repute during the subversive activities inquisitions of the 1950s, especially the Red scare witch-hunts of Senator Joe McCarthy.

THE PRESIDENCY

The US president is simultaneously prime minister and head of state, and it is here that American ambivalence concerning authority is focused. A nation as diverse as the United States hungers for leadership to hold it together while, at the same time, its ethos of individualism provokes scepticism of power. The pomp and circumstance surrounding the White House occupant's symbolic embodiment of the nation skews the perception of his merely managerial functions.

The president is elected for a four-year term (the next election is in 2000) and can serve only two terms in total. Since the whole House and one-third of the Senate stands for election every two years, every presidential election coincides with the election of the new House and one Senate class.

As the nation's chief administrative officer, the president commands several million civilian employees in nearly 100 separate departments, agencies and bureaus. The most important of these are the 14 Cabinet departments, of which the four key and original ones are Foreign Affairs (now State), War (now Defense), Treasury, and Justice (formally, the Attorney General). Each department head, with the exception of the Attorney General, is referred to as the 'Secretary'.

Cabinet secretaries and other major executive branch officers may be elected officials (in which case they would resign their previous offices), but can be chosen from any field. They are subject to approval by the Senate but rarely rejected. Lesser officials and employees of the executive branch – some 85 per cent of the total – are career civil servants exempt from dismissal through a change of regime.

The Constitution's description of presidential powers is surprisingly limited. In addition to the role of commander-in-chief of the armed forces, the president receives foreign ministers and grants federal pardons. The president's annual State of the Union address includes recommended legislation and the president can veto legislation – but his veto can be overridden by a two-thirds vote of both houses of Congress. The president negotiates foreign treaties – but their approval requires a two-thirds vote in the Senate. The president appoints federal judges – but that also requires the Senate's 'advice and consent'. Presidents have nominal leadership of their political party but may face a Congress that is under the control of the opposition party – as has frequently been the case in the post-war era.

Since presidents are elected by the nation at large, they are expected, realistically or not, to rise above partisanship. The framers of the Constitution envisioned the chief magistrate as a check upon legislative excess. But with America's emergence as a world power and the rise of the 'Imperial Presidency', that equation has been stood on its head.

Filibusters

One of the peculiarities of the Senate for many years was its rule of 'unlimited debate'. Since Senators could hold the floor for an unlimited period of time, those in a minority position on an issue could block consideration of bills for as long as they could stand and talk. This practice came to be known as the 'filibuster', derived from a Dutch word for freebooter.

The filibuster was practised as far back as the 1840s and reached epidemic proportions in the late nineteenth century. A 'cloture' (closure) rule, adopted in 1917, provided that a two-thirds vote of the Senate could cut off debate but was rarely enforced. In addition to interminable oratory, wily parliamentarians could obstruct legislation through the introduction of one after another trivial and/or arcane parliamentary motions.

The modern practice of the filibuster has been by Southern senators attempting to block passage of civil rights legislation. Strom Thurmond, the centenarian South Carolina senator, holds the record for the longest such effort, holding forth for over 24 hours in an around-the-clock session in the summer of 1957.

Senate rules do not require that floor speakers address the topic under consideration, so it is not unusual for practised filibusterers to wander far afield. In 1935, Louisiana senator Huey 'Kingfish' Long sprinkled a 15-hour speech with recipes for Southern-style cooking and 'pot likker', and an Idaho senator of the 1940s livened up an eight-hour stand with observations on such unrelated topics as fishing, baptism and Wall Street manoeuvring.

For example, Congress has the exclusive power to declare war, but the president is commander-in-chief and he alone treats directly with foreign nations. After the US became a global power, the effective understanding was that 'politics stops at the water's edge', and Congressional dissent ended when American forces went into combat.

Consequently, throughout the twentieth century, American troops, at the president's directive and without Congressional authorisation, have frequently gone into action throughout the world. This balance righted itself somewhat when domestic political discontent over Vietnam finally emboldened Congress to reassert its prerogatives and limit presidential war-making authority with the War Powers Act of 1973. Still, the executive retains enough leeway that Ronald Reagan was free to invade Grenada and Bill Clinton to police Somalia.

Presidential power has evolved over time in step with the immense growth of the federal government, but it is also a highly personalised affair that varies in accordance with the character of the individual.

Media-savvy JFK utilised star power in the 1960s; a dour, paranoid Richard Nixon dabbled in intrigue; and the experienced professional pitchman Ronald Reagan perfected the art of image manipulation as the Great Communicator.

THE COURTS

The judicial branch of American government consists of three levels of tribunals. Numerous district courts are seated throughout the states, an intermediate level of appellate courts sits in 'circuits' above them, and the **Supreme Court** – consisting of a chief justice and eight associate justices – sits in Washington, DC. The number of justices has varied from six to ten but been steady at nine for nearly a century.

The federal courts do not rule directly on law, but on cases arising under the law. Any dispute that hinges on matters in which federal law is at issue or where an aggrieved party claims an infringement of constitutionally specified rights can be heard in these courts. As cases make their way up this legal ladder, the constitutional validity of particular acts of Congress or the executive may be determined.

The Court aspires to an Olympian detachment, but since its decisions frequently touch on fiercely contested matters – abortion rights, racial issues – it is an inescapably political institution. During the 1960s and '70s, it was social conservatives who decried the Court's 'judicial activism' – school desegregation orders, for example – but, in the 1930s, it was FDR who damned the 'nine old men' and tried to pack the court with new appointees more to his liking.

Selection for the court is through nomination by the president and confirmation by the Senate. Since appointments are for life (with the proviso of 'good behaviour', an exception rarely invoked) it is during the confirmation process that controversies around the Court become most heated. The battle over the nomination of Clarence Thomas in 1991 was only the most recent but far the ugliest, touching on questions of both race and gender.

Presidents of the USA

George Washington
Served: 30 April 1789 – 3 March 1797
Elected from: Virginia
Born: 22 February 1732
Died: 14 December 1799
Political party: Federalist
Vice President: John Adams (1789-97)
Known as 'Father of Our Country'. Leading member of Southern plantation aristocracy. Military commander of US revolutionary forces. Presiding officer of Constitutional Convention. Only unanimous selection (twice) to chief executive position. Warned against the formation of political parties and foreign entanglements.

John Adams
Served: 4 March 1797 – 3 March 1801
Elected from: Massachusetts
Born: 30 October 1735
Died: 4 July 1826
Political party: Federalist
Vice President: Thomas Jefferson (1797-1801)
Political philosopher with autocratic tendencies. War hysteria over difficulties with new French republic leads to Alien and Sedition Acts, in violation of rights of habeas corpus and free speech.

Thomas Jefferson
Served: 4 March 1801 – 3 March 1809
Elected from: Virginia
Born: 13 April 1743
Died: 4 July 1826
Political party: Democratic-Republican
Vice Presidents: Aaron Burr (1801-05); George Clinton (1805-09)
Free-thinking polymath and author of Declaration of Independence. Sends US Navy into battle against Barbary Coast pirates. Purchases Louisiana from French, more than doubling size of US territory. Losing dispute with Supreme Court establishes power of judicial review.

James Madison
Served: 4 March 1809 – 3 March 1817
Elected from: Virginia
Born: 16 March 1751
Died: 28 June 1836
Political party: Democratic-Republican
Vice Presidents: George Clinton (1809-12); Elbridge Gerry (1813-14)
Leading architect of Constitution. Maritime dispute with Britain, coupled with expansionist dreams of annexation of Canada, leads to inconclusive War of 1812 (known in Britain as American War of Independence), during which New England Federalists contemplate secession and British capture Washington, DC, torching the White House. American victory at Battle of New Orleans (fought after peace treaty signed) assuages national pride.

James Monroe
Served: 4 March 1817 – 3 March 1825
Elected from: Virginia
Born: 28 April 1758
Died: 4 July 1831
Political party: Democratic-Republican
Vice President: Daniel D Tompkins (1817-1825)
Last Revolutionary-era figure to occupy White House. Formulates Monroe Doctrine, closing western hemisphere to European intervention. US turns inward, focusing on domestic growth and infrastructure matters. Slavery question comes to fore over admission of new states, but Missouri Compromise forestalls ultimate resolution.

John Quincy Adams
Served: 4 March 1825 – 3 March 1829
Elected from: Massachusetts
Born: 11 July 1767
Died: 23 February 1848
Political party: Democratic-Republican
Vice President: John C Calhoun (1825-29)
'Boston Brahmin' and son of second president. Served as secretary of state under Monroe, negotiating acquisition of Florida and Oregon Territory. Captures presidency in ballot by House of Representatives, after none of four candidates gains majority in either popular or electoral vote. Initiates extensive canal and highway construction programme.

Andrew Jackson
Served: 4 March 1829 – 3 March 1837
Elected from: Tennessee
Born: 15 March 1767
Died: 8 June 1845
Political party: Democratic
Vice Presidents: John C Calhoun (1829-1832); Martin Van Buren (1832-1837)
Military leader at Battle of New Orleans and subjugator of south-east Indian tribes. Combative backwoods lawyer ('Old Hickory'), becomes first commoner to rise to presidency. Introduces spoils system of bureaucratic appointments. Makes frequent use of veto power, most prominently to prevent creation of national bank. Challenges orders of Supreme Court. Threatens use of troops over South Carolina's attempt to nullify federal law.

Martin Van Buren
Served: 4 March 1837 – 3 March 1841
Elected from: New York
Born: 5 December 1782
Died: 24 July 1862
Political party: Democratic
Vice President: Richard M Johnson (1837-41)
One of the first 'machine' politicians, rising to US Senate seat with support of New York political organisation. Panic of 1837 throws country into five years of severe economic depression and cripples administration.

William Henry Harrison
Served: 4 March 1841 – 4 April 1841
Elected from: Ohio
Born: 9 February 1773
Died: 4 April 1841
Political party: Whig
Vice President: John Tyler (1841)
Another veteran of the War of 1812 and assorted Indian suppression campaigns. Delivers longest inaugural address on record, promising not to run for a second term. Contracts pneumonia and dies the same spring, thus having the shortest presidential term.

John Tyler
Served: 6 April 1841 – 3 March 1845
Elected from: Virginia
Born: 29 March 1790
Died: 18 January 1862
Political party: Whig
Vice President: none
Popularly known as 'His Accidency', first president elevated to presidency because of death of the chief executive. First subject of impeachment inquiry, as a result of tariff dispute. Encourages settlement of Northwest Territories (present-day Midwest) and annexes Texas.

James Knox Polk
Served: 4 March 1845 – 3 March 1849
Elected from: Tennessee
Born: 2 November 1795
Died: 15 June 1849
Political party: Democratic
Vice President: George M Dallas (1845-1849)
Protégé of Andrew Jackson and an ardent expansionist. Negotiates present-day boundary with Canada in

the Pacific Northwest. Provokes war with Mexico that results in conquest of American Southwest and California. New territories reignite dispute over expansion of slavery.

Zachary Taylor

Served: 5 March 1849 – 9 July 1850
Elected from: Louisiana
Born: 24 November 1784
Died: 9 July 1850
Political party: Whig
Vice President: Millard Fillmore (1849-50)
Career army officer, Indian fighter and commander in Mexican War. Slave-owning Southerner, presses for admission to US of California and New Mexico despite their status as free territories, to the dismay of Southern states. Threatens use of force to hold the Union together. Dies from complications after a bout of indigestion following Fourth of July festivities.

Millard Fillmore

Served: 9 July 1850 – 3 March 1853
Elected from: New York
Born: 7 January 1800
Died: 8 March 1874
Political party: Whig
Vice President: none
Another product of New York state machine politics. An opponent of slavery but a supporter of states' rights. Approves Compromise of 1850, which admits California as a free state and abolishes slave trade in Washington, DC, but strengthens fugitive slave laws. Authorises Commodore Perry's expedition to Japan.

Franklin Pierce

Served: 4 March 1853 – 3 March 1857
Elected from: New Hampshire
Born: 23 November 1804
Died: 8 October 1869
Political party: Democrat
Vice President: William R King (1853-57)
Personally engaging but distracted by family tragedy. Opposed to both abolitionism and sectionalism. Fails to cope with consequences of Kansas-Nebraska Act, which reopens slavery issue and provokes bloodshed on the plains. Practises gunboat diplomacy in Nicaragua and hatches schemes to annex Cuba.

James Buchanan

Served: 4 March 1857 – 3 March 1861
Elected from: Pennsylvania
Born: 23 April 1791
Died: 1 June 1868
Political party: Democrat
Vice President: John C Breckinridge (1857-61)
Veteran legislator and diplomat, ran on 'Save the Union' theme but fails to reconcile contending factions. Manages Kansas's admission to the Union as a free state but still offends both sides. Staves off hostilities despite secession of seven Deep South states.

Abraham Lincoln

Served: 4 March 1861 – 15 April 1865
Elected from: Illinois
Born: 12 February 1809
Died: 15 April 1865
Political party: Republican
Vice Presidents: Hannibal Hamlin (1861-65); Andrew Johnson (1865)
Tall and gangly, self-educated and folksy, a renowned public speaker with a streak of melancholy, 'Honest Abe' holds a mythic status in American life rivalled only by George Washington. Rose from frontier poverty to lead the nation through Civil War. His 'Emancipation Proclamation' of 1 January 1863 abolishes slavery in the rebellious states. Murdered within days of the war's conclusion.

Andrew Johnson

Served: 15 April 1865 – 3 March 1869
Elected from: Tennessee
Born: 29 December 1808
Died: 31 July 1875
Political party: Democratic
Vice President: none
Humble artisan inspired to political engagement by Jacksonian egalitarianism. Conciliatory approach to former rebel states draws wrath of Congress. First president to be impeached by the House.
Acquitted in Senate by a one-vote margin. His secretary of state's purchase of Alaska becomes known as 'Seward's Folly'.

Ulysses Simpson Grant

Served: 4 March 1869 – 3 March 1877
Elected from: Illinois
Born: 27 April 1822
Died: 23 July 1885
Political party: Republican
Vice Presidents: Schuyler Colfax (1869-73); Henry Wilson (1873-75)
Rough-hewn, hard-drinking commanding general of the Union army. Two terms in office rife with financial scandal. Policy towards the South does nothing for freed blacks. Foreign policy includes botched effort to annex Santo Domingo (now Dominican Republic).

Rutherford Birchard Hayes

Served: 4 March 1877 – 3 March 1881
Elected from: Ohio
Born: 4 October 1822
Died: 17 January 1893
Political party: Republican
Vice President: William A Wheeler (1877-81)
Progressive Republican who came into office through disputed election settled with the appointment of a special commission. Withdraws armed federal support of 'carpetbag' governments in South, ending Reconstruction. Initiates federal civil service reform.

James Abram Garfield

Served: 4 March 1881 – 19 September 1881
Elected from: Ohio
Born: 19 November 1831
Died: 19 September 1881
Political party: Republican
Vice President: Chester A Arthur (1881)
Last president born in a log cabin. Efforts at further civil service reform and more enlightened policy toward Latin America stillborn. Assassinated after just six months in office.

Chester Alan Arthur

Served: 19 September 1881 – 3 March 1885
Elected from: New York
Born: 5 October 1830
Died: 18 November 1886
Political party: Republican
Vice President: none
Bon vivant and man about town. Product of an especially corrupt New York political machine led a surprisingly clean administration that culminated in final enshrinement of merit system of appointments. Many other initiatives stymied by Congressional resistance.

Grover Cleveland

Served: 4 March 1885 – 3 March 1889 and 4 March 1893 – 3 March 1897
Elected from: New York
Born: 18 March 1837
Died: 24 June 1908
Political party: Democrat
Vice Presidents: Thomas A Henricks (1885-89); Adlai E Stevenson (1893-97)
Reform-minded New York politician reasserted presidential authority vis-à-vis Congress. Lost first re-election effort in campaign marked by blatant vote-buying on both sides. Second term, four years later, clouded by economic depression following Panic of 1893. Federal troops crush Pullman railroad strike of 1894 and imprison union leaders.

Benjamin Harrison

Served: 4 March 1889 – 3 March 1893
Elected from: Indiana
Born: 20 August 1833
Died: 13 March 1901
Political party: Republican

Vice President: Levi P Morton (1889-93)
Descendant of prominent colonial family and grandson of President William Harrison. Advocate of high tariffs and a two-ocean navy. Sherman Antitrust Act forbids corporate collusion in restraint of trade.

William McKinley

Served: 4 March 1897 – 14 September 1901
Elected from: Ohio
Born: 29 January 1843
Died: 14 September 1901
Political party: Republican
Vice Presidents: Garret A Hobart (1897-99); Theodore Roosevelt (1901)
Prominent advocate of hard money and high tariffs, better remembered for foreign adventures. Spanish-American War results in the annexation of Puerto Rico and occupation of Cuba and the Philippines. 'Open Door' policy in China leads to armed intervention in Boxer Rebellion. Assassinated early in second term.

Theodore Roosevelt

Served: 14 September 1901 – 3 March 1909
Elected from: New York
Born: 27 October 1858
Died: 6 January 1919
Political party: Republican
Vice President: Charles W Fairbanks (1905-09)
Kiplingesque scion of prominent New York merchant clan. 'Square Deal' regulation of corporate monopoly power. 'Big-stick' diplomacy projects American power globally. Engineers Panamanian Revolution to assure US control of future Canal Zone.

William Howard Taft

Served: 4 March 1909 – 3 March 1913
Elected from: Ohio
Born: 15 September 1857
Died: 8 March 1930
Political party: Republican
Vice President: James S Sherman (1909-12)
Elephantine first US governor-general of the Philippines. Tepid administrator split with Roosevelt wing of Republican party. Served as chief justice of the Supreme Court in the 1920s.

Woodrow Wilson

Served: 4 March 1913 – 3 March 1921
Elected from: New Jersey
Born: 28 December 1856
Died: 3 February 1924
Political party: Democrat
Vice President: Thomas R Marshall (1913-21)
Professional academic whose moralistic zeal led to domestic fiscal and social reform and repeated foreign intervention in Latin America. Entry into World War I assured German defeat. Idealistic post-war foreign policy founders on Congressional isolationism.

Warren Gamaliel Harding

Served: 4 March 1921 – 2 August 1923
Elected from: Ohio
Born: 2 November 1865
Died: 2 August 1923
Political party: Republican
Vice President: Calvin Coolidge (1921-23)
Small-town newspaper editor and tool of Ohio political machine. Deferred to Congressional leadership and the influence of poker-playing cronies. Numerous corruption scandals erupted shortly after his death in office.

Calvin Coolidge

Served: 3 August 1923 – 3 March 1929
Elected from: Massachusetts
Born: 4 July 1872
Died: 5 January 1933
Political party: Republican
Vice President: Charles G Dawes (1925-29)
Famously taciturn 'Silent Cal' (apocryphal quip, to a dining companion who bet she could get him to say more than two words: 'You lose'). Presided over domestic economic boom of the Roaring Twenties. Negotiated 1928 Kellogg-Briand international non-belligerence pact.

Herbert Clark Hoover

Served: 4 March 1929 – 3 March 1933
Elected from: California
Born: 10 August 1874
Died: 20 October 1964
Political party: Republican
Vice President: Charles Curtis (1929-33)
Dour professional engineer and post-World War I international relief director. Determinedly laissez-faire economic policies proved inadequate to Crash of '29 and Great Depression that followed. Maintained isolationist foreign policy, but supported disarmament efforts of 1930 London Naval Conference.

Franklin Delano Roosevelt

Served: 4 March 1933 – 12 April 1945
Elected from: New York
Born: 30 January 1882
Died: 12 April 1945
Political party: Democrat
Vice Presidents: John N Garner (1933-41); Henry A Wallace (1941-45); Harry S Truman (1945)
Scion of Hudson Valley gentry, same line as Theodore Roosevelt. Master of bonhomie (despite ill health), wins unparalleled four terms in office. Leads unprecedented expansion of federal power in response to Great Depression of 1930s and World War II. Lays groundwork for post-war social welfare policies and United Nations.

Harry S Truman

Served: 12 April 1945 – 20 January 1953
Elected from: Missouri
Born: 8 May 1884
Died: 26 December 1972
Political party: Democrat
Vice President: Alben W Barkley (1949-53)
Feisty product of Kansas City political machine. Authorised use of nuclear weapons against Japan. Initiated cold war 'containment' policy in Europe and armed intervention in Korean conflict. Domestic policies blocked by Congressional resistance and domestic anti-communist hysteria.

Dwight David Eisenhower

Served: 20 January 1953 – 20 January 1961
Elected from: New York
Born: 14 October 1890
Died: 28 March 1969
Political party: Republican
Vice President: Richard M Nixon (1953-61)
Avuncular former military leader presides over maturation of middle-class consumer society. Effects cessation of Korean military conflict. Prosecutes cold war through threat of 'massive retaliation'. Warns against power of domestic 'military-industrial complex'.

John Fitzgerald Kennedy

Served: 20 January 1961 – 22 November 1963
Elected from: Massachusetts
Born: 29 May 1917
Died: 22 November 1963
Political party: Democrat
Vice President: Lyndon B Johnson (1961-63)
Telegenic scion of Irish-American tycoon is the US's first Catholic president. Authorises manned space exploration programme. Avid cold warrior, bungles invasion of Cuba and approaches brink of nuclear war over Soviet missile emplacements on that island. Extends American commitment to South Vietnamese regime. Assassinated in Dallas.

Electing the president

The president is elected on the basis of a nationwide popular vote, but it is an indirect election. Although in most states only the names of the presidential candidates appear on the ballot papers, voters are actually choosing their state's representatives in the Electoral College, which choses the president and vice president in a majority vote. Electoral candidates are pledged to support their party's presidential nominees, and while they are, in theory, free to cast their vote for whoever they wish, through time and custom they almost invariably accede to the voters' direction and go with party affiliation.

Each state is allotted a number of Electors equivalent to the combined total of their representatives and senators.

Representation is not proportional; Electoral candidates affiliated to the party whose presidential hopeful gets most votes assume all the places in the College. This means that it is possible for the winning candidate to have less than a majority of the popular vote. That was the case with Kennedy in 1960, Nixon in 1968 and Clinton in 1992 and 1996. This skews the concerns of candidates toward those states that have the largest number of electors – California, New York, Texas and Florida – since even a slender majority in any state garners all of that state's votes. There have been repeated efforts through the years to reform the system but the consensus has been that, despite its flaws, there is no obviously superior alternative.

Lyndon Baines Johnson

Served: 22 November 1963 – 20 January 1969
Elected from: Texas
Born: 27 August 1908
Died: 22 January 1973
Political party: Democrat
Vice President: Hubert H Humphrey (1965-69)
Effusive Texan institutes ambitious Great Society social welfare programme and advances civil rights legislation. Deepens US involvement in Vietnamese civil war. Widespread domestic racial unrest and cultural ferment.

Richard Milhous Nixon

Served: 20 January 1969 – 9 August 1974
Elected from: New York
Born: 9 January 1913
Died: 22 April 1994
Political party: Republican
Vice Presidents: Spiro T Agnew (1969-73); Gerald R Ford (1973-74)
Anti-communist crusader of the 1950s oversees beginning of US withdrawal from Vietnam. Opens dialogue with People's Republic of China. Resigns in disgrace after impeachment by House for domestic political crimes collectively known as Watergate.

Gerald Rudolph Ford

Served: 9 August 1974 – 20 January 1977
Elected from: Michigan
Born: 14 July 1913
Political party: Republican
Vice President: Nelson A Rockefeller (1974-77)
Affable Midwesterner functions as interim leader following Nixon débàcle. Congress reasserts itself, cuts off funds for South Vietnamese and exposes illicit activities of CIA.

James Earl Carter Jr

Served: 20 January 1977 – 20 January 1981
Elected from: Georgia
Born: 1 October 1924
Political party: Democrat
Vice President: Walter F Mondale (1977-81)
Southern liberal institutes foreign policy keyed to human rights questions. Fumbles question of American dependence on foreign oil. Quandary over Iranian siege of American embassy in Teheran proves political undoing.

Ronald Wilson Reagan

Served: 20 January 1981 – 20 January 1989
Elected from: California
Born: 6 February 1911
Political party: Republican
Vice President: George Bush (1981-89)
Professional actor and TV pitchman. Leads conservative effort to dismantle post-war social welfare policies. Huge increases in military spending drive national debt to unprecedented heights, but also bankrupt Soviet regime. Flirts with impeachment over illegal arms deals in Middle East and covert operations in Latin America (Iran-Contra affair).

George Herbert Walker Bush

Served: 20 January 1989 – 20 January 1993
Elected from: Texas
Born: 12 June 1924
Political party: Republican
Vice President: J Danforth Quayle (1989-93)
Eastern patrician and moderate conservative whose party was under control of Sunbelt hard right-wing. Laid basis for North American Free Trade zone. Authorised military intervention in Panama. Irresolute Middle Eastern policy followed by inconclusive Gulf War.

William Jefferson Clinton

Served: 20 January 1993 – present
Elected from: Arkansas
Born: 19 August 1946
Political party: Democrat
Vice President: Albert Gore, Jr (1993-present)
First baby boomer president. Leads Democratic party to political right on welfare, crime and other social issues. First post-cold war president. Authorises military interventions in Haiti, Somalia and former Yugoslavia. Squabble over personal life (Lewinsky affair) leads to impeachment by House. Senate fails to convict.

Further Reading

Non-fiction

Jonetta Rose Barras
The Last of the Black Emperors: The Hollow Comeback of Marion Barry in a New Age of Black Leaders
A critical look at the career of infamous DC Mayor Marion Barry, from his beginnings as a civil rights leader to his drug-induced fall to his improbable rebirth.

Carl Bernstein & Bob Woodward
All the President's Men
The story behind the reporting that subsequently forced President Richard Nixon to resign and forever changed the American presidency.

David Brinkley
Washington Goes to War
Highly rated history of the capital city during World War II, under the presidency of FDR, charting its move on to the international stage.

Cynthia Connolly
Banned in DC: Photos and Anecdotes from the DC Punk Underground
Photo-heavy, first-person accounts of DC's hardcore punk heyday.

Katherine Graham
Personal History
The autobiography of the erstwhile publisher of the *Washington Post*, undoubtedly one of the most powerful women of her time.

Harry Jaffe & Tom Sherwood
Dream City: Race, Power and the Decline of Washington, DC
An in-depth look at how race and power-lust corrupted local politics in Washington.

PJ O'Rourke
Parliament of Whores
America's most scabrous and hilarious right-wing commentator gets to grips with the US political system, as practised in Washington. Very funny.

Bob Woodward
Shadow: Five Presidents & the Legacy of Watergate
Recent (1999), thought-provoking bestseller by scoopmeister Woodward on how the Watergate affair affected subsequent presidential scandals, culminating in an entertaining, fly-on-the-wall account of Monicagate.

Fiction

Anonymous
Primary Colors
A temperamental, philandering Southern governor becomes president of the US with the help of an ambitious wife and morally questionable campaign tactics. Sound at all familiar? The author was eventually identified as journalist and Washington insider Joe Klein.

William Peter Blatty
The Exorcist
The infamous 1970s horror story of the possession of a teenage girl (subsequently turned into a very very scary film) was based around Georgetown University.

Christopher Buckley
Thank You for Smoking
Send-up of TV pundits and political special interest groups; a political cartoon drawn with words.

John Grisham
The Pelican Brief
Bestselling legal/conspiracy mystery (made into a film with Julia Roberts and Denzel Washington) kicks off

Resources

The cradle of satire

Washington is the seat of American government, but not the seat of American culture, and Americans tend to see life inside the Beltway as somehow foreign to American life generally. Consequently, the city remains something of a specialised sideshow in American literature.

Allen Drury's 1959 melodramatic blockbuster *Advise and Consent* remains the all-time Washington bestseller, while Gore Vidal's five-volume American Chronicle series offers the biggest, least sugar-coated, contemporary canvas of the capital and its place in American history. Vidal is from a prominent American political family (which includes the current vice president) and writes with the advantage of an insider's knowledge of Washington ways.

Usually, however, when writers turn their pens to Washington, the result is satire. The cartoonish exaggerations of American politics' main stage beg for it. The flavour of the work changes with the tenor of the times – buffoonish, bitter, surreal – but the edge is always there. The major literature of the manners and morals (such as they are) of the national capital includes:

Mark Twain's The Gilded Age (1873); Henry Adams' Democracy (1880)

A set of *romans-à-clef*, both featuring Washington in the grip of the Robber Barons, with offices and legislation blatantly auctioned off to the highest bidder. Twain's sprawling, broadly sensationalistic novel gained more of an audience than Adams' more sober approach, and the Gilded Age came to serve as a standard historical name for the period.

Sinclair Lewis's It Can't Happen Here (1935); Nathanael West's A Cool Million (1954)

Washington is the setting for studies of the emerging threat of fascism. Nobel Prize winner Lewis and elegant miniaturist West both imagine victorious fascist campaigns for the presidency. Lewis's book is straightforward with the assassination of two Supreme Court judges.

Ward Just
Echo House
The story of three generations of a powerful Washington family written by a former *Washington Post* reporter and foreign correspondent.

Carole Marsh
Chill Out! Scary Washington, DC Stories based on Frightening Washington, DC Truths!
Fictional stories based on true DC events, this book aims to help kids become interested in the capital.

Brad Meltzer
The Tenth Justice
Bestselling thriller based on the travails of an ambitious young clerk to a Supreme Court justice.

George P Pelecanos
King Suckerman
A hard-boiled literary homage to blaxploitation films that takes place during the bicentennial celebration in Washington, DC.

Elliott Roosevelt
Murder in the Map Room (and other titles)
Series of White House murder mysteries written by FDR's son, with First Lady Eleanor Roosevelt as the problem-solving sleuth.

Gore Vidal
Empire
A historical novel based on Theodore Roosevelt's Washington, Vidal's epic brings America during the Gilded Age into vivid focus. Vidal's other books in the same American Chronicle series, tracing the history of the US, are *Burr, Lincoln, 1876* and *Washington DC.*

Walt Whitman
Drum-Taps
Whitman's war poems were directly influenced by his work in Civil War hospitals in Washington. *Leaves of Grass* (first edition 1855) lost him his job at DC's Bureau of Indian Affairs when the Secretary of the Interior objected to it.

Reference

Holly Bass, Arthur Frommer, Ann Berta & Theodore Fischer
Frommer's Irreverent Guide to Washington, DC (2nd edition)
Off-beat guide.

Sandra Fitzpatrick & Maria R Goodwin
The Guide to Black Washington
Sights, places and events, located by area, of significance to DC's African-American heritage.

Cynthia Hacinli & William Connor
Romantic Days and Nights in DC
Ideas and information for romantic excursions in and around the DC area.

Phyllis C Richman
The Washington Post 1999-2000 Dining Guide
Eating guide written by the *Post*'s restaurant critic

Pamela Scott & Antoinette J Lee
Buildings of the District of Columbia
Detailed architectural history of DC, from the Revolutionary War to post-World War II, with 360 photos, drawings and maps.

Christopher Weeks
AIA Guide to the Architecture of Washington, DC
Concise descriptions and photos of DC's most notable structures, including 100 built since the mid-70s.

Tom Weil
America's South: The Atlantic States
Historical/cultural guide to Virginia, North and South Carolina, Georgia and Florida, including Civil War sites.

and polemical, West's a bitterly funny twist on Horatio Alger.

Norman Mailer's Superman Comes to the Supermarket (1960) & Armies of the Night (1968)

Two classics of the 1960s New Journalism. The first, a seminal *Esquire* article, brilliantly dissected the Democratic Party and its presidential nominating convention of that year. The article was particularly noteworthy for its analysis of the character and abilities of the eventual Democratic candidate, young John Kennedy, and it probably swayed more than a few wavering liberals into an accommodation with the stylish patrician. Towards the decade's end, Mailer's impassioned reportage of the 1968 anti-war March on the Pentagon (and his own participation in it), won the author his first Pulitzer Prize.

Hunter S Thompson's Fear and Loathing on the Campaign Trail (1972)

Gonzo journalism, Hunter Thompson's drug-fuelled, hallucinatory version of campaign reportage was original, comic and unpredictable. What other writer would have detailed the joys of a late-night discussion with Richard Nixon on the deep strategies of American football? Or reported that the mood swings of future secretary of state Edmund Muskie were due to his addiction to the African psychoactive plant, ibogaine.

Nixoniana

The politician American intellectuals loved to hate provoked the imaginations of some of America's leading novelists . From Philip Roth's acid pen came *Our Gang* (1971), about the manoeuvres of a deceitful and larcenous President Trick E Dixon. Kurt Vonnegut turned out two Washington novels, *Slapstick: Or Lonesome No More!* (1976), the fictional memoirs of a future American ex-president, and *Jailbird* (1979), whose protagonist is a fictional Watergate felon. Joseph Heller's *Good as Gold* (1979) recounted the misadventures of a middle-aged Jewish academic caught up in Washington's bureaucratic underbrush.

A-Z of politikspeak

A is for Acronym
Washingtonian bureaucratic shorthand, such as SALT (Strategic Arms Limitation Treaty).

B is for Boondoggle
Wasteful or corrupt project involving government funds; any such project occurring in a legislative district not the speaker's own or that of his political allies.

C is for Camelot
Mythical Kennedy White House, where all the men were Ivy League intellectuals and dinner music was by Pablo Casals. Those who recall legislative drift and foreign policy fumbling refer to it as 'Camelittle'.

D is for Demagogue
Any political figure whose oratorical talents arouse the general population in ways not favoured by the observer. If compatible with the observer's beliefs, a great leader.

E is for Executive Privilege
President's legal authority to withhold information from Congress when such disclosure would impair their ability to perform the functions of office or reveal violations of domestic and international law.

F is for Foggy Bottom
Sometimes used for the State Department. Derived from the district it occupies, formerly a swampy, industrial area. Not a comment on the diplomatic state of mind.

G is for Gridlock
Procedural confusion and/or conflict in which legislative activity grinds to a halt. Also a frequent occurrence in District traffic.

H is for the Hill
The White House rests on land that is 55ft above sea level; the Capitol on a rise that is 33ft higher. There are places of greater elevation in DC, but only one Hill.

I is for Incumbency
In a city where politics is the common religion, the holding of office is the Holy Grail, enlightenment, state of grace and sign of divine favour.

J is for Junket
Congressional fact-finding mission to foreign locales. Usually in winter, to warm climes with deluxe hotels and intensive dining and recreational opportunities.

K is for Kitchen Cabinet
An advisory council of presidential political cronies and poker-playing buddies, functioning outside the routes of Congressional oversight.

L is for Leak
An unauthorised disclosure of information, or deliberate disclosure in such a manner that its source can be disavowed. Richard Nixon created his secret counter-intelligence team, the Plumbers, to prevent leaks.

M is for McCarthyism
From the smear tactics of the anti-Communist, rabble-rousing senator of the early 1950s. The attempt to drive Bill Clinton from office for adulterous behaviour was called 'sexual McCarthyism'.

N is for Neoconservatives
Formerly mildly leftish policy mavens whose abhorrence of 1960s counterculture drove them to right of political spectrum. 'A liberal who's been mugged.'

O is for Officialese
Gobbledygook designed to keep officeholders' mouths moving, their followers engaged and information stifled.

P is for Pork
Short for 'pork barrel' legislation, from the Southern practice of feeding slaves from such. A form of bacon that legislators strive to bring home, though if found in other's districts, is a boondoggle (*see above* **B**).

Q is for Quagmire
What the Pentagon found itself in in Vietnam. Now used for any sticky political situation, though George Bush preferred the term 'deep doo-doo'.

R is for Rose Garden
Secluded area on the White House grounds where presidents relax, meditate and hide from the press while their aides field questions. Thus, 'Rose Garden strategy'.

S is for Situation Room
Area of the White House basement used for high-strategy meetings of presidential national security advisors preparing next quagmire (*see above* **Q**).

T is for Teflon
The ability to remain untouched by the scandalous muck that adheres to one's close aides. First used of Ronald Reagan's 'Teflon Presidency'; Clinton's, conversely, was the 'Velcro' one.

U is for Uncle Tom
Republican of African-American descent; also, 'Oreo' (black outside, white inside). Analogues include Hispanic 'coconut', Asian 'banana' and native American 'apple'.

V is for Voodoo
George Bush's description of Ronald Reagan's trickle-down economics, which he went on to support as Reagan's vice president, leading one observer to remark that he was 'giving voodoo a bad name'.

W is for Watergate
Hotel/office complex. Site of 'two-bit burglary' that unseated Richard Nixon. All subsequent scandals now require some form of '-gate' designation: Koreagate, Travelgate, ad infinitum, ad nauseam.

X is for 'Mr X'
Pseudonym used by diplomat George Kennan as author of seminal 1947 paper that shaped early cold war American foreign policy.

Y is for Yellow Dog Democrat
Southernism, from statement 'Ah'd vote fer a yeller dog if he wuz on the Democrat ticket.' Zoological curiosity: conservative Southern Dems (a disappearing breed) were 'boll weevils'.

Z is for Zoo Plane
Adjunct to presidential aircraft White House One, to which lesser journalistists are relegated on campaigns.

Index

Page numbers in **bold** refer to sections containing key information on a subject. *Italics* indicate illustrations.

g

h

i

j

k

l

Advertisers' Index

Please refer to the relevant sections for addresses/telephone numbers

Maps

Trips Out of Town

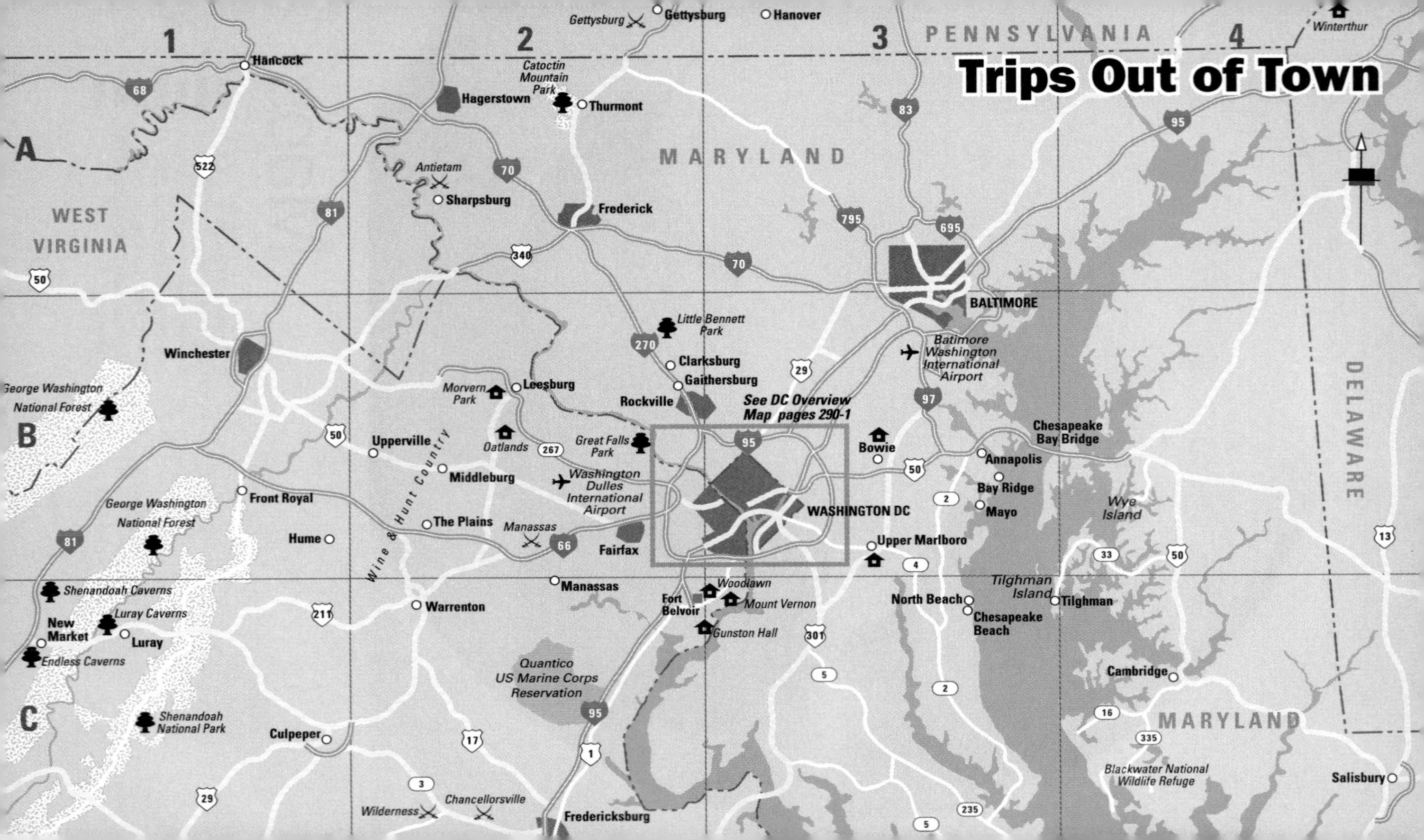

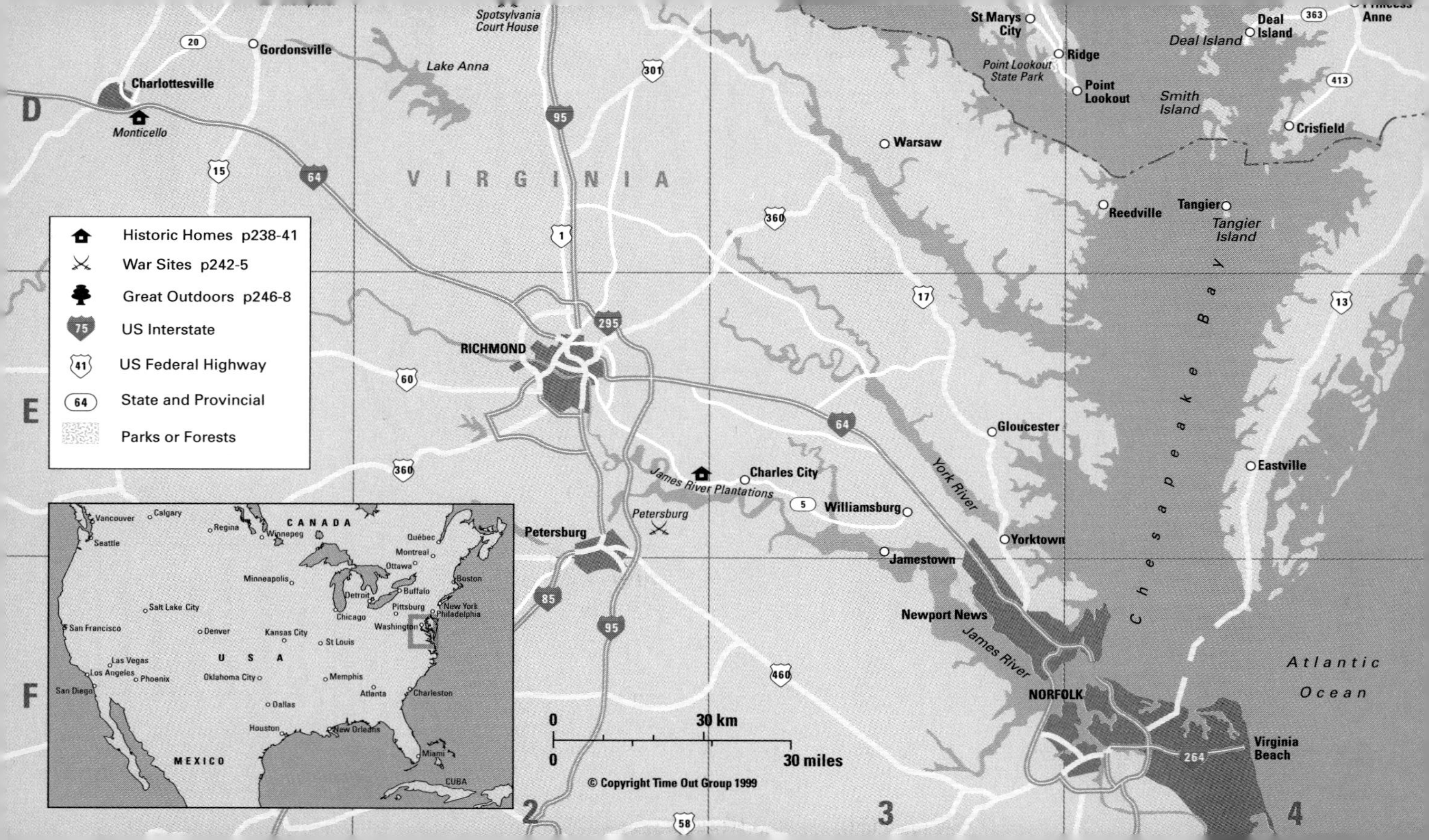
Historic Homes p238-41
War Sites p242-5
Great Outdoors p246-8
US Interstate
US Federal Highway
State and Provincial
Parks or Forests
VIRGINIA
Charlottesville
Monticello
Gordonsville
Spotsylvania Court House
Lake Anna
RICHMOND
Petersburg
James River Plantations
Charles City
Williamsburg
Jamestown
Warsaw
Gloucester
Yorktown
York River
Newport News
James River
NORFOLK
Virginia Beach
St Marys City
Point Lookout State Park
Ridge
Point Lookout
Reedville
Tangier
Tangier Island
Smith Island
Deal Island
Crisfield
Princess Anne
Eastville
Chesapeake Bay
Atlantic Ocean
CANADA
USA
MEXICO
CUBA
30 km
30 miles
© Copyright Time Out Group 1999

DC Overview

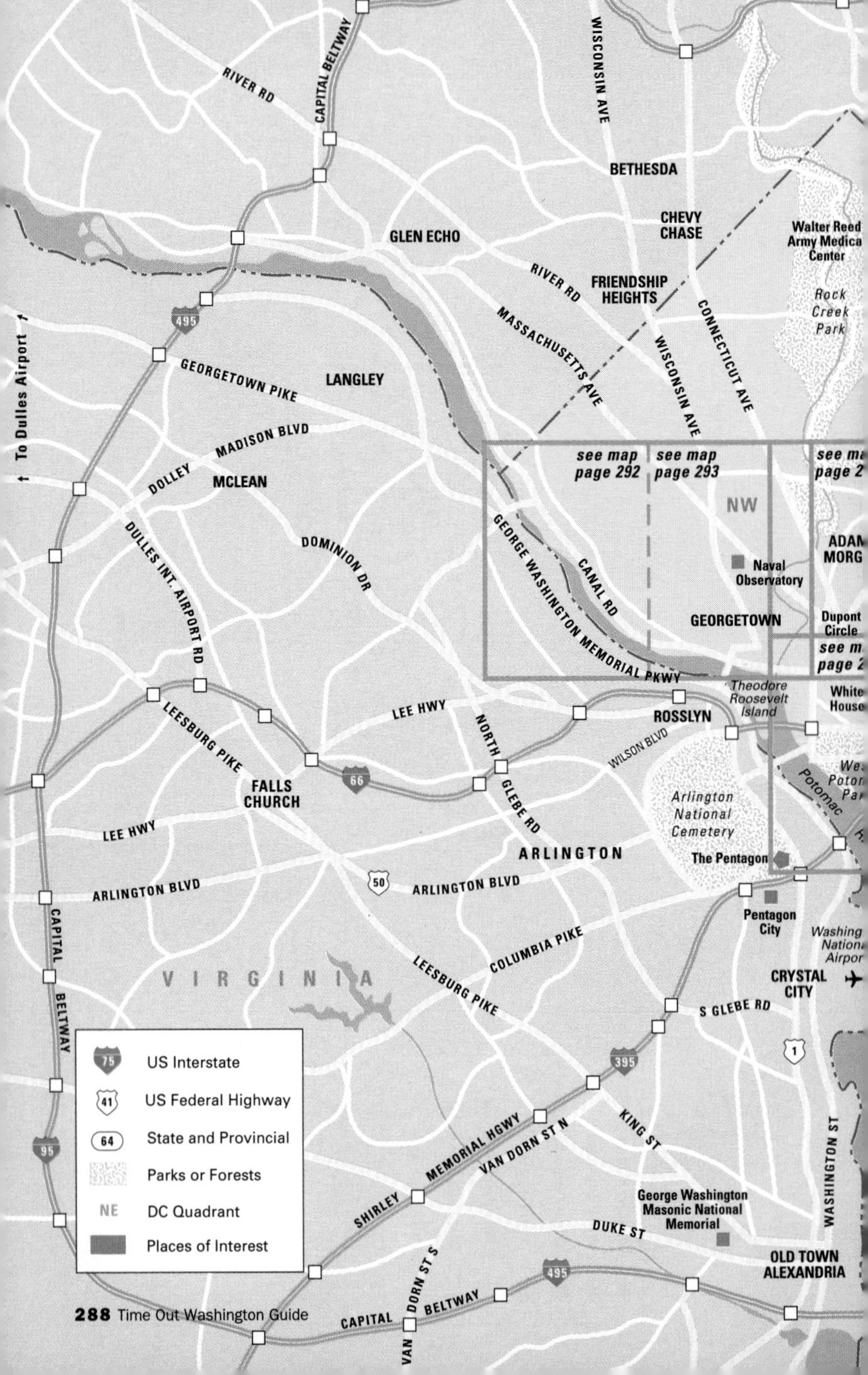

To Dulles Airport
RIVER RD
CAPITAL BELTWAY
WISCONSIN AVE
BETHESDA
CHEVY CHASE
GLEN ECHO
Walter Reed Army Medica Center
RIVER RD
FRIENDSHIP HEIGHTS
Rock Creek Park
MASSACHUSETTS AVE
WISCONSIN AVE
CONNECTICUT AVE
GEORGETOWN PIKE
LANGLEY
MADISON BLVD
DOLLEY
MCLEAN
see map page 292
see map page 293
NW
DULLES INT. AIRPORT RD
DOMINION DR
GEORGE WASHINGTON MEMORIAL PKWY
CANAL RD
Naval Observatory
GEORGETOWN
Dupont Circle
Theodore Roosevelt Island
White House
LEESBURG PIKE
LEE HWY
NORTH GLEBE RD
ROSSLYN
WILSON BLVD
FALLS CHURCH
Potomac
Arlington National Cemetery
LEE HWY
ARLINGTON
The Pentagon
ARLINGTON BLVD
ARLINGTON BLVD
Pentagon City
CAPITAL BELTWAY
COLUMBIA PIKE
VIRGINIA
LEESBURG PIKE
CRYSTAL CITY
S GLEBE RD
KING ST
SHIRLEY MEMORIAL HGWY
VAN DORN ST N
WASHINGTON ST
George Washington Masonic National Memorial
DUKE ST
VAN DORN ST S
OLD TOWN ALEXANDRIA
CAPITAL BELTWAY
US Interstate
US Federal Highway
State and Provincial
Parks or Forests
NE
DC Quadrant
Places of Interest

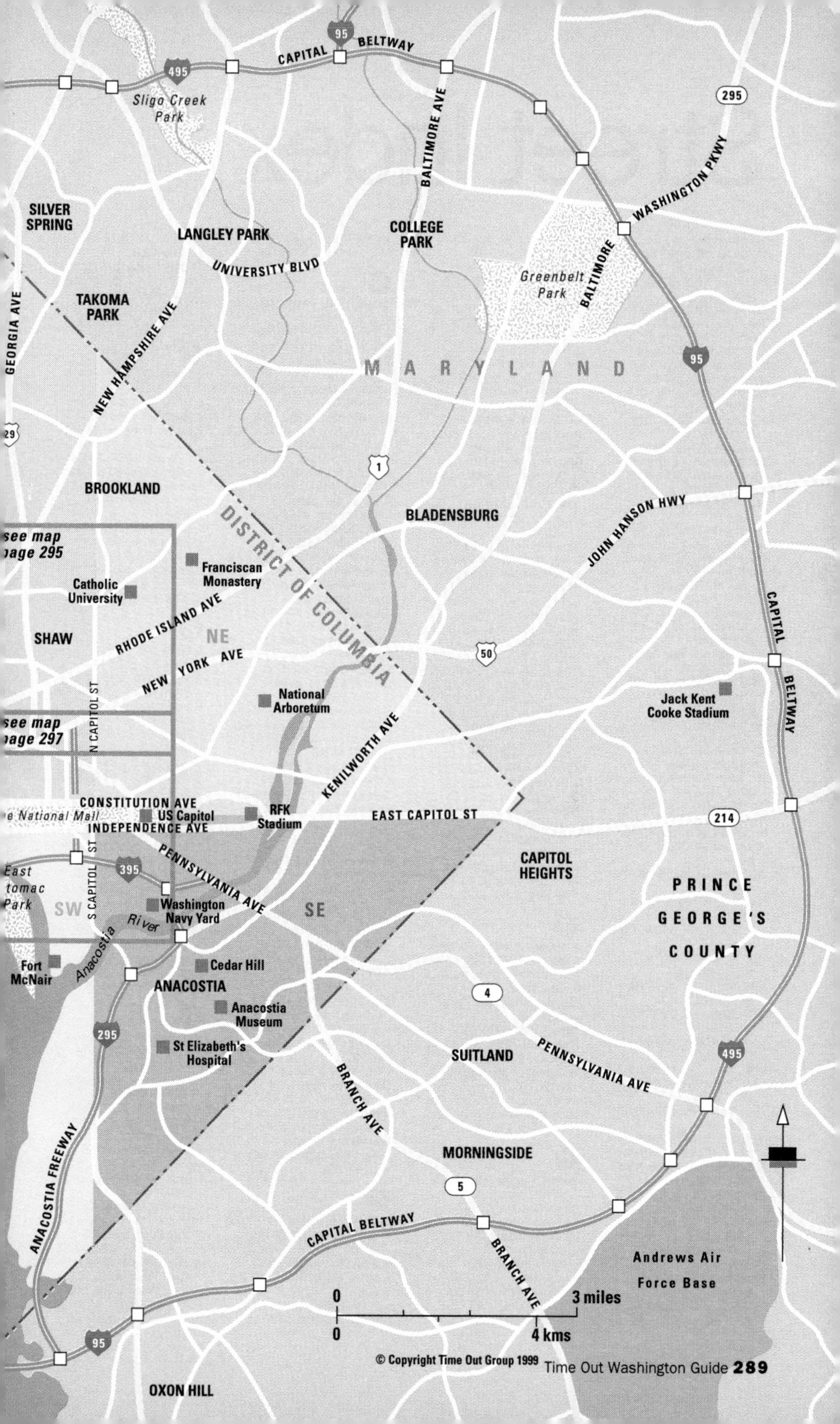
CAPITAL BELTWAY
95
495
Sligo Creek Park
BALTIMORE AVE
295
WASHINGTON PKWY
SILVER SPRING
LANGLEY PARK
COLLEGE PARK
UNIVERSITY BLVD
BALTIMORE
Greenbelt Park
TAKOMA PARK
GEORGIA AVE
NEW HAMPSHIRE AVE
MARYLAND
29
1
BROOKLAND
BLADENSBURG
DISTRICT OF COLUMBIA
JOHN HANSON HWY
see map page 295
Franciscan Monastery
Catholic University
CAPITAL BELTWAY
RHODE ISLAND AVE
SHAW
NE
NEW YORK AVE
50
National Arboretum
Jack Kent Cooke Stadium
N CAPITOL ST
see map page 297
KENILWORTH AVE
CONSTITUTION AVE
The National Mall
US Capitol
RFK Stadium
EAST CAPITOL ST
214
INDEPENDENCE AVE
PENNSYLVANIA AVE
395
CAPITOL HEIGHTS
East Potomac Park
S CAPITOL ST
SW
Washington Navy Yard
SE
PRINCE GEORGE'S COUNTY
River
Anacostia
Fort McNair
Cedar Hill
ANACOSTIA
4
Anacostia Museum
St Elizabeth's Hospital
SUITLAND
PENNSYLVANIA AVE
BRANCH AVE
MORNINGSIDE
ANACOSTIA FREEWAY
5
CAPITAL BELTWAY
BRANCH AVE
Andrews Air Force Base
0
3 miles
0
4 kms
95
OXON HILL

Street Index

NW: West of the Park

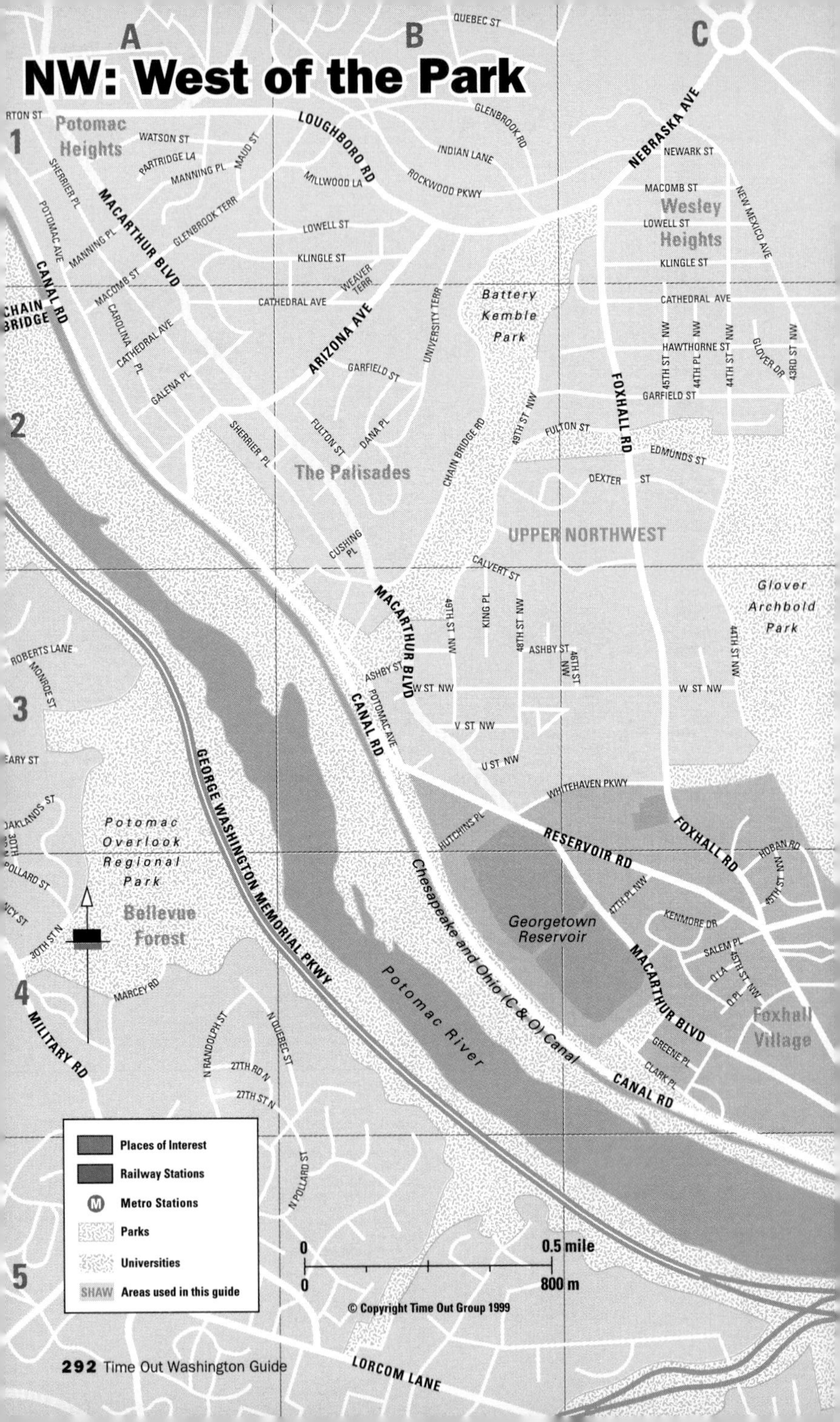

D
E
F
QUEBEC ST
ROWLAND PL
Melvin Hazen Park
PORTER ST
IDAHO AVE
35TH ST NW
39TH ST NW
Cleveland Park
Cleveland Park
ORDWAY ST
NEWARK ST
34TH PL NW
HIGHLAND PL
30TH ST NW
ORDWAY ST
WILLIAMSBURG LA
36TH ST NW
WISCONSIN AVE
MACOMB ST
KLINGLE AVE
IDAHO AVE
LOWELL ST
33RD PL NW
UPPER NORTHWEST
38TH ST NW
WOODLEY RD
DEVONSHIRE PL
MASSACHUSETTS AVE
Washington National Cathedral
KLINGLE RD
National Zoological Park
CATHEDRAL AVE
CORTLAND PL
CONNECTICUT AVE
CLEVELAND AVE
HAWTHORNE ST
BELLEVUE TERR
GARFIELD ST
29TH ST NW
28TH ST NW
27TH ST NW
CATHEDRAL AVE
32ND ST
Woodley Park
FULTON ST
34TH ST NW
35TH ST NW
34TH PL NW
31ST PL
WOODLEY RD
TUNLAW RD
36TH PL NW
36TH ST NW
35TH PL NW
FULTON ST
29TH PL NW
Woodley Park-Zoo
WOODLEY PL
EDMUNDS ST
WOODLAND DR
24TH ST NW
DAVIS PL
DAVIS ST
OBSERVATORY
CALVERT ST
41ST ST NW
NORMANSTONE DR
28TH ST NW
Glover Park
TUNLAW RD
Naval Observatory
Normanstone Park
BENTON ST
OBSERVATORY PL
37TH ST NW
Rock Creek Park
40TH PL NW
40TH ST NW
39TH PL NW
HUIDEKOPER PL
CIRCLE
30TH ST NW
BENTON PL
W ST NW
W PL NW
Rock Creek
Whitehaven Park
WHITEHAVEN ST
KALORAMA CIRCLE
BELMONT RD
Dumbarton Oaks Park
KALORAMA RD
Kalorama
WYOMING AVE
Burleith
TRACY PL
T ST NW
CALIFORNIA ST
Montrose Park
Glover Archbold Park
S ST NW
BANCROFT PL
R ST NW
RESERVOIR RD
ROCK CREEK AND POTOMAC PKWY
AVON PL
Georgetown University Medical Center
DENT PL
SHERIDAN CIRCLE
32ND ST NW
31ST ST NW
Q ST NW
VOLTA PL
GEORGETOWN
P ST NW
44TH ST NW
Georgetown University
37TH ST NW
36TH ST NW
35TH ST NW
34TH ST NW
33RD ST NW
POTOMAC ST
O ST NW
DUMBARTON ST
N ST NW
CANAL RD
PROSPECT ST
Georgetown
OLIVE ST
M ST NW
23RD ST
26TH ST NW
25TH ST
24TH ST
Potomac River
KEY BRIDGE
GRACE ST
SOUTH ST
31ST ST NW
T JEFFERSON ST
Washington Harbour
K ST NW
WASHINGTON CIRCLE
Foggy Bottom-GWU
George Washington University
22ND ST
21ST ST
Rosslyn
Theodore Roosevelt Island
Watergate Complex
1
2
3
4
5

NW: East of the Park

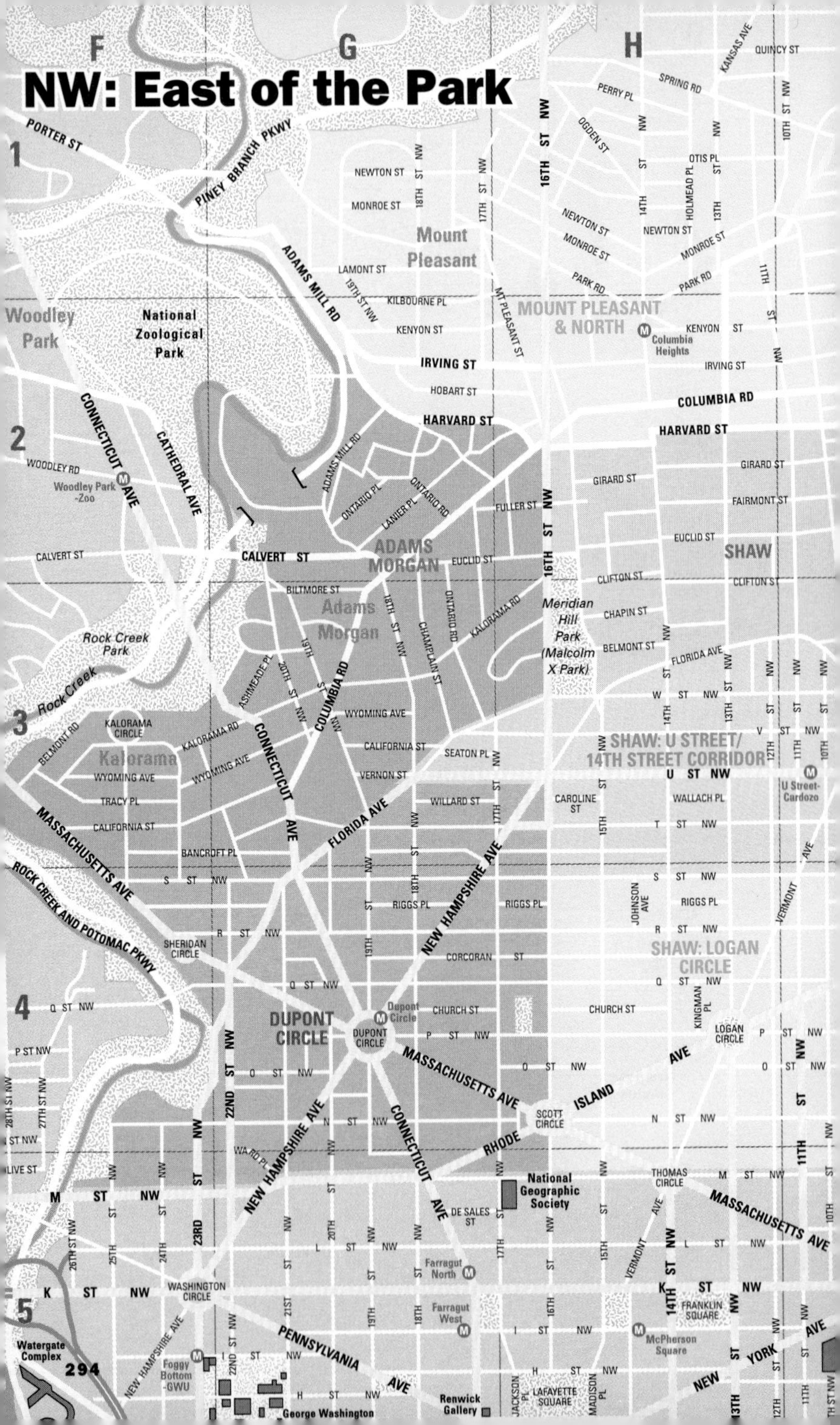

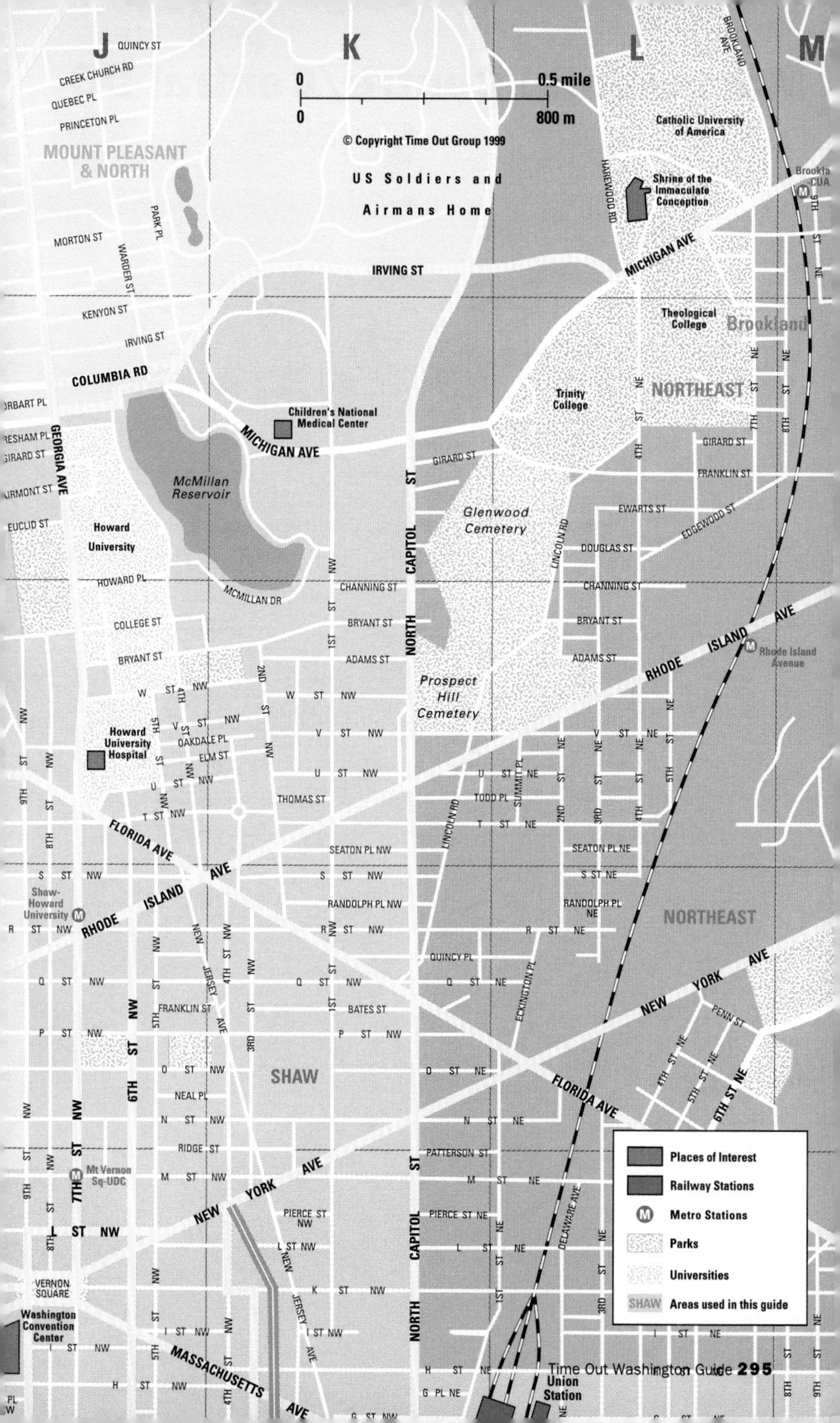
J
K
L
M
0
0.5 mile
0
800 m
© Copyright Time Out Group 1999
MOUNT PLEASANT & NORTH
US Soldiers and Airmans Home
Catholic University of America
Shrine of the Immaculate Conception
Brookland CUA
Theological College
Brookland
Trinity College
NORTHEAST
Children's National Medical Center
McMillan Reservoir
Howard University
Glenwood Cemetery
Prospect Hill Cemetery
Howard University Hospital
Rhode Island Avenue
Shaw-Howard University
SHAW
Mt Vernon Sq-UDC
VERNON SQUARE
Washington Convention Center
Union Station
QUINCY ST
CREEK CHURCH RD
QUEBEC PL
PRINCETON PL
MORTON ST
PARK PL
WARDER ST
KENYON ST
IRVING ST
COLUMBIA RD
GEORGIA AVE
MICHIGAN AVE
HAREWOOD RD
BROOKLAND AVE
NORTH CAPITOL ST
GIRARD ST
FRANKLIN ST
EWARTS ST
EDGEWOOD ST
DOUGLAS ST
CHANNING ST
BRYANT ST
ADAMS ST
LINCOLN RD
MCMILLAN DR
HOWARD PL
COLLEGE ST
OAKDALE PL
ELM ST
THOMAS ST
TODD PL
SUMMIT PL
SEATON PL NW
SEATON PL NE
RANDOLPH PL NW
RANDOLPH PL NE
QUINCY PL
ECKINGTON PL
BATES ST
FRANKLIN ST
NEAL PL
RIDGE ST
PATTERSON ST
PIERCE ST NW
PIERCE ST NE
FLORIDA AVE
RHODE ISLAND AVE
NEW YORK AVE
NEW JERSEY AVE
DELAWARE AVE
PENN ST
MASSACHUSETTS AVE
6TH ST
7TH ST
Places of Interest
Railway Stations
Metro Stations
Parks
Universities
SHAW Areas used in this guide

Monumental Centre/Central DC

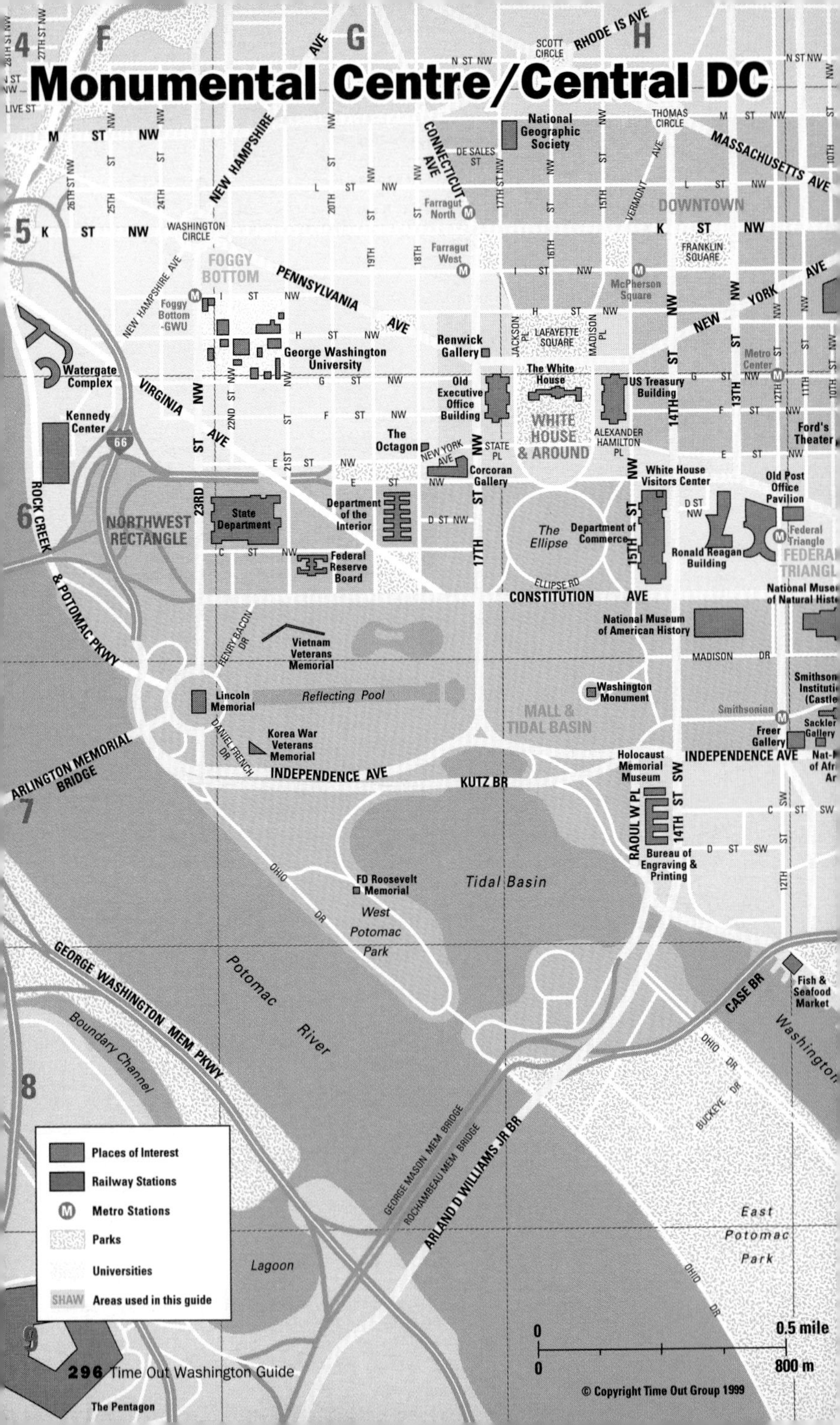

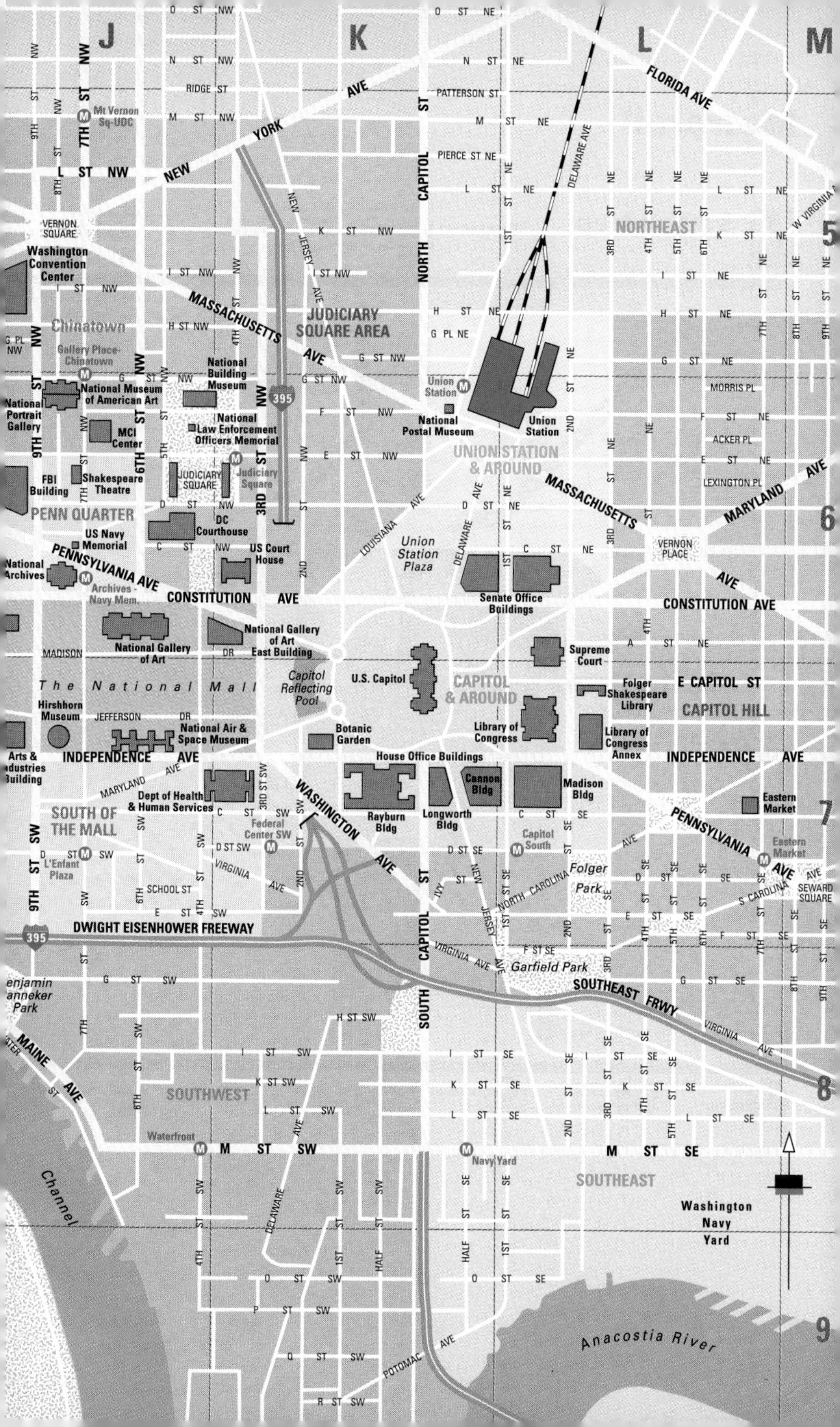
J
K
L
M
5
6
7
8
9
NEW YORK AVE
FLORIDA AVE
Mt Vernon Sq-UDC
7TH ST NW
L ST NW
VERNON SQUARE
Washington Convention Center
Chinatown
Gallery Place-Chinatown
National Museum of American Art
National Portrait Gallery
MCI Center
FBI Building
Shakespeare Theatre
PENN QUARTER
National Building Museum
National Law Enforcement Officers Memorial
JUDICIARY SQUARE
Judiciary Square
DC Courthouse
US Navy Memorial
US Court House
National Archives
Archives-Navy Mem.
PENNSYLVANIA AVE
CONSTITUTION AVE
MASSACHUSETTS AVE
NEW JERSEY AVE
JUDICIARY SQUARE AREA
NORTH CAPITOL ST
DELAWARE AVE
NORTHEAST
Union Station
National Postal Museum
UNION STATION & AROUND
LOUISIANA AVE
Union Station Plaza
Senate Office Buildings
MARYLAND AVE
VERNON PLACE
National Gallery of Art
National Gallery of Art East Building
MADISON DR
The National Mall
Capitol Reflecting Pool
U.S. Capitol
CAPITOL & AROUND
Supreme Court
Folger Shakespeare Library
E CAPITOL ST
CAPITOL HILL
Library of Congress
Library of Congress Annex
Hirshhorn Museum
JEFFERSON DR
National Air & Space Museum
Botanic Garden
House Office Buildings
Arts & Industries Building
INDEPENDENCE AVE
Dept of Health & Human Services
Rayburn Bldg
Longworth Bldg
Cannon Bldg
Madison Bldg
Eastern Market
SOUTH OF THE MALL
L'Enfant Plaza
Federal Center SW
WASHINGTON AVE
VIRGINIA AVE
Capitol South
Folger Park
NORTH CAROLINA AVE
S CAROLINA AVE
SEWARD SQUARE
DWIGHT EISENHOWER FREEWAY
395
SOUTH CAPITOL ST
Garfield Park
SOUTHEAST FRWY
MAINE AVE
SOUTHWEST
Waterfront
M ST SW
Navy Yard
M ST SE
SOUTHEAST
Washington Navy Yard
Channel
DELAWARE AVE
POTOMAC AVE
Anacostia River

Metrorail

metro
System Map
Legend
Red Line • Glenmont/Shady Grove
Orange Line • New Carrollton/Vienna/Fairfax-GMU
Blue Line • Addison Road/Franconia-Springfield
Green Line • Branch Avenue/Greenbelt
Yellow Line • Huntington/Mt. Vernon Sq-UDC
Commuter Rail
Transfer Station
Parking
Station in Service
Future Station
RED LINE
Shady Grove
Rockville
Twinbrook
White Flint
Grosvenor
Medical Center
Bethesda
Friendship Heights
Tenleytown-AU
Van Ness-UDC
Cleveland Park
Woodley Park-Zoo
Dupont Circle
Farragut North
Glenmont
Wheaton
Forest Glen
Silver Spring
Takoma
GREEN LINE
Greenbelt
College Park-U of Md
Prince George's Plaza
West Hyattsville
Fort Totten
Georgia Ave-Petworth
Columbia Heights
U Street-Cardozo
Shaw-Howard U
Mt Vernon Sq-UDC
Brookland-CUA
Rhode Island Ave
New Carrollton
Landover
Cheverly
Deanwood
Minnesota Ave
McPherson Sq
Rosslyn
ORANGE LINE
Vienna/Fairfax-GMU
Dunn Loring-Merrifield
West Falls Church-VT/UVA
East Falls Church
Ballston-MU
Virginia Sq-GMU
Clarendon
Court House
Foggy Bottom GWU
Farragut West
Metro Center
Federal Triangle
Smithsonian
Archives-Navy Mem'l
Gallery Pl-Chinatown
Judiciary Sq
Union Station
L'Enfant Plaza
Benning Road
Capitol Heights
Addison Road
Stadium-Armory
Potomac Ave
Eastern Market
Capitol South
Federal Center SW
Waterfront-SEU
Navy Yard
Anacostia
Congress Heights
Southern Ave
Naylor Road
Suitland
Branch Ave
Arlington Cemetery
Pentagon
YELLOW LINE
Pentagon City
Crystal City
National Airport
Braddock Road
King Street
Eisenhower Ave
Huntington
Van Dorn Street
BLUE LINE
Franconia-Springfield
Capital Beltway
Montgomery Co
District of Columbia
Prince George's Co
Fairfax Co
Arlington Co
Alexandria
N
© COPYRIGHT 1998
WASHINGTON METROPOLITAN
AREA TRANSIT AUTHORITY
No Smoking
No Food or Drinks
No Animals (except guide dogs)
No Audio or Video Devices (without earphones)
No Litter or Spitting
No Dangerous or Flammable Materials

Time Out Washington, DC Guide Please let us know what you think

(FIRST EDITION)

About this guide...

1. How useful did you find the following sections?

	Very	Fairly	Not very	
In Context	❑	❑	❑	(5)
Sightseeing	❑	❑	❑	(6)
Accommodation	❑	❑	❑	(7)
Eating & Drinking	❑	❑	❑	(8)
Shopping	❑	❑	❑	(9)
Arts & Entertainment	❑	❑	❑	(10)
Trips Out of town	❑	❑	❑	(11)
Resources	❑	❑	❑	(12)
Maps	❑	❑	❑	(13)

2. Did you travel to Washington: (17)

Alone? ❑ With partner? ❑
As part of group? ❑ With children? ❑
On business? ❑ I live here. ❑

3. How long was your trip to Washington? (18)

Less than three days ❑
Three days to one week ❑
One to two weeks ❑
Over two weeks ❑

4. Did you visit any other destinations in the USA? If so, which ones?

5. Where did you get additional travel information from? (19)

Tourist board ❑
Internet ❑
Travel agents ❑
Another guide book (please specify)

Other

(20/22)

6. Is there anything you'd like us to cover in greater depth?

7. Are there any places that should/should not be included in the guide?

8. How many other people have used this guide? (23)

none❑ 1❑ 2❑ 3❑ 4❑ 5+❑

About other Time Out publications...

9. Have you ever bought/used Time Out magazine? (24)

Yes ❑ No ❑

10. Have you bought any other Time Out City Guides? (25)

Yes ❑ No ❑

If yes, which ones?

(26/28)

11. Have you ever bought/used other Time Out publications? (29)

Yes ❑ No ❑

If yes, which ones? (30)

Film Guide ❑
Kids Out magazine ❑
London Eating & Drinking Guide ❑
London Pubs & Bars Guide ❑
London Visitors' Guide ❑
ici Londres ❑
Paris Eating & Drinking Guide ❑
Paris Free Guide ❑
London Shopping Guide ❑
Student Guide ❑
Book of Country Walks ❑
Book of London Walks ❑

(31)

Book of New York Short Stories ❑
Time Out New York magazine ❑
Time Out Roma ❑
Time Out Diary ❑
www.timeout.com ❑

About you...

12. First name:
Surname:
Address:

Postcode:
13. Year of birth (32)

14. Sex: male ❑ female ❑ (43)

15. Are you: (44)

employed full-time ❑
employed part-time ❑
self-employed ❑
unemployed ❑
student ❑
homemaker ❑

16. At the moment do you earn: (45)

under £10,000 ❑
over 10,000 and up to £14,999 ❑
over £15,000 and up to £19,999 ❑
over £20,000 and up to £24,999 ❑
over £25,000 and up to £39,999 ❑
over £40,000 and up to £49,999 ❑
over £50,000 ❑

❑ Please tick here if you don't want to receive further information on related promotions or products.

2

Time Out Guides

FREEPOST 20 (WC3187)
LONDON
W1E 0DQ